Encyclopedia of
CAPITALISM

Volume II
H–R

SYED B. HUSSAIN, Ph.D.

GENERAL EDITOR

☑®
Facts On File, Inc.

Encyclopedia of Capitalism

Library of Congress Cataloging-in-Publication Data

Encyclopedia of capitalism / Syed B. Hussain, general editor
         p. cm.
    Includes bibliographical references and index.
    ISBN 0-8160-5224-7 (alk paper)
       1. Capitalism—Encyclopedias.   I. Hussain, Syed B.

    HB501.E558 2004
    330'.03—dc22   2003064170

GOLSON BOOKS, LTD.

Geoff Golson, President and Editor
Syed B. Hussain, Ph.D., General Editor, Encyclopedia of Capitalism
Kevin Hanek, Design Director
Brian Snapp, Copyeditor
Gail Liss, Indexer

PHOTO CREDITS
Bank of Sweden Prizes in Memory of Alfred Nobel: Pages 20, 193, 281, 320, 380, 488, 553, 614, 735, 780. Kenneth Gabrielsen Photography: Pages 11, 14, 27, 52, 60, 72, 75, 137, 139, 150, 152, 160, 188, 189, 212, 217, 238, 243, 248, 249, 275, 278, 281, 329, 372, 391, 413, 422, 495, 527, 556, 596, 617, 656, 659, 669, 674, 696, 708, 709, 758, 765, 768, 784, 801, 818, 831, 841, 872, 883, 889. PhotoDisc, Inc.: Pages 55, 133, 214, 269, 310, 355, 408, 433, 469, 516, 546, 675, 870, 934. U.S. Senate: 442.

Printed in the United States of America

VB PKG 10 9 8 7 6 5 4 3 2 1

This book is printed on acid-free paper.

Contents

List of Contributors

Abugri, Benjamin
Department of Economics and Finance
Southern Connecticut University

Aka, Arsène
The Catholic University of America

Azari-Rad, H.
Department of Economics
State University of New York, New Paltz

Balak, Benjamin
Department of Economics
Rollins College

Barnhill, John
Independent Scholar

Batchelor, Bob
Independent Scholar

Becker, Klaus
Texas Tech University

Berkley, Holly
Department of History
Hardin-Simmons University

Bhattacharya, Tithi
Department of History
Purdue University

Bishop, Elizabeth
Institute for Gender and Women's Studies
American University in Cairo, Egypt

Blankenship, Cary
Department of History, Geography, Political Science
Tennessee State University

Block, Walter
Loyola University, New Orleans

Boettcher, Susan R.
Department of History
University of Texas

Borden, Timothy G.
Independent Scholar

Bradley, Robert L., Jr.
Institute for Energy Research

Braguinsky, Serguey
Department of Economics
State University of New York, Buffalo

Caplan, Bryan
Department of Economics
George Mason University

Carton, Joel
Department of Economics
Texas Tech University

Cawley, John H.
Department of Economics
Cornell University

Chen, Shehong
University of Massachusetts, Lowell

Chung, Wai-keung
Department of Sociology
University of Washington

Coelho, Alfredo
University of Montpellier, France

Cruz, Laura
Department of History
Western Carolina University

Cundiff, Kirby R.
Hillsdale College

Dadres, Susan
Department of Economics
Southern Methodist University

DeCoster, Karen
Walsh College

Dolenc, Patrick
Department of Economics
Keene State College

Dompere, Kofi Kissi
Department of Economics
Howard University

Douglas, R.M.
Department of History
Colgate University

DuBose, Mike
American Culture Studies
Bowling Green State University

Dynan, Linda
Independent Scholar

Elvins, Sarah
Department of History
University of Notre Dame

Erickson, Christian
Roosevelt University

Evrensel, Ayşe Y.
Department of Economics
Portland State University

Ewing, Bradley T.
Department of Economics
Texas Tech University

Ferguson, William
Institute for Experiential Living
Grinnell College

Foster, Kevin R.
City College of New York

Fowler, Russell
University of Tennessee, Chattanooga

Fuming, Jiang
Charles Sturt University, Australia

Gabriel, Satya J.
Department of Economics
Mount Holyoke College

Gallois, William
American University of Sharjah
United Arab Emirates

Geringer, Joseph
Essays On History

Gerlach, Jeffrey
Department of Economics
College of William & Mary

Grassl, Wolfgang
Department of Economics
Hillsdale College

Haworth, Barry
University of Louisville

Hill, Kirstin
Merrill Lynch & Company
London, England

Holst, Arthur
Widener University

Howell, Chris
Red Rocks College

Hussain, Akmal
Institute of Development Economics
Pakistan

Hussain, Syed B.,
General Editor of the Encyclopedia

Işcan, Talan
Department of Economics
Dalhousie University, Canada

Jacobson, Katherine
Department of History
Metropolitan State University

Jeitschko, Thomas D.
Department of Economics
Michigan State University

Kinni, Theodore
Independent Scholar

Kline, Audrey D.
University of Louisville

Klumpp, Tilman
Economics Department
Indiana University

Kosar, George
Brandeis University

Kozlov, Nicholas N.
Economics Department
Hofstra University

Kucsma, Kristin
Economics Department
Seton Hall University

Kypraios, Harry
Rollins College

Laberge, Yves
Institut Québécois des
Hautes Études Internationales, Canada

Larudee, Mehrene
Department of Economics
University of Kansas

Lawrence, Taresa
Howard University

Lawson, Russell M.
Independent Scholar

Lewis, David
Citrus College

Luque, Emilio
UNED University, Madrid, Spain

MacKenzie, D.W.
George Mason University

Mahmud, Tayyab
Ohio State University

Malik, Farooq
Pennsylvania State University, Berks

Matheson, Victor
Department of Economics
Williams College

Matraves, Catherine
Department of Economics and Management
Albion College

Mattson, Kevin
Department of History
Ohio University

Mazzoleni, Roberto
Department of Economics and Geography
Hofstra University

McGee, Kevin
University of Wisconsin

McGregor, Michael
Fannie Mae

Mitchell, David
George Mason University

Mocnik, Josip
Bowling Green State University

Moiz, Syed
Marian College

Moore, Karl
McGill University, Canada

Motluck, Mark E.
Anderson University

Mozayeni, Simin
State University of New York, New Paltz

Nesslein, Thomas
Urban and Regional Studies
University of Wisconsin, Green Bay

Neumann, Caryn
Department of History
Ohio State University

Odekon, Mehmet
Skidmore College

Ornelas, Emmanuel
University of Georgia

Paas, David
Hillsdale College

Palmer, Scott
RGMS Economics

Papageorgiou, Chris
Department of Economics
Louisiana State University

Petrou, Linda L.
Department of History
and Political Science
High Point University

Phelps, Chris
Ohio State University

Prieger, James E.
Department of Economics
University of California, Davis

Prono, Luca
University of Nottingham, England

Pullin, Eric
College of Business
Cardinal Stritch University

Purdy, Elizabeth
Independent Scholar

Rabbani, Mahbub
Temple University

Raman, Jaishankar
Department of Economics
Valparaiso University

Reagle, Derrick
Department of Economics
Fordham University

Robinson, Charles
Brandeis University

Rodríguez-Boetsch, Leopoldo
Portland State University

Rubel, Shawn
Independent Scholar

Saeed, Agha
University of California, Berkeley

Sagers, John
Department of History
Linfield College

Schrag, Jonathan
Harvard University

Schuster, Zeljan
School of Business
University of New Haven

Silver, Lindsay
Brandeis University

Sorrentino, John A.
Department of Economics
Temple University

Subramanian, Narayanan
Brandeis University

Sullivan, Timothy E.
Department of Economics
Towson University

Swanson, Paul
Department of Economics
and Finance
William Patterson University

Syed, Aura
Department of Political Science
Northern Michigan University

Thompson, Mark A.
Sephen F. Austin State University

Traflet, Janice
Columbia University

Troy, Michael J.
Michigan State University

Turdaliev, Nurlan
Department of Economics
McGill University

Vavrik, Ursula
Vienna University of Economics, Austria

von Ende, Terry
Texas Tech University

Walsh, John
Shinawatra University, Thailand

Weed, Charles
Department of Social Science
Keene State College

Weston, Samuel
Economics Department
University of Dallas

Whaples, Robert
Department of Economics
Wake Forest University

Wu, Xiadong
University of North Carolina, Chapel Hill

Young, Derek Rutherford
Department of History
University of Dundee, Scotland

Young, Ronald
Georgia Southern University

Zaccarini, Cristina
Adelphi University

List of Articles

Encyclopedia of
CAPITALISM

VOLUME II

H

Haavelmo, Trygve (1911–99)

THE NORWEGIAN ECONOMIST Trygve Haavelmo began his career as a student of Ragnar FRISCH at the University of Oslo. He went to the United States in 1939 as a Fulbright scholar, where he ended up staying until 1947. Haavelmo spent much of his sojourn at the Cowles Commission, before returning to Oslo.

Haavelmo was awarded 1989 Nobel Prize in Economics for his clarification of the probability theory foundations of ECONOMETRICS and his analyses of simultaneous economic structures.

The field of econometrics is concerned with estimating economic relations and testing whether postulated relations conform fully to reality. In an article in *Econometrica* in 1943 and in his doctoral thesis entitled, "The Probability Approach in Econometrics" (1944), Haavelmo showed that the results of many of the methods used thus far had been misleading. Earlier methods did not sufficiently account for the fact that real economic development is determined by the interaction of a multitude of economic relations and that economic laws are not strictly rigorous. For example, he demonstrated that an economist could not gauge the impact of a change in tax rates on consumer spending without using sophisticated statistical methods.

In his thesis, Haavelmo presented a new and groundbreaking approach to the estimation of economic relations by applying methods used in mathematical statistics. His work established the foundations for a new field of research, which came to dominate the study of estimating complex economic relations.

In his review of Haavelmo's doctoral thesis, the British Nobel laureate Richard STONE wrote that it was a brilliant contribution to econometrics, which would have a revolutionary effect on the degree of success in estimating economic relations. After he became professor at the University of Oslo, Haavelmo's research interests turned to economic theory. His book, *A Study in the Theory of Economic Evolution* (1954), was a pioneering study of the possible reasons for economic underdevelopment of a country in relation to other countries, long before other economists became seriously engaged in development research.

Haavelmo also made a valuable contribution to the theory that determines the extent of investments in a country. His book, *A Study in the Theory of Investment* (1960), introduced theories that have been of fundamental importance in subsequent research. Numerous theoretical and empirical studies of investment behavior have been inspired by his work.

Many of Haavelmo's other studies, such as a monograph on environmental economics that appeared long before such research came into vogue, have been an inspiration to other researchers. "Haavelmo had a tremendous influence on me and on many other young econometricians in the 1940s," said Lawrence KLEIN, 1980 Nobel Laureate for his work in the field.

Haavelmo has also had a decisive influence on economics in Norway, not only as a researcher but also as a teacher. During his active years at the Institute of Economics at the University of Oslo, he was the leading teacher in the field. He covered numerous areas of economic theory and many of his students and assistants received their first instruction in authorship by writing expositions based on his lectures, under his stimulating guidance. No less inspiration was given to the many research recruits for whom Haavelmo served as advisor.

BIBLIOGRAPHY. Trygve Haavelmo Biography, www.nobel.se; Trygve Haavelmo Biography, www.cepa.newschool.edu; T.

Haavelmo, *A Study in the Theory of Economic Evolution* (Augustus M. Kelley, 1991).

SYED B. HUSSAIN, PH.D.
UNIVERSITY OF WISCONSIN, OSHKOSH

Hamilton, Alexander (1755–1804)

ALEXANDER HAMILTON IS BOTH a character on the stage of American capitalism and one of its main theorists. Hamilton's story is one of upward mobility. He emerged from a bankrupt family to become one of the most influential politicians in 18th-century America. At the age of 12, because of the failure of the family business, Hamilton entered the workforce as a clerk and apprentice at the counting house of Cruger and Beekman. Three years later, he was running the business, although the ambitious Hamilton was certainly not satisfied: "I would willingly risk my life, though not my character, to exalt my station," he wrote when he was 14 years old.

His station in life suddenly changed as he joined a patriot volunteer corps in the AMERICAN REVOLUTION and became George WASHINGTON's personal secretary and aide. After independence, Hamilton left the military career and turned to politics and economics: he was a delegate to the Constitutional Convention of 1787, an author of the *Federalist Papers*, and the first secretary of the Treasury from 1789 to 1795.

While an upward-mobile character in the plot of American capitalism, Hamilton was also one of the system's main theorists and is considered the father of the U.S. financial and banking system. As U.S. Treasury secretary, Hamilton developed an economic system that would help the expansion of the new nation. He focused on the repayment of the American Revolution debt, and on the expansion of commerce both through the establishment of trade relations among the states with European countries, as well as through the exploration of the *terra incognita* west of the Mississippi River.

In addition to the well-known *Federalist Papers*, Hamilton's political and economic legacy is clearly expressed in the four reports that he authored as Treasury secretary and presented to Congress between 1790 and 1791. These four reports on public credit, the establishment of a mint, the establishment of a national bank, and manufactures stand in sharp contrast with the economic theories espoused by Hamilton's contemporary Scottish theorist Adam SMITH. The four reports conceive an interaction between the nation's development into political unity and economic prosperity—into an "em-

pire" in Hamilton's own words—and its economic institutions. Public and private interests are interrelated, as are politics and markets.

In particular, Hamilton's "Report on Manufactures" represents a rejection of Smith's LAISSEZ-FAIRE capitalism and recurrently argues that economics is mutually dependent on state power, thus outlining a plan for governmental support of American industry. Hamilton wanted a protective tariff so that imports were taxed and foreign goods would be more expensive than American products. It did not seem plausible to him that a nation of farmers could compete against the industrial strength of Europe. He argued that the United States could only assure its political independence by maintaining economic independence. Hamilton rejected the idea that "the systems of perfect liberty to industry and commerce were the prevailing systems of nations," and disputed "that industry, if left to itself, will naturally find its way to the most useful and profitable employment," according to Smith's policies. Hamilton's elaborate plan for tariffs and support of American growing industries was the only part of his program that was not initially supported by Congress.

The report also stands in contrast with Thomas JEFFERSON's view of America as a society built on an agrarian economy and the most eloquent opposition to Hamilton's proposals came, not surprisingly, from him. Jefferson believed that the growth of manufacturing threatened the values of an agrarian way of life. Hamilton's vision of America's future directly challenged Jefferson's ideal of a nation of farmers in communion with nature and maintaining personal freedom through land ownership. Like slaves, Jefferson feared, factory workers would be controlled by their masters, who would make it impossible for them to think and act as independent citizens.

While his personal story is about individual success and rise from poverty to political influence, Hamilton's political economy is anchored in the belief that the state had an important part to play in sustaining the process of industrial growth. In addition, this process could be employed to reach a "General Welfare," in Hamilton's phrase, going beyond mere individual wealth.

BIBLIOGRAPHY. Samuel H. Beer, *To Make a Nation: the Rediscovery of American Federalism*. (Harvard University Press, 1993); Alexander Hamilton, *The Papers of Alexander Hamilton* (Columbia University Press, 1961-79); Alexander Hamilton, James Madison, and John Jay, *The Federalist Papers* (Bantam, 1982); V. Hart and S.C. Stimson, eds., *Writing a National Identity: Political, Economic and Cultural Perspectives on the Written Constitution* (Manchester University Press, 1993); Cathy D. Matson and Peter S. Onuf, *A Union of Interests: Political and Economic Thought in Revolutionary America* (University of Kansas Press, 1990); Shannon C.

Stimson, *The American Constitution in the Law: Anglo-American Jurisprudence before John Marshall* (Princeton University Press, 1990).

LUCA PRONO, PH.D.
UNIVERSITY OF NOTTINGHAM, ENGLAND

Hancock, John (1737–93)

ALTHOUGH THE HISTORICAL legacy of John Hancock is often overshadowed by some of the more prominent Founding Fathers, Hancock was one of the most important political leaders in colonial America. By the mid-18th century, Hancock had become the wealthiest man in the North American colonies, and Great Britain's financial impositions on the colonists incited the former British loyalist to become a revolutionary. But in spite of his social status and financial comfort, Hancock's appreciation of the ideals of liberty earned him the admiration and trust from ordinary men who would ultimately unite in the colonial militia.

Hancock's evolution from Tory to revolutionary leader was in part due to his ability to appeal to the elite merchant class as well as the working class and farmers. He became a critical player in both Massachusetts and, later, national politics and nation-building during the era and the aftermath of the AMERICAN REVOLUTION.

Hancock was born in Braintree (now Quincy), Massachusetts to the Reverend Thomas Hancock and his wife Mary Hawke. The Hancocks were prominent Congregational clergymen in Boston and young Hancock enjoyed a privileged early childhood. However, in the spring of 1744, Reverend Hancock fell ill and died, leaving his wife and children facing a life of poverty. Shortly following his father's death, Hancock was sent for by his extremely wealthy and childless uncle, another Thomas Hancock, who desired an heir to the fortune he had amassed under the title, "The House of Hancock."

Living under the wing of his uncle's good fortune, Hancock developed a love and appreciation of the finer, richer things that money afforded. He also had the opportunity to attend the finest educational institutions: Hancock enrolled in Boston Latin School and later Harvard College. Following his graduation from Harvard, Hancock opted to enter the colonial merchant world of trade and commerce and he became formally apprenticed to his uncle who soon made Hancock his official business partner and sole heir. When his uncle died during the summer of 1764, Hancock, at the age of 27, became one of the wealthiest men in the colonies.

Though Hancock would become a popular figure in Boston politics, he spent much of life alone, living only with his widowed aunt in his isolated Beacon Hill mansion. Years later, he would marry Dorothy Quincy, a woman from a prominent family. They had two children, a daughter and a son but neither lived to see adulthood.

Well known for his success in commerce, Hancock formally entered political life in 1765 when he was elected to the position of Boston selectman. As anger brewed in the colonies over the British Parliament's unfair policies of taxation such as the Stamp Act (the first internal tax levied on the colonies), Hancock became acquainted with Sam Adams, who led much of the opposition to Britain. By 1768, with the imposition of British taxes on paper, glass, paint, and tea, Hancock's camaraderie with Adams and other revolutionaries steered him toward becoming a leader of resistance against the British.

That same year, British customs agents invaded and investigated Hancock's ships but he took a stand against the agents; the incident propelled him to hero status overnight.

Elected to the Massachusetts legislature, Hancock's skills as an orator rallied the colonists, particularly in the wake of the 1770 Boston Massacre, when British soldiers fired upon a hostile, unarmed crowd and killed five people. When the American Revolution began just five years later, Hancock was charged with the responsibility of organizing the Boston militia. His role made him as reviled by the British as he was revered by the colonists. Hancock's reputation primed him for the position as president of the Second Continental Congress that convened to assume the responsibilities of coordinating the revolution. On July 4, 1776, the Congress formally adopted the Declaration of Independence. It was upon that document that Hancock left his elaborate, famous signature; it was a mere representation of the indelible mark he would leave on the nation.

In 1780, Hancock returned to Massachusetts and received an enthusiastic homecoming from Bostonians who elected him governor later that year. During his first term, Hancock faced a state financial crisis brought on by the devaluation of Continental money. Congress continued to print worthless paper dollars and colonists grew outraged at such irresponsible economics. In Massachusetts, farmers and soldiers alike rallied against the worthless money and demanded back payments. The culture of debt and credit that was inherent to the colonial economy exacerbated the tensions among the classes.

Although his health had markedly declined, Hancock was continually re-elected governor of Massachusetts during the first half of the 1780s. Throughout his term, the state was plagued by internal conflicts stemming from western farmers' demand to abolish the requirement that property taxes be paid in hard currency. Although Hancock took measures to appease the parties, even his political and business acumen were not enough to alleviate the fiscal crisis. Hancock had at one time been able to bridge the divide between the wealthy merchant class and the working class, but in the era after the revolution, economic issues made it much harder for him to appeal to both sides.

Exhausted by age and frustration and fearing heightened economic tensions, Hancock chose not to seek re-election in 1785 and 1786. His decision would prove clairvoyant: in 1786–87, Daniel Shays, a former captain in the Continental army, led farmers and debtors in a series of armed rebellions against state and local authorities who enforced tax collection and imprisonment for debt. The Massachusetts state militia ultimately suppressed the insurrection but the incident revealed the lack of essential legislative powers that characterized the weak American government under the Articles of Confederation.

In 1787, Hancock was re-elected as governor of Massachusetts. Although Shay's Rebellion had been a largely unsuccessful episode for farmers, Hancock was careful not to punish the colonists who had rallied behind Shays and the Massachusetts' uprising became an important point in the debates over the United States Constitution.

Hancock recognized the need for a stronger central government, but he was very committed to adding a Bill of Rights to the Constitution document in order to give the anti-Federalists, those who were against centralized power, a stake in their government. Hancock's mediation skills were critical to the Constitutional convention; in 1791 the Bill of Rights became part of the U.S. Constitution.

Although he continued to serve as the governor of Massachusetts, Hancock lived his remaining years in very poor health. He spent much of his personal fortune rebuilding the city of Boston and accordingly, historians have recognized him as American's first great humanitarian and philanthropist.

BIBLIOGRAPHY. Herbert S. Allan, *John Hancock: Patriot in Purple* (Macmillan, 1948); Paul D. Brandes, *John Hancock's Life and Speeches* (Scarecrow Press, 1996); William M. Fowler, Jr., *The Baron of Beacon Hill: A Biography of John Hancock* (Houghton Mifflin, 1980); Harlow Giles Unger, *John Hancock: Merchant King and American Patriot* (John Wiley & Sons, 2000).

LINDSAY SILVER
BRANDEIS UNIVERSITY

Harding, Warren G. (1865–1923)

POPULAR MYTHS COLOR the memory of President Warren G. Harding's brief administration and mysterious death. Generally thought to be one of the most corrupt and ineffective presidents, Harding served only two years in office during which time he was subject to the influence of ambitious and crooked Republican operatives.

Warren Gamaliel Harding was born on November 2, 1865 in Blooming Grove, Ohio, a region dominated by the Republican Party. He spent his formative years in small, rural communities and attended Ohio Central College, graduating in 1882. Upon earning his degree, Harding moved to Marion, Ohio, where he worked for a short time as a teacher before joining the reporting staff of the Marion *Mirror*, the local newspaper. Yet, his determination to become a successful businessman drove him to purchase a different newspaper, the Marion *Star*, just one year later. Encouraged by the burgeoning industrial capitalist spirit, and armed with an affable and enthusiastic personality, Harding quickly transformed the dying publication into a powerful, small-town newspaper by developing it as a Republican journal. His success in business would have a permanent impact on his views and understanding of the American economy during an era of industrial growth and change.

In 1891, at the age of 25, Harding married Mrs. Florence Mabel King DeWolfe, a divorcée five years his senior. Generally believed to be a marriage of convenience, the couple had no children though they did share the responsibilities of running the *Star*. His wife's attention to business afforded Harding time for an active social life characterized by drinking and gambling. His illicit personal activities also included a series of affairs, one of which produced an illegitimate child. However, such behavior was kept hidden from the public and did not affect his social standing, or his increasing political power within the ranks of the Ohio Republican party.

Harding's popularity propelled him to the Ohio State Senate, where he served for two years, before being elected lieutenant governor of Ohio in 1904. Despite an unsuccessful run for governor, Harding was elected to the U.S. Senate in 1914 and in 1919, his name was proposed as the Republican nominee for president. Considered a dark-horse candidate, Harding nevertheless put forth the economic creed that had made him successful: "American business is everybody's business." Believing that business would save the country, and promising Americans a "return to normalcy" in the wake of WORLD WAR I, Harding defeated Democratic candidate James Middleton Cox, also of Ohio, to become the 29th president of the United States.

President Harding's rags to riches story and commitment to business made him a very appealing figure to Americans in the post-World War I era. By 1923, the postwar depression seemed to be giving way to a new wave of economic prosperity. His victory had been made possible in large part because of his powerful Republican friends, and he repaid their friendship by appointing many of them to his cabinet—a fateful mistake. Rumors soon circulated that some of his friends and advisors were involved in illicit activities such as graft, bribery, and other malfeasance.

In an attempt to defend his administration against such charges, Harding embarked on a talking tour across the country in the summer of 1923. It was during his travels that he became ill with food poisoning, then suffered a heart attack and died on August 2, 1923 in San Francisco.

BIBLIOGRAPHY. Robert K. Murrary, *The Harding Era: Warren G. Harding and his Administration* (American Political Biography Press, 1969); Andrew Sinclair, *The Available Man: The Life Behind the Masks of Warren Gamliel Harding* (Macmillan, 1965); David Williamson, *Presidents of the United States of America* (Salem House, 1991); *Biography of Harding*, www.whitehouse.gov/history/presidents.

LINDSAY SILVER
BRANDEIS UNIVERSITY

Harrison, William Henry (1773–1841)

THE NINTH PRESIDENT of the UNITED STATES, William Henry Harrison was born in the wealthy Tidewater section of Virginia. His father served in the Continental Congress and was governor of Virginia. In 1791, Harrison began studying at the University of Pennsylvania Medical School. However, when his father died, he could not afford to continue his studies. He received a commission in the army and began a military career.

Harrison fought as an officer in the Indian Wars of the Northwest Territories (present-day Ohio, Indiana, Michigan, Illinois, and Wisconsin). In 1800, President John ADAMS appointed him territorial governor. During the WAR OF 1812, Harrison commanded U.S. forces in the Northwest Territories. Later, Harrison served in the U.S. House of Representatives and Senate, elected from Ohio, and as ambassador to Colombia under President John Quincy ADAMS.

President Andrew JACKSON refused to renew the charter for the Second Bank of the United States, resulting in its termination in 1836. State banks filled the demand for credit and currency, but this was dependent on the financial soundness of the institution that issued the notes. If people lost faith in a bank, there would be a run on the bank to cash in their notes for specie (gold or silver). Those left holding notes when a bank ran out of specie and suspended payments were left with worthless pieces of paper.

During the westward expansion of the 1830s, speculators borrowed money to buy land that they hoped to resell to pioneers moving west. In 1836, the federal government began requiring gold or silver as payment. This caused the contraction of credit as people scrambled for gold and silver to make their land payments. Banks quickly ran out of specie and had to suspend payments. At the same time, a collapse in the price of cotton crippled the south, where many farmers were unable to make mortgage payments. This led to a severe RECESSION, the Panic of 1837, which lasted well into the 1840s.

The Whigs, who had elected only one president so far in the 19th century, were eager to capitalize on the crisis. Henry Clay was the favorite, but his Masonic membership caused opposition from the anti-Masonic wing of the party. Harrison was nominated because he was a man of the people and a war hero: two images that called to mind the popular former President Jackson. Harrison used the nickname "Tippecanoe," a reference to his military victory against the Indians in 1811 and spoke of being born in a log cabin.

The Harrison campaign also supported a higher tariff, which appealed to northern manufacturers. The tariff and a stable financial system were key issues of the campaign. Harrison received only 53 percent of the popular vote, but carried 80 percent of all electoral votes, doing well in all regions of the country.

Harrison never had a chance to do much as president. He contracted pneumonia after giving a long inaugural address in freezing weather, and died 30 days later.

BIBLIOGRAPHY. Reginald Charles McGrane, *The Panic of 1837* (University of Chicago Press, 1924); James McPherson, ed., *To the Best of My Ability* (DK Publishing, 2000); Norma Lois Peterson, *The Presidencies of William Henry Harrison & John Tyler* (University Press of Kansas, 1989).

THOMAS D. JEITSCHKO, PH.D.
MICHIGAN STATE UNIVERSITY

MICHAEL J. TROY, J.D.

Harrod, Sir Roy F. (1900–78)

ANY UNDERSTANDING OF Roy Harrod's theory would be impaired by the belief that he had anything to do with the "Harrod-Domar Growth Theory" bowdlerized by some economics textbooks. Harrrod attempted to create a model of an unstable economy that regularly underwent booms and busts.

His mathematical model derived from the basic identity that savings must equal investment, S = I. Assume that savings is a fixed fraction of income, so s = (S/Y), and divide both sides of the equation by Y. Then take the right-hand side and multiply by (dY/dY) and get (S/Y) = (dY/Y)(I/dY), or s = GC (in Harrod's terms), where G = (dY/Y) is the growth rate of national income and C = (I/dY) is the incremental capital-labor ratio (remember that Investment is the change in the capital stock, so I = dK). So this equation, s = GC, is as much a tautology as S = I.

The theory only enters with some modest behavioral assumptions: if growth is faster than expected, then this can only occur if C is lower than expected. If firms, seeing their desired capital-output ratio decline, respond with more investment, then the system is clearly unstable. An unexpected increase in income growth will increase investment, or vice versa. The economy will not be dynamically stable but will be on a "knife edge" so that chance deviations will set in motion cumulative processes (similar to Knut Wicksell's theories).

Most economists learned about Harrod's work only after WORLD WAR II, and then only in tandem with a paper by Evsey Domar that used similar analytical structures in questions of long-run growth. This vein of business-cycle research was transmogrified into neo-classical growth theory: Robert SOLOW's and almost every modern macroeconomic growth theory can trace roots back to Harrod. (Still growth theorists talk of "Harrod-neutral technological change" that leaves C constant.) Harrod's original essay stimulated an enormous amount of research, following up on his basic point that John Maynard KEYNES' simple model did not take adequate account of the effect of investment on future capacity.

Harrod was an early Keynesian, one of the group of young economists who clustered about the influential man (however Harrod was at Oxford not Keynes' Cambridge). Harrod made other important contributions beyond his dynamic theory: with Joan ROBINSON, he was one of several innovators establishing the concept of "Marginal Revenue" for a firm with market power. Harrod wrote an early biography of Keynes, from the perspective of a young disciple who had proofed early versions of both the *Treatise* and *General Theory*.

BIBLIOGRAPHY. H.P. Brown, "Sir Roy Harrod: A Biographical Memoir," *The Economic Journal* (March, 1980); R.F. Harrod, "An Essay in Dynamic Theory," *The Economic Journal* (March, 1939); R.F. Harrod, *Toward a Dynamic Economics* (St. Martin's Press, 1960); R.F. Harrod, *The Life of John Maynard Keynes* (Augustus Kelley, 1953).

KEVIN R FOSTER, PH.D.
CITY COLLEGE OF NEW YORK

Harsanyi, John (1920–2000)

HUNGARIAN-AMERICAN philosopher, economist, and Nobel Laureate, John Harsanyi was born in Budapest, HUNGARY. He began studies in pharmacy at the University of Budapest in 1937, but was sent to a forced-labor camp during WORLD WAR II. He escaped his captors just before his unit was about to be transferred to a concentration camp in Austria. After the end of the war, Harsanyi re-enrolled at the University of Budapest in 1946 and graduated with a Ph.D in philosophy in 1947. He served at his alma mater as a faculty member until 1948, at which time he was forced to resign for his outspoken criticism of the communist regime.

Harsanyi emigrated to Sydney, AUSTRALIA, in 1950. He obtained an M.A. in economics from the University of Sydney in 1953, and a Ph.D. in economics from Stanford University in 1957 while on a visiting appointment. He served in several academic departments in Australia and the UNITED STATES, before accepting a professorship at the University of California, Berkeley, in 1964.

In his research, Harsanyi showed how strategically behaving individuals can make optimal choices even when their knowledge of each other's objectives is imperfect. He extended GAME THEORY and the methods of predicting non-cooperative games, pioneered by John NASH in the 1950s, to situations of incomplete information. For his path-breaking achievements, Harsanyi was awarded the Bank of Sweden Prize in Economic Sciences in Memory of Alfred Nobel in 1994. He shared the prize with Nash of the United States, and Reinhard SELTEN of Germany.

Harsanyi demonstrated that games of incomplete information can be analyzed by introducing an auxiliary player (nature) who, through chance moves, determines the other player's objectives. If the probabilities of nature's moves are common knowledge among all other players, the techniques of Bayesian statistical inference allow players to make predictions and optimal choices under uncertainty. Harsanyi extended Nash's equilibrium concept to games with chance moves, so that each player's strategies are optimal when taking into account both the uncertainty of the situation and the choices made by the opponents.

Harsanyi published his results on incomplete information games in a series of articles in 1967 and 1968. His work had an immediate and profound impact on the state of economic analysis. Today, Harsanyi's work is the foundation for what is known as Information Economics. Its applications range from the theory of contracts, to the optimal design of auctions, to advice for individuals in bargaining situations and negotiations, to name just a few.

BIBLIOGRAPHY. J.C. Harsanyi, "Autobiographical Essay," The Nobel Foundation (1994); J.C. Harsanyi, "Games with Incomplete Information Played by Bayesian Players," *Management Science* (v.14, 1967–68); The Nobel Foundation, Prize in Economic Sciences Press Release (1994).

TILMAN KLUMPP, PH.D.
INDIANA UNIVERSITY, BLOOMINGTON

Hayek, Friedrich August von (1899–1992)

FELLOW NOBEL LAUREATE Vernon L. SMITH called Friedrich von Hayek the "leading economic thinker of the 20th century." Born in Vienna, Hayek, winner of the 1974 Nobel Prize in Economics, served in the Austro-Hungarian army during the latter part of WORLD WAR I and returned to AUSTRIA in 1918 to begin his studies at the University of Vienna, where he was introduced to the ideas of the AUSTRIAN SCHOOL of economics. Hayek earned two doctorates, in law and political science, and after a year in the UNITED STATES, became director of the Austrian Institute for Business Cycle Research in 1927.

Hayek's analysis of business cycles led him to forecast an impending economic crisis, specifically in the United States. He argued that increases in the money supply sent misleading signals to the market, creating an unsustainable expansion followed inevitably by economic collapse. His lectures on the subject at the London School of Economics (LSE), which were published as *Prices and Production* in 1935, were a great success and Hayek became a professor at LSE.

In 1944, Hayek published *The Road to Serfdom*, which became a surprise bestseller in England and the United States. He warned against the dangers of both FASCISM and SOCIALISM, arguing that state control over the economy led inexorably to totalitarianism, and concluded that "only capitalism makes democracy possible." According to Hayek, "Economic control is not merely control of a sector of human life which can be separated from the rest: It is the control of the means for all of our ends." Hayek published "The Use of Knowledge in Society" in 1945, an article in which he described the price system of competitive markets as a "marvel" that allows society to use its resources efficiently. Market prices, he argued, act to coordinate the separate actions of many different people, providing them with information about how to respond best to economic changes. According to Hayek, "The mere fact that there is one price for any commodity . . . brings about the solution which . . . might have been arrived at by one single mind possessing all the information which is, in fact, dispersed among all the people involved in the process."

Hayek moved to the United States in 1950 and became a professor at the University of Chicago. He returned to Europe in 1962, first as a professor at the University of Freiburg, and later, the University of Salzburg. Hayek received the Nobel Prize for his work on business cycles, the problems of centralized planning, and his analysis of how competitive markets incorporate widely dispersed information. He continued to write and lecture throughout the 1970s and 1980s, and, at the age of 89 published his last great work, *The Fatal Conceit: The Errors of Socialism*.

BIBLIOGRAPHY. Friedrich August von Hayek, *The Fatal Conceit: The Errors of Socialism* (University of Chicago Press, 1988); Friedrich August von Hayek, *The Constitution of Liberty* (University of Chicago Press, 1960); Friedrich August von Hayek, *The Road to Serfdom* (Routledge, 1944); Friedrich August von Hayek, "The Use of Knowledge in Society," *American Economic Review* (1945); Alan O. Ebenstein, *Friedrich Hayek: A Biography* (St. Martin's Press, 2001).

JEFFREY R. GERLACH
COLLEGE OF WILLIAM AND MARY

Hayes, Rutherford B. (1822–93)

THOUGH THE HISTORY of the 19th president is tainted by the controversy surrounding his 1876 election, Rutherford B. Hayes' handling of the Great Railway Strike of 1877 ultimately played an important role in shaping the relationship between capitalistic business and the presidency.

Hayes spent his early life in Ohio as the youngest child of Rutherford and Sophia Birchard Hayes. His father passed away before he was born and his mother was frequently ill, but Hayes nevertheless flourished as a student and a civic leader. Graduating as valedictorian of his class at Kenyon College, he went on to Harvard Law School, and successfully practiced law in Cincinnati, Ohio, until he joined the Union Army. Returning to

Ohio following his army service, Hayes was elected to the House of Representatives and also served three terms as governor of Ohio before being nominated for president on the Republican ticket in 1876.

The presidential election of 1876 remains one of the most controversial elections in American history. The country was still engulfed in Reconstruction and both the Democrats, who opposed the Reconstruction regime, and the Republicans, who supported it, stood widely divided and eager for power. Neither Hayes nor Samuel J. Tilden, the Democratic Party nominee, gained the 185 electoral votes necessary for election.

Despite Tilden's 200,000-vote popular majority, both candidates claimed to have won the electoral college. Congress established an electoral commission consisting of eight Republicans and seven Democrats; the commission voted along party lines and pushed Hayes into the White House. To appease the Democrats, upon entering the White House, Hayes astutely withdrew federal troops from the South, ostensibly ending Reconstruction.

Hayes' previous political experience and even temperament proved to be important assets when he faced the great Railway Strike of 1877. Beginning in West Virginia but quickly spreading to other states, strikers resorted to violence and state militia could not control the discontent.

Although economic indicators, such as the Panic of 1873 that greatly hurt the RAILROADS, might have anticipated such a crisis, the strike represented the first major confrontation between labor and capital. President Hayes responded by issuing a series of proclamations warning strikers against further lawless action. Ultimately, Hayes was compelled to use federal troops to quell the strikers. By using his executive authority against labor interests, Hayes both set the tone for the era of big business and established a precedent for executive intervention in industrial capitalism at the end of the 19th century.

Hayes decided against seeking a second term. He spent the remaining years of his life at Speigel Grove, his elaborate Ohio residence, and died there on January 17, 1893.

BIBLIOGRAPHY. Harry Barnard, *Rutherford B. Hayes and His America* (Russell & Russell, 1954); Kenneth E. Davison, *The Presidency of Rutherford B. Hayes* (Greenwood Publishing Group, 1972); Ari Hoogenboom, *Rutherford B. Hayes: Warrior and President* (University Press of Kansas, 1995); Ari Hoogenboom, *The Presidency of Rutherford B. Hayes* (University Press of Kansas, 1988).

LINDSAY SILVER
BRANDEIS UNIVERSITY

Hazlitt, Henry (1894–1993)

NEVER TRAINED AS an economist, Henry Hazlitt nevertheless goes down in history as the author of one of the best-selling books on economics of all time, *Economics in One Lesson,* first published in 1946. Meant to be a satire, nothing more, *Lessons* derides the government's ill uses of its own economy, but in preaching this message, Hazlitt inadvertently helped set the basic rules mandating government policy spending.

A man of many talents, Hazlitt, throughout his 98 years, was a journalist, literary critic, economist, and philosopher. At an early stage in life he had determined that a lack of formal education was not going to prove a barrier to his success. He wanted to learn, to use what he learned.

Drifting through a series of menial jobs in his youth, Hazlitt eventually decided to be a newspaperman. In 1915, he landed a job as a stenographer with the *Wall Street Journal.* At the same time, and attesting to the brilliance already stirring within him, he had a book published. It was a philosophical retrospect entitled *Thinking as a Science.* He was 21.

Throughout the 1920s, Hazlitt wrote for a number of popular New York newspapers, among them the *Evening Mail,* the *Sun* and the *Evening Post.* He also published a second book, the psychoanalytical *Way to Will Power.* This book, in particular, a deep and sometimes searing analysis of the errors rampant in Freudian psychology, is a tribute to the author who never completed a university education.

At this point, Hazlitt began to earn a number of well-known admirers who found his straight-to-the-point style a refreshing transition from so-much heavy-handed prose from other, more notable writers. One admirer was the British philosopher Bertrand Russell who, for a time, considered writing Hazlitt's biography.

Hired by *Nation* magazine to write hard-hitting essays on an assortment of subjects, Hazlitt stumbled on the subject of American economics, the direction it was taking, the changes, the basic laws of economics affecting the public. The more he researched it, the more convinced he became that government intervention was hurting the national public life. Spurred on by the social evils caused by the 1930s DEPRESSION, Hazlitt began attacking Franklin Delano ROOSEVELT's presidency, particularly his NEW DEAL program. Despite warnings from the pro-Roosevelt *Nation* magazine, Hazlitt's tirades didn't cease. He was fired.

Over the next couple of decades, Hazlitt's left-wing views on the economy brought him in contact with others like him, who respected his openness on any conceivable topic. In the 1930s, he took over as editor of the *American Mercury* magazine whose founder, the critical

H.L. Mencken, called Hazlitt "one of the few economists in human history who could really write." But, much of what he produced was for the *New York Times*, then beginning to take on a radical transformation.

Cooling his tone somewhat, Hazlitt accepted a job with *Newsweek* in the 1940s, writing a widely read and quoted financial column called "Business Tides." Simultaneously, he wrote *Economics in One Lesson*. Soon after, he penned *Will Dollars Save the World*, attacking the post-World War II MARSHALL PLAN.

The 1950s and 1960s saw Hazlitt manifesting other successful literary ventures. While serving as editor of *Freeman* magazine, he compiled the best of his past satire into the analogous *Wisdom of Henry Hazlitt*. As well, he published a resource guide, *The Failure of the New Economics*; a study of psychology, *The Foundations of Morality*; and a novel, *The Great Idea*. The latter relates, in a unique story-telling fashion, the progression of socialism into market economics.

Reaching his 70th birthday in 1964, his work slowed down. Yet his messages remain in many of his works that continue to be regarded by economists as, to quote Ludwig von MISES, "the economic conscience of our country and our nation."

BIBLIOGRAPHY. Henry Hazlitt, *Conquest of Poverty* (Arlington House, 1973); Henry Hazlitt, *Foundation of Morality* (Van Nostrand, 1964); Llewellyn J. Rockwell, "Biography of Henry Hazlitt," Ludwig von Mises Institute, www.mises.org/hazlittbio.

JOSEPH GERINGER

SYED B. HUSSAIN, PH.D.
UNIVERSITY OF WISCONSIN, OSHKOSH

health

IN THE CANONICAL ECONOMIC model of health developed by Michael Grossman (1972), health is a durable capital stock that yields an output of healthy years of life. Individuals are born with an initial endowment of health stock, which depreciates with age but can be increased through investments. Death occurs when the health stock falls below some minimal level.

People demand health because it provides them with utility, either on the extensive margin by increasing lifespan, or on the intensive margin by increasing the quality of a fixed lifespan. On each of these margins, health is valuable both as a consumption good (one is happier when one is alive and healthy) and as an investment good (it determines the amount of time available for market and household production).

In the economic model of health capital, people produce their own health by combining time (for sleep or exercise) with market goods such as pharmaceuticals and food. People would not demand medical care except as inputs to the production of health; for this reason, the demand for medical care is a "derived" demand. This model of health capital has the intriguing feature that individuals both demand and produce health.

This economic model also provides the interesting insight that people to some extent choose the length of their life. When deciding whether to smoke tobacco, drink alcohol, take drugs, eat cholesterol-rich food, skydive, or engage in any risky behavior, individuals weigh the utility benefits of the risky behavior against the utility costs of the behavior in terms of lost length and quality of life.

This is a radically different perspective on health and health behaviors than those that dominate the fields of medicine and public health. Medicine typically studies the role of exogenous factors like genetics, bacteria, and viruses on health and longevity. The public health literature often engages in advocacy; those in the field of public health typically believe that individuals should act to maximize their health. For example, public-health officials frequently issue guidelines stating that a certain activity lowers health, and therefore people should not participate in that activity. In contrast, economists believe that individuals seek to maximize their overall utility. Since health is one determinant, but not the only determinant, of utility, economists accept that people may rationally decide to participate in an activity that lowers their health and shortens their life.

There is a strong, positive correlation between socioeconomic status and health. Education appears to have a stronger correlation with health than any other measure of socioeconomic status, including occupation and income. There are three possible explanations for this correlation:

1. education increases health

2. people with better health invest in more education because they have longer lifetimes over which the investment can pay off

3. unobserved factors (such as genetics or household influences) lead some people to be healthy and well-educated and others to be unhealthy and poorly educated.

Arguments that education increases health can be classified into two categories. The first is that education increases allocative efficiency in the production of health (i.e., better educated people, presumably because they have access to better information, choose a different set of inputs that allows them to produce more health). The second is that education increases productive efficiency

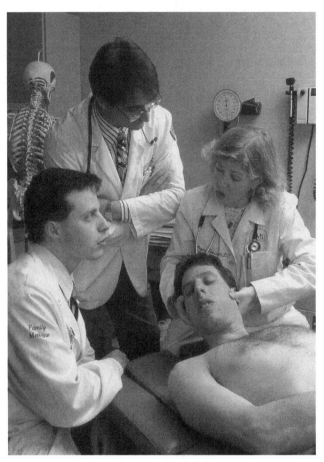

In economics, health is viewed as a capital stock that can yield an output of productive years.

(that is, better-educated people can produce more health using the exact same inputs). The strong correlation between education and health is still not well understood, and it is not yet clear whether education increases allocative efficiency or productive efficiency or has no role in the production of health.

Failures in health care markets. Five factors differentiate the study of health from the study of other GOODS and services. First, consumer demand for health care is a derived demand. Second, there are many EXTERNALITIES in health markets. Third, consumers suffer a severe lack of information in health markets. Consumers must visit physicians (sometimes, multiple physicians) to learn which, if any, health care goods and services they should consume. Fourth, there is considerable uncertainty, both on the part of patients and physicians, about the benefits and costs of various health-care goods and services. Fifth, the person who consumes health-care goods and services often pays little of the total price.

Some of these characteristics are also found in other markets, but health-care markets are special in exhibiting so many potential market failures. The complications in-

herent in markets in which patients consume medical goods and services on the advice of their doctors, with the bill paid by an insurer or the government, has led one commentator to ask how well would restaurants work if one person ordered the meal, a second prepared it, a third ate it, and a fourth person paid for it.

Externalities abound in markets for health care. For example, when a person receives an influenza vaccine, everyone in that person's community enjoys a positive externality, because the spread of the flu has been hindered; every person's risk of contracting the flu has fallen thanks to the inoculation of one individual. The socially optimal quantity of vaccines has been provided when the marginal social costs of the vaccine equal the marginal social benefits. Market failure occurs because when individuals decide whether to get vaccinated, they take into account only their marginal private benefits; they do not tend to take into account any benefits to others. For this reason, consumption of vaccines and other treatments for infectious diseases tend to be lower than what is socially optimal. Governments seek to solve this market failure by subsidizing vaccines and/or requiring them by law.

Consumers face considerable uncertainty about their future health care expenditures. One is always at risk of exogenous health shocks, such as being hit by a car. Because many people are risk-averse, health insurance is very attractive. Health insurance allows people to transfer the financial risk of health shocks to insurance companies. Health insurers are willing to assume this risk because as long as the health shocks of their enrollees are independent, insurers can spread the risk of health shocks over large numbers of enrollees and enjoy considerable confidence about the amount of future claims.

A difficulty for private markets in individual health insurance is that enrollees may have private information about their future health care expenses. People with private knowledge of high future expenses will be more likely to buy insurance that is actuarially fair for the population, whereas people with private knowledge of low future expenses will be less likely to buy such insurance. From the perspective of the insurer, this is adverse selection; the people selecting the insurance are those the insurer least wants to enroll, those who are the most unexpectedly costly.

Such adverse selection results in insurers paying higher-than-expected claims, and then raising premiums in the next period. This can lead to a death spiral in insurance premiums; as they rise, only those with the highest expected health-care costs increasingly buy the insurance, causing costs to rise further and forcing additional premium hikes. At the extreme, only the very sickest are covered and the insurance market disappears.

To alleviate the risk of such adverse selection, the governments of many developed countries sponsor universal health insurance. In such programs, adverse selection is impossible because selection is impossible; participation is mandatory. The UNITED STATES is unusual among developed countries for not offering universal health insurance. Instead, most Americans receive their health insurance through an employer. Specifically, employers sponsor group health insurance. Risks are pooled among the employees, and insurers set premiums based on their previous experience with similar pools of employees. The total cost of the employer-sponsored insurance is divided between employer and employees. To some extent this arrangement lessens the opportunity for adverse selection because to select into a specific health insurance plan one must be hired by an employer sponsoring such a plan. A significant percentage of Americans lack health insurance because they are not covered by employer-provided health insurance and do not qualify for government health insurance programs for the elderly (Medicare) or poor (Medicaid).

The consumer's lack of information introduces a principal-agent problem into markets for health care. The agent is the physician, and the two principals are the patient and the payer (whether a private health insurance company or a government insurance program). The patient wants the physician to provide treatment, prescriptions for drugs, and referrals for specialist care to the extent that the patient's out-of-pocket cost equals the patient's benefit. The interest of the patient differs from that of the payer, who wants to minimize its long-run costs. It has been alleged, with weak empirical support, that physicians are capable of exploiting consumer ignorance by inducing demand, that is, convincing patients to purchase goods or services that they do not need but that enrich the physician.

Some payers have tried to solve the principal-agent problem by giving the physician a fixed per-patient (or capitated) payment, in most cases based on patient health status. A physician is allowed to keep whatever amount is left after treating the patient; this pay structure can align the incentives of the physician with those of the payer.

MORAL HAZARD is another complication in health-care markets. Insured patients do not bear the full financial cost of medical care, which creates an incentive for patients to invest less in avoiding illness, and to consume more medical care, than is socially optimal. The socially optimal consumption of medical care occurs when the marginal social benefits of consumption equal the marginal social costs. The complication is that with insurance, patients' out-of-pocket costs are often far less than the marginal social costs, and as a result, patients have an incentive to consume an amount greater than is socially optimal. Insurers seek to restrain such moral hazard by covering only health care expenditures beyond some large initial deductible, and/or by requiring

patients to pay a certain amount, called a co-payment, for each covered good or service consumed.

Managed care is a popular solution to the information asymmetries and other market failures inherent in health markets. A managed-care organization (e.g., a health-maintenance organization) regulates the relationship between health-care providers and the insured, either by setting conditions under which services will be covered, limiting access of the insured to a set of providers, or creating financial incentives for providers to act in a manner that minimizes long-term costs.

Managed care has spread rapidly in the United States since the early 1980s; today the vast majority of Americans with health insurance are enrolled in a managed-care plan. While managed care developed in the private insurance markets of the United States, the public health insurance programs of other developed countries have adopted methods of managed care. From the perspective of the insured, managed care can be less attractive because it tends to limit the choice of providers. Also, patients fear that the financial incentives for providers to act in a manner that minimizes the long-term costs of the payer will encourage the provider to provide less care than is socially optimal.

However, it has been argued that there is a benefit from managed care's tendency to offer better coverage for preventive services; managed care organizations have an incentive to provide preventive care to the extent that it decreases long-term costs.

Information asymmetries also exist with respect to the efficacy of certain treatments. In the 19th century, hucksters roamed the United States, touting elixirs as cures for a variety of ailments. In the 20th century, most developed countries began to regulate the market for pharmaceuticals, requiring proof from manufacturers that DRUGS were both safe and efficacious before allowing them to be sold. In designing such regulations, governments face a trade-off between requiring lengthy review periods to guarantee efficacy and safety before allowing drugs to be sold, and allowing potentially beneficial drugs to reach market as quickly as possible.

Another strategy governments have used to improve the flow of information to consumers in health markets is to sponsor public health departments, which disseminate information about preventing the spread of communicable disease and the health consequences of certain behaviors.

The RAND Health Insurance Experiment. Much of what economists know about moral hazard and insurance comes from the Health Insurance Experiment (HIE), which was funded by the U.S. Federal Government and conducted by the RAND Corporation, lasted from 1974 to 1982, and has been described as the largest randomized experiment in the history of economics.

Two of the major objectives of the HIE were to determine: 1) the effect of cost-sharing between the insurer and the insured on costs and patient health; 2) the extent to which lower utilization of health care services by enrollees of health maintenance organizations (HMOs) was due to either favorable selection (that is, healthier people joining HMOs) or to HMO enrollees receiving fewer health-care services than people of equal health status in traditional health-insurance plans.

The HIE was a randomized field trial; approximately 2,000 families were assigned to various insurance plans. The insurance plans differed in two dimensions. The first was the co-insurance rate (the fraction of the total health-care bill paid by the insured), which was set at 0 percent (free care), 25 percent, 50 percent, or 95 percent. The second dimension was the maximum out-of-pocket expenditure per year (after which the insurance plan covered 100 percent of charges), which was set at 5 percent, 10 percent, or 15 percent of family income, up to a maximum of $1,000. Some participants were randomized into HMOs that had zero cost-sharing. Seventy percent of the participants were enrolled for three years and the remainder for five years.

The results of the HIE indicate that cost-sharing matters; the more families had to pay out-of-pocket, the fewer services they used. This was true even for services one might consider necessities, such as hospital admissions. An exception, however, was hospital admissions for children: these were not sensitive to out-of-pocket cost. The decreased use of health-care services that accompanied cost-sharing did not result in worse health for the average person. However, those who at time of enrollment were both poor and sick enjoyed health gains if they were randomized into the plan offering completely free care.

The HIE also found that there was no evidence of favorable selection into HMOs; people who voluntarily enrolled in HMOs had similar utilization to those who were randomized into an HMO. Managed care appeared to result in lower utilization; those randomized into an HMO had 39 percent fewer hospital admissions and 28 percent lower estimated expenditures than comparable people randomized into the zero co-payment plan (free care). With the possible exception of those who at time of enrollment were both sick and poor, this reduced service use did not appear to have negative health effects. However, patients randomized into HMOs tended to report lower satisfaction with their health care plan than those randomized into traditional insurance plans.

The findings of the HIE have been tremendously influential in policy circles and the health-insurance industry. The findings generated optimism that managed care could reduce utilization and spending without worsening enrollee health. Moreover, the results confirmed the importance of cost-sharing for insurers and payers seeking to reduce utilization and costs without affecting enrollee health.

Health policy for special populations. Policymakers have shown special interest in the health care provided to three groups in society: children, the elderly, and the disabled. Children are treated as special because early childhood health has been linked to health and welfare throughout later life. Out of a sense of fairness, policymakers often seek to establish a minimum threshold of health for children, to ensure that all citizens have roughly equal opportunity in life. Furthermore, while policymakers often are concerned that adults may seek government health-insurance coverage to avoid paying for insurance out of their own pocket, children are incapable of such calculating behavior. For these reasons, virtually all developed countries guarantee prenatal care for pregnant women and health care for infants.

Policymakers also take special interest in the health of the elderly. The market for health care to the elderly is characterized by the extra complication that some elderly individuals suffer from Alzheimer's disease or dementia, and are not always capable of making rational decisions. This, combined with the fact that individuals are credit-constrained toward the end of their lives, suggests that the elderly are among the most vulnerable in society. A political economy explanation for the interest of policymakers in providing health care to the elderly is that the elderly tend to be a powerful and influential voting bloc. For these reasons, virtually all developed countries guarantee health-insurance coverage to elderly individuals.

Disability is loosely defined as the inability to work for pay because of poor physical or mental health. Disability policies are designed to achieve one or more of the following goals: offset lost earnings through income transfers; require employers to accommodate disabled individuals in the workplace; and retrain disabled individuals for jobs in which their limitations would not prevent employment. In essence, disability benefits represent a social insurance policy; all taxpayers contribute to those unfortunate enough to become disabled. Policymakers, concerned about the incentive to feign disability in order to receive income transfers, typically require physician certification of disability and waiting periods before benefits may be received.

Many of the discussions regarding health policy focus on issues of fairness and equity of access and care. While the tools of economics can be effectively used to assess the efficiency impacts of alternate health-care policies, the discipline of economics is silent on normative questions of equity.

BIBLIOGRAPHY. Michael Grossman, "On the Concept of Health Capital and the Demand for Health," *Journal of Political Economy* (1972); Joseph P. Newhouse and the Insurance Experiment Group, "Free for All?: Lessons from the RAND Health Insurance Experiment," (1993); A. J. Culyer and J. P. Newhouse, eds., *Handbook of Health Economics* (v.1A, 1B, North Holland, 2000).

JOHN CAWLEY, PH.D.
CORNELL UNIVERSITY

Heckman, James (1944–)

LABOR ECONOMIST AND econometrician, James Heckman pioneered the study of the econometric problem of selection. Economists often wish to know the relationships between variables in the population, and because of selection, they are forced by necessity to measure the relationships using samples, which are in some important ways, non-representative of the population.

For example, suppose one wanted to know how age affects WAGES. The problem is that at higher ages many people choose to drop out of the labor force. The people who stay in the labor force are likely those able to earn the highest wages. This is a problem of missing data on wages for certain individuals.

Heckman perceived that this problem of missing data is due to calculated decisions (selection) on the part of the individuals involved. In this example, people decide whether to stay in the labor force based on the costs and benefits. People who calculate that their utility is maximized by working will work, and people who calculate that their utility is maximized by retiring will retire. If one were to naively estimate the effect of age on wages by regressing wages on age for all workers, that calculation would suffer from selection bias, because at high ages, wages are likely only observed for people who have the highest earning potential.

The challenge for the researcher is to find some way to adjust the estimates derived from a select sample to account for the selectivity of the sample. Heckman developed techniques to correct the econometric problems associated with sample selection. Perhaps the most widely used technique created by Heckman is the two-stage procedure dubbed the "Heckit."

In the example given above, the first stage would consist of estimating the probability that an individual works as a function of age and other variables using a sample that includes both people who work and those who do not work. In the second stage, one would estimate wages as a function of age and a function of the estimated probability that the individual works that was calculated in the first stage, using the sample of workers. In essence, the coefficient on age in the naive regression of wages on age suffered from omitted variable bias; Heckman's solution is to add a variable reflecting the probability that the observation appears in the sample.

Heckman has applied these methods to program evaluation, in which one must estimate how government programs have affected individuals when one does not know how the participants would have fared if they had not been enrolled in the program. His techniques have also been widely applied in the study of education, choice of occupation, and job training. His research also spans the econometrics of duration models, with a particular emphasis on the unobserved heterogeneity that causes some people to spend more time unemployed than others.

Heckman was born in Chicago, Illinois. He studied mathematics at Colorado College and earned a Ph.D. in economics from Princeton University. He has served on the faculties of Columbia University, Yale University, and the University of Chicago. In 2000, he was awarded the Bank of Sweden Nobel Prize in Economics "for his development of theory and methods for analyzing selective samples" that "are now standard tools, not only among economists but also among other social scientists."

BIBLIOGRAPHY. James J. Heckman, "Shadow Wages, Market Wages and Labor Supply," *Econometrica* (1974); James J. Heckman, "Sample Selection Bias as a Specification Error," *Econometrica* (1979): James Heckman and Burton Singer, "A Method for Minimizing the Impact of Distributional Assumptions for Duration Data," *Econometrica* (1984): James Heckman and Burton Singer, "The Identifiability of the Proportional Hazard Model," *Review of Economic Studies* (1984): James J. Heckman and Jeffrey Smith, "Assessing the Case for Social Experiments," *Journal of Economic Perspectives* (1995).

JOHN CAWLEY, PH.D.
CORNELL UNIVERSITY

Hecksher, Eli (1879–1952)

A SWEDISH ECONOMIST and a very influential thinker of his time, Eli Hecksher was a prolific writer and had to his credit over a thousand publications. His educational background took him from training under David Davidson at Uppsala University to Gustav Cassel at Stockholm University. Hecksher, however, decided to pursue economic research on his own terms.

Among his publications, Hecksher's work on MERCANTILISM accorded him some notoriety. Originally published in 1931, and later translated into German and then into English in 1934, this work drew a lot of attention, as it presented a case for the origins of mercantilism in the formation of nations in Europe and their expanding influence over the rest of the world. Hecksher presented a case for mercantilist policies as the logical extension of the process of colonization pursued by the European countries.

Hecksher wrote a paper in 1919 titled "The Influence of Foreign Trade on the Distribution of Income." This paper became the basis for the writings of Bertil OHLIN, who went on to receive the Nobel Prize in Economics in 1977. When Hecksher was a Professor at the Stockholm School of Business, Ohlin was his student.

Together Hecksher and Ohlin are credited with explaining how international trade takes place, in a manner that refined trade theories of the 18th and 19th centuries. This theory focused on the ability of a nation to produce a commodity using the most abundant factor of production. Thus, trade between countries would not simply look at the comparative cost of producing commodities, but instead factor the endowment of different countries. A labor-abundant country would produce a commodity that uses labor intensively, and a capital-abundant country would produce a commodity that uses capital intensively. This theory also spawned some of the seminal work of the 20th century, such as Factor Price Equalization by Paul SAMUELSON.

BIBLIOGRAPHY. John J. McCusker, Book Review, www. eh.net/lists/archives/hes; Beth Yarbrough and Robert Yarbrough, *The World Economy: Trade and Finance*; (Dryden, 1997); Michael Todaro and Stephen Smith, *Economic Development* (Addison Wesley, 2002); History of Economic Thought, cepa.newschool.edu.

JAISHANKAR RAMAN, PH.D.
VALPARAISO UNIVERSITY

Hegel, Georg W.F. (1770–1831)

GEORG WILHELM FRIEDRICH HEGEL goes down in history as one of the world's greatest thinkers and philosophers, yet his philosophies are brooding and often meandering juxtapositions of harshness and even darkness. His writings, albeit extremely complex in nature, earned him the title of "Father of the German Idealist School of Thought." This train of thought, generalized, is called the Dialectic Branch of Philosophy.

Author Peter Landry attempts to define Hegel's philosophy in layman's terms. Hegel, says Landry, "departed from the earlier Fichte-Schelling analysis by stating that it was reason that should take over, not your reason or my reason, but the World Reason, Universal Consciousness; an Absolute. This Absolute, while it governs the individual (the Ego) and all the world around the individual (the non-Ego) . . . is synonymous with Reason (Ego) and Reality (non-Ego)."

Hegel's Dialectic Logic stems from this premise. Based on a reasoning-and-disputing approach, it is based in part on Plato's and Socrates' teachings, urging "absolute contraries" in order to find inaccuracies in all arguments. Through various steps including the Theory, then the Antithesis of that Theory, a conclusion or a truth could be arrived at—perhaps by finding the most practical factors and melding them together (or "Synthesizing" them) into a conclusion.

Hegel spent almost his entire adulthood diagnosing the most complex of philosophies and adjusting them to his own rationale and beliefs—the existence of man and his fundamental being; the world that developed through a series of events (or economic stages). For example, he saw mankind as having evolved through four episodes in its history: from subservience (the Oriental Empire), to a more republic-oriented state of the individual (the Greek Empire), to a political subservience (the Roman Empire), and finally to a condition where individual and state become one (the Germanic Empire).

Unwavering and severe, Hegel's views resemble something of a political survival of the fittest. "Since a political unit must act through the wills of individuals," Hegel wrote, "the hero represents the Spirit in its march through history, no matter how unconscious he may be of his mission or how unappreciated his deeds are by his fellow men."

Examining this statement, which is a crux to the Hegelian School, it is not surprising to learn that Adolf Hitler was a devout Hegelian. In Landry's estimation, "If one needs an example of a philosophy which can lead millions of people to ruin, then one need look no further than the philosophy of Hegel."

Hegel was the son of a Stuttgart (GERMANY) civil servant and a mother whose devotion to Protestant piety was unwavering. Both parents encouraged Hegel, in his early years, to study for the clergy but his mind had already become infatuated with the airy and colorful philosophies of Greek and Roman poets. Nevertheless, in 1788, he entered the Tubingen Seminary to please his parents.

At the seminary, Hegel befriended two fellow students who would prove to impact his future direction. One, Friedrich Holderlin, would become a world-famous romantic poet of aesthetic leanings; the other, Friedrich W. von Schelling, would make his mark as one of Germany's luminary philosophers. "These friendships clearly had a major influence on Hegel's philosophical development," explains the *Stanford Encyclopedia of Philosophy*, "and for a while the intellectual lives of the three were closely intertwined."

By the time Hegel received his degree in philosophy and theology from the seminary in 1792, he had already abandoned his pursuit of the ministry. At Tubingen, he had been enraptured by the limitless horizons of philosophy, a field that he felt stretched with no direction, begging (he felt) for some definition—at least some guide-posting on its perimeter to lead others to follow with a compass into the unknown. He moved to Berne, SWITZERLAND, where, for the next nine years, he obsessively threw himself into the deepest recesses of the mysterious subject. During this time, he was forced to tutor an ongoing number of students to allow him funds for lodging and food.

When his father passed away (early 1800), Hegel received a small fortune, which was large enough for him to be able to dismiss his students and concentrate on the cultivation of philosophy.

"Hegel's aim was to set forth a philosophical system so comprehensive that it would encompass the ideas of his predecessors and create a conceptual framework in terms of which both the past and future could be philosophically understood," explains the Encarta Learning and Research Center. "Such an aim would require nothing short of a full account of reality itself." Over the following 30 years of his life, Hegel strove to frame that "reality," what he called the Absolute—to define it, to demonstrate its purpose in nature and history, and to communicate its infiniteness.

The first decade of the 19th century brought Hegel through various stages in not only his advancing independent research, but also in his professional and private life. From 1801 to 1806, he taught and lectured at the University of Jena (Germany), while turning out exhaustive writings on his studies. Much of his findings up to that time were put under one cover when he published *The Phenomenology of Spirit* in 1807. *Spirit* was, simply put, an explanation of what he saw as Reason.

Fleeing the devastation caused by the invading French Army under Napoleon, Hegel fled to the Bavarian Alps. There, in Bamberg, he edited the local newspaper, *Zeitung*. When the war calmed, he relocated to northern Germany, accepting a job as headmaster and philosophy professor at the Nuremberg Preparatory College in 1808. He would remain with the school until 1818, in between marrying, siring four children, and writing another book, *The Science of Logic*.

Actually a series of three books—published respectively in 1812, 1813, and 1816—*Science* refines his statements made earlier in *The Phenomenology of Spirit*. The triad explores his developments on three interrelated doctrines, "Being," "Essence" and "Concept," and is rather a transcendental look at the nature of man.

According to Hegel, "the state is the living God and individuals but passing shadows in which conflict and war are affirmations of the vitality of the state." This pseudo-militaristic philosophy was put to the test in Hegel's native Germany much later in world wars.

In 1818, Hegel accepted the chair of the philosophy department at the famed Heidelberg University, then two years later, took a similar position at the University of Berlin. He compiled the thrust of his knowledge in the compendium, *Encyclopaedia of Philosophical Sciences*, following it up with what would be his final major work, *Elements of the Philosophy of Right*. This, considered by many to be his masterpiece, interweaves the philosophy of law, politics and sociology with the philosophy of history.

Although his life came to an end when he died from a cholera plague at the age of 61, his work continues to be studied today for its efficiency, depth, and diverse views of the human animal.

BIBLIOGRAPHY. Frederick C. Beiser, *The Cambridge Companion to Hegel* (Cambridge University Press, 1993); Peter Landry, "Georg Wilhelm Friedrich Hegel," www.blupete.com; Microsoft Encarta Learning and Research Center Online, www.connect.net; *Stanford Encyclopedia of Philosophy*, www.stanford.edu.

JOSEPH GERINGER

SYED B. HUSSAIN, PH.D.
UNIVERSITY OF WISCONSIN, OSHKOSH

hegemony

FIRST DEVELOPED BY THE Italian Marxist theorist Antonio Gramsci during the late 1920s and 1930s while he was in prison because of his opposition to fascism, the concept of hegemony has enjoyed a vast popularity throughout the 20th century. Coined in his *Prison Notebooks* due to Gramsci's intellectual search for the reasons why the Italian working-class had deserted democracy and yielded to fascism, the term has not remained restricted to political theory but it has been widely applied to a number of cultural fields and disciplines: from history to literary studies, from media to film theory.

Hegemony defines the winning of consent to unequal class relations, which it makes instead appear as natural and fair. Dominant elites in society, including but not limited to the ruling class, maintain their dominance by securing the consent of subordinate groups, such as the working class. This produces a split consciousness in the members of a subordinate group. In Gramsci's words, the "active man-in-the-mass" has one consciousness "which is implicit in his activity and which in reality unites him with all his fellow-workers in the practical transformation of the real world." Yet, at the same time, he holds another consciousness which, "superficially explicit or verbal, . . . he has inherited from the past and uncritically absorbed."

The process of hegemony "holds together a specific social group, it influences moral conduct and the direction of will, with varying efficacy but often powerfully enough to produce a situation in which the contradictory state of consciousness does not permit any action, any decision, or any choice, and produces a condition of moral and political passivity." Hegemony, therefore, does not function mainly by coercion: subordinate groups are dominated through their consensus and collusion thanks to their desire to belong to a social, political, and cultural system.

The central focus of hegemony is not the individual subject but the formation of social movements and their leadership. As Michael Denning has explained, the construction of hegemony is a matter "of participation, as people are mobilized in cultural institutions—schools, churches, sporting events—and in long-term historic projects—waging wars, establishing colonies, gentrifying a city, developing a regional economy." The participation in such a movement depends on how the patterns of loyalty and allegiance are organized, conveying specific cultural practices in a new historical bloc, by offering new values and world visions, such a historical bloc "creates the conditions for a political use or reading of cultural performances and artifacts, the conditions for symbolizing class conflict."

In theorizing the concept of hegemony, Gramsci was clearly concerned to modify the economic determinism typical of Marxist social theory. Class struggle must always involve ideas and ideologies and historical change is brought about by human agency; economic crises in themselves would not be able to subvert capitalism. Gramsci shows that there is a dialectic between the process of PRODUCTION and the activities of consumption.

Hegemony is not exclusive property of the bourgeoisie. The working class can develop its own hegemony as a strategy to control the state by taking into account the interests of other oppressed groups and social forces and finding ways of combining them with its own interests. Working for the formation of a counter-hegemonic discourse implies considering structural change and ideological change as part of the same struggle. The labor process may well be central for the class struggle but it is no less crucial to address the ideological struggle if the masses of the people are to reject their internalized "false consciousness" and come to a consciousness allowing them to question the political and economic assumptions of the ruling elites.

However, this process of consciousness formation requires time and intellectual strengths as people have in-ternalized the assumptions of ideological hegemony: what is happening in society is common sense or the only way of running society. The basic beliefs and value system at the base of capitalist society are seen as either neutral or of general applicability in relation to the class structure of society. In the establishment of a counter-hegemony that can break the hold of the elites over subordinate groups, Gramsci reserved a relevant role to intellectuals. The creation of a mass consciousness was an indispensable premise for the mass participation in the future revolution and, to this effect, that there should be a strong unity between the intellectuals and the population. Critical self-consciousness requires the creation of an intellectual elite as the human mass cannot become independent without organizing itself.

Intellectuals must be "organic" to the masses: they should work out and make coherent the principles and the problems raised by the masses in their activity, thus forming a cultural and social bloc. This unity and mutual dependence is at the core of what Gramsci describes as "the philosophy of practice." It does not tend to leave "the simple [people] in their primitive philosophy of common sense, but rather to lead them to a higher conception of life. If it affirms the need for contact between intellectuals and simple [people] it is not in order to restrict scientific activity and preserve unity at the low level of the masses, but precisely in order to construct an intellectual-moral bloc which can make politically possible the intellectual progress of the mass and not only of small intellectual groups."

Gramsci's concept of hegemony crucially advanced Marxist theory by showing that Karl MARX was inaccurate in assuming that social development always originates form the economic structure and that the revolution could be the result of the spontaneous outburst of revolutionary consciousness among the working class. The usefulness of hegemony, however, is not limited to Marxist theory, alerting us, as it does, to the routine structures of everyday common sense, which work to sustain class domination and tyranny.

BIBLIOGRAPHY. Michael Denning, *The Cultural Front: The Laboring of American Culture in the Twentieth Century* (Verso, 1997); Joseph V. Femia, *Gramsci's Political Thought: Hegemony, Consciousness, and the Revolutionary Process* (Clarendon Press, 1993); Benedetto Fontana, *Hegemony and Power: On the Relation between Gramsci and Machiavelli* (University of Minnesota Press, 1993); Antonio Gramsci, *Selection from the Prison Notebooks* (International Publishers, 1971); Jackson Lears, "The Concept of Cultural Hegemony: Problems and Possibilities," *The American Historical Review* (v.90, 1985); Roger Simon, *Gramsci's Political Thought: An Introduction* (Lawrence and Wishart, 1991).

LUCA PRONO, PH.D.
UNIVERSITY OF NOTTINGHAM, ENGLAND

Hewlett-Packard

IN A GARAGE IN PALO ALTO, California, engineers William Hewlett and David Packard started a company with $538 in 1939. Today, Hewlett-Packard (HP) operates in 120 countries, produces almost 30,000 technology products, and was ranked as the 70th largest company in the world by *Fortune* magazine. Hewlett and Packard first developed testing devices for clients such as Walt Disney, but HP's pioneering products include the oscilloscope, handheld scientific calculators, business computers, and LaserJet printers.

In 1977, chief executive John Young led Hewlett-Packard into the computer age. Young presided over the introduction of HP's early desktop mainframe computers, LaserJets, and personal computers.

Despite a 60 percent share of the laser-printer market, dominance in the ink-jet printer market, a $13-billion valuation, and a great reputation for reliability, HP's revenues dropped in the 1980s, as did those of competitor IBM. Adaptation to the global economy was needed. Young retired and Lewis Platt took over in 1992. A 1984 Cannon partnership led to reaching LaserJet and ink-jet markets globally.

After the death of founder Packard in 1996, Hewlett-Packard paid $1.3 billion to acquire Verifone, a leading manufacturer of credit-card authorization systems and devices. The move marked the full-scale HP entry into the most sacred area of capitalism, its medium of exchange, or money. In 1999, Hewlett-Packard spun off its testing, measurement, and medical technology unit as Agilent Technologies. More recently, HP has merged with Compaq Computers, one of the early leaders in producing clones of IBM PC computers in the 1980s.

HP Labs played a key role in developing the JPEG (Joint Photographic Experts Group) standard for the transfer of digital images over the internet, for instance—the payoff comes in the form of licensing rights to their intellectual property. HP used its background in measurement and standards testing to help develop EISA, or Extended Industry Standard Architecture after 1988. As one of the founding nine technology companies, HP had a strong input into how the standards for future technology integration would look. In the new millennium, HP continues to stir up the market with mergers, spin-offs, and acquisitions.

BIBLIOGRAPHY. www.hp.com; D. Packard, *The HP Way: How Bill Hewlett and I Built Our Company* (HarperBusiness, 1996); D. Zell, *Changing by Design: Organizational Innovation at Hewlett-Packard* (Ilr Press, 1997).

CHRIS HOWELL
RED ROCKS COLLEGE

Hicks, Sir John R. (1904–89)

AWARDED THE 1972 NOBEL PRIZE in Economics, Sir John Richard Hicks pioneered contributions to the general economic EQUILIBRIUM theory and the WELFARE theory. He shared the award with Kenneth J. ARROW.

Hicks' classic work, *Value and Capital* (1939) attests to the economic forces that, in his theory, balance one another rather than merely reflect trends. The content is widely used by public and private sectors and utilities to determine foreign trade, investment policies and prices. "The trail of the eternally eclectic John Hicks is found all over the economic theory," explain economists at New School University. For example, in looking at the role of the earlier-established accelerator theory in affecting growth and income, Hicks concluded that the accelerator theory may induce various fluctuations in the level of output. Using that base as a foundation to subsequent perceptions, he then developed the IS-LM model. This model provides a frame for equilibrium in the economy by looking at equilibrium in the goods and services markets (the IS curve) and equilibrium in the money markets (the LM curve). Where both these markets meet—or are in equilibrium—is the true level of output.

In short, the IS-LM model, which was one of the main components in his winning the Nobel Prize, compares output against rate of interest. This model focuses on the assumptions concerned with investment, savings and supply-and-demand, pinpointing a cross-section where all elements meet.

Aside from winning the Nobel Prize, Hicks was knighted by Queen Elizabeth II in 1964 for his academic contributions as a subject of Great Britain.

Hicks was born in Warwick, England. The son of a columnist on a local newspaper, he grew up in a very erudite way, taught to see the world in an exciting manner, a world offering many possibilities for success. A brilliant student early on, he attended Clifton College from 1917 to 1922, then Balliol College, Oxford, between 1922 and 1926. An expensive education, most of it was made possible through scholarships that he successively earned for his achievements.

Hicks felt that his interests in literature and history—most likely incited by his father's literate background—needed to be addressed. The study of philosophy interested him, as well, so much so that in 1923 he changed his course of study to philosophy, politics and economics. The combining elements of these three subjects were being woven into a new school of focus at Oxford.

After receiving his degree, he accepted a lectureship at the London School of Economics in 1927, simultaneously serving as a labor economist, and conducting research on industrial relations. In 1930, after the London School began a resurgence of new ideas and thoughts

ation. With his wife, he traveled abroad in order to research articles that he eventually wrote on applied economics in developing countries. In 1950, he became a member of the Revenue Allocation Commission in Nigeria, and in 1954 he freelanced as financial consultant to Jamaica.

Besides being a recipient of a host of honors—as fellowship with the British Academy, as a member of the Accedemia del Lincei in Italy, as president of the Royal Economic Society, and many more—Hicks is the author of a large number of additional notable works. Among them are *Taxation and Wealth* (1941), *The Problem of Budgetary Reform* (1949), *A Revision of Demand Theory* (1956) and *Capital and Growth* (1965).

BIBLIOGRAPHY. "Autobiography of Sir John R. Hicks," www.nobel.se/economics; "History of Economic Thought," Department of Economics, www.cepa.newschool.edu; Nobel Prize Internet Archive, www.almaz.com/nobel/economics.

JOSEPH GERINGER

SYED B. HUSSAIN, PH.D.
UNIVERSITY OF WISCONSIN, OSHKOSH

Sir John R. Hicks, son of an erudite writer, who brought new conceptions to economics, such as the IS-LM model.

closer to what Hicks believed, he accepted a full-time teaching position as professor of economics.

With new conceptions of economics occupying his interest, Hicks felt he needed time away from teaching to "put it all together," as he explains in his autobiography. "[When] an opportunity arose for a university lectureship at Cambridge, I took it." At that time, he also introduced his conjectural variations hypothesis as a way of uniting various theories of the imperfect condition syndrome. This theorem was the threshold to the work that would earn him many admirers.

During his Cambridge years (1935–38), Hicks focused on compiling his research findings, readjusting and realigning them, so that by 1939 he published his *Value and Capital.*

Hicks spent the next eight years as professor at the University of Manchester (England), broadening his scope on welfare economics and its association with social accounting. The year 1946 saw him back at Oxford—where he would remain through 1971—first as a research fellow of Nuffield College, then as Drummond Professor of Political Economy, and lastly as a research fellow of All Souls College.

During his latter Oxford years, and after retirement, he wrote on international trade and growth and fluctu-

Hitachi, Ltd.

BEGUN IN 1910 AS A SINGLE mechanic's shop in Tokyo, Hitachi, Ltd. has since risen to become one of the world's largest and most identifiable technology companies. Some 95 years later, now with more than 300,000 employees, it ranks as number 32 on *Fortune* magazine's 2002 list of Global 500 largest companies in the world. The company's values are encompassed in its promise to customers of the new millennium: "Reliability and Speed."

The founder of Hitachi, Ltd., Namihei Odaira, designed the Hitachi trademark logo even before the establishment of the company in 1910. It was his belief that a mark was necessary to win the trust and confidence of the people as a symbol of quality products.

Odaira used the two Chinese characters *hi*, meaning "sun" and *tachi*, meaning "rise" to form the mark by superimposing one character on the other and enclosing them in a circle. The four barbs protruding at the four points of the compass signify the sun's rays. The mark was designed to capture Odaira's vision of a man standing before the rising sun, planning a better future for all.

To meet the ever-changing demands of the times, the corporate structure of Hitachi, in the early 2000s, was undergoing a re-mapping, according to its president and director, Etsuhiko Shoyama. The changes are, he says, "brought about by the rapid pace of the progress of digital technology, information systems technology and network technology."

Hitachi reported revenues of almost $64 billion in 2001, derived from the following seven product and service areas: Information & Telecommunications Systems (i.e., systems integration); Electronic Devices (i.e., medical electronics equipment); Power & Industrial Systems (i.e., nuclear power plants); Digital Media & Consumer Products (i.e., microwave ovens); High Functional Materials & Components (i.e., printed circuit boards); Logistics & Service (i.e., general trading); and Financial Services.

BIBLIOGRAPHY. "2002 Global 500:The World's Largest Corporations," *Fortune* magazine (July, 2002); Hitachi's annual report, www.hitachi.co.jp; Hitachi's "High Technology Products," www.hitachidisplays.com.

JOSEPH GERINGER

SYED B. HUSSAIN, PH.D.
UNIVERSITY OF WISCONSIN, OSHKOSH

Hobson, John Atkinson (1858–1940)

ECONOMIST AND JOURNALIST, the author of more than 40 books, principally on economic and social questions, John Hobson stands in the ranks of British economists of the early 20th century second only to J.M. KEYNES, upon whom he had an important influence. His contemporary reputation, however, rests mainly upon his status as one of the earliest and most significant theorists of IMPERIALISM as a political phenomenon.

Born in Derby in northern England, the son of a provincial newspaper proprietor, Hobson was educated at Oxford University and worked as a schoolteacher and university extension lecturer. His conventional political views were transformed firstly by his exposure to the works of John Ruskin and Herbert Spencer, and subsequently by his membership of the moderate socialist Fabian Society. His involvement in Fabianism led him to the systematic study of political economy, and in 1889 he published his first major work, *The Physiology of Industry*, with A.F. Mummery. This book contained the first systematic exposition of Hobson's "under-consumptionist" thesis, which he was to spend much of his life attempting to defend.

Under-consumptionist theories were by no means new to 19th-century economic thought, but Hobson's was one of the more sophisticated and persuasive examples of the genre. Market economies, he maintained, were not self-regulating as classical political economy had assumed, but tended to result in the accumulation of excessive amounts of capital in the hands of a wealthy elite. This "mal-distribution" of income was the principal cause of slumps, depriving as it did the masses of purchasing power and manufacturers of profitable markets for their goods.

Over-saving and over-investment, in Hobson's view, could best be prevented by state regulation of the economy, in particular by means of redistributive taxation. The transfer of wealth from the richest to the poorest members of society was not only desirable on ethical grounds, but would create a steady source of demand and smooth out oscillations in the trade cycle. The raising of the average standard of living was thus as much in the interests of the well-to-do class as of the working class, especially as it offered the only practical method of avoiding a destructive clash between the classes.

After the Boer War (1899–1902) Hobson extended his under-consumptionist thesis to the field of foreign affairs. In the book for which he is best known, *Imperialism: A Study* (1902), he drew connections between the vast expansion of the British Empire from the 1880s onward and the export of British capital overseas. Because the wealth-monopolizing classes were unable to find profitable investment outlets at home, they increasingly looked to African and Asian lands for suitable opportunities, and applied pressure on the government to annex these territories to protect their assets.

Hobson acknowledged that imperial trade contributed little to national prosperity: It was nonetheless, he contended, highly profitable for the small minority of well-connected investors engaged in it. The costs—in the form of colonial wars, bloated military establishments and legions of unproductive imperial administrators—were borne by the rest of the community, that derived no overall benefit from the possession of empires. Hobson's proposed solution was the same as in the previous instance: the raising of living standards at home to absorb surplus wealth and expand the domestic market.

Hobson's importance lies in a catalyzing influence upon the ideas of others, rather than as the founder of a school of his own. His theory of imperialism, for example, was taken up in 1916 by V.I. LENIN, who used it to explain why the inevitable crisis of capitalism—a notion to which Hobson himself did not subscribe—had failed to occur. Similarly, his insistence on the need to stimulate demand and raise the purchasing power of the masses was echoed by Keynes, who nonetheless rejected Hobson's proposition that over-saving rather than under-investment was to blame for economic depressions. But as a theorist who stressed the interconnectedness of economics, politics, international relations and ethics, Hobson helped to lay the foundations for a more holistic and interdisciplinary approach to social science, an emphasis that has led to a recent revival of interest in his ideas.

BIBLIOGRAPHY. P.J. Cain, *Hobson and Imperialism* (Oxford University Press, 2002); J.A. Hobson, *Imperialism: A Study* (Nisbet, 1902); J.A. Hobson, *Confessions of an Economic Heretic* (George Allen & Unwin, 1938); J. Pheby, ed., *J.A. Hobson After Fifty Years* (St. Martin's Press, 1994). J. Townshend, *J.A. Hobson* (Manchester University Press, 1990).

R.M. DOUGLAS, PH.D.
COLGATE UNIVERSITY

Hodgskin, Thomas (1787–1869)

THOMAS HODGSKIN'S CONTRIBUTIONS to political economy and his influence on socialist and anarchist thought were the subject of renewed interest in the 1990s, not least because they resist a neat classification into any specific school of thought. An associate of Jeremy BENTHAM and James Mill, he influenced an entire generation of progressive and radical thinkers, most notably Karl MARX.

Throughout his life, Hodgskin had been an important advocate for educational reform and especially for the diffusion of practical science among the working class. He edited (with J.C. Robertson) the *Mechanics Magazine,* which was instrumental in launching numerous Mechanics Institutes (first founded in Glasgow in 1806 and London in 1810) in which an inexpensive, modern education could be obtained. Mechanics Institutes quickly opened in several Scottish cities, and by the 1820s, there were many institutes throughout Britain. Hodgskin published *Popular Political Economy* in 1827 based on his lectures at the London Mechanics Institute. In 1824-5, Hodgskin edited *The Chemist* in which he attacked the scientific establishment's exclusion of the working classes from scientific knowledge and education.

Hodgskin's first book was an anarchistic critique of naval discipline (*An Essay on Naval Discipline,* 1813) which he experienced first-hand during the Napoleonic Wars. Following suit with a book on Germany (*Travels in the North of Germany,* 1820), Hodgskin then directed his attention to political economy with what is probably his most well-known work: *Labor Defended Against the Claims of Capital* (1825). It is here that he articulated his critique of capitalism which, together with *Popular Political Economy* (1827), was an important influence on Marx. Furthermore, the latter book has often been considered to be the first textbook of socialist economics.

Hodgskin was certainly a radical and an anti-capitalist, but his views significantly diverge from those of the proto-socialists of the Chartist movement; he did not argue for a classless society and directed his critique at the specific practices of capitalist employment that gave rise to urban squalor. Hodgskin held that economic justice requires political freedom—no dictatorship of the proletariat here—and that both depend on markets unhindered by government intervention. It should be noted, however, that unlike most of today's advocates of LAISSEZ-FAIRE, Hodgskin saw government as intervening on behalf of the capitalists who control it, and not as a check on free markets or a provider of a social safety net. Be that as it may, he must be credited with the extension of classical labor theory-of-value to industrial capitalist labor markets with the concept of exploitation. Marx explicitly used Hodgskin's work in developing his own theory, but "de-ethicized" it by showing that exploitation inevitably arises from the political economic system itself, and not from specific unethical practices of capitalists.

His last book (excluding published lectures and periodicals), *The Natural and Artificial Right of Property Contrasted* (1832), is the key to recasting Hodgskin as an early neo-liberal, but his commitment to liberty and the free market can be traced throughout his texts. While maintaining his concern with unequal exchange between employers and employees, Hodgskin locates the source of the problem in the "artificial" privileges associated with political power as it is applied in the economic sphere. Specifically, he applies the LIBERTARIAN nonaggression principle to argue against economic privileges resulting from government intervention on behalf of well-connected and influential individuals. This allows him (along with John Wade and other so-called Ricardian Socialists) to develop a philosophical position that ethically supports fair exchange while economically supporting free markets and strong property rights.

Hodgskin's commitment to the education of the masses eventually led to his co-authorship (with James Wilson) of THE ECONOMIST periodical from its launch in 1843. Initially published by the Anti-Corn-Law League, the renowned weekly newspaper was the voice of the laissez-faire movement, but soon became an influential voice of classical 19th-century liberal thought in general. In 1857, Hodgskin left *The Economist,* which had probably become, by then, too conservative for him.

BIBLIOGRAPHY. Élie Halévy, *Thomas Hodgskin 1787–1869* (1903, Peter Smith Publications, 1956); David Stack, *The Life and Thought of Thomas Hodgskin, 1787–1869* (Royal Historical Society, 1997); Michael Davis, ed., *Radicalism and Revolution in Britain, 1775–1848* (Palgrave Macmillan, 1999); Noel Thompson, *The Real Rights of Man: Political Economies for the Working Class, 1775–1850* (Pluto Press, 1998); Marx Karl, *The Grundrisse* (Notebook VI, 1858,

1939), *Theories of Surplus Value* (Ch. III, 1863), & *Capital* (Vol. II, Ch. XIII, 1885); E.K. Hunt, "Value Theory in the Writings of the Classical Economists, Thomas Hodgskin, and Karl Marx," *History of Political Economy* (Fall, 1977); J.A. Jaffe, "The Origins of Thomas Hodgskin's Critique of Political Economy," *History of Political Economy* (Fall, 1995).

BENJAMIN BALAK, PH.D.
ROLLINS COLLEGE

Home Depot

WHEN BERNARD MARCUS, Arthur Blank, and Ronald Brill found themselves unemployed from Handy Dan's home center, their creative solution was to do what most cut-rate retail operations, like their former employer, could not do.

They would appeal to the majority of the building-supply industry's buyers by offering more than double the 10,000 different items normally sold, and knowledgeable, accessible salespeople who would take the mystery out of how to use the products. This concept allowed the three men to acquire the financing necessary to open the first Home Depot outlets in Atlanta, Georgia, and eventually become the largest home-center retailer in the UNITED STATES, ranking as the 46th-largest company in the world by *Fortune* magazine in 2002. Home Depot was incorporated in 1978.

Creative customer amenities, plumbers and electricians on staff, and contractors giving workshops led to large profits; however, in the 1980s, attempts to expand into new areas brought an increase in the cost of sales that cut profits, and sent stock prices plummeting significantly.

Marcus shifted to a more conservative approach, emphasizing reducing existing debts with a stock offering of 2.99 million shares, the build-up of existing markets rather than expansion to new areas, and the development of a satellite data-communications network to link existing stores together.

The chain's ability to more accurately assess market changes led to its continued success. By the 1990s, it added 75 stores in the northeast to its operations in 19 states, and by 2000 it had over 1,300 stores. In 2002, Home Depot reported sales of $53.5 billion, ranking it as the 46th largest company in the world.

BIBLIOGRAPHY. Ron Zemka and Dick Schaaf, *The Service Edge: 101 Companies that Profit from Customer Care* (Penguin, 1990); Chris Roush, *Inside Home Depot* (McGraw-Hill, 1999); Lisa Gibbs, *Money* (March, 2002).

CRISTINA ZACCARINI, PH.D.
ADELPHI UNIVERSITY

homo economicus

TRANSLATED INTO ENGLISH AS "economic man," homo economicus is the name given to the abstract concept of the human being who behaves in ways typical of mainstream economic models. According to these mainstream models, human actions and choices are motivated solely by the pursuit of one's own self-interest, and are selected optimally to maximize one's own level of satisfaction, or utility.

The expression homo economicus first appeared in 1909 in the writings of Vilfredo Pareto. Weighing in on a contemporary debate about the proper approach to the study of social science, Pareto proposed that specialized social sciences such as economics should develop by focusing on abstractions from the real phenomena that they investigated.

While the actions of real humans reflected varied motives, including economic, moral, and religious, the study of economics, or ethics, or religion, should concern themselves with abstractions (homo economicus, homo ethicus, or homo religious) whose behavior reflects only the motives of critical interest to the relevant social science. Just what were the economic motives that Pareto refers to? And how did they differ from moral motives, if at all?

Pareto's concept of homo economicus reflected a more-than-a-century long debate over the subject matter of economics and the ethical foundations of economic behavior. In the course of that debate, philosophers and economists struggled to provide a satisfactory account of how selfishness and moral principles motivated human behavior. Thus, in his book on the Theory of Moral Sentiments, Adam SMITH recognized the power of selfishness, but made sure to add that:

> How selfish soever man may be supposed, there are evidently some principles in his nature, which interest him in the fortune of others, and render their happiness necessary to him, though he derives nothing from it except the pleasure of seeing it.

These principles, referred to as "sympathy," tempered Man's hedonistic pursuit of personal happiness and pleasure, a central aspect of utilitarian philosophy. Its recognized father, Jeremy BENTHAM, proposed the principle of utility according to which human behavior's "only object is to seek pleasure and to shun pain," feelings that could be associated with behavior in accordance with morals and codes of conduct.

While accepting the principle of utility, later economists aimed at separating the study of political economy from concerns about the morality of human behavior. Thus, Stanley JEVONS, a pioneer of contemporary microeconomic theory, argued that the pursuit of utility was driven either by higher motives (responding to mental and moral feelings) or by lower motives (responding to the desire for physical objects). The latter should be the exclusive concern of economics because their intensity had a critical and quantifiable influence on the determination of prices.

Alfred MARSHALL shared Jevons' view that economics should concern itself with those aspects of behavior resulting from motives whose intensity could at least indirectly be measured. Unlike Jevons, however, Marshall identified the scope of economics in the normal actions of humans whether dictated by higher or lower motives, a distinction that he thought to be of no consequence from the viewpoint of economics. Marshall was also critical of the emerging characterization of homo economicus as behaving in accordance with rational calculations of utility, arguing that "people do not weigh beforehand the results of every action, whether the impulses to it come from their higher nature or their lower."

Subsequent development leaned precisely toward the abstract view of human behavior as self-interested, materialistic, and perfectly rational. While Pareto laid scorn on simplistic attempts to understand concrete phenomena, as if the actions of real humans were solely driven by their economic motivations, later economists such as Lionel Robbins, Milton FRIEDMAN, or Gary BECKER, have provided different, and on the whole, positive assessments of the usefulness of the concept of homo economicus in economic theorizing. In contrast with Pareto's concern about defining narrow boundaries for its intellectual habitat, homo economicus has spread to an increasingly broad range of topics in the social sciences. To mention but a few, homo economicus has been adopted as a model of individual behavior in the study of political processes, and in the development of GAME THEORY and its application to the social sciences.

This record of success notwithstanding, homo economicus has been the focus of intense criticism and controversy. A growing contingent of economists has denounced the lack of moral bearings in economic discussions of human behavior, describing homo economicus as a "hedonistic sociopath."

Herbert SIMON has been perhaps the most influential critic of the assumption of perfect rationality and, at least since the 1960s, homo economicus has been under fire from a growing body of literature in cognitive psychology, associated with Amos Tverski and Daniel KAHNEMAN, that emphasizes the role of heuristics in human problem-solving and the resulting failures of rationality. While several of these critics of homo economicus have been the recipients of the Nobel Prize in economics, the demise of homo economicus is yet to come.

BIBLIOGRAPHY. Adam Smith, *The Theory of Moral Sentiments* (1790, Prometheus Books, 2000); Jeremy Bentham, *The Theory of Legislation* (1802, Prometheus Books, 1988); Stanley Jevons, *The Theory of Political Economy* (Transaction Publishing, 1911); Alfred Marshall, *Principles of Economics* (Prometheus Books, 1920); Vilfredo Pareto, *Manuel d' Economie Politique* (AMS Press, 1904).

ROBERTO MAZZOLENI, PH.D.
HOFSTRA UNIVERSITY

Honda Motor Company, Ltd.

HONDA HAS LONG PURSUED QUALITY through customer-convenient products. Since 1948, when it built only bicycles, it has developed into a mammoth industry leader of nearly 200,000 employees who produce technologies for a diverse marketplace. The company concentrates on products with a strong public demand—from small utility engines to sports cars. From its 300 subsidiaries throughout the world (including its native Japan) spring major products that include small-sized and mini-automobiles, motorcycles and motorbikes, and power products such as tractors, hedge trimmers, and snow removal equipment.

Some 110 manufacturing facilities in 31 countries produce the products that serve 11 million customers each year. Major plants are located throughout Japan, Africa, Asia, the Caribbean, Europe, the Middle East, North and South America, and Australia. Of its vast product line, its automobile output has become the most visible and identifiable on the streets of the world, from the Honda Overview to the Honda Accord to the Honda S2000. The Honda "H" is one of the automotive industry's most familiar logos.

While its assembly lines roll all over the world, Honda also actively pursues an image in the community market—to be a good corporate citizen by focusing on safety standards and environmental issues. For instance, Honda's "Green Factories" focus on carbon-dioxide reduction and fuel efficiency.

Honda was ranked number 41 on *Fortune* magazine's 2002 Global 500 list of the largest companies of the world, with revenues of $58 billion.

BIBLIOGRAPHY. "Global 500: The World's Largest Companies," *Fortune* (July, 2002); "Honda Motor Corporate Profile," www.honda.com; "Honda Motor" www.world.honda.com.

JOSEPH GERINGER

SYED B. HUSAIN, PH.D.
UNIVERSITY OF WISCONSIN, OSKKOSH

Honduras

PART OF SPAIN'S VAST EMPIRE in the New World, Honduras became an independent nation in 1821. Located in Central America, Honduras borders the Caribbean Sea between Guatemala and Nicaragua, and the Pacific Ocean between El Salvador and Nicaragua. After two-and-a-half decades of mostly military rule, a freely elected democratic constitutional republic came to power in 1982. During the 1980s, Honduras proved a haven for anti-Sandinista contras fighting the Marxist Nicaraguan government and an ally to Salvadoran government forces fighting against leftist guerrillas. It is one of the poorest and least developed countries in Latin America with an economy based on agriculture, mainly bananas and coffee.

Honduras depends on world prices for the exportation of bananas, leaving the country at the mercy of market fluctuations. Hondurans are banking on expanded trade privileges under the Enhanced Caribbean Basin Initiative and on debt relief under the Heavily Indebted Poor Countries (HIPC) initiative. Honduras lacks abundant natural resources and its manufacturing sector has not yet developed beyond simple textiles. In early 2003, Honduras was still coping with the catastrophic effects of 1998's Hurricane Mitch that caused $3 billion in damage.

Honduras is a trans-shipment point for illegal drugs and narcotics and an illicit producer of cannabis, cultivated on small plots and used principally for local consumption. Corruption and bribery are cited by international agencies as major problems facing the Honduran government. In addition, there is expanding deforestation as a result of logging and the clearing of land for agricultural purposes. There has been uncontrolled development and improper land-use practices, such as farming of marginal lands, and mining activities, leading to further land degradation and soil erosion.

With a population of approximately 6.5 million people, Honduras had a GROSS DOMESTIC PRODUCT (GDP) of $17 billion in 2001.

BIBLIOGRAPHY. The Department of State Background Note, www.state.gov; *CIA World Factbook* (2002); "Honduras, A Country Study," The Library of Congress, lcweb2.loc.gov.

LINDA L. PETROU, PH.D.
HIGH POINT UNIVERSITY

Hong Kong

A POWERHOUSE OF capitalist enterprise under British rule until July 1997, when Hong Kong reverted to Chinese control, the territory has remained capitalistic (if not as democratic) under CHINA's communist party direction. China has promised that, under its "one country, two systems" formula, China's socialist economic system will not be imposed on Hong Kong.

In 2003, having managed to rise from a two-year period of economic doldrums, Hong Kong's free-market economy improved—but not to the point that it might be called stable. Moving into a new millennium, problems persist; the economy is a dichotomy of good figures and bad.

Hong Kong was one of the first east Asian territories to experience explosive economic growth and its consequences in the ASIAN FINANCIAL CRISIS, due to a strong dependence on international trade. Hong Kong's per capita GROSS DOMESTIC PRODUCT (GDP) growth, before 1998, averaged 5 percent, peaking between the years 1989 and 1997. With the fallout of the Asian Financial Crisis, 1998 saw Hong Kong's economy hard hit, with GDP tumbling 5 percent. But by 2000, GDP had risen 10 percent; five percent in 2001. Yet, with a slow global economy in the early 2000s, Hong Kong carries a 7.5 percent unemployment rate.

The majority of Hong Kong's industry is in electronics, textiles and garments, printing, publishing, machinery, fabricated metal goods, plastics, and watches and jewelry.

While it is argued that the economy of pre-China Hong Kong was more stable, many determined Chinese entrepreneurs would not agree.

MariMari, an Asian-based travel company that monitors the region's economies, writes in its report that, "Hong Kong's business sector was [once] an arena for British companies like Jardine Matheson, Wheelock Marden, Hutchison Whampoa and the Swire Group. Since then, enterprising Chinese groups with investments in shipping, property, and the textile industry have risen to compete with some of the British-founded concerns."

Chinese counterparts have demonstrated a competitive nature just as strong, if not more aggressive, than the British capitalists who preceded them. Because of the present "Chinese connection," China dominates Hong Kong's trade in merchandise at 40 percent of total trade. Behind JAPAN and the UNITED STATES, Hong Kong is China's third largest trading partner.

China's official policies for Hong Kong include low taxation, free and fair market competition, an orthodox legal and financial framework, a fully convertible and secure currency, an efficient network of transport and communication, a skilled workforce (that includes an enterprising spirit), a large degree of internationalization, and cultural openness. "The private sector deals with business decisions and is usually left intact by the government," reports MariMari. "The taxation system is simple, a corporate tax rate at 16.5 percent."

Supporting the organized corporate/business structure are financial institutions: Hong Kong is the world's fifth largest banking center, formulating itself as a major international trade and financial arena. The territory impressively houses 80 of the world's top 100 banking corporations. Links between Hong Kong and mainland China-based banks and financial institutions have been slowly but surely solidifying. The Bank of China is currently the second-largest banking group in Hong Kong, behind the British-owned Hong Kong Bank.

James E. Thompson, chairman of the American Chamber of Commerce in Hong Kong, remains economically optimistic. He told the Xinhua News Agency he sees the economic integration of Hong Kong and the Chinese mainland as an opportunity for expanded growth. "Actually," he said, "one can see that the integration process has taken a life of its own. All the partners in the process start to look for better ways to work together for their common interests."

The Hong Kong Trade Development Council agrees with Thompson's predictions for eventual recovery if exportation can succeed. The inconsistent ratios of consumer spending should not regulate the output, explains the Council. The real matter is productivity—how good or how bad, how successful or unsuccessful.

Economist Alex Leonardo, a writer for the *Hong Kong Voice of Democracy*, explains, "If productivity in manufacturing or services keeps pace with rising business costs (the result will be) profitable returns . . . If Hong Kong's economic woes are due to a lack in productivity to justify or sustain high operating costs, then the way to return to market equilibrium will be through both productivity improvement and asset deflation."

BIBLIOGRAPHY. Hong Kong Trade Development Council, "Economy Moving Toward Gradual Recovery" and "Hong Kong Economic Outlook for 2003: Muddling Through to Recovery," www.tdctrade.com; Alex Leonardo, "The Fundamental Weakness of the Hong Kong Economy," *Hong Kong Voice of Democracy* (April 5, 2002); MariMari, "Economy of Hong Kong," www.marimari.com; "Hong Kong Economy to Rebound in 2003," www.china.org.

JOSEPH GERINGER

SYED B. HUSSAIN, PH.D.
UNIVERSITY OF WISCONSIN, OSHKOSH

Hoover, Herbert (1874–1964)

THE 31ST PRESIDENT of the UNITED STATES, Herbert Hoover is remembered as one of the least effective and least popular executives. But, Hoover's legacy may be as much a product of historical circumstances as it is a reflection of his inadequacies as president.

In office at the onset of the Great DEPRESSION, Hoover's commitment to 19th-century economic ideals of efficiency, enterprise, opportunity, individualism, substantial laissez-faire, personal success, and material welfare made him ill-equipped to handle the financial crisis that swept the country following the STOCK MARKET crash in 1929. Although his business acumen and firm beliefs had made him both a self-made success and a well-liked American figure, his social and economic philosophy hampered his ability to provide essential leadership and relief as the country endured unprecedented financial hardship.

Hoover was born in West Branch, Iowa, to Jesse Clark Hoover and his wife Hulda Randall Minthorn. Hoover would become the first president to be born west of the Mississippi River. His father passed away in 1880, and his mother died less than three years later leaving Hoover an orphan at the age of 9. Hoover and his siblings lived briefly with other relatives in Iowa before moving to Oregon to live with their mother's brother, Dr. John Minthorn. Dr. Minthorn had amassed a fortune though the Northwestern land boom and Hoover enjoyed his first forays into business by working as an office boy for his uncle.

Educated in the local Oregon schools, Hoover was later encouraged to apply to Stanford University, a then-new institution dedicated to providing higher education to residents on the west coast. Once at Stanford, Hoover excelled as a student of mathematics and the sciences. In 1895, he graduated from Stanford as a member of the university's first graduating class.

Following graduation, Hoover took a job in a mine near Nevada City. In a short time, he had advanced his career to hold more responsible positions assisting prominent western engineers. As the mining industry expanded into national and international markets, Hoover made a career for himself as an engineer and international businessman. By the time he was 40, he had become a multimillionaire and was the director of engineering companies in several countries around the world. By the early 20th century, Hoover's self-made success had imbued him with an appreciation of and commitment to the ideals of American capitalism and individual enterprise.

Early political career. Hoover achieved international fame and recognition at the outbreak of WORLD WAR I in 1914. A Quaker dedicated to humanitarianism, Hoover initiated a massive undertaking of war relief by providing food, clothing, and shelter to thousands of war refugees. When the United States joined the war three years later, Hoover's reputation preceded him and President Woodrow WILSON placed him in charge of food distribution both in the United States and abroad. Wilson continued to seek counsel from Hoover during the peace negotiations. The two men shared a commitment to American liberal capitalism and thus had the same vision for a reconstructed European economy. Hoover's position as one of Wilson's economic advisors during the Versailles peace conference made him into a prominent political figure.

Although Hoover initially had no strong party affiliation, by 1920, he announced that he would be seeking the Republican nomination for president. Hoover lost the Republican nomination to Warren G. HARDING but he remained a powerful personality within the ranks of the Republican Party. When Harding won the presidency he appointed Hoover as the secretary of commerce, a position Hoover would continue to hold through the subsequent Calvin COOLIDGE administration.

During his tenure as commerce secretary, Hoover's popularity and fame continued to rise. The 1920s were an era of big business, and Hoover was able to strike an important political balance between the interests of business leaders and consumers. He also encouraged greater investments and trade abroad in an attempt to increase American economic opportunities in foreign markets. Hoover believed that America's emergence as a leading world power was due to the American economic creed of free enterprise and "rugged individualism." He believed that government interference in business impinged on personal liberty and progress, and argued that the government's role in the economy should be strictly limited to levying high tariffs and low taxes, and also maintaining a balanced budget. The flourishing economic conditions of the "Roaring 1920s" solidified Hoover's economic beliefs as he advanced further into the political foreground.

Presidency and the Great Depression. At the 1928 Republican National Convention in Kansas City, Missouri, Hoover was the clear nominee. Running against Democrat Alfred E. Smith, the first Roman Catholic to run for the office, Hoover won an easy victory and was inaugurated on March 4, 1929. Just over six months later, in October 1929, the values of the stock market fell abruptly. This crash represented the beginning of the Great Depression, a period in which levels of production, prices, profits, employment, and wages declined so dramatically that Americans were quickly plunged into a period of economic despair.

When the nation entered the Depression, Hoover believed that the economy was basically sound and would eventually recover, as it had from previous depressions and recessions, through the naturally correcting mechanisms of the American system of capitalism.

Nevertheless, to halt the depression, Hoover took some limited initiatives. He requested business leaders to voluntarily maintain employment, wage scales, and capital investment; however, faced by falling prices, production, and profits, businesses were unable to do so—rather, companies were trying to avert bankruptcy. Economic conditions continued to worsen and in the 1930 congressional elections, the Democratic Party made huge gains in the face of Hoover's declining popularity.

Going against his economic principles, Hoover tried to take limited action to alleviate the failing economy. He secured an increase in appropriations for a limited federal public works program and he also tried to stimulate the economy through increased government spending. Then, in December, 1931, Hoover requested that Congress create the Reconstruction Finance Corporation. Known as the RFC, the institution was meant to provide federal loans to banks, life insurance companies, railroads, and other businesses in financial trouble. Hoover further tried to alleviate the country's economic problems through domestic legislation. In 1929, the passage of the Agricultural Marketing Act was an attempt to raise farm prices by establishing a Federal Farm Board with funds to purchase surplus produce. And the Hawley-Smoot Tariff, passed in 1930, raised tariffs to their highest levels. However, Hoover's efforts proved inadequate to stop the Depression, which reached its lowest depth in the years 1932 and 1933.

Hoover's failure to implement relief measures was a reflection of his personal opposition to government intervention in the economy. For example, he opposed the proposals for direct federal relief to unemployed workers; he was against such government handouts because they were in direct conflict with his belief in "rugged individualism." He also rejected the request of unemployed veterans for immediate payment of their World War I bonuses (not due until 1945). Known as the Bonus March of 1932, the Veterans' request of their bonuses caused trouble for Hoover and exacerbated his relationship with veterans, who had been staunch supporters of him just three years earlier.

Hoover ultimately ordered the U.S. Army to remove groups of veterans from the Anacostia neighborhoods of Washington, D.C., where they had gathered to pressure the government for their bonuses. Hoover's seeming insensitivity made him a target for thousands of suffering Americans, searching to blame for their frustrations. But even as the country continued to suffer desperate economic conditions, Hoover remained faithful that the economy would recover and that "prosperity was right around the corner."

Although some of his greatest personal successes had come through his international dealings, as president, Hoover's forays into foreign affairs were nearly as unsuccessful as his domestic policies. At the 1930 London Naval Conference, the United States, England, and

JAPAN agreed to continue limiting the size of their navies for five years. One year later, the Japanese government invaded the Chinese northern province of Manchuria, breaking its pledge to resist imperialist impulses and avoid war in east Asia. Hoover's secretary of state, Henry L. Stimson, informed Japan that the United States would not recognize the Japanese seizure of Manchuria, or any of other coerced acquisition of land. This policy was known as the Hoover-Stimson doctrine and was viewed unfavorably as an ineffective measure to protect American security interests in Asia.

Additionally, in the Western Hemisphere, Hoover refused to intervene in Latin America to protect American economic interests, thus rejecting dollar diplomacy, or the offer of full military and diplomatic support to American business interests in the Caribbean and Latin America. Consistent with Hoover's lack of diplomatic support in Latin America, in 1933, he withdrew American marines from Nicaragua.

During Hoover's four years in office, unemployment increased to 13 million people, nearly 25 percent of the American workforce. The high increase in unemployment was mirrored by the decline in business production, hurting huge American industries, such as steel, but also small businesses and family farms. Hunger and homelessness rose to all-time-high levels. Because of the problems that plagued Americans, there were instances of rioting and violence. However, Americans, in general, remained faithful to the country's traditions and patiently awaited the presidential election of 1932.

Although the country blamed Hoover for the depression, the Republican Party re-nominated him at the convention in 1932. His Democratic opponent was the governor of New York, Franklin Delano ROOSEVELT. The two men stood in direct opposition to each other over economic issues: While Roosevelt believed that it was the government's duty to intervene in the American economy, Hoover remained firm in his belief that the government's proper role in the economy should be a very limited one.

Although Hoover's vision of the economy had served him well, the years of Depression had rendered obsolete his commitment to non-government action. The American people were ready for a change in government and in economic philosophy and they elected Roosevelt in an overwhelming victory. The Democrats also achieved a substantial majority in both houses of Congress. Thus began the era of the NEW DEAL, a period of great transformation for the American political tradition.

Hoover enjoyed the longest post-presidential career in American history thus far. He left the White House in 1932 and lived outside of the public eye for the following 31 years. Over the years, he was able to earn respect for his conservative views. The government called upon him for advice on more than one occasion and he willingly provided it. He wrote books, chaired a variety of commissions, and worked to restore his reputation as a worthy and venerable American statesman.

Although he would never enjoy the popularity that had ushered him into the White House in the late 1920s, when Hoover died on October 20, 1964, at the age of 90, his body lay in the U.S. Capital Rotunda before burial. He was remembered as a man of high integrity whose commitment to his ideals and beliefs were as much his weaknesses as they were his strengths. Hoover's presidency is not likely to ever be regarded favorably by historians and economists, but in the decades following the Great Depression and World War II era, some experts began to assess and understand Hoover as a product of an economic doctrine that proved incompatible with the circumstances surrounding his administration and the new era.

BIBLIOGRAPHY. Kendrick A. Clements, *Hoover, Conservation and Consumerism* (University Press of Kansas, 2000); Richard Hofstader, *The American Political Tradition and the Men Who Made It* (Vintage, 1989); James M. McPherson, ed., *To the Best of My Ability: The American Presidents* (Dorling Kindersley, 2000); George H. Nash, *The Life of Herbert Hoover* (W.W. Norton, 1983); Harris Gaylord Warren, *Herbert Hoover and The Great Depression* (Oxford University Press, 1959); David Williamson, *Debrett's Presidents of the United States of America* (Salem House, 1989).

LINDSAY SILVER
BRANDEIS UNIVERSITY

housing

IN THE ECONOMIC HISTORY of American capitalism, few industries play as central a role as housing. American capitalism is an economic system with private OWNERSHIP of LAND and CAPITAL, an individual's right to his or her own labor, and the existence of competitive markets that determine prices and quantities for goods, services, and for factors of production (land, raw materials, labor and capital). It is often defined as free enterprise, or LAISSEZ-FAIRE, describing an economy in which government plays a limited role. Until the Great DEPRESSION of the 1930s, housing construction was a local activity and the federal government adopted a laissez-faire policy. But by the Depression, the laissez-faire policy was rejected in favor of an interventionist approach. After the 1930s, the U.S. federal government used housing policy to address social problems of postwar America. This new approach significantly impacted the structure of the 21st-century housing market.

The nature of the market. Before discussing housing in specific periods, it is important to understand the nature of the housing market. Builders generally tend to extol Adam SMITH's philosophy of production for progress and the benefits of hard work. In housing, the greatest advances have always been the result of inventiveness, research, enterprise, and a favorable financial climate. Public housing has usually failed, while private building has produced wanted homes, aided by federal financial agencies such as the Federal Housing Administration (FHA), Veterans Administration (VA) and quasi-government agencies such as Federal Home Loan Bank (FHLB), FANNIE MAE and Freddie Mac.

The actual construction of houses is carried on in thousands of isolated sites or on small lots in and around more than 20,000 towns and small communities, as well as in an infinite number of scattered locations in suburbia, exurbia, and rural areas. The result of this vast dispersion of labor, materials, and land has been to discourage large-scale production. Home building is a profession of individuals. Anyone with energy, initiative, and a small amount of expertise can get ahead, or as often happens, go broke. Many builders get started by building one house—if it sells at a profit, they build another, if not, they sometimes move in. The housing industry testifies to the strength of a private enterprise system that allows housing to function as independently as it does.

The housing industry is one of the last places where a small entrepreneur, a carpenter, a bricklayer, or a gifted college student can start from nowhere and become great. From 1880 to 1990, these individual homebuilders produced approximately 102 million homes, whether single-family homes or multifamily apartment complexes.

Housing history. Despite an extended depression in the 1890s and later short recessions, the "pre-modern" era lasting from 1880 to 1916 was generally an era of rapid economic and urban growth, and heavy immigration in which the United States emerged as the world's leading industrial nation. Important technological innovations were introduced during this era that directly impacted the housing market, including improved building techniques, the street car, the automobile and the generation of electric power. These developments all contributed to a relatively high and stable level of housing production with minimal direct government involvement.

By 1916, about 11 million dwelling units had been added to non-farm housing stock since 1880. The quality of the housing stock was substantially better in 1916 than in 1880, particularly in the cities. From 1880 to 1916, there was an estimated increase of 4.5 million units. The ratio of homeownership went up from a roughly esti-

mated 36 percent to 40 percent. While this may seem like a relatively small increase in the ratio over a full generation, it should be kept in mind that the country had absorbed a massive inflow of poor immigrants; despite their economic progress most families still could not afford to own their own homes. Mortgage credit was limited compared with later periods.

The period from 1880 to 1916 incorporated the Progressive Era, and housing reform was an integral part of this movement, with special emphasis on the elimination of tenement houses, which crowded the land and lacked proper light, ventilation, fire protection, and rudimentary sanitary facilities. Commercial builders speculatively built tenements for low-income renters at an earlier time during strong population growth and rising land values. Enactment of building and housing codes specifying minimum standards for both new and existing construction was the principle objective of this "restrictive" legislation. Enforcement of the codes was reasonably effective with regard to new construction, one result of which was to raise the cost of new housing beyond the reach of poor families. Enforcement of existing-housing regulations was less vigorous, partly because requiring strict compliance, even where feasible, would make minimum housing prohibitively expensive.

The second or "transition" period in housing history begins in 1917 and ends in 1956. During the transition period, housing production was very uneven due to the tumultuous events of the period. Housing production fell to exceptionally low levels during wartime and Depression periods and attained unusually high levels during the postwar booms. The housing market was rarely in equilibrium during this era. By 1956, the United States transformed itself from a laissez-faire economy to one in which the federal government had a predominant involvement, including extensive intervention in the housing market. The drastic change was attributable to the political consequences of the Great Depression and World War II.

Housing production in World War I dropped to a level not seen since the depressed 1870s. Housing starts declined from 437,000 units in 1916 to 240,000 units in 1917 and 118,000 units in 1918, due to rising costs and the diversion of capital and materials to war production. The reduced rate of production during the war, coinciding with a time of rising income, produced a severe housing shortage, estimated at 1 million units in 1920. The federal government became directly involved in housing construction, outside government reservations, as a war measure during World War I under the Emergency Fleet Corporation and United States Housing Corporation. The former acted as mortgagee while retaining control over rents and prices; the latter assumed direct responsibility for construction. These organizations provided over 15,000 new family dwelling units as well as other accommodations in defense production centers.

After World War I, the federal government returned to its policy of laissez-faire. The 1920s witnessed one of the greatest housing booms in U.S. history. The period from 1921 to 1928 was the first, since at least 1880, in which the number of homeowners increased significantly more than the number of renters. Homeowners increased by 2.8 million, or 61 percent of the total increase in households, and renters by 1.8 million. The homeownership ratio went up by 4 percentage points from 41 percent in 1921, nearly equaling the increase of the preceding 40 years. This change was due to several developments. The 1920s was a decade of rising real income during a period of sustained high-level prosperity, generating a larger volume of mortgage credit than ever before at moderate and stable interest rates with consumers more willing to assume the burden of debt.

The Great Depression. The laissez-faire policies of the federal government ended with the onset of the Great Depression and the election of Franklin ROOSEVELT and his NEW DEAL policies to return the unemployed to work and allow homeowners to remain in their homes.

The stock market crash of 1929 changed the course of U.S. housing and affected it for many years. On October 29, 1929, the stock market crashed with the selling of 16 million shares of stock. The consequences were significant. Builders stopped working overnight, mortgage finance dried up, housing starts plunged, millions of building laborers were thrown out of work, and more than 1.5 million homes were foreclosed. Housing starts plummeted from 330,000 in 1930 to 254,000 in 1931; 134,000 in 1932; and to the irreducible minimum of 93,000 in 1933, still an all-time low, and a 90 percent drop from 1925. No funds were available to builders to finance anything—not a house or even the tiniest remodeling job. Huge mortgage bond defaults on real-estate projects approached scandalous proportions.

In December 1932, President Herbert HOOVER recognized the desperate plight of housing by calling his President's Conference on Home Building and Ownership. More than 400 housing specialists took part. One of these urged an improved mortgage-credit system "to make it easy to buy a house as a car." But this was far too radical an ideal for Hoover, and little came of the conference.

One Hoover achievement was the passage of the Federal Home Loan Bank Act in 1932, creating 12 regional banks with capital of $125 million to act as a reserve system for savings and loan associations and thrift home-finance firms. Under Roosevelt's New Deal, the Federal Home Loan Bank was expanded and a subsidiary, the Home Owners' Loan Corporation, was set up to refinance and save more than a million foreclosed homes.

Federal intervention. The New Deal acts, laws, legislation, and programs had an important impact on housing. Together with the restoration of confidence in the economy, these acts produced a remarkable expansion in building. The three direct major contributors to the revival of this industry were the Home Loan Bank Board (FHLB), the Home Owners' Loan Corporation (HOLC), and the extremely successful Federal Housing Administration's FHA program, a new concept in low-cost, long-term amortized home-mortgage finance.

FHLB was organized in 1932, operating through 12 regional banks, and acted as a reserve system similar to the FEDERAL RESERVE. It brought stability and liquidity to thousands of saving and loans, savings banks and thrift institutions. It chartered hundreds of new Federal Savings and Loan Associations that brought added funds into the hard-pressed home finance field. The result was that funds began to flow once more into thrift institutions, and they were able to resume making loans for new home construction.

The HOLC operation was a classic example of the well-managed use of the financial power of central government. HOLC raised billions for the refinancing operation by selling low-interest bonds. It then offered to pay off the short-term, high-interest mortgages of distressed homeowners and replace them with one long-term, amortized loan at 3 percent interest. The program was an immediate success. By September 1934, HOLC had refinanced 492,700 mortgages, totaling $1.48 billion. The program rescued more than a million homeowners, and brought solvency and strength to the savings and loans and thrift institutions of the country. The Home Loan Bank enabled the financing of home construction to resume, and paved the way for a sharp increase in housing in later years.

Roosevelt signed the Federal Housing Act putting FHA into business in June 1934, but FHA achieved much more. It revolutionized finance with its long-term amortized mortgage, and it changed the structure of the housing industry.

The result of this revolution in housing finance, wrought by the federal government's direct intervention in housing finance, was that private builders, both large and small, went back to work, and housing starts and sales began to accelerate rapidly in 1936.

Housing during the 1940s focused on building desperately needed defense homes and a better-housed, postwar America. The ultimate achievement of the decade was the production of an astounding 7,443,000 homes for war veterans and other Americans. Independent builders constructed 96 percent of the total.

With the 1950s came social and cultural advances, economic growth, vast highway expansion, new concepts for better living, and, of course, building advances. A record 15.1 million homes were constructed, and they were markedly better built, better planned, and better equipped, larger in size, and gave higher value than had ever been achieved in this or any other nation. And housing research, planning, and design reached new heights, paving the way for still further improvements.

Creation of suburbia. Perhaps nothing in the 1950s had a greater impact on the lives and housing of Americans than the highway-building programs that the U.S. Congress initiated. The national interstate program brought thousands of miles of roads, expressways, thruways, and urban and suburban development to towns and cities in every corner of the land. It was a major stimulant to building projects in cities, suburbs, and outlying areas, spawning thousands of new home communities, shopping centers, motels, and vacation-home projects. With the initiation of the national interstate-highway building system, housing entered the modern period of 1956 to 1990.

The 1960s was a time of remarkable housing growth, and it saw more than 14.42 million homes provided by American builders. Each of the three U.S. presidents of this decade took office on a wave of political promises to aid housing and urban development. The cold statistics, however, show that the greatest housing advances of the decade came in the private sector. Of the 14.42 million total starts, only 357,000 were in public housing, less than 3 percent. The dream of great urban development and redevelopment to restore the decaying central cores of the cities simply did not materialize.

Housing history in the 1970s reflected the tumultuous, turbulent, and sensational life of America in those years. Home buyers and home builders were rocked by tight money, double-digit inflation, sky-high interest rates, the energy crunch, and a drastic building depression in 1973–75 that bankrupted 1,500 building firms. Yet the years, 1970–79 were a great decade for the housing industry: 17.8 million housing units were built—the largest number in U.S. history. Even more astonishing, the single-family home—the epitome of the American dream—became reality to millions of Americans.

Homeowners fared extremely well in that decade. The value of their homes increased faster than inflation, and the average home that sold for $25,000 in 1970 was selling for $68,000 or more in 1979. The inventory of occupied housing (single family, condominiums, co-ops, and apartments) rose to 88 million units, and Americans continued to be better housed than citizens of any other nation The soaring equity values of older homes became a powerful aid to new home buying in the 1970s.

The Fed's influence. Of all the forces at work on housing and builders during the decade, the most powerful were the monetary policies of the federal government.

Dr. Arthur Burns, chairman of the Federal Reserve System for many years, was the prime villain to most building industrialists. They saw housing starts rise or crash, time after time, as a result of the Fed's actions. Perhaps the most drastic was the tight-money, building depression that brought U.S. starts tumbling from 1973's 2,058,000 level to 1,171, 400 in 1975. Hundreds of building, real estate, and financial firms were forced into bankruptcy and the losses were in the billions. Again, many economists say the culprit was government spending funds it did not have.

During the 1980s, the economy was dominated by the Federal Reserve's frontal attack on inflation in 1981 and 1982, which raised interest rates and unemployment. Housing production fell, reflecting the limited demand due to the long-term decline in annual population increases. Production totaled 17.3 million units for the period, averaging 1.7 million annually.

Mortgage-interest rates rose to unprecedented heights and thrift institutions experienced a dis-intermediation crisis. Housing production, including mobile homes, sank to 1.3 million units in each year, the lowest production totals since 1946. Single-family starts were 50 percent below the peak levels of the late 1970s and multifamily starts were off by 35 percent.

New deposits turned negative in the first half of 1981 and continued so through 1982. Money-market mutual funds diverted deposits from thrift institutions in very large amounts. The growth rate of outstanding mortgage debt declined drastically. The profitability of savings and loan associations and mutual savings banks as a whole was negative in both years. In these two years, 843 federally insured savings and loan associations and 39 mutual savings banks failed or merged.

Multifamily apartment complexes are among the 102 million homes built in the United States from 1880 to 1990.

To return deposits to savings and loans, Congress enacted legislation that authorized thrift institutions to offer money-market deposit accounts at market interest rates with federal deposit insurance. This attracted a very large inflow of funds in a very short time. With the ending of high rates of inflation and the slowing-down of income growth, the burden of mortgage debt continued to rise. The financial health of the savings and loan industry continued to deteriorate.

After the flush years of 1983 and 1984, new deposits virtually dried up. The Federal Savings and Loan Insurance Fund was bankrupt, and a large portion of the industry was on the verge of collapse. A deadly combination of deposit insurance, relatively high interest rates, adverse economic conditions in the southwest, mismanagement by some institutions of the new powers accorded a deregulated industry, numerous instances of blatant fraud involving criminal prosecutions, and ineffective, if not irresponsible oversight by the federal government produced some of the largest loan losses in U.S. history.

To address the problems of the savings and loan, through the 1990s Congress enacted legislation that would provide the capital and organization required for closing the many insolvent institutions whose losses were steadily mounting, and to end abuses that had developed in the 1980s by establishing stricter standards for the remaining institutions while retaining deposit insurance. By the late 1990s and early 2000s, continued drops in interest rates to levels not seen in 40 years propelled the housing market while much of the rest of the American economy slid into recession.

BIBLIOGRAPHY. Mason C. Doan, *American Housing Production 1880–2000: A Concise* History (University Press of America, 1997); Gertrude S. Fish, ed., *The Story of Housing* (Macmillan, 1979); Saul B. Klaman, *The Postwar Residential Mortgage Market* (Princeton University Press, 1961); Joseph B. Mason, *History of Housing in the U.S., 1930–1980* (Gulf Publishing, 1982); J. Paul Mitchell, *Federal Housing Policy and Programs* (Rutgers University, 1985); Gwendolyn Wright, *Building the Dream: A Social History of Housing in America* (Pantheon Books, 1981).

MICHAEL MCGREGOR
FANNIE MAE

HSBC Holding

LONDON-BASED HSBC HOLDING is ranked among the 10 largest banks in the world. Branded as "the world's local bank," HSBC is the parent company of a global network of financial services institutions serving 32 million customers in 81 countries. In 2002, the bank reported assets of $746 billion.

Founded in 1865 as the Hongkong and Shanghai Banking Company, Ltd. by Thomas Sutherland, a shipping-line manager with no banking experience, and financed by HONG KONG's business leaders, HSBC was the then-British colony's first locally owned bank. It grew steadily through regional branch expansion until the 1950s, when it began to form subsidiaries and make acquisitions in the UNITED STATES, INDIA, and the Middle East. The expansion accelerated as Hong Kong's future became evermore uncertain and in 1993, four years before the colony was returned to China, the bank was renamed HSBC Holdings and relocated to London.

In step with the emergence of the global banking industry, HSBC's acquisition strategy continued throughout the 1990s. After buying major banks in the UNITED KINGDOM and FRANCE, it became Europe's largest bank. It also continues to grow in North and South America and remains positioned strongly in Asia, where it hopes to participate in the economic opening of CHINA.

BIBLIOGRAPHY. Frank H.H. King, *The History of the Hongkong and Shanghai Banking Corporation* (Cambridge University Press, 1987–91); Theodore B. Kinni and Al Ries, *Future Focus* (Capstone, 2000); The HSBC Group: A Brief History, www.hsbc.com (2000).

THEODORE B. KINNI
INDEPENDENT SCHOLAR

Hume, David (1712–76)

IN RETROSPECT, DAVID HUME is considered a notable figure among 18th-century Scottish philosophers. Hume passed through academic courses at the University of Edinburgh, where he devoted himself to the study of Scottish laws. Whether from the modesty natural to one of great merit, from a consciousness of his deficiency in elocution, or from a happy indolence of a temper that was little fitted for the Bar's agon, he never put on an advocate's gown. "Few men, even among the learned, had ever less of that spirit than the honest, easy, indolent, but philosophic Hume. His life, consequently, affords few of those occurrences which are commonly supposed to give interest to a biographical narration," Edinburgh newspapers said in his obituaries.

Other studies than the law attracted him. Hume rested all his hopes of fame and fortune on his merit as an author. He applied himself to metaphysical inquiries early in his career: He perceived, or claimed to identify, defects within former systems of thought. His reputation grew slowly until he became acknowledged as one of Britain's principal men of letters. Adam SMITH, writing of Hume after his death, noted "upon the whole, I have always considered him, both in his life-time and since his death, as approaching as nearly to the idea of a perfectly wise and virtuous man, as perhaps the nature of human frailty will admit."

Hume settled down to a life of literary work at his residence in Edinburgh. In 1739, he published the two first volumes of his *Treatise of Human Nature*, with a third emerging from the presses the following year. The author's purpose in that work, as he informs his readers in the preface, was "to introduce the experimental method of reasoning into moral subjects." In such a fashion, Hume employed the empirical techniques of the scientific revolution for the study of humans as social and moral creatures. In this work, Hume stated: "The sole end of logic is to explain the principles and operations of our reasoning faculty, and the nature of our ideas: morals and criticism regard our tastes and sentiments; and politics consider men as united in society, and dependent on each other. In these four sciences, logic, morals, criticism, and politics, is comprehended almost every thing, which it can any way import us to be acquainted with, or which can tend either to the improvement or ornament of the human mind."

Many readers have since cited portions among Hume's work to complement Smith's idea that an "invisible hand" guides market transactions. Both authors' ideas converge in the observation that individuals' actions can promote economic distribution—and, presumably, social harmony—without the deliberate coordinating efforts of institutions acting in the public interest. However, Hume's *Treatise of Human Nature,* while in no way inferior to any other rumination on the moral or metaphysical kind in any language, was largely overlooked at the time of its publication, or decried, except among a few liberal-minded men.

In 1741, Hume published two small volumes of moral, political, and literary essays. On the whole better received than the former publication, Hume later noted in an autobiographical volume "the work was favorably received, and soon made me entirely forget my former disappointment." His small patrimony having been almost spent, Hume was glad to return to his essays. As he noted to a correspondent, "You must know, that Andrew Millar is printing a new Edition of certain Essays, that have been ascrib'd to me; and as I threw out some, that seem'd frivolous and finical, I was resolv'd to supply their Place by others, that shou'd be more instructive," (1748).

Eventually, Hume supervised the printing of approximately 47 different compilations between this first trial and his death. In 1751, Hume published *Political Discourses*, which he remembers in his autobiography as "the only work of mine that was successful on the first

publication. It was well received abroad and at home." During his lifetime, printers in London, Amsterdam, and Utrecht published Hume's philosophical works in French. Editions were printed in Hamburg, Biesterfeld, Leipzig, and Copenhagen for German readers, and in Venice for Italian readers.

Political Discourses included such topics of interest to scholars of capitalism as "of Money," "of the Balance of Trade," "of Commerce," "of Interest," "of Taxes," and "of Public Credit." Taken all together, these followed the continental PHYSIOCRATS' rejection of MERCANTILISM, with the counter-argument that national wealth derived not from gold but agricultural surplus. Hume's economic essays, particularly those "of Money" and "of the Balance of Trade," merited critical responses from Robert Wallace, James Steuart-Denham, Josiah Tucker, and Smith.

Even after Hume's death, his economic ideas continued to be discussed by John Weatley, David RICARDO, and Dugald Stewart. Later commentators turned to Hume's economic essays for a metaphor drawn from the natural sciences to describe the circulation of specie: Just as gravity causes a fluid to seek its own level through interconnected chambers, increased supply of money in one country speedily disperses to other countries. When fluid is removed from one chamber, fluid will be drawn from the surrounding chambers. If Great Britain were to receive new specie, this would drive up Britons' labor prices and the cost of British goods. On finding that other nations' labor and goods are cheaper, Britons would import, in effect sending their money to foreign countries.

From contemporary politics, toward which he had now made a considerable contribution, Hume turned his inquiries to history, and completed a first volume for the *History of Britain Under the House of Stuart,* which reached the printers in 1750. This initial contribution received little notice; the success of a second volume was by no means considerable; yet by the time of their publication, Hume could happily announce, "notwithstanding the variety of winds and seasons, to which my writings had been exposed, they had still been making such advances, that the copy-money given me by the booksellers, much exceeded any thing formerly known in England; I was become not only independent, but opulent." In this way, Hume served as an example of how the values of a commercial society, that he defended in his own essays, could be compatible with a philosopher's life. Indeed, such a philosopher could thrive in the new world of global trade in goods and ideas.

Hume's life was also a consequence of his relationships with friends and antagonists. Smith, although close to Hume, made little effort on the latter's behalf when he attempted to secure an appointment at the University of Glasgow: "I should prefer David Hume to any man for a colleague; but I am afraid the public would not be of my opinion; and the interest of the society will oblige us to have some regard to the opinion of the public," Smith wrote to a colleague. The celebrated Jean Jacques Rousseau, whom Hume brought over to England with him in 1766, and for whom he procured the offer of a pension from the king, will long be noted for the vigor with which he waged a campaign of animosity toward Hume. Hume spent his last years trying to protect his name from calumny in Rousseau's forthcoming memoir, and completing his own memoir only months before his death in 1776.

BIBLIOGRAPHY. David Hume, *Essays and Treatises on Several Subjects* (1753, Thoemmes Press, 2002); David Hume, *Four Dissertations* (1757, St. Augustine Press, 2001); David Hume, *Essays, Moral Political and Literary* (1758–77, Liberty Fund, 1985).

ELIZABETH BISHOP, PH.D.
AMERICAN UNIVERSITY

Hundred Years' War

A DISPUTE OVER ENTANGLED feudal property rights in FRANCE evolved into the Hundred Years' War, lasting from 1337 to 1453. The war, complemented by the plague, destroyed more than two centuries of gains in both population and living standards in western Europe. It was to increase the incentives for a more centralized government and army, and to alter the way wars were financed.

The feudal system of fielding and funding the military quickly became inadequate and the longevity of the conflict required a standing army. Such an army relied on merchants and their emerging towns to supply the taxes and loans necessary for its upkeep. The inability of the feudal warrior class to achieve a decisive victory was to lessen their political power, and kings began to bypass the nobility and to economically rely on, and nourish, the merchant class which would become the necessary source of funding for a national government and army—prerequisites of the modern state. The new armies of commoners loyal to the Crown, added to this shift from feudal obligations to a spirit of nationalism.

Western Europe had reached a stage of relative prosperity by 1337, and with its rich soil and increased agricultural productivity (improved field rotation, heavier plows, horse harnesses, and water mills), it experienced significant increase in population and income. Trade had increased substantially with a variety of trade fairs in which instruments of CREDIT and bills of exchange were used. Newly chartered towns, with trade guilds and merchants, accelerated the movement away from the self-sufficiency of the manorial economy toward a greater degree of economic specialization.

Politically, Europe was still feudal with land still the principal form of wealth and, thus, land was the foundation of military and economic power. The property of the nobility was like a mosaic spanning different kingdoms. In 1337, the English king, Edward III, had a claim to the throne of the French kingdom through maternal lineage, and was also the Duke of Aquitaine, a province under the domain of the king of France. Skirmishes became particularly intense in the sole English duchy of Aquitaine, England's main source for wine. Given this system of overlapping political jurisdictions, appeals were made to either the French or English royal courts, depending on where one was likely to get the most favorable ruling. Conflicts were ultimately resolved by whose military was in command of the area under dispute.

Both kings, however, had limited military and financial resources to engage in military expeditions. By the late Middle Ages, the feudal levy system was in decline, especially in England. It required the nobles to send troops in defense of the realm for 40 days, at their own expense, at the king's call. Given the mosaic of land ownership, important nobles faced a dilemma. Siding with either king would result in the forfeiture of land in the other kingdom. This created incentives for nobles to not hear the king's call to arms, or answer it only in part.

War expenses outran the kingdoms' government revenues from the very start. The first 10 years of war used up 18 years of English government revenues, most of which were generated by an export tax on wool, and special war taxes. These measures, however, decreased the funds available to the nobility, and therefore their ability to fund the war.

Usually, however, the effective use of war propaganda by the kings led to a rising national consciousness (especially among the merchants) and the tax was granted. To supplement the tax, the English resorted to voluntary and sometimes forced loans, requisitions (especially ships and sailors), and the manipulation of the lucrative wool trade, which was used to leverage political and military alliances, and as collateral for loans and credit. The revenue from the wool-export tax was about twice the value of all other sources of government revenue.

The French supplemented war taxes with repeated manipulations of the value of coinage, from which they could earn a 30 to 40 percent profit. They also resorted to loans, confiscation of the funds of a planned crusade, and the sale of a princess as a wife for the Duke of Milan.

By the time the war began, England's feudal levy had been replaced by a system of indenture. This was a system where military combatants were paid according to the feudal military hierarchy based on the types of weapons and armor that the combatants would provide (mounted knight, squire, archer, and so on to the footman).

The demise of the feudal levy in England was partly due to necessity because knights were scarce in relatively small England, and the feudal levy was restricted for domestic defense. Furthermore, recent defeats in the Scottish wars had forced reorganization in military strategy. The mounted cavalry charge was now replaced with the dismounted knight, the archer, and better field tactical control. The English army was therefore a volunteer force, serving for pay and spoils of war, and willing to serve abroad.

The French *chevalier* was still the most formidable warrior on the continent, but the limitations of the feudal levy were becoming apparent as armies were sometimes withdrawn mid-siege when the 40-day period elapsed. French royal ordinances were issued to develop a royal army much like the English, but the French nobility's distaste for the lower classes and belief in the nobility of combat hampered this effort.

There were only three pitched land battles in the first 100 years, all won by the English use of the archer. In that same period of time, the French belief in their superiority as warriors led them to continue the mounted charge with little discipline, into the arrows of these well-trained commoners. The repeated defeats at the hands of commoners diminished the social superiority that the noble had enjoyed throughout the Middle Ages. Ultimately, by 1450, the French royal army, with commoners at its core, was able to defeat the English in a fourth battle.

The fact that there were only three major pitched battles reflects, in part, the costs of these armies. It, however, does not imply that the ravages of war did not continue throughout the period. The most effective way of controlling costs was to dismiss the army the day the battle was over. This transferred the costs from the king to the local population. The dismissed army would reorganize into smaller groups of armed men that would approach a town or province, demand food and money, and destroy the area if (as often was the case) their demands were not satisfied. The destruction of rural and urban property in the French kingdom continued for decades and resulted in famine and flight. The fact that, with the exception of some coastal raids, the war was fought on French soil was a tremendous economic advantage for the English.

The persistence of war taxes led to peasant and urban revolts against the farmers and the nobility, but interestingly not against the kings. The oppressive taxes, military reverses, and general economic depression were ascribed to the incompetence and greed of the nobility.

The kings were seen as victims with popular sentiment rallying around them. The peasant uprisings were violently suppressed, while the urban revolts were sometimes appeased by royal concessions that further increased the power of the merchant class in both the local and national governments.

Although most of the French kingdom was affected by this war, it was too large to be completely enveloped by it. Regions that were less affected rallied to the king's cause with revenue and men. The rise of nationalism, driven by the desire to defeat the English, concentrated power in the hands of the king.

Both the French and English kingdoms were about to be temporarily eclipsed by SPAIN and PORTUGAL during the age of exploration, but their economies were irreversibly altered by the war. The rise of the merchant class (particularly in England) and the concentration of power in the hands of the king (particularly in France) formed their subsequent histories as nation states.

BIBLIOGRAPHY. C.T. Allmand, *Society at War* (Oliver & Boyd, 1973); Anne Curry, *The Hundred Years' War* (Osprey, 1993); Edouard Perroy, *The Hundred Years' War* (1965); David Potter, *A History of France, 1460–1560—The Emergence of a Nation State* (Palgrave Macmillan, 1995); Jonathon Sumption, *The Hundred Years' War: Trial by Battle* (University of Pennsylvania Press, 1991).

HARRY KYPRAIOS, PH.D.
ROLLINS COLLEGE

Hungary

THE REPUBLIC OF HUNGARY borders Slovakia to the north, UKRAINE to the northeast, Romania to the east, Serbia and Montenegro, and Croatia to the south, Slovenia to the southwest, and AUSTRIA to the west. Budapest is the capital.

Hungary's population is approximately 90 percent Magyar, with Roma, Germans, Slovaks, Croats, Serbs, Romanians, and others making up the rest. Hungarian, or Magyar, is the official language. German and English, as well as other languages, are also spoken. About two-thirds of the population lives in urban areas, with Budapest significantly larger than any of the other cities. Due to a higher death rate than birth rate, Hungary has a negative population growth rate.

Hungary was part of the Austro-Hungarian Empire, which endured until its defeat in WORLD WAR I. After WORLD WAR II, Hungary fell under communist rule directed by the SOVIET UNION. In 1956, Hungary revolted and attempted to withdraw from the Warsaw Pact. The Soviet Union suppressed the revolt by sending in its military. During Mikhail Gorbachev's years as the head of the Soviet Union, Hungary was the leading advocate for dissolving the Warsaw Pact and shifting toward a multiparty democracy and market-oriented economy. After the Soviet Union's collapse in 1991, Hungary developed close economic and political ties to Western Europe. In 1999, Hungary became a member of the North Atlantic Treaty Organization (NATO).

Industry accounts for about a third of Hungary's GROSS DOMESTIC PRODUCT (GDP), services 62 percent, and agriculture the rest. After the collapse of communism, Hungarian industries were ill-equipped to compete in the international marketplace and, during the first half of the 1990s suffered substantial economic fallout. One industry that has grown substantially is tourism. Hungary's currency is the forint. The National Bank of Hungary is the central bank and is responsible for issuing currency and maintaining checking and savings accounts. The Foreign Trade Bank services enterprises trading abroad and the State Development Institution finances large-scale investment projects. In 1990, the Budapest Stock Exchange opened.

In 2002, Hungary's exports were valued at approximately $31.4 billion annually and its imports at $33.9 billion. Exports include machinery and equipment, chemicals, agricultural products, and wine. Imports include machinery and equipment, fuels and electricity, consumer goods, and raw materials.

Hungary was unprepared for the competitiveness of the international marketplace and developed a large trade deficit that it covered via foreign loans. In order to repay these loans the country had to use much of its export earnings.

Hungary continues to show strong economic growth and is expected to join the EUROPEAN UNION (EU). In 2000, its sovereign debt was upgraded to the second-highest rating among central European transition economies.

BIBLIOGRAPHY. Stephen Sisa, *The Spirit of Hungary: A Panorama of Hungarian History and Culture* (Vista Court Books, 1991); Miklos Molnar, *A Concise History of Hungary* (Cambridge University Press, 2001); *CIA World Factbook* (2002).

S.J. RUBEL, PH.D.
INDEPENDENT SCHOLAR

Hypovereinsbank (HVB Group)

TWO GERMAN BANKS, Bayerische Hypotheken und Wechsel Bank founded in 1835 and Bayerische Vereinsbank founded in 1869, merged in 1998 and became the HVB Group. After the acquisition of Bank Austria Creditanstalt in 2001, the HVB Group became one of the five largest banking groups in Europe, with a commanding position in central Europe.

The HVB Group has more than 66,500 employees, with 2,100 branch offices and approximately 8.5 million customers. Their core geographic markets are Germany, where HVB is number two (2002 revenues were ⃞4.2 billion), Austria, where they are the market leader, and the rapidly growing markets in central and eastern Europe (2002 revenues were ⃞3.1 billion). The "corporates and markets" business segment accounted for ⃞2.5 billion in 2002, providing the corporate customer with an integrated one-stop shopping solution for financing, risk management, and other services. HVB's strategic aim is to focus on retail and corporate banking, and to recover from their first loss ever of ⃞858 million in 2002 through an ambitious cost-cutting exercise and restructuring via the disposal of non-core activities, such as the spinning-off of the commercial real estate group into an independent entity. Despite the loss in 2002, HVB Group still ranked among the top 100 of the largest companies in the world.

BIBLIOGRAPHY. "Investor Relations," www.hypovereinsbank.com; "Global 500: World's Largest Companies," *Fortune* (July, 2002).

CATHERINE MATRAVES
ALBION COLLEGE

I

imperialism

AS A SOCIAL CONCEPT, imperialism became part of the political vocabulary as recently as the late 19th century, but empires have existed since ancient times. It can be argued that imperialism refers to the stage in the historical development of capitalism when it became a global system, from the 19th century onward. There has been an extensive scholarly debate on the phenomenon of imperialism, which was sharpened by the fact that its conclusions became important to Marxist political movements during the 20th century (even though Karl MARX never used the term).

After the INDUSTRIAL REVOLUTION in Britain in the late 19th century, the continuously expanding process of investment, technical change, production, and trade led to the emergence of a globalized economy. It involved a new international specialization of production in which the economies of a number of countries of Asia, Africa, and Latin America were restructured to export raw materials to, and serve as markets for the manufactured goods of the industrial economies. This phenomenon was associated with a division of the world among the major capitalist powers into a set of colonies and spheres of influence. For example, as Eric Hobsbawm points out, between 1876–1915 about one quarter of the globe's land surface was distributed in the form of colonies among half a dozen states.

It is undeniable that the division of the world (as much as its integration) since the late 19th century and the strategic projection of state power (as much as international collaboration) have had an economic dimension. Like the systems of power, the ideologies that legitimized the political imperatives of imperialism and those that impelled revolt, were also modulated by the expanding capitalist economy. Indeed, this new division

of the world reached into the very heart of humanity. The colonized people were ruptured from their history, language, and culture, as they internalized the image of the native, an image that was constructed by the settlers charged with a civilizing mission. Thus, it was not only the economy of the colonized peoples that was restructured but their very psyche. As Aime Cesaire, in his discourse on colonialism, points out: "I am talking of millions of men who have been skillfully injected with fear, inferiority complexes, trepidation, servility, despair, abasement."

The dynamic of growth and inequality. The new world that was shaped by the development of capitalism from the Industrial Revolution to the contemporary period was marked by dramatic improvements in TECHNOLOGY, and in the growth of output and incomes. Just as dramatic was the increase in the inequality of incomes and the availability of basic public services between the industrialized countries on the one hand, and the countries that became under-developed on the other. For example, the share of world income accruing to the advanced capitalist countries in 1850 was only 35 percent while the share of what are now called the less-developed countries was 65 percent.

Over the next 100 years there was a dramatic change in the relative economic fortunes of these two sets of countries brought about by the uneven impact of capitalism. Thus, by 1938, the share of world income accruing to the advanced capitalist countries had increased to 76 percent while the share of the less-developed countries fell to 24 percent. The disparity in income shares subsequently continued to increase rapidly.

The question is, what is it in the nature of the industrialization process, within the framework of capitalism, that imparts to it such tremendous dynamism and such a powerful mechanism of inequality? In the late 18th and early 19th centuries, the shift from handicraft production to factory manufacturing represented perhaps a watershed in the history of man's relationship with nature. Throughout the preceding ages, it was the human hand that wielded the implement of production. There was, therefore, a close ceiling to the growth of productivity because it depended on the strength of the human hand and the quickness of the human eye. With the onset of large-scale factory production in capitalism, the implement of production was transferred into a machine, thereby opening up unprecedented possibilities of productivity growth. Now the speed with which the implement could be wielded was determined no more by the human hand, but by the development of science and its systematic application to machine design. Income inequality could therefore be expected to grow rapidly between industrialized and non-industrialized countries.

The capitalist growth process had a tendency for continuous expansion due to its social organization of production: Individual capitalists (later management-controlled corporations) were pitted in competition with each other within a market framework, where survival required not only increasing profit but reinvesting it continuously. In the process of reinvestment, if profit was to increase, an increase in productivity had to be achieved. It was this imperative of continuous reinvestment, expansion of profits, and the systematic application of science to production that imparted to capitalism an unprecedented dynamism.

At the same time, the fact that this process was powered by those who could acquire the initial investment resources, command labor, and secure access to raw materials and markets for finished goods, meant that there was an inherent tendency for inequality both at the national and global levels. The town-dwelling burghers, who started life as merchants supplying goods and finance to feudal estates in Europe, had by the end of the 17th century emerged as a political power in England. Such was the interplay between politics and a dynamic capitalist growth process, that by the end of the 18th century, the bourgeoisie had become a major political force in FRANCE, and by the end of the 19th century, the dominant political power in the world.

Imperialism and the development of capitalism. In the process of capitalist expansion after the Industrial Revolution, four distinct phases in the structure of the global capitalist economy can be identified. A brief discussion of these phases would indicate the dynamics of imperialism in the context of the changing relationship between the dominant capitalist countries and the dependent countries.

From the 16th century to the mid-18th century, there was direct appropriation of resources. This precursor stage to the Industrial Revolution was characterized by the coercive extraction of resources from Asia, Africa, and South America on the basis of organized, though selective, use of military force and administrative measures. As Ernest Mandel argues, the appropriation of resources in this period by Europe from the countries of the East was "the outcome of values stolen, plundered, seized by tricks, pressure or violence, from the overseas peoples with whom the Western world had made contact."

In this pre-industrialization phase, trade consisted of imports into Europe of luxury goods from the east such as silk, cotton and fabrics, spices, and jewelry and precious stones. Trade in this period was neither conducted within free markets nor were norms of fairness in fashion at the time. The resources extracted from the countries of the East during this period, were not only substantial, but may have played an important direct or indirect role in the process of investment and economic growth in Europe. According to a conservative estimate by a senior colonial official, Sir Percival Griffiths, £100 to £150 million was plundered from INDIA alone during the period 1750–1800. Its significance can be judged from the fact that the British National Income in 1770 was only £125 million, and the total investment that had been made in the whole of Britain's modern metallurgical industry (including steel), by 1790, was only £650,000. According to another estimate, gold and silver valued at 500 million gold pesos were exported from Latin America during the period 1503–1660. Similarly, profit obtained from the slave labor of the Africans in the British West Indies amounted to over £200 million.

From the late-18th century to the mid-19th century, there was a period of export of European manufactures. Following the Industrial Revolution in Britain (which subsequently spread to Europe), the imperative of capitalist expansion was for each of the new industrial countries to secure sources of raw materials and exclusive markets for their manufactured goods. This involved not only sovereign control over the colonized countries of Asia, Africa, and Latin America, but a restructuring of their economies to enable systematic resource extraction through the market mechanism. Specifically this consisted of rupturing the link between domestic agriculture and handicrafts industry, which was the basis of the self-sufficiency of many of these countries. This domestic disarticulation laid the basis of integrating the colonized economy into the global capitalist economy.

The undermining of the domestic industry of the colony was, in many cases, conducted through protectionist measures. For example, even as late as 1815, Indian cotton and silk goods were 50–60 percent cheaper than similar British goods, thereby making Indian exports more competitive than the British. Accordingly, Indian exports to Britain were subjected to an import duty of 70–80 percent for a long period. Moreover on at least two occasions (in 1700 and 1720), import of Indian cotton textiles into Britain was prohibited altogether.

The domestic economy of the colonies was restructured to specialize in the export of cheap raw materials for the emerging European industry on the one hand, and import of its expensive manufactured goods on the other. Thus, the economy of the colony became structurally dependent on, and a source of resource extraction for, the European economy: The economies of Asia, Africa, and Latin America became part of world capitalism, yet the accumulation of capital that characterizes the system, occurred essentially in the dominant industrial countries. Thus, while the global economy was integrated, its gains were divided unequally between what Samir Amin calls the metropolitan and peripheral countries, respectively.

The late 19th century to the mid-20th century was characterized by the export of capital. Joseph SCHUMPETER describes "gales of creative destruction," that swept away the inefficient firms; the efficient firms, through new products and manufacturing processes, rapidly increased their market share. By the 19th century, large national corporations emerged as an important production unit in the dominant capitalist countries. This enabled considerable monopolistic profits to be made. Soon there was the attendant problem of re-investing these within the European market, which set the stage for the DEPRESSION of the 1870s. This crisis impelled an historically unprecedented export of European capital. During the period 1870–1914, large investments were made in CANADA and AUSTRALIA. Apart from this, rapid development of COMMUNICATION technologies (steam ships, railways, and telegraphy) enabled export of capital to a number of countries in Asia, Africa, and Latin America for building economic infrastructure to facilitate the export of raw materials, and the import of European manufactured goods.

The growth of large national corporations during this period resulted in intense rivalry and occasional conflict between the dominant industrial countries, as their respective national corporations sought to secure sources of raw materials, and markets for their goods and capital in the rest of the world. These tensions constituted one of the underlying factors leading to WORLD WAR I.

The mid-20th century to the present can be called the era of multinational corporations, the information revolution, and the financial sector. After WORLD WAR II, a new era of globalization and (after the end of the Cold War) a new structure of power relations emerged whose specific features are just beginning to be manifested. At least three characteristics distinguish the globalized economy at the end of the 20th century from that of the late 19th century. These are:

1. In the late 19th century, the globalized process of extracting raw materials, manufacture, and sale of goods was conducted by large national corporations. This induced a contention between the dominant industrial countries. Since World War II, the multinational corporations have emerged as the predominant production unit. Within this framework there has been an inter-penetration of capital among the advanced industrial countries. Consequently the earlier rivalry and conflict between the advanced industrial countries has been replaced by the possibility of growing collaboration in the economic and political spheres, ensuring the conditions of growth and stability in the global economy.

   After more than 200 years of economic growth within the advanced capitalist countries and their dependent territories, a much more integrated globalized economy may be emerging in the world. It is a world where economic boundaries and, indeed, the sovereignty of nation states is eroding, although more for the weaker than for the stronger states. The doctrine that the free market mechanism at the global level is the most efficient framework of resource allocation, production, and distribution of GOODS is resurgent. It is being translated into national economic policies of various countries through the loan conditions imposed by multilateral institutions such as the WORLD BANK and the INTERNATIONAL MONETARY FUND (IMF), which emerged after World War II. More recently, the "open economy" policy framework has been embodied into a set of international trade agreements under the auspices of the WORLD TRADE ORGANIZATION (WTO). Under these circumstances those developing countries, which do not have the institutions, economic infrastructure, and resources to compete in the world market, are vulnerable to rapid economic deterioration, debt, and impoverishment. This could become a new factor in accentuating international economic inequality.

2. The revolution in information technology (IT) has created the potential of a new trajectory of technological growth. Its consequences may be as far-reaching as the Industrial Revolution in the late 18th century. The Industrial Revolution involved the systematic application of science to machine-manufacture and thereby laid the basis of rapid productivity growth. Now artificial intelligence, embodied in interactive computers, can become an aid to human intelligence itself, and can therefore help achieve an unprecedented acceleration in technological change.

   As knowledge-intensive industries, particularly the IT industry, become the cutting-edge of growth, the economic gap between countries with a highly trained human capital base and those without such a base is likely to grow rapidly. While this fact has opened new opportunities for developing countries to achieve affluence (for example, the newly industrializing countries), it has also created a grave danger of rapidly increasing poverty for those countries that are not positioned to meet the challenge of knowledge-intensive growth.

3. The financial sphere in the second half of the 20th century has grown much more rapidly than the sphere of production, so that the volume of international banking is greater than the volume of trade in goods and services in the global economy. For example, international banking in 1964 was only $20 billion compared to $188 billion worth of international trade in goods and services. By 1985, the relative position of the two sectors had reversed with international banking valued at $2,598 billion and the value of traded goods and services worldwide being lesser, at $2,190 billion.

The predominance of the financial sector, internationally integrated financial markets, and the previously unimaginable speed with which financial transfers can be effected, have combined to introduce into the global economy a new fragility. Exogenous shocks (such as terrorist attacks, regional wars, and political instability in raw-material producing countries) can be transmitted much more rapidly through the globalized economic network. Therefore, the world's real economy that underlies the financial sphere and spawns production, employment, and standards of living in individual countries, is prone to instability. Economic instability in the real economy is likely to have a relatively greater adverse impact on poorer countries than on the rich, thereby further accentuating poverty and inequality.

Future challenges. Through much of history, hunger and deprivation had pitted individuals and states against each other and therefore constrained the human quest of actualizing the creative potential of the individual. Capitalism, with its capacity for a rapid improvement in the material conditions of society based on science and individual freedom, created the possibility of human liberation. Yet the very process through which historically unprecedented improvements in technology and levels of material production were achieved, also created a world order based on dominance and dependence. While it provided hitherto unimaginable material well-being to a relatively small population, it engendered the conditions of systemic poverty, human misery and conflict for a large section of the world's population.

Today, after over 300 years of capitalist development, of the world's 6 billion people, almost half (2.8 billion) live in poverty (earning less than $2 a day per person). In poor countries, where the majority of the world's population resides, as many as 50 percent of children below the age of five are malnourished, thereby stunting their mental and physical growth. While there has been an impressive growth in technologies and production, the gains are grossly unequal. The average income in the richest 20 countries is 37 times the average in the 20 poorest countries, a gap that has doubled in the last 40 years. The poor countries are, in many cases, under such a heavy debt burden that the debt-servicing expenses are greater than their foreign-exchange earnings, so that debt servicing itself has become a mechanism of resource transfer from the poor countries to the rich.

The rapid and continuous growth of production over the last three centuries has been associated with environmental damage, affecting the life support systems of the planet. At the same time economic destitution, illiteracy, or in some cases a sense of political injustice is tearing apart the fabric of society in some countries and giving rise to extremist tendencies that violate human values and threaten the economic and political stability of the world.

The problems of mass poverty, debt, and environmental degradation threaten the sustainability of growth (see SUSTAINABLE DEVELOPMENT) in a highly integrated global economy, which we have suggested, is both fragile and unstable. Overcoming poverty and debt will not only require changes in institutions and the structures of the economies of poor countries, but will also require large net-resource transfers from the developed to the developing world, and rectifying the asymmetry of global markets with respect to the rich and poor countries. These changes can only occur through international collaboration based on a shared human responsibility toward the global community and its future.

The problem of environmental degradation results from a level and composition of economic growth that is based on a private profitability calculus that does not adequately take account of the social costs of production. A market-based regime of tax incentives and disincentives, together with regulatory institutions, is, of course, necessary for reducing the environmental cost of growth. Equally important is the rapid development and adoption of environmentally gentle ("green") technologies. Yet this may not be enough. The level of growth itself may need to be adjusted to make it consistent with the conservation of the environment. In view of the fact that currently almost 85 percent of the world's resources are being consumed by less than 10 percent of the world's population, the burden of reduced growth in per capita consumption may have to be borne by the rich countries. This will require a new sensibility characterized by a responsibility of the individual toward the present and future human community, and new forms of social life.

BIBLIOGRAPHY. Samir Amin, *Accumulation on a World Scale* (Monthly Review Press, 1978); Frantz Fanon, *Black Skin White Masks*, Paladin, 1970); Robert Heilbroner, *21st Century Capitalism* (W.W. Norton, 1993); Eric Hobsbawm, *The Age of Empire* (Abacus, 1997); Karl Marx, *Capital* (Progress Publishers, 1887); Gerald Meier, *Leading Issues in Economic Development* (Oxford University Press, 1970); Joseph A. Schumpeter, *Capitalism, Socialism and Democracy* (Harper, 1942); "Attacking Poverty," *World Bank Report 2000/2001* (Oxford University Press, 2002).

AKMAL HUSSAIN, PH.D.
PAKISTAN INSTITUTE OF DEVELOPMENT ECONOMICS

income

THE LIFEBLOOD OF A capitalistic society is the diversity of income, the variety of ways it can circulate within society. From the rent of houses to the salary of workers or the royalties of copyright, securing the rights to a certain type and flow of income are the name of the game under capitalism. But income means more than a purely economic relationship: social and political structures are built around it, at least from the point of view of classical political economy, and later Marxian economists. When classical economists, such as Adam SMITH or David RICARDO, spoke of class, they conceived of it as the set of people receiving a particular type of income. Feudal lords of the land and serfs, masters and slaves, obviously made their living in different ways.

What about a capitalistic society? We would find three main classes in the classical economists' description. CAPITAL, made up of capitalists whose gain is originated in their property of the means of production (think of a pin-factory owner), and the PROFIT obtained after the expenses of production have been accounted for; LABOR, comprising workers whose income comes in the way of wages (such as those people working in the pin factory), and land-owners, whose income is the rent of their fields to farmers. As agriculture has diminished in importance as the main productive activity, the former two classes have remained the most important, even if many would argue that social conflict is not really found along the lines defined by types of income. In some political economy accounts, however, how labor and capital divide the total product in a society, how income is shared or appropriated, determines its development in the long run.

Now, if income were associated with more or less material possessions and nothing else, perhaps we should not be overly worried. The problem is that other more important traits are linked to income stratification. In the well-known Whitehall Study that surveyed 17,000 British civil servants, it was found that mortality rates were three times as high among the lowest grade workers (messengers, doorkeepers) than among the highest grade civil servants (administrators). In 1995, American people below the poverty level were three times as likely as those above twice the poverty level to report fair or poor health status. In hundreds of reports, the most powerful predictor of educational achievement is consistently the social class background of the students and their parents, usually driven by income level.

An international map of income per capita. Although the source of income is surely important, the amount of total national income and its distribution are certainly decisive for a great number of factors affecting quality of life, such as health or cultural and political participation. GNI, or Gross National Income (also known as GNP, GROSS NATIONAL PRODUCT), is a very good indicator of a country's place under the sun. The WORLD BANK defines GNI as the sum of value added by all resident producers plus taxes and receipts of compensation of employees and property income from abroad. In 2001, according to the *CIA World Factbook*, INDIA's GNI was $2.66 trillion, SWEDEN's was $227.4 billion, and the U.S. GNI topped the world's ranking at $10.1 trillion.

But the number of people adding value to India's GNI is certainly higher than the number of Swedes adding value to their GNI. So we need to divide the GNI by the population, in order to get the picture of the income available to the average resident (we shall see that inequality greatly affects this "average"), and a very good indicator of the stage of economic development and modernization of that country. We can expect to find good health care services and basic education granted to all citizens of countries above $10,000 per capita, which was exactly that of CHILE in 2001, measured in purchasing power parity (that is, adjusted to what you really can buy with the same amount of money in different places). This GNI per capita was also highly unequal in its international distribution, such as $2,540 in the case of India, to follow with our example, $25,400 for Sweden, and $36,300 in the United States. Very low per-capita-income countries are to be found in Africa, such as poverty-ravaged Sierra Leone, with $500 per capita. These low-income levels are usually associated with high mortality rates, especially infant mortality, and low education levels.

It has been argued that this distribution is no accident, but is the result of a highly unfair world-system, where trade policies, financial structures and skewed international arrangements maintain a flow of wealth from poor countries (the periphery) into rich countries (or core), the United States in particular, and increase within-nation inequality. How can this happen? Take corn as an example. Thanks to large subsidies and industrialized production systems (for instance, how fertilizers are used can be optimized through satellite imagery of large-scale crops), American corn producers are able to outsell farmers in Mexico (where corn, incidentally, was turned into a crop around 7,000 years ago). This eventually leads unemployed laborers out of the countryside and into cities. Corn subsidies in the Dakotas may, in this way, have a devastating impact in the slums of Mexico City. This is another, and less obvious, side of GLOBALIZATION.

Measuring income inequality. Income is not evenly distributed, a fact we know all too well. Inequality of income is one of the main ways to understand the fundamental workings of a society, the joint result of its legal, social, and political institutions, and also a cottage industry in the social sciences. Among other problems, it is not an easy task to know just how unequally income is distributed in a given country at a given moment. Say that we divide the population into five parts, and then we compare the income accruing to the top 20 percent (or quintile), to that earned by the bottom quintile. That is the 80th/20th ratio, and looks good as a measure of inequality. Now see how it has changed in recent American history. In 1967, that richer fifth of the population got 3.95 times more income than the poorer 20 percent. But in 2001, they got an income 4.65 times greater than their poorer fellow countrymen, which means that inequality (measured this way) had grown around 18 percent.

But what if the growth in inequality was really concentrated in the upper rungs in the income ladder? What if only the very rich had grown truly richer? In that case we may have needed to look at other places in society, for example the top five percent of the distribution, and how their income compares to the bottom 20. What we see now in this 95th/20th indicator is a different story: it goes up from 5.97 in 1968 to 8.38 in 2001. That is a 40 percent increase. Whatever has been going on in the growth of income inequality in America, it has mainly taken place among the very rich.

Another indicator, probably the best known of inequality measures, is called the Gini coefficient. To understand how it is calculated, start with some (social) science-fiction. Imagine a society where income is distributed in a perfectly equal way. If we took the first percentage of people in the population, they would also have one percent of the total income. Five percent of people, five percent of the income, and so on. If we drew that in a graph showing the different fractions of total population (horizontal axis) and their accumulated share of total income (vertical axis), a graph called the Lorenz curve, we would end up with a straight line from 0:0 to 100:100, running at an angle of exactly 45 degrees from the bottom left corner of the graph.

Real life is not like that. The poorest first percent of the people have much less that one percent of the nation's income, perhaps 0.1 percent or probably less. The poorest 20 percent have maybe 5 percent of total income, but this goes on up to the upper rungs. Take the less rich 95 percent of the country, and they have still have less than 80 percent of total income. That is because the richest 5 percent has more than 20 percent of it, in case you had not guessed.

The trend is more or less clear: increasing income inequality in all countries, but at a much faster pace in the United States and the UNITED KINGDOM, less so in CANADA, and a mild growth in Sweden. This clearly points out that policy choices and institutional structures (such as redistributive measures) have a deep impact in income inequality: the Thatcherite and Reaganite conservative revolutions (led by Margaret THATCHER and Ronald REAGAN), with their market-oriented reforms, led to more income inequality than European welfare states.

But let us say that we know perfectly well how income is distributed in a given society. Does that mean we have a perfect picture of social structure, e.g., we know how and when to intervene to prevent health or educational differences? It is important to underline that income is only one of the factors we need to take into account. Money is only part of the story: EDUCATION (human capital), connections (social capital) or other assets (real estate, for instance), have a great impact in life chances.

But is income inequality a bad thing, something that is perhaps inevitable or even fair, or in and of itself, is it a social wrong? Some think it is a very necessary evil, or not an evil at all if compared to the alternatives. If people desire an ever-greater income, and this income can be increased as a result of their investment in human or physical capital, their ambition would push them toward ever-greater productivity and better use of productive and technological possibilities.

Taken together, all those individuals striving for greater incomes would push the society as a whole toward more productive states. This is more or less the basis for what Bernard Mandeville, an 18th-century philosopher, famously called "private vices, public virtues." In fact, according to this view, only fear of want may keep the slack and lazy in motion, or as Mandeville stated in his *Fable of the Bees*, "[t]hose that get their living by their daily labor . . . have nothing to stir them up to be serviceable but their wants which it is prudence to relieve, but folly to cure." This idea, in a more palatable guise, underpins the incentive theory of the positive effects of inequality.

A more sophisticated argument for differences in income is the contention that the market needs those differences as "signals," that direct activity in ways that cannot be calculated by some central authority. This is in line with Friedrich von HAYEK's ideas, developed in opposition to socialist economists' plans for a centralized system. Hayek argued, in what has become one of the most powerful rationales in favor of capitalism as a market-based economy, that economic signals such as PRICES (wages are prices of labor in this sense, too) are in fact the best way to cope with the essentially incomplete and fragmented knowledge of the state of things. Prices tell us, in condensed form, about the conditions of production of goods we could never know in detail.

Income, productivity, and the winner-take-all economy. But what determines who gets what—or how much? Economic theory, in its now dominant neoclassical version, gives a very clear answer: What we earn depends on what we produce. This is called the marginal productivity theory of income. In theory, that is, if all the necessary conditions hold (most important of all, that no agent can manipulate prices of the factors of production), workers get a wage that is exactly proportional to the value they add. Imagine that a pin factory worker is able to make 1,000 pins per day. According to neoclassical economics, we would expect him, all other things being equal, to earn twice the salary of another worker who makes 500 pins per day, since in equilibrium no one would be willing to pay more than that to the less productive worker. As in other accounts of neoclassical economics, any other outcome is the result of a distortion, for example, if workers are unionized and control the supply of work, or "hide" individual productivity levels in collective arrangements.

But, as we have seen, we find a much higher degree of inequality than what absolute differences in productivity could account for. Perhaps it is relative differences in productivity that matter, as the so-called tournament theory claims. Small differences may get huge rewards if being first is the only valid goal.

Michael Jordan helped the Chicago Bulls score a few more points than their rivals, but that made all the difference, and that's why he got such a high compensation. Astonishing salaries (and stock options) of corporate CHIEF EXECUTIVE OFFICERS (CEOs) may also tie to this winner-take-all economy.

BIBLIOGRAPHY. A.B. Atkinson and F. Bourguignon, eds., *Handbook of Income Distribution* (North Holland-Elsevier, 1998); Census Bureau, United States Department of Commerce, www.census.gov; Friedrich Hayek, "The Use of Knowledge in Society," *American Economic Review* (v.35/4, 1945); Luxembourg Income Study, www.lisproject.org; Ingrid H. Rima, *Development of Economic Analysis* (Routledge, 2001); Edward N. Wolff, *Economics of Poverty, Inequality, and Discrimination* (South-Western, 1997); World Bank, www.worldbank.org; *CIA World Factbook* (2003).

EMILIO LUQUE, PH.D.
UNED UNIVERSITY, SPAIN

income distribution theories

IN CLASSICAL ECONOMIC theory there were three factors of production—LABOR, CAPITAL, and LAND. In modern economic theory a fourth factor of production, entrepreneurship, is often added. The concept of labor is fairly self-explanatory. It refers to the human input into production, the process of working itself. Capital refers to the tools, machinery, and all non-human (excluding natural) material with which labor works to produce output. Land refers to land itself, as well as other natural resources that are needed to produce goods and services. By introducing a fourth factor, entrepreneurship, the services of those who initiate, oversee, and control production are separated out from the first human factor, labor.

In the process of production these factors are combined to produce the myriad goods and services within an economy. The factors are then paid for their productive services, so that the total output is divided among them, either according to what they have contributed to production or according to their position within economic society. The study of how and why the total output is divided the way it is among the factors of production is called the theory of income distribution.

Economists from different perspectives have addressed the issue of income distribution in many different ways. This is not surprising, given the political import of how the theory is developed. If, for example, we argue that labor is paid less than what it contributes to output, then the inevitable conclusion is that workers are exploited, and capitalism is an unjust system. If, on the other hand, we say that labor, and all the other factors of production, are paid what they create, then we can conclude that capitalism is a just and fair economic system. The main theoretical positions on income distribution over the years include the following: classical, Marxist, marginal productivity, post-Keynesian, and neo-Ricardian.

We will discuss the two most important theories below. The first, developed by Karl MARX in the 19th century, takes the position that labor, in opposition to capital (which is owned by capitalists), is exploited under a capitalist system. The second, developed primarily in the 20th century, argues that all factors of production are paid according to their contribution to production and thus the capitalist system is fair.

Marxist theory of income distribution. Marx's primary concern in his theory of distribution was how output was divided between capitalists and workers. He considered these two factors of production—capital and labor—as the two great classes under capitalism, and an explication of the relationship between them as crucial to an understanding of the laws of motion of capitalism. It was particularly important for Marx to view workers as members of the working class, and not as isolated individuals who happened to be working for capitalists. Because they are members of this class they enter into certain social relationships with the capitalist class and it is this class relationship that is paramount for an understanding of income distribution.

In order for production to begin, the capitalist hires the worker to work for a particular period of time, say one day. The worker, of course, expects to get paid by the capitalist in exchange for his or her labor. The question for a theory of distribution is then, how much should this worker receive for his or her effort? How are wages, in general, determined in a capitalist economy?

Marx based his answers to these questions on his theory of the value of commodities. Put simply, the value of any commodity (a good or service that is produced for exchange, not for the use of the producer) is determined by the amount of labor necessary to produce it. This means that each commodity embodies a certain proportion of the total labor expended by society. Marx then argued that commodities would exchange with each other on the market according to these socially necessary proportions. As more labor was bestowed on a commodity, its value would increase, and it would exchange for a larger value in the market; in a competitive system, equal value would exchange for equal value.

Capitalist firms are in business to produce commodities. The whole point is to produce goods and services for sale at a price that will both recover the expenses laid out by the firm (for labor and all the non-human materials) and leave enough for a profit. But where can this profit be generated if all commodities are exchanged at equal value?

Marx answered this question with his theory of SUR-PLUS value. The key was to consider the ability to work, what he called labor-power, as a commodity. Even though this ability to work—which is embodied in workers—is not produced by firms, it is bought and sold on the (labor) market, and so becomes a commodity like all other commodities. Its value is determined, as for all commodities, by the labor necessary to produce it, or in this case, the labor necessary to reproduce the worker. Marx writes: "For his maintenance [the worker] requires a given quantity of the means of subsistence . . . [thus] the value of labor-power is the value of the means of subsistence necessary for the maintenance of the laborer." The amount of the means of subsistence, or in other words, the worker's standard of living, is historically determined, depending on "the degree of civilization of a country."

So the capitalist buys labor-power for a day at its value as determined above. Let us say that this value is 6 hours (i.e., the value of what the worker consumes is 6 hours). If the working day is 8 hours, then there are 2 hours left over, in which the worker produces value beyond what the capitalist paid the worker. The worker creates what Marx called surplus value in these 2 extra hours. Because the capitalist owns anything produced by the firm, this surplus value—profit—accrues to the capitalist. We see that workers create more output in a day than is distributed back to them, meaning that a part of their day is spent creating value for capitalists.

Marx thought that this manner of distribution of output between workers and capitalists showed the exploitative nature of capitalism. Workers spend a portion of every day creating value for which they receive no compensation, with this value going to capitalists simply because they own the productive resources and therefore control production. Even though distribution is based on market exchange at equal values, workers are exploited by capitalists in the distribution of income between capital and labor.

Marginal-productivity theory of income distribution. The neoclassical marginal-productivity theory of income distribution, which was developed in the early 20th century, and which has become the dominant theory accepted by economists, stands in stark contrast to the Marxist theory. In this theory, capital and labor are seen as equal factors of production, each contributing to production, with each receiving their just reward. In particular, these two factors are not seen as representing the two great classes in capitalism, i.e., capital and labor are simply technical factors of production, and the sense of class, which is so important for Marx, is completely missing in this conception. The focus in neoclassical economics is always on the individual, who as the owner of a factor of production enters into the production process as an isolated unit, not representing a class in any way. Rather, capital and labor face each other as equals in the distribution of output, where exploitation does not occur, contrary to Marx where capital clearly has the upper hand and is able to exploit labor.

To understand the neoclassical theory we must first explain what is meant by the "value of the marginal product." One aspect of marginalism (the general concept of which is central to all of neoclassical theory) is that the marginal product of a factor can be defined as the added increment to total output which can be attributed to the addition of one unit of a factor to the production process. For example, if one more worker is hired (with all other factors remaining the same), and the total output of chairs rises from 49 units to 51 units, the marginal product of labor at that point would equal 2. The value of the marginal product is then defined as the marginal product multiplied by the price of the commodity being produced. In this case, if the price of a chair were $120, then the value of the marginal product would be $240.

From this concept of marginal product, neoclassical theorists then developed a general theory of the distribution of income between the factors of production. Not surprisingly, this theory is a form of SUPPLY and DEMAND theory, not unlike the neoclassical theory of prices. The supply of any factor is calculated to be positively sloped, while the demand is calculated to be negatively sloped, with the market price determined by the intersection of the supply and demand curves.

In the theory of the distribution of income, the firms would demand a productive service so that the value of the marginal product would equal the factor price, for example, the wage. What this means is that a certain amount of output (the marginal product) can be said to be produced by a worker, and that the wage paid to the worker will exactly equal the value of that extra output (the value of the marginal product). Thus, the worker receives as payment exactly what he or she produced. This conclusion can be generalized to all of the other factors so that each one of them also receives exactly what it has produced.

By treating all factors of production in the same way, neoclassical theory removes the political dimension from the theory of income distribution. Each factor simply becomes a technical component in the process of production, with distributive shares determined precisely by contribution to production. As long as competitive market forces work freely, exploitation does not exist. Rather, the conclusion one draws from this theory is that income distribution under capitalism is ethical just because each factor receives back as payment exactly what it contributed to production.

Conclusions. Because of their inherent political component there are many theories of income distribution. We have discussed here the two main ones that are current today. These two theories of income distribution give distinctly different views of the capitalist economic system. The first, derived from Marx, sees capitalism as an exploitative system, squeezing surplus value out of workers, who receive minimal wages unrelated to their productive contributions. Capitalists receive profits not because they have contributed anything to production, but because they own the productive resources and are able to hire workers (who are defined precisely as that

group which does not own the productive resources and therefore must work for others) to labor for them.

Neoclassical theory, on the other hand, sees capitalism as a system in which all of the factors of production voluntarily come together to produce output, which is then distributed back to them in a fair and just manner. Capitalism is seen as a system in which individuals, as owners of the factors of production, but not as members of classes, enter into the productive process on an equal basis, and receive payments because of their productive contributions. Capitalism, far from being an exploitative system, rewards individuals who are productive members of society.

BIBLIOGRAPHY. Athanasios Asimakopulos, ed., *Theories of Income Distribution* (Kluwer Academic, 1988); Mark Blaug, *Economic Theory in Retrospect* (Cambridge University Press, 1978, third edition); C. E. Ferguson, *Microeconomic Theory* (Irwin, Inc., 1972); Michael C. Howard, *Modern Theories of Income Distribution* (St. Martin's Press, 1979); Karl Marx, *Capital* (International Publishers, 1967); Bradley R. Schiller, *The Macro Economy Today* (McGraw-Hill, 2000); Paul M. Sweezy, *The Theory of Capitalist Development* (Monthly Review Press, 1970).

PAUL A. SWANSON
WILLIAM PATERSON UNIVERSITY

income statement

ALSO CALLED THE statement of income, statement of earnings, or statement of operations, the income statement reports the revenues and expenses for a period. The excess of revenues over expenses is called net income. An ACCOUNTING principle, called the matching concept, is applied in recognizing the revenues and expenses for the period. The term PROFIT is also widely used for this measure of performance, but accountants prefer to use the technical terms, net income or net earnings. If the expenses used in generating the revenue exceed the revenue, the excess is the net loss for the period.

An income statement is the primary measure of performance of a business, during a period. The accounting period used to measure the income can be a month, a quarter, or a year. Usually, one year is the most widely used period of measurement.

GENERALLY ACCEPTED ACCOUNTING PRINCIPLES (GAAP) require that financial statements should be prepared in accordance with accrual-basis accounting principles. The matching concept is the essence of accrual-basis accounting. Therefore, an understanding of the matching concept is important to grasp the concept of accrual-basis accounting. In its simplest form, matching concept requires that all the expenses incurred to generate a period's revenue should be recorded (matched) in the same period regardless of when paid. Conversely, if the expenses of the next accounting period are paid in the current period, they cannot be deducted in the current year; they need to be deducted (matched) with the revenues of the next year. Accrual-basis accounting also requires that revenues should be recorded when earned, regardless of the timing of the cash receipts.

There is another form of accounting, called cash-basis accounting, which is usually used by very small businesses. It is based on the actual cash receipt and payment system. Therefore, under this system, revenue would not be recognized (included) in the income statement until actually collected. Similarly only those expenses, which have actually been paid, are recorded as expenses. Because, by choosing the timing of the payment of expenses or collection of revenues, income of the business can be manipulated, GAAP does not recognize the cash method of accounting as an acceptable method of reporting income.

Components of the income statement. Business entities earn revenues from the sale of goods and services to customers. It is immaterial if cash has been received. If the business substantially has done all that it was supposed to do to have a right on the agreed-upon revenues from customers, revenue should be recognized in the period when it was earned, regardless of the timing of the collection.

Expenses represent the dollar amount of resources the entity used to earn revenues during the period. In accordance with the matching principle, again the timing of the payment of expenses does not matter. It is the timing of the obligation to pay for the expenses that counts. Thus, revenues are not necessarily the same as collections and expenses are not necessarily the same as payments to suppliers, landlord, utility company, or employees. It follows that because of this timing difference, net income normally does not equal the cash generated by operations. Expenses are further divided into two main categories, selling expenses and general and administrative expenses.

Merchandising or manufacturing companies first calculate the gross profit on sales as an intermediary step before calculating the net income. Gross profit is the excess of the selling price (revenue) over the cost of the product sold. From the gross profit, total expenses are deducted in order to arrive at the net income number.

GAAP requires providing the user of the financial statement a detailed breakdown of the sources of income, so that the user can evaluate the quality of the income. Therefore, operating income resulting from the entity's main activity and from its day-to-day operations is separately calculated, and shown in the income statement. Income arising from non-frequent or ancillary activities of the business is separately calculated. The presentation of the income statement (and supported by detailed notes) in this manner helps a user to assess the long-term earning power of the company and not be misguided by one-time or infrequent income or loss items. For example, if there was loss on the sale of the textile division of the company, it will be separately reported as "other revenues and gains" (and not as part of the operating income). Similarly, if there was a loss due to an earthquake, it will be reported under the category called "extraordinary items," within the income statement.

GAAP also requires that companies calculate earnings per share (EPS) and show it on the face of the income statement. EPS is the net income divided by number of common stock shares in hands of the shareholders. It needs to be separately calculated for different income numbers such as income per share from continuing operations, loss per share from discontinued operation, and so on.

Users of income statements. Prospective or existing owners/investors, financial analysts, bank loan officers, income tax authorities, customers, and suppliers—all of these people need to use the income statement to analyze the company's performance over a period of time. Management of an entity needs it to compare the actual results to the budgets and take appropriate corrective measures, if needed. Investors are interested in the income statement of the company to evaluate the company's performance and divest if necessary.

The preparation and the use of the income statement is not limited to the business or for-profit companies. Not-for-profit entities such as American Cancer Society would need to prepare an income statement and other financial reports for its donors, management, and for the governmental agencies. An income statement for a not-for-profit entity would include a breakdown of various sources of revenues and how much and in what categories money was spent. It would also show what was the fund balance in the beginning and at the end of the year.

BIBLIOGRAPHY. Libby, Libby, and Short, *Financial Accounting* (McGraw-Hill, 2004); Kieso, Weygandt, and Warfield, *Intermediate Accounting* (John Wiley & Sons, 2001); Warren, Reeve, and Fess, *Financial Accounting* (South-Western, 1999).

SYED MOIZ, PH.D.
MARIAN COLLEGE

incorporation

THE LEGAL CREATION of an entity having an existence separate from its owners is termed incorporation. Examples are business corporations, NONPROFIT corporations, professional corporations, limited partnerships, limited-liability companies, limited-liability partnerships and business trusts. Opposed to such entities are sole proprietorships and general PARTNERSHIPs that are not legally separate from their owners.

An incorporated entity has three advantages: continuity of existence, centralized management, and the ability to accumulate large amounts of capital. Large business enterprises require large amounts of capital; even medium-sized corporations today require more capital than is owned by any individual except the rare billionaire. An incorporated entity allows for the pooling of investments from a large number of individuals.

Incorporated entities have continuity of existence, with most having a perpetual life. The capital accumulated in such entities will continue to be used for various purposes even though the individual owners die or sell their ownership interests.

This is unlike a sole proprietorship or a general partnership whose business existence terminates when the owners die or decide to leave the business.

Incorporated entities have the advantage of centralized management. Individual owners are not required to participate in day-to-day management and can hire professional managers whose expertise is more likely to make the enterprise profitable. This is different from sole proprietors and general partners who have full management rights.

People who invest in incorporated entities also gain advantages. First, they normally have limited liability for the debts and liabilities of the business. The statutes under which these entities are formed usually stipulate that the investors are liable only for the amount of money they promised to pay for their interest in the entity. Second, investors normally have the right to freely transfer their interests in the business. The business entity itself is not affected by the transfer and the investor does not need the permission of the managers of the entity before making the transfer.

Sole proprietors and general partners have unlimited liability for the debts and liabilities of their businesses. Moreover, if a sole proprietor or a general partner attempts to transfer his or her ownership interest in the business, this business normally terminates.

Very small incorporated entities often lose or give up some of these advantages. The shareholders of a very small corporation are often so few in number that all of them are directors and the principal employees of the corporation. Such shareholders often agree to restrict the free transferability of interests in the corporation to avoid having outsiders take over the business. These shareholders often do not have limited liability since they actively participate in management and may be required to personally guarantee the debts of the corporation.

The creation and operation of incorporated entities is governed by statute. Although there are some federally chartered corporations in the UNITED STATES, the vast majority are created under state law. The normal state statute requires the filing of documents with a central office such as the secretary of state or the department of commerce. If the entity is to be a business corporation, the document is called the corporate charter or the corporate articles of incorporation.

Management of the business is turned over to a small group such as the directors of a business corporation, a management committee of a limited-liability company, or some other such group. These people are responsible for the general business policy of the entity and often delegate some of their authority to officers and high-level employees. The responsibilities of directors, officers, and high-level employees are often spelled out in by-laws, resolutions of the directors, and other documents.

The managers of the business are also in charge of selling ownership interests in the business to various investors. In a corporation, these owners are shareholders. In other entities they may be limited partners or members. In many cases, owners have some control over the incorporated entity because they are allowed to vote on whom will be managers. Most business corporation acts require an annual meeting of shareholders where these shareholders have the right to elect a new board of directors. Similar rights exist with respect to other kinds of incorporated entities.

One area of major concern is the relationship between managers and investors. The law states that managers owe a fiduciary duty to the investors. Since investors have very little control over the managers, it is often possible for managers to conduct the affairs of the business in such a way as to damage the interests of the investors. Once ownership and control are separated, the possibility of abuse easily arises. The history of American business can be written around scandals where managers have abused the trust of the owners, and enriched themselves at the expense of the owners and employees of the business. Law and business ethics have struggled with various mechanisms to avoid or limit breaches of fiduciary duties by management.

BIBLIOGRAPHY. John Alexander and Harry Henn, *Henn and Alexander's Handbook on Corporations* (West Group, 1986); Adolf Berle and Gardner Means, *The Modern Corporation and Private Property* (Macmillan, 1932).

DAVID PAAS, J.D., PH.D.
HILLSDALE COLLEGE

India

LOCATED ON THE SOUTH Asia peninsula with the Indian Ocean and the island of Sri Lanka to the south and the Himalayan Mountains to the north, India has a tropical monsoon climate except in the mountains. Major rivers include the sacred Ghanges and Bhramaputra in the north, the Indus in the west, and the Namarla, Godavari, Krishna, and Kaveri Rivers in the center and south.

The country has a population of over one billion people rivaling CHINA as the largest in the world. Unlike China, India has been unsuccessful in controlling population growth. Natural resources have been heavily denuded to support this growth, especially natural forests and topsoil, as well as coastal marine resources. India has surprisingly few cities with populations over 10 million people, but they include its capital New Delhi in the north, its major west coast port Mumbai (Bombay), and its major east coast port Kolcata (Calcutta).

Over 70 percent of the population is rural and a big economic problem is adequate rainfall at the right time and place for a bountiful harvest. India's official languages include Hindi (derived from ancient Sanskrit), English (from the British colonization of India until 1947), Punjabi (in the western provinces), and 15 major and 1,600 minor additional languages. Major ethnicities include 72 percent northern Indo-Aryans and 25 percent southern Dravidians. Religiously, 83 percent are Hindus, 10 percent Muslim, 2.6 percent Christian, 2 percent Sikh, 1 percent Buddhist, and 1 percent Jain. Such variety is largely due to an endless historical stream of invasions and migration into the region.

The Hindu caste system, derived from the Indo-Aryan migrations into north India over 3,000 years ago, is still the major organization of Indian society, with some 60 percent of the population designated as low-caste or *dalit*. About 15 percent of the Hindu population consists of the *Brahmin* priestly caste, who are often Indo-Aryan and wealthy. India has a population density of 277 inhabitants per square kilometer, and over 15 million people who live and work overseas.

The current, multi-linguistic, ethnic, and religious identity of India is represented in India's ruling group the National Democratic Alliance (NDA). India's socialist past, which helped it gain independence from the British Empire in 1947 under the leadership of Ghandi, is represented by the main opposition party, the Indian National Congress (INC). Together, the NDA and INC struggle for control of an economic system rooted in colonial MERCANTILISM, independence-period SOCIALISM, and new-millennium global capitalism.

Beginning with the 4,500-year-old Indus River valley civilization of the Punjab, the subcontinent of India has been at the center of Afro-Eurasian trade, migration, and invasion routes by land and sea because of its central geographic location and highly prized natural resources such as spices and jewels. Civilizations from the ancient Sumerians to the Han Chinese to the Romans have sought land- and sea-trade routes to India and today, these linkages continue. Well-educated, English-speaking Indians often leave India for jobs around the world, while Asian, Western, and Middle Eastern industries seek the inexpensive labor pool within India to keep costs down. Despite such global linkages, during the 1990s India had persistent 10-percent unemployment and inflation rates, foreign debt of close to $200 billion, and gross domestic and national production of less than $500 per person. Despite recent indications of political and social reform as evidenced by the 1997 election of Kocheril Raman Narayanan as president, the economic outlook for India's move toward capitalism is mixed.

Recent attempts to modernize the rail system have not led to a national transportation and communication infrastructure. Air and ship travel are still best between cities while a haphazard mixture of telephone, telegraph, and telex suffice for communication. India's debt-straddled, multi-interest state is only able to spend about $9 per person for education. This does not compare favorably with other rising east Asian, state-run economies that serve as a model for India, where spending is often 10 times more.

India's population is frugal, saving over 22 percent of its rupees (Indian currency) but unreliable rainfall forces many of India's 700 million rural inhabitants to borrow money at high rates of interest to buy food. Government efforts to remedy the food situation are hampered by high inflation prices and poor transportation. Additionally, the privatization of state-run businesses by selling them off or trying to make them competitive by encouraging joint foreign ventures, has

The Taj Mahal, a symbol of eternal love, also attests to the wealth of the emperor who built it for his late wife.

only led to foreign-owned but Indian-administered industry that seeks profitable global markets rather than developing Indian markets.

India is the world's largest producer of tea, mangoes, sugar, and jute, but it also does well in rubber, tobacco, textiles, spices, and gems. India is self-sufficient in rice, grain, and dairy products but earthquakes, monsoon storms, droughts, poor storage, and transport cause great fluctuation in its staple products and food supply at a regional level. In manufactured products, India produces and exports clothing and textiles often made of native cotton. India is rich in mineral resources such as iron ore, bauxite, and chromite, leading to steel, chemical, rubber, and heavy machinery exports. This is offset by India's need for hydrocarbons in the form of oil as energy for its privatizing industries. Current consumption is over two billion barrels of crude oil per day compared with only 643,000 barrels of crude oil production per day within India. Many rural residents rely heavily upon wood for power but the forest reserves are now decimated. Increasing production of natural gas, thermal, and hydroelectric sources must happen quickly to relieve the energy situation. Unfortunately, this appears unlikely as major foreign power- and energy-investors include troubled transnational companies, such as the collapsed ENRON. Such foreign companies have an abysmal record in India and now are looked upon with suspicion and distrust by the majority of the labor force.

Although a stock market and banking system has existed in India since the days of the Dutch and British EAST INDIA companies, government debt, public poverty, and distrust of foreign corruption have led to an increasing reliance on a strong central bank and regional stock markets for funding the growth of capitalistic enterprises. The Reserve Bank of India now firmly controls India's banking system. Even private banks must contribute to national initiative projects. Since 1986, the Bombay Stock Exchange has also helped fund this growth but foreign-derived corruption scandals involving banks and shares have hurt the Indian banks and stock exchanges in 2001.

A more promising sign is the establishment of information technology (IT) enterprises in India, with the second-largest "Silicon Valley" being Bangalore in the south of the country. These IT firms present enormous potential for generating local employment and earning foreign exchange.

Many economists believe India must first negotiate power relationships between various groups with differing belief systems inside and outside of India. Then a civilization infrastructure of transport, communication, and education can be addressed. Only afterward can India move beyond a patchwork of local economic systems. Conflict between Hindu, Sikh, or Muslim, between PAKISTAN, China, or India, only masks the more

serious social economic issues within India due to its fascinating past and future population growth.

BIBLIOGRAPHY. G. Das, *Indian Unbound: The Social and Economic Revolution from Independence to the Global Information Age* (Knopf, 2001); India Department of Commerce, www.nic.in/eximpol; P. Maitra, *The Globalization of Capitalism in Third World Countries* (Praeger, 1996); B. Nevaskar, *Capitalists Without Capitalism: The Jains of India and the Quakers of the West* (Greenwood Publishing Group, 1971); A. Sen and J. Dreze, *India: Economic Development and Social Opportunity* (Oxford University Press, 1996).

CHRIS HOWELL
RED ROCKS COLLEGE

Indonesia

A NATION OF ISLANDS, Indonesia consists of eight major and over 17,000 smaller islands. Situated in the Indian Ocean between Asia and Australia, the unique natural resources of the area have played a significant role in its economic development. The earliest settlers to the islands were attracted, perhaps, by the stores of metallic ores including tin, nickel, copper, gold, and silver. In the 2nd century, the Greek geographer Ptolemy reported that the islands possessed a relatively advanced economy, including the use of special dyes for their *batik* clothing, the production of metal wares, and metal coinage. The islanders were active traders and participated in elaborate trading networks with southern INDIA, Persia, southeast Asia, and later CHINA and JAPAN.

Exotic spices were another important natural resource. Cinnamon, mace, and nutmeg were rumored to have medicinal or magical properties. Lured by such rumors (and high profits), several European countries came to these spice islands in the 1500s. Control over the luxury trade was hotly contested between the Portuguese, the British, and the Dutch who ultimately prevailed. The secret of the Dutch success was the unification of the efforts of individual traders and trading companies under one umbrella organization, the Dutch East India Company (*Verenigde Oost Indische Compagnie*), or VOC, which became one of the world's most powerful company. Using funds raised from issues of stock, the VOC set up their headquarters in the city of Jakarta. Either as a private company or a branch of the government, Dutch interests would dominate the Indonesian economy until independence in 1949.

While the Dutch maintained a fairly effective monopoly in the native spices, they were not able to keep competitors out of the more lucrative pepper market, and they began to introduce new crops in an effort to offset the costs incurred in the defense and maintenance of their colony. The most successful of these was coffee, introduced to the island of Java in 1723. Despite these efforts, the VOC was beset by high costs, corruption, and poor management. By the latter part of the 18th century, its profitability was steadily declining. In 1800, the VOC was disbanded and the Dutch presence in Asia was assumed directly by a newly created government agency.

In 1830, the agency instituted a radical new policy called the *cultuurstelsel*, or Cultivation System. Under its auspices, Dutch overseers managed agricultural output in the islands to maintain a balance between subsistence crops for the natives and profitable export crops. Farmers were assigned quotas of each and had to sell to the Dutch state at fixed prices and to ship them on Dutch ships. The system quickly became very profitable and constituted as much as approximately one-third of the state's revenue throughout the nineteenth century.

Not everyone was pleased. In 1860, a former colonial official, using the alias Multatuli, published *Max Havelaar: The Coffee Auctions of the Dutch Trading Company*, a scathing condemnation of the Cultivation System that exposed the brutal exploitation of Javanese peasants upon which it rested. The government bowed to public pressure fueled by the book and instituted a series of reforms, such as public education and irrigation, that were collectively called the Ethical Policy. By the end of the century, most economic regulations had been removed and the local economy prospered.

In the 20th century, the Indonesian economy benefited from the presence of rich oil and gas reserves. Possession of such strategic commodities was less helpful during WORLD WAR II, as the islands became a frequent target for bombing raids, but the two fuels constitute the bulk of Indonesian export income to the present day. The other major export, timber, is in increasing jeopardy because of deforestation. Since World War II, the Indonesian economy has had periods of prosperity but faces serious problems in the form of chronic political instability, corruption, and massive debt.

Indonesia is the most populous Muslim country in the world, with a GROSS DOMESTIC PRODUCT (GDP) of $687 billion (2000) for a population of 231 million.

BIBLIOGRAPHY. Anne Booth and W.J. O'Malley, *Indonesian Economic History in the Dutch Colonial Era* (Yale University Press, 1990); Anthony Reid, *Southeast Asia in the Age of Commerce 1450–1680: The Land Below the Winds* (Yale University Press, 1990); M.C. Riklefs, *A History of Modern Indonesia Since c. 1200* (Stanford University Press, 2002); Bernard M. Vlekke, *The Story of the Dutch East Indies* (AMS Press, 1973); *CIA World Factbook* (2003).

LAURA CRUZ
WESTERN CAROLINA UNIVERSITY

industrial organization

AS ECONOMIST Kaushik Basu notes, the importance of a field becomes evident when it usurps the acronym of another. For a long time, a mention of "IO" in economics would certainly be taken as a reference to input-output analysis. Today, however, "IO" is for certain to be taken as a reference to industrial organization (or industrial economics, as it is called in Europe).

In short, industrial organization is the study of the functioning of markets or industries. Studies in industrial organization have influenced, and are continuing to influence, the formulation and implementation of public policy in such areas as regulation and deregulation, the promotion of competition through antitrust policy and merger guidelines, and the stimulation of innovation and technological progress through subsidies and granting of PATENTS.

Industrial Organization is not a new subject. The field's foundations are traceable to Adam SMITH (1776), Antoine Cournot (1838), Alfred MARSHALL (1879), and Joseph Bertrand (1883), who are viewed by many as pioneers of industrial organization. However, it took a long time and two waves of interest for industrial organization to become what it is today, one of the major fields in MICROECONOMICS.

The first wave, known as classical industrial organization, is best characterized by the famous structure, conduct, performance approach. The basic idea of this approach is that market structure (i.e., the number of firms in a market, the degree of product differentiation, the cost structure, the degree of vertical integration, and so on) determines market conduct or pricing, research and development activities, investment, advertising, and so on. Market conduct then yields market performance that is measured by cost efficiency, price-cost margins, product variety, and innovation rates.

One can think of a profit-maximizing MONOPOLY as a theoretical model relying on the structure-conduct-performance approach. Assuming that the monopolist maximizes profit by choosing the level of output, the first order necessary condition for a maximum implies that the percentage deviation of price from marginal cost be equal to the inverse of the absolute value of the price elasticity of demand. Strictly speaking, this EQUILIBRIUM condition does not imply anything regarding causality, however it seems natural to view causality flowing from the demand elasticity to the price, the cost margin. Thus, from the basic conditions (DEMAND) via structure (MONOPOLY) we move to conduct (profit maximization) and performance (price cost margin). The structure-conduct-performance approach, although plausible, often rested on "loose" theories and emphasized case studies and empirical studies of industries. In fact, during this first wave of interest, industrial organization became synonymous with empirical studies of industries.

Typically, some measure of industry profitability was regressed on some measures of industry concentration, barriers to entry, and other proxies for structural variables of the industries under consideration. These regressions were run on cross-sectional data for a large sample of industries. Ignoring measurement problems, such regressions produced an array of stylized facts or regularities. However, the "links" between variables must be interpreted as correlations or descriptive statistics, not as causal relationships. The absence of causal interpretation is unsatisfactory from a theoretical perspective.

The finding that the price-cost-margin increases with the concentration in an industry suggests that firms in concentrated industries have market power and that the performance of these industries is not optimal. However, it does not reveal anything about the causes of market power and does not provide any guidelines for public policy aimed at improving market performance. Nevertheless, the first wave (i.e., the empirical tradition with its regressions and case studies) set an agenda for industrial organization. It also has to be noted that the first wave, or classical industrial organization, did not completely ignore economic theory. Still, growing dissatisfaction with the limitations of the empirical analysis and its lack of theoretical foundations gave rise to the second wave, that many have labeled the new industrial organization.

This second wave of interest started in the 1970s and was primarily fueled by the fact GAME THEORY imposed itself as a unifying methodology to the analysis of strategic interaction in markets. To a degree, the second wave re-launched the research started by Cournot and Bertrand. The new industrial organization utilizes the tools of microeconomic theory and game theory to analyze strategic interactions among firms in markets that are between the extreme cases of perfect competition and pure monopoly.

As a result, new solution concepts such as John NASH's equilibrium, dominant strategy equilibrium, sub-game perfect equilibrium, to mention a few, have been applied. Non-cooperative, as well as cooperative game theory, are used to explain behavior of firms operating under specific market conditions. Furthermore, dynamic analysis has in many instances replaced the old static approaches to the analysis of market structures. The New Industrial Organization has successfully formalized some of the informal stories and rejected others that were used to explain the results of the regressions analysis of the structure-conduct-performance approach. The theoretical contributions of the second wave have also fed back to empirical analysis. Cross-sectional studies of particular industries have been complemented by time-series analysis of the same industry, as well as comparisons of different industries. Advances in industrial organization, brought about by the new industrial organization, have also led to changes in other fields in economics.

Models of perfect competition are being replaced with models of imperfect competition in international trade and macroeconomic theory. In fact, one can argue that the new industrial organization was at the forefront of a drastic change that is going on in economic theory (i.e., re-examining all economic interactions as strategic interactions).

BIBLIOGRAPHY. Kaushik Basu, *Lectures in Industrial Organization Theory* (Blackwell, 1993): F.M. Scherer, *Industrial Market Structure and Economic Performance* (Rand McNally, 1980); Richard Schmalensee and Robert D. Willig, *The Handbook of Industrial Organization* (v. 1, North Holland, 1989). William G. Shepherd, *The Economics of Industrial Organization* (Prentice Hall, 1985); Oz Shy, *Industrial Organization: Theory and Applications* (MIT Press, 1995); Jean Tirole, *The Theory of Industrial Organization* (MIT Press, 1989).

KLAUS G. BECKER, PH.D.
TEXAS TECH UNIVERSITY

Industrial Revolution

THE WORDS "Industrial Revolution" have been used to describe the most extensive change the world has ever experienced. The term was coined by English philosopher John Stuart MILL (1806–73) but was brought into popular use by English historian Arnold Toynbee (1889–1975). The most significant aspect of the Industrial Revolution was that it changed much of the world from a collection of separate agrarian communities into interconnected industrialized cities.

In the process, much of the work that had been done by human hands for centuries began to be performed by machines, which were faster and more efficient than humans could ever be. While many scholars accept 1760–1850 as the official period in which the Industrial Revolution took place, it actually continued into the 20th century in parts of the world and continues to evolve in developing nations into the 21st century.

Pre-Industrial Revolution. When the Industrial Revolution began in Europe, most people supported themselves from agriculture in some way. Agricultural practices had changed little since the Middle Ages. Families not only grew the food they ate but also made their own tools, clothing, and household items. Many workers did not own the land they farmed. Sometimes land was divided into strips that were farmed by different workers. Agriculture production was often inefficient because farmers did not understand the best way to use the land.

A common practice, in the early part of the 17th century, was to grow winter wheat one year, plant summer wheat the following year, and then allow the land to remain idle during the third year. Animals used fallow land for grazing, which upset nature's way of caring for arable land. Either famine or drought frequently destroyed crops, and whole communities went hungry when crops failed. Life was hard, and the mortality rate was high because diseases were common. Medical knowledge was often nonexistent, unavailable, or inadequate. Education was rare among the working and lower classes. Since people rarely traveled, many of them knew little of the world beyond their immediate areas.

The only sources of power on most farms were human muscles and animal strength. On a farm, human work generally included planting seed, gathering and chopping firewood, harvesting crops, and threshing grain. Horses, mules, or oxen usually pulled plows and transported goods. As knowledge advanced, people began using wind and water as sources of power to grind flour, pound cloth, saw timber, and crush stones. Villages might also have blacksmiths, carpenters, and wheelwrights. Women sometimes worked alongside the men in the fields, but were still expected to perform essential household tasks. Additionally, some women worked in their homes producing hand-made goods that could be sold to help support the family. Cloth-making was a major industry in Europe, and much of it was produced by women working in their homes.

Early stages of the Industrial Revolution. As the 18th century began, Europe was on the brink of enormous changes that would alter the entire world. Industrialization progressed faster in England than the rest of Europe because it was a land that possessed many essential resources, such as coal and iron. The population was rapidly growing to meet the needs of additional workers, and both the physical climate and the political climate were relatively stable. Between 1700–1850, the population of Europe doubled, while the population of England tripled. The North American population grew from one million to 26 million during this same period. As TECHNOLOGY and innovation grew, agricultural knowledge expanded accordingly. New and better ways of using the soil made agriculture more efficient and productive. The Dutch developed improved methods of rotating crops that did not exhaust the land so rapidly, and the number of agricultural products expanded when North Americans began to grow potatoes, tomatoes, beans, and corn for the first time. Farmers began to concentrate on growing special products rather than on trying to grow everything they needed or could sell from a limited number of acres. New machines were developed that improved farming still further. In England, for instance, Robert Ransome invented a self-sharpening plow; and in the UNITED STATES, John Deere invented a steel plow. Both inventions saved time for farmers that could be used elsewhere, making them more productive.

By the beginning of the 18th century, England had become the center of the cloth-making industry; and as industrialization progressed, the demand for all kinds of cloth products increased. Advances in machinery brought this industry into factories and away from the cottage industries that had sprung up earlier to meet the ever-growing need for cloth. Cotton replaced wool as the most commonly used textile because it was cheaper and it uses were more varied. New inventions, such as the flying shuttle, the "Spinning Jenny," combing and carding machines, and the power loom improved both efficiency and production in textile mills.

The iron industry also grew rapidly as the Industrial Revolution progressed. Iron was used to build railroads, steamships, machinery and bridges. New ways of producing purer iron of higher-quality resulted in additional uses for iron, such as farm implements, moving parts for factory machines and steam engines. However, it was the discovery of the process by which iron could be turned into steel that revolutionized the iron industry. In the mid-18th century, Henry Bessemer in England and William Kelly in the United States learned how to make steel by injecting air into molten ore. Steel became cheaper and more durable with this process; and thereafter, steel was used in making railroads, bridges, and buildings. This process paved the way for skyscrapers that would dominate cities in the following centuries.

Industrialization also brought about increased demand for coal to be used as fuel, which was needed to stoke the furnaces that produced steel. Once methods of mining were developed that allowed coalminers to dig deep into the earth, safety was a questionable issue. New ways of providing light and pumping water from the mines made mining safer, but then new problems developed. Small children were put to work bringing the coal to the surface, and what would later become known as black-lung disease developed among mine workers from breathing cold dust in confined spaces. Critics claimed that Great Britain became the world's manufacturing center by exploiting workers who were required to work long hours for little pay and under poor working conditions. Child labor became a major political issue, partly because of the practice of buying children from orphanages and workhouses to work in mills in Great Britain's cities.

Great Britain in the UNITED KINGDOM was the undisputed leader of manufacturing and technology in the early days of the Industrial Revolution. A full 75 percent of British exports were manufactured goods. Then, other European countries, such as GERMANY and FRANCE, began to covet Great Britain's success. At first, the countries simply sent representatives to England to observe the processes of industrialization. Afterward, these countries tried to entice industrialists, inventors, and workers to their countries. As a result, industrialization expanded throughout Europe. Inventors both in Europe and North America began flooding various industries with improvements, and Great Britain became afraid of losing industrial superiority. The country passed laws in 1774 and again in 1781 in an attempt to retain control over the spread of technology. Once expansion of industrialization became inevitable, Great Britain began to voluntarily export technology to countries such as RUSSIA and AUSTRIA. As industrialization spread, so did the need for raw products. These products were supplied from around the world. The United States, CANADA, AUSTRALIA, NEW ZEALAND, ARGENTINA, INDIA, and JAPAN all became major exporters.

Industrialization in the New World. Alexander HAMILTON (1755–1804), then serving as the first secretary of the Treasury, called for the Industrial Revolution to begin in the United States. He believed that the country would be left behind if the changes taking place in Europe were to bypass the New World. America was ripe for the Industrial Revolution because of its abundance of rich soil and available land. The country was new, and its citizens were eager for progress. Additionally, the American system was stable with a shared language and a citizenry who believed in equal opportunities and hard work, and who had a healthy respect for the law.

Foreign investors had been interested in the United States since the end of the AMERICAN CIVIL WAR, so CAPITAL was readily available for building factories, refineries, and mills. Once begun, the Industrial Revolution would progress much more rapidly in the United States than in other areas. American industrialists expanded an idea developed in Switzerland concerning the use of moveable parts for factory machines. They found that parts could be constructed so that moveable parts from one machine were interchangeable with moving parts from another machine. American industrialists also learned that continuous process manufacturing put out goods more quickly. Profits grew, and some of the money that was saved was spent on innovation, which in turn made even more money. The American economy was further transformed by the discovery of gold in California in 1848, and government revenues rose from $29 million in 1844 to $73 million in 1854.

New inventions and better ways of doing things guaranteed continued progress in the United States. In 1833, Obed Hussey developed a mechanical reaper, and the following year Cyrus McCormick patented an improved version that was widely used. In the American

The invention of the steam locomotive was one of the engines that pushed forward the Industrial Revolution.

West, cattle ranchers began to fence land to grow cattle, and range wars between the farmers and the ranchers became commonplace. In the South, rubber, coffee, sugar, and vegetable oil were grown for export. The major impact on Southern agriculture was Eli WHITNEY's invention of the cotton gin, which became instrumental in convincing farmers to switch from growing rice and tobacco crops to growing cotton. In the South, cotton became "king," and the result was that SLAVERY flourished throughout the region. The issue of slavery continued to divide the North and South until the AMERICAN CIVIL WAR, and its aftermath would create problems for the next one hundred years.

In 1785, Claude Berthollet discovered a way to bleach cloth, and the textile industry boomed as patterns printed on cloth made cotton even more versatile and desirable. Elias Howe and Isaac Singer invented the sewing machine almost simultaneously, providing more efficient ways of turning the cloth into other products. In 1789, Samuel Slater left England and brought his skills as a textile worker to the United States, where he designed the first spinning mill. Hamilton's ambitions had become reality. Over the course of the next century, countless numbers of immigrants would come to the United States seeking better lives and greater opportunity. Most of them came from Great Britain and IRELAND, but others left Italy, Germany, RUSSIA, and POLAND to swell their ranks. All of them would bring an element of their own culture into the "melting pot" that the United States had become.

The new industrial workers. The influx of women into the factory system began as the demand for workers resulted in recruitment of farm women who were used to hard work. Males were sometimes given bonuses for recruiting women workers. The women were often clustered together in boarding houses where they could be supervised during their time away from the factories. In factories such as those in Lowell, Massachusetts, women worked 14-hour days from 5 A.M. to 7 P.M. with 30-minute breaks twice a day for breakfast and dinner. Some of the workers were as young as 10, and they came from as far away as Canada. Although the work was hard, overall working conditions in the United States were better than those in Europe. Since the class system was more open and political rights were more readily available, workers were less likely to feel alienated from the system. This would change to some extent in the next century when battles between labor and management became common.

During the early part of the 20th century, industrialization continued to change life in the United States in major ways. Inventions of the past began to be used more commonly and to greater effect. Benjamin Franklin's experiments with electricity had identified its potential use as early as the 1740s, and by the late 1880s, some large cities had begun to develop utility systems. However, it was not until the 20th century that electricity became commonly used. Ilatian Alessandro Volta developed the first battery, and Michael Faraday learned how to generate electricity through coiled wire. In 1844, Samuel Morse invented the telegraph and transmitted the message "What God hath wrought" from Baltimore, Maryland, to Washington, D.C. These inventions were followed by Alexander Graham Bell's invention of the telephone in 1876 and Thomas EDISON's construction of the electric light bulb in 1879. By the turn of the century, Guglielmo Marconi had developed his work with transmitting electric signals to the point that instantaneous communication around the world was possible.

Petroleum, which was already a major industry in the United States, was changed forever when Gottlieb Daimler built the first gasoline-powered car in 1886. Henry FORD revolutionized the automobile industry when he modernized the process by which cars were assembled, producing the Model-T in 1908 at a cost of $825. By 1928, the price of an automobile had dropped to $399. In 1857, Frederick Winslow Taylor began to understand the principles of time and motion. Using a stopwatch, Taylor observed and timed workers, then used the information to develop more productive ways of accomplishing particular tasks. Improved transportation made it easier to send food products across the country and around the world. The food industry was further modernized through new processes of canning, preservation, and refrigeration. Agricultural researchers, such as Booker T. Washington, began to develop derivative products from existing foods. For instance, Washington discovered 325 products that could be made from peanuts and over 100 products that could be made from potatoes.

Industrialization had created corporate giants in the United States such as STANDARD OIL in the petroleum industry and the American Tobacco Company. These industries became so powerful that the federal government successfully sued them for forming monopolies. Industrialist and philanthropist Andrew CARNEGIE used the Bessemer process to produce steel and built the first modernized steel mill in Pittsburgh, Pennsylvania. As a result of the cheaper steel, American output increased from 19,000 tons to 10,000,000 at the turn of the century, and the United States began producing more steel than Great Britain and Germany combined. Further advances were made when interchangeable parts began to be used in guns, sewing machines, electrical equipment, calculators, cash registers, typewriters, and bicycles, making them all cheaper to produce and repair. With each new innovation, labor costs dropped further. By 1919, the United States was producing 35.8 percent of the world's capacity of goods. Its closest competitor was Germany at 15.7 percent, and Germany was reeling from the aftermath of WORLD WAR I.

Life had changed drastically for American women, and many began to demand the right to vote. This right was given in 1920 with the 19th Amendment to the U.S. Constitution. During World War I, women began to work in industries that had previously been closed to them, and they later dominated in many fields. This dominance led to the prominence of women in the early days of the labor movement. For example, in Elizabethton, Tennessee, two rayon plants were built that together employed around 5,000 mostly female workers. In 1929, 500 workers led a walkout, the first of many that would take place in textile mills across the country over the next decade. African-American women were hampered in their attempts for a better life because of legal segregation in the South and discrimination throughout the country. Many of them traded the hardships of the rural South for low-paying service jobs in the North. Industrialization was also a time of change for African-American men in the United States. Educator Booker T. Washington founded Tuskegee Institute in Tuskegee, Alabama, and began to educate African-Americans.

Advances in transportation continued to make the world much smaller during the Industrial Revolution. In

1763, James Watt improved on the earlier ideas of Thomas Newcomen and produced the internal-combustion steam engine, and by the early part of the 19th century, steam was used for sources of power all over the world. The invention of steam engines improved the RAILROADS to such an extent that they began to be used for travel as well as for transporting goods. Reduced travel time made travel more inviting. For example, in 1830, it took three weeks to travel from New York to Chicago, By 1857, the trip could be done in two days. Railroad mileage increased in all major industrial areas. In Great Britain, railroad mileage grew from 6,621 miles in 1850 to 23,387 in 1910. Germany's railroad mileage increased from 3,637 to 36,152 in the same period. The increase was even more dramatic in the United States. From 1840–1910, railroad mileage increased from 9,021 to 249, 902. Intercontinental travel by rail became a reality. In the 1800s, Robert Fulton and Patrick Bell developed the use of steamships for commercial use. In 1837, the Great Western carried passengers from England to the United States. Once ships were in common use, it became necessary to develop quicker routes, and the SUEZ CANAL was built to link the Mediterranean Sea and the Indian Ocean. By 1920, the construction of the PANAMA CANAL opened a shorter passageway between the Caribbean Sea and the Pacific Ocean. The world had truly become smaller place and was now irrevocably linked through travel, communication, economics, and politics.

BIBLIOGRAPHY. John Bowditch and Clement Ramsland, eds., *Voices of the Industrial Revolution* (University of Michigan Press, 1963); Henry Dale and Rodney Dale, *The Industrial Revolution* (Oxford University Press, 1992); Sara M. Evans, *Born Free: A History of Women in* America (The Free Press, 1989); John Steele Gordon, "The Business of America," *American Heritage* (June 2001); Andrew Langley, *The Industrial Revolution* (Viking, 1994); Brink Lindsey, "The Decline and Fall of the First Global Economy," *Reason* (December 2001); "Lowell Mill Girls," www.fordham.edu; Natalie McPherson, *Machines and Economic Growth* (Greenwood Press, 1994); Paul A. Samuelson, *Economics* (McGraw-Hill, 1973); Peter N. Stearns, *The Industrial Revolution in World History* (Westview Press, 1998); Gary M. Walton and Hugh Rockoff, *History of the American Economy* (Dryden, 1998); "What Was It Really Like to Live in The Middle Ages," www.learner.org; "Workhouse Children," www.spartacus.schoolnet.co.uk.

ELIZABETH PURDY, PH.D.
INDEPENDENT SCHOLAR

inflation

A CONTINUAL RISE in the general level of prices of goods and services is termed inflation. The inflation rate equals the percentage rate of increase in the price level within a certain period of time, usually a year. The two most widely used measures of the price level are the GROSS DOMESTIC PRODUCT (GDP) deflator and the Consumer Price Index (CPI). The former measures the average level of prices of goods and services included in GDP and is defined as follows:

GDP deflator = nominal GDP / real GDP

CPI measures the average level of prices of goods and services purchased by a typical consumer in the economy.

Why should we care about inflation? If the inflation rate is, say, 6 percent, and all prices and wages increase by 6 percent, why would it cause any major cost? The problem is that during inflation not all prices change proportionately; some prices (and wages) rise faster than others. Therefore, inflation can redistribute income from those who raise their prices to those who do not. It seems that despite this income redistribution, the economy as a whole does not become poorer as a result of higher inflation. However, inflation is usually associated with some undesirable consequences. Economists usually talk about the following costs of inflation:

1. A higher inflation rate leads to a higher interest rate and thus increases the opportunity cost of holding money. As a result, people will try to minimize their holdings of money and increase their trips to the bank. This cost of additional trips to the bank is called *shoe-leather cost*.

2. When prices are stable, it is easier for people to compare prices and make the right choices; when inflation is high, this kind of calculation becomes increasingly difficult. This argument is supported by evidence gathered by both psychologists and economists.

3. Since prices rise unevenly, inflation distorts efficiency of economic allocations.

4. Higher inflation is usually more variable. This makes financial assets riskier and increases uncertainty.

Inflation at moderate level has its benefits too. For example, the CENTRAL BANK may want the real interest rate to be negative, say, when the economy is in recession. The idea is that a low or negative interest rate makes investment spending attractive and may boost the economic performance. Recall that the real interest rate is the difference between the nominal interest rate, which cannot be negative, and inflation rate. If inflation rate is zero then the real interest rate cannot be negative and the central bank has very limited ability to help the economy.

High inflation, also called hyperinflation, is always a pathology. Two classical instances of hyperinflations are those in GERMANY in 1922–23 and in HUNGARY in 1945–46. The average monthly inflation rate during the German hyperinflation was around 320 percent, whereas the figure in Hungary was 19,800 percent. Hyperinflations are stopped through what is called a stabilization strategy. It is necessary to impose some control on wages to cut through the wage-price spiral. This is referred to as an incomes policy, which may require less frequent wage indexation, or an agreement between firms and workers about lower real wages. The recent examples of successful stabilizations include Bolivia in 1985, MEXICO in 1989, ARGENTINA in 1992, and BRAZIL in 1996. As the events in Argentina and Brazil suggest, stopping a hyperinflation is a very complex task. It takes government credibility for a stabilization policy to work.

It is widely believed that in developed countries, the optimal inflation rate is somewhere between 0 percent and 3 percent. Those who advocate price stability prefer 0 percent, whereas those who emphasize the benefit of small positive inflation prefer 3 percent.

Economists believe there is a short-run trade-off between inflation and unemployment. This relationship is called the PHILLIPS CURVE, after British economist A.W. Phillips who first observed a negative relationship between the inflation rate and the unemployment rate. The current version of this relationship can be described through this equation:

$$\pi = \pi^e - b(u-u^n) + \varepsilon, \, b>0$$

According to this relationship, the actual inflation rate π exceeds the expected rate of inflation π^e if the actual unemployment rate u exceeds the natural rate of unemployment u^n. (The role of the random term ε is discussed below.) It is clear that if a policymaker wants to decrease inflation there will be a price to pay in the short run (i.e. a higher unemployment rate and thus lower output). Economists use the notion of sacrifice ratio to measure the cost of lowering inflation. The sacrifice ratio is the percent deviation of output when the inflation rate is lowered by 1 percent. For the UNITED STATES and CANADA this ratio has been estimated to average around 2.4 and 1.5 over the 1960s, 1970s, and 1980s.

If inflation is not desirable, why do governments allow inflation to occur? Almost all cases of hyperinflation occur because of fiscal problems. Governments run large budget deficits and finance them through printing money. This argument is best supported by the so-called quantity theory of money. At the center of the theory is the quantity equation:

(percent change in M) + (percent change in V)
= (percent change in P) + (percent change in Y)

where M is the stock of money in the economy, V is the transaction velocity of money and measures how fast money circulates in the economy, P is the price level, and Y is real GDP. The percentage change in GDP Y depends on the factors of production and technological progress and thus taken as fixed. It is also assumed that velocity V does not change in the short run. Then the quantity theory of money states that the percentage change in the money stock changes one-to-one with the percentage change in the price level, which is inflation.

In other words, this theory claims that the central bank is in control of inflation. If it wants increases in money supply then inflation will pick up. If the central bank wants the price level to be stable, it should keep the money supply stable.

The two terms in the Phillips Curve equation, $b(u-u^n)$ and ε, can explain how the inflation rate may change. The first term implies that if the unemployment rate exceeds its natural level, this will put upward pressure on inflation. This is called demand-pull inflation for the source of the upward pressure comes from high aggregate demand. High unemployment puts downward pressure on inflation.

The second term, ε, indicates that inflation may go up and down as a result of supply shocks. An example of such a shock could be the oil price increase in the 1970s. This is called cost-push inflation for adverse supply shocks are responsible for higher production costs and eventually higher inflation.

BIBLIOGRAPHY. Laurence Ball, "What Determines the Sacrifice Ratio?" *Monetary Policy* (University of Chicago Press, 1994); Olivier Blanchard and Angelo Melino, *Macroeconomics* (Prentice Hall, 1999); Milton Friedman, "The Role of Monetary Policy," *American Economic Review* (v.58/1, 1968); Thomas Sargent, *Rational Expectations and Inflation* (HarperCollins, 1993); Eldar Sharif, Peter Diamond, and Amos Tversky, "Money Illusion," *Quarterly Journal of Economics* (v.112/2, 1997).

NURLAN TURDALIEV, PH.D.
MCGILL UNIVERSITY

information revolution

THE INFORMATION REVOLUTION is a phrase we use to refer to the dramatic changes taking place during the last half of the 20th century in which service jobs (ranging from high-technology, highly skilled professions to low-skill jobs) are more common than jobs in manufacturing or AGRICULTURE. The product of skilled professionals is the information or knowledge they provide. It is still early enough that no one knows precisely what all of the implications of the information revolution will be for social life. But clearly changes such as the information superhighway permitting people to communicate using computers all around the globe, fax machines, satellite dishes, and cellular phones are changing how families spend their time, the kind of work we do, and many other aspects of our lives.

At the end of WORLD WAR II, the first electronic digital computer, ENIAC, weighed thirty tons, had 18,000 vacuum tubes, and occupied a space as large as a boxcar. Less than 40 years later, many hand-held calculators had comparable computing power for a few dollars. Today most people have a computer on their desk with more computing power than engineers could imagine just a few years ago.

The impact of computers on our society was probably best seen in 1982 when *Time* magazine picked the computer as its "Man of the Year," actually listing it as "Machine of the Year." This perhaps shows how influential the computer had become in our society. The computer has become helpful in managing knowledge at a time when the amount of information is expanding exponentially. The information stored in the world's libraries and computers doubles every eight years. In a sense the computer age and the information age seem to go hand in hand.

The information revolution began with the invention of the integrated circuit or computer chip. Those chips have revolutionized our lives, running our appliances, providing calculators, computers, and other electronic devices to control our world.

Information revolution and the "new economy." There exists a general consensus among economists and noneconomists alike that information technology is creating an economy that is "new." Information technology is indeed revolutionizing the economy: creating new opportunities, allowing old tasks to be done in different ways, shifting relative costs. What is driving or shaping this change in business and economics? There is no simple answer to this very large question, but certainly very important is the ability of firms to obtain or transmit information at rates never before thought possible. Companies now have the ability to go from ideas to the production line within weeks. Investors have (almost) complete information in making important financial decisions. Students can use the internet to more effectively research a topic. Scientists around the world can better coordinate their efforts to combat the spread of disease. The information revolution created a new economy that is significantly more productive and significantly more efficient than anyone had ever thought possible.

The revolutionary impact of the information revolution is just beginning to be felt in the first decades of the 21st century. But it is not only information that fuels this impact, nor is it only artificial intelligence. It is also the effect of computers and data processing on decision-making, policymaking, and strategy. It is something that practically no one foresaw or, indeed, even talked about until the mid-1990s: e-commerce, that is, the explosive emergence of the internet as a major, perhaps eventually some predict, the major worldwide distribution channel for goods, for services, and, surprisingly, for managerial and professional jobs. This is profoundly changing economies, markets, and industry structures; products and services and their flow; consumer segmentation, consumer values, and CONSUMER BEHAVIOR; jobs and labor markets. But the impact may be even greater on societies and politics and, above all, on the way we see the world and ourselves in it.

Of course, these are only predictions. But they are made on the assumption that the information revolution will evolve as several earlier technology-based "revolutions" have evolved over the past 500 years, since Gutenberg's printing revolution in the mid-15th century. In particular, the assumption is that the information revolution will be like the INDUSTRIAL REVOLUTION of the late 18th and early 19th centuries. And that is, indeed, exactly how the information revolution has been progressing during its first decades.

Industrial Revolution vs. information revolution. The information revolution is now at the point at which the Industrial Revolution was in the early 1820s, about 40 years after James Watt's improved steam engine was first applied, in 1785, to an industrial operation, the spinning of cotton. And the steam engine was to the first Industrial Revolution what the computer has been to the information revolution, its trigger and its symbol. Almost everybody today believes that nothing in economic history has ever moved as fast as, or had a greater impact than, the information revolution. But the Industrial Revolution moved at least as fast in the same time span, and probably had an equal impact if not a greater one. Moore's Law asserts that the price of the information revolution's basic element, the microchip, drops by 50 percent every 18 months. The same was true of the products whose manufacture was mechanized by the first Industrial Revolution. The price of cotton textiles fell by 90 percent in the 50 years spanning the start of the 18th century.

Like the Industrial Revolution two centuries ago, the information revolution so far (that is, since the first computers, in the mid-1940s) has only transformed processes that were here all along. In fact, many argue that the real impact of the information revolution has not been in the form of "information." Almost none of the effects of information envisaged 40 years ago have actually happened. For example, there has been practically no change in the way major decisions are made in business or government. But the information revolution has mechanized traditional processes in a remarkable number of areas.

Information technology and income differences across nations. How does the information revolution affect the income differences between developed countries? There is a debate among economists about how likely it is that the information revolution will provide satisfactory explanations for differences among advanced industrial economies, between, say, the UNITED STATES and western Europe. Advanced economies have access to the same technologies. Yet the degree to which these technologies have been adopted, the purposes to which they are put, and their apparent consequences for business and economic life vary significantly from one country to another. It has been suggested that differences in national policies—encouraging or discouraging private investment in information technology, facilitating or hindering economic restructuring to take advantage of new technologies, shaping private attitudes towards risk-taking, and so on—may be the underlying reasons that different economies have exploited technology in different ways, and that technology has affected economies differently.

Perhaps a more important question is how will the information revolution affect developing and less-developed countries? The answer to this question lies in these countries' ability to effectively adopt existing technology. The work of R. Nelson and E. Phelps (1965), R. Findlay (1978) and more recently J. Benhabib and M. Spiegel (1994) has shown that technology imitation can be a remarkable source of economic growth and development in less-developed nations.

However, technology imitation is not at all trivial as poor countries have neither the human capital nor the infrastructure necessary to make productive use of these technologies. Indeed, one of the recent puzzles in GROWTH theory is why we do not observe more imitation of existing technologies and readily available information by poor nations. It has been suggested by many economists that if poor countries do not start taking advantage of the information revolution, there will be a substantial increase in income inequality within and across countries.

The nature of information. The difference between the value of information (just like technology) on the one hand, and factors of production such as physical and human capital on the other, can more formally be described as follows: If a conventional factor of production is being used by one person, it cannot be used by another. Exactly the opposite is true of information in general; the fact that one person is using information does not prevent others from using it just as effectively.

This non-rivalry of information means that in studying it, researchers have to focus much more on transfers (between firms or between countries) than is the case with more traditional factors of production.

In many cases, this transferability can be a disadvantage. The fact that new information can be easily replicated often (but not always) means that the person (firm or country) who has created it will not be able to reap most of the benefits from its creation. This, in turn, means that the incentives for creating technology are diminished.

To see evidence of the role of readily accessible information in economic growth all we have to do is to look around. Growth in living standards is so wrapped up with technological progress that often the two seem indistinguishable. We consume goods that did not even exist 50 years ago. Modern inventions, ranging from the obviously important to the minor, have changed the way in which goods are produced, and have enabled workers to produce immensely more than they did a few generations ago.

One of the main sources of information technology is RESEARCH AND DEVELOPMENT (R&D). R&D (public or private) results in the production of ideas (information) that is then easily distributed to the rest of the economy at low costs. The nature of information is very unique as it is different from most other economic goods.

Most R&D is conducted by private firms that seek to maximize profits. However, the unique nature of technology has long led governments to play a role in research.

For example, in 1714 the British government offered a prize of £20,000 for the creation of a sea-going clock accurate enough to measure longitude. In the United States in 1997, 30.5 percent of R&D was sponsored by the government, although a good deal of this was aimed at military, rather than business applications. And lest we forget, the internet was created and nurtured under government auspices. The most important way in which government aids R&D, however, is by providing inventors with legal protection against having others copy their work, in the form of a PATENT.

Private firms engage in R&D in the hope of inventing something: a new product, or a new, more efficient way of producing some existing product. If the firm is successful in its research, it will be able to raise its profits. In the best case (from the firm's point of view), its invention will give it a MONOPOLY on the sale of some product, allowing it to earn super-normal profits. Alternatively, a new invention may give the firm a means of producing the same product that is being sold by other firms, but at a lower price. In either case, the extra profits that arise from this competitive advantage are the incentive that makes the firm perform R&D in the first place. The larger the profits associated with having invented something, the more the firm is willing to spend in the effort to invent it.

The process by which new inventions create profits for firms, by which these profits serve as the incentive to engage in research in the first place, and by which eventually the new technologies so created are replaced by yet newer technologies, was given the name "creative destruction" by the economist Joseph SCHUMPETER. Although we often celebrate the new technologies, such a perspective ignores the dislocations suffered by those firms and workers who are displaced by new technologies. History is full of examples of technologies (and people) that have been displaced by technological progress.

Many recent models of economic growth emphasize the key role that R&D plays in the production of information and economic development. For example P. Romer (1990), P. Aghion and P. Howitt (1992), and C. Jones (1995), among others, have contributed to our understanding of the unique nature of technological goods and services by constructing economic models in which the production and dissemination of technology/information by private firms results in increased aggregate output and economic growth. The effect of "R&D growth models" in the economics literature is so great that these models are an integral part of teaching at the undergraduate and graduate level. In addition, understanding the economics of information technology using R&D growth models is now a common practice in the literature and a hot topic among economics researchers.

Potential costs associated with the information revolution. There are several costs associated with the information revolution. First, there are computer crimes involving malicious intent of individuals for financial gain (hacking). Second, there are programming breakdowns and failures involving bad programming, operator error, and accidental failure. Third, there is the risk of cyber terrorism and information warfare that involve malicious intent of (political) groups and states. All of these potential drawbacks of the information revolution are serious with very costly consequences to individuals, firms, and the economy.

There are many measures (in fact, markets) in place that try to deal with these problems and try to mitigate their effect. However, as with any other major innovation, we do not know exactly what the future holds and how large these costs may really be. One thing is for sure (and ought to be highlighted more often) and that is that the benefits from the information revolution grossly outweigh the costs.

BIBLIOGRAPHY. P. Aghion and P. Howitt, "A Model of Growth Through Creative Destruction," *Econometrica* (v.60, 1992); J. Benhabib and M. Spiegel, "The Role of Human Capital in Economic Development: Evidence from Cross-Country Data," *Journal of Monetary Economics* (v.34, 1994); C. Jones, "R&D-Based Models of Economic Growth," *Journal of Political Economy* (v.103, 1995); R. Findlay, "Relative Backwardness, Direct Foreign Investment and the Transfer of Technology: A Simple Dynamic Model,'" *Quarterly Journal of Economics* (v.92, 1978); R. Nelson and E. Phelps, "Investment in Humans, Technological Diffusion, and Economic Growth," *American Economic Review* (v.56, 1966); P. Romer, "Endogenous Technological Change," *Journal of Political Economy* (v.98, 1990).

CHRIS PAPAGEORGIOU
LOUISIANA STATE UNIVERSITY

ING Group

A GLOBAL FINANCIAL institution, ING Group N.V. offers banking, insurance, and asset management to almost 50 million private, corporate, and institutional clients in more than 60 countries, and is based in Amsterdam, the NETHERLANDS. As a whole, ING is the result of a merger that took place in 1990, between Nationale-Nederlanden and NMB Postbank Groep. Its 1991 acronym means International Netherlands Group.

This financial institution comprises a broad spectrum of companies that are known under the ING brand. Since 2000, ING also includes ReliaStar, Aetna Financial Services, and Aetna International. The company's products and services include private banking, current accounts, savings and investments, individual loans and individual insurance. The company has subsidiaries and affiliates on five continents.

ING's stock is traded in Amsterdam, Brussels, Frankfurt, Paris, New York City, and Switzerland. ING has almost 2 billion shares outstanding. Its market capitalization is around $25 billion, about the same size as DEUTSCHE BANK in GERMANY or FleetBoston Financials in the United States. As a true international company, its Annual Report is published in three versions: Dutch, French and English. ING was ranked as the 20th largest company in the world in 2002 with $83 billion in revenue.

BIBLIOGRAPHY. ING Group, www.ing.com; ING *Annual Report* (Amsterdam, 2001); ING *Rapport Annuel* (Amsterdam, 1998); "Global 500: World's Largest Companies," *Fortune* (July 2002).

YVES LABERGE, PH.D.
INSTITUT QUÉBÉCOIS DES
HAUTES ÉTUDES INTERNATIONALES

insider trading

BROADLY, INSIDER TRADING refers to the practice of corporate insiders such as officers, directors, and employees, buying and selling stock in their own companies. In the UNITED STATES, all such trades must be reported to the SECURITIES AND EXCHANGE COMMISSION (SEC), which publishes a monthly compendium of trades in its "Official Summary of Securities Transactions and Holdings."

While such trades may be perfectly legal, insider trading is most frequently used in relation to versions of such trades that are deemed illegal. In these cases, insider trading refers to the practice of trading in a security, while in possession of material, non-public information about it, violating a fiduciary duty or other relationship of trust and confidence in the process. Examples of illegal insider trading would include:

1. An officer of a firm buying the company's stock just prior to release of its financial results, knowing that the news will lead to an increase in the share price.

2. An investment banker trading on the basis of confidential information on a corporate client acquired in the course of his duties for the client.

3. An employee "tipping" information about a company to friends and family members in advance of its public release, so that they might trade on that information.

4. An employee of a printing firm trading on the basis of information gained from documents being printed for a client regarding a corporate merger.

5. "Front Running," a practice in which a stock broker purchases (or sells) stock in a company just prior to executing a large "buy" (or "sell") order for a mutual fund.

Insider trading is frequently viewed as unfair and not conducive to free and efficient markets. Such a practice is characterized as fraudulent in many countries, punishable under civil and criminal law. In the United States, sections 10(b) and section 16 of the Securities Exchange Act of 1934 are applicable to insider trading. Section 16 prohibits "short-swing profits" in the company's own stock by corporate insiders, defined as the officers and directors of the company and shareholders with greater than 10 percent holdings. Short-swing profits are profits realized through purchase and sale of the company's stock within a six-month period. Section 10(b) contains provisions against fraud in securities transactions.

The Securities and Exchange Commission, which was created by the Act, promulgated Rule 10b5 speci-fying the circumstances in which section 10(b) of the Act was applicable. Rule 10b5 is a rule with broad anti-fraud provisions, making it unlawful to engage in fraud or misrepresentation in connection with the purchase or sale of a security, and therefore applicable to insider trading cases as well. Further legislation has since been enacted to tighten the law and provide appropriate penalties. The Insider Trading Sanctions Act of 1984 provides for penalties up to three times the profit gained or the loss avoided by the insider trading. In 1988, following several high-profile cases of insider trading, the law was further augmented through the passage of the Insider Trading and Securities Fraud Enforcement Act of 1988.

In interpreting and applying SEC Rule 10b5, an argument that is frequently invoked is the "misappropriation theory." Under this theory, when a person misappropriates confidential information for securities trading purposes in breach of fiduciary duty, he or she defrauds the principal of the exclusive use of the information. The person therefore commits fraud in connection with a securities transaction, violating section 10(b) of the Securities Exchange Act of 1934 and SEC Rule 10b5.

Rule 10b5 has been bolstered by several other rules to take into account special cases occurring in securities markets. The "disclose or abstain rule" covers outsiders who are in a special relationship with a company that gives them access to confidential information regarding its affairs, such as its consultants, lawyers, auditors and bankers. Such outsiders are termed "temporary" or "constructive insiders." As per the rule, corporate insiders, as well as temporary or constructive insiders, who possess material nonpublic information must disclose it before trading or abstain from trading until the information is publicly disseminated.

Rule 14e3 removes the fiduciary-duty requirement in the case of tender offers. Under the rule, it is illegal for anyone to trade on the basis of material nonpublic information pertaining to tender offers provided that they were aware that the information had emanated from an insider. Regulation FD (Fair Disclosure) provides that when a firm discloses material nonpublic information to certain specific persons such as stock analysts, it must also make a public disclosure of that information.

Rule 10b5-1 clarifies the circumstances under which a person would be deemed to have traded "on the basis of" material nonpublic information. Under the rule, it is merely sufficient for the trader to have been aware of material non-public information when making the purchase or sale, in order for the trade to be deemed to have been made on the basis of such information. There are a few exceptions to the rule. These pertain to situations where it is clear that the information that the trader was aware of was not a factor in the decision to trade. For example, the trade could have been made pursuant to a pre-existing plan or contract.

Rule 10b5-2 specifies that a person receiving confidential information under certain circumstances would owe a duty of trust or confidence and thus be liable under the misappropriation theory. These circumstances include:

1. When the person agreed to keep information confidential

2. When the persons involved in the communication had a history, pattern, or practice of sharing confidences that resulted in a reasonable expectation of confidentiality

3. When the person who provided the information was a spouse, parent, child, or sibling of the recipient, unless it could be shown that there was no reasonable expectation of confidentiality in such a relationship.

In the United States, the law on insider trading has evolved through several landmark cases such as *SEC v. Texas Gulf Sulphur Co.* (1968), *Chiarella v. United States* (1980), *United States v. Newman* (1981), *Dirks v. SEC* (1983), *United States v. Carpenter* (1986) and *United States v. O'Hagan* (1997).

In other countries, the law on insider trading is still in a developmental stage. In 1989, the Council of the European Communities promulgated the European Economic Community Directive Coordinating Regulation on Insider Trading, coordinating insider trading regulations within the community and setting minimum standards that must be met by all members. The directive prohibits insiders from using inside information either by themselves or by tipping others. Article 1 of the directive defines "inside information" as "information of a precise nature about the security or issuer which has not been made public which, if it were made public, would likely have a significant effect on the price of the security."

The directive does not require a fiduciary duty to be violated in order for a trade to be deemed illegal. Several member countries have since passed legislation to apply the principles of the directive. The statutes in these countries are usually more specific about what constitutes material nonpublic information. Also, many of these countries define insider trading, not on the basis of fiduciary duty, but on the basis of "access" to information. In general, those who have unequal access to the material nonpublic information are prohibited from trading on the basis of that information, regardless of whether they have a fiduciary duty or not. Thus, even "tippees" who receive information from insiders or others who have privileged access to such information, are liable under this principle.

Over 80 countries have laws in place to regulate insider trading. However, the pace of enforcement of these laws varies widely across countries, with fewer than 40 countries having seen any proceedings under such regulations.

BIBLIOGRAPHY. Thomas C. Newkirk and Melissa A. Robertson, "Insider Trading: A U.S. Perspective," U.S. Securities & Exchange Commission, 16th International Symposium on Economic Crime (Cambridge University, 1998); Securities And Exchange Commission, "Final Rule: Selective Disclosure and Insider Trading," www.sec.gov; Marc I. Steinberg, "Insider Trading, Selective Disclosure and Prompt Disclosure; A Comparative Analysis," *Journal of International Economic Law* (v.22/3, Fall, 2001); Utpal Bhattacharya and Hazen Daouk, "The World Price of Insider Trading" *Journal of Finance* (v.57/1, February, 2002).

NARAYANAN SUBRAMANIAN, PH.D.
BRANDEIS UNIVERSITY

insurance

IF A PERSON EXPERIENCES diminishing marginal utility of wealth (i.e., an extra dollar provides more utility when one is poor than when one is rich) then a fair bet, which has an expected value of zero, will lower the person's utility. Even though the bet has an expected value of zero, it has an expected utility that is negative because losing the bet would cause more disutility than winning the bet would provide in increased utility. For this reason, people who experience diminishing marginal utility of wealth are called risk-averse and they often seek to eliminate future risks to their wealth using insurance.

An insurance policy is a contract with the following characteristics. The insured pays a premium to the insurer before a specific risk is resolved. The specific risk might involve the possibility of an auto accident, sickness, or death. For simplicity, assume there are only two possible outcomes: a good state of the world (e.g., no auto accident, healthy, or alive), and a bad state of the world (e.g., crash, illness, or death). After the risk is resolved and the state of the world is known, the insurer will pay the insured if the bad state of the world occurred, and will pay nothing if the good state of the world occurred. Thus, insurance is a way that individuals can transfer their risk to an insurance company in exchange for a fee and allows individuals to smooth their wealth over possible future states of the world.

Risk assumption. An insurance company is willing to assume applicants' risks because if the insurance company has insured a large number of people, and if the risks of the people they insure are independent, the insurance company can enjoy great confidence in the amount they will have to pay in claims in the next period. If, however, the risks of applicants are highly correlated, then the insurer cannot benefit from risk-pooling and will be reluctant to assume the risks. Insurers tend to only insure risks that are diversifiable and not to offer insurance for non-diversifiable risks, such as war.

Insurance is actuarially fair if the premium is exactly equal to the expected value of the gamble. For example, if an applicant has a 50 percent chance of perfect health and zero medical costs and a 50 percent chance of illness that will cost $100, then an actuarially fair premium for a policy that would cover the $100 cost of illness would equal (.5 * 0) + (.5 * $100) = $50. If insurance is actuarially fair, risk-averse individuals will fully insure; that is, they will buy enough insurance to eliminate all variance in wealth across possible future states of the world. For example, consider risk-averse people who face two possible states of the future (good and bad) who fully insure. If the good state of the world occurs, they will keep their current wealth less the insurance premium. If the bad state of the world occurs, they will receive an insurance settlement that will bring their wealth to the same level it would have been in the good state of the world.

In practice, insurance is never actuarially fair. There are many costs to an insurance company besides paying benefits to the insured; they must hire a sales staff, comply with state regulations, pay rent on their office space. As a result, the premiums charged to applicants exceed the expected value of the gamble. Faced with premiums that are actuarially unfair, even risk-averse individuals may choose to less than fully insure. The amount that risk-averse individuals are willing to pay for insurance, above and beyond the actuarially fair premium, is called the risk premium.

Insuring against natural disasters is one way to avert the risk of catastrophic future events.

Hedging is the use of forward contracts to insure against future price movements. It is commonly used by farmers, who must plant crops well before they know what the price of the crops will be at harvest. In order to eliminate the risk of price fluctuations, farmers may hedge by entering into a forward contract, in which they promise to deliver the crops at a future date in exchange for a price agreed upon today. Farmers wishing to insure against a future price fall contract with crop buyers who wish to insure against a future price rise.

Insurance markets. Markets for insurance are to some extent affected by the problems of adverse selection and MORAL HAZARD. Adverse selection occurs when there exists asymmetric information between the insurance company and an applicant for insurance; specifically, when individuals have private knowledge about their risk that insurers cannot obtain. If insurers price their policies according to the average risk in the population, their policies will be unattractive to those of lower-than-average risk, and very attractive to those of higher-than-average risk.

As a result, those who sign up for the insurance will be those of the highest risk, and the insurer will pay out greater than expected claims. In response to paying higher than expected claims, the insurer will likely raise the premium, further limiting the pool to the unobservably high-risk. A "premium death spiral" can result, in which the customers of low risk cancel their insurance, premiums rise, more customers cancel their insurance, and the shrinking insurance pool increasingly consists of the high-risk. Fearing that adverse selection may lead to breakdown in private insurance markets, many developed countries have compulsory, publicly sponsored markets for old-age annuities, such as Social Security in the United States, and compulsory, publicly sponsored health insurance programs. Because participation is mandatory in such programs, adverse selection is impossible.

It has been shown that, in theory, adverse selection could be eliminated under certain conditions through a separating equilibrium. Suppose there exist two groups in the population, high risk and low risk, and insurers cannot distinguish between them; it may be possible for insurers to offer two different insurance contracts that cause the two groups to voluntarily choose the contract that indicates their risk type; this is the origin of the term "separating equilibrium." If insurers structure the contracts correctly, a policy that offers a small quantity of insurance at a low price per dollar of coverage will attract the low risk, and a policy that offers a large quantity of insurance at a high price per dollar of coverage will attract the high risk. This theoretical result may not conform to how actual insurance markets operate, however. There is evidence that, contrary to the prediction of this model, those who buy larger contracts, all else equal, are charged lower prices per dollar of coverage by insurers and are of lower risk.

The extent to which adverse selection impedes the functioning of insurance markets is unclear. Insurance companies seek to minimize the impact of adverse selection by collecting information about the expected risk of the applicant (through medical examinations and collecting detailed family medical history), a process called underwriting. When this information is combined with the insurance company's estimates of expected payouts associated with certain characteristics that are based on the insurance company's previous experience, insurance companies may know more about applicants' risks than applicants themselves, greatly limiting the possibility of adverse selection.

The United States is one of the few developed countries that has not instituted a compulsory, publicly provided health-insurance program. In America, most people receive their health insurance coverage through an employer. The heavy reliance on employer-provided health insurance is an artifact of tax policy that allows employers to deduct from their taxes health insurance costs for their workers.

Moral hazard occurs when people take fewer precautions because they know that they are insured against bad outcomes. Moral hazard can occur *ex ante* or *ex post*. Ex ante moral hazard occurs before the risk is resolved if people take fewer precautions against the loss occurring. For example, people may drive somewhat more carelessly if they have auto insurance because they know that if they do get into an accident, they won't have to pay the full price of the damage. Insurance policies seek to limit *ex ante* moral hazard through the use of exclusion clauses, which state that the insurance policy is invalid if the harm seems to have been caused through negligence.

Ex post moral hazard occurs after the risk is resolved and when the insured has the opportunity to influence the total amount of the claim. For example, an insured person who has been in a car accident might choose to stay an extra night in the hospital because she doesn't pay the full cost. Insurers try to limit *ex post* moral hazard by imposing deductibles and co-insurance rates that create disincentives for the insured to increase costs. A deductible is an amount that the insured must pay before an insurance company will pay anything. The co-insurance rate is the percentage of the total bill after the deductible that the insured must pay; however, the co-insurance rate often drops to zero after an insured has reached a specified amount of out-of-pocket spending that is called the stop-loss.

The best evidence on the effectiveness of such cost-sharing mechanisms comes from the RAND Health Insurance Experiment. In this experiment, individuals were randomized into an insurance plan with varying degrees of cost sharing. The experiment found a price elasticity of demand for medical care of –0.2, which is consistent with co-payments decreasing moral hazard.

Insurance markets are also characterized by the principal-agent problem. In such a problem, a principal's welfare depends on actions taken by the agent, but the principal can only imperfectly monitor the actions of the agent. The possibility that the agent may not take the action desired by the principal is raised by the fact that the agent's utility function may differ from that of the principal. Applied to insurance, a health-insurance company would like physicians to minimize the costs of treatment, but physicians have an incentive to maximize their earnings (and minimize their chances of being sued for malpractice). Insurers can only imperfectly monitor whether physicians are over-prescribing care or inducing demand. Patients may go along with an over-prescription of care because they, too, lack perfect information and they may derive some utility from the treatments. Managed-care organizations have attempted to solve the principal-agent problem by attempting to monitor or influence physician practices and by providing physicians with financial incentives to reduce costs.

BIBLIOGRAPHY. Michael Rothschild and Joseph Stiglitz, "Equilibrium in Competitive Insurance Markets: An Essay on the Economics of Imperfect Information," *Quarterly Journal of Economics* (v.90/4, 1976); John Cawley and Tomas Philipson, "An Empirical Examination of Information Barriers to Trade in Insurance," *American Economic Review* (1999); Peter Zweifel and Willard G. Manning, "Moral Hazard and Consumer Incentives in Health Care," *Handbook of Health Economics* (v.1A, 2000); David M. Cutler and Richard J. Zeckhauser, "The Anatomy of Health Insurance," *Handbook of Health Economics* (v.1A, 2000).

JOHN CAWLEY, PH.D.
CORNELL UNIVERSITY

Inter-American Development Bank

ESTABLISHED IN 1959, the Inter-American Development Bank (IDB) was the first regional development bank. Originally composed of 19 Latin American nations and the UNITED STATES, its membership has expanded to include 26 borrowing members from Latin America and the Caribbean (all the Latin American nations except CUBA) and 20 non-borrowing members including JAPAN, CANADA, the United States, ISRAEL and 16 European nations. Washington, D.C., serves as the banks' headquarters, but there are offices in all borrowing member nations as well as Paris, FRANCE and Tokyo, JAPAN.

The idea of a regional development institution goes back to the First Inter-American Conference held in Washington, D.C., in 1890, but the IDB was conceived much later to complement the lending efforts of the WORLD BANK in Latin America. Over time the IDB has become the largest source of multilateral funds to the region, with $110 billion in outstanding loans and loan guarantees, and $7.9 billion in new loans and guarantees in 2001.

Unlike other multilateral regional banks, borrowing countries hold a majority of shares in the IDB. Latin American and Caribbean nations have a majority representation in the board of governors, but most functions are relegated to the board of executive directors that approves the loans negotiated between banks' staff and the governments of the borrowing nations. The IDB has been very responsive to U.S. interests in the region as was evident in the refusal to grant new loans to the administration of Salvador Allende in CHILE during the early 1970s, and the switch to market-oriented reforms in the 1980s.

IDB loans were traditionally directed to large infrastructure projects such as dams and roads. The debt crisis of the 1980s in Latin America pointed to the shortcomings of large-project financing for development and threatened the financial soundness of the bank. The IDB responded with a significant shift towards policy-based lending, that is, projects whose objective is to redirect domestic economic policy into compliance with the "Washington Consensus" including administrative reform of the state, trade liberalization, and privatization. Loans for the reform and modernization of the state in 2001 accounted for 30 percent of all loans that year, whereas they were only 17 percent for the period 1961–2001. Other innovations include setting aside up to 5 percent of the bank's portfolio for private sector lending without government guarantee and the establishment of a $10 billion special operations fund to lend to lesser-developed nations at lower-than-market rates.

The IDB gives priority to projects that enhance competitiveness, integration into the global economy, modernization of the state and social development, a strategy that purportedly leads to its two primary objectives, SUSTAINABLE DEVELOPMENT and poverty reduction. The marked adoption of neo-liberal strategies has made the IDB the target of protests more commonly associated with the World Bank and the INTERNATIONAL MONETARY FUND (IMF).

The weakness of Latin American economies since the mid-1990s has placed the bank in a difficult position. When ARGENTINA briefly ceased payments to multilateral organizations in late 2002, the IDB faced the possibility of having its credit rating downgraded given an exposure of 15.1 percent of its loan portfolio in that country. Sluggish growth in BRAZIL and MEXICO, the other two largest borrowers, represents a constant danger to the creditworthiness of the organization.

BIBLIOGRAPHY. Inter-American Development Bank, www.iadb.org; "Not Much Spice in Latin America," *Businessweek* (January 6, 2003).

LEOPOLDO RODRÍGUEZ-BOETSCH
PORTLAND STATE UNIVERSITY

interest rate

THE PRICE PAID FOR the use of credit or money, expressed either in money terms or as a rate of payment, interest is payment for use of funds over a period of time, and the amount of interest paid per unit of time, as a fraction of the balance, is called the interest rate. As with any other PRICE, the rate of interest can be analyzed in the normal framework of demand and supply analysis.

Classical economists argue that the rate of interest is a real phenomenon. The interest rate is determined by the demand for investment funds and by thrift, supply of funds in the form of SAVING. The primary objective of borrowing is investment, that is, the addition to productive capital of machines, buildings, and inventories. The basic factor underlying the demand schedule is the productivity of additions to capital, or, the marginal productivity of capital. The downward sloping of the demand for capital goods reflects the principle of diminishing marginal returns, that is, the larger the use of capital goods, the less the increment of production from their further use, or, the greater the use of capital, the smaller the marginal product of capital.

The saving schedule reflects savers' impatience, the increasing marginal disutility of abstinence or time preference. A positive rate of interest is necessary to produce saving, and a rising rate of interest is necessary to secure increasing amounts of saving, thus reflecting the upward sloping supply schedule. The EQUILIBRIUM interest rate is determined at the intersection of the supply and demand schedule, that is, at the point where saving and investment were equal. At the interest rate higher than equilibrium rate, saving and lending would exceed borrowing and investment. Savers unable to find a borrower would accept lower return and bid the rate down. If, on the other hand, an actual interest rate was below equilibrium level, investors would seek more funds than savers would provide. The ensuing competition among borrowers would push the interest rate up.

John Maynard KEYNES, on the other hand, regarded the rate of interest as a purely monetary phenomenon, reflecting the supply and demand for money. In the Keynesian system, money supply is exogenously determined, while demand for money materializes from the speculative, precautionary, and transaction motives. Transaction demand for money comes from individuals' desire to purchase goods and services, and precautionary demand for money materializes from individuals; aspiration to meet unforeseen expenditures. The speculative demand for money comes from people's propensity to hold money as a store of wealth. The cost of holding wealth in the form of liquid money is the rate of return that could be earned on the alternative financials assets, such as BONDS. Since the bond prices were inversely related to interest rate, Keynes deduced that speculative demand for money also was inversely related to the interest rate. He argued that the interest rate is not the price that brings into equilibrium the investment demand with saving; rather the interest rate is the price that equilibrates the desire to hold wealth in the form of cash with available quantity of cash.

The classical economists argued that a unique market rate of interest would be established by the tendency of the rate of returns on physical and financial assets to equate. Keynes emphasized that the speculation in the bond market would stabilize the interest rate, which could differ from the rate of return on physical assets, which may lead to a shortfall in investment and insufficient aggregate demand.

Unlike classical economists, Keynes and his followers argued that interest rate is affected by time preference and liquidity preference (i.e. that interest rate is both a real and monetary phenomenon). However, monetarists, like their classical predecessors, continue to uphold the view that interest rate is a real phenomenon, and that rate of return on physical and financial assets would tend to equality in the long run.

For the sake of simplicity, economists often refer to interest rate as a single number. They assume that only one interest rate prevails in the economy due to simultaneous sale and purchase of an asset (i.e., ARBITRAGE). In fact, at any point of time there are many prevailing interest rates. The actual rate would depend on numerous factors, such as maturity of the loan, credit worthiness of the borrower, the amount of collateral, etc. Financial institutions charge higher interest rates to borrowers and pay lower interest rates to lenders. In addition, due to the risk inherent to lending, lenders will ask for a risk premium, thus charging the higher than market rate of return.

[Editor's Note: In the end analysis, the social significance of the interest rate translates into the privilege that a moneyed individual does not have to work for a living. His or her money (earning interest) works for the individual, a fantastic social arrangement, indeed.]

BIBLIOGRAPHY. Graham Bannock, R.E. Baxter, and Evan Davis, *The Penguin Dictionary of Economics* (Penguin Books, 1998); E. Brigham and J. Houston, *Fundamentals of Financial Management* (South-Western, forthcomimng); John Eatwell, Murray Milgate, and Peter Newman, eds., *The New Palgrave: A Dictionary of Economics* (Stockton Press, 1991); I. Fisher, *The Theory of Interest* (Macmillan, 1930); Roger LeRoy Miller and David VanHoose, *Money, Banking, and Financial Markets* (South-Western, forthcoming); David William Pearce, *The MIT Dictionary of Modern Economics* (MIT Press, 1992).

ZELJAN SCHUSTER, PH.D.
UNIVERSITY OF NEW HAVEN

International Monetary Fund (IMF)

A SPECIALIZED AGENCY of the United Nations (UN), the IMF was founded by treaty in 1945 to promote international monetary cooperation. The organization is headquartered in Washington, D.C., and is governed by a board of governors that consists of representatives of 184 member states. The statutory purposes of the IMF are to promote the balanced growth of world trade, the stability of EXCHANGE RATES, and the orderly adjustment of member-countries' balance of payments.

Overseeing the international monetary system. In 1944, representatives of 45 countries met at a United Nations conference in BRETTON WOODS, New Hampshire, to establish the IMF. The main purposes of the new organization included overseeing the international monetary system, promoting the elimination of exchange restrictions, and the stability of exchange rates. Under the Bretton Woods system of exchange rates that existed between 1945–71, members of the IMF agreed to keep their exchange rates fixed against the U.S. DOLLAR and change them only to correct a "fundamental disequilibrium" in the balance of payments. The U.S. dollar was pegged to gold during that period. After 1971, when the United States suspended the convertibility of the U.S. dollar into gold, each country chose its own method of determining the exchange rate. Among them are a free float (when the exchange rate is determined by the supply and demand), a managed float (when the monetary authority may occasionally intervene to influence the exchange rate), and a pegged exchange system (when the monetary authority promises to peg its currency's exchange rate to some other currency).

The 1944 conference also founded the WORLD BANK to promote sustained economic development. The two organizations have complementary functions. If the IMF is mostly concerned with macroeconomic issues, the main activities of the World Bank include providing loans to finance the reform of particular sectors of the economy and infrastructure projects.

The IMF is headed by the board of governors. All countries are represented on the board. The day-to-day operations, however, are carried out by the executive board that consists of 24 executive directors. Eight directors represent CHINA, FRANCE, GERMANY, JAPAN, RUSSIA, SAUDI ARABIA, the UNITED KINGDOM, and the UNITED STATES. The remaining 16 directors are elected for two-year terms and represent certain groups of countries. The executive board selects the managing director who is appointed for a five-year term and supervises the IMF staff of about 3,000 employees. The managing director is traditionally a European.

The sources of the fund come mostly from the contributions (called quotas) of its members. The size of a quota broadly depends on the size of the country's economy. The quota also determines the voting power of a country. For example, the United States' contribution to the fund is approximately 18 percent of total quotas. This entitles the U.S. to 18 percent of the total votes.

Three most important areas of IMF assistance to its members are:

1. Monitoring and advising countries on economic policies

2. Lending hard currency to members of the fund

3. Technical assistance and training.

At the country level, an IMF team visits an individual member of the fund and collects economic data, as well as holds discussions with the government. The findings of the team are reported to the executive board, the opinion of which is then given to the country's government. An example of the fund's global monitoring is the publication of a semi-annual *World Economic Outlook* report.

If a member country faces a balance of payments problem (i.e., if it needs to borrow to make external payments without having to take hard measures), it always can immediately withdraw up to 25 percent of its quota. If the country needs more, the IMF assesses the situation and decides the size of the additional loan. The IMF first has to agree with the country's authorities on a specific program aiming to restore financial and monetary stability and promote economic growth.

For short-term balance of payments problems the IMF uses stand-by arrangements that form the core of the fund's lending policies. Loans are given for 12–18 months. If a country has a balance of payments problem that takes structural changes to fix, the fund uses the extended fund facility where loans are for three to four years. The structural program may involve privatization of public enterprises and tax and financial reforms. The poverty reduction and growth facility has been used to help the poorest countries achieve sustainable economic growth and improve living standards.

It should be pointed out that IMF loans are not given to finance projects. The foreign exchange provided by the fund is deposited with the country's central bank to give balance of payments support. Moreover, the IMF ties its loans to certain policies the country has to follow to solve its problems. Loans are divided into several portions, and the next portion is conditioned on meeting goals for the previous stage. Loans must be repaid and borrowing countries pay interest rates and service charges. The typical interest rate charged on a loan is 4.5 percent.

Starting in the mid-1960s, the IMF has provided technical assistance to its member countries. This complements policy advice and financial assistance. With the aim of strengthening countries economic policies, the IMF staff regularly meets with representatives of member countries and provides assistance in central banking, tax policy, monetary and exchange policy. If in the 1960s and 1970s this assistance was given to newly independent countries, the lion's share of such assistance in the 1990s was directed to the countries of eastern Europe and the former Soviet Union. These countries, central-planning economies, were moving toward market-based systems. The IMF helped them to improve their financial systems, to strengthen banking regulation and supervision, and to improve their legal systems.

The IMF and globalization. The IMF faces new challenges that emerge with globalization. The major problem is financial crises that showed weaknesses in the international financial system. The financial crises of the 1990s demonstrated that once alarmed, investors may withdraw very quickly leading to a financial crisis that may rapidly spread to other countries. In order to confront this problem, the IMF works on strengthening countries' financial systems, promoting internationally accepted standards related to countries' statistical practices and codes of good practice in fiscal, monetary, and financial policies. It also encourages openness and timely publication of economic and financial data. The fund has taken steps to increase the organization's transparency. In particular, increased information on the fund's activities and policies is found on its website. External evaluations of the IMF policies and their publications are an evidence of its increased accountability.

The effectiveness of the IMF policies and their impact on the world economy is a subject of debate. Some believe that the IMF conditions on loans exacerbate the recipient country's crises and reduce economic growth. Some even believe that the IMF should cease its lending activity altogether and leave this task to the central banks of the major economic powers.

BIBLIOGRAPHY. V.V.Chari and Patrick Kehoe,"Asking the Right Questions About the IMF," *The Region* (The Federal Reserve Bank of Minneapolis, 1998); Martin Feldstein, "Refocusing the IMF," *Foreign Affairs* (v.77, 1998); "What Is the International Monetary Fund?" www.imf.org.

NURLAN TURDALIEV, PH.D.
MCGILL UNIVERSITY

International Trade Centre

CREATED IN 1964 by the GENERAL AGREEMENT ON TARIFFS AND TRADE (GATT) the International Trade Centre (ITC) is the focal point used by the United Nations (UN) to foster technical cooperation in trade promotion with developing countries. Acting at the request of the countries concerned, ITC projects are implemented by ITC specialists working in liaison with local officials and, depending on what is required, the length of individual projects may vary from several weeks to several years.

In terms of strategy, the ITC has set as its overriding objective the development of national capacity for improving the trade performance of business. In order to achieve this strategy the ITC assists developing countries to expand exports and improve their import operations by providing assistance in the following six core areas. Product and market development advises on product development and international marketing in order to expand and diversify these countries' exports; development of trade support services is aimed at the enhancement of foreign trade support services at the national and regional levels. Trade information assists in the establishment of trade information services that are designed to allow the effective dissemination of information on products, services, markets, and functions. Human resource development is aimed at the strengthening of existing institutional capacities for foreign trade training and organization of direct training in importing. International purchasing and supply management works by strengthening the advisory services provided by national purchasing organizations; and needs assessment and program design are provided in order to reinforce the link between trade policy and the implementation of trade promotion.

ITC operates by coordinating its work programs with other organizations such as the Food and Agricultural Organization of the UN. In order to allow developing countries to develop the skills required to operate independent of any supporting organization, the ITC produces a range of information sheets on subjects as diverse as *How to Approach Banks*, *Export-led Poverty Reduction Program*, *Product-Network Approach*, and *Jute Geotextiles Promotion Program*, all of which are readily availably to the countries involved.

Over the years, ITC has provided a diverse range of services and these now include market analysis services that collates national trade statistics and details the trade performance of 184 countries by sector or by product; market briefs that are concise market reports on export products likely to be of interest to developing countries; market news service which provides up to date market intelligence on product prices on a range of goods such as pharmaceutical products, fruit and vegetables, and spices; international trade statistics which can be accessed by country or by product group.

BIBLIOGRAPHY. Rudy Kortbech-Olesen and Tim Larsen, *The U.S. Market for Organic Fresh Produce* (ITC 2001); Morten Scholer, *Coffee—Organic Certification and Labeling* (ITC 2000); www.intracen.org.

DEREK RUTHERFORD YOUNG, PH.D.
UNIVERSITY OF DUNDEE, SCOTLAND

investment

See CAPITAL; VENTURE CAPITAL; BANKING, INVESTMENT.

invisible hand

See SMITH, ADAM.

Iran

THE NATION OF IRAN is located in southwest Asia and borders the turbulent Middle East. The Caspian Sea and Caucasus Mountains are to the north, IRAQ is to the west, Turkmenistan, AFGHANISTAN, and PAKISTAN are to the east, and the Persian Gulf is to the south. Summers are hot and dry, with winters bitter and cold. The massive Iranian Plateau dominates the landscape; scarce water comes from the forested Zagros Mountains to the north.

Iran has a population of 63 million with most living in the northwest. Tehran, the capital, is the center of industry with 8 million people. Farsi (Persian) is the official language and 55 percent are of Persian ethnicity. Shi'a Islam is the religion of 95 percent of the population. This more conservative belief system of Islam has dominated the politics and economy of Iran since the revolution of 1979. President Mohammed Khatami's limited reforms have not changed Iran's economy or political system significantly to date in the middle of 2003. The STATE still controls 85 percent of the GROSS DOMESTIC PRODUCT (GDP), centered on OIL exports.

GDP per capita is $1,604 (1999) with a growth rate of 2.5 percent. Unemployment and inflation are both over 15 percent annually in real terms. Foreign debt is over $10 billion but recent trade balances have approached $6 billion due to the end of the Iranian war with Iraq, high oil prices, and increased exports of oil to RUSSIA. A substantial black market, perhaps 40 percent of GDP reportedly exists.

In 2001, the projected budget expenditure for 2002 was $56.4 billion with $38 billion going to state organizations. Most private businesses are located in the non-oil sector and are likely tied to the black market.

Development and buy-back agreements between Iran and GERMANY, NORWAY, Russia, and JAPAN will help develop oil and gas production, nuclear power, and petrochemicals. In drought years, Iran must import food, and is not yet consistently energy independent. While these projects will allow for energy independence and an influx of combined state and private sector capitalism, the buy-back agreements mean that these partial capitalism ventures will again become state-controlled by the Tavinar electric organization.

Banking and stock-exchange systems are state-controlled and foreign investment is limited to partnerships with state energy-development projects. During the 20th century, decades of capitalistic growth were followed by revolutions, wars, and Middle East strife leaving Iran with a truncated legacy of capitalistic ventures. The strict enforcement of conservative Muslim beliefs allows for only small internal consumption. Its estimated labor force of 18 million so far, interacts mainly through the oil industry with the global economy. Until state control of the oil economy becomes privatized, private enterprise will be restricted to only about 10–20 percent of the GDP. State sponsored privatizing attempts in industry have had little impact to date.

BIBLIOGRAPHY. P. Alizadeh, H. Hakimian, and M. Karshenas, eds., *The Economy of Iran: Dilemmas of an Islamic State* (I.B. Tauris & Co. Ltd, 2001); C. Bina and H. Zangeneh, eds., *Modern Capitalism and Islamic Ideology in Iran* (Palgrave Macmillan, 1991); www.salamiran.org; Bizhan Jazani, *Capitalism and Revolution in Iran* (Zed Books, 1981).

CHRIS HOWELL
RED ROCKS COLLEGE

Iraq

THE NATION OF IRAQ borders TURKEY to the north, IRAN to the east, SYRIA and Jordan to the west, and SAUDI ARABIA and KUWAIT to the south. Baghdad is the capital. [Editor's note: At the time of this writing, July 2003, Iraq was under U.S. military occupation, with efforts being planned for new economic and political policies.]

Iraq's population is approximately 24 million, with about 75 percent Arab, 15 to 20 percent Kurd, and the rest made up of Jews, Turkmens, and Yazidis. Arabic is the official language. Kurdish and other minority languages are spoken, and English is spoken in commerce. Almost 75 percent of the population lives in urban areas, with almost a third living within 90 miles of Baghdad. Much of the rural population lives in tribal communities, leading nomadic or semi-nomadic existences. Due to migration from rural areas, the proportion of urban dwellers continues to rise.

Called Mesopotamia in classical times, Iraq was home to the world's earliest civilizations, and was later part of the Ottoman Empire. In 1932, Iraq gained formal independence, and in 1945 was a founding member of the League of Arab States. In 1958 Iraq was proclaimed a "republic," but in reality a series of military dictators have been in power, the most recent being Saddam Hussein. In the 1980s, Iraq fought an eight-year war with Iran. Due to war expenditures, Iraq incurred financial difficulties, which led the government to impose austerity measures, borrow heavily, and later reschedule debt repayments. In the end, Iraq lost more than $100 billion.

In August 1990, Iraq invaded Kuwait. United Nations (UN) coalition forces expelled Iraq from Kuwait during the Gulf War of January-February, 1991. Following this war, the UN required Iraq to destroy all weapons of mass destruction and long-range missiles, and allow verification of such by inspectors. Iraq failed to comply in full and in response the UN-imposed trade sanctions that remained in effect until the United States and coalition military action (the Iraq War) in 2003. In 1996, the UN implemented the oil-for-food program, which enabled Iraq to export oil in exchange for food, medicine, and necessary infrastructure supplies.

Petroleum is Iraq's most valuable natural resource. In the 1970s, all foreign oil companies were nationalized, and their operations were turned over to the Northern Petroleum Organization and the Iraq National Oil Company. Other natural resources include natural gas, phosphates, coal, gold, copper, and silver.

Approximately 13 percent of Iraq's land is used for agriculture. Crops raised include wheat, rice, figs, olives, and dates, with Iraq's harvest of dates accounting for a large share of the total world cultivation. Livestock raised include cattle, sheep, goats, chickens, and Arabian horses. Timber resources are minimal. In 1983, private rental of land from the Ministry of Agriculture and Agrarian Reform was allowed. In 1987, the government sold or leased all state farms.

Approximately 80 percent of Iraq's roads are paved and there are links with neighboring countries. There are railway connections through Syria with Turkey and Europe. In 1984, Iraq and neighboring countries formed the Middle East group of the International Union of Railways with an eye toward further integration of their rail systems. Domestic air travel is slight, but has been rising. There are international airports at Baghdad and Basra. Rivers, lakes, and channels are used for local transportation, and river steamers navigate the Tigris River. In some rural regions, camels, horses, and donkeys are still a means of transportation. Iraq's oil exports are transported via pipelines, which pass through neighboring countries to reach Mediterranean ports.

Since the mid-1970s, Iraq's industrial sector has rapidly developed, but still accounts for less than 15 percent of the GROSS DOMESTIC PRODUCT (GDP). Services account for more than 80 percent of the GDP and agriculture the rest. Petroleum and natural gas products are the major industries. Other industries include textiles and clothing, cigarettes, and construction material.

Thermal plants produce more than 95 percent of Iraq's electricity. There are hydroelectric facilities along the Tigris River and its tributaries, but generating capacity is below its potential. Iraq's labor force is approximately 4.4 million. About one-quarter of the work force belongs to the General Federation of Trade Unions, Iraq's main labor organization.

Iraq's currency is the Iraqi dinar (IQD). In 1964, all banks and insurance companies were nationalized. The Central Bank of Iraq is responsible for issuing currency. Iraq's exports are valued at approximately $15.8 billion annually and its imports at $11 billion. Petroleum exports account for approximately 90 percent of the earnings. The latest figures (2001) show Iraq had a GDP of $59 billion, with a per capita income of $2,500.

BIBLIOGRAPHY. Majid Khaddouri, *The Gulf War: The Origins and Implications of the Iran-Iraq War* (American Philological Association, 1988); Hans W. Maull and Otto Pick, eds., *The Gulf War: Regional and International Dimensions* (Palgrave Macmillan, 1990); Helen Chapin Metz, *Iraq: A Country Study* (Government Printing Office, 1990); Efraim Karsh, *The Iran-Iraq War 1980–1988* (Osprey Publishing Company, 2002); *CIA World Factbook* (2003).

S.J. RUBEL, J.D.
NEW YORK CITY

Ireland

EIRE, OR IRELAND, is an island country located at the west edge of Europe in the northern Atlantic Ocean. Summers are mild and winters can be cold but rain is present year round. Rivers and lakes keep the hilly terrain well watered and green. The Irish Sea separates Ireland from Scotland, Wales, and England. Irish ports abound and helped fuel the growth of the "Celtic Tiger" in the 1990s.

The Republic of Eire has 3.8 million people with Dublin, the capital at over 1 million. It is 95 percent Roman Catholic with both Irish Gaelic and English as official languages. Politically, Ireland has a bicameral government with a president and ministers. Economically, it is a mix of capitalist and socialist policies.

Eire's history is one of both isolation and invasions by Celtic, Viking, Norman, and Anglo-Saxon tribes. External trade is evident at least 2,000-years ago in Ptolemaic maps of Irish trading ports. During the Middle Ages, Eire was a haven for Christian scholars and emerging Roman Catholicism after the fall of the Roman Empire. However Eire's Catholic ties drew it into conflicts with Protestant neighbors in Europe, especially England. Eire effectively became a colony of expanding mercantile empires after 1690, and lost further power as it was divided into capitalistic English estates in the 18th and 19th centuries.

After a century of revolution and revolt, the 26 counties of the Republic of Ireland achieved full political if not economic independence in 1949. In the 1980s and 1990s, Eire became economically independent as well, with the incredible growth of the Celtic Tiger economy. Agriculture, industry, technology, and shipping led the way, with averages of 10 percent GROSS DOMESTIC PRODUCT (GDP) real growth, 4 percent UNEMPLOYMENT, $25,000 GDP per capita, 5 percent INFLATION, and trade balances of $25 billion.

In 2001, Eire joined the EUROPEAN UNION (EU) and its currency converted from the Irish punt to the EURO. Its fiscal policies are currently under direction of the EU banks in Frankfurt, Germany. Current problems due to the growth include political scandals and limited success of the social-partner model of the public sector, employers, and unions. The government response has been a controversial expansionary budget that hopes to reduce inflation rates that are twice that of EU neighbors. The republic also exerts increasing influence over Northern Ireland and takes its foreign policy direction from the EU.

The GROSS NATIONAL PRODUCT (GNP) rate of 8 percent growth annually since 1993 is transforming rural, Irish Gaelic-speaking, farming and fishing villages. Urban areas with foreign, especially German-owned industry are growing in Dublin and Cork. Tourism and a return to Ireland by those of Irish ancestry make up a significant component of the economy. A third of U.S. investment in the EU goes directly to the island and now, numerous traditional, Irish businesses, such as alcoholic beverages, crystal, and clothing, are being exported to the United States.

Eire has an inexpensive and educated workforce of over two million, and a low tax regime for business. Tax cuts and a growing Irish Stock Exchange (ISEQ) along with its labor force should allow the Republic of Ireland to continue to attract foreign investment, industry, and tourism. This is key for a healthy economy as major road and energy production projects continue to modernize the country.

Internally, the country's economy is thriving, fueled by consumer consumption. Exports consist of farming and fishing products to Europe, and a growing textile and manufacturing sector to the EU and United States. Mining and electronic-engineering industries are also in a growth pattern.

BIBLIOGRAPHY. R. Crotty, *Ireland in Crises: A Study in Capitalist Colonial Undevelopment* (Brandon Books, 1987); P. Keating and D. Desmond, *Culture and Capitalism in Contemporary Ireland* (Avebury, 1993); P. Maitra, *The Globalization of Capitalism in Third World Countries* (Praeger, 1996); D. O'Hearn, *Inside the Celtic Tiger: The Irish Economy and the Asian Model* (Pluto Press, 1998).

CHRIS HOWELL
RED ROCKS COLLEGE

Islamic banking

THE INNOVATION OF Islamic banking has taken on considerable significance since the 1970s. The accumulation of vast reservoirs of cash in the Arab Muslim nations as a result of OIL price increases led to a lively debate regarding the institutional modalities of savings and investment options. The Muslim orthodoxy revived the notion of Islamic banking as a religiously sanctioned and socially responsible alternative to capitalist, interest-based banking. As the Institute of Islamic Banking proclaims, "the basic principle of Islamic banking is the prohibition of Riba (usury—or interest)." This necessitates the development of alternative instruments of financial transactions. Following are some of the innovations proposed to circumvent the role of interest in the new model of banking.

Profit and loss sharing accounts. In these accounts, depositors are not allowed any interest on deposits. Instead, they participate in the profit or loss of the bank's transactions which, in turn, include only interest-free assets such as government commodity operations, bills of import, export, etc. At times, the banks implicitly, and when necessary, explicitly guarantee a minimum rate of return on deposits. The religious scholars consider this as quite objectionable since the guaranteed rate of profit looks suspiciously like an INTEREST RATE.

Musharaka model. Two or more partners contribute to the capital fund and share profits or losses in strict ratio of their contributions.

Muzaraba companies. These companies could issue specific and general purpose certificates to raise capital to invest the funds in Shariat (religious law)-approved projects. The profits (losses) are shared in a predetermined ratio between the partners.

Participation-term certificates are allowed as a means for corporate finance instead of debentures. The certificates are both transferable and negotiable with the proviso that unlike debentures, the holders of certificates would share in the profit (loss) of the companies instead of a given interest.

Housing finance is carried out through banks that would own the building, charge a rent premium till they recovered their loan capital plus a markup; or on a rent-sharing basis with co-ownership where a share of the rent is imputed as return to the bank.

The central bank is allowed to issue hire-purchase leases where the bank would purchase (own) physical commodities and hire them out for a rent premium.

The banks are allowed to advance interest free loans and charge administrative costs at negotiated rates.

It may be noted that foreign transactions are generally allowed on an interest-rate basis to keep the complications to a minimum. Also, the two systems, interest-based and interest-free banking are allowed to operate side-by-side for a period of initial introduction. The interesting thing about this whole project is that some Islamic courts have disbanded the variety of financial instruments and arrangements that were being used in the place of interest. The most obvious is the case of markup. The Islamic Development Bank defines the markup as "the margin added as a profit in addition to the real cost of the commodity sold as in installment sale. . . . Markup is different from interest in that it is related to machinery, etc. . . . whereas interest is related to money." This sounds suspiciously like interest in a new guise.

The limited use of other interest-free innovations is due to the fact that the banks are unable to predict their return in advance and the businesses fear the intrusive role of banks in their daily operations. To get around these difficulties, a complex web of subterfuge seems to have been developed to charge interest to borrowers and pay interest to lenders using Islamic nomenclature, which even the proponents of Islamic banking cannot abide.

The impasse has led to a further refinement of a technical nature among the followers of the Islamic School—an ever-expanding industry of ingenious innovations to circumvent the use or appearance of the use of interest. A more assertive approach is characterized by an attack on the institution of interest as the embodiment and source of all ills, economic and otherwise, like unemployment, inflation, and international exploitation in the defense of devising different interest-free strategies to advance and extend credit service. Another line of argument in the mix has been advanced by the secularist scholarship at various times. This is meant to validate the modern interest-based banking after formally addressing the concerns of Islamic scholars regarding the ill effects of interest.

Interest or usury? It is posited that indeed the role of interest-based loans in ancient times led to exploitation in the form of loan bondage. The Riba (usury) "played a double role in the social and economic structure of (pre-Islamic) Mecca by allowing the concentration of huge amounts of wealth in the hands of a few and by reducing the social status of other." Hence the justified injunctions against the charging of interest. However, in the modern age, interest-based banking encourages SAVINGS, rations CAPITAL and extends the roundabout production of capitalism that benefits consumers. And since banks make large loans to capitalists and landlords, abolition of interest would be a windfall to the ruling elites at the expense of the workers and peasants. The distinction is between interest and usury—the latter being the unusually high rate of interest charged by the rich elite leading to loan bondage of poor people. This might appear as an easy way out of the controversy on interest and usury but the mainstream of Islamic banking proponents find it not to be very meritorious.

Regardless of the acceptability or efficacy of this argument as a whole, it has led to a closer examination of the conceptual definition and practical role of interest in the affairs of humanity, current and ancient. In the mainstream literature of economics there is a long tradition of the exegesis of interest. Eugen von BÖHM-BAWERK, "the bourgeois Karl MARX," in his theory of interest formulates the concept in a way that justifies the receipt of interest (and profit) by capitalists as a reward for abstinence or, as Knut Wicksell explained, how the rate of interest tends to equal social marginal productivity of real capital—meaning that interest is the rightfully earned claim of capital (i.e., the capitalist).

To Irving FISHER, the interest rate helps adjust the time flow of INCOME receipts. The neoclassical theory maintains that interest functions as the equilibrating mechanism between savings and investment. Pre-classical thinking characterized interest as a return for permitting others to use the property accumulated in the form of MONEY. As important as these theoretical formulations are, what is really paramount and long-lasting is the accompanying philosophic social change. The values and ethical norms for economic life in the Christian perspective emphasize the primacy of justice to be measured by how the community treats its poor and the powerless, whether or not the social institutions permit all persons a measure of dignity and active social participation regardless of station in life, where there is a strong presumption against inequality of wealth and income.

The secularist theoreticians, by a process of selective inclusions and exclusions, move the debate away from issues of justice and fair play and toward concerns of productive efficiency and hierarchical social organization. A very similar process is under way in the Islamic economic formulations. The orthodoxy of Islamists is intent on a reformulation of the issue and a change in focus through theorizing their way out of the injunction against interest in Islam, and yet give it the name of Islamic banking. The opponents of this mode of banking propose a different solution—distinguish between interest and usury, have the sanction be directed at usury however characterized and leave the institution of interest intact.

However another reading of the injunction is that interest is unearned income and hence leads to a fundamental introduction of injustice in the community. Money is not fecund in its own right, does not by itself create value. Interest is a social mechanism to transfer value from those who create it through human endeavor to those who have control over money—an apparent case of exploitation. Since the spirit of Shariat in Islam is governed by a strong sense of social justice, fraternity, equality and cooperation, it is possible to argue the logic of inadmissibility in Islamic social schema of an exploitative distributive mechanism such as interest. The abolition of rent and interest—the twin categories of unearned income—may threaten the rentier classes that thrive on them. The debate, it seems, has to be elevated to articulate a system of social relations that encompasses the entire gamut of production, distribution, and consumption, as well as the reproduction of the system itself.

The main features that will have to be addressed are the distribution of property rights, the organization of decision-making arrangements, the setting up of the agenda of social objectives, defining the roles of the state and the market, the individual and the collective, identification of moral and material incentives, prescribing the limits of the permissible and impermissible in the human project. The Islamic concept of oneness—a mode of looking upon all beings as unity—dictates a value prescription of fairness, justice, and equity for all. All economics, including banking—Islamic or otherwise—will have to be tested against this dictum before we can fully overcome the age-old problem of economic injustice perpetually fed by categories of unearned income like the interest rate.

BIBLIOGRAPHY. F. Nomani and A. Rahnema, *Islamic Economic Systems* (Zed Books, 1994); T.S. Zaher and M.K. Hassan, "A Comparative Literature Survey of Islamic Finance and Banking," *Financial Markets, Institutions and Instruments* (Blackwell, forthcoming); Islamic Development Bank, "Islamic Modes of Financing and Shariat," www.isdb.org (2002); Shaikh M. Ahmad, *Man and Money: Toward an Alternative Basis of Credit* (Oxford University Press, 2002); National Conference of Catholic Bishops, *Pastoral Letter on Catholic Social Teaching and the U.S. Economy* (November 1986).

SYED B. HUSSAIN, PH.D.
UNIVERSITY OF WISCONSIN, OSHKOSH

Israel

LOCATED ON THE eastern Mediterranean Sea, Israel borders Lebanon to the north, SYRIA and JORDAN to the east, and EGYPT to the south. Of Israel's more than six million people, 80 percent are Jewish. The remaining 20 percent of the population is 80 percent Muslim, 10 percent Christian, and 10 percent Druze. In the late 20th century, a notable change to this mix has been the one million people who have immigrated to Israel since 1989.

The State of Israel was founded on May 14, 1948, on the basis of a United Nations Partition plan to create separate Jewish and Arab states, with the city of Jerusalem to be administered by the United Nations. In the fifty years preceding the 1948 proclamation of the State of Israel, growing numbers of Jews emigrated to Palestine. The main impetus to this emigration was the Zionist movement, led by its founder Theodore Herzl, a Hungarian-born Jewish journalist. This political form of Zionism, which viewed being Jewish as a nationality by itself, aimed to create a Jewish state in Palestine.

In 1917, toward the end of WORLD WAR I, Britain's foreign secretary Lord Balfour issued a declaration on behalf of the British government promising to support the creation of a Jewish homeland in Palestine. As a result of its loss in World War I, the Ottoman Empire lost control of its Arab lands, and the League of Nations granted a mandate to Great Britain to administer Palestine. Although the Balfour note promised "nothing shall be done which may prejudice the civil and religious rights of existing non-Jewish communities in Palestine," Arab inhabitants of Palestine opposed the subsequent immigration of Jews.

This influx increased in 1919, after the end of World War I, and grew significantly with the rise of Adolf Hitler to power in Germany by 1933. Great Britain, which had been supporting the rise of Arab nationalism, found itself in an intractable situation. It permitted continued Jewish immigration, but set quotas on the number of Jews who could settle in Palestine. The result was that no one was satisfied. After WORLD WAR II, Britain relinquished its mandate, leading to the 1947 United Nations-sponsored Plan of Partition.

Immediately after the Israelis' declaration of independence in May 1948, the Arab states of Egypt, IRAQ, Jordan, Lebanon, and Syria attacked Israel, refusing to recognize the new state. Israel won what it has since called its War of Independence, in the process increasing its territorial size by 50 percent. Jordan took over the central area of PALESTINE, the West Bank of the Jordan River, as well as East Jerusalem. The resulting situation was very different for Jews and Palestinians: The half million Palestinian Arabs who had fled or left their homes during the war were left with nowhere to go and were not accepted by the Arab states; meanwhile, Israel offered citizenship to any Jew who wanted to emigrate to the new state.

By 1967, the military forces of Syria and Egypt began to threaten Israel's borders to an increasing degree. In response, that year Israel attacked the Egyptian, Jordanian, and Syrian armies. After six days, the Arabs and Israelis agreed to a cease-fire, but Israel's accomplishments provided a new source of conflict. It had seized the West Bank of the Jordan River and East Jerusalem (previously controlled by Jordan), had taken the Golan Heights from Syria, and occupied the Sinai Peninsula and Gaza Strip, both previously held by Egypt. Israel had more territory, but it also now had to rule over one million more Arabs and still had not succeeded in getting the Arab states to recognize its existence.

In an effort to solve the Israeli-Palestinian conflict, the United Nations Security Council adopted Resolution 242, which provided a formula of "land for peace." This proposed solution has remained a central element in the Mideast peace process, and calls on Israel to return territory to the pre-1967 borders, prior to that year's Six-Day War. In return, borders were to be secure and the sovereignty of all nations, including Israel, was to be respected.

The Yom Kippur War of 1973, which took place on October 3, when the Egyptian and Syrian armies attacked Israel on the Jewish Day of Atonement, initially surprised the Israeli Defense Forces. Eventually, however, the Israelis were able to expand (with U.S. arms supplies) the amount of territory they controlled in the Sinai Peninsula. In two ways this war showed how the Israeli-Palestinian conflict reached around the world.

First, Cold War geopolitics—the desire of the United States and Soviet Union to expand their influence worldwide, at the expense of the other—led both superpowers to help conclude the war. Second, oil-producing Arab states used embargoes to drive up the price of oil, thereby hoping to force the United States and Western Europe to have Israel remove its forces from occupied territories. A peace treaty between Israel and Egypt in 1979 led to the removal of the Israeli army from the Sinai Peninsula and the Gaza Strip.

Hope for a comprehensive peace, however, remained remote until 1993, when negotiations conducted in secret in Norway led to a breakthrough: Israel permitted limited Palestinian self-rule in the West Bank and accepted the Palestine Liberation Organization (PLO) as a representative of the Palestinian people; the PLO, for its part, recognized the legitimate existence of the State of Israel. In 1994, Israel began to transfer ruling authority to the Palestinians, at first in places such as the town of Jericho on the West Bank. Since then, however, acts of violence on both sides have harmed efforts to establish peace through the "land for peace" formula.

The Palestinian intifada, or uprising, and extremist suicide bombings have made it difficult to focus on peace. At the same time, militant Israelis harm the process as well, such as the Israeli settler Baruch Goldstein who gunned down Palestinians praying in a mosque in Hebron in 1994, or the right-wing Jewish radical who assassinated Yitzhak Rabin, the Israeli prime minister who had signed the landmark peace agreement in 1994 with PLO Chairman Yasser Arafat.

By the turn of the century, with a population just over 6 million people, democratic and capitalist Israel was suffering through economic challenges driven by the intractable Palestinian situation. Drops in tourism, high technology, and other primary industries have led to negative growth for the $119 billion GROSS NATIONAL PRODUCT (GDP).

BIBLIOGRAPHY. H.M. Sachar, *A History of Israel: From the Rise of Zionism to Our Time* (Knopf, 1976); Sydney D. Bailey, *Four Arab-Israeli Wars and the Peace Process* (St. Martin's Press, 1990); Thomas L. Friedman, *From Beirut to Jerusalem* (Doubleday, 1995); *CIA World Factbook* (2002).

GEORGE KOSAR
BRANDEIS UNIVERSITY

Italy

AS FABRIZIO BARCA has correctly summarized, the judgment on Italian capitalism has constantly wavered between two opposite evaluations, though these have

The centuries-old canals of Venice, Italy, contributed to the growth of trade and capitalism among the merchant class.

co-existed in the public mind. On the one hand, Italian capitalism remains an anomaly and is negatively influenced by several factors from its beginning: The low standard of living of the middle and working classes, the social and economic impasse of the southern regions of the country, the ambiguous role of the STATE in industrial production, and the inefficiency of the state's bureaucracy. On the other hand, the Italian capitalist system is nonetheless considered capable of assuring one of the most sustained economic developments within industrialized countries.

Origins of capitalism. The origins of Italian capitalism can be traced back to the 1830s when Italy was only a geographic area, fragmented into a myriad of small, independent states. From that decade, the Italian peninsula witnessed new forms of banking activities with the establishment of offices open to the general public. These increasingly replaced the varied class of people who had supported commercial activities and investments until then: merchant-bankers, usurers, and charitable banks such as the *Monti di Pietà*. From the 1830s onward, Italian banking assumed a progressively public dimension, which substituted the contracts between private parties typical of the previous decades. The *casse di risparmio* were by far the most successful type of this new phenomenon, public banks.

The unification of the Kingdom of Italy between 1859 and 1860 accelerated the spread of banks. The number of towns and cities with bank branches tripled, and the credit system became a source of investment. If the phenomenon of the *casse di risparmio* had been predominantly a public one, the protagonists of this "banking revolution," as Franco Bonelli calls it, were instead private bankers, businessmen, capitalists, and landowners. The private banking sector, throughout the 1860s, also marked the beginning of an enduring phenomenon of Italian capitalism, big banks supplying money to the biggest firms and to whole core sectors of the Italian economy.

During the 1910s, Italy had to face the developments of international capitalism and the second industrial revolution without adequate technical and social structures. The country was struck by the 1907 RECESSION that stopped the growth of the industrial sector and consolidated the hegemony of financial capital. During the 10 years of governments led by the liberal Giovanni Giolitti (1903–14), Italy would try to enter the international markets through the unsuccessful colonial war against Libya (1911–12). These years also witnessed the birth of an important debate that came to endanger the very nature of Italian capitalism. While the government was led by a liberal coalition, the Socialist Party and the Catholic movement were getting increasingly stronger and more organized. Despite their clear ideological differences, both forces aimed at the transformation of the capitalist society into one based on a collective and cooperative structure. This points to a lasting feature of Italian capitalism, the bourgeoisie's and the capitalists' inability to promote social and political reforms. After WORLD WAR I, Italy entered another recession, due to the transition from a war economy to a peace economy, and was shaken by several important strikes.

Rise of Fascism. Because of the inability of Italian liberal governments, linked to conservative beliefs, to innovate and reform, FASCISM could present itself as a movement for the reform of Italian society and its economic structure. The Fascist regime, led by the dictator Benito Mussolini from the mid-1920s to the mid-1940s, adopted two main policies to reinvigorate Italian capitalism, monetary deflation and a re-launch of Italian agriculture by breaking up large agricultural estates and putting them on the market. The process of deflation was intended to expand industrial production, while the agricultural project was designed to distinguish Fascism from the previous liberal governments: the "attack on the large agricultural estates," as Fascists called their agricultural policy, implied the improvement of backward agricultural structures, putting on the market properties which were managed unproductively, and reclaiming malarial and marshy lands.

The Fascist state conceived itself to be a strong, modern nation-state, accepting both the ideas of capitalism in the socio-economic sphere and a syndicalist state, which brought about a forced union of labor and capital. Yet traditional unions were replaced by the Fascist corporations as the sole representatives of the workers with the Palazzo Vidoni Pact signed in 1925. Already weakened by Fascist violence, traditional trade unions, both of Catholic and socialist/communist orientations,

were denied their very reason for existence, the right to negotiate wages and working conditions on behalf of their members.

The Fascist regime had to face the 1929 international economic crisis and its aftermath. In Italy, the DEPRESSION became apparent in 1930. At the end of the year, industrial unemployment rose by 70 percent, while agricultural unemployment increased by 50 percent. Significantly, unemployment statistics stopped to be published after 1932. The measure to counter the crisis was somewhat surprising and was not pursued by any other European government except in GERMANY: the Fascist government favored a reduction of salaries (up to 25 percent) and of prices, thus continuing its policy of monetary deflation. In a famous speech in the Senate, Mussolini declared that the Italians' ability to endure hardships was due, paradoxically, to the country's underdeveloped economic system. "Fortunately, Italian people are not accustomed to eat much and they feel the privation less than others," Mussolini declared.

The result of this policy was to increase the mergers of different firms and, thus, the creation of a national economy that was even more dependent on monopolies. The regime also increased spending on public works, social welfare, and armaments. The most original Fascist contributions to the social and economic fields were also dictated by the impact of the Depression, and the difficulties experienced by the banks due to business failures. IMI, a business-credit bank, was founded in 1931, and IRI (Industrial Reconstruction Institute) was established in 1933. Through these organizations, the state intervened to prevent the collapse of banks and of manufacturing companies.

Though Italy recovered sooner than other, more industrialized countries from the Depression, the Fascist government soon had to face another economic crisis resulting from the sanctions imposed on Italy by the League of Nations following its invasion of Ethiopia. Mussolini thus inaugurated the policy of AUTARKY or economic self-sufficiency, tending to reduce imports from other countries. The result, however, was far from successful and produced a closed economy, which had neither the power to import nor to autonomously produce all supplies. As economic historian V. Zamagni puts it, while "the Fascist period did not represent a standstill in the industrialization process . . . nevertheless Fascism failed to bridge the gap between Italy and the other industrialized countries."

The Italian Republic. Most of the Fascist-state apparatus was swept away after WORLD WAR II and the Italian Republic was established by a 1946 referendum. Yet there was a major aspect of continuity between Mussolini's dictatorship and the postwar democratic governments in their economic policies: the huge public sector.

Until a program of PRIVATIZATION started during the 1990s, 40 percent of the Italian manufacturing industry and 80 percent of all banking operations were controlled by the state. Such a massive state presence in the national economy had both positive and negative effects. In the 1950s and 1960s, state intervention played a major role in creating the material conditions of the so-called Italian "economic miracle."

The state succeeded in establishing several new chemical, engineering, and ENERGY industries in which private Italian capitalism had been unwilling to risk its own resources. But the vast intervention of the state in the national economy has also caused one of the characterizing features of the Italian economic system in the second half of the 20th century, CORRUPTION. The governing parties, especially the Christian Democrats and, in the 1980s, the Socialists took direct hold of the public sector and supplied jobs in exchange for votes. In addition, the funds of public companies were often used to fund political parties and their onerous structures while public contracts were awarded to private business after the politicians in charge of the decision had been bribed.

Despite the complications of privatization and corruption, Italy remains a powerful economy. With a population of 58 million (2002), the country's GROSS DOMESTIC PRODUCT (GDP) was $1.5 trillion with a per capita purchasing power of $25,000.

BIBLIOGRAPHY. F. Barca, ed., *Storia del capitalismo italiano dal dopoguerra a oggi* (Donzelli, 1997); John Pollard, *The Fascist Experience in Italy* (Routledge, 1998); A. Polsi, *Alle origini del capitalismo italiano: Stato, banche e banchieri dopo l'Unità* (Einaudi, 1993); L. Villari, *Il capitalismo italiano del Novecento* (Laterza, 1993); V. Zamagni, *The Economic History of Italy, 1860–1990: Recovery after Decline* (Oxford University Press, 1993).

LUCA PRONO, PH.D.
UNIVERSITY OF NOTTINGHAM, ENGLAND

J

Jackson, Andrew (1767–1845)

THOUGH HE WOULD BECOME the seventh president of the UNITED STATES, Andrew Jackson was not from a prominent, aristocratic family and had little formal education. Born in the Waxhaw Settlement of South Carolina to Irish-immigrant parents, Jackson rose to national prominence after he directed the victory in the Battle of New Orleans during the WAR OF 1812. Jackson's humble origins and military heroics earned him enormous popularity with the "common" people and he remained sincere in his desire to curtail the elitism and financial privilege inherent to what had become the American system of government. Thus, the evolution of the United States during the antebellum era from a republic to a popular democracy has been labeled the period of Jacksonian Democracy.

After minimal education in the Waxhaw schools, Jackson joined the AMERICAN REVOLUTION's Continental Army at the age of 13. He was captured in 1781 and brutally slashed on the hand and forehead by a British officer whose boots he refused to clean. Jackson contracted smallpox in prison before a prisoner exchange afforded his release and his subsequent recovery.

In 1784, he began to pursue a legal career in North Carolina. There he met divorcée Rachel Donelson Robards, the daughter of a prominent Tennessee family, whom he married in 1791 against rumors that her divorce was not finalized. Due to the circumstances surrounding their matrimony, the couple had a second marriage ceremony in 1794.

His marriage into the Donelson family and his thriving legal career catapulted Jackson into the political spotlight. He served as a delegate to the Tennessee Constitutional convention and was elected the state's first U.S. Representative in 1796. In 1797, the legislature elected him to the Senate, but after serving just a few months he resigned to become judge of the Superior Court of Tennessee.

During the early 19th century, Jackson proved instrumental in military efforts against Native Americans, concerning territory disputes, and against the British during the War of 1812. On January 8, 1815, Jackson led a vastly outnumbered American army unit to defeat British military forces in the Battle of New Orleans. Given the importance of New Orleans to American trade in the interior, control over the city was critical and the victory established Jackson as a national hero and one of the most popular men in the country.

Riding the groundswell of popularity, Jackson challenged John Quincy ADAMS, Henry Clay, and William H. Crawford of Georgia in the election of 1824. Although Jackson won the plurality of both the popular and the electoral vote, he did not earn the necessary majority and the election was sent to the House of Representatives who chose Adams as president. Labeled the "corrupt bargain," Adams' election incensed Jackson and intensified his hatred of the elites. Four years later, in the bitter election of 1828, Jackson was handily elected behind the support of a unified Democratic Party. But despite Jackson's victory, the year ended sadly for him when Rachel Jackson died of a heart attack that December.

The events of Jackson's first term in office foreshadowed the growing sectionalism in the United States. In 1828, Congress had imposed a tariff on imported goods that Southerners felt benefited the Northeast's burgeoning industrial capitalist economy over their more agrarian society. In an 1832 Ordinance of Nullification, the state of South Carolina declared the tariff null and void and threatened to secede from the Union. Exercising the extents of his presidential authority, Jackson rejected nullification and secession as powers of the states. Though the crisis was resolved by a compromise tariff in 1833, Jackson became the first president to deem secession an act of treason.

However, the most significant event of Jackson's administration was the controversy surrounding the Second National Bank. Established as a depository for federal funds and a source of credit for businesses, the Second National Bank angered Andrew Jackson, for he believed that it provided the wealthy with unfair financial advantages.

In 1832, Congress renewed the bank's charter, but Jackson vetoed the bill and the conflict over the bank quickly became the focus of that year's presidential campaign. Although Jackson's stance alienated northeastern business interests, his popularity with farmers and artisans afforded him a handy victory. After the election, he took measures to destroy the bank.

But without a national banking system, the country was soon plagued by enormous inflation. Maintaining his commitment to a policy of hard money (gold and silver), in 1836, Jackson issued the Specie Circular, prohibiting the use of paper money in the use of federal lands. He believed that requiring hard currency for land purchase would end the frenzy of land speculation. However, in 1837, a financial panic seized the nation and Congress overturned the Specie Circular issuance.

Thus, during the course of his administration, Jackson maintained his desire to remove financial privilege from the government. He and his followers feared the concentration of economic and political power and believed that government intervention in the economy benefited special-interest groups and created corporate monopolies, both of which favored the rich.

Jackson wanted to restore the financial independence of the individual, the yeoman farmer and the artisan, by ending federal support of banks and corporations and by limiting the use of paper currency, which they distrusted. Jackson's opponents charged him with abusing presidential power and accused him of destroying the economy. But historians have associated him with the rise of liberal capitalism that would nurture the growth of American business and industry over the course of the 19th century.

When Jackson left office in 1837 and later died on June 8, 1845, in Nashville, he remained the hero of the common people, of "rural capitalists and village entrepreneurs" who believed in their right to expanding economic opportunities.

BIBLIOGRAPHY. Donald B. Cole, *The Presidency of Andrew Jackson* (Lawrence: University Press of Kansas, 1993); Richard Hofstader, *The American Political Tradition and the Men Who Made It* (Vintage, 1989); James M. McPherson, ed., *"To the Best of My Ability": The American Presidents* (Dorling Kinder-sley, 2000); Marvin Meyers, *The Jacksonian Persuasion: Politics and Belief* (Stanford University Press, 1957).

LINDSAY SILVER
BRANDEIS UNIVERSITY

Japan

A COUNTRY OF ISLANDS in the Far East, Japan is known as the land of the rising sun. It has a population of 127 million people and a GROSS DOMESTIC PRODUCT (GDP) of $3.55 trillion in purchasing power parity (2002). A very high level of human capital, especially in industrial technology, has allowed Japan to become one of the richest countries in the world, with a GDP per capita of $28,000 (2002), despite having a territory slightly smaller than California, rugged and mountainous terrain, and virtually no natural resources. Japan is one of the world's largest and technologically advanced producers of motor vehicles, electronic equipment, machine tools, steel and nonferrous metals, ships, chemicals, textiles, and processed foods.

Early industrialization and the birth of Japanese capitalism. Prior to starting the transition to capitalism in the second half of the 19th century, Japan had gone through almost 250 years of self-imposed isolation from the outside world. In 1854, the UNITED STATES' warships arrived at Japanese ports and demanded the opening of trade. Overwhelmed by the display of western technology and military might, the feudal-military rulers of Japan yielded first to the Americans and then also to other major powers. These events precipitated an acute political crisis. A coalition of rebellious provinces emerged, challenging the government and demanding that the emperor, who had been deprived of political power for several centuries, be restored as the supreme ruler. In 1868, the central government relinquished power in a bloodless restoration of the emperor's rule; this became known as the Meiji restoration.

Amazingly, the new government quickly abandoned the existing ultra-nationalistic stance and embarked instead on a program of profound social and economic reform and rapid Westernization. According to most historical accounts, the changes, that were nothing short of revolutionary, appear to be a result of just a handful of intellectuals persuading the new leaders that, in order to successfully defend the country's independence, it needed to modernize, both economically and politically. If true, these accounts suggest that human capital played the crucial role in shaping the development of Japanese capitalism from its cradle. In a matter of a couple of decades Japan became a constitutional monarchy with an elected parliament and competing political parties; it also embraced free markets, and the concept of civil rights.

Modern capitalist production started in Japan in the late 19th century in the cotton textile industry. This was the first industry to be set up in countries that had gone through industrialization prior to Japan, and its rise in Japan marked the first completely successful instance of Asian assimilation of modern Western manufacturing techniques. For example, Japanese firms introduced new technology of ring-spinning frames faster than any country in the world: in 1910 98.5 percent of Japanese spinning frames were rings as compared to 82.4 percent in the United States, 51.6 percent in RUSSIA, and only 16.6 percent in the UNITED KINGDOM.

In the middle 1880s, Japan still imported over 80 percent of its domestic consumption of cotton yarns. Then, during 1888–1900, domestic production of cotton yarn increased more than 20 times. Exports began in 1890, and the value of exports exceeded that of imports in 1897. By the early 1930s, the three largest cotton-spinning firms in the world were all Japanese. This remarkable success came about as a result of private entrepreneurial initiative and not through government protection.

Initially, the government, lacking an opportunity to impose protective TARIFFS, attempted to assist the process of industrialization by means of publicly subsidized firms. The experiments produced only a budgetary deficit and failed on all accounts, so that in the mid-1880s the policy was abandoned, and fiscal austerity and LAISSEZ-FAIRE in private business became the prevailing mode of economic policy. It was precisely at that time that an internationally competitive textile industry emerged and began to flourish. This historical episode contains a lesson not only for many developing countries and countries in transition to a market economy, but also for the economic problems facing Japan itself at the turn of the 21st century.

As manifested by the example of the textile industry, the institutional system of early Japanese capitalism that made possible this success had very little in common with some widespread notions about it. Until the 1930s, government intervention into the economy was limited. Even the banking system was almost unregulated, and it did not play an important role in financing industrial development anyway. Successful Japanese firms relied on equity issuance to finance investment. Shares were purchased by wealthy people with high reputations in the business community, who personally knew and monitored the management and the engineering personnel of firms they owned. This hands-on style by reputable owners, and the prospect of high dividends, encouraged small investors to also purchase shares, creating the basis for business expansion.

The tragedy of narrow nationalism. The development of Japanese capitalism was interrupted by a resurgence of narrow nationalism in the 1930s. Although some of the contributing factors came from global economic problems stemming from the Great DEPRESSION and isolationist trends in other countries, Japan's own history was probably more important. Ever since the Meiji government adopted the policy of modernization and Westernization, the country had a legacy of considering economic prosperity not as an end in itself, but rather as a means to an end, which was the creation of a strong state and armed forces.

As economic problems mounted, the civilian government gradually became politically paralyzed, and the real power slipped away from it and into the hands of the military. Civil liberties were curtailed, and in the run-up to war economic liberties were curtailed as well. Private businesses were forced to merge and were brought under government control. A group of old business leaders from the Meiji era left in disgust. The rest embraced the military rule. On December 7, 1941, Japanese warplanes attacked Pearl Harbor. WORLD WAR II began, and it was a war that Japan could not hope to win.

U.S. occupation and postwar recovery. Yasuzaemon Matsunaga, founder and president of one of Japan's largest electrical power companies was one of the most influential business leaders in the 1920s and 1930s. He was also one of the "old guard" who strongly disagreed with what he considered to be a policy headed toward disaster, so he quit all his posts in early 1942 and retired from public life.

When, on August 15, 1945, Japan announced its unconditional surrender, the 71-year old Matsunaga stunned his family and friends by declaring, "As of today, I am starting my own war against America!" With many active business leaders discredited by their cooperation with the military regime, Matsunaga was appointed head of the committee that was to decide on the organization of the postwar Japanese electrical power industry. His proposal, calling for splitting the government monopoly into nine independent regional companies and introducing the forces of competition, met with fierce opposition within the committee and from Japanese politicians but was upheld by the U.S. occupational authorities, which left the government with no choice but to implement it.

It was thus a combination of the vision of the best Japanese business leaders and U.S. economic advisors that played a key role in introducing vital reforms that changed the face of Japanese capitalism. After its defeat,

Japan became a truly democratic country under civilian rule. Article 9 of the new constitution explicitly prohibited Japan from establishing offensive military capability and eliminated any political power of the military. Land was given to the peasants, government-sponsored monopolies were shattered, and independent labor movement emerged. In 1949, an American advisor, Joseph Dodge, put an end to postwar government budget deficits, price controls, and run-away inflation. The Americans also provided funds to import U.S.-grown raw cotton and other raw materials in exchange for cotton textile and other manufactured products. Helped also by special demand related to the KOREAN WAR, the Japanese economy, in the early 1950s, was finally on the road to recovery.

Years of rapid growth. In the early 1950s, very few people could still imagine that the recovery would be nothing short of an economic miracle. As it turned out, Japan's GDP grew by an average of 9.6 percent per year during the 19 years from 1953 to 1971. For comparison, the U.S. economy, for which those were also very good years, grew by an average of 3.6 percent a year. By the early 1970s, Japan was a major economic power again and its competition was threatening U.S. manufacturers in various key industries, from automobiles to electronics. Matsunaga's friends may have laughed at the old man when he declared the start of his own "war" on America on the day of the Japanese surrender. When Matsunaga died in 1971 at the age of 97, he had witnessed some significant victories scored by the Japanese in the economic war.

A common perception of the post–World War II Japanese economic miracle is that it happened as a result of very close cooperation between the government and business, with the leading role in establishing what is often called "Japan Inc." played by the Ministry of International Trade and Industry (MITI). In reality, the story is much more complicated. The following is just one, although an extremely important illustration.

In October 1945, Masaru Ibuka rented a utility room that did not even have glass in its windows and started a radio repair shop in war-devastated Tokyo. On May 7, 1946, a new company called Tokyo Tsushin Kogyo was officially born, with shareholders' capital of 190,000 yen (several thousand dollars). The new firm had no capital equipment and whatever tools its employees used were handmade.

Fifty years later, in 1996, the shareholders' capital of the same company stood at 1,459,332,000,000 yen, or about $15 billion, with a comparable figure representing the market value of its plants, capital equipment, and other capital assets. The company employed 151,000 people and had 998 subsidiaries worldwide, including the United States. Long before

that, in 1957 the company also officially changed its name to SONY.

The biggest breakthrough in company's history came in the 1950s when it became the first Japanese firm to produce transistor radios. In order to do so, Sony had to purchase patent rights from Western Electric, but the transaction required approval from MITI. Sony's initial request for such an approval was flatly rejected on the grounds that other, much larger firms were unanimous in their opinion that there was not enough indigenous technology in Japan to produce its own transistors. It took Sony almost a year to overcome the bureaucratic red tape, and it certainly did not receive any support from the government. Then, a few years later a famous episode made headlines, in which 4,000 only Sony-made transistor radios were stolen from a warehouse in Long Island. The burglars did not take radios made by any other company. In other words, the brand name of Sony had already become a synonym for excellent performance and quality.

The transistor technology example seems to be just one of many cases in which MITI blundered in arbitrarily designating winners, and in picking the direction of development for an industry. Another famous episode is the entry of HONDA MOTOR COMPANY into auto manufacturing. Just about the time Honda was contemplating starting automobile production in addition to producing motorbikes, MITI policy-makers decided that Japan did not need more automobile companies, and were pushing legislation that would have banned any new entry into the industry. Fortunately, the legislation was defeated in parliament. It is hard even to imagine where the Japanese economy would stand 50 years later without Sony and Honda.

True, in some cases, coordination by the government did play an important role (for example, helping Japanese construction-equipment manufacturers and computer producers to become internationally competitive). But the main driving force for the Japanese economic success in the 1950s to early 1970s, just as almost a century before that, mostly came from private initiative and spurring technological innovation based on entrepreneurial spirit and high human capital. Japan was also helped by the overall favorable business conditions in the world economy, low energy prices, expanding international trade, as well as by the fact that it didn't have to spend almost anything on military build-up.

Japan as number one? The advent of complacency. In 1971, President Richard NIXON abandoned the BRETTON WOODS fixed exchange-rate system. In the years following that decision the Japanese yen gained more than 100 percent in value versus the U.S. dollar, from 360 yen for one dollar to the temporary peak of less than 180 yen for the dollar in 1978. In the early 1980s, the Japanese became the biggest holders of U.S. government bonds and Japanese investors were aggressively buying real estate in the United States, including the famous deal to purchase Rockefeller Center in New York City.

More and more people on both sides of the Pacific and elsewhere were starting to believe that Japanese capitalism was inherently superior to its versions in the United States and Europe, and that the 21st century would be the century of Japan. A book entitled *Japan as Number One* by Ezra Vogel became a bestseller.

Complacency and self-satisfaction is a great enemy not only of individuals but also of nations. Precisely at the time the Japanese started flattering themselves with their economic success, problems started mounting.

The biggest problem was with the Japanese financial sector. As Japan grew rapidly in the 1950s and 1960s, private investment demand was so high, compared to the amount of savings that the economy could generate, that the government had to step in aggressively to support the market for corporate loans. The financing of investment by Japanese firms relied heavily on the country's banking system, while the BANK OF JAPAN acted as a lender of last resort to commercial banks, regulated and protected by the Ministry of Finance. Protection and regulation were not limited to banks. They encompassed most of the infrastructure (construction, transport) and wholesale and retail trade. Behind the shadow of highly efficient and internationally competitive manufacturing industries a "second economy" was hiding, where waste of resources, lack of responsibility, and corruption were rampant.

As the era of high industrial growth based on real investment and export demand neared its end in the 1970s, the distortions of the "second economy" started taking a heavy toll. Government budget deficit re-emerged in the 1970s for the first time since it was abolished by the "Dodge line" in 1949. The share of bank loans in the external financing of large corporations had shrunk from more than 80 percent in early 1970s to less than 40 percent in mid-1980s and continued to slide. Instead, large corporations in manufacturing industries themselves became large investors in financial assets. This shift from lending to internationally competitive firms in manufacturing industries to the government and smaller businesses, mostly in inefficient sectors of the economy, proved detrimental, although this was not widely recognized at that time. Instead, a temporary speculative bubble emerged that conveyed a false impression of continued prosperity but resulted only in lowering the morale of the working Japanese.

The systemic crisis and challenges for the 21st century.
On the last day of trading in 1989 the stock price index (NIKKEI) at the Tokyo stock exchange reached its all-time peak of 38,916 yen. (Thirteen years after that, on the last day of trading in 2002, it was down 78 percent at 8,579 yen). In the next year the bubble burst, leading to the most protracted depression in the history of the Japanese economy, with the real growth rate averaging a meager 1.4 percent over the "lost decade" of the 1990s.

The burst of the bubble and the resulting economic slump exposed problems in Japanese capitalism that had not been apparent until the economy stumbled. At the turn of the new century, Japan faced a full-scale systemic crisis of severe magnitude. For various reasons, Japan was slow to apprehend the new reality, and to devise its way out of the crises for much of the 1990s. The inertia of more than 30 years of almost uninterrupted economic success proved initially to be too strong for both the business sector and the government.

Japan had to dismantle the outdated system of government guarantees to banks and other inefficient industries, to abandon its implicit life-time employment guarantees for workers regardless of their productivity, and to introduce more disclosure and market competition, but this process moved painstakingly slowly, if at times at all. Investors hung on to their assets in futile hopes of a quick turn-around; as a result, when they eventually did sell, they got back just a fraction of the original value. Fearing the social cost of unemployment, the government tried to bail out inefficient firms, which only prolonged the misery. The government budget deficit eventually took on levels unseen in any other developed economy. Coupled with the aging of the population, this put the country's social security and pension system on the verge of bankruptcy. Many economists believe Japan badly needs to implement a comprehensive restructuring of its economy at the industry and firm level, reform the government and the social security system as well as find innovative ways to compete against the rapidly growing neighboring economies of CHINA and South KOREA.

Still, Japan remains the world's second most powerful economy, and its potential of human capital is as strong as ever. It has also proven more than once in its history that it is capable of strongly recovering from challenging economic times.

BIBLIOGRAPHY. Masahiko Aoki and Gary Saxonhouse, eds., *Finance, Governance and Competitiveness in Japan* (Oxford University Press, 2000); Thomas Cargill, ed., *Financial Policy and Central Banking in Japan* (MIT Press, 2001); *CIA World Factbook: Japan* (2002); David Flath, *The Japanese Economy* (Oxford University Press, 2000); Yoshiro Miwa, *Firms and Industrial Organization in Japan* (New York University Press, 1996); Ezra Vogel, *Japan as Number 1: Lessons for America* (Harvard University Press, 1979).

SERGUEY BRAGUINSKY, PH.D.
STATE UNIVERSITY OF NEW YORK, BUFFALO

Jefferson, Thomas (1743–1826)

THE ARCHITECT OF THE American Declaration of Independence and the third president of the United States (1800–08), Thomas Jefferson was also a scientist, philosopher, politician, writer, and Renaissance man, and he emerged at the same time as the ascendancy of capitalism in world history. His extraordinary legacy in writing and his actions in life have been interpreted in myriad fashion. Nowhere is this truer than Jefferson on capitalism.

Jefferson's life of hard work seemed to echo that of Benjamin FRANKLIN, and his concepts of individual liberty seemed in line with those of Adam SMITH. His obsession with debt, both personal and national, seems reminiscent of today's fiscal conservatives. Yet Jefferson, the LIBERTARIAN and equalitarian, defies categorization and maybe always will.

Jefferson's economic policy and thought centered on balancing economic inequalities in the complex linkages of agrarian, mercantilist, and capitalist economies that

Thomas Jefferson sought a personal and national balance between agrarian, mercantilist, and capitalist forces.

were all present in the early UNITED STATES. Agrarian economies were based on land, mercantile economies upon colonies, and capitalist economies upon surplus capital, and each represented different dynamics. Jefferson himself was an agrarian practitioner who had gone into debt in a mercantilist system, and experienced bankruptcy in the emerging capitalist United States in his later years. It is no wonder he sought balance of economic inequality based on his own and the nation's early debt experiences.

As president and private businessman in the early 19th century, Jefferson sought personal and national economic balance in the trichotomy of an agrarian, mercantilist, and capitalist U.S. economy. Here stems some of the confusion surrounding Jefferson and capitalism. In the 20th century, the three broad paradigms of dealing with economic inequality had emerged. Socialists advocated government ownership; social democrats (known as liberals in the United States) wanted the welfare state and power sharing between capital, government, and labor; and classical liberals (known as conservatives in the United States) wanted personal freedom and responsibility in a free-market context. However, such 20th century concepts do not necessarily directly correlate with the economic systems of Jefferson's time. Moreover, Jefferson's prolific writing career is often contradicted by his actions in life. The Jefferson adage, "Do you want to know who you are? Don't ask. Act! Action will delineate and define you," suggests we should examine his actions as well as his words.

Jefferson has been referred to as the American sphinx, difficult to interpret and impossible to pin down. His seemingly contradictory views and actions are befuddling even in their own historical context. At times, Jefferson appeared to be led by compromise, by vision, by influence, or by all three. In politics, he was influenced by John LOCKE's idea of individual natural rights and Charles de MONTESQUIEU's diffusion of government power in a mixed republic with judicial, executive, and legislative branches. Friend and future U.S. president, James MADISON influenced Jefferson as they fought for balanced government and individual rights in the U.S. Constitution and Bill of Rights, yet kept slaves in a failing slave-plantation economy. Jefferson and Madison also acted for religious thought and freedom of expression, especially if Christianity was involved.

Amid this sea of change and thought in early America, came the emergence of capitalism as espoused by Smith in 1776, the same year Jefferson penned the Declaration of Independence. Jefferson witnessed firsthand early farming colonies in North America transition from agrarian economics to small cottage industries to urban capitalism. At times he tried to direct, interact with, or just get out of the way of the rise of capitalism in his personal and public life. The enormous volume of written material he left leaves a mixed legacy concerning his thoughts and actions on capitalism.

Jeffersonian capitalism is often interpreted as economic policies that can redistribute ownership of productive capital to individuals and small groups. Such a policy should be promoted efficiently by a government that is accountable to the electorate. The result would be an egalitarian economic system of decentralized activities in competitive markets by individuals.

Such an interpretation stems from Jefferson's 1776 draft of the Virginia Constitution. Jefferson advocated free-born male suffrage or voting rights with a qualification of ownership of 25 acres of land. Those who did not own land would be allotted 50 acres and thus suffrage. Though suffrage was not universal (slaves and women were excluded), the idea of combining both political power via the vote, and economic power via the most valued possession of the time, land, was significant to say the least.

Proponents of small government and big capitalism today often quote Jefferson, who wrote, ". . . government is best which governs the least, because its people discipline themselves." Yet Jefferson, as an agrarian, was wholly against what he called "monied corporations," or banks and believed much of the wealth of a nation should always reside in the hands and lands of its people, not banks, stock markets, or capitalist enterprises. Jefferson was supportive of individualism to the extreme, but this did not necessarily translate to support of capitalistic banks and corporations. Jefferson saw the individual, free male landowner as citizen, soldier, money-issuer and keeper of liberty, who, through education and action, would control the power of government and corporations.

He even considered banking corporations a greater threat to personal liberty than armed force or the government. Jefferson and Madison both contested formation of centralized banking in the United States. Jefferson stated, "I believe that banking institutions are more dangerous to our liberties than standing armies. Already they have raised up a monied aristocracy that has set the government at defiance. The issuing power should be taken from the banks and restored to the people to whom it properly belongs." Jefferson also stated, "I hope we shall crush in its birth the aristocracy of our monied corporations which dare already to challenge our government to a trial by strength, and bid defiance to the laws of our country."

Such stances have been interpreted in the modern era as indicating Jefferson was against centralized capitalism with money as the key source of power, and that the law of the land along with individual thought and action should be the guiding mechanisms, not supply and demand. Yet Jefferson defies such simplistic interpretation by any side in debates on capitalism.

Jefferson's purchase of the Louisiana territory from a cash-poor Napoleonic FRANCE in 1804 is also open to multiple interpretations. He purchased it with funds the fledgling United States did not have, a purchase on debt if you will. As soon as possible, he made the land available for settlement, despite the presence of large numbers of settled and nomadic Native American communities. His vision was of the land as the key component for individual liberty as well as economic and political stability at the expense of national debt.

Additionally, Jefferson's own debt in what had been a largely mercantilist economy of slave plantation production of cash crops, such as tobacco, has been given multiple interpretations. Jefferson felt strongly those monied institutions, whether banks or government, represented a serious threat to liberty through debt. Jefferson envisioned political power as a means to redress economic power in the grasp of creditors. He has been called a poor capitalist who needed venture capital to fund his research and development projects in science and invention, the AMERICAN REVOLUTION war debt, and the national debt. Alternatively, he has been portrayed as a successful agrarian and mercantilist who failed only due to the rise of capitalist monied institutions. Some suggestions go so far as to indicate the debt of the landed aristocracy of the colonies owed to creditors in the British Empire mercantilist economy led to their participation in the American Revolution, and to guarded approaches to any future credit and debt system such as financing in capitalism.

Finally, Jefferson's vision of an educated populace acting for its own destiny via government-funded public education has been interpreted as socialist, social-democratic, and democratic, to name but a few labels. Jefferson's suggestion was to "Educate and inform the whole mass of the people. . . . They are the only sure reliance for the preservation of our liberty." However, as should be evident by now, Jefferson is not easy to label nor are his beliefs simplistic. Perhaps that is why his complex messages still have relevance today, no matter the perspective and interpretation.

BIBLIOGRAPHY. J. Ellis, *American Sphinx: The Character of Thomas Jefferson* (Vintage Books, 1998); T. Jefferson, (A. Koch, and W. Peden, eds., *The Life and Selected Writings of Thomas Jefferson* (Modern Library, 1998); T. Jefferson, (L. Cappon, ed.,) *The Adams-Jefferson Letters: The Complete Correspondence Between Thomas Jefferson and Abigail and John Adams* (University of North Carolina Press, 1988); H. Sloan, *Principle and Interest: Thomas Jefferson and the Problem of Debt* (University Press of Virginia, 2001).

CHRIS HOWELL
RED ROCKS COLLEGE

Jevons, William Stanley (1835–82)

BEST KNOWN FOR HIS DEVELOPMENT of the concept of marginal utility and his introduction of mathematics into the field of economics, William Stanley Jevons was born in Liverpool, England, the ninth of 11 children of a prosperous family. His father, Thomas, ran the family business, Jevons & Sons, and his mother, Mary Anne, was an accomplished poet. The family's fortunes changed in 1845 when Jevons' mother died following a prolonged illness. Three years later, a collapse in the RAILROAD industry forced Jevons & Sons into BANKRUPTCY, and the family never recovered financially.

At the age of 15, Jevons entered the Junior School of University College, London, and continued on to the University College the following year. In London, he lodged with his cousin, Henry (Harry) Enfield Roscoe, who later became one of Britain's most eminent chemists. In 1853, Roscoe arranged a lucrative position for his cousin at the newly established Sydney mint in AUSTRALIA. Jevons worked at the mint until 1859 when he returned to University College to complete his studies. He became a tutor at Owens College in Manchester in 1863 just as his first book, *A Serious Fall in the Value of Gold*, began to gain recognition.

Three years later, he became a professor at Owens College, and the following year, married Harriet Ann Taylor, the daughter of the owner of the *Manchester Guardian*, a prominent newspaper. The couple had three children, one of whom, Herbert Stanley, followed in his father's footsteps and became an economist. Jevons remained at Owens College for 10 years until he returned to University College, London, as Professor of political economy in 1876. Poor health forced him to resign his position in 1881, and, during a family holiday in August, 1882, Jevons drowned off the coast of Devon.

Jevons first became known in Great Britain for *The Coal Question*, which was published in 1865. He predicted that Britain would soon exhaust its supply of coal and, as a result, relinquish its position as the world's leading industrial power to the UNITED STATES, which had a nearly inexhaustible supply of coal. His prediction about the United States proved correct, but he was far too pessimistic about the prospects for Britain's future. Jevons' analysis failed to account for the development of alternative energy resources such as oil or natural gas, the discovery of new sources of coal, and the incentive to use coal more efficiently as its price increased.

In 1871, Jevons published the *Theory of Political Economy*, which included his most important contributions to economics. Like Carl MENGER and Leon WALRAS,

each of whom worked independently of the others, Jevons challenged the view of classical economics that the cost of production determines value: "Repeated reflection and inquiry have led me to the somewhat novel opinion, that value depends entirely upon utility."

Jevons used the example of water to illustrate the subjective nature of value, pointing out that "a quart of water per day has the high utility of saving a person from dying in a most distressing manner." As the quantity of water available increases, though, an additional unit of water provides less utility. Beyond a certain quantity, the utility of additional water gradually sinks to zero. For virtually everything that humans consume, Jevons concluded, "all our appetites are capable of satisfaction or satiety sooner or later."

These observations led Jevons to articulate the idea that later became known as the principle of diminishing marginal utility: "We may state as a general law, that the degree of utility varies with the quantity of commodity, and ultimately decreases as that quantity increases."

Jevons realized that value depended not on total utility, but on the "final degree of utility" of a particular good. This insight allowed Jevons to develop his well-known principle of exchange, which holds that the "ratio of exchange of any two commodities will be the reciprocal of the ratio of the final degrees of utility of the quantities of commodity available for consumption after the exchange is completed." For example, consider a consumer whose marginal utility of oranges is 2 units and whose marginal utility of apples is 4 units. If she gives up 1 apple, she loses 4 units of utility and would require 2 oranges to offset the loss. Thus, the ratio of exchange, 2 oranges for 1 apple, equals the reciprocal of the ratio of the marginal utility of oranges to apples.

In addition to developing marginal analysis, Jevons was also instrumental in introducing mathematics into the field of economics. He pioneered the use of index numbers and believed that "all economic writers must be mathematical so far as they are scientific at all."

BIBLIOGRAPHY. William Stanley Jevons, *The Theory of Political Economy* (Palgrave, 1871); Sandra Peart, *The Economics of W.S. Jevons* (Routledge, 1996); Margaret A. Schabas, *A World Ruled by Number: William Stanley Jevons and the Rise of Mathematical Economics* (Princeton University Press, 1990).

JEFFREY R. GERLACH
COLLEGE OF WILLIAM AND MARY

Jiang Zemin (1926–)

A VIRTUAL UNKNOWN UNTIL 1989, when he was picked as the next general secretary of the Chinese Communist Party (CCP), Jiang Zemin can best be described as traditional, a devoted communist, and Western in his economic orientation.

Jiang's roots are traditional: As a young child, he was given up for adoption as male heir to the family of an uncle killed in combat after joining the CCP. His firm background in revolutionary martyrdom positioned Jiang to rise in the CCP: In 1943 he participated in the CCP students' movement, joining the party in 1946. One year later, at age 21, he graduated with an electrical-engineering degree from a Shanghai University.

During the tumultuous Cultural Revolution, he kept a low profile; however, as the pragmatic Deng Xiaoping rose to power and began to liberalize CHINA's economic policies, Jiang began to gain influence. He was elected a member of the CCP Central Committee at the Twelfth CCP National Congress in 1982, oversaw the development of Shanghai's first stock exchange, and was appointed China's electronics industry minister in 1983. Two years later, as mayor of Shanghai, he brought in venture capital from HONG KONG, JAPAN, and the West.

Jiang's economic liberalism was matched by his political conservatism. For supporting suppression of Tiananmen Square protestors, he was appointed in 1989 to the powerful post of chairman of the Central Military Commission, and president of the PRC by 1993.

Soon after having emerged from an elite group after Deng's's 1997 death, Jiang expounded the importance of the party to China through his Three Represents theory, that dictated that the CCP should lead China to modernize its economy, develop its own culture (albeit accepting appropriate Western ideas), and represent all people, rather than only the workers and peasants.

Jiang's theory and policy was affirmed in November 2002, with his announcement of the succession of vice-president Hu Jintao as chief of the CCP, and the invitation that capitalists join the party, thus breaking a long tradition of exclusion. Like his predecessor, Hu vowed to continue to promulgate not only Jiang's Three Represents theory, but also his strict political control. Thus, the resulting mixture of continued political totalitarianism with some aspects of capitalism provides a unique model of non-democratic capitalism. Whether it succeeds in the long run has yet to be seen.

BIBLIOGRAPHY. Bruce Gilley, *Tiger on the Brink: Jiang Zemin and China's New Elite* (University of California Press, 1998); June Teufel Dreyer, *China's Political System, Modernization and Tradition* (Addison-Wesley Longman, 2000); British Broadcasting Company, "The Legacy of Jiang Zemin," www.news.bbc.co.uk.

CRISTINA ZACCARINI, PH.D.
ADELPHI UNIVERSITY

Jobs, Steve (1955–)

A PIONEERING FIGURE in the personal computer industry and co-founder of Apple Computer, Inc., Steven Paul Jobs was born and raised in the heart of Silicon Valley, California. Jobs attended Reed College for a time but dropped out in 1974 to design video games for the Atari Corporation. Shortly thereafter, Jobs reconnected with a high-school friend, Steve Wozniak, who had been working on developing his own computer logic board design. Jobs took an interest in his innovative work and the two formed a business venture. Jobs and Wozniak dubbed the logic board design, the Apple I, and the two founded Apple Computer on April 1, 1976.

A refined version in a more stylish enclosure, the Apple II, was finished in 1977. It became an immediate success in the fledgeling personal-computer industry. Apple's fortunes soared over the next several years, as it became one of Americas most high-profile computer companies. In 1983, Jobs lured PepsiCo Chief Executive Officer John Sculley to run Apple, in part with the famous line, "Do you want to spend the rest of your life selling sugared water or do you want a chance to change the world?"

Inspired by the concept of a graphical user interface developed at Xerox-Parc (and seen by Jobs on a controversial visit in 1979), Jobs oversaw Apple's efforts to develop a new consumer computer. The 1984 introduction of the resulting Macintosh was a public-relations coup, and a pioneering case of "event marketing." But while the Macintosh proved an instant icon in American business history and popular culture, sales did not match expectations immediately, and Jobs bore considerable blame for this, leading to his dismissal from Apple in 1985 (a move engineered by Sculley).

After leaving Apple, Jobs founded NeXT in 1985 with the goal of matching fine design and superior function in high-powered workstation computers for education markets. The high price of initial models, however, doomed NeXT to a minor position in the computer industry of the early 1990s. Jobs then bought Pixar Animation Studios in 1986, building it into a major Hollywood design studio, responsible for the first full-length computer-generated motion picture, "Toy Story" (1995).

Jobs, by now undeniably a marketing and public-relations expert, accepted an offer to return to Apple in 1997 after it acquired NeXT for $400 million. He resumed leadership of the company several months later, with the typically atypical title of "interim CEO" or "iCEO." With Apple at its lowest fortunes, Jobs made a number of organizational moves to turn the company around, the most dramatic and successful of which included a partnership with MICROSOFT in 1997 and the introduction of the radically revised consumer computer, the iMac, in 1998. In early 2003, Jobs remained at the helm of Apple and one of the more enigmatic and charismatic figures in modern capitalism.

BIBLIOGRAPHY. Lee Butcher, *Accidental Millionaire: The Rise and Fall of Steve Jobs at Apple Computer* (Paragon, 1988); Alan Deutschman, *The Second Coming of Steve Jobs* (Broadway, 2000); Scott Rosenberg, *Machine Dreams* (Salon Media Group, 2001); Randall Stross, *Steve Jobs and the NeXT Big Thing* (Macmillan, 1993).

CHARLES ROBINSON, PH.D.
BRANDEIS UNIVERSITY

Johnson, Andrew (1808–75)

THE 17TH PRESIDENT of the UNITED STATES, Andrew Johnson, was born in Raleigh, North Carolina. His father died when Johnson was three years old. Johnson became a tailor's apprentice at 14; he never attended school but taught himself to read and write.

At age 18, Johnson headed west, setting up a tailor shop in Greenville, Tennessee, where he became inspired by Jacksonian Democracy. At that time, power in the southern United States lay with the large plantation owners. Johnson supported the small farmers and professionals who often had opposing interests. In 1829, he challenged the local leadership to win election to town council, and later mayor.

After serving in the Tennessee state legislature, Johnson was elected to the U.S. Congress in 1843. Being gerrymandered out of his district in 1852, Johnson was elected Tennessee governor and after two terms, returned to Washington, D.C., as a senator in 1857.

Although Johnson was a Democrat, he frequently clashed with party leaders in Tennessee. He proposed a homestead law that provided free western land up to 160 acres, opposed by slave owners. In 1860, he supported Stephen Douglas who thought territories should decide whether they would be slave states or free states. Most Southerners were arguing that they had the right to take their slaves anywhere.

While he supported slavery, Johnson staunchly opposed the idea of secession. After Tennessee voted to secede, Johnson refused to recognize its status. He was the only Southern senator to remain in the U.S. Senate after his state voted to secede.

When Union armies recaptured Tennessee in 1862, President Abraham LINCOLN appointed Johnson military governor. In the 1864 presidential election, Lincoln selected Johnson as his vice-presidential running mate. By choosing a Southerner and a moderate who had remained loyal to the Union, Lincoln hoped to pull the nation closer together.

When Lincoln was assassinated a few weeks into his second term, Johnson became president. From the outset of his presidency, there may never have been a more hostile relationship between a president and Congress. Johnson had always been a strict constructionist, who believed in limited government. Although he had accepted emancipation, he wanted to leave it up to the states to decide how to deal with the new freedmen. He saw military occupation of the South as a temporary measure and wanted to return to democratic government as soon as possible.

Johnson's critics pointed out that his policies left the new freed-men at the mercy of a hostile white majority, and that quick removal of the military would turn these states back to people who had been traitors just a few years earlier.

Nevertheless, Johnson opposed measures designed to protect the rights of African-Americans, including the proposed 14th Amendment to the Constitution. Congress overruled most of his vetoes and the relationship between Congress and the White House remained hostile.

Congress passed the Tenure in Office Act over Johnson's veto, taking away his right to fire his cabinet members without Senate approval. When Johnson fired Secretary of War Henry Stanton, the House voted to impeach him. After a lengthy trial, the Senate failed by a single vote to reach the two-thirds majority necessary to convict him. Johnson finished his final year in office and left town.

Thanks to a highly competent secretary of state, Johnson had a relatively successful foreign policy, acquiring Alaska from RUSSIA, and getting the French to abandon MEXICO. Johnson remained relatively popular in Tennessee. In 1874, he was re-elected to the Senate but died only a few months after taking office.

BIBLIOGRAPHY. Nathan Miller, *Star-Spangled Men* (Scribner, 1998); Milton Lomask, *Andrew Johnson: President on Trial* (Octagon Books, 1960); Hans L. Trefousse, *Andrew Johnson: a Biography* (W.W. Norton, 1989).

THOMAS D. JEITSCHKO, PH.D.
MICHIGAN STATE UNIVERSITY
MICHAEL J. TROY, J.D.

Johnson, Lyndon B. (1908–73)

LYNDON BAINES JOHNSON, born in southwestern Texas, became the 36th president of the UNITED STATES after an exemplary political career that spanned four decades. Throughout his career in politics, Johnson maintained a composure that became one of his legacies. His ability to compromise and push the Democratic Party's agendas through the toughest of political arenas is well known, as was his dedication to civil rights legislation.

These skills led him to the vice presidency under John F. KENNEDY. After the tragic assassination of President Kennedy, Johnson assumed the commander-in-chief position and used it to pass some of the broadest social legislation the United States had ever seen. His ability to negotiate through political quagmires was pushed to the extremes when the conflict in South Vietnam escalated to a boiling point in 1964. Ultimately, it was the VIETNAM WAR and its repercussions that would allow those who opposed Johnson to maneuver for political advantage against him.

Johnson grew up in a rural farming community. His parents were not wealthy. His father served five terms in the Texas legislature, setting young Johnson up for political connections, but his parents could not fully support his finances. Johnson graduated from Johnson City high School in 1924. In 1927, Johnson attended Southwest Texas State Teachers College in San Marcos. Although he was involved in a significant number of school activities, he was able to graduate in just 312 days. This kind of drive and ambition was the primary trait that would propel Johnson up the political ranks and into power.

Johnson had his first experience in the public arena in 1931 when he campaigned for Richard M. Kleberg, and was appointed as the newly elected congressman's secretary. Now in Washington, D.C., Johnson used his amiable and energetic personality to make his way into the social circles of the House of Representatives. He became known to President Franklin D. ROOSEVELT, Congressman Sam Rayburn, and Vice President John Nance Garner.

Johnson was elected to Texas' 10th congressional district in 1937 in the face of five anti-NEW DEAL Democratic opponents. Using his new Washington acquaintances, Johnson jockeyed for position and made his way onto committees where he could benefit his district. He was interested in such problems as public power, flood control, reclamation and public housing. Also a member of the Naval Affairs Committee, Johnson stood firmly in his opinion that power in international affairs was the correct route to take in the unfolding conflict that would become WORLD WAR II.

Prior to 1941, Johnson had known nothing but political success and direct vertical ascension into the ranks of the U.S. government. But in 1941, Johnson ran against W. Lee O'Daniel for U.S. senator. At the time, Texas Democrats were split between those who supported President Roosevelt and those who opposed him. Johnson had full support of the president, yet lost to O'Daniel, who ran on the anti-Roosevelt platform.

After losing the senate race, Johnson joined the U.S. Navy in December 1941. He was awarded the Silver Star from General Douglas MacArthur for his service in the Pacific theater and returned to Washington, D.C., in 1942 at the order of Roosevelt. Johnson concentrated his legislative efforts on the military during the remainder of World War II.

The post-war political atmosphere was in significant contrast to the environment that was prevalent before the war. Many Americans, and their representatives, began to lean more toward the right in policy and legislative action. After the war, Johnson no longer supported an expansion of the New Deal, but did look after the maintenance of Roosevelt's social reform. Furthering his own tendency to lean toward the right, Johnson supported the Taft-Hartley Act of 1947 that helped to lessen the power of strong labor forces moving throughout the country.

In 1948, it was clear that Johnson had made the correct political decisions to gain the support of the state of Texas, and defeated his Republican opponent for the senator's seat in the U.S. Senate. In his initial years in the Senate, Johnson maintained a right-leaning platform and supported President Harry TRUMAN in the intervention in KOREA. Johnson was directly opposed to communism and its expansion out of Korea, VIETNAM, CHINA, RUSSIA, and CUBA.

Through some fortunate turns of events, Johnson became the Senate's Democratic Party leader in 1953. Johnson's political ambitions were further realized when, in 1954, the Democrats gained control of the Senate and, in 1955, he won the bid for majority leader for a second time. After the political chess match in which he grasped the position of senate majority leader, Johnson had now to prove his effectiveness in pushing legislation through a partisan legislature.

One of Johnson's key methods of directing legislation through the Senate was to selectively support the Republican president, Dwight EISENHOWER. Johnson did not, however, support the president's policies of not exploring space or developing military technology. On foreign-policy matters, Johnson urged the Democrats to support Eisenhower in most initiatives.

As November 1960, and the presidential election closed in, Johnson aimed to present a more liberal approach to legislation in an attempt to balance his appearance to the public as well as his colleagues. He supported two civil rights bills that came through the Senate; one in 1957 and another in 1960. Coming out of World War II as a near-conservative, Johnson had moved back to nearly his original political platform.

Johnson would have liked to run for president in 1960, but he did not have the necessary national support. He got the next best thing. Appointed as Kennedy's running mate and defeating Richard NIXON, Johnson took his seat as vice president in 1961.

Johnson was active during his vice presidency and took on a more liberal platform than he had in the past. He was the chairman of the President's Committee on Equal Employment Opportunity. This position enabled

Johnson to further prove to the public that he was pro-civil rights and in full support of Kennedy's social reforms. Kennedy gave Johnson assurances that he would remain on the presidential ticket in the 1964 election. On November 22, 1963, however, Kennedy was assassinated. Johnson was sworn in as president aboard Air Force One.

Johnson continued to further the Kennedy agendas in Congress. Prior to the assassination, Congress was reluctant to pass Kennedy's civil rights and tax legislation, but now there was no problem passing the legislation. In 1964, Congress passed an enormous amount of social bills, including the Tax Reduction Act and the Civil Rights Act.

The 1964 presidential election was essential for Johnson to further his ambition of establishing a "Great Society." Johnson chose Hubert H. Humphrey as a running mate and defeated Senator Barry Goldwater in November 1964. The Democratic Party had a huge victory in the 1964 election, winning 37 new seats in the House, bringing the total to 295 out of 435, and they held 67 out of 100 seats in the Senate. After the Democrats resounding victory, Johnson was in a position to push a tremendous amount of new legislation. Bills included the Voting Rights Act of 1965 that removed restrictions on the right to vote, two new federal departments including the Department of Housing and Urban Development and the Department of Transportation, an "unconditional war on poverty," and legislation that liberalized unemployment, expanded the food stamp program, and opened up opportunities for youth employment.

With the escalation of the Vietnam War came the decline of Johnson's power and public opinion. Caught between his principles of quelling communism from North Vietnam, public opposition to the war, and a growing number of political opponents, Johnson announced his intentions to not run for another term of office on March 31, 1968, the same day he ordered that almost all bombing in North Vietnam be ceased.

Johnson left office January 20, 1969, and dedicated his final few years to peace resolution.

BIBLIOGRAPHY. Robert A. Caro, *Master of the Senate: The Years of Lyndon Johnson* (Knopf, 2002); *Encyclopedia Americana,* Lyndon B. Johnson, www.grolier.com; White House, "Lyndon B. Johnson," www.whitehouse.gov.

ARTHUR HOLST, PH.D.
WIDENER UNIVERSITY

Jordan

THE HASHEMITE KINGDOM of Jordan is located between Israel and Saudi Arabia. A small nation with a small population, it lacks adequate supplies of national resources such as water and oil. The PERSIAN GULF WAR of 1990–91 aggravated Jordan's serious economic problems, forcing the government to stop most debt payments.

In 2000 B.C.E. Semitic Amorites settled around the Jordan River in the area called Canaan. Over the centuries many different groups invaded and settled the region, ending with the British. At the end of WORLD WAR I after the breakup of the Ottoman Empire, the League of Nations awarded the mandate over this territory (which included ISRAEL, the West Bank, Gaza, and Jerusalem) to the UNITED KINGDOM. In 1922, the British established the semiautonomous Emirate of Transjordan to be ruled by the Hashemite Prince Abdullah (who was assassinated in 1951). This mandate ended on May 22, 1946. Three days later, the country became the independent Hashemite Kingdom of Transjordan.

In 1948, Jordan assisted Palestinian nationalists in their attempt to prevent the creation of Israel, leading to war. An armistice agreement was reached on April 3, 1949, and as a part of this agreement, Jordan had control of the West Bank. In June, 1967, Jordan participated in the war between Israel and an array of Arab states including SYRIA, EGYPT, and IRAQ. During the war, Israel gained control of the West Bank, and by 1988, Jordan renounced all claims to the area. During the October 1973 Arab-Israeli conflict, Jordan sent a brigade into Syria to fight Israel.

By the outset of the Persian Gulf War in the early 1990s, Jordan had had enough of conflict and turned toward the role of peacemaker, attempting to mediate between Iraq's Saddam Hussain, other Arab nations, and the West. In 1994, with the aid of the UNITED STATES, Jordan's King Hussein signed a peace treaty with Israel.

Today, Hussein's son, King Abdallah, continues peaceful relations with Israel and has focused his government on economic reform. Jordan has signed agreements with the INTERNATIONAL MONETARY FUND (IMF), practiced careful monetary policy to ensure membership in the WORLD TRADE ORGANIZATION (WTO), and has made agreements with the EUROPEAN UNION (EU). Productivity has improved in Jordan to the point the country enjoys growing foreign investment. In 2001, Jordan had a population of 5.3 million and a GROSS DOMESTIC PRODUCT (GDP) of $21.6 billion.

BIBLIOGRAPHY. "The Department of State Background Note," www.state.gov; *CIA World Factbook* (2002); "Jordan, A Country Study," The Library of Congress, lcweb2.loc.gov; Chaim Herzog, *The Arab-Israeli Wars* (Random House, 1982).

LINDA L. PETROU, PH.D.
HIGH POINT UNIVERSITY

J.P. Morgan Chase & Co.

RANKED AS THE 54TH LARGEST company in the world in 2002 by *Fortune* magazine, J.P. Morgan Chase & Co. was formed in December 2000, after the Chase Manhattan Corporation acquired J.P. Morgan & Co., Inc. Both were leading banking firms, with the former a commercial and retail bank and the latter an investment bank. This acquisition became possible through the Gramm-Leach-Bliley Financial Services Modernization Act of 1999, federal legislation that repealed the main provisions of the NEW DEAL's Glass-Steagel Act. This 1933 law had prohibited a company from offering both investment banking and commercial banking. Once the federal government lifted this ban, a number of mergers and consolidations between commercial banks and investment banks occurred.

Chase's acquisition of J.P. Morgan strategically combined the two firms' strengths and was based on the belief that capital size was related to the size of investment banking transactions. J.P. Morgan & Co. could handle larger investments with the added capital of Chase Manhattan and Chase could cross-market J.P. Morgan's investment services to its many commercial banking clients. In addition, the newly created bank could achieve economies by staff reductions in support areas. Results in the first two years after the acquisition did not live up to pre-acquisition expectations.

The histories of these firms that merged to form the second largest financial services company in the UNITED STATES are integral to America's economic and commercial history.

J.P. Morgan & Co. traces its history to the early 19th century. George Peabody, an American businessman, opened a London merchant banking house in 1838. Junius S. Morgan became Peabody's partner in 1854 and in 1864 took over the firm and renamed it J.S. Morgan & Co. In 1861, J. Pierpont Morgan, Junius' son, opened a New York office of his father's firm and named it J.P. Morgan & Co. In 1895, J.P. Morgan consolidated all of the family's holdings, including European operations, and became senior partner. During the 1890s and early 20th century, J.P. Morgan was one of the most powerful bankers in America. During the DEPRESSION of 1893 President Grover CLEVELAND asked Morgan for a personal loan to help the United States avoid defaulting on its obligations. In 1901, Morgan bought Carnegie Steel and merged 200 steel operations into the new United States Steel Corporation, America's first billion-dollar company that controlled more than three-fifths of the nation's steel production.

When Morgan died in 1913, his son J.P. Morgan, Jr. replaced him as senior partner. The Glass-Steagel Act of 1933 forced banks to divide their commercial and investment banking operations. In 1935, J.P. Morgan & Co.'s American investment operations formed a new investment-banking firm, Morgan Stanley & Co., while it concentrated on commercial and retail banking. Until 1989, J.P. Morgan & Co. targeted the upper income sector. That year the Federal Reserve Bank granted it the right to once again deal in corporate underwriting. J.P. Morgan made a strategic decision in 1996 to concentrate on investment banking, competing with Wall Street firms. In 2000, J.P. Morgan & Co. accepted an offer from Chase Manhattan Corporation to form J.P. Morgan Chase & Co.

Chase Manhattan Corporation in 2000 resulted from numerous mergers of famous banks in New York City. The earliest entity was the Manhattan Company, founded in 1799 by Alexander HAMILTON, the first U.S. Treasury secretary, and Aaron Burr, vice president in the Jefferson administration. The precursor of Chemical Bank of New York was established in 1823. Hanover Bank was founded in 1851 and eventually became Manufacturers Hanover Bank. In 1877, Chase National Bank was created and named after President Abraham Lincoln's Treasury Secretary Salmon P. Chase. In 1930, Chase National Bank bought Equitable Trust Company from the Rockefellers, making them among the largest stockholders in the merged firm. In 1955, Chase bought the Manhattan Banking Company and became Chase Manhattan Bank. Hanover Bank acquired Manufacturers Bank in 1961 to create Manufacturers Hanover Trust Company. In 1991, Chemical Bank bought Manufacturers Hanover, and in 1996 acquired Chase Manhattan Bank and assumed its name. It became the largest bank-holding company in the country. In 2000, when Chase Manhattan Bank bought J.P. Morgan & Co. and formed J.P. Morgan Chase & Co. it became the second largest financial services company in America after Citigroup. The company reported revenues of over $50 billion in 2001.

BIBLIOGRAPHY. Ron Chernow, *The House of Morgan: An American Banking Dynasty and the Rise of Modern Finance* (Touchstone Books, 1991); John Donald Wilson, *The Chase: The Chase Manhattan Bank, N.A., 1945–1985* (Harvard Business School Press, 1986); www.jpmorganchase.com; Global 500, *Fortune* (July 2002).

CARY W. BLANKENSHIP, PH.D.
TENNESSEE STATE UNIVERSITY

K

Kahneman, Daniel (1934–)

AMONG THE TWO RECIPIENTS of the 2002 Nobel Prize in Economics (the other was Vernon L. SMITH), Daniel Kahneman was awarded "for having integrated insights from psychological research into economic science, especially concerning human judgment and decision-making under uncertainty."

Kahneman, regarded as a psychologist despite winning the prize traditionally given to economists, used his keen understanding of human psychology to develop a theory of how economic decision-makers function. Using a series of studies, Kahneman and his colleagues, including the late Amos Tversky, whom Kahneman credits for being his collaborator on his prize-winning work, were able to conclude that under certain decision-making circumstances, where complex data is used and future consequences are undetermined, people are more likely to disregard some important data and rather rely on "a rule of thumb," or analytical shortcuts to make the decision. In one experiment, two groups of people were chosen, one given a coffee mug and the other nothing. The first group was given the choice of keeping the mug or trading it in for money. The second group was given the choice of a mug or money. Results showed that those without the mug were willing to accept less money than those who were required to give it up.

Born in Tel Aviv, ISRAEL (PALESTINE at the time) in 1934, Kahneman lived in FRANCE during WORLD WAR II and returned to Israel in 1946, where he began his formal education. Studying at Hebrew University in Jerusalem, Kahneman received his B.A. in psychology and mathematics in 1954, and then served in the Israeli Army, where he pioneered a new-recruit interview process, before receiving his Ph.D. in psychology at the University of California, Berkeley, in 1961.

Kahneman's early work was not limited to a select number of fields, as he studied various forms of psychology including vision, attentiveness, the study of counterfactual human emotions, and psychophysiology. It wasn't until the late 1970s that his most significant work was accomplished by collaborating with Tversky as they contributed a number of general psychological analyses dealing with judgment and choice. Together, they would win the Distinguished Scientific Contribution Award of the American Psychological Association in 1982, as the new field of economic behavioral science began to win over more and more adherents.

In the 1990s, Kahneman continued his research while a professor at Princeton University, where he held the dual positions of the Eugene Higgins Professor of Psychology and Professor of Public Affairs at the Woodrow Wilson School of Public and International Affairs. In 2000, Kahneman and Tversky published *Choices, Values, and Frames* elaborating further on their research into economic choices and studies of CONSUMER BEHAVIOR.

BIBLIOGRAPHY. "Daniel Kahneman Biography," www.nobel.se; Daniel Kahneman and Amos Tversky, *Choices, Values, and Frames* (Cambridge University Press, 2000); Faculty Biography, www.princeton.edu.

SYED B. HUSSAIN, PH.D.
UNIVERSITY OF WISCONSIN, OSHKOSH

Kantorovich, Leonid (1912–86)

LEONID KANTOROVICH IS, in all likelihood, the only Lenin Prize-laureate included in this *Encyclopedia of Capitalism.* Considered by many to have founded Soviet ECONOMETRICS, the use of mathematical and statistical methods to solve economic problems, Kantorovich shared a 1975 Nobel Prize in Economics prize with Dutch-born Tjalling KOOPMANS, for independent "contributions to the theory of optimum allocation of resources." Koopmans, a wartime statistician at the Combined Shipping Adjustment Board in Washington, D.C., before joining the economics faculty at Yale University, developed a linear programming technique in order to minimize transportation costs. As Koopmans' conclusions were similar to Kantorovich's earlier, published work, the Nobel Committee attributed innovations in linear programming to both.

When Kantorovich was awarded the prize, a journalist from the Soviet news agency TASS asked him why the Nobel Committee, in a capitalist country such as Sweden, would honor the contributions of a researcher in socialist economics. Kantorovich's answer firmly fixed his research in the economics of socialism: While such work was applicable to "any economically developed country," mathematics "must be considered most valuable and more appropriate for the socialist system of economy, where scientific planning plays an immeasurably greater role."

Following his assertion, it would be most appropriate to place Kantorovich's contributions to economics in the chronology of the SOVIET UNION's state economy. Kantorovich's biography extends from establishment of Soviet authority in industrialized urban communities, through nation-wide industrial transformation, economic planning for national defense during the World War II, and the extension of state research institutes during the postwar era. The same year that Kantorovich was awarded the economics prize, Soviet physicist A. Sakharov received the Nobel Peace Prize for his extended unofficial campaigns on behalf of human rights and disarmament.

As Kantorovich wrote in his citizen's formulaic autobiography or *anketa,* "I was born in Petersburg (Leningrad) on January 19, 1919. My father, Vatilij Kantorovich, died in 1922 and it was my mother, Paulina (Saks), who brought me up." During the privation of World War I, Kantorovich's family removed themselves to Byelorussia; their son returned and entered Leningrad State University's Mathematical Department at the age of 14. Kantorovich held a professorship in the same institution between 1944–60. In 1960, he left his academic chair to become director of mathematical economic methods at the prestigious, newly formed Siberian Division of the Soviet Academy of Sciences. He was awarded the Lenin Prize in 1965, and the Order of Lenin in 1967. In 1971, he was appointed laboratory head within the Institute of National Economic Management, in Moscow.

In 1938, while a lecturer at Leningrad State University, Kantorovich consulted in applied mathematics for the Plywood Trust's laboratory. Responding to challenges in raw materials deliveries, Kantorovich demonstrated that many problems of economic allocation could be understood as maximizing a function subject to constraints, maximizing linear functions on a convex polygon. This work was published as *The Mathematical Method of Production Planning and Organization,* the following year. John HICKS (Britain) and Paul SAMUELSON (United States) independently demonstrated that certain equation coefficients could be regarded as input prices in capitalist economies; Samuelson, like Kantorovich, showed that certain coefficients in the equations should be input prices.

Published during socialism's economic liberalization of the early 1960s, Kantorovich's most widely recognized book, *The Best Uses of Economic Resources* (1965), developed a common vocabulary for economic planners in socialist states and in market economies. According to Kantorovich, even centrally planned economies should use prices to allocate limited resources. As trade-offs between present and future costs concerned planners in socialist economies, then interest rates were as necessary to economic calculations under socialism as in capitalist economies.

In developing a mathematical solution for the transport problem, Kantorovich demonstrated that many problems of economic allocation should be restated in mathematical terms. Unknowingly, Kantorovich's mathematical solution for distribution of transport flows contributed to A. Tolstoy's approximation of the Monge problem from 1930, later developed by F. Hichcock as the Hichcock Transportation Problem. By the time the Nobel Committee recognized Kantorovich's work, it—along with that of Dantzig and Von Newman—had come to be considered the basis for theories of linear programming. The Central Bank of Sweden established an Alfred Nobel memorial economics prize in 1968, following Kantorovich's most significant contributions by a number of years.

Kantorovich was buried in the cemetery of Moscow's Novodevichy convent, appropriately among Soviet intellectual and political leaders. His neighbors in death include near-contemporaries N.S. Khrushchev and D.D. Shostakovich. Kantorovich was honored with publication of a memorial volume, *Functional Analysis, Optimization and Mathematical Economics,* published in 1990—as the history of the Soviet Union drew to a close.

BIBLIOGRAPHY. L.V. Kantorovich, *Approximate Methods of Higher Analysis,* Curtis D. Benster, trans. (Interscience, 1964); L.V. Kantorovich, *Functional Analysis and Applied Mathematics,* Curtis D. Benster, trans. (National Bureau of Standards, 1952); L.V. Kantorovich, *The Best Use of Economic Resources*, P.F. Knightsfield, trans. (Harvard University Press, 1965); www.nobel.se.

ELIZABETH BISHOP, PH.D.
AMERICAN UNIVERSITY

Kennedy, John F. (1917–63)

IN POPULAR MEMORY, the assassination of President John F. Kennedy remains a painful scar on the American past. The first president born in the 20th century, Kennedy brought youth, energy, and charisma to the White House. Though his administration lasted just over 1000 days, and though historians have carefully revealed the complexity of his character, Kennedy's personality and political initiatives left a permanent mark on American culture.

The second son of the wealthy and powerful Joseph Patrick KENNEDY and his wife, Rose Elizabeth Fitzgerald, Kennedy enjoyed a privileged childhood. Educated at the prestigious Choate School in Connecticut, Kennedy went on to Princeton University until he had to withdraw for health reasons. He later enrolled at Harvard University and graduated *cum laude* in 1940. Following his graduation, as America closely monitored the escalating military conflict in Europe, Kennedy entered the U.S. Navy.

While serving in the Solomon Islands in 1943 during WORLD WAR II, his boat was sunk by a Japanese destroyer. Although he suffered serious and permanent injuries to his back, Kennedy managed to lead his fellow survivors to safety.

Returning from military service, Kennedy entered politics through the ranks of the Democratic Party. In 1945, he was elected to the House of Representatives, where he served until he was elected to the Senate in 1953. Not long after becoming a senator, Kennedy married Jacqueline Lee Bouvier, a socially prominent woman 12 years his junior. Also, during his first term as senator, Kennedy achieved national fame when his book, *Profiles in Courage*, won the Pulitzer Prize in History. He was re-elected to the Senate in 1958 as speculation grew about a potential bid for the presidency in 1960.

At the Democratic National Convention in 1960, Kennedy gained the nomination for president. Millions of Americans watched him and his Republican opponent, Vice-President Richard M. Nixon, in the first nationally televised presidential debate. In one of the closest popular votes in American history, Kennedy gained the necessary majority of electoral votes and won the election. At age 43, he was the youngest man and the first Roman Catholic elected to the office.

With his inspiring inaugural address that told Americans to "ask not what your country can do for you, ask what you can do for your country," Kennedy reinvigorated the American spirit. Labeling the new age of scientific technology and social relations the "New Frontier," Kennedy dared Americans to rise to the challenges of the 20th century.

But much of Kennedy's initiatives, foreign and domestic, can be seen as functions of the international hostility known as the Cold War. The Cold War originated immediately after World War II as a struggle between Western, capitalist nations, led by the United States, and the communist nations, led by the Soviet Union. American leaders feared that the expansion of Soviet power would be a threat to the rest of the world but also predicted that peaceful competition would lead to the triumph of societies committed to democracy and capitalism. To bolster American might in the event of military conflict, Kennedy improved U.S. infrastructure through increased support of engineering, education, and corporations.

Kennedy's support of civil rights, though undoubtedly a genuine interest, can also be understood within the context of the Cold War. Concerned that the Soviet Union could use American internal strife as a form of propaganda, Kennedy intensified improvements to the status of African-Americans. Moved by the brutal televised images of Southern racism, Kennedy ordered federal troops to the University of Mississippi to end anti-desegregation rioting in September 1962. And on June 11, 1963, on national television, he declared the segregation of the University of Alabama to be "moral issue." His concerns for civil and human rights also extended beyond domestic borders. In 1961, he created the Peace Corps, a program that sent skilled and idealistic Americans into third-world countries to develop their public health and agricultural procedures.

Consistent with his capitalist imperatives, Kennedy introduced economic programs that helped launch the United States into its longest period of sustained growth since World War II. He expanded Social Security coverage and benefits, raised the minimum wage, furthered public HOUSING initiatives, increased measures to clear the slums, and lowered tariff barriers.

Kennedy's 1961 Area Redevelopment Act directly benefited economically depressed areas and the 1962 Manpower Development and Training Act retrained destitute farmers and unemployed workers. Despite these legislative successes, Kennedy faced serious opposition from the conservative coalition in Congress on issues relating to tax reduction, federal aid to education, medical care to the elderly, and civil rights.

However, Kennedy's administration is particularly remembered for its foreign affairs, especially the incidents that reflected the Cold War. Kennedy's first foray into the international conflict occurred in April, 1961, when he authorized American-trained Cuban exiles to invade Cuba at the Bay of Pigs and overthrow Fidel Castro's communist regime. The invaders were quickly repulsed. Soon after the Bay of Pigs disaster, Kennedy made a poor showing at the Vienna Conference and led Soviet Premier Nikita Khrushchev to believe that the young president could be easily manipulated.

Khrushchev thus stepped up the Soviet Union's campaign against West Berlin. Kennedy responded to Khrushchev's aggression by offering support to West Berlin. The heightened hostilities between the Soviet Union and the United States over Germany culminated on August 13, 1961, with the erection of the Berlin Wall, which divided the communist bloc of East Berlin from West Berlin. The wall symbolized the ideological differences and sharp tensions between the two superpowers—tensions that were further played out through the Cuban Missile Crisis.

In October 1962, American spy planes discovered that the Soviet Union was building missile sites in Cuba. Kennedy ordered a naval quarantine on all offensive weapons bound for Cuba. For two weeks, the world teetered on possible nuclear war until Kennedy's stand forced the Soviets to back down and remove their missiles from Cuba. Not since the WAR OF 1812 had an American president faced such a tangible threat from a foreign nation. Kennedy's leadership during the Cuban Missile Crisis was a critical moment of his presidency and it demonstrated his commitment to curtail the threat of nuclear war. To this end, Kennedy negotiated the 1963 Limited Nuclear Test Ban Treaty in which the United States, Great Britain, and the Soviet Union agreed to ban all but underground nuclear tests.

Kennedy's policies in southeast Asia, however, left a far less favorable effect. In an attempt to curtail the influence of communist Soviet Union and China, Kennedy increased military aid to the government of South Vietnam, which was struggling against a communist insurgency from North Vietnam. By late 1963, Kennedy's policies in South Vietnam laid the groundwork for what was to become one of America's most tragic foreign-policy failures, the VIETNAM WAR.

On November 22, 1963, Kennedy was assassinated, and though the circumstances and motives behind his murder continue to arouse debate, his death resulted in an outpouring of grief across the globe. Unflattering details about his private life and his health have emerged in recent years, but many historians believe Kennedy was on the threshold of political greatness. By re-energizing American ideals and committing the United States to the opportunities of the 20th century, Kennedy seemed to many to embody the best image of American liberty and democratic capitalism.

BIBLIOGRAPHY. Frank Freidel, *The Presidents of the United States of America* (White House Historical Association, 1985); Doris Kearns Goodwin, *The Fitzgeralds and the Kennedys: An American Saga* (Simon & Schuster, 1987); James M. McPherson, ed., "To the Best of My Ability," *The American Presidents* (Dorling Kindersley, 2000); Richard E. Neustadt, *Presidential Power and the Modern Presidents: The Politics of Leadership from Roosevelt to Reagan* (The Free Press, 1990); Theodore C. Sorensen, *Kennedy* (Harper and Row, 1966).

LINDSAY SILVER
BRANDEIS UNIVERSITY

Kennedy, Joseph P. (1888–1969)

BORN THE SON OF A saloon keeper and ward boss in Boston, Massachusetts, Joseph P. Kennedy became the patriarch of the politically powerful and wealthy Kennedy family. He showed his ambition early on, delivering papers and doing chores in the neighborhood. He attended Catholic schools and Harvard University, where he was popular, successful in the classroom, and refused entry into the elite clubs due to his Irish-Catholic background. His Harvard experience motivated him to become a millionaire and to show up the Protestants who rejected him. By age 25, he was president of a small bank, comfortable but not yet rich.

He had help from his wife, Rose Fitzgerald, daughter of Boston's mayor, and the political connections the marriage brought. Married in 1915, they had their first son, Joe, Jr., later that year. Rose and nannies reared the nine Kennedy children while Joe was becoming wealthy in commercial and investment banking, motion-picture production and distribution, and shipbuilding. Kennedy was known as a womanizer, and at one point, during his highly publicized affair with actress Gloria Swanson, had her as a guest in the family home.

During WORLD WAR I, Kennedy was the number-two man in a shipyard that employed more than 2,000 workers. After the war, he became a stockbroker. He was adept at insider trading and stock manipulation, especially the then-legal stock pool in which traders worked together to inflate a stock's value, selling out when the bubble was about to burst. Kennedy also sold his movie interests just in time to avoid the industry's consolidation, clearing $5 or $6 million in the process. And he withdrew from the stock market before the 1929 crash, sold short, and made money from a collapsing market.

Scholars disagree over the extent, but generally agree that Kennedy smuggled illegal LIQUOR from Europe to the UNITED STATES during Prohibition. His father, after all, was in the liquor business, and, whether or not he was a high-dollar rum-runner, he unquestionably set himself up in the liquor-importing business just before repeal of Prohibition.

Kennedy was not extremely rich prior to WORLD WAR II. Still, he had enough wealth to be respectable. And he was politically active. He supported the Democratic presidential candidate, Franklin D. ROOSEVELT, in the election of 1932. Roosevelt appointed him the first chairman of the SECURITIES AND EXCHANGE COMMISSION (SEC) in 1934, where he served until 1935. In 1936 and 1937, he was chair of the Federal Maritime Commission. In 1938, Roosevelt appointed him the first-ever Irish-American, Catholic ambassador to Great Britain. Kennedy's presidential aspirations seemed realizable.

Kennedy was an isolationist and probably an appeaser of Hitler. He wanted the United States to be neutral in any British-German conflict. He supported the position of British Prime Minister Neville Chamberlain. His views were not palatable to many British, especially Winston Churchill, and Kennedy resigned under pressure when war was inevitable in 1940.

The war years took the lives of two of his children. Joe, Jr. died as a pilot over Germany, and Kathleen, the eldest daughter, died in a plane crash shortly after the war. Another Kennedy daughter, Rosemarie, had problems that led Kennedy in 1941 to authorize a prefrontal lobotomy; it went poorly, and reduced her to the level of an infant. In later years, Kennedy revealed he suffered from this decision.

Kennedy's presidential aspirations died with the American entry into the war, and his hopes for Joe Jr. died over Germany. Kennedy focused his ambitions on his second son, John Fitzgerald, war hero, soon-to-be senator from Massachusetts.

Though his domestic life suffered, Kennedy continued to have success in business, especially in real estate, amassing a fortune upward of $100 million. And his philanthropic interests took much of his time. His main philanthropy was the Joseph P. Kennedy, Jr., Memorial Foundation. The foundation's purposes were to improve society's manner of dealing with the mentally retarded and to find and disseminate methods of preventing the causes of mental retardation. Emphasizing the multiplier effect, the foundation provided seed money for projects demonstrating innovative and new service and support capabilities. It stressed that both research and individual service were vital. Kennedy also authored *I'm for Roosevelt* (1936.)

In the close election of 1960, Kennedy's money may well have provided the difference that brought his son to the White House. Kennedy was able to see John become the United States' first Roman Catholic president, but shortly thereafter he had a series of disabling strokes that forced him to watch helplessly as his dreams died with the deaths of sons John and Robert and the destruction of son Edward's presidential aspirations at Chappaquidick (a scandal involving the death of one of Edward's girlfriends). Kennedy died in 1969 at the age of 81.

BIBLIOGRAPHY. Doris K.Goodwin, *The Fitzgeralds and the Kennedys* (Touchstone Books, 1991); Joseph P. Kennedy, Jr. Foundation, www.jpkf.org; Ronald Kessler, *The Sins of the Father: Joseph P. Kennedy and the Dynasty He Founded* (Warner Books, 1997).

JOHN H. BARNHILL, PH.D.
INDEPENDENT SCHOLAR

Kenya

A REPUBLIC IN EAST AFRICA, Kenya is a member of the Commonwealth of Nations. With its capital at Nairobi, Kenya is located on the Indian Ocean neighboring ETHIOPIA to the north, Tanzania to the south, and Uganda to the west. Kenya covers approximately 225,000 square miles of land.

Nearly all of Kenya's 31 million people are African. Europeans, Arabs, and Asians make up only 1 percent of the population. The population density is 53 people per square mile and, with an annual population increase of about 3.4 percent, it is one of the highly populated countries in the world. Sadly, even with such a high birth rate the country has a young population; 50 percent of Kenya's population is under the age of 15, and life expectancy in the country is 47 years old.

Geologically, Kenya has many features worth noting. The country is volcanic and faulting has split the land. The best-known fault is the Eastern Rift of the Great Rift Valley. Topographically, the country has several zones as well. Beginning at the coastline, which is fringed with coral reefs, then coastal plains and tropical forest, and, as you go west, the terrain rises through a series of plateaus gaining elevation from sea level to 10,000 feet. The Equator also runs through the country from east to west. Also worth noting, Lake Victoria, the second-largest freshwater lake in the world, after Lake Superior in the United States, sits at the southwest corner of Kenya.

Kenya's main natural resource is its land: 30 percent of the land is covered in forest. The country has many rivers that provide hydroelectricity; 8 percent of the land, mostly in the southern areas, is being used for cultivation.

Upon Kenya's great lands roam some of the world's most exotic animals. Kenya is best known for its game parks that protect wildlife. These reserves attract large numbers of tourists and create state revenue.

In 2002, Kenya had a GROSS DOMESTIC PRODUCT (GDP) of $31 billion with a population of 31 million, making per capita purchasing power $1000. While suffering through numerous droughts over the past decade, Kenya has had substantial help from the INTERNATIONAL MONETARY FUND (IMF) which has cut off aid periodically as Kenya's economy struggled with anti-corruption measures.

BIBLIOGRAPHY. David Cohen, *A Day in the Life of Africa* (Publishers Group West, 2002); Tepilit Ole Saitoti, *Maasai* (Abradale Press, 1990); *CIA World Factbook* (2002).

SHAWNA ELLIOT
RED ROCKS COLLEGE

Keynes, John Maynard (1883–1946)

JOHN MAYNARD KEYNES, the most influential economist of the 20th century, was born in 1883 to an English family that prized intellectual pursuit. His father taught political economy and logic at Cambridge University, and his mother was a celebrated writer and social reformer. His parents provided him with tutors in addition to his general education; and by the age of 11, Keynes was winning prizes for mathematics. He entered Eton in 1897 at the age of 14. After obtaining a degree from King's College Cambridge, Keynes worked in the India Office and became an expert on the Indian monetary system. He decided to continue his academic studies and returned to King's College in 1909. Keynes later maintained that a master economist should be a mathematician, a historian, a salesman, and a philosopher.

At the age of 30, Keynes was named secretary of a Parliamentary commission on Indian Finance and Currency, but the following year WORLD WAR I began. Keynes hated the war, which changed his life forever. He wrote that civilization had become a "thin and precarious crust." By 1915, Keynes was working for the British Treasury as a deputy for the chancellor of the exchequer in the Supreme Economic Council. It was as a Treasury representative that he attended the Versailles Peace Conference to help negotiate a peace agreement. Keynes resigned in 1919, convinced that the government was demanding reparations from GERMANY that the country could never repay. In *The Economics of the Peace*, Keynes reminded the Allies that they had agreed not to seek retributions or punitive damages from the Germans. He blamed French Prime Minister Georges Clemenceau (1841–1929) for trying to totally destroy the Germans. It should be understood that France suffered considerably more financial losses than any other Allied country. Keynes estimated French losses at $4 billion. Keynes believed that the key to reparations, however, was to re-establish Germany as a producer of goods so that they would be able to make reparation payments. Some people believe that WORLD WAR II could have been avoided if the world had listened to Keynes in Versailles.

Keynes lost favor with the British government because of his views on war and peace, but he regained prominence with his "Treatise of Probability" in 1921, which some consider to be his most significant work. Others, however, contend that Keynes' *General Theory of Employment, Interest, and Money* is more important because of its continued impact. Keynes was particularly determined to counteract the influence of Jean-Baptiste SAY's (1767–1832) theory that supply creates its own demand. Keynes' writings on the economy signaled a shift in the perceptions of economists, academia, government, and the general public.

After World War I, Keynes became intrigued with developing ways for governments to function in the new world order; and by the 1930s, Keynes had come to believe that government was obligated to take an active role in the economy in order to maintain stability. The resulting clash between Keynesians and anti-Keynesians continued throughout the 20th century. The introduction of the social welfare state in the UNITED STATES as part of President Franklin ROOSEVELT's NEW DEAL policies established the importance of Keynes' economic theories to the American political and economic systems, to the point that President Ronald REAGAN's reliance on the economic theories of Milton FRIEDMAN could not totally dislodge them. Keynes believed that economic cycles are constantly changing, and each cycle has a distinct impact on INCOME, employment, prices, and output. He pointed out that individuals are different, as are their economic needs and habits. Some people put their money in banks while others choose to invest. He believed they acted from different motives and expected different results. If people lost trust in the economic system, he argued, they would begin to hoard money, and the ripple effect would create high unemployment and economic crisis. Therefore, the government had a responsibility to increase its own spending and reduce taxes to stimulate the sluggish economy. For example, if the government spends money on a construction project, new workers are employed who then spend more money, which improves the economy for everyone.

Before the United States entered World War II, Keynes served as an advisor to the lend-lease deals whereby Roosevelt supported Great Britain's war effort with essential war materials. Keynes was honored for his contributions to Great Britain and was named to the British peerage in 1942. His voice was also well respected in international circles, and Keynes served as a representative to the BRETTON WOODS Conference in Bretton Woods, New Hampshire, and was instrumental in establishing the INTERNATIONAL MONETARY FUND (IMF) and the WORLD BANK created by the conference. This 1944 conference, attended by 44 nations, also established the International Bank for Reconstruction and Development.

The politics of Margaret THATCHER, British prime minister, who led the Conservative Party from 1979–87 signaled a rejection of Keynesianism, but the politics of Prime Minister Tony Blair of the Labour Party revived them to some extent in 1997. Scholars do not agree on the validity of Keynes' work. Supporters, such as Keynesian scholar Robert Skidelsky, believe that Keynes was a "beacon of light in a benighted world," while critics argue that his ideas were unsound and chaotic. No one can argue that he continued to affect economics around the world long after his death from a heart attack in 1946.

BIBLIOGRAPHY. Peter Clark, "Keynes and Keynesianism," *Political* Quarterly (July/September, 1998); David Felix, *Keynes: A Critical Life* (Greenwood Press, 1999); John Fender, *Understanding Keynes: An Analyses of the General Theory* (John Wiley & Sons, 1981); John Maynard Keynes, *Collected Writings* (Macmillan, 1971–1989); John Maynard Keynes, *The Economics of the Peace* (Penguin Books, 1971); Robert Lekachman, *The Age of Keynes* (Random House, 1966); Robert Skidelsky, *John Maynard Keynes, Fighting for Britain, 1937–1946* (Macmillan, 1983); Robert Skidelsky, "Keynes," *Three Great Economists* (Oxford University Press, 1997).

ELIZABETH PURDY, PH.D.
INDEPENDENT SCHOLAR

Keynesian economics

A BODY OF ECONOMIC theory that draws from the insights of John Maynard KEYNES (1883–1946) has evolved into Keynesian economics. Keynes, generally regarded as the greatest economist of the 20th century, played a pivotal role in the foundation of the branch of economics (macroeconomics) that focuses on national economic issues such as INFLATION and UNEMPLOYMENT. Though it no longer enjoys the consensus it once commanded, Keynesian economics remains to this day one of the major schools of macroeconomic thought.

Background. Although all strands of Keynesian economics trace their origins to *The General Theory of Employment, Interest, and Money* (Keynes' 1936 masterpiece), there is a surprising degree of controversy regarding what actually constitutes "Keynesian economics." Indeed, an assortment of schools of Keynesian economists have emerged with names such as "neo-Keynesian," "post-Keynesian," and "new-Keynesian." Though the various kinds of Keynesians are in disagreement as to what Keynes "really" meant, they all agree that market forces cannot always be trusted to deliver full employment, and therefore markets may benefit from active government intervention in times of economic crisis. This general view shared by all Keynesians stands in sharp contrast to the classical assumption that the invisible hand of the marketplace will best deliver the socially optimal result if left to its own devices. This latter view is commonly associated with a laissez-faire (or "leave markets alone") role for government policy.

Keynes wrote his *General Theory* at a time of global economic malaise. By 1936, the UNITED STATES had spent over half a decade in DEPRESSION. Unemployment had averaged over 20 percent for each year since 1930, and the GROSS NATIONAL PRODUCT (GDP) had fallen more than 30 percent from the start of the Great Depression in 1929 to its low point in 1933.

Indeed, unemployment in the United States would remain above 10 percent each year until 1941. Great Britain's economic woes dated back even further, in large part due to the 1920s effort to return to the GOLD STANDARD. From 1922 to 1936, the British unemployment rate was above 9.5 percent every single year.

Keynes contended the prevailing economic theory of his time was mistaken in its belief that full employment was the norm and any economy that departed from full employment would quickly return to that optimal state simply by relying on the invisible hand of the market. His challenge to the prevailing laissez-faire mentality was one of the most important characteristics of Keynes' *General Theory*.

The neo-Keynesians. Unfortunately, Keynes did not develop a formal model in *The General Theory*, leaving that task to others. This explains the widespread disagreement that ensued among economists persuaded by Keynes' message. Some of the earliest and most widely accepted models of Keynesian economics were developed by the neo-Keynesians who sought to integrate the insights of Keynes into traditional (or neoclassical) economics, particularly in the context of models that generate an equilibrium state. The neo-Keynesian perspective is sometimes referred to as the Neoclassical Keynesian Synthesis.

Neo-Keynesian models emphasize overall demand for goods and services in the economy as the driving force for determining the economy's performance. Examples of these models include Paul SAMUELSON's Keynesian Cross model and the IS-LM framework developed by John HICKS and Alvin Hansen.

Samuelson's Keynesian Cross model, a standard component of introductory economics textbooks for decades, focuses on the various categories of spending (i.e., consumer spending, business investment, government spending, and exports) that comprise aggregate demand. In this model, aggregate (or total) demand determines national output (i.e., gross domestic product) as well as the level of employment. Consequently, any effort to alter the level of employment requires manipulating the level of aggregate demand, either explicitly through changes in government spending, or by encouraging greater levels of consumer spending or business investment (through tax policy.) Both government spending and tax policy represent categories of FISCAL POLICY, a favorite tool of neo-Keynesians in the early decades following WORLD WAR II.

An earlier but more complicated attempt to integrate Keynes with neoclassical economics was offered by Hicks in his 1937 paper "Mr. Keynes and the 'Classics:' A Suggested Interpretation." In this paper, Hicks constructed the IS-LM model that was to become the standard interpretation of Keynesian economics for generations. The IS-LM model also emphasizes aggregate demand, but unlike the Keynesian Cross, this model explicitly incorporates a market for money. The IS-LM model identifies equilibrium values of the interest rate and the level of output such that both the market for goods and services (the IS component) and the market for money (the LM component) are each in a state of balance. From this position of equilibrium, IS-LM theorists demonstrate how various fiscal and monetary policies can be used to manipulate the two separate (i.e., product and money) markets and thereby alter the overall level of output (and hence employment.)

The Phillips Curve. By manipulating aggregate demand through fiscal-policy tools (government spending and tax policy) or monetary-policy tools (i.e., increasing or decreasing liquidity in the banking system to alter the magnitude of the money supply), neo-Keynesians believed it was possible to fine-tune the performance of the economy. This belief was strengthened by the discovery (mid-1950s) and application (early 1960s) of the PHILLIPS CURVE. The original curve uncovered an empirical relationship between changes in employment and the rate of wage inflation. Subsequent research by Samuelson and Robert SOLOW extrapolated these findings to a relationship between unemployment and the rate of inflation.

When Samuelson and Solow discovered a stable, negatively sloped relationship in 25 years of U.S. data, they concluded the Phillips Curve could be used to identify macroeconomic policy options. Indeed, the empirical findings of the curve made a strong case for the demand-oriented approach and active role for government the neo-Keynesians advocated. As a result, neo-Keynesian economics enjoyed widespread acceptance by the end of the 1960s. Indeed, U.S. President Richard NIXON remarked in 1970 that, "We are all Keynesians now." Ironically within a decade this widespread consensus would fall apart because of three challenges, two theoretical and one empirical.

Challenges. The first theoretical challenge came in the form of the natural rate hypothesis. Milton FRIEDMAN, long a critic of Keynesian economics, published an important critique in 1968 (similar insights were developed and published at the same time by Edmund Phelps.) In his work "The Role of Monetary Policy," Friedman claimed that active government intervention to manipulate the BUSINESS CYCLE might enjoy temporary successes (primarily by acting contrary to the public's expectations) but the policy would fail to permanently alter the economy's level of unemployment (because eventually public expectations would adjust to the new policy direction).

Dubbed the "Fooling Model" (because government success required "fooling" the public), this new approach contended that government policy efforts paid a high price for their temporary gains against unemployment: the gains came with accelerating inflation. Friedman claimed this relative ineffectiveness of government policy was because the economy had a "natural rate of unemployment" around which market forces would gravitate. He predicted that the active government policies of the 1960s would not have a permanent effect on unemployment levels although they would result in higher levels of inflation. Friedman's prediction was to prove accurate. In addition to raising serious doubts about the neo-Keynesian approach, it also cast a permanent shadow on the use of fiscal policy to alter the performance of the macroeconomy.

Friedman's approach was also important because it uncovered an apparent weakness in the neo-Keynesian approach, the absence of "microfoundations." While Friedman's model carefully considered the role of individual decisions, the neo-Keynesian approach had largely ignored individual behavior (or MICROECONOMICS), in developing its macroeconomic insights. Keynesian economists operating within the mainstream of the economics profession would henceforth feel compelled to develop microfoundations to accompany their macroeconomic models.

The second theoretical challenge came in the form of "rational expectations." This view had its origins in a 1961 article by John Muth but achieved prominence with the work of Robert LUCAS in the 1970s. Lucas, like Friedman before him, emphasized microeconomic decision-making in modeling and analyzing macroeconomic policy. The rational expectations hypothesis contends that economic agents effectively utilize all available information and therefore can never be systematically "fooled." Labeled the "Lucas Critique," this approach went further than the Friedman model by suggesting that "fooling" the public was not even an option in the short run.

The empirical challenge to the neo-Keynesian consensus came in the form of two periods of simultaneously high levels of inflation and unemployment. This phenomenon, known as stagflation, occurred in 1974 and again in 1979–80. Because the aggregate demand analysis employed by the neo-Keynesians could explain either rising inflation or rising unemployment, but not both simultaneously, this new development cast serious doubt on the ability of the neo-Keynesian theorists to successfully manage the macroeconomy. Indeed, stagflation was not possible according to the Phillips Curve tradeoff between inflation and unemployment.

The timing of stagflation's first appearance could not have been better for Friedman, delivering the results he had predicted several years earlier: rising inflation without evidence of permanent decreases in the unemployment rate. In fact, the simplest way to explain stagflation was by focusing on "supply shocks," shifting the analysis from the demand-side of the economy (the Keynesian approach) to the supply-side (a more classical orientation).

The combination of Friedman's natural rate hypothesis, the rational expectations hypothesis, and stagflation paved the way for the resurgence of classical economics and a supply-oriented approach to macroeconomics in the late 1970s and 1980s. This theoretical challenge to Keynesian economics resulted in the emergence of the "new classical" approach to macroeconomics.

New-Keynesians. Since the neo-Keynesian models had totally dominated the textbook versions of Keynes, the demise of the neo-Keynesian view was widely viewed as the end of Keynesian economics. This prognosis proved to be premature. Although new classical economic thought flourished in the 1980s, within a decade a resurgence of Keynesian theories had returned, this time in the form of new-Keynesian economics.

New-Keynesians also rely on an equilibrium approach to macroeconomic analysis. Unlike their neo-Keynesian counterparts, these theorists embrace the rational expectations hypothesis and acknowledge the natural rate hypothesis Friedman developed. As a result, new-Keynesians are far less enthusiastic about the active use of fiscal policy such as government spending to counter downturns in the business cycle.

In response to the new classical criticisms, new-Keynesians have integrated micro-foundations into their work. This task has been accomplished by modeling wage and price "stickiness" (i.e., failure to adjust completely) to explain why markets sometimes fail to clear. A variety of specific models have been developed using concepts such as relative wages, efficiency wages, implicit contracts, long-term labor contracts, menu costs, and increasing returns to scale to explain price rigidities.

Wage and price rigidity (or stickiness) is the key component in new-Keynesian models that combine rational expectations with macro market failures. Just as the neo-Keynesians of an earlier era attempted to synthesize neoclassical general equilibrium theory with insights from Keynes, the modern new-Keynesians have sought to integrate the rational expectations hypothesis with Keynesian thought.

Like the neo-Keynesians before them, the new-Keynesians accept the classical notion that money is "neutral," particularly over the long run. If money is neutral then changes in the money supply will not affect the long run magnitudes of output nor employment (both output and employment are real variables), but instead monetary changes will only affect the overall price level (i.e., inflation.) This assumption of money neutrality is one of the important areas of disagreement between the two Keynesian schools already examined and the post-Keynesians.

Post-Keynesians. With a view of Keynesian economics very different from the frameworks developed by the neo-Keynesians and the new-Keynesians, post-Keynesians, in large part, reject neoclassical economics and rational expectations. Post-Keynesians believe the key to understanding Keynes is to recognize we live in a "monetary production economy," where money is not neutral because it provides a vital link between an unchangeable past and an unknowable future. In the post-Keynesian tradition, money has important and unique properties, uncertainty is more than probabilistic risk, and disequilibrium processes merit more attention than equilibrium states.

Post-Keynesians adopt an endogenous view of money, contending economic conditions determine changes in the money supply rather than central bank policy.

They believe central banks are obliged to accommodate the monetary needs of the economy and thus lack precise control over the money supply. Consequently, the post-Keynesians are skeptical of the effectiveness of monetary policy, instead seeing the money supply as an economic outcome rather than as a policy tool.

Conclusion. Today, the new-Keynesian paradigm strongly influences macroeconomic discussion, though it does so against relatively strong new classical forces. Post-Keynesian analysis continues to develop, though largely outside the mainstream of the economics profession and rarely receiving attention in textbooks. All three perspectives (new-Keynesian, new classical, and post-Keynesian) operate on the assumption that they each have the correct set of assumptions and models that best describe the workings of the macroeconomy. Given the complex and evolving nature of the economy as well as the phoenix-like quality of the business cycle, this continued struggle between theoretical approaches is likely to persist for the foreseeable future.

BIBLIOGRAPHY. Lester V. Chandler, *America's Greatest Depression: 1929–1941* (Harper & Row, 1970); Paul Davidson, *Controversies in Post Keynesian Economics* (Edward Elgar, 1991); Milton Friedman, "The Role of Monetary Policy," *American Economic Review* (March 1968); J.K. Galbraith and W. Darity, Jr., *Macroeconomics* (Houghton Mifflin, 1994); Robert J. Gordon, "What is New-Keynesian Economics?," *Journal of Economic Literature* (September 1990); J.R. Hicks, "Mr. Keynes and the 'Classics:' A Suggested Interpretation," *Econometrica* (April 1937); J.M. Keynes, *The General Theory of Employment, Interest, and Money* (Harcourt Brace Jovanovich, 1964); Gregory N. Mankiw, "A Quick Refresher Course in Macroeconomics," *Journal of Economic Literature* (December 1990).

PATRICK DOLENC, PH.D.
KEENE STATE COLLEGE

Klein, Lawrence (1920–)

WHEN MANY PEOPLE meet an economist, they immediately ask him or her to predict where the economy is headed. How fast will it grow or shrink? What will be the inflation rate? These questions are the legacy of Lawrence Klein, winner of the 1980 Nobel Prize in Economics, who pioneered the application of statistical methods to understanding and forecasting the behavior of the macroeconomy.

Klein's experience of growing up during the Great DEPRESSION had a deep impact on his professional career, drawing him to the study of economic fluctuations. After studying economics and mathematics at the University of California, Klein completed a Ph.D. in economics at the Massachusetts Institute of Technology (MIT) in 1944, under the direction of Paul SAMUELSON. His dissertation became *The Keynesian Revolution* (1947), which attempted to reveal the genesis of John Maynard KEYNES' economic ideas and to interpret them into a more precise mathematical model.

As Klein put it: "The Keynesian economic system is essentially a machine which grinds out results according to where the several dials controlling the system are set. The functional relations are the building-blocks of the machine, and the dials are the parameters (levels and shapes) of these functions."

The book became very influential in Keynesian circles, but critics panned it as ideologically extreme and naively technocratic. In his early writings, Klein even suggested that "capital accumulation in relation to the profit motive, a purely capitalist phenomenon, is the root of all economic evil," contrasting it with the "smooth operation of a socialist economy." It was during this period that Klein briefly became a member of the U.S. Communist Party, a mistake that he later attributed to "youthful naivete." Ironically, later in his career he worked for the nation's leading business school and advised major corporations.

After MIT, Klein became a research associate for the Cowles Commission at the University of Chicago, where he joined a team that put together one of the first econometric models of the American economy. Klein's task was to translate the Keynesian model into statistical terms. His accomplishment was to build "the original Model T Ford," the first useful model of a national economy that others subsequently copied and adapted. Klein's lifelong work became building successively larger, more sophisticated macroeconomic models, which estimated a series of simultaneous equations representing relationships and feedbacks between economic forces and sectors.

These models were then used to explain economic events and outcomes, simulate the impact of policies (such as tax cuts) and events (such as wars), and forecast the economic future. His journal essay, "A Post-Mortem on Transition Predictions of National Product" (1946), grabbed professional attention by explaining why the American economy didn't return to massive unemployment after World War II. During an appointment with the Survey Research Center at the University of Michigan, he expanded this work with *Economic Fluctuations in the United States, 1921–42* (1950), published a pioneering textbook in econometrics (the application of statistical methods to the empirical estimation of economic relationships), and developed (with Arthur Goldberger) the Klein-Goldberger model which brought macroeconomic modeling into mainstream practice.

Klein left Michigan for political reasons and found his permanent academic home, after a stint in Europe, at the University of Pennsylvania in 1958. There he became the first editor of the *International Economic Review*, and extended his modeling activities to make quarterly forecasts which included a role of expectations. He established the Wharton Econometric Forecasting Unit (1963), which provided economic forecasts to business clients, plowing revenues back into funding research and student support. The capstone of Klein's modeling program is Project LINK, which he co-founded (1968) and directed. It explores the international transmission of economic forces by developing and linking econometric models of over 40 nations and regions.

In 1976, Klein served as the chief economic advisor to Jimmy CARTER's presidential campaign. While he turned down Carter's invitation to head the COUNCIL OF ECONOMIC ADVISORS, he continued to advise the administration and wrote columns for leading newspapers and magazines.

Critics contend that Klein's modeling exercises have spread the wrong message about how the economy works—that these models are too ad hoc and are divorced from the microeconomic decisions of households and businesses—and that they don't have a very good track record in forecasting economic events. For these reasons, macroeconomic forecasting has lost much of its prestige among economists and the public. However, it is still an important tool, and its practitioners, including the FEDERAL RESERVE, can trace their models directly back to the work of Lawrence Klein.

BIBLIOGRAPHY. R.J. Ball, "On Lawrence R. Klein's Contributions to Economics," *Scandinavian Journal of Economics* (v. 83, 1981); Lawrence Klein, *Lives of the Laureates: Seven Nobel Economists*, William Breit and Roger Spencer, eds. (MIT Press, 1986).

ROBERT WHAPLES, PH.D.
WAKE FOREST UNIVERSITY

kleptocracy

THE TERM *KLEPTOCRACY*, sometimes also spelled *cleptocracy*, literally means rule by theft. It was originally coined to refer to the regime of Mobutu Sese Seko, the Zairian dictator, who, over three decades, carefully transformed the public resources of Zaire into private wealth, while using CORRUPTION, coercion, and violence to thwart all movements for change. Zaire's debt at the end of his rule had increased to $5 billion, a sum almost equivalent to the dictator's personal fortune. Kleptocracy often implies the impoverishment of the people, the destruction of the national infrastructure and the enrichment of leaders and their officials. The methods include diverting international funds to the dictators' supporters, bribing foreign governments and officials, and seizing foreign and local assets to increase personal wealth.

Because of its original association with Mobutu's regime, the term was first applied to dictatorships, especially in developing and Third World countries, which originally prospered thanks to the political climate of the Cold War. Yet, despite its recent origin, the term has enjoyed vast currency, and almost every nation is exposed as being ruled by different forms of kleptocracy. With the rise of anti-global movements in the 1990s, kleptocracy has become a synonym of global capitalism and Western economic imperialism.

Even the writings on kleptocracy that still focus on Third World countries have finally started to take into account that corruption requires two parties, the briber and the bribed. Thus, political and economic analysts have called attention to the complacency of the so-called developed and industrialized nations with the system of corruption in Third World countries. For example, Steve Askin and Carole Collins have argued that hundreds of millions of dollars have disappeared annually from the treasury of Zaire under Mobutu "without even an indication of how, when, or why the funds were taken. A 1989 World Bank study showed that fully 18 percent of the year's state expenditures went on unexplained 'other goods and services'; in 1986 these absorbed $269 million. According to World Bank experts who have examined Zairian state financial records, much of this money appears to have been spent on luxury purchases or superfluous military hardware."

Despite this knowledge, though, loans were still given to Mobutu's as well as to other dictatorial regimes. Because of this the activity of the WORLD BANK has been challenged by important analysts such as the Nobelprize winner Amartya SEN: "An integrated analysis of economic, social, and political activities, involving a variety of institutions and many interactive agencies are needed. The roles and interconnections between certain crucial instrumental freedoms, including economic opportunities, political freedoms, social facilities, transparency guarantees and protective security need to be examined when providing assistance."

Askin and Collins complement their description of the regime that gives kleptocracy its name by stating clearly the connivance of Western governments: "Western governments and multilateral institutions have known at least since the mid-1970s that money lent to the Mobutu regime was likely to disappear without explanation." In spite of their knowledge, European countries and the UNITED STATES continued to support Mobutu for many years and agreed to loans to the dictator in exchange for his political and military favors: in 1983, to name but one of the numerous events of this kind, Zaire sent troops to defend U.S.-backed Chadian President Hissen Habre. Mobutu earned President Ronald REAGAN's praise for what the American president described as a "courageous action."

The example of Mobutu's regime is representative of the active interests that Western countries have to keep Third World kleptocratic governments alive. In face of this fact, the various meetings on poverty and industrial development held in New York (2000), Genoa (2001), and in the Canadian Rocky Mountains (2002) have come under strong criticism as ineffectual and expensive summits to ease the West's post-imperial conscience and win domestic contracts. The financial aid that Western countries give to Third World regimes does nothing to stop their corruption as it often does not go any further than the officials' bank accounts. Western countries still display an imperial mentality and treat Third World countries as still infant political economies to which they are willing to give aid, but not trade. The resources of so-called developing countries, from diamonds to oil, are often prey to the rapacious behavior of Europe and the United States. As Simon Jenkins has put it, "[. . .] the poorest on Earth can take their aid and say thank-you. But they must stay poor."

Radical analysts have also pointed out that the international consensus of the left and the right seems to be supporting the continuation of looting and corruption, both favoring those policies that reward the practitioners of self-enrichment, and particularly those who use absolutist power to pile up personal wealth for themselves and members of their circles.

Yet, the capitalist solution calling for PRIVATIZATION of public resources does not offer a better solution. Two realities must be taken into account, considering privatization, that undermine the efficacy of the process. First, the sale of public resources to private interests usually takes place for less than the actual value of the resource. Second, the sale is often, if not exclusively, to those who are well connected to the regime in power. In addition, once the resource has been sold, it is no longer a resource to the public, and becomes a resource to a private interest. The end result of both of these policies is the provision of enormous personal fortunes to dictators and dictatorial regimes, and their associates, at the expense of citizens in developing and developed countries alike.

People in Western democracies are often scandalized by the plight of poor Africans under Mobutu, of Philippinos exploited by Ferdinand Marcos, of Iraqis by Saddam Hussein, or of Central Americans oppressed by Baby Doc Duvalier or military juntas. Yet, they do not always have to look that far to be scandalized. Some experts say Western powers have vested interests in keeping these regimes alive and, as the economic scandals of the early 2000s might indicate, global capitalism may soon be replacing democracy with kleptocracy, corruption, and corporations.

BIBLIOGRAPHY. Steve Askin and Carole Collins, "External Collusion with Kleptocracy: Can Zaïre Recapture its Stolen Wealth?" *Review of African Political Economy* (v.20/57, 1993); Loren Fox, *Enron: The Rise and Fall* (John Wiley & Sons, 2002); Rachel Neumann and Emma Bircham, eds., *Anti-Capitalism: A Field Guide to the Global Justice Movement* (The New Press, 2003); Simon Jenkins, "Don't Patronize Africa: Give Trade, Not Aid," *The Times* (June 26, 2002).

LUCA PRONO, PH.D.
UNIVERSITY OF NOTTINGHAM, ENGLAND

Knight, Frank H. (1885–1972)

ONE OF THE PIONEERING economists of the early 20th century, Frank H. Knight's insights have appeared in more than 100 published works in his lifetime. His most famous theory, written early in his career in *Risks, Uncertainty, and Profit* (1921), made an economic distinction between insured and uninsured risks in a capitalist market. In his preface, he said, "There is little that is fundamentally new in this book. It represents an attempt to state the essential principles of the conventional economic doctrine more accurately, and to show their implications more clearly, than has previously been done. That is, its object is refinement, not reconstruction; it is a study in 'pure theory.'" Knight's "pure theory" would be studied in economic courses several generations later, and other economists would later use derivations of it to formulate new economic theories.

Born in McLean County, Illinois, Knight had a humble farming childhood until 1911 when he received his B.A. in economics at Milligan College in Tennessee. Knight studied at the University of Tennessee and earned his Masters, then moved on to Cornell University where he received his Ph.D. in economics. It was at Cornell that professors inspired and molded Knight's beliefs into the ideas that would make up the bulk of his many books.

At the outset of his 30s, Knight's educational opportunities had peaked, so he sought to inspire future economists. He began teaching at the University of Chicago and soon was heading the Department of Economics, which gained so much prestige during the 1920s and 1930s that it became simply known as the CHICAGO SCHOOL. The department would feature future Nobel laureates Milton FRIEDMAN, James BUCHANAN, and George STIGLER, all of whom had been students and had attended Knight's lectures and speeches.

Despite Knight's great penchant for understanding an economy, much of the economic doctrines that he created were rooted in his philosophical and societal beliefs. During a time when President Franklin D. ROOSEVELT was restructuring America's economy with public works programs and governmental intervention in the economy, Knight opposed the idea of the NEW DEAL, saying that the economy is a very fragile and unstable thing, and that government programs were too simplistic to grasp and adhere to the complexities of a capitalist system. LAISSEZ-FAIRE economics, he argued, were necessary because of the individual freedoms it guarantees, and that the removal of such freedoms would be disastrous.

Knight continued to publish works involving topics not necessarily related to economy, branching out into such subjects as the ethics of LIBERALISM, the effect of religion on the economy, and political doctrines. His last book, *Laissez-Faire: Pro and Con*, was published in 1967.

BIBLIOGRAPHY. Frank Knight and David E. Jones, *Risks, Uncertainty and Profit* (Beard Books, 2002); Frank Knight and Ross B. Emmett, *Laissez-Faire: Pro and Con* (University of Chicago Press, 1999); "Frank H. Knight Biography," www.econlib.org.

SYED B. HUSSAIN, PH.D.
UNIVERSITY OF WISCONSIN, OSHKOSH

Koopmans, Tjalling Charles (1910–85)

ECONOMIST, PHYSICIST, and author, Tjalling Koopmans of the NETHERLANDS won the Nobel Prize in Economics in 1975 for his contributions to the theory of optimum allocation of resources. His work stemmed from his many years' researching the field of theoretical physics as applied to economics. He shared the 1975 prize in economics with the Russian mathematician, Leonid KANTOROVICH, whose work somewhat paralleled Koopman's.

The third son of schoolteachers Sjoerd and Wijtske, Koopmans was born in Gravelands, the Netherlands. He grew up in a poor but scholastic atmosphere. "School was Bible," he later recalled. At age 14, he received a study stipend from the St. Geertruidsleen of Wijmbritseradeel fund, awarding him monies to continue his education.

Attending the University of Utrecht at age 17, he initially sought a degree in mathematics. But, swayed by the intellectual and curious upheavals of the Netherlands at the time, he began reading external literature, mostly of a philosophical nature. Searching for a field more appropriate to his nature and thirsting for a field closer to his mathematical training, he chose theoretical physics. His idol became Hans Kramers, a well-known theorist and one of the university's teachers; Kramers nurtured Koopmans' interest and mentored him along the way. As the months passed, the student became more aware of the tenuous nature of the economy and, in brief, the possibilities existing to stabilize the science of economics.

He graduated from college in 1933 and went on to complete his graduate degree in physics. While engaged in pursuing his doctorate, he wrote the first of what would be a long series of major scientific/economic essays. The first, popularly called Koopmans' Theorem, presents an analysis of quantum mechanics still in use today.

After receiving his doctorate in 1936, he married Truus Wannigen, whom he tutored in mathematics. That same year he and his wife relocated to Geneva, Switzerland, where he constructed a BUSINESS CYCLE model for the League of United Nations. When WORLD WAR II broke out, his project was discontinued. Fearing for his family's safety in a Europe fraught with Nazism, he moved to the United States.

During the war, Koopmans worked as a statistician for the British Merchant Shipping Mission in Washington, D.C., then as an economist with the Cowles Commission of the University of Chicago from 1944–55. When the Commission relocated in 1955, he followed it to Yale University, where he was appointed professor of economics. He retired in 1981.

BIBLIOGRAPHY. T.C. Koopmans, *Three Essays on the State of Economic Science* (Augustus M. Kelley, 1991); "Biographical Memoirs: Volume 67," *National Academy Journal* (National Academy Press, 1995); Thayer Watkins, "Tjalling Koopmans, Physicist and Economist," San Jose State University, www.sjsu.edu.

JOSEPH GERINGER
SYED B. HUSSAIN, PH.D.
UNIVERSITY OF WISCONSIN, OSHKOSH

Korea, North

IN 1946, NORTH KOREA'S Communist Party, the Korean Worker's Party (KWP), was formed under the leadership of Kim Tubong and Kim Il Sung. In 1948, the Democratic People's Republic of Korea (DPRK) was proclaimed and Kim Il Sung was named its first premier. In 1949, he became the chairman of the KWP and served in that capacity until his death in 1994.

North Korea's population is approximately 22.3 million and is one of the most homogenous in the world. After the Korean War, the population roughly doubled in size between 1953 and 1980. Although the rate of population increase has slowed since 1970, it is nearly twice that of South KOREA. North Korea, however, can be considered underpopulated by east Asian standards, with an overall density of about two-fifths that in the south.

The population, however, is unevenly distributed, with most living near the coastlines and only sparse settlement in the interior. Exacerbating this imbalance has been the government's emphasis on industrialization, which has led to rapid urbanization, with approximately two-thirds of the total population living in urban areas. This industrialization has also produced a severe farm-labor shortage.

North Korea's economy is a command or centralized economy, which means that the government controls production and sets the economic development plans. Since 1954, a series of national economic plans have determined the economic policy. Early on, the plans gave high priority to reconstruction and developing heavy industries. Subsequent plans focused on resource exploitation and improving infrastructure, technology, and mechanization. Until the 1970s, little attention was paid to AGRICULTURE and only in the late 1980s has any effort been made toward improving the quality and quantity of consumer goods.

The country has failed to meet its stated economic goals and the production statistics the government quotes are often inflated. In the first decade after the Korean War the economy grew rapidly, but since then growth has been slow or imperceptible. By the early 1990s, North Korea was in the midst of an economic decline, due largely to the demise of the SOVIET UNION and Europe's communist nations, all of whom had been the country's major trading partners. At present, North Korea faces dire economic conditions. As a result of years of under-investment and spare-parts shortages, its industrial capital stock is nearly beyond repair and its industrial and power output has similarly declined. Thus, despite its stated policy of self-reliance, North Korea has had to import essential commodities and open up the economy to limited foreign investment and increased trade. Since 1995–96, massive international food aid has allowed the nation to escape mass starvation, but the population continues to be vulnerable to extensive malnutrition and deteriorating living conditions.

BIBLIOGRAPHY. Ralph N. Clough, *Embattled Korea: The Rivalry for International Support* (Westview Press, 1987); Eui-Gak Hwang, *The Korean Economies: A Comparison of North and South* (Clarendon Press, 1994); Joungwon Alexander Kim and Chong-Won Kim, *Divided Korea: The Politics of Development 1945–1972* (Hollym International Corporation, 2000); *CIA World Factbook* (2002).

S.J. RUBEL, J.D.
INDEPENDENT SCHOLAR

Korea, South

IN 1948, THE REPUBLIC of Korea, or South Korea, was created. It occupies the southern half of the Korean Peninsula, while North Korea occupies the north. It is separated from North Korea by a demilitarized zone (the DMZ) that runs for roughly 150 miles and can be found at the 38th parallel. South Korea occupies about 45 percent of the Korean Peninsula.

The population of South Korea is approximately 48.3 million. Like North Korea, the population is highly homogenous. However, in urban areas the number of foreigners is increasing, especially from CHINA and southeast Asia. The South Korean constitution guarantees freedom of religion and there is no national religion. Modern Korean culture stems from a melding of shamanism, Buddhism, and Confucianism, and was strongly influenced by the Chinese. Every effort is made to respect and preserve this culture. However, as South Korea continues to build relationships with the West, this has become more difficult.

The majority of South Korea's population can be found in the coastal areas to the south and west. While the population has more than doubled since 1950, the annual rate of increase has declined from more than 3 percent in the 1950s to less than 1 percent by the mid-1990s. During this period, there was a vast shift in South Korea's population demographics away from rural areas and to developing and expanding urban regions. Thus 75 percent of South Korea's population can be classified as urban with the majority living in the country's six largest cities. This accounts for South Korea having a population density about two-and-a-half times greater than North Korea's.

Prior to World War II, large numbers of Koreans (both North and South) emigrated to Manchuria and Japan. After the war, about half of the Koreans living in Japan returned to South Korea. Shortly after the establishment of North Korea, approximately two to four million North Koreans immigrated to South Korea. This high number was offset somewhat by the emigrations of South Koreans, mainly to JAPAN and the UNITED STATES. As South Korea's economy and political conditions began to improve, the emigration rate slowed and many of those that emigrated began to return.

In 1950, in an effort to unify the Korean Peninsula, North Korea, with the aid of China, invaded South Korea. In order to defend itself, South Korea called upon the support of United States and United Nations armed forces. President Rhee used the military to force the legislature to conduct popular elections for president, and in 1952 he was re-elected. In 1953, South and North Korea signed an armistice that created the DMZ, thus dividing the peninsula in two. Even with aid from the United States, the years shortly after the war saw a slow recovery on the part of South Korea. Rhee, though, was able to use his power to win re-election in 1956 and again in 1960. In 1960, however, Rhee was forced to resign amid numerous protests and allegations, proven true, of widespread election malfeasance.

After Rhee's resignation, power was transferred to the office of Prime Minister Chang Myon. Though the Chang regime initiated numerous efforts at reform, the economy still lagged. Chang was unable to stabilize

South Korea's political arena and to form a majority of support for his regime. In 1961, and before a complete program of reforms could be launched, a coup was staged by military elements within the government.

Park Chung Hee and his military junta dissolved the National Assembly, banned political activity, imposed martial law, and governed by decree until 1963, at which time he was elected president. Park instituted vigorous economic reforms and, despite hefty opposition, entered into a treaty with Japan that, in exchange for economic aid, dropped demands for war reparations. Soon thereafter, Japanese capital began to come into South Korea. During the VIETNAM WAR the country also sent troops and workers to the aid of the United States. The effect was a rapid increase in industrialization and economic growth.

Park and his Democratic Republican Party closely controlled funds and, via surveillance and intimidation, overwhelmed all opposition. In 1972, Park declared martial law and instituted a new constitution (Yushin or "revitalizing reform") that allowed him to stay in office indefinitely. Numerous emergency measures were imposed which restricted civil liberties and removed political opposition. In 1978, Park was re-elected president. Though the economy continued to grow at a spectacular rate, political dissatisfaction and unrest increased throughout Park's tenure.

In 1979, Park was assassinated. Under the Yushin Constitution, Prime Minister Choi Kyu became acting president and later that year was formally elected president. However, General Chun Doo Hwan seized control and instituted martial law. In May 1980, through the use of severe violence, Chun thwarted major demonstrations by dissidents and students and ousted Kyu as president.

In August 1980, Chun was elected president. In 1981, martial law was lifted and a new constitution went into effect that retained many of the Yushin control mechanisms, but also called for one seven-year term. Chun's regime was marked by numerous successes, including being designated the host of the 1988 Summer Olympics and having Japan pledge $4 billion in low-interest loans to help finance development. However, it was also marred by several scandals and events, including the North Korean bombing in Burma that killed several members of South Korea's government, and the shooting-down of a Korean Air Lines jet by the SOVIET UNION. By the mid 1980s, relations with North Korea had improved enough for the border to be opened to allow family visits for the first time since the Korean War.

By 1987, dissatisfaction with the government was prevalent. Chun was forced to accept a constitutional reform program that re-established the basic civil rights and institutions that martial law had taken away. The new constitution also reduced the presidential term from seven to five years and called for a direct popular presidential election. Chun lost the election to Roh Tae Woo and opposition parties captured the majority of the National Assembly.

In 1990, Roh successfully merged competing political parties to create the Democratic Liberal Party (DLP), which commanded a vast majority in the National Assembly. In 1991, local elections were held for the first time in 30 years. Later that year, North and South Korea were admitted to the United Nations as separate countries. Three months later, North and South Korea entered into a non-aggression pact. In 1992, the Japanese Premier, Miyazawa Kiichi, visited South Korea and apologized for actions undertaken toward Koreans during the Japanese occupation. During this time, Roh also established diplomatic ties with Hungary, Poland, Yugoslavia, and the Soviet Union, and was able to establish full diplomatic ties with China as well.

In 1992, amid allegations of election wrongdoing, Roh stepped down as head of the DLP. Later that year, Kim Young Sam was elected president and instituted an anti-corruption reform program. In 1993, the government opened the Korean rice market to imports. In 1995, Kim renamed the DLP the New Korea Party (NKP) in an effort to disassociate it from the regimes of Chun and Roh. Also, in 1995 Chun and Roh were arrested and, in 1996, were convicted. In 1996, Kim admitted that he had accepted political donations but denied that they were bribes. Subsequently, a former aide to Kim was arrested for bribery, thus casting doubt on Kim's anticorruption efforts only weeks before the elections. Though the NKP lost control of the National Assembly, it was able to recruit enough independent legislators to regain its majority. In 1997, new scandals rocked the government and led to a cabinet reshuffling.

In 1996, North Korea declared that it would no longer comply with the armistice that ended the Korean War and sent armed troops into the DMZ. South Korea and the United States proposed a four-party peace negotiation, with China and the United States serving as mediators. South Korea agreed to invest in North Korea and to provide food aid. In 2000, South Korea's President Kim Dae-Jung and North Korea's leader Kim Chong-il participated in the first South-North summit. Later that year, Kim Dae-jung was awarded the Nobel Peace Prize for his commitment to democracy and human rights in Asia.

Between the early 1960s and 1990s, South Korea's economy grew at an average rate of 9 percent, its gross national product more than doubled, and its per-capita income increased more than one hundredfold. South Korea, along with Singapore, Hong Kong, and Taiwan, is now considered one of East Asia's "Four Tigers." However, it was not always this way.

Prior to the early 1960s, South Korea's economy was predominantly agrarian and undeveloped. In the early 1960s, however, the military junta committed the government to economic development. This economic expansion was driven in large part by the development of export-oriented industries, initially through the development of textile and light manufacturing, then through the development of heavy industries such as chemicals and steel, and still later, via the development of, among others, shipbuilding, bioengineering, aerospace, automobile, and electronic industries.

In order to maintain control over industrial development, the government gave most of its support to giant-size conglomerates, or chaebols, that were emerging. The result was that smaller, privately managed industries had difficulties finding financing and became dependent on the chaebols for survival. At the expense of consumer goods, the government promoted the import of raw materials and technology and encouraged savings and investment over consumption. By 1980, the government was gradually removing itself from direct involvement in industry and these anti-consumer policies began to be reversed. In the 1980s, labor unions gained significant wage increases, which contributed to the growth in consumer consumption.

As South Korea converted to an urban, industrialized nation, its farm population decreased to the extent that less than one-quarter of its land is cultivated and the percentage of the national income derived from agriculture is a fraction of its 1950s percentage. Increasing farm productivity has been hampered by several factors, including a shortage of farm labor due to an aging rural population, and the fact that fields are typically small and mainly cultivated via manual labor. Rice is the most important crop and constitutes, in value, about 40 percent of all farm production. Barley, wheat, soybeans, potatoes, cabbages, garlic, and maize, among others are also important crops, and it is not uncommon for double-cropping to occur.

Though its deposits of graphite and tungsten are among the worlds largest, South Korea's mineral resources are scarce. And most of its crude oil and metallic mineral needs are imported.

In the 1960s, South Korea nationalized all banks, but by the early 1990s this was reversed, with most banks being returned to private ownership. The Bank of Korea is owned by the government and is the county's CENTRAL BANK. It oversees all banking activities and issues currency. In 1992, foreigners were allowed to trade on the Korea Stock Exchange.

After 1960, South Korea drastically expanded and improved its transportation system. It built a modern highway network and established a nationwide air service. Prior to 1960, rail travel was the predominant means of travel, but now the bulk of passenger travel and freight transport is via road transport. Since the early 1960s, internal air transportation has increased, with most major cities having connections. With the growth in trade, port facilities have undergone substantial expansion.

To fuel its industrial expansion, South Korea borrowed heavily from international financial markets, much of which was repaid because of the success of its exports. However, Asia's financial crisis of 1997–99 exposed longstanding weaknesses in South Korea's financials. Growth plunged in 1998, but recovered to post significant growth in 1999 and 2000. However, in 2001 growth again declined due to the slowing global economy, falling exports, and the sense that South Korea's corporate and financial reforms had stalled.

BIBLIOGRAPHY. Harold C. Hinton, *Korea Under New Leadership: The Fifth Republic* (Praeger Publishers, 1983); Frank B. Gibney, *Korea's Quiet Revolution: From Garrison State to Democracy* (Walker and Company, 1993); Bruce Cumings, *Korea's Place in the Sun: A Modern History* (W.W. Norton & Company, 1998); *CIA World Factbook* (2002).

S.J. RUBEL, J.D.
INDEPENDENT SCHOLAR

Kroger

A PIONEERING GROCERY retailer founded by Barney Kroger in Cincinnati, Ohio, in 1883, Kroger supermarkets became the largest American grocery chain. To better serve its customers, Kroger established quality assurance programs, opened the first grocery-run bakery, became the first grocer to offer an in-store meat department, and employed the first electronic scanner checkout system.

Bernard Henry "Barney" Kroger (1860–1938), the son of German immigrants, began selling groceries in Cincinnati as a door-to-door salesman for the Great Northern and Pacific Tea Company. After flourishing for several years, Kroger noticed that his sales were dropping and traced the problem to the store-owner cutting quality while continuing to charge full price for inferior goods. This experience taught Kroger that people could not be fooled by food and that goods must be priced in keeping with the level of their quality. These principles would shape the course of his career.

In 1883, Kroger joined with a friend to open the Great Western Tea Company and offered about 300 items, typical for a grocery of that day. He soon gained a reputation for being a demanding buyer who pretested his products to guarantee the quality of the goods. Kroger bought out his partner in 1884 and began to expand into new locations. By 1893, Kroger owned 17 stores, all of which showed substantial profits in that depression year.

Kroger saw an opportunity to increase his income by manufacturing the products that he sold (today, a common practice known as private label), as well as a chance to improve the quality of his groceries. In 1901, he became the first grocer to operate a bakery. In the following year, the firm incorporated as The Kroger Grocery and Baking Company with 40 stores and $1.75 million in annual sales. In this era, customers typically bought meat only at butcher shops, but in 1904, Kroger bought a meatpacking house and a butcher chain to begin selling both meat and groceries under one roof. The move brought much opposition from butchers who had been accustomed to a considerable amount of independence in setting their own working conditions and their own prices, often perhaps with the aid of a thumb on the scale.

In the early days of the company, Kroger followed a long-established pattern by having clerks personally assist customers as they shopped. In 1916, the firm became the first grocery business to adopt self-service. Kroger would open its first supermarket style of gigantic self-service stores in 1935. In the 1950s, the company attracted national attention with a "merchandising democracy" program that allowed customers to vote on store-by-store marketplace decisions. Technological innovations would continue through the years, with the introduction of symbol-reading scanners in 1972.

As it expanded, Kroger continued to focus on quality. It became the first grocer to establish strict specifications for its private-label products. To ensure that these standards were met, it opened its own quality-assurance laboratories for testing products sold under the Kroger label. Samples of Kroger products, made for the company by outside food manufacturers, would be removed from store shelves and tested on a regular basis. The first food retailer to establish a consumer-research department, Kroger learned that its customers wanted nutritional labeling. In 1972, the company placed such labels on Kroger-brand goods.

Through a series of mergers, Kroger emerged as the largest food-retailer in the United States by the end of the 20th century. The company's emphasis on quality and customer service reached throughout the industry while its innovations were much copied. In 2002, Kroger ranked as number 56 on *Fortune* magazine's *Global 500* (largest companies in the world) with revenues of over $50 billion.

BIBLIOGRAPHY. George Laycock, *The Kroger Story: A Century of Innovation* (1983); Martin M. Pegler, *Designing the World's Best Supermarkets* (Visual Reference, 2003); www.kroger.com.

CARYN E. NEUMANN, PH.D.
OHIO STATE UNIVERSITY

Krugman, Paul (1953–)

EDUCATED AT YALE University and the Massachusetts Institute of Technology (MIT), Paul Krugman has made valuable contributions in the area of international economics. His first contribution was to provide a theoretical explanation of the phenomenon of intra-industry trade in differentiated products. Intra-industry trade cannot be explained using traditional trade models. Long before Krugman, some economists had pointed out the possibility that this type of trade could arise from product differentiation. Krugman acknowledges their contributions but offers a more tractable, simple, and elegant model. Another contribution was to create what is now called the "new trade theory." The new trade theory is a mixture of industrial organization and international trade theory based on the concepts of increasing returns and imperfect competition.

Krugman has also contributed to international finance with theories about target zones. A target zone is an exchange-rate regime that allows the exchange rate to vary only within a specific range. When the exchange rate ventures outside the range because of market forces, the monetary authority (mostly in coordination with other central banks) intervenes in the foreign-exchange market to bring back the exchange rate within the range. Krugman showed that a target zone provides a framework for exchange-rate stabilization, since the volatility of the exchange rate (in the presence of monetary shocks) in a target zone is smaller than would be the case if it were allowed to float free.

Krugman's final major theoretical contribution has to do with the creation of the field of economic geography, which he defines as "the location of production in space." Economic geography is, at its core, about the concept of multiple equilibria and increasing returns. This field attempts to provide an explanation of why some economic activities are clustered in cities and regions; Krugman shows that producers enjoy an economy of scale as long as they are clustered within the same region or city. He argues that the emergence of economic activity is not random but chaotic; that is, there is an underlying pattern to economic activity, though this pattern is based on the principles of non-linear dynamics (i.e., chaos). For example, in the case of high-tech clusters, the availability of transportation and communication systems, of core competencies, and of the adequate research infrastructure are variables that confer a self-reinforcing set of advantages on a certain area.

Krugman has also contributed to our understanding of economic policy. He showed that there is almost no gain for a country to engage in industrial policy, which is basically done by closing some key domestic industries to foreign competition through trade protection. It is worth pointing out that Krugman did reach this conclusion on empirical grounds only, using the case of Japan. On a theoretical note, he did however show that granting protection to an industry could promote export under certain conditions.

In 1991, Krugman wrote *The Age of Diminished Expectations*, addressing issues such as the productivity slowdown in the United States, INFLATION, UNEMPLOYMENT, and the DOLLAR among many others. He explained to a general audience why the gap in the distribution of income widened in the previous two decades, despite the robust economic growth of the Clinton era. Unlike some prominent economists who believe that the answer lay with globalization, Krugman proposed the reason had to do with productivity. Indeed, some economists believe that with the increased globalization, U.S. trade with countries where labor is cheap has put downward pressure on wages in the United States. Krugman partially shares this view but believes that the bulk of the answer lies in new technologies that require more well-educated, well-paid workers and less of the unskilled.

As a writer for *The New York Times*, Krugman is sharing his views with a broader audience. With all his important contributions, he was awarded the prestigious Bates Clark medal in 1991, a prize given every two years to a "brilliant economist under the age of forty who is believed to have made a significant contribution to economic knowledge." He is also viewed as a possible future Nobel-Prize laureate for his contribution in international trade.

BIBLIOGRAPHY. Warren J. Samuels, *American Economists of the Late Twentieth Century* (Edward Elgar Publishing Company); Avinash Dixit, "In Honor of Paul Krugman: Winner of the John Bates Clark Medal," *Journal of Economic Perspectives* (American Economic Association, 1993).

ARSÈNE A. AKA, PH.D.
CATHOLIC UNIVERSITY OF AMERICA

Kuwait

LOCATED AT THE HEAD of the Persian Gulf bordering IRAQ and SAUDI ARABIA, Kuwait's modern history began in the 18th century with the founding of the city of Kuwait by a section of the Anaiza tribe who had wandered north from Qatar.

Fearing that the Ottoman Empire would tighten-up its regional authority, the head of Kuwait, Mabarek al-Sabah, signed a treaty with Great Britain in 1899 that made the small territory a British protectorate. This relationship persisted until 1961 when Kuwait gained its independence from Great Britain. At the time of independence, Iraq stated that Kuwait was historically part of Iraq based on old Ottoman records. The only obstacle that prevented the Iraqi government from acting was the presence of British military forces.

In 1963, Iraq recognized Kuwait's independence but it did not totally renounce any claims to Kuwaiti land. During the eight-year Iran-Iraq War in the 1980s, the government of Kuwait supported Iraq. Due to its location, Kuwait has always been vulnerable to regional disputes and disruptions. On August 2, 1990, Iraqi troops stormed into Kuwait. While the Iraqis claimed they were only retaking territory that was historically theirs, in reality the invasion was due to Iraqi economic problems.

Iraq owed a significant debt to Kuwait, which Kuwait refused to forgive. In addition, Kuwait was exceeding its oil production quota as set by the ORGANIZATION OF PETROLEUM EXPORTING COUNTRIES (OPEC). The resulting low global oil prices did not help Iraq recover from its economic troubles. After the invasion, Iraq announced that it was annexing Kuwait; it would become Iraq's 19th province.

Through U.S. efforts, a multinational coalition of nearly 40 nations was assembled, and, under UNITED NATIONS auspices, initiated military action against Iraq to liberate Kuwait. Many Arab states supported Kuwait by sending troops to fight with the coalition, or donated equipment and financial support to the Kuwait cause. By early March 1991, the U.S.-led coalition force had driven the Iraqi army from Kuwait and occupied much of southern Iraq. After the conclusion of the war, the multinational coalition helped with the reconstruction of Kuwait.

Before the Iraqi invasion, Kuwait had a small military force, most of which was destroyed by the Iraqis, but since then Kuwait has made significant efforts to increase the size and modernity of their armed forces. The government has also improved their defense arrangements with other Arab states, as well as with the UNITED STATES. Though Kuwait is a small country, it has massive oil reserves. In the 1970s, Kuwait benefited from the dramatic rise in oil prices. The economy suffered from the triple-shock of a 1982 securities-market crash, the mid-1980s drop in oil prices, and the 1990 Iraqi invasion. The Kuwait government-in-exile depended upon its $100 billion in overseas investments during the Iraqi occupation.

With a GROSS DOMESTIC PRODUCT (GDP) of $31 billion and a population just over 2 million, the government has sponsored social welfare, public works, and development plans financed with oil revenues. But as a desert country, Kuwait must import or distill 75 percent of its potable water. Despite calls for political reform, the ruling family continues to hold all major ministerial posts and severely limits women's rights and suffrage.

BIBLIOGRAPHY. "The Department of State Background Note," www.state.gov; *CIA World Factbook* (2002); Chaim Herzog, *The Arab-Israeli Wars* (Random House, 1982); Tarq Y. Ismael, *The Middle East in World Politics* (Syracuse University Press, 1974).

LINDA L. PETROU, PH.D.
HIGH POINT UNIVERSITY

Kuznets, Simon (1901–85)

WINNER OF THE 1971 Nobel Prize in Economics, Simon Kuznets is noted as one of the architects of national income accounts and for an "empirically founded interpretation of economic growth which . . . led to new and deepened insight into the economic and social structure and process of development," according to the Nobel citation. Kuznets was born in Russia, of Jewish parents. He fled to the UNITED STATES during the RUSSIAN REVOLUTION and completed his education with a Ph.D. in economics from Columbia University in 1926. After graduation, he joined the research staff of the National Bureau of Economic Research (NBER), remaining affiliated for over three decades. His first academic appointment was at the University of Pennsylvania (1931–54), followed by professorships at Johns Hopkins University (1954–60) and Harvard University (1960–71).

At the NBER, Kuznets worked on a pioneering series of BUSINESS CYCLE studies. *Cyclical Fluctuations* (1926) analyzed the cyclical patterns of wholesale and retail trade as the economy goes through expansions and recessions. It presented a theory of how business cycles are transmitted, with changes in consumer demand magnified both by the speculation of retailers and wholesalers, and by the existence of lags and differences in their responses. *Secular Movements in Production and Prices* (1930) looked at long-term cyclical changes in the American economy beginning with the Civil War, while *Seasonal Variations in Industry and Trade* (1933) examined causes and solutions to economic fluctuations from season to season.

In 1933, Kuznets wrote a groundbreaking article that carefully considered how to define and measure national income. The article led the U.S. Department of Commerce to construct official estimates of national income for the first time, with Kuznets overseeing the project. His subsequent work on historical national income showed that the long-term ratio of consumption to income remains nearly constant, and led to the development of modern theories about the behavior of consumption, such as those by Milton FRIEDMAN and Franco MODIGLIANI.

During World War II, Kuznets worked with his former student Robert Nathan at the War Production Board, using his extensive knowledge of the economy to locate areas of slack that could be switched over to the munitions program, directing the flow of materials, and scheduling production to maximize wartime output. Some historians conclude that the Kuznets-Nathan team played a key role in expanding output during the war.

During the last half of his career, Kuznets turned his focus to the nature and causes of historical economic growth and inequality. His work was noted for its relentless quantification, carefully handling each piece of data "with the delicate patience of the archeologist," and for broadening the normal scope of economic investigation to include analysis of demographic, political, and institutional factors. Culminating in works such as *Modern Economic Growth: Rate, Structure and Spread* (1966) and *Economic Growth of Nations: Total Output and Production Structure* (1971), Kuznets codified a new understanding of the patterns and process of economic growth around the world.

He concluded that economic growth requires both technological change and institutional response within each society and that it often initially triggers increasing

Simon Kuznets' work on national income and business cycles led to modern theories about the behavior of consumption.

economic inequality (and with it political instability) before it spreads the benefits of progress to all, and inequality subsides—known as the Kuznets U hypothesis.

Another important Kuznet finding was that, contrary to Malthusian pessimism, rising population does not seem to harm economic growth, perhaps because it increases the number of talented individuals and, thus, opportunity for technological advance.

BIBLIOGRAPHY. Vibha Kapuria-Foreman and Mark Perlman, "An Economic Historian's Economist: Remembering Simon Kuznets," *Economic Journal* (1995); Vibha Kapuria-Foreman, "Simon Kuznets," in *Business Cycles and Depressions: An Encyclopedia* (Garland Publishing, 1997).

ROBERT WHAPLES, PH.D.
WAKE FOREST UNIVERSITY

L

labor

THE FACT THAT human beings work in order to create the world around them is not the most unusual proposition to make. Indeed, this proposition forms the universal basis of most moralistic claims under capitalism. Poverty, homelessness, starvation, lack of education, are all explained, with common sense, as an individual's (or a community's) incapacity or unwillingness at some stage of life to be hard-working. Given the importance accorded to work in social consciousness, it would be only natural to assume that the idea that human labor forms the basis of wealth in society would be easily acceptable under capitalism. It is, however, completely inadmissible in public rhetoric. The "provider of work" is seen as the source of wealth as opposed to the person who actually performs the work. How did this inversion in perception come about?

There is an inversion regarding labor at the very heart of capitalism. A human being's capacity to labor, to work upon nature in order to change it, has formed the basis for human history. Human labor, consequently, has taken a variety of forms through time. Hunting and gathering, agriculture, the herding of animals, are all, in this basic sense, the same as attaching wheels to the body of an automobile, in that they are all forms of labor. All pre-capitalist societies, however, differed from capitalism in one vital respect as far as work was concerned. The goal of work in pre-modern societies was the immediate satisfaction of people's needs. Granted that the needs of the ruling elite took priority over the those of the great majority of people, it still remains true that the slave, peasant, or handicraft worker worked to produce goods that would immediately be used either by themselves or by the elite. Under capitalism, however, very little production is for immediate use. The Ford autoworker does not produce cars for her own immediate use or even for the immediate use of her managing director. She produces cars so that they can be sold. Goods under capitalism thus have a strange peculiarity: before they can be used, they have to be exchanged against money, which in turn can then be exchanged for other GOODS.

It is this act of exchange for money that transforms "goods" into "commodities" under capitalism. The appreciation of goods lies in their exchange value thus inverting the basic logic of normal production. No longer are goods valued for their intrinsic qualities but for the amount that they fetch when exchanged. Labor embodied in the goods becomes the invisible quotient that goes perpetually unnoticed and consequently disregarded.

The scrutiny of work. With the rise of the new discipline of political economy in 18th-century Europe, work, as a theoretical concept, came under renewed scrutiny. Between the *Tableau économique de la France* (1759) of Francois QUESNAY, founder of the PHYSIOCRATS, and Adam SMITH's *Wealth of Nations* (1776), there emerged the idea of work in general, that is, work considered separately from all its particular forms in agriculture, manufacturing, or commerce.

Karl MARX is given most credit for having rediscovered the hidden value of commodities to be the labor of human beings. Marx, in *Capital*, asks what it is that two very different objects that cost the same amount of money have in common, say a pair of socks and a loaf of bread. The answer cannot lie in their respective qualities (weight, color, shape, utility), but would have to be sought elsewhere. According to Marx, the item that both have in common was the amount of labor that went into making them, and this labor actually was something that determined their values.

Marx did not chance upon this explanation on his own; 18th- and 19th-century economists, Smith and David RICARDO in particular, drew partially similar conclusions before Marx. Smith argued that "the proportion between the quantities of labor necessary for acquiring different objects," was "the only circumstances which can afford any rule for exchanging them for one another." This claim is further consolidated by Smith with the famous example of the beaver and the deer:

> If among a nation of hunters . . . it usually costs twice the labor to kill a beaver which it does to kill a deer, one beaver should naturally exchange for or be worth two deer. It is natural that what is usually the produce of two days or two hours labor, should be worth double of what is usually the produce of one day's or one hour's labor.

Ricardo introduced in this mix the question of ownership of the means of producing wealth:

> All the implements necessary to kill the beaver and deer might belong to one class of men, and the labor employed in their destruction might be furnished by another class; still their comparative prices would be in proportion to the actual labor bestowed, both on the formation of capital, and on the destruction of the animals.

The separation of the worker from the means of creating wealth is yet another novel development under capitalism not experienced by either the peasant or the slave in previous eras. In Europe in the late Middle Ages and throughout Africa and Asia at the time of European colonization in the 18th and 19th centuries, most people had some direct access to the means of creating a livelihood. Peasants grew food on their own land and craftsmen made goods in their own workshops.

The rise of capitalism was initiated by a primeval act of robbery, some economists say, where masses of people were forcibly de-invested of control over the means of production. Acts such as the "enclosures" in England and Wales, the "clearances" in Scotland, or the "Permanent Settlement" in India were all part of the same historical process to bring about the separation of a large and growing proportion of the laboring population from means of production that could provide them with an adequate subsistence. This was by no means a gradual, harmonious process but involved force, suffering, and popular resistance.

British proponents of enclosure, for instance, were remarkably forthcoming. Common rights and access to common lands, they argued, allowed a degree of social and economic independence and thereby produced a lazy, dissolute mass of rural poor. Once deprived of the commons, wrote one Mr. Bishton in a report prepared for the Board of Agriculture in 1794, "the laborers will work every day in the year, their children will be put out to labor early" and "that subordination of the lower ranks which in the present times is so much wanted, would be thereby considerably secured."

Labor, under capitalism, was thus historically freed in two crucial ways: It had been freed from the control of the feudal landowners; it had also been freed from any access to the means of production and hence free to sell its labor power to the highest bidder.

In Marx's account of capitalism, the essential nature of the system is defined by a unique relationship of production: that between "owners of money, means of production, means of subsistence" on the one hand, and "on the other hand, free workers, the sellers of their own labor-power, and therefore the sellers of labor." Labor power, a term coined by Marx, refers to the human being's capacity to work, as opposed to the work that they actually perform. Labor power depends on physical and mental sustenance to be able to labor. Smith put it succinctly:

> There is a certain minimum below which it is impossible to reduce for any considerable time the ordinary wages of even the lowest species of labor. A man must always live by his work, and his wages must be enough to maintain him. They must even on most occasion be somewhat more; otherwise it would be impossible for him to bring up his family and the race of his workmen could not last beyond the first generation.

The wage or salary of the worker hence is directly related to the cost of replenishing labor power. Smith is unconsciously paraphrased in our daily media everyday. "Many managers realize," the *Financial Times* reported in 1995, "that unless their staff take their holidays and maintain a life outside work they will fail to perform effectively."

The value of labor. Like all commodities under capitalism, the value of labor power depends on the amount of labor needed to produce it. But the amount of labor needed to produce the goods for sustenance (food, shelter, clothing) for a worker, is substantially less than the amount of labor performed on any given work day by an average worker. Herein, according to Marx, lies the root of profit. It may take four person-hours of society's total labor to produce one family's food, shelter and clothing. But most people put in more than eight hours of work every day. The surplus labor hours that the worker puts in for "free" for her employer, was baptized by Marx as surplus value: the source of profit, rent, and interest.

The history of capitalist development is punctuated by the history of the development of the labor movement. The latter has tried, successfully or unsuccessfully, at every instance to resist the development and growth of the former at its expense. Theoretical concepts such as labor power and surplus value, outlined above, have been and continue to be, best illustrated by the actual struggles and trials of working men and women.

Since the dispossession of peasants and artisans from the means of production was a precondition for capitalist development, 17th-century England saw a series of struggles waged by small peasants, artisans, and laborers against rural magnates to secure for a time the survival of many small holdings and common rights. Landless or near-landless peasants struggled to retain their common rights in order to avoid becoming completely dependent on wages and losing their independent way of life. The agitations among the rank and file of the London artisan guilds and companies in the 1640s and 1650s were a major element in the English revolution. They addressed class-conscious manifestos to the rich merchants of the city, in tone and content pre-empting Marx's theory of labor power:

> You of the city that buy our work must have your tables furnished, and your cups overflow; and therefore will give us little or nothing for our work, even what you please, because you know we must sell for monies to set our families on work, or else we famish. Thus our flesh is that whereupon you rich men live, and wherewith you deck and adorn yourselves.

The 19th century saw the slow but steady emergence of worker's own organizations, or trade UNIONS. This, despite the fact that with the sole exception of Britain, trade unions and strikes were legally prohibited almost everywhere in Europe. Trade unions in the loose sense of the word were to be found in Britain as far back as the 17th century. One of the earliest instances of a permanent trade union was in tailoring, in 1720. In the first half of the 19th century, many trade unionists were inspired by the utopian socialism of Robert Owen and the demands for democratic rights embodied in the People's Charter of the Chartist movement.

The turbulent changes and the economic instability of the early stages of the INDUSTRIAL REVOLUTION encouraged militant trade unionism and revolutionary politics. Some unions, such as the Amalgamated Society of Engineers (1852) and the Amalgamated Society of Carpenters and Joiners (1860) in Britain, even commanded membership on a national scale.

Socialist labor. By the middle of the 19th century, the industrial proletariat had created for itself a permanent niche in world historical development along with an ideology that was to be enduringly associated with it, namely SOCIALISM. The International Workingmen's Association (1864–72), founded in London under the leadership of Marx and Friedrich ENGELS, propagated international solidarity among all working people in the famous slogan "workingmen have no country."

The International formed, in part, the inspiration for the first mass working-class political party, the powerful Social Democratic Party (SPD) of Germany in 1875. The International, however, was much more effective in strategizing and leading movements. From 1868 onward, a wave of labor unrest swept through Europe either led or inspired by members of the International. A surge of industrial actions led to strikes in almost all the leading European countries: RUSSIA (1870), GERMANY (1868), FRANCE (1868), BELGIUM (1869), ITALY (1871) and the UNITED KINGDOM (1871–73). The crest of the wave, undoubtedly, was the Paris Commune of 1871, the first display of insurrectionary governance by ordinary workers.

Workers' movements have been historically involved in a collective problem-solving activity. Various leaderships and members have shaped and reshaped their forms of organization, their own capacities, and the tasks they set for themselves. All the while, they were practically testing various theories concerning the nature and possibilities of their own movement and the character, interests and the capabilities of their antagonists. It is worth mentioning that the leading theories about labor or labor movements are in actuality the direct generalization of the real experiences of the working class. Marx reformulated his theory of the "dictatorship of the proletariat" in the *Communist Manifesto* after the Paris Commune. In the Commune, it was revolutionary workers themselves, who demonstrated for Marx some of the basic principles of a worker's democracy: payment of all officials at workers' wages; election and recall of all delegates; replacement of the standing army by armed workers; and so on.

The Commune lasted for less than two months, and more than 30 years were to pass before the working class experimented yet again with methods of governance, this time in the form of the soviets or workers councils, in Russia during 1905. The soviets were yet another instance of the working class creating its own mode of organization and protest well ahead of theoreticians and leaders.

By the early 20th century, it had become customary, in western Europe, for workers and their organizations to see a division between the fight against the state for political change, and the trade union struggle to win economic improvement from employers. In Russia, on the other hand, no such separation existed due to the repressive nature of the Tsarist regime. Even the most "bread-and-butter" trade union struggles came under severe surveillance and coercive tactics. In such a political climate trade unions grew up fully conscious of the fact that the overthrow of the autocracy was a basic precondition for the improvement of worker's fortunes.

The soviets, or workers' councils, set up by the workers of Petrograd during the revolution of 1905, were uniquely suited to the expression of workers' power. The fact that its formation came straight from the shop floor, and not from any theoretical leader, cannot be over-emphasized. The majority of the Bolsheviks, with the exceptions of Leon Trotsky and Vladimir LENIN, were actually opposed to the workers' soviets. The great merit of the soviet was that it was based not on the worker as an individual citizen in a geographical area, but on the worker as a part of a collective in the work place, or the unit of production. The soviets also expressed a fusion of economic and political demands that was common to the whole of the Russian labor movement. One of the main slogans of the 1905 revolution, "Eight hours and a gun," combined the ideas of both the economic struggle for a shorter working day and the political struggle against the Tsarist regime.

Workers' revolution. The October Revolution of 1917, that finally swept the Bolsheviks into power, has been either celebrated or reviled as the singular instance of workers' power in the history of capitalism. For our purposes, suffice to say that it was certainly a mass uprising that ended in the horror of the civil war (1918–21), the isolation of the Revolution, and the gradual and tragic substitution of the actual working class by the Bolshevik party. From the point of view of the majority of workers, except for the brief heady days of October, the Revolution was far from a bed of roses. The immediate aftermath of the Revolution was the invasion by some 16 armies of the leading European countries intent on crushing the Bolsheviks.

Approximately eight to 10 million people died in the ensuing civil war between the defenders of the revolution and the remnants of the Tsarist regime, and from hunger and disease that came in its wake. The crisis can be seen at its deepest in Petrograd, once the crucible of the revolution. The population of the town fell from 2.4 million in 1917 to 740,000 in 1920, a fall of nearly 70 percent. The numbers in the industrial working class fell even more. Most had to leave work to go and fight in the Red Army. As a class, the Russian workers had practically ceased to exist. The grotesque transformation of the revolution into the Stalinist dictatorship was the final cruel irony that history had to offer to the Russian labor movement.

Since 1917, there have been a series of revolutionary experiences for the modern working class: Germany from 1918–23; SPAIN during the civil war from 1936–37; HUNGARY against the Stalinist regime in 1956; POLAND under *Solidarnosc* from 1980–81; to name a few. They have been relatively protracted processes, involving retreats and advances, skirmishes and confrontations. Not until the 1980s, however, was the entity of the working class as a whole denied existence in both the popular media and also academic writing.

The Financial Times, in 1981, welcomed the emergence of the Social Democratic Party in Britain as an "example of the political system beginning to catch up with societal change. . . . There is a new class which [now] outnumbers either the stereotypes of working class or capitalists." The 1980s saw a series of developments that were seen by many as the final triumph of capitalism.

In Britain and the United States the electoral victories of Margaret THATCHER (1979) and Ronald REAGAN (1980) ushered in an era of aggressive neo-conservatism. Welfare benefits were cut to the levels of 50 years earlier or even abolished in some American states. The 1970s carried unpleasant memories of industrial militancy for capital, and both Thatcher and Reagan became symbols to soothe the fears of "union power" for big business.

Average output per head in the 1980s grew at less than half the rate of the early 1960s. Unemployment reached virtually unimaginable levels, commonly staying above 10 percent for years at a time, and rising close to 20 percent in places such as Spain and IRELAND. Lower rates in the United States in the early 1980s and late 1990s were driven by welfare cuts, which forced people to take jobs at poverty wages, the poorest 10 percent earning 25 percent less than the equivalent group in Britain.

Labor strikes. Contrary to popular opinion about the 1980s being the era of the "yuppie," the decade actually saw some very big, and sometimes violent, class confrontations as workers tried to prevent the decimation of jobs in old established industries. Some of the more remarkable of them were the struggles by steel workers in France and Belgium, the year-long strike of over 150,000 miners in Britain, and a strike of similar length by 5,000 British print workers, a five-day general strike in DENMARK, public-sector strikes in the NETHERLANDS and a one-day general strike in Spain.

The more spectacular triumph for the neo-liberals was the collapse of eastern Europe and the SOVIET UNION. The actual spectacle of the fall of the Berlin Wall, or the execution of the Romanian dictator by his own generals, seemed to signal the ultimate victory of Western capitalism in terms of ideology as well as material reality. The war between capital and labor seemed to be truly over according to the media pundits, no doubt to the advantage of the former.

What did this "victory" for capitalism translate as in real terms? Across Asia, Africa, and Latin America, bureaucrats and politicians who had made their careers sponsoring versions of eastern Europe and Russia, switched over to praise free markets. Most third-world governments showed their commitment to this new approach by signing up to the "structural adjustment program" of the WORLD BANK and the INTERNATIONAL MONETARY FUND (IMF). Seventy-six countries implemented adjustment program on "free market" criteria in the 1980s. In 1990, 44 percent of Latin America's population was living below the poverty line according to the United Nations economic commission, which concluded that there had been "a tremendous step backwards in the material standard of living." In Africa, more than 55 percent of the rural population was considered to be living in absolute poverty by 1987.

The unleashing of the forces of the global market was to have global consequences by the end of the 1990s. The first indication of this was the ANTI-GLOBALIZATION protest in Seattle, Washington, in November 1999, that succeeded in shutting down a session of the World Bank. The significant presence of labor unions at the protest was only the first signal that the post-Cold War Washington consensus was not as consensual as it appeared. The war between capital and labor, yet again, seemed not to have been won.

After Seattle, similar protests took place in Washington, D.C., Melbourne, Quebec City, Prague, and most recently in Genoa. Two elements common to these protests stand out in their significance. The first is regarding the holistic nature of the opposition. For the first time perhaps in the history of capitalism, there were protests taking place at various corners of the world that were against the system as a whole. The new generation of activists styled themselves as anti-capitalists. The second relevant development for this movement is the increasing involvement of organized labor. There have been large contingents of trade unionists at most of these protest gatherings since Seattle. Italy had its very own general strike soon after the demonstration at Genoa at the G8 SUMMIT. Labor was also central to the explosion of protests against World Bank and IMF policies in the global south in the year after Seattle. Large numbers of organized workers either struck or demonstrated against PRIVATIZATION and austerity program in ARGENTINA, Bolivia, BRAZIL, COLOMBIA, Nigeria, Paraguay, and SOUTH AFRICA to name a few.

E.P. Thompson, in his seminal work on the English working class, remarked that "[The working class] did not rise like the sun at an appointed time. It was present at its own making." The history and theory of the labor movement, like the class itself, is one that is always in the making. There exists an enormous gap today between the objective existence of a world working class and its becoming an active political force of the kind hoped for by the leaders of the labor movement. The confluence of events of the recent decades, however, in no way suggests that it is an impossible project.

BIBLIOGRAPHY. Adam Smith, *An Inquiry into the Nature and Cause of the Wealth of Nations*, E. Cannnan, ed., (Methuen, 1961); David Ricardo, *The Works and Correspondence of David Ricardo*, P. Sraffa, ed., with M.H. Dobb (Cambridge University Press, 1951–73); J.L. Hammond and Barbara Hammond, *The Village Labourer* (Longman, 1978); Karl Marx, *Capital*, Ben Fowkes, trans., (v.1, Penguin, 1976): D.M. Wolfe, ed., *Leveller Manifestoes of the Puritan Revolution* (Prometheus Books, 1944); J. Petras and M. Morley, *Latin America in the Time of Cholera* (Routledge, 1992); E. P. Thompson, *The Making of the English Working Class* (Penguin, 1968).

TITHI BATTACHARYA, PH.D.
PURDUE UNIVERSITY

Laffer Curve

ARTHUR LAFFER, AN ECONOMIST from the University of Southern California, was having dinner at a restaurant. The discussion turned to high tax rates. It was 1974 and, at that time, the highest marginal federal individual income tax rate was 70 percent. Laffer started sketching a graph on a napkin. Laffer's drawing depicted the relationship between tax rates and the total revenue generated by the federal government. The graph indicated that the revenue generated by the federal government rises gradually with the higher tax rates until a certain threshold is reached. Upon reaching this threshold, the curve reverses its direction, and total revenues fall. This tax paradox applies to all tax rates above the threshold. However, no one knows where the optimum point is located or the actual shape of the curve itself.

Laffer wasn't the first economist to claim that tax cuts would increase government revenue. In 1776, economist Adam SMITH stated, "High taxes, sometimes by diminishing the consumption of the taxed commodities and sometimes by encouraging smuggling, afford a smaller revenue to government than might be drawn from more moderate taxes."

Although the term "Laffer Curve" is not widely known outside of economic circles, Laffer is credited with being the chief architect behind President Ronald REAGAN's supply-side economic plan, dubbed "Reaganomics." The Laffer Curve was the cornerstone of the plan.

The Keynesian demand-management policies dominated economic thinking from WORLD WAR II until the early 1970s. The Keynesian theory, named after its originator, John Maynard KEYNES, was conceived during the

Great DEPRESSION of the 1930s. It is based upon the demand side explanation of business cycles. Keynes believed that a recession is created when there is a decrease in aggregate demand. As the country's consumption and investment spending declines, so does production and employment. To stimulate demand, government should increase spending and cut taxes across the board.

Both Presidents John F. KENNEDY and Lyndon JOHNSON wholeheartedly adopted the Keynesian philosophy. President NIXON declared himself a Keynesian in 1971. Beginning in the 1970s, the country was hit with "stagflation." That is, a combination of stagnation and INFLATION. During this period, there was slow economic growth, rising prices, and rising unemployment. Economists attributed this phenomenon to an excessive expansion in the money supply coupled with sharp increase in resource costs, especially oil. Economists concluded that Keynesian demand-side was unable to solve the stagflation problem. This opened the door for supply-side economics.

The roots of supply-side economics can be traced back to French economist Jean Baptiste Say, who provided the original logic behind the classical school of economics. Underlying SAY'S LAW was the maxim, supply creates its own demand. "The modern application of the law can be seen in the argument that an increase in savings, induced by tax cuts, will not only stimulate an increased supply of goods and services, but also create sufficient demand to purchase them."

When Reagan took office in 1981, he embraced supply-side economics. Supply-siders reasoned that the U.S. progressive tax system provided a great disincentive to work, save, and invest. Lowering the tax rate would stimulate savings and production. It would also result in an increase in federal government revenue as demonstrated by the Laffer Curve.

The reduction in marginal tax rates does not bode the same for middle-class taxpayers or the poor. To begin with, these groups have a lower marginal tax rate. They are not proficient savers, and the lowering of the marginal tax rate does little to stimulate savings or production. This gave ammunition to opponents of supply-side economics. They blasted it as a proposal to solely benefit the rich.

Supply-siders argued that the middle class and the poor indirectly benefited from lowering the top marginal tax rates. The increased government revenue would stimulate production and jobs. This would benefit the middle-class and the poor. Opponents of supply-side economics derogatorily labeled this as the "trickle-down economic theory."

Whether Reaganomics was a success or not is subject to debate. The primary goal of Reaganomics was to stimulate economic growth. For the years 1981–88, the growth rate averaged almost 3 percent, less than the Reagan administration forecast of 3.9 percent. However, it did exceed the growth rate averaged for the previous seven years, which was 2.7 percent.

Reagan lowered the highest marginal tax rate from 70 percent to 35 percent. This did result in a large increase in disposable income. Consumer optimism rose and as a result, personal savings actually dropped. The increased spending resulted in an additional 13 million jobs. The unemployment rate fell to less than 6 percent.

When Reagan assumed office, inflation was a staggering 12.1 percent. It dropped to 4.8 percent in 1988, a 60 percent decrease. Interest rates also dropped by approximately 31 percent.

The federal budget deficit soared in the 1980s. Reagan's plan was in addition to a tax reduction, to reduce federal spending, and decrease government regulation. Reagan's plan called for a large increase in defense spending, while keeping social security payments intact. However, Congress did not match spending cuts with the tax cuts, and the deficit ballooned.

The debate continues. However, both economists and politicians agree to a much greater extent that higher marginal income tax rates have a negative impact, albeit marginal, on incentives.

BIBLIOGRAPHY. V.A. Canto and A.B. Laffer, *Monetary Policy, Taxation, and International Investment Strategy* (Quorum Books, 1990); T. Karier, *Great Experiments in American Economic Policy: From Kennedy to Reagan* (Praeger, 1999); H.G. Morissen, "Exploration of the Laffer Curve," www.gmu.edu/jbc (1999); M.H. Spencer, *Contemporary Economics* (Worth Publishers, 1990).

MARK E. MOTLUCK, PH.D.
ANDERSON UNIVERSITY

laissez-faire

A FRENCH PHRASE that literally means "let do," and translates better as "let a person alone," laissez-faire was applied to economics by English and French thinkers of the 17th and 18th centuries. The phrase generally applies to the same conditions in modern as in pre-modern times. Proponents of laissez-faire believe that government controls on economic behavior—trade, competition, prices, wages—curtail the freedom of the individual, not just in his economic life, but in all aspects of life, since economics is often closely tied to social status, moral behavior, and religious beliefs. Laissez-faire philosophy has been associated with both liberal and conservative political philosophies depending on whether it is the liberal, or the conservative thinker, of a given time who puts the most emphasis on liberty in economic matters.

Early proponents of laissez-faire. The origins of the phrase are unclear except that it was apparently in use by the time Adam SMITH (1723–90) wrote *The Wealth of Nations* in 1776. Indeed, Smith became one of the early proponents of the doctrine. Previous to Smith, one finds isolated remarks by English and French observers that MERCANTILISM hampers natural liberty. Mercantilism was (and is) the doctrine where a government imposes rules on trade, particularly international trade. A famous example of mercantilism involves the control of the trade of the British-American colonies in the colonial period before 1776. The British government passed a series of Navigation Acts that curtailed the freedom by which an American producer could export his crop. As a result, farmers in the American south were forced to sell their produce to English merchants at a reduced price. Clearly such restrictions seemed to curtail economic potential and the freedom of the individual producer to exchange goods for the best price. Under mercantilism, the British were less apt to restrict domestic trade, which could reveal to any insightful observer the advantages of such liberty.

John LOCKE (1632–1704), the English philosopher of the Glorious Revolution anticipated Smith, the greatest proponent of laissez-faire economics, in his *Second Treatise of Civil Government*. Locke argued that humans, though concerned with self-interest, tend to do good, and join together into governmental or economic associations for mutual benefit, but not at the expense of natural liberty. The earth is, as it were, a public domain set aside by God for all humans to enjoy equally. The apparently endless plenty of nature allows for each person to acquire sufficient materials for his needs. Excess is against the plan of the Creator, hence immoral. Competition among humans for their share of the public domain is natural, yet not harmful, as long as there is more than enough to satisfy every person's needs. Private property, one of Locke's fundamental natural rights shared by all humans, derives from a person putting forth labor to acquire goods from the public domain. Private property is therefore not evil, rather a good, as is the competition and labor that results in its acquisition.

Another group that anticipated Smith was the group of diverse intellectuals known as the PHYSIOCRATS. During the mid-18th century the French economy was still very much beholden to the old-regime economy of aristocratic landowners and peasant laborers. The Physiocrats believed that such a dominant, almost feudal, structure limited the exchange of goods and use of capital in the French countryside. Part of the problem they identified was the extensive impositions by the French government on trade and the heavy taxes imposed on farmers. By removing restrictions and reducing taxes, that is by the government accepting a "hands off" or laissez-faire policy, exchange of goods and capital would flow more freely in FRANCE; economic liberty would be commensurate with more political liberty.

Smith observed as much, agreed with the Physiocrats that government policies should give way to the natural liberty of economic production and trade, and agreed with Locke that private property is a sanctified right as a consequence of human labor, and that competition, even for private interests, is valuable and good. Smith despised the contrast of mercantilist policies with free trade. Smith believed that human self-interest is not a barrier to altruism because humans use reason to temper their acquisitiveness. This rational self-interest meant that economic competition would occur according to natural laws of human behavior instructed by reason. There was no justification, therefore, for government to impose restrictions on economic behavior. Such restrictions would be necessary only if humans irrationally engaged in destructive competitive behavior, which was clearly not true to the Enlightenment-mind of Adam Smith.

Smith is usually identified as a proponent of economic LIBERALISM, because he combined his optimistic view of economic competition and restrained self-interest with the liberal assumptions of man's inherent goodness and collective goal to work for the interests of the common good. Unlike modern liberals, Smith believed that economic behavior did not require government intervention to achieve the maximum good for society. Goodness could not be imposed, but rather would be a natural consequence of human behavior.

American laissez-faire. The 18th-century American counterpart to Locke, the Physiocrats, and Smith was Thomas JEFFERSON (1743–1826). Jefferson was the epitome of the Renaissance man, talented in architecture, music, philosophy, government, history, literature, and economics. He was one of the most complex men of his time, being simultaneously one of the great liberal thinkers of all time yet a slave owner, a proponent of laissez-faire economics yet the president who pushed for the trade embargo of 1808, a believer in limited government yet one of the architects of the UNITED STATES. Jefferson epitomized 18th-century economic liberalism in his advocacy of limited government-involvement in economic affairs, his ideas of free trade among all nations, his opposition to protectionism and tariffs, and his support of the agricultural way of life.

To Jefferson, as he wrote in his *Notes on the State of Virginia* (1784), the farmer is the most virtuous of humans because of the inherent liberty of the farming way of life. The farmer pursues self-interest but not at the expense of the common good. The farmer is the best republican because he votes his mind and believes that what is good for him is good for the whole. Jefferson feared the INDUSTRIAL REVOLUTION because he feared a nation of entrenched urban wage-earners who could not exercise their natural liberty in economic matters, and who would become aggressively self-interested without a thought for the common good because of the intense competition waged for limited resources.

Jefferson's powerful ideas came to be adopted by many 19th-century liberals in America. Jeffersonianism became synonymous with laissez-faire liberalism. It must be said, however, that the Jeffersonian philosophy was altered over the course of the 19th century.

Interpretations of laissez-faire. The aggressive competition and exploitation consequent upon the Industrial Revolution in Europe and America resulted in a host of philosophies that contradicted classic economic liberalism. Karl MARX (1818–83), for example, reacted to the perceived class competition between the proletariat and bourgeoisie by advocating (in the *Communist Manifesto*, co-written with Friedrich ENGELS in 1848) the abolition of the free market and the embracing of government controls over the economy. At the opposite spectrum, English and American philosophers reacted to Darwin's theories of natural selection and survival of the fittest by developing a theory to explain human competition. Social Darwinism advocated the notions of the free market and the common good built upon the victory of the strongest and fittest over the weakest. Some Social Darwinists, such as Andrew CARNEGIE, tempered these ideas by arguing that the strongest, hence wealthiest, should eventually give back to the community by means of philanthropic behavior.

One of the strangest interpretations of laissez-faire philosophy involved the Populists of the 1890s. The Populists were a political party made up of farmers of the American South and Midwest. Suffering from the exploitation of railroad monopolies that set high prices for transporting farm produce, the Populists advocated government intervention to establish a society and economy consistent with Jeffersonian principles and economic liberalism. In other words, the Populists believed that economic self-interest among farmers resulted in activities for the common good, but corrupt industrialists, monopolists, and politicians were thwarting traditional American economic liberalism. The situation could be remedied only by involvement of the federal government in the economy by means of government ownership of railroads and other utilities, a rejection of the monetary GOLD STANDARD, and the adoption of a national income TAX.

The Populist political program only succeeded with the rise to political power and socio-economic influence of the Progressives. The Progressives possessed the heritage of American economic liberalism but at the same time realized and wanted to address the varied problems brought about by the Industrial Revolution. It was under the influence of the Progressives that the first two decades of the 20th century in America witnessed the onset of the income tax, legislation putting restrictions on business practices and monopolies, a constitutional amendment to make United States senators more directly answerable to the people, the creation of the FEDERAL RESERVE, and the achievement of women's suffrage.

Similar occurrences marked English politics of the 19th and early 20th centuries. Jeremy BENTHAM (1748–1832) and John Stuart MILL (1806–73), the two most important English utilitarian philosophers, mitigated the classical laissez-faire theory of Smith to take account of industrialization and its negative consequences. The utilitarians believed that private interest working for the common good—the essence of laissez-faire economics—should continue to be the driving principle behind the relationship of government to the economy. But sometimes the common good demanded government intervention to aid the plight of the poor, to restrict unfair corporate practices, and the like.

Laissez-faire and politics. The ironic twist that laissez-faire took around the turn of the 19th century is best illustrated by the example of American political parties. The Republicans, formerly the Whigs and before that the Federalists, had long advocated government involvement in the economy. Alexander HAMILTON, for example, proposed the federal support of investment in the economy, the accumulation of federal debt (assuming it from the 13 states), and the promotion of manufacturing. The Whigs of the 1830s advocated the American system of federal investment in America's infrastructure. Abraham LINCOLN, and the early Republicans, promoted the interests of American corporations and sought a strong and united economic union. But industrial changes and the growing protests of wage-earners and the poor put the Republicans into a defensive posture, so that they increasingly returned to a defense of laissez-faire economic policy to prevent government restrictions on American capitalists. The hands-off policy of the American government reached a climax during the 1920s and the Republican administration of Calvin COOLIDGE.

The Democrats, on the other hand, who had long promoted the interests of the individual and the state, by 1900 demanded the tempering of laissez-faire economics with government intervention. The initial programs of the Populists and Progressives bore fruit during the 1930s with the Franklin Delano ROOSEVELT administration. The Democrat Roosevelt, who cut his political teeth on Progressive and Wilsonian politics, realized that the Great DEPRESSION symbolized the bankruptcy of laissez-faire economics.

The NEW DEAL of the 1930s followed by the Fair Deal of the 1940s and 1950s, and the New Frontier and

Great Society of the 1960s, revealed the commitment of the Democratic party to government taking over the pursuit of the common good. Twentieth-century philosophers such as John Maynard KEYNES declared that the once positive assumptions of economic liberalism had fallen short, that private interest did not somehow miraculously work for the common good, that it was up to government to temper private interest for the good of all people.

The Great Depression of the 1930s and its effects were the watershed in the history of laissez-faire economics. The Depression caused such panic and anxiety, weakened and destroyed the economies of great nations, that no Western industrial government would advocate a return to the principles of laissez-faire. Even the conservative Republicans of American politics and the Tories in the UNITED KINGDOM were forced to concede the failure of economic liberalism. Pure laissez-faire economics had come to an end, for now.

BIBLIOGRAPHY. Robert L. Heilbroner, *The Worldly Philosophers: The Lives, Times, and Ideas of the Great Economic Thinkers* (Time Incorporated, 1962); Robert B. Ekelund, Jr. and Robert F. Hebert, *A History of Economic Theory and Method* (McGraw-Hill, 1975); Thomas Jefferson, "Notes on the State of Virginia," *The Life and Selected Writings of Thomas Jefferson* (Modern Library, 1944); Richard Hofstadter, *The Age of Reform: From Bryan to FDR* (Knopf, 1981).

RUSSELL LAWSON, PH.D.
BACONE COLLEGE

land

ATTEMPTS TO EXPLAIN the dominant global economic position of modern Western civilization are many and varied. Most arguments center on the emergence of capitalism in the 19th and 20th centuries and cite Adam SMITH's *The Wealth of Nations* in 1776 as the model. The role of resources, especially land, is a key component of the model. A historical overview of the role of land and the emergence of capitalism provides insight into the complex relationship between the two.

Arguments used to explain the emergence of capitalism in the West, and not elsewhere, include technology advancement, seafaring superiority, the gunpowder revolution, the INDUSTRIAL REVOLUTION, cultural traits or belief systems, slave labor, and colonialism to name a but a few. All the arguments have some drawbacks: For example, the Chinese first invented printing and gunpowder weapons before 1000 C.E., experienced a military and industrial revolution around 1000 C.E. and

launched huge sailing expeditions with large economic impact by 1400 C.E. The rise of Japanese and other east Asian economies has been cited to refute cultural arguments, or to argue for their adaptation as the reason for success. Slave labor and colonial arguments are often argued against because of the failure of certain slave-labor colonies to become economically dominant, such as those of Latin America.

Whatever position one takes, the role of land and the emergence of capitalism it seems, is always just beneath the surface of the argument. So what role did land play historically in the rise of capitalism?

First, there was land. From the start of human history, land has been the key resource of human societies, cultures, and civilizations. Everything associated with our survival and success is also tied to the land in one way or another. Water, flora, fauna, minerals, marine resources, even air, are accessed by land. So land control, in the form of access and OWNERSHIP, is a key foundation of western civilization's rise of capitalism that is based on consumption and production of those resources.

Most early humans were nomadic as hunter-gatherers, pastoralists, or fishing folk, and accessed the land and its resources on a timely basis. Later, as farming became the norm for sedentary groups, land control moved from access to ownership and conflict between nomadic and sedentary groups became common. This conflict played an important role in the emergence of capitalism, with its need for surplus production only possible on a large scale with more sedentary practices.

During ancient history, land was often controlled by a few elites, usually associated with political and religious institutions. Peasants and slave labor were used to access product from land resources in these agrarian economies. In the medieval period, land ownership was often dispersed among lesser elites and nobility, or controlled by local institutions such as churches or peasant villages. FEUDALISM in a broad sense was prevalent around the globe and governed land ownership and access. Communal lands for the use of all became common, as a means to balance private ownership and ensure access to needed land. This concept remains in the modern world, as evidenced by one-third of all land in the United States being publicly owned (federal, state, and local).

The spread of western civilization by sea, led to colonization of new lands in the Americas, AUSTRALIA, Africa, and Asia. Eventually the seafaring, global colonial empires, with Western mercantile economies, replaced Asian empire markets for global dominance. Examples include the Portuguese, Spanish, Dutch, English, and French between 1500 and 1800.

Control of land was achieved by conquest and assimilation, as nomadic forms of land-access in parts of the Americas, Africa and Australia was replaced with land ownership. Mercantilism involved the colonies harvesting and shipping back land resources to the colonial mother countries in Europe. Elsewhere, sedentary empires were conquered and their agrarian economies transitioned to mercantilism. Examples include the Spanish conquest of the Inca and Aztec Empires in the Americas, the British and French conquest of the Mughal Empire in India, the Kingdom of the Congo in Africa, the collapse of the Ottoman Turkish Empire in Africa and Asia, and the Manchu Chinese Empire in Asia. Native-American, African, and Asian labor was used to harvest the land resources while much of the wealth and resource flowed back to Europe.

Other European groups such as the Portuguese and Dutch became known as middlemen in the mercantilism economic period. The Dutch especially, helped form a new system of economics that would become known as capitalism. Banks, mediums of exchange with set rates, stock markets, private enterprise companies, shipping of goods, and private land ownership, as well as personal freedoms all became common in this period, at least for some segments of Western civilization.

Colonial strife, competition, and rebellions eventually brought an end to mercantilism but not to land ownership and land-access issues. The American, French, and Industrial Revolutions in Western civilization all involved issues of land resources as part of the change they embodied. The Industrial Revolution in particular, relied heavily upon land resources. Production for subsistence or survival and trade wealth for a very few had been the norm. During the Industrial Revolution, the mass production of all types of products, led to a surplus of goods available for an emerging middle class. Labor was freed from the land by the mass surplus production, and more time-saving products available than ever before. Local-market, agrarian-economy barter systems tied to the land began to be replaced with banks, stock markets, and urban market stores.

The new center for civilization was no longer the land and rural villages, but the emerging urban areas with industry as the core. Most people no longer needed the land for subsistence; industry now needed the land for raw resources such as minerals and fuels. From the Industrial Revolution came surplus production, a diffusion of labor-saving products, and the shifting of humans from land ties toward industry ties. Complex financial, production, and delivery-system needs led to the development of a civilization infrastructure of unrivaled complexity in world history. Capitalism had arrived and the role of land was changed forever.

During the 20th century, land changed from a needed resource for survival to the key natural resource in surplus production of finished goods for early capitalistic societies. Land was now needed for cities to grow upon, industrial and post-industrial resources to be harvested from, and goods to be moved across. Most industrial economies of the last century saw land-based agriculture, as a share of GROSS DOMESTIC PRODUCT (GDP), drop from 60 percent or more to less than 15 percent, on average. In some extreme cases, as in Germany, agriculture accounts for as little as 1 percent of the GDP today. Correspondingly, industry share of the GDP rose exponentially to over 60 percent in some industrialized countries during the 20th century.

American land. In the UNITED STATES, the history of land ownership is representative of these mercantilist changes. Early English colonies in North America were allotted by kings as land grants to powerful or disaffected groups in England. Native-American losses of eastern seaboard territory during wars, such as the Pequot War of 1637 and King Philip's War of 1676, resulted in gains of land in the Appalachian Mountains for many English settlers. It also meant the native groups lost control of port areas where European ships exchanged goods. Now, European merchants could dictate economic terms to native groups for native products such as tobacco, fur, and timber. The growing population of the English colonies soon meant loss of production control of key native crops and resources, often completely excluding the native people from the emerging mercantilist system of the colonies.

In 1620, there were approximately 25,000 people of European descent in North America, by 1700 there were over 250,000, and by 1776 there were approximately 2 million European people mostly in the 13 English colonies, the Spanish colonies in Florida and New Mexico, and the French colonies around Québec in Canada. Tobacco plantations with first native slave labor, and later African slave labor became the major economic variable in the middle colonies such as Virginia. Cotton plantations with first native slave labor, and later African slave labor became the major economic variable in the southern colonies such as South Carolina. In both areas, production of Indian crops, including corn (maize), tomatoes, peppers, chiles, and much more also formed a key export. In the New England colonies, timber for ships and rich fishing areas became key cogs in their regional economic systems. Fur trade and fruit production in French Québec, sugar plantations in the English colonies of the Caribbean Sea, Brazilian food plantations controlled by the Portuguese, and Latin American *encomiendas* or Spanish land grants producing silver, potatoes, chiles, manioc and other food stuffs, rounded out the emerging mercantile economic system of new-world colonies. Most importantly, these European colonies were linked to other European empire possessions around the globe by seafaring.

Known as the Columbian Exchange, the exchange of products, goods, ideas, and people around the globe changed the balance of economic power from Asia to the Americas, from the western Pacific and Indian Ocean to the Atlantic Ocean. New-world chiles showed up in food from India; Andean potatoes in European diets; and liquor, Southeast Asian bananas, and rubber trees in the Amazon.

SLAVERY also became a tragic economic factor with indigenous slaves often replaced by African slaves in the Americas, after terrible disease episodes eradicated much of the native population. Elsewhere, slaves from India were imported to South Africa, China, and Indonesia. Chinese workers, effectively in near-slave status, eventually were spread across parts of the globe as well. The toll on human life is best summed up by statistics from the Americas. Up to 90 percent of the native peoples died from farm-animal diseases between 1492–1800. The pre-Columbian Americas had only turkey, llamas, and dogs to domesticate, and farm animals of the old world like cows, sheep, goat, and chickens were unknown. The diseases the farm animals spread to humans were well known and genetically adapted to in the old world but not in the new world of the Americas. To replace this lost labor, slave traders (e.g., Portuguese) and slave sellers (e.g., Dutch and English) brought over 10 million Africans to South America, 1 million to the Caribbean colonies and several hundred thousand into North America.

The Columbian Exchange. The list of exchanged flora, fauna, disease, and human lives from the Columbian Exchange is enormous. For better or for worse, the mercantile system, predecessor to capitalism, was built on the back of this exchange. It laid the groundwork for capitalism by emphasizing bullion and treasure (silver, gold, rubies, emeralds, etc.) cash crops (tea, spices, fruits, rubber, etc.) and farm animals as well as addictive products like tobacco, opium, and liquor over simple agrarian economies that had dominated the medieval period. The slave and servant based system of mercantile labor also changed labor relations and ruined local economies where slaves were from. In some cases, political power was used to manipulate the economic system so that the expanding European empires could gain control. Examples include opium trade between India and China, the flooding of African markets with mass-produced European cloth, and guns that were made inferior to European guns and traded to local groups.

The key to all of this exchange of global power and the emerging mercantile economy was land. It is what the Europeans acquired in the Americas, or New World, and what the Asian and African peoples lost control of in the Old World. On the land were the raw materials that fueled the global trade. Mercantilism

had some of the earmarks of capitalism with trade goods of high value emphasized in a global market and complex monetary systems to handle the exchange. Dutch banks and credit houses, private enterprises such as the DUTCH WEST INDIA COMPANY rounded out the capitalistic field.

However, the mercantile system of colonial land-based goods flowing back to the European countries had a flaw. Control of colonial lands far across the seas was only possible if the colonies were economically dependent on the mother countries for finished products. In a purely capitalistic sense, it was not efficient to harvest raw materials from your own colony, ship them back to Europe for production as finished goods, then have the good shipped back to you, where you then paid for the finished product. Mercantile empires attempted to control their colonies by restricting finished-good production, requiring shipping only on empire ships, and forbidding trade with unfriendly mercantile empires and colonies even if they were next door with needed products.

This was only possible by military force and control of vital necessities such as food production. In the well-documented North American case, the English mercantile empire attempted to keep the 13 colonies in North America dependent on food produced in the Caribbean Sea English colonies. Eventually the growing populations of the 13 colonies made this unfeasible; meanwhile the colonies became self-sufficient in food production, finished goods, and military forces. The AMERICAN REVOLUTION that followed helped spur economic and social changes in the mercantile system that would lead to capitalism, in part due to another revolution in the West, the Industrial Revolution of the 19th century.

A similar collapse occurred in the Spanish Empire with its Latin American colonies. The pattern has been repeated numerous times since in world history, leading to the end of mercantilist economies and opening the door for capitalism as the dominant economic system. Both types relied heavily upon land as the foundation resource.

Land capitalism. The U.S. economy is an excellent example of the rise of land capitalism. Agrarian at first, then mercantile, and finally capitalist with the importing of the Industrial Revolution from Europe, it grew fast and furious under President Thomas JEFFERSON in the early 1880s. The survey and land-grant policy of the U.S. government was used to promote the growth of the nation westward to the Mississippi River by awarding lands to settlers, albeit lands indigenous groups still occupied. These land grants allowed settlers to establish farm and homesteads. The lands were usually well watered, fertile, and forested. These land-based resources became the backbone of early agrarian economics in the

United States. Even as the nation began expanding westward after the Revolution and the War of 1812 to the Mississippi River, the Industrial Age of the nation began to emerge in the eastern seaboard.

Cities such as Boston, New York City, Philadelphia, and Charleston became urban hubs for rural cottage industries such as textiles and gun-making. The seaboard ports moved fibers, including cotton and hemp from the southern, slave-based plantation economic system to the northern textile mills near ports. Inland, the river systems of the Ohio and Mississippi moved goods from the homestead land grants out to the Gulf of Mexico at New Orleans, an international port by the 1830s.

The Great Lakes between CANADA and United States along with the St. Lawrence River moved goods east to the Atlantic Ocean through French and Huron Indian territory, that became British-controlled after the Seven Years' War (French-Indian War) of 1756–63. President Andrew JACKSON (1824–32) fueled further growth west of the Mississippi River. Huge land acquisitions were made with the annexation of Texas in 1845, the spoils from victory in the MEXICAN-AMERICAN WAR of 1848, and the acquisition of Alaska and Hawaii by the end of the 19th century. In the interior of the U.S., farms and ranches came into conflict over land use, as was the case in Australia.

Farm sizes in the United States went from 160-acre tracts granted by the federal government with the Northwest Ordinance to over 350 acres on average by the end of the 19th century. The Industrial Age of the east with its power equipment of internal-combustion engines (tractors and trains) was catching up with the agrarian economy of the west. Soon mining interests had replaced the agrarian farm and ranch conflicts in the west of the United States. The economy was now linked as three regions. The rural, agrarian, slave plantation in the south providing cotton to textile mills in the north, and the west providing raw materials from mines to the industries of the north and east. This strained economic relationship between the three regions eventually helped spawn the AMERICAN CIVIL WAR of 1861–65. The economic use of the land was a key component as witnessed by the number of business professionals who were associated with Lincoln's cabinet. The war was a case study in the industrialized, capitalistic economy of the North *vs.* the agrarian, mercantilist economy of the South. Capitalism, with its emphasis on surplus production through industry, persevered and set the U.S. economy on course toward full-scale capitalism that would spread around the globe in the 20th century.

Cattle barons, industrial farms, railroad magnates, the linkage between political power and the economy, urbanization, and civilization infrastructure of rail, road, car, skyscraper, self-powered ships, mass produc-
tion and mass consumption, and the middle class all followed in the 19th and early 20th centuries in the United States. Big business under Andrew CARNEGIE, big finance under J.P. MORGAN, and government intervention under President Theodore ROOSEVELT all signified the age. WORLD WAR I and II just added further evidence that capitalistic economies in the Industrial Age had gained control of the reigns of power globally.

The United States, JAPAN, and Great Britain all emerged from World War I as evidence of this while old agrarian-based economies like the Ottoman Turkish Empire, the Manchu Chinese Empire and the Russian Empire collapsed.

Through all of this change, land has maintained its value and importance because of its pre-eminent position as the resource for civilization and humanity. While the way capitalistic and post-industrial civilizations view land has changed from mercantile and agrarian times, the value of land as a resource inextricably tied to civilization has remained. Examples today include the stock market REITS (Real Estate Investment Trusts) that create profit by large real-estate holdings and the surplus income produced. The consistent rise of the cost of housing in the United States for the entire 20th century is another example. Land as the physical resource for civilization, tends to rise steadily in value in a capitalist system. Although this relationship may eventually change, the role of land as the stabilizer in all economic systems past and present, including capitalism, will not soon be usurped.

Until humans figure out how to manufacture land, and lots of it, land is a finite resource covering about a fourth of the planet; 60 percent of Earth's land is in poor-climate regions or poor-soil regions, lacking suitable qualities for civilization. So the remaining sectors will always be highly valued by a human population that is approaching 7 billion people.

BIBLIOGRAPHY. R. Behan, *Plundered Promise: Capitalism, Politics, and the Fate of the Federal Lands* (Island Press, 2001); C. Cipolla, *Between Two Cultures: An Introduction to Economic History* (W.W. Norton, 1992); C. Cipolla, *Before the Industrial Revolution: European Society and Economy 1000–1700* (W.W. Norton, 1994); J. Diamond, *Guns, Germs, and Steel* (W.W. Norton, 1999); D. Landes, *The Wealth and Poverty of Nations* (W.W. Norton, 1999); P. McMichael, *Settlers and the Agrarian Question: Capitalism in Colonial Australia* (Cambridge University Press, 1984); J. Martin, *Feudalism to Capitalism: Peasant and Landlord in English Agrarian Development* (Prometheus Books, 1983); S. Plotkin, *Keep Out: The Struggle for Land Use Control* (University of California Press, 1987).

CHRIS HOWELL
RED ROCKS COLLEGE

Latvia

THE REPUBLIC OF LATVIA has a population of 2.42 million, and is located on the Baltic Sea and bordered by ESTONIA, RUSSIA, Belarus, and LITHUANIA. With a rich and long history of changing governments and populations, Latvia currently has a parliamentary democracy centralized in Riga, the capital. Comprised of 26 counties and seven municipalities, the country gained its independence from the Soviet Union on August 21, 1991.

Latvia's GROSS DOMESTIC PRODUCT (GDP) in 2001 was $18.6 billion and its major capitalistic industries are buses, vans, street and railroad cars, synthetic fibers, agricultural machinery, fertilizers, washing machines, radios, electronics, pharmaceuticals, processed foods, and textiles.

Latvia is poised to join the EUROPEAN UNION (EU) in 2004. The country has been and continues to be a major trade route between what are now western Europe and Russia. Latvia's major trading partners are Russia, GERMANY, the UNITED KINGDOM, SWEDEN, and Finland.

Latvia is expected to enter into the ranks of the North Atlantic Treaty Organization in 2004. Although NATO is primarily a military and political organization, countries that join usually experience an economic boost and a greater sense of "well being." Small countries, such as Latvia, are vulnerable to world markets and global military movements. However, when Latvia is formally introduced into NATO, it will become part of a larger whole that includes such partners as the United Kingdom, France, Spain, Germany, Turkey, the United States, Greece, Denmark, and Canada. With these strong military and trading partners in place, the Latvian economy is expected to steadily rise in the coming decades.

BIBLIOGRAPHY. Central Intelligence Agency, *CIA World Factbook* (2002); *Destination Latvia* (Lonely Planet World Guides, 2002); Embassy of Latvia, www.latvia-usa.org.

ARTHUR HOLST, PH.D.
WIDENER UNIVERSITY

Lenin, Vladimir (1870–1924)

VLADIMIR ILYICH ULYANOV, WHOM HISTORY would later baptize Lenin, was the second son of a school inspector, Ilya Nikolaevich Ulyanov. When Lenin was born, RUSSIA was a country with only two major cities, St. Petersburg and Moscow, hardly any industry, and only a small middle class. Under the Tsarist regime, there were no elections, no freedom of press, right of assembly or right to strike, much of which had been already won by this time in western Europe. The Ulyanov family lived in Simbirsk, a small town on the banks of the river Volga. The area was not without a revolutionary history: Simbirsk was witness to an enormous peasant revolt a century earlier ending in the public execution of its leader Pugachev in Moscow. Lenin's childhood, compared to the past of the town and his own future, was comfortable and relatively uneventful.

In 1887, a 17-year-old Lenin first came face to face with the realities of the Tsarist autocracy. His elder brother Alexander was arrested and hung for his part in a plot to assassinate the Tsar, Alexander III. Lenin never let it be known in later life what his reactions were to his brother's death, but there seems no doubt that the incident left its mark.

At the end of June 1887, the Ulyanov family moved to Kazan where Lenin started to study law at the university. This undertaking, however, was cut short, as he took part in a student demonstration and was expelled from the university and the city for his efforts. Four years were to pass before the young Lenin was allowed back into a university, this time at St. Petersburg.

Lenin arrived in St. Petersburg in the autumn of 1893 and joined a Marxist study circle. At the time, the industrial working class was only just beginning to form and organize in St. Petersburg. Large textile mills and engineering factories were being built and, throughout the 1890s, Russian industry began to develop rapidly.

It was with these factory workers in the Russian capital that Lenin, in the period 1893–95, gained his first political experience. He began a study circle, wrote leaflets, and distributed them outside the factory gates. Workers joining these circles (*kruzhki*) showed an insatiable thirst for knowledge. A leading Marxist of the time Plekhanov, described the sort of worker who came to such groups:

> After working at the factory 10 to 11 hours a day, and returning home only in the evening, he would sit at his books until one o'clock at night. . . . I was struck by the variety and abundance of the theoretical questions which concerned him. . . . Political economy, chemistry, social questions, and the theory of Darwin all occupied his attention. . . .

Lenin adapted himself to the needs of industrial agitation. Krupskaya, his wife-to-be, recounted in her memoirs how many of the intellectual Marxists of the time "badly understood the workers" and Lenin would read them "a kind of lecture." Lenin did not shrink from the more difficult tasks of education, instead he read Karl MARX's *Capital* with the workers in the study circle. He also published a number of pamphlets on strikes, factory acts, fines, and industrial courts that related theory to practice and Marxist ideas to worker conditions.

At the end of 1895, the Tsarist police caught up with Lenin and after a year in prison he was sentenced to three years' exile in Siberia, the barren far east of Russia where political militants were sent. Krupskaya soon received a similar sentence, and while they were both in Siberia they got married.

Upon his release, Lenin decided to leave Russia. He had joined the Russian Social Democratic Workers' Party, and he saw his principal task as writing and producing the Party's paper, *Iskra* (Spark). This was an impossible task within Russia so Lenin and Krupskaya lived in Munich, then London and Geneva, indeed anywhere, where the police would leave them to work uninterrupted.

In 1903, at the second congress of the infant Social Democratic Party, the party split into two sections: the Bolsheviks, meaning the majority, and the Mensheviks or the minority. This historic split contained seeds of several arguments that, in later years, were to distinguish both Lenin as an individual and the Bolsheviks as an organization. Lenin's idea of the new party was of a tightly knit organization whose members were subject to its discipline. The Mensheviks were happy with a looser structure. It is perhaps worth mentioning that Lenin insisted, as far as conditions allowed, on tolerance for opposition and political discussion within the Bolshevik Party.

Both the Bolshevik and Menshevik idea for a revolutionary organization was to be put to a real historical test very shortly. In January 1905, a peaceful procession of workers bearing a petition signed by thousands marched through the capital toward the Tsar's residence, the Winter Palace. The petition demanded an eight-hour working day, the recognition of workers' rights, and a constitution. The Tsar ordered his troops to shoot at the demonstration, and the incident became known as Bloody Sunday. It sparked off a revolution. There were general strikes in St. Petersburg and Moscow and many sailors in the Russian Navy came over to the side of the revolution. The army, however, remained loyal and Tsar Nicholas II, having at first made concessions, brutally crushed the movement killing over 15,000 people and imprisoning 79,000 others.

The Bolsheviks had been unable to have any decisive influence on the events of 1905. Lenin had to flee for his life pursued by the secret police. The most outstanding occurrence of the revolution was the emergence of the soviets, or workers' councils. The first of these were set up by ordinary workers in St. Petersburg at the height of the revolution. It was a new and unique expression of working-class governance linking the production process from the shop floor to the highest level of decision-making in the state by transparent democratic methods of election and recall.

The aftermath of the failed revolution of 1905 was perhaps the most difficult period in Lenin's life. Party membership dropped and it became difficult to keep any organization going. Even so, Lenin continued to work, from Geneva and Paris, trying to hold a movement together.

The period 1911–14 saw a great revival of militancy in Russia and a corresponding growth in the Bolshevik Party. Trade Unions grew rapidly as did Bolshevik influence in them. By the outbreak of the WORLD WAR I, the Russian labor movement was stronger than ever.

The Russian rulers entered the war with hopes of being able to stave off revolution at home by victory abroad. By 1917, these hopes had been dashed. Lenin, unlike the vast majority of European socialists, had been a strident opponent of the war. He took the initiative to unite socialists who held similar antiwar views, and in so doing emerged as a leader of international significance. Even so, he was no prophet, and could certainly not foresee how dramatically Russia was to change. In February 1917, in a speech to a Swiss audience, he said, "We the old shall not live to see the revolution." Two weeks later the RUSSIAN REVOLUTION broke out. The army this time supported the workers' riots in St. Petersburg and the Tsar fell from power.

At the age of 47, Lenin was faced with the decisive months of his life. Everything he had done up to this point had been in preparation for the situation that now faced him. In Russia, a bourgeois government had been established with the support of all the left-wing parties. But side by side with this government, and disputing its authority were the soviets that had sprung up all over Russia. It was a situation of "dual power."

Lenin managed to get back to Russia in April 1917, and in his famous April Thesis declared that the Bolsheviks did not recognize the middle-class government and that the way was open for the workers to seize power. He stressed that a proletarian revolution could be achieved, provided the peasantry supported them and the Russian Revolution set off similar revolutions in western Europe. Lenin's two most influential slogans: "all power to the soviets" and "bread, peace, and land" summed up the revolutionary situation in terms of both its theoretical orientation and tactical moves.

By September 1917, the Bolsheviks had a majority in the Petrograd Soviet and popular feeling was in their favor across the country. By the beginning of October, Lenin judged the moment to be right for revolution and won a majority on the decision at the Bolshevik Central Committee. With the support of the workers and soldiers of Petrograd and the backing of the city soviet, the Bolsheviks stormed the Winter Palace and seized power. Lenin went to address the All-Russia Congress of Soviets and, to thunderous applause, leaning over the rostrum said: "Comrades, we shall now proceed to construct the socialist order."

Lenin now had less than six years before his death in which to turn his famous words into reality. Though the soviet state made a costly peace with Germany at Brest-Litovsk, it faced invasion from foreign powers intent on restoring the monarchy. The remnants of the Tsarist regime assembled the White Army to regain power. Lenin himself narrowly escaped death when a would-be assassin shot at him.

The survival of the Bolshevik Revolution through these severe counter-currents carried a very high price. Russia emerged from the civil war in chaos. Industrial production had fallen drastically and the working class had been decimated. The communists had increasingly taken on state power and the party had replaced the soviets as the decision-making body. The fear of a peasant revolt forced Lenin to introduce the New Economic Plan in 1921 by which capitalism was restored to certain sectors of the economy.

The reality contrasted sadly with the hopes that Lenin had held in 1917. His health gave way and in May 1922, he suffered a severe stroke and was partially paralyzed. Between 1922 and 1923 he wrote his last notes and articles, including his controversial will, in which he warned the party against Josef Stalin and advised them to find a new general secretary. In March 1923, Lenin suffered a final stroke and died 10 months later, at the age of 53. His place in history as the leader of the first successful socialist revolution was firmly established.

BIBLIOGRAPHY. Tony Cliff, *Lenin: Building the Party* (Pluto Press, 1975); Marcel Liebman, *Leninism Under Lenin* (Merlin Press, 1985); Alfred Rosmer, *Moscow Under Lenin* (Monthly Review Press, 1971).

TITHI BHATTACHARYA, PH.D.
PURDUE UNIVERSITY

Leontief, Wassily (1906–99)

IN 1973, WASSILY LEONTIEF won the Nobel Prize in Economics for his development of the input-output method and its application to important economic problems. The method he created analyzes how changes in one sector of the economy affect others. Since its formulation, the input-output has been considered a mainstay of economics and economic policy throughout the world. One example of his legacy includes the fact that introductory textbooks in international economics include a section on Leontief's Paradox, a result of his work that questioned the conventional wisdom of countries exporting commodities that exploit their resources.

Leontief was in St. Petersburg, Russia, where he spent his youth amid the turbulence of the aftermath of the RUSSIAN REVOLUTION. Despite riots in the streets, shouts of angry insurgents and their angry bullets and angrier posters, Leontief dreamed of a better life away from the hands of the new and austere communist government. In retrospect, his future calling seemed mandated, as his father taught economics in the city. When a mere 15 years of age, Leontief entered the University of Leningrad. At first studying philosophy and sociology he eventually switched his major to economics, receiving his degree of Learned Economist in 1925.

After being forced to leave St. Petersburg because of his anti-communist sentiments, Leontief traveled to Berlin, Germany, where he pursued his Ph.D. There, his mentors and peers began to note his individuality. The subject that Leontief chose for his thesis focused on the derivation of statistical demand-and-supply curves. This train of thought would later blossom into the formula that would earn him his Nobel award 40 years later. In his paper, Leontief concluded (as he later wrote), "that so-called partial analysis cannot provide a sufficiently broad basis for fundamental understanding of the structure and operation of economic systems."

After receiving his doctorate in 1929, Leontief planned to take the concept introduced in his thesis a step further, but for the moment accepted a position as advisor to the Ministry of Railroads in China. Throughout his 12-month tenure as a freelance economics advisor, he consulted with the Chinese government on a series of wide-ranging transportation-related projects. The relationship he helped create garnered him high respect and esteem from grateful Chinese officials.

Western counterparts were equally taking notice. Leontief, returning to Berlin, received an invitation to join the National Bureau of Economic Research in New York City. Once in the United States, a country he says he immediately loved, Leontief moved on to a staff position with the department of economics at Harvard University in 1932. Leontief would remain with the university for many years, culminating in his appointment as professor of economics in 1946.

Leontief's ambition to formulate a general-equilibrium theory capable of a universal input-output spectrum never wavered. While still with the Bureau of Economic Research in 1931, he received a long-term grant to compile the first input-output tables, using as its basis the American economy for a 10-year period, 1919–29.

In his autobiography Leontief recollects, "I began to make use of a large-scale mechanized computing machine in 1935." As well, he worked with the Mark I, the very first electronic computer.

With the publication of his *Structure of the American Economy, 1919–1929*, Leontief resumed his research to implement his main concept, a working input-output theory with real-time applications.

The model sought by Leontief would show "the extensive process by which inputs in one industry produce outputs for consumption or for input into another industry," explains *The Concise Encyclopedia of Economics*. The matrix devised by Leontief in 1941—the accomplishment for which he would win the Nobel Prize—did indeed show the effects of a change in production on the demand for inputs.

Leontief found an inclusive method of determining a real value in machine production. Thanks to his efforts, industrial nations were now able to more accurately forecast their production (output) and plan their results ahead of time. The input-output scales opened a new door for PLANNING in economics.

Leontief was a man of simple tastes and his thirst for his work never interfered with a private life he cherished. In 1932, he married poetess Estelle Marcks, and had a daughter, Svetlana (now a professor of history). Away from his academic life, Leontief's passion was fishing.

He remained with Harvard for 44 years, until 1975, then accepted the directorship of the Institute for Economic Analysis of New York University. Even after retirement in the early 1990s, he continued to teach, almost daily until his death at age 93 in February 1999.

Leontief, throughout his lifetime, was an active member of many organizations, including the American Economists' Association and the Academy of Arts and Sciences. An author of hundreds of journal articles, he also wrote several books, still consulted by economists today.

BIBLIOGRAPHY. Wassily Leontief and Faye Duchin, *The Future Impact of Automation* (Oxford University Press, 1986); Wassily Leontief, *Essays in Economics: Theories and Theorizing* (M.E. Sharpe, 1977); Wassily Leontief Autobiography, www.nobel.se; *Concise Encyclopedia of Economics*, (Liberty Fund, Inc., 2002).

JOSEPH GERINGER
SYED B. HUSSAIN, PH.D.
UNIVERSITY OF WISCONSIN, OSHKOSH

leverage

THE TERM *LEVERAGE* MEANS to measure a company's debt against its assets. It refers to a company's capital structure and is often considered synonymous with gearing. A company is able to access capital through various sources such as EQUITY, preference shares, debentures, and long-term DEBT. The two main sources of capital can be classed as debt and equity. Capital structure refers to the weight given to each of these sources as a proportion of the company's total capital. A firm is considered highly leveraged if its debt is a large proportion of its assets or total capital, because the use of debt capital acts as a lever of sorts that allows the equity capital to access more than its weight in assets.

There is a significant debate about the existence of an ideal division of capital between debt and equity, such that a company has the lowest possible cost of capital. The Modigliani-Miller Theorem plays a significant role in this discussion. According to Franco MODIGLIANI and Merton H. MILLER, a company's leverage decision is irrelevant to its cost of capital. This argument can be illustrated with the example of Company X, whose capital is composed entirely of equity, and Company Y whose capital is evenly dividend between debt and equity. Company Y pays Z percent annual interest on its debt capital. In this example, Company X and Company Y generate the same net operating income (or profit) each year of $1000. If an individual buys 5 percent of the equity capital in Company X, his annual return will equal 5 percent * $1000 = $50. If an individual buys 5 percent of the equity capital and 5 percent of the debt capital (DC) of Company Y, his annual return will equal 5 percent * ($1000 – Z percent * DC) + 5 percent * (Z percent * DC) = $50. The return on each investment is equal. Miller once used a simpler example: if you cut a pizza into 4 slices you have the same amount of pizza as if you cut it into 8 slices or left it whole.

The Modigliani-Miller Theorem relies on several assumptions, and ignores several factors, that have subsequently caused its conclusions to be challenged. The most frequently discussed of these factors are the consequences of corporate taxation and the costs of bankruptcy or financial distress. In the case of corporate taxation, it is argued that interest deductibility can motivate leverage decisions that favor greater levels of debt rather than equity capital. On its own, this argument would suggest that the optimal capital structure would consist entirely of debt financing. However, it is noted that the advent of corporate taxation did not cause an increase in corporate-debt financing. In fact, the level of corporate long-term debt as a proportion of total capital remained the same after WORLD WAR II as it was in the first decade of the 20th century, prior to the introduction of corporate taxation. Moreover, this conclusion ignores the greater risks inherent in debt versus equity financing. These risks are best exemplified by the costs of bankruptcy or financial distress. In countries where these costs are not as high, such as JAPAN, corporate leverage is often observably higher.

Other discussions of corporate leverage take into account individual investors and the motivations behind their investment decisions. Some scholars maintain that it is necessary to consider the effects of personal taxation on investors' holdings. This theory claims that individual investment decisions are determined by the net income generated post everything, including personal taxes on equity income, capital gains, and debt income. For example, in its simplest form, the individual's return on debt will equal 1 less the personal tax on debt income. The individual's return on equity will equal 1 less the personal tax on equity income * 1 less the corporate tax (this takes into account a firm's opportunity cost in choosing equity financing versus deductible-debt financing). Therefore, in an environment where heterogeneous tax rates exist, there is not necessarily an advantage for investors in higher corporate leverage. Separately, it is argued that individual investment decisions can be motivated by factors other than returns, in particular diversification and risk.

In 1974, Joseph STIGLITZ wrote a proof for the Modigliani-Miller theorem. His proof requires three major limitations: no bankruptcy, personal borrowing must be a perfect substitute for corporate borrowing, and differing capital structure or leverage decisions must not affect individual investors' expectations of futures earnings or prices. This last assumption, that investors must believe that a firm's future profit is not related to or determined by a firm's financial structure, has subsequently been challenged. The existence of asymmetric information is acknowledged (the likelihood and magnitude of the firm's future profit or loss is not common knowledge, but is known by the firm's management). However, it is argued that investors can take corporate-leverage decisions as an indication of the managements' expectation of future returns. A management of a company is more likely to choose higher leverage if their expectations of future returns are high.

Leverage can refer not only to capital structure, but also to the characteristics of certain financial instruments such as options, futures, and forwards. Options, futures, and forwards are securities that allow an investor to buy or sell something at a specified future date and price. In the case of futures and forwards, this purchase or sale is unconditional, while for options it is conditional (or optional). As a consequence, futures and forwards may have negative values, while options may not. These instruments provide the investor with leveraged exposure to the underlying instrument. Because the initial investment of capital is small, the absolute return on the investment is magnified as a proportion of invested capital.

In 1973, the Chicago Board of Exchange (CBOE) established the first organized options market for options on single stocks. The initial success of this market eventually caused the expansion of option underlyings to fixed income securities, commodities, stock indices and currencies. These instruments and all their variations are more broadly called DERIVATIVES, and they are a specialized but increasing proportion of financial market trading. Derivatives are not the only way for investors to achieve leveraged exposure to financial markets. The ability to trade on margin also provides a similar magnification of risk and return.

These instruments and their consequences meet with a mixed reaction within the financial community. Their proponents argue that they allow investors to better meet their risk-return preferences, generate greater investment into information gathering and financial analysis, and therefore create more efficient asset pricing and more liquid financial markets. However, their detractors argue that they often contribute to financial market instability by creating speculative bubbles, and are not backed by sufficient capital to prevent solvency problems during market instability or corrections.

Although options are still a relatively small proportion of financial markets, option-pricing theory is more generally applicable to financial and economic theory. In the simplest example, shares in a company that are partially financed by debt have a payoff structure similar to a call option. Moreover, it is possible to value different elements of a company's capital structure (leveraged equity or various permutations of corporate debt) using option-pricing theory. In this way it is possible to see the connection between leverage in its different forms: financial instruments and capital structure.

BIBLIOGRAPHY. A.J. Auerbach and M.A. King, "Taxation, Portfolio Choice and Debt-equity Ratios: A General Equilibrium Model," *Quarterly Journal of Economics* (v.98/4, 1983); A.J. Auerbach, "Real Determinants of Corporate Leverage," *Corporate Capital Structures in the United States* (University of Chicago Press, 1985); F. Black and M. Scholes, "The Pricing of Options and Corporate Liabilities," *Journal of Political Economy* (v.81, 1873); M.H. Miller, "Debt and Taxes," *Journal of Finance* (v.32/2, 1977); David W. Pearce, ed., *The MIT Dictionary of Modern Economics* (MIT Press, 1996); F. Modigliani and M.H. Miller, "The Cost of Capital, Corporation Finance, and the Theory of Investment," *American Economic Review* (v.48, 1958); J.E. Stiglitz, "On the Irrelevance of Corporate Finance Policy," *American Economic Review* (v.64, 1974).

KIRSTIN HILL
MERRILL LYNCH & COMPANY

Lewis, Sir Arthur (1915–91)

MUCH OF THE RESEARCH of Sir Arthur Lewis focused on the economics of development, clearly a major concern to a majority of the world's population. The central question is why some countries are successful at initiating, and then sustaining, rising productivity and living standards whereas other countries are caught in a vicious cycle of poverty from which no sustained progress is made. Yet until the 1950s, the economics of underdevelopment was an intellectual backwater within the discipline of economics. For his pioneering work that did much to rectify this situation, Lewis was awarded, along with Theodore SCHULTZ of the University of Chicago, the Nobel Prize in Economics in 1979.

Such an auspicious scholarly achievement is not usually expected of one from such humble origins. Lewis was born on the island of St. Lucia, British West Indies, to parents of very modest means, both of whom were schoolteachers. He was further disadvantaged because his father died when he was seven years old, leaving a widow to care for five children. A disciplined and brilliant student, Lewis completed high school at 14 and began work as a clerk in the civil service. From there, he succeeded in winning a scholarship to the London School of Economics, taking a first class honors degree in 1937. His scholarly promise was quickly recognized at the London School and he was awarded a scholarship to study

Sir Arthur Lewis' work focused on improving economic theories relating to growth in underdeveloped countries.

for a Ph.D., completing the degree in 1940. From 1938 to 1947, Lewis was a lecturer at the London School and quickly made his way up the academic ladder. In 1948, at age 33, he was made a full professor at the University of Manchester. In 1959, Lewis accepted a position as principal of University College of the West Indies. In 1963, he accepted a professorship at Princeton University, remaining there until his retirement in 1983.

Lewis was awarded the Nobel Prize in recognition for his leading role in improving economic theory relating to underdeveloped economies. Specifically, in articles and his classic book *The Theory of Economic Growth* (1955), he developed two relatively simple, but highly innovative theories that offer significant insights into the workings of Third World economies. The first is Lewis's theory that seeks to elucidate the process by which underdeveloped, essentially subsistence agricultural economies, are transformed to more modern urban economies with substantial production and employment in the manufacturing and service sectors. In large measure, Lewis employs a neoclassical theoretical framework but makes an important departure in one respect. Unlike standard neoclassical models where rising LABOR productivity leads to proportionate increases in wages, Lewis sets forth a model in which, at least for a long period, the close link between rising labor productivity and wages is broken. According to Lewis, poor economies should be seen as having a distinctly dual nature, a small but relatively high productivity industrial sector in conjunction with a large, overpopulated subsistence agricultural sector characterized by zero marginal labor productivity. In other words, agricultural labor is assumed to be in surplus since workers can be withdrawn effectively with no decrease in output. Based on this assumption, underdeveloped economies are characterized by an "unlimited supply of labor" that is available to flow into the industrial sector at a constant wage linked to the low productivity existing in the backward agricultural sector.

The essence of development in this context is that the unlimited supply of cheap labor to the industrial sector allows high profits to be reaped in the industrial sector. High profits, in turn, are assumed to finance increasing industrial investments, leading to rising production and employment growth in the industrial sector over time.

Lewis also saw a dual nature to the world economy and the trading relations between rich and poor countries. In his view, a strong tendency exists for international trade to favor rich countries. Again, Lewis uses the assumption of unlimited supply of agricultural labor to model the determinants of the terms of trade—the ratio of a country's average export price to its average import price—between the rich industrial countries and the poor, subsistence economies. The surplus labor assumption gives rise to a model where the terms of trade between a rich and a poor country depend upon the relative productivity of agriculture in the rich versus the poor country. In essence, the unlimited supply of labor in many Third World economies results in cheap agricultural prices for their exports on the world market, and deteriorating terms of trade over time.

Lewis' theoretical research was motivated by his intense interest in improving the economic policies implemented in Third World economies. In particular, his research made him strongly critical of the kind of agricultural policies pursued in most of the Third World. He was critical of the failure by policymakers to recognize the importance of economic incentives and entrepreneurship in agriculture, even in the poorest, most distressed economies.

BIBLIOGRAPHY. Sir Arthur Lewis, *Autobiography* (1979); Robert Lalljie, *Sir Arthur Lewis: A Biographical Profile* (1996); W. Arthur Lewis, *The Theory of Economic Growth* (1955), *Development Planning* (Unwin Hyman, 1966), *Tropical Development 1880–1913* (Northwestern University Press, 1971), "Economic Development with Unlimited Supplies of Labour," Manchester School (v.22, 1954).

THOMAS S. NESSLEIN
UNIVERSITY OF WISCONSIN, GREEN BAY

liberalism

GENERALLY SPEAKING, liberalism refers to a system of thought that focuses on the good of the whole of society as opposed to its neglect in the service of the restricted few. Liberalism began at a time of rejection of traditional feudal values, structures, and institutions; the opposition to hierarchical forms of government; and the attack on aristocratic privilege. Liberals have supported modernizing change as leading to increased freedoms for the individual, the establishment of democratic governments worldwide, and the development of the idea of government as a guide and protector of human happiness.

Liberalism's first great apostle was the English philosopher John LOCKE (1632–1704). Conflict, crisis, and civil war dominated the political history of England during the 17th century. In 1660, after more than a decade of exile, Charles Stuart was restored to power in England as King Charles II. Thomas Hobbes, the English philosopher, defended the Restoration of the monarchy in England. Humans, sinful by nature, require the strong imposition of government authority, Hobbes argued. Strong central government is necessary to corral the passions of humans, to impose order upon chaos. Hobbes' vision was fulfilled during the reign of Charles

II. It was a different story for his successor James II. Parliament, representing the English people, forced James from power in what the English called the Glorious Revolution. A new king, William, agreed to limitations upon his power. Centuries of struggle by the English people had come to a conclusion in the conquest of royal oppression and the accession of law as the true ruler of England.

The Glorious Revolution. Locke was the philosopher of the Glorious Revolution of 1688. He had experienced the vast changes that England underwent during the 17th century, not only in politics but in the English economy and thought as well. The power of the landed English aristocracy was slowly waning in light of the continued expansion of manufacturing and trade. Merchants involved in rudimentary corporations employed workers intent on achieving material success. The English economy was breaking away from a landed, agrarian base toward a money economy rich in opportunity for entrepreneurs willing to take risks with capital to invest and to build. Some investors supported colonies in America and Asia; hard-working commoners traveled to such far away places to make their fortune. Political philosophers worked out the theory of MERCANTILISM to justify colonial expansion, arguing that colonies would provide raw materials and serve as markets for English goods. Capitalistic expansion and the consequent attack on the old aristocratic, feudal structures was reflected in politics. After centuries of struggle the English Parliament of the 17th century, representing the people of England, stood equal to the King.

Locke's *Second Treatise of Civil Government* provided the philosophical underpinning for the dramatic political, social, and economic changes occurring in England. Locke sought from the beginning to distance himself from the thinking of his predecessors, particularly Hobbes, who in Locke's words believed "that all government in the world is the product only of force and violence, and that men live together by no other rules but that of beasts, where the strongest carries it, and so lay a foundation for perpetual disorder and mischief, tumult, sedition, and rebellion." On the contrary, Locke argued that government is not an angry paternal authority, rather an extension of the goodness of human nature itself. Humans in the state of nature, Locke believed, are competitive but not violent toward one another. They discover soon enough that by joining together they can more successfully take what they need from nature to survive. This mutual need for greater survival, even happiness, is the basis of government.

Locke's theory of property was as follows: He believed that God the Creator endowed the world with sufficient resources to care for all humans. Locke thought that humans should use care with the creation, practice economy with the world's resources, use only what is necessary and spare the rest for another's use. Private property was one of Locke's natural rights (the others being life, liberty, and health). Since humans are inherently free and equal, the resources of creation are therefore equally available for the use of all humans. When, however, a person forages for an item of food, such as acorns, which are initially in the public domain, upon retrieving the acorns by one's own labor, the acorns become a possession of the one who retrieved them. Labor toward the accumulation of goods that are initially open to all human use is the basis of private property. The entrepreneur is the one who expends the most labor to accumulate the most goods. But Locke was adamant that one must labor to achieve only what is necessary, and nothing more.

Early American liberalism. England's Glorious Revolution, as Locke understood it, stood for freedom, equality, liberty, the open society, the good of society and of man, and a government that works for the people rather than to accentuate its own power. These were precisely what Thomas JEFFERSON, the early American philosopher, third president of the UNITED STATES, founder of the University of Virginia, and architect of the Declaration of Independence, believed about the rights of Americans living under the British government. Jefferson, and other Americans, believed that King George III and the English Parliament had, by 1776, generally rejected the principles of its own government as defined by Locke and implemented during the Glorious Revolution.

Jefferson followed Locke's thinking closely when he proclaimed: "We hold these truths to be self-evident, that all men are created equal; that they are endowed by their Creator with certain unalienable rights; that among these are life, liberty, and the pursuit of happiness. That, to secure these rights, governments are instituted among men, deriving their just powers from the consent of the governed; that, whenever any form of government becomes destructive of these ends, it is the right of the people to alter or to abolish it, and to institute a new government, laying its foundation on such principles, and organizing its powers in such form, as to them shall seem most likely to effect their safety and happiness." There is no better statement of liberal philosophy than these words of the Declaration of Independence.

Actions do not, however, always follow the precise meaning of grand words. Jefferson, for all of his great ideas, was a slave-owner throughout his life, not manumitting his slaves until his death 50 years later in 1826.

French liberalism. More striking is the example of the FRENCH REVOLUTION. French thinkers such as Jean Jacques Rousseau were inspired by Locke to press for a government and society in France based not on the privilege of birth, but on human equality. The French people broke the compact with the French monarchy in 1789, creating, in time, a government based on the principles of equality. The Declaration of the Rights of Man and Citizen, echoing Jefferson and Locke, proclaimed that "men are born and remain free and equal in rights. Social distinctions can be based only upon the common good." Freedom, unfortunately, can sometimes reduce itself to anarchy, as American and French conservatives often feared. The French Revolution degenerated into a power struggle and blood bath that had hardly anything to do with the rule of law, so dear to Jefferson and Locke.

English liberalism. Liberalism in England continued to focus on the ideas of Locke even as Great Britain fought to retain its empire. Adam SMITH, a Scottish philosopher who wrote *The Wealth of Nations* in 1776, argued that self-interest among humans resulted in healthy competition that did not need government regulation. This was in contrast to the British mercantilist system of the 16th and 17th centuries, the advocates of which believed in strict government supervision of trade.

Nineteenth-century liberals continued to voice the concerns and develop the ideas of the 18h-century Enlightenment. In England, Jeremy BENTHAM and John Stuart MILL expanded on the moral thinking of Smith, creating the philosophy of utilitarianism, which sought the greatest good for the greatest number in a society. The INDUSTRIAL REVOLUTION and new technology deriving from changing ideas of science inspired the same sense of optimism and dedication toward continued progress among 19th-century thinkers that had defined previous expressions of liberalism.

Liberal thinkers generally embraced the opportunities for social and cultural change suggested by the new philosophies of the 19th and early 20th centuries. The social and behavioral sciences became important professional fields for those who sought ways to reform social structures, institutions, and human behavior. The challenges of the Industrial Revolution—such as the increasing poverty; class disparity between bourgeosie and proletariat; and urban crowding, crime, and pollution—were treated as challenges incumbent upon the process and progress of modernization. Socialists such as Sidney and Beatrice Webb, Progressives such as Jane Addams and Woodrow WILSON, and humanists such as Bertrand Russell and John Dewey, embraced new ideas and their implications for society. Naturalism, the philosophy inspired by Charles Darwin; behaviorism, inspired by Sigmund Freud; materialism, the product of Karl Marx; relativism, the offshoot of the theories of Albert Einstein; existentialism, the vague catalog of ideas identified with Soren Kierkegaard and Friedrich Nietzsche; and the dada movement and other such nihilist philosophies, tended toward the aim of the common good, social justice, free will and freedom, a rejection of traditional ideas and assumptions, and the value of diverse, open societies.

Political liberalism. Politics and economic policies reflected the changes in modern society. In both England and America, conservative politics (signified by the Republicans in America, and the Tory party in Great Britain) gave way after the turn of the century to the liberal politics of reform—the Democrats in America and the Labor party in England. LAISSEZ-FAIRE economic policy was slowly discarded as liberal politicians, such as David Lloyd George and Ramsay McDonald in England and Woodrow Wilson and Franklin Delano ROOSEVELT in America, adopted interventionist policies wherein government would have a more direct role in economic development and bring government into the fight of the common person for good wages, good working conditions, help when ill or aged, and the general promise of a satisfying material existence.

Roosevelt's NEW DEAL, for example, began decades of social and economic reform conforming to a liberal agenda of broadened government policies and agencies to help the poor, disadvantaged, unemployed, retired, and disabled. The New Deal was in direct response to the Great DEPRESSION, which caught the Republican Herbert HOOVER administration by surprise. The Democrat Roosevelt further implemented the initial liberal policies of Wilson to fight the Depression of the 1930s. Roosevelt's consequent "alphabet soup" of acronyms for a dizzying number of social and economic programs still inspires today's liberal politician. The New Deal churned out the Banking Act, creating the Federal Deposit Insurance Corporation (FDIC) to back investor's deposits in case of bank runs and closures. Farmers were helped with the Agricultural Adjustment Act (AAA), which paid farmers to destroy crops and increase land lying fallow so to lessen agricultural supplies and raise farm prices.

The New Deal helped the unemployed with a variety of programs. The Civilian Conservation Corps (CCC) brought young men out of the urban areas into the countryside to work on conservation and forest projects in return for a bed, three square meals a day, and a little money. The Works Progress Administration (WPA) and Public Works Administration (PWA) provided government funds to employ men in public works projects, helping to build the infrastructure of America and helping the confidence of fathers and husbands who were glad once again to bring home good wages to wives and children. The Social Security Act (SSA) created the Social Security Administration (and the Social Security Number and Social Security Card) to protect America's senior citizens from ever knowing the same degree of want as had older Americans during the Great Depression.

Subsequent liberal presidents were inspired by the New Deal to continue its policies and programs. President Harry TRUMAN's Fair Deal and President John KENNEDY's New Frontier culminated in President Lyndon JOHNSON's Great Society, which brought to America the liberal vision of civil rights. These Democratic presidents were not so successful in foreign policy. Johnson's decision to escalate the war in Vietnam resulted in the dawn of the New Left, the venue for student radicals.

Today's liberal continues to embrace issues and actions that conservatives find offensive and controversial, but which to the liberal seem appropriate for people concerned with individual rights and government leadership of social and economic reform. The liberal continues to embrace modernization and its consequences, finding in relativism and secularism opportunities for continued human progress.

BIBLIOGRAPHY. Daniel Aaron, *Writers on the Left* (Avon, 1961); Ronald Berman, *America in the Sixties: An Intellectual History* (Free Press, 1968); Louis Hartz, *The Liberal Tradition in America* (Harcourt Brace Jovanovich, 1955); Robert L. Heilbroner, *The Worldly Philosophers: the Lives, Times, and Ideas of the Great Economic Thinkers* (Time Incorporated, 1962); John Locke, *Treatise of Civil Government* (Irvington Publishers, 1979).

RUSSELL LAWSON, PH.D.
BACONE COLLEGE

Liberia

LOCATED ON THE northwestern coast of Africa, Liberia is bordered by Sierra Leone and Guinea, Côte D'Ivoire, and the Atlantic Ocean to the west. The capital of Liberia is Monrovia and the official currency is the Liberian dollar, which has been exchanged equally for the U.S. dollar since 1940.

Founded in the 1800s by freed American slaves, they now make up less than 5 percent of the local population. The vast majority of Liberians are indigenous Africans who comprise a dozen different ethnic groups. Most people live in coastal cities and towns.

Liberia has an agricultural economy; minerals and forest products are its most important resources. Rich in biodiversity, Liberia was almost entirely forested until recent decades. The forest and woodlands now cover about 36 percent of the land. The country is suffering from deforestation, water pollution from mining, and soil erosion. In the late 1980s plans for conservation of land was put on hold due to a civil war.

Civil war from 1989-96 destroyed much of Liberia's economy and infrastructure in and around Monrovia.

Prior to the war, Liberia was developing its rich natural resources, however, without foreign investors the economy has slowed to a halt. Revenue has been reduced to a small amount generated by registering merchant ships. The principal port reopened in 1993 and the export of rubber and timber resumed.

Principal trade partners for export were BELGIUM and LUXEMBOURG, UKRAINE and the NETHERLANDS. Leading sources for import were SOUTH KOREA, JAPAN, and FRANCE. In 2001, Liberia had 3.2 million people and a $3.6 billion GROSS NATIONAL PRODUCT (GNP).

BIBLIOGRAPHY. Adekeye Adebajo, *Liberia's Civil War: Nigeria, Ecomog, and Regional Security in West Africa* (Lynn Rienner, 2002); J. Gus Liebenow, *Liberia: The Quest for Democracy* (Indiana University Press, 1987); Catherine Reef, *This Is Our Dark Country: The American Settlers of Liberia* (Clarion, 2002); *CIA World Factbook* (2002).

CHRIS HOWELL
RED ROCKS COLLEGE

libertarian

IN THE MODERN WORLD, political ideologies are largely defined by their attitude toward capitalism. Marxists want to overthrow it, liberals to curtail it extensively, conservatives to curtail it moderately. Those who maintain that capitalism is an excellent economic system, unfairly maligned, with little or no need for corrective government policy, are generally known as libertarians.

Libertarians hasten to add that by "capitalism" they mean LAISSEZ-FAIRE capitalism, not the status quo economic system of the UNITED STATES. Unlike conservatives, who primarily resist new forms of government intervention, libertarians advocate a massive rollback of existing intrusions into the free market, an across-the-board program of privatization and deregulation. Libertarians typically favor the abolition of Social Security, Medicare, welfare, public education, quality and safety regulation, tariffs, immigration restrictions, subsidies, antitrust laws, narcotics prohibition, pro-unions laws, and, of course, the minimum wage. The most common libertarian position is minarchism, the view that government should be limited to its "minimal" or "night watchman" functions of police, courts, criminal punishment, and national defense, but many libertarians endorse a somewhat broader role for government, and a vocal minority of "anarcho-capitalists" insist that the functions of the minimal state should be privatized as well.

An overwhelming majority of the world's voters would obviously reject such proposals out of hand. But libertarianism enjoyed sharp growth over the past 50 years, largely because it generated many knowledgeable and articulate advocates, such as Milton FRIEDMAN, Ayn RAND, Robert Nozick, Ludwig von MISES, Murray Rothbard, David Friedman, Charles Murray, Thomas Sowell, Walter Williams, and a long list of fellow travelers including Nobel laureates F.A. HAYEK, Gary BECKER, George STIGLER, and James BUCHANAN.

Much of the libertarian case for laissez-faire is rooted in standard economics. Many economists recognize that competition tends to align private greed and the public interest, given appropriate circumstances. Libertarians go further by minimizing the exceptions to this rule. Even when the number of competing firms is small, libertarians believe that new entry and potential competition provide effective discipline. Though most acknowledge the existence of externalities, libertarians argue that their magnitude and extent is overstated. They are similarly optimistic about markets' ability to function in spite of imperfect information. Even when they concede that the free market falls short, libertarians point out that government exacerbates its failings rather than solving them. For example, libertarians see great irony in the antitrust laws' effort to "increase competition," when other branches of the government are busily restricting competition with tariffs, licensing, and price supports.

Other prominent arguments point to the moral superiority of laissez-faire capitalism. Libertarians heavily emphasize the voluntary nature of the market, appealing to two related moral intuitions: First, that an individual has the right to do what he wants with his own person and his own property so long as he does not violate others' rights to do the same; second, "violation" should be interpreted narrowly as use or threat of physical force.

Libertarian ethicists also frequently appeal to merit. Those who are financially successful under laissez-faire earned what they have and deserve to keep it. While libertarians are not opposed to private charity, they believe that the worse-off are presumptuous to angrily demand "their share of the wealth." The free market already gave them their share. If they are unhappy with its size, they should figure out a way to raise their own productivity instead of complaining that the market mistreats them.

Libertarians routinely highlight the hypocrisy of government programs to "help the poor." Progressive tax systems at most transfer income from, for example, the American rich to the American poor. By world standards, though, the American poor are well-off. If helping "the poor" is the real objective, why not send welfare checks to Haiti instead of America's inner cities? Instead, U.S. immigration restrictions deliberately close off the opportunities the free market provides the Haitian poor to better their condition. A low-skill U.S. job would pay vastly more than they could ever hope to earn in Haiti. Libertarians conclude that the "hard-hearted" 19th-century policy of free immigration and minimal welfare did more for the truly poor than any government has done since.

The 20th century was marked by a great debate between social democrats who wanted to reform capitalism and socialists who sought to abolish it. The collapse of Communism and revelations of its massive inefficiency and brutality have settled this question. If the 21st century has a great debate, it will probably be between social democrats who want to "reinvent" government, and libertarians who maintain that laissez-faire is not only more efficient but also more just.

BIBLIOGRAPHY. David Boaz, *Libertarianism: A Primer* (The Free Press, 1997); David Friedman, *The Machinery of Freedom: Guide to a Radical Capitalism* (Open Court, 1989); Milton Friedman, *Capitalism and Freedom.* (University of Chicago Press, 1982); Ludwig von Mises, *Liberalism: The Classical Tradition.* (Foundation for Economic Education, 1996). Charles Murray, *What It Means to Be a Libertarian: A Personal Interpretation* (Broadway Books, 1997).

BRYAN CAPLAN, PH.D.
GEORGE MASON UNIVERSITY

Libya

LOCATED IN NORTH AFRICA on the Mediterranean Sea, Libya shares a large eastern border with EGYPT, a western border with ALGERIA, a southern border with Chad, and minor borders with Tunisia, Niger, and Sudan. With a population of 5.5 million people, most reside in north-coast cities such as the capital city of Tripoli (1.5 million) or Benghazi (750,000). Although association with terrorism brought worldwide economic sanctions against Libya in the 1990s, cooperation by leader Muammar Al-Qadafi has led to a lifting of sanctions and resurgence in the oil-based, Libyan economy since 2000.

In 2002, the Arabic speaking, Berber Muslim nation had a per capita GROSS DOMESTIC PRODUCT (GDP) of $5,000, but 30 percent unemployment and 24 percent inflation have taken their toll on the economy. Foreign debt sits at $3.8 billion but heavy investment in oil and gas projects by companies such as the Italian ENI, French TOTALFINAELF, and British Lasino are equal to that debt and promise to keep Libya fiscally sound despite its troubles in international politics.

Oil exports make up 95 percent of Libya's export wealth and 50 percent of all government revenue. Together mining and hydrocarbon extraction account for

35 percent of GDP and employ 10 percent of the workforce. Libya is the second-largest oil producer in Africa behind NIGERIA with proven oil reserves of 30 billion barrels of high quality, light crude. Agriculture is limited to only 1.2 percent of all land but accounts for 8 percent of the GDP and employs 20 percent of the workforce. The "Great-Man-Made River Project" takes water from underground in the Sahara Desert and brings it to the agriculture oases and coastal ports to support this workforce. Small industries now make up 18 percent of GDP and employ 15 percent of the workforce. A $5 billion investment in building up the tourist infrastructure is scheduled for completion in 2005. Railroads, coastal tourist resorts, and developed ancient ruins such as the Roman town of Leptis Magnus promise to increase this component of the Libyan economy. However, the negative perception of Libya in international politics, despite recent efforts at image control, are expected to limit tourism.

The Libyan economy is run ad hoc despite state control of industry, banking, and development that ranks among the best in Africa. Continued sanctions by the United States against large investment in Libyan oil still have an impact on EUROPEAN UNION (EU) countries that are Libya's largest trading partners. Since 2000, Egyptian construction contractors have been steadily replaced by European contractors, but U.S. sanctions have led to many small contracts and a slower pace of development in Libya.

BIBLIOGRAPHY. Judith Gurney, *Libya: The Political Economy of Oil* (Oxford University Press, 1996); Leslie Mackenzie, *Nations of The World* (Greyhouse Publishing, 2002); Chris Scott, *Sahara Overland* (Trailblazer, 2000).

CHRIS HOWELL
RED ROCKS COLLEGE

Liechtenstein

THE PRINCIPALITY OF Liechtenstein is a small state in central Europe, situated between AUSTRIA and SWITZERLAND. Though its geographical location and diminutive size make it a somewhat anonymous state, its independent political climate gives rise to an exemplary model for the study of political and economic phenomena.

Once a part of the Holy Roman Empire, Liechtenstein gained its sovereignty in 1806 when it was admitted as a member of the Confederation of the Rhine. It rose to the status of an independent state in 1866, and as a result, it became the master of its own fate. Its standing army was abolished in 1868, and this marked the beginning of its long-standing neutrality position within Europe's geopolitical ambit.

Upon its independence, Liechtenstein's interests abroad were maintained by Austria until the collapse of the Austro-Hungarian Empire in 1918. At this time, Liechtensteiners recognized that a break with the politically unstable Austria was imminent, and so they turned toward their neighbors to the west in Switzerland. The fiercely independent principality sustained its neutrality throughout WORLD WAR I, and shortly thereafter, it adopted the Swiss currency and entered into a customs agreement with Switzerland, and since that time, Switzerland has represented Liechtenstein in international matters.

This German-speaking principality is governed by a hereditary constitutional monarchy, and in fact, it is often referred to as a representative republic. According to its modern constitution, state power proceeds from the ruling prince and the people. With its 11 municipal areas and a population of 33,000, its constitutional neutrality proviso requires that it refrain from all foreign aggression and political alliances.

In the post-WORLD WAR II era, Liechtenstein underwent an industrialization in which it developed into one of the world's wealthiest countries. Its refusal to bow to rigorous banking regulatory oversight, while maintaining the secrecy of its financial institutions, has made Liechtenstein into a prospering financial haven along the lines of neighboring Switzerland.

Finally, its magnificent wealth creation is helped along by a lack of public debt and low tax rates. Minimal taxes are imposed on multinational corporations, making it a popular refuge for international business headquarters. In spite of the low tax rates, the government of Liechtenstein derives much revenue from its authentication as a thriving financial and business center.

BIBLIOGRAPHY. Pierre Raton, *Liechtenstein: History and Institutions of the Principality* (1970); Encyclopedia Britannica, *Almanac 2003* (2002); Central Intelligence Agency, *CIA World Factbook* (2002); BBC News, "Timeline: Liechtenstein" www.bbc.co.uk.

KAREN DE COSTER
WALSH COLLEGE

Lincoln, Abraham (1809–65)

THE 16TH PRESIDENT of the United States, Abraham Lincoln was born in rural Kentucky. His family moved to Indiana a few years later and moved again to Illinois when he was 21. Like the children of most poor frontier families, Lincoln received almost no formal education. However, he did learn to read, write, and do basic math. He became an avid reader, always looking for new books to borrow from friends and neighbors.

For much of his childhood, Lincoln worked on his family farm. When there was not much work, his father hired him out as a manual laborer to neighbors. When he was older, Lincoln ran a flatboat down the Mississippi River to New Orleans, and later worked as a store clerk. His athletic ability and storytelling made him quite popular in his community.

Lincoln enlisted in a volunteer regiment being created to fight Native Americans in 1832. He was elected captain but his unit never saw any service. After returning from the war, Lincoln ran for election to the state legislature with the Whig party but lost. He tried again two years later and won. In office, Lincoln tended to support the party line on most issues, including the Bank of the United States, high tariffs, and infrastructure improvements. He also drafted a resolution on slavery that reflected his early views: "The institution of slavery is founded on both injustice and bad policy; but that the promulgation of abolition doctrines tends rather to increase than to abate its evils." Further, "the Congress of the United States has no power, under the constitution, to interfere with the institution of slavery in the different states."

This moderate position was criticized by Abolitionists before the war and by future generations who thought any compromise with slavery was unacceptable. But while Lincoln was clearly an enemy of slavery, he recognized that Abolitionists would only force slaveowners to become more intractable and prevent any solution. Lincoln recognized, and later said while running for U.S. Senator in 1858, that "this government cannot endure permanently half slave and half free" and that "it will cease to be divided. It will become all one thing, or all the other." By preventing its expansion, Lincoln hoped to lay the foundation for a time when the antislavery forces would far outweigh the pro-slavery forces and allow for slavery's extinction.

Lawyer and congressman. While serving in the legislature, Lincoln studied law and began to practice in 1836. Because no state courts met permanently year-round, the judges and lawyers traveled together around the state trying cases. During these years Lincoln developed his oratory, logic, and his reputation for honesty. In 1843, he left his job in the legislature and practiced law full time, also remaining active in politics.

Lincoln first considered running for the U.S. Congress after the 1840 elections. There were three young Whig politicians who wanted the position. They came to an understanding that each would serve one term. When Lincoln's turn came in 1846, the incumbent decided to run for re-election. Lincoln, however, out-maneuvered him and won the nomination and election anyway.

During his one term in Congress, Lincoln voiced strong opposition to the MEXICAN-AMERICAN WAR, although he did vote for appropriations to support the soldiers in the field. While he opposed the war, he did recognize the legitimacy of Texas' earlier decision to secede from Mexico. In a speech opposing the war, he made the following statement:

> Any people anywhere, being inclined and having the power, have the right to rise up, and shake off the existing government, and form a new one that suits them better. This is a most valuable, a most sacred right—a right, which we hope and believe, is to liberate the world. Nor is this right confined to cases in which the whole people of an existing government, may choose to exercise it. Any portion of such people that can, may revolutionize, and make their own, of so much of the territory as they inhabit.

The war was popular in Lincoln's district, so his opposition hurt him politically. At the end of the war, he supported the Wilmot Proviso, which prohibited slavery in the territories ceded by Mexico. This was consistent with his longstanding view that the evils of slavery should not be allowed to expand into new territories.

In 1848, Lincoln campaigned for Zachary TAYLOR for president in hope of getting a job with his administration. However, when nothing of interest arose after the election, he returned home to resume his private practice.

Return to politics.

In 1854, Illinois Senator Stephen Douglas engineered a repeal of part of the Missouri Compromise to allow slavery in northern territories if those living in the territories supported it. Lincoln campaigned heavily against these measures and was therefore considered for the U.S. Senate that year. Senators were selected by the state legislature. The anti-slavery Whigs and anti-slavery Democrats had enough combined votes to defeat the pro-slavery candidate. While Lincoln was the favorite for the nomination, when the anti-slavery Democrats refused to support him, he had his supporters vote for the anti-slavery Democrat John Trumbull rather than let their division cause the seat to go to the pro-slavery candidate.

By 1856, it was clear that the Whig Party was dead. Lincoln joined the new Republican Party where he was briefly considered for the vice-presidential nomination. In 1858, Lincoln challenged Senator Douglas for his Senate seat. The two held a series of seven famous debates, primarily over the expansion of slavery. While Lincoln had more popular support, Douglas' support in the legislature allowed him to win re-election.

Abraham Lincoln guided the abolition of slavery through the course of the American Civil War.

The debates, however, brought Lincoln to national prominence. In February 1860, he gave a speech at the Cooper Union in New York City to meet eastern leaders of the anti-slavery movement. His speech opposing expansion of slavery was wildly popular. A few months later, he received the Republican presidential nomination.

In the general election, the Democratic Party fractured: northern Democrats favored Stephen Douglas while southern Democrats supported John Breckenridge. The Constitutional Union Party nominated John Bell. Lincoln received the electoral votes of all free states except New Jersey and no slave state votes. But that was enough for an electoral majority.

Secession and Civil War.

After his election but before he could take office, Southern states began to secede from the Union. In his inaugural address, Lincoln tried to appeal to the South to reconsider, that while he was opposed to the expansion of slavery into the territories, he would not interfere with it in the states: "I have no purpose, directly or indirectly, to interfere with the institution of slavery in the states where it exists. I believe I have no lawful right to do so, and I have no inclination to do so." He also made clear that he did not consider secession legal and that, unless it was withdrawn, civil war would be the result.

A few weeks later, Southern troops fired on federal soldiers who refused to surrender Fort Sumter in Charleston harbor. The nation was at war, the AMERICAN CIVIL WAR. Although President Lincoln had hoped to resolve the secession issue peacefully by appealing to the South, he showed no hesitation in prosecuting the war effort in both the North and the South.

Political leaders who opposed Lincoln's policies were frequently arrested and imprisoned without charges. Newspapers opposed to the war were closed by military order. For the first time income taxes were levied and a military draft was enacted to support the war effort, both considered constitutionally suspect at the time. As the war dragged on and casualties reached unprecedented numbers, he was frequently (falsely) criticized for being callous to the suffering and death caused by the war.

Since Lincoln's entire presidency was consumed by the war, it is impossible to say how his administration would have acted in peacetime. Lincoln's overriding concern throughout his presidency was keeping the Union intact, no matter the cost.

There were certain barriers he would not cross, however. Many supporters called for Lincoln to suspend the 1864 presidential elections. They feared he would lose re-election and the winner would make peace by permitting the Confederacy to secede. Despite dim prospects for re-election, Lincoln permitted the elections to proceed. The Republicans had lost heavily in the 1862 mid-term elections. For a time, it seemed he might not even receive his own party's nomination. However, by the fall of 1864, a string of Union victories convinced most that the war would soon be won, and Lincoln won all states still in the Union except for Delaware, New Jersey, and Kentucky.

The Emancipation Proclamation. Throughout the first years of the war, Northerners debated whether the war should be about slavery or simply to preserve the Union. Many Northerners either did not object to slavery or believed, as Lincoln had often said, that the federal government had no authority to do anything about it. Among these people was General George McClellan, commander of the Union Army. Four states loyal to the Union still permitted slavery. Many working-class Northerners also feared that emancipated slaves would migrate to northern cities and compete for their jobs.

For at least a year, Lincoln focused on preserving the Union and keeping slavery from becoming a war issue. When several generals proclaimed that they would free any slaves owned by rebels that fell into Union control, Lincoln quickly countermanded those orders and issued public statements that federal policy would protect slavery in those states where it was legal. The primary concern seemed to be keeping the four border states from seceding, which—with Maryland being one of them—would have left Washington, D.C., well behind enemy lines. During this same time, Lincoln advanced several proposals to pay those states to free their slaves gradually, and to be compensated for property losses as a result of emancipation. State leaders firmly rejected those proposals.

However, at least by early 1862, Lincoln was already considering forcible emancipation. He distributed a draft proclamation to his cabinet in July. Yet, he did not make the draft public based on Secretary of State William Seward's argument that because the Union had lost most of the major battles to that point, the Proclamation might be seen as an act of desperation by the losing side.

When, on September 17, 1862, the armies clashed at the battle of Antietam/Sharpsburg and the Confederacy was forced to withdraw, Lincoln used that victory to issue the Proclamation five days later. The Proclamation actually freed no slaves since it only applied to areas not under federal control. However, after the Proclamation was issued it became hard to imagine a conclusion to the war without universal emancipation.

The immediate effect of the measure was to keep the UNITED KINGDOM and FRANCE from supporting the Confederacy. Although both countries would have benefited from a weaker and more divided North American continent, strong anti-slavery sentiment in both countries prevented them from supporting the Confederacy, once the main war issue became slavery.

Some have argued that emancipation was designed to disrupt the Southern economy by encouraging slaves to flee northward. If this was a goal, it failed since slaves were unable to leave in any significant numbers. Some have also argued that it was meant to help solidify support for the war in the North. However, in some cases it had the opposite effect. Most Abolitionists already supported the war. On the other hand, emancipation upset many Northerners who supported the war, but believed the government had no authority over slavery. They saw the Proclamation as a move toward unconstitutional despotism. Indeed, the Proclamation was a factor in the draft riots in northern cities. Moreover, some of the heavy losses of the Republicans in the Congressional elections, held two months after the Proclamation was issued, may be attributed to the issuance of the Proclamation. There was also little support for the Proclamation in the west and among high-ranking democratic appointees in the officer corps of the Union Army.

The politically astute Lincoln was aware of the political consequences and acted in spite of them. By the end of the war, popular support favored Lincoln's emancipation policies and the states ratified the 13th Amendment, permanently outlawing slavery in the United States.

Plans for Reconstruction. As the war came to a close, many in the North wanted to punish the South for starting such a costly conflict. Proposals were made to confiscate all land from former slave-owners and anyone else who participated in the rebellion, to deny voting rights to former rebels, and to maintain military control of the South indefinitely. Lincoln, however, recognized that if the Union was to remain a democracy, the South had to be rebuilt and brought back into the fold as a full partner. He chose a Democrat from the Southern state of Tennessee, Andrew JOHNSON, as his vice president and sought a quick return of the former Confederate states back to their full status within the Union.

We will never know for certain the direction Lincoln's postwar policies would have taken. In particular, Lincoln's views on suffrage are somewhat in doubt. It is not known how the president, who had advocated colonization for freed slaves before the war, would have approached this issue in the wake of the war. Days after the South surrendered, Lincoln and his wife attended a play at Ford's Theater. There, an actor and Southern sympathizer named John Wilkes Booth shot the president in the head. Lincoln died later the following day, never having regained consciousness.

Johnson became president. Although he seemed to have shared some of Lincoln's views on Reconstruction, the radical Republicans in Congress were in no mood to work with a Southern Democrat. Congress overrode numerous vetoes. Military occupation of the South would remain for 12 years.

Legacy. The Civil War profoundly changed the nation. The federal government, empowered by the 14th and 15th Amendments, gained much more control over state governments. The abolition of slavery ended a major sectional rift, as well as provided a true birthright of freedom to all Americans. Although always controversial during his presidency, in death, Lincoln took on a heroic, if not a messianic status. He is consistently ranked as one of the greatest presidents in America's history.

BIBLIOGRAPHY. David Herbert Donald, *Lincoln* (Touchstone, 1995); George M. Fredrickson, "A Man but Not a Brother: Abraham Lincoln and Racial Equality," *The Journal of Southern History* (v.41/1, 1975); Ludwell H. Johnson: "Lincoln's Solution to the Problem of Peace Terms, 1864-1865," *The Journal of Southern History* (v.43/4, 1968); Mark M. Krug: "Lincoln, the Republican Party, and the Emancipation Proclamation," *The History Teacher* (v.7/1, 1973); Stephen B. Oates, *With Malice Towards None: The Life of Abraham Lincoln* (Perennial, 1994); Carl Sandburg, *Abraham Lincoln: The Prairie Years and The War Years* (Harvest Books, 2002); Abraham Lincoln, *Collected Works,* www.hti.umich.edu/l/lincoln.

MICHAEL J. TROY, J.D.
THOMAS D. JEITSCHKO, PH.D.
MICHIGAN STATE UNIVERSITY

liquor

AN ALCOHOLIC BEVERAGE that is made through the process of distillation, liquor is the strongest of alcoholic beverages. Alcoholic beverages such as beer and wine are made using the process of brewing and fermentation, and as such they are not considered liquors. However, many distilled liquors may be made from other alcoholic beverages that contain a lower alcohol content. An example of this is brandy, a liquor made from wine.

Though fermented alcoholic drinks such as wine and beer are not liquors, their history is important to understanding the development of the industry of distilled alcoholic beverages. The presence of wine can be traced back to the Neolithic period. In the northern Zagros Mountains of Iran a vessel used to contain wine has been found in a building dating to ca. 5400–5000 B.C.E. By at least the third Dynasty (ca. 2700 B.C.E.) there was a royal winemaking industry in Egypt. Wine production was controlled by the nobility and most commonly enjoyed by the ruling class and in religious ceremonies. By 1700 B.C.E., the Greeks had developed a process that made locally produced wine viable. Because the drink was now open to the common people it was used on a more regular basis. People consumed the drink at social gatherings, as an integral part of daily meals, and wine was used as a medicine to treat pain.

The cultivation of vines was introduced to the Italian peninsula most likely by Greek settlers. Wine had become the Romans' most popular beverage by the 1st century B.C.E. It was not only a favorite drink, but wine was also a staple of the Roman economy. Wine became one of Rome's most important domestic industries and was an important source of government revenue. The making and selling of wine was not a privately owned industry; the government had control over production and trade. For example, Roman emperor Domitian, fearing the overproduction of wine, enforced a program that decreased the number of vineyards, thus stabilizing Rome's wine industry.

During the early Middle Ages, only monasteries had the stability, security, and economic resources to enable the large-scale production of wine. The monks were able to improve upon the wines of old and to produce high-quality beverages. Franciscan monks were also responsible for beginning the California wine industry: The monks brought their knowledge and history of winemaking to California when they established the first missions in the 1700s.

The process of distilling alcohol was first recorded by Abul Kasim, an Arabian physician, in the 10th century. Though the process had been known for some time, it was only introduced to Europe around 1250. Distilled alcoholic beverages, or liquors, did not become popular until the 1700s. The first liquors were produced and sold in small quantities by apothecaries, monks, and physicians, mainly as medicines.

Water of life. One French professor of medicine, Arnald of Villanova, referred to distilled spirits as *aqua vitae* or water of life and encouraged the use of wine and spirits for medicinal purposes. Spirits were used as protection against the plague, as painkillers, energy boosts, and as a way to keep healthy in damp and cold environments.

Soon drinking liquor primarily for medicinal purposes faded and consuming liquor as a social pastime became common. The tavern, an institution seen as early as the ancient Greeks, re-emerged in the towns and cities of Europe. These taverns became social centers where the drinking of liquor was not only tolerated but encouraged. One of the reasons for the success of the taverns was the increased variety of liquors: brandy, gin, rum, vodka, and whiskey. In these early times, a method for testing the strength of liquor was developed. A sample of the liquor being tested was mixed with an equal amount of gunpowder. This mixture was then burned and observed. If the flame produced from the burning was steady and blue it was considered proved. This is the origin of the term proof that is used today when discussing and classifying liquor. Later, more advanced tests were used to prove that liquor is made up of about 50 percent alcohol, which is considered 100 proof.

Different types of liquors are achieved by distilling other organic materials. Brandy, one of the first liquors to be developed, is produced by the distillation of grape wine and is then matured by aging in wooden casks. Gin is distilled from grain and gains its flavor predominantly from the addition of juniper berries to the distillation process. Rum is made by distilling various fermented cane sugar products, the most common being molasses or sugar combined with water. Vodka is usually distilled from a wheat mash. Whiskey, whose name is derived from terms meaning "water of life," is distilled from the fermented mash of cereal grains.

As time progressed new advances in technology allowed liquors to be produced in mass quantities. Because liquor could now be made in such large quantities and fairly cheaply it could be sold to a large market of people. The drinking of liquor became excessively popular and formed a large market, a market ripe for capitalist producers. With the growth of the liquor industry came profits, and with these profits came taxes from governments who wished to control the growing problems associated with the overindulgence of alcohol, and to have a part in the money being made.

Liquor and taxes. In 1736, England's government passed the Gin Act, making the favored liquor prohibitively expensive. There was a high duty placed on gin per gallon, and the government raised the cost of a spirit license. Many opposed the act, including some people in high government positions who feared the act could not be enforced against the will of the common people. This fear was accurate. The Gin Act of 1736 led to riots and the gin trade went underground. Within the six years that the act was in place, only two gin licenses were sold, yet production of gin increased 50 percent. As a result of the widespread and open breaking of the law, in 1743 the government loosened the restrictions.

In 1791 the UNITED STATES government placed an extremely high tax on all whiskey sold in the country. This angered many private-farm owners, because whiskey was a commodity produced and sold by the citizens themselves, and accounted for much of their profits. By 1794, the resistance had reached such a point that the national government chose to get involved. President George WASHINGTON ordered a militia to be formed and was able to put down the rebellion. This was the first time that a militia was called into federal service, and the incident entered the history books as the Whiskey Rebellion.

As time progressed and the consumption of alcohol increased, worries began to develop surrounding the morals of drinking alcohol. In the United States by the 1820s, each person was drinking, on average, seven gallons of pure alcohol per year. A growing group of religious and political leaders were coming to see drunkenness as a national curse. Many states passed laws to restrict the consumption of alcohol but during the AMERICAN CIVIL WAR, from 1861 to 1865, many of these laws were repealed or ignored. When the Civil War ended there were more than 100,000 saloons in the country. Because there was so much competition in the saloon business entrepreneurs began to offer other services as well. To lure customers, saloons began to offer gambling and prostitution along with alcohol, feeding an increase in public unruliness and violence.

American Prohibition. By the early 1900s, millions of U.S. citizens shared a hostility toward saloons and came to think of the consumption of liquor as a threat to society. The Anti-Saloon League of America (ASL) was formed in Ohio and was able to lead such people into political action, helping to back congressional members who supported Prohibition. By 1917, members of Congress who supported Prohibition outnumbered those who opposed it by more than two-to-one. Using this majority, supporters of Prohibition pushed for an amendment to the Constitution that would ban the production and sale of liquor except for religious ceremonies and medicinal purposes. In January 1919, the 18th Amendment to the Constitution was ratified prohibiting the manufacture and sale of intoxicating beverages in the United States.

America was not the only country to try to repress the sale of liquor. Most Protestant nations had come to view the drinking of alcohol as a social sin, and the British government passed laws that made it illegal to sell alcoholic drinks except during a few early-evening hours. The citizens of towns and villages in Scotland had the option to vote out drinking establishments. In SWEDEN, the movement against liquor had been strong since the 1830s. The government was astute in realizing one of the problems with the abundance of liquor was that there was such a high profit in it for the private producers. In 1922, Sweden took care of this motivation to sell liquor by nationalizing the production and sale of it. Sweden then went a step further by restricting sales of liquor to one liter per family per week. CANADA also had several laws passed restricting the use of alcohol.

There were many unintended side effects of Prohibition in the United States. A new UNDERGROUND ECONOMY was created and tremendous profits were made by smuggling and selling liquor. Bootlegging, the practice of illegally transporting or selling intoxicating liquors, became a profitable business: Prohibition laws made the supply of liquor decrease and yet the demand still remained. Because there was no equilibrium between supply and demand, high prices could be charged. Speakeasies, places where people gathered to imbibe the illegal beverages, began to pop up throughout the nation. Entrepreneurial salesmen started to sell garter flasks, hollow heels and books where illegal liquor could be hidden.

Liquor produced in Canada could be snuck in to the United States fairly easily. Canada had repealed its laws against liquor before Prohibition was enacted in the United States. A major reason for this was economic pressures: Canada recognized the abundance of economic opportunities stemming from selling liquor to the "dry" United States.

Many people, including those who had previously been law-abiding citizens, took up home-brewing to make a profit. As in the case of Britain's Gin Act of 1736, officials learned that it was impossible to fully enforce laws that went against the will of the common people.

Another side effect of Prohibition in the United States was the emergence of organized crime. GANGSTERS such as Al Capone took advantage of the market created

by Prohibition to make vast fortunes. Many gangsters cornered the market on bootlegged liquor and the facilities that served it before branching out into prostitution, drugs, and racketeering.

Finally, by the late 1920s most citizens of the United States realized Prohibition was not working and, in fact, was probably causing more harm than good. Many other countries that had laws restricting liquor production had lessened the restrictions and repealed some of their laws. In the early years of the Great DEPRESSION, an economic, rather than moral argument was brought to bear: It was argued that Prohibition limited the number of jobs to be had, and decreased the amount of revenue the government and individuals could be collecting. Prohibition came to be seen as a contributor to economic stagnation. Other arguments against Prohibition stressed that the government was encroaching on the tradition of individual freedom, a cornerstone of the American capitalist economic system.

The 21st Amendment to the Constitution, proposed in February 1933, gave control of the liquor traffic back to the individual states. By December, a majority of the states had ratified the Amendment and it became part of the Constitution. Prohibition had come to an end.

Prohibition and capitalism. Though Prohibition in the United States was a failure it did have some unplanned positive results to many capitalist ventures. The Seagram Company, Ltd., is one capitalist company, as an example, that owes some of its success from profits made during Prohibition. Today, Seagram is the leading manufacturer and distributor of distilled liquor and fruit drinks. The company sells more than $2 billion worth of liquor each year and it has 600 brands marketed in more than 175 countries.

The Seagram Company's origins can be traced back to two separate Canadian liquor companies. One company was owned by Joseph Emm Seagram who, in 1883, purchased a distillery in Waterloo, Ontario. His company was named Joseph E. Seagram & Sons and, by 1900, was one of the leading whiskey distillers in Canada. In Montreal, another capitalist had begun his career in the beverage industry. Samuel Bronfman purchased the Bonaventure Liquor Store Co. in 1916. Bronfman and his brother joined together to form Distillers Corporation Limited in 1924. This move allowed them to operate their own distillery. The Bronfman brothers benefited greatly by Prohibition in the United States during the 1920s: They were able to smuggle a great amount of liquor and earn large profits. Only in 1934, after Prohibition ended, were members of the Bronfman family caught by Canadian officials for smuggling, but even then, they were not convicted.

In 1928, the Bronfman's Distillers Corporation Limited purchased Joseph E. Seagram & Sons, and the new company was renamed Distiller Corporation-Seagrams Limited. The new company focused its marketing campaigns toward highlighting its smooth, blended whiskeys. By the 1930s, the Distillers Corporation-Seagrams had grown to such a size it needed to expand. Several U.S. distillers were bought by the company. In 1939, a new type of whiskey was created by Samuel Bronfman named Crown Royal whiskey. It was named in honor of the British royal family's visit to Canada that same year.

The Distillers Corporation-Seagrams continued its growth. In the 1940s, the corporation purchased wine, champagne, and rum companies. As the corporation grew so did its interests. In the 1950s, the company began to branch out by purchasing different types of businesses such as shopping malls, supermarkets, and petrochemical enterprises. In 1975, the corporation was renamed as The Seagram Company. Continuing its growth, Seagram bought Tropicana in 1988 and Dole's juice business in 1995. Seagram then merged the two businesses and formed Tropicana Juice Beverages.

To further spread out its interests, in 1994 Seagram bought 80 percent of Universal Studios, then known as MCA. In 1997, the company bought out USA Networks and went into a joint venture with another company concerning USA Networks, retaining a large stake in the venture. In recent years, The Seagram Company has had some difficulties resulting from mergers yet it still remains a major player in the business field. The Bronfman family still operates one of the largest family-controlled capital pools in the non-Arab world. The Seagram Company's success is a good example of how a small business, in this case a liquor business formed because of Prohibition, can grow to be a large force in a capitalist economy.

Seagram is not the only liquor business that has flourished in a capitalist economy. The Brown-Forman Corporation was founded in Louisville, Kentucky, in 1870. In 2002, it employed 6,550 people and earned $1.6 billion in sales. Another example of the capitalist economic system at work can be found in the story of Distillers Company. Based in Edinburgh, Scotland, it was once one of the most powerful and important companies in the UNITED KINGDOM. The company controlled almost 75 percent of the world's market in scotch whiskey. The company ran into problems, though, as competition became more aggressive and its markets began to shrink. In 1986, the company could no longer continue running independently and was purchased by Guinness.

A capitalist economy highly favors competition. This characteristic encourages innovations and benefits the consumer by keeping prices down. This characteristic also makes businesses highly motivated to make their products as visible as they can in the market. This is why advertising plays such a large role in the success of any business. When a consumer is faced with a choice between two products that are of equal price and quality the consumer usually chooses the product that they are most acquainted with. The importance of advertising is at the center of an ongoing struggle between hard-liquor companies and the broadcast media.

Selling liquor. In the modern United States, a debate continues over whether or not hard liquor should be advertised in all areas of the broadcast media. The debate involves moral issues and what modern-day American society deems acceptable. In many states, it is illegal for radio and television stations to have liquor advertised on their programs. Opponents of advertising explain advertisements for liquor would encourage underage drinkers to break the law. Proponents of liquor advertising view the question another way. They feel that liquor is a legally produced product and should be allowed to advertise as any other common product. Many point out that malt beverages, such as beer, are the most common alcoholic beverages consumed by underage drinkers. Yet, malt beverages are allowed to advertise in the broadcast media.

Many liquor producers are getting creative to circumvent this debate, introducing malt beverages that carry their brand and logo. Most distillers deny that the introduction of these new products is a plan for the name-brand recognition to carry over to the distilled liquors and boost sales. However, most do admit that this would be a pleasant side benefit.

The sale of liquor has generated billions of dollars for governments around the world. Throughout history, governments have raised money by taxing the sale of liquor. In the United States, almost half the price of an average bottle of liquor is taxes put in place on the federal, state, and local levels. Though such a huge sum of money is made by the sale of liquor, most governments regulate how it is distributed and sold. Studies have shown that alcohol can distort a person's thinking and reasoning skills, and in some cases lead to violence. Many governments impose taxes on liquor hoping to reduce and control alcohol abuse. Age limits are also enforced hoping to curtail the drinking of alcoholic beverages by the young. Most experts agree that young people are less able to moderate their drinking and are more vulnerable to the harmful effects that can occur from the overindulgence of alcohol.

In the American capitalist economy there are many privately owned businesses that deal with liquor. These businesses are highly regulated by both state and local governments, including types of retail outlets, hours of sale, and minimum age for consumers. In some states, and in certain nations, the government actually operates retail liquor stores. Regulations on the liquor industry also come from the federal government under the jurisdiction of the Bureau of Alcohol, Tobacco, and Firearms. The bureau is in charge of controlling the production, labeling, and advertising of alcohol products. The agency also regulates the relationships between producers, wholesalers, and retailers who deal with alcohol, and is in charge of protecting consumers against alcohol products that may be impure, incorrectly labeled, or have some other irregularity.

The largest producers of liquor in the world are the United States, the United Kingdom, Canada, RUSSIA, and JAPAN. All of these countries, excluding Russia, export a great deal of the liquor they produce. Because of the great varieties of alcohol concentrations in different liquors it is hard to determine an accurate amount of alcohol consumed in the world. One survey, conducted by the Industry of Distilled Drinks, looked at 45 countries and their relationships with liquor. It was found that liquor is only responsible for about one fourth of the alcohol consumed. The United States was ranked 22nd in the total alcohol consumed per capita and 11th for liquor consumption. The nations with the highest rates of liquor consumed per capita in 1991 were listed as GERMANY, HUNGARY, POLAND, Czechoslovakia (before its breakup), and Bulgaria. The countries with the lowest consumption were TURKEY, ARGENTINA, ITALY, MEXICO, and PORTUGAL.

BIBLIOGRAPHY. Thomas Babor, *Alcohol Customs and Rituals* (Chelsea House, 1986); William J. Baumol, *Market Innovation Machine: Analyzing the Growth Miracle of Capitalism* (Princeton University Press, 2002); Edward Behr, *Prohibition: Thirteen Years that Changed America* (Arcade, 1997); Thomas Brennan, *Burgundy to Champagne: The Wine Trade in Early Modern France* (Johns Hopkins University Press, 1997); Norman H. Clark, *Deliver Us from Evil: An Interpretation of American Prohibition* (W.W. Norton, 1985); James C. Fernald, *The Economics of Prohibition* (2002); William Grimes, *Straight Up or on the Rocks: A Cultural History of American Drink* (Simon & Shuster, 1993).

CHRIS HOWELL
RED ROCKS COLLEGE

Lithuania

THE REPUBLIC OF LITHUANIA has a population of approximately 3.6 million (2002) and borders Belarus, LATVIA, the Kaliningrad portion of RUSSIA and the Baltic Sea. It has a parliamentary democracy, and is divided into 10 counties. Lithuania declared its independence from the SOVIET UNION on March 11, 1990, but it was not until September 6, 1991, that the Soviet Union officially recognized its secession.

In 2001, Lithuania's GROSS DOMESTIC PRODUCT (GDP) was approximately $27.4 billion. During the same year, its GDP real growth rate was 4.8 percent, due in part to Lithuania's membership in the WORLD TRADE ORGANIZATION (WTO). Lithuania is also set for membership in the EUROPEAN UNION (EU) and the North Atlantic Treaty Organization (NATO) in 2004. The country's largest industries are metal-cutting machine tools, electric motors, television sets, refrigerators freezers, petroleum-refining, shipbuilding, furniture-making, and textiles.

Lithuania's largest trading partner is Russia. Due to the country's economic dependency on Russia, Lithuania felt the full force of the Russian economic downturn in 1998. Lithuania has bounced back well from the recession and is in a position to potentially become a growing service-based economy.

BIBLIOGRAPHY. *CIA World Factbook* (2002); Lonely Planet World Guide, www.lonelyplanet.com; *Lithuanian Tourism Product Manual 2002* (Lithuanian Department of Tourism).

ARTHUR HOLST, PH.D.
WIDENER UNIVERSITY

Lloyd, Henry Demarest (1847–1903)

DRAWING ATTENTION TO the activities of the industrial elite, and in particular, to the threat that MONOPOLY posed to the welfare of the nation, Henry Demarest Lloyd gained fame as a crusader for justice during the late 19th century. Born in New York City, he attended Columbia University and Law School. He worked at various jobs that allowed him to develop the skills he would use in his reform efforts.

As a field agent of the American Free-Trade Association, he canvassed the public, distributed pamphlets, wrote newspaper articles and advertisements, and became an outspoken advocate of tariff reform. In the early 1870s, he became active in a movement to lower the dues and increase the hours of the New York public libraries, and worked against the corruption of Tammany Hall leader "Boss" Tweed. He then moved to Chicago and joined the staff of the *Chicago Tribune*, where he eventually became chief editorial writer.

After more than a decade at the newspaper, however, Lloyd ultimately decided to leave to independently pursue writing and research. His article "The Story of a Great Monopoly" appeared in *The Atlantic Monthly* magazine in 1881. Lloyd's analysis of the business practices of Standard Oil and its collusion with the Pennsylvania Railroad became a model of this type of journalistic exposé. The article, the first of a series critiquing laissez-faire capitalism and the dubious ethics of the "robber barons" of the Gilded Age, gained national acclaim and that issue of the magazine went through six reprints.

Lloyd described the dangers of such a concentration of wealth and power, arguing, "In less than the ordinary span of a life-time, our railroads have brought upon us the worst labor disturbance, the greatest of monopolies, and the most formidable combination of money and brains that ever overshadow a state . . . Americans as they are, they ride over the people like a juggernaut to gain their ends."

Lloyd was notable for his willingness to take up any cause, to attempt to right any wrong. He and his wife Jessie opened their home in Winnetka, Illinois, to a varied group of reformers, intellectuals, and artists. In 1886, Lloyd attended the trial of eight anarchists accused of setting off a bomb during a labor rally in Haymarket Square in Chicago. The trial was one of the most controversial of the era, and after the defendants were sentenced to death Lloyd actively campaigned to the governor for clemency for the condemned men. He also became an outspoken advocate of trade unionism, believing that it was one of the only defenses against the power of big business. Lloyd gave speeches at rallies for the Eight Hour Movement, and wrote about the abuses suffered by locked-out coal miners in Spring Valley, Illinois. He became involved in the settlement house work of Jane Addams at Hull House, and also worked to bring the message of the rural Populist Party to urban audiences, particularly workers.

Yet even as he pursued these disparate projects, Lloyd remained fascinated by the problem of monopoly. He returned to the subject in a book-length examination of Standard Oil, *Wealth Against Commonwealth*, published in 1894. The 600-page tome used four case-histories of the victims of Rockefeller's companies, including a poor widow, an independent businessman, and an old inventor. Critics charged that his prose was sentimental and moralistic, but Lloyd managed to rally his readers against the "oil trust" that raised the price of commodities.

Lloyd's style of writing inspired others to draw the public's attention to scandal and corruption in business and government with the hope of correcting abuses. For this reason, he has been called "the first of the muckrakers," a term given to Progressive Era journalist-reformers by Theodore ROOSEVELT. In some ways, he was slightly ahead of his time: the debate over trusts in the American economy that he prompted would continue well into the 20th century. Lloyd died on September 17, 1903, while organizing another campaign against monopoly, this time advocating municipal ownership of the Chicago Streetcar Company.

BIBLIOGRAPHY. Richard Digby-Junger, *The Journalist as Reformer: Henry Demarest Lloyd and Wealth Against Commonwealth* (Greenwood Press, 1996); E. Jay Jernigan, *Henry Demarest Lloyd* (Twayne Publishers, 1976); John L. Thomas, *Alternative America: Henry George, Edward Bellamy, Henry Demarest Lloyd and the Adversary Tradition* (Harvard University Press, 1983).

SARAH ELVINS
UNIVERSITY OF NOTRE DAME

Locke, John (1632–1704)

THE ELDEST SON OF a landowner, John Locke's life, as well as much of his philosophy, parallels the rise of the middle class. He attended Oxford University, where he also lectured in Greek and moral philosophy. He studied medicine on his own initiative and became interested in politics and economics through a friendship with Anthony Ashley Cooper, who later became the first Earl of Shaftesbury.

Locke entered civil service, and was soon spending more time in London than in Oxford. Though he was not associated with the business world in any way, he became acquainted with practical matters of trade, and was appointed as secretary to the Council of Trade and Plantations, and eventually commissioner for promoting colonial trade. As a cautious supporter of the opposition to King James II, Locke was deprived of his academic appointment in 1683, and was briefly driven into exile. He found refuge in Holland until William and Mary had assumed the crown following the Revolution of 1688–89. By the time Locke returned to England, he was already an established scholar. He spent the remaining years of his life writing, including the *Essay Concerning Human Understanding* (1690) and *Two Treatises on Government* (1690) while holding minor government positions and occasionally advising political leaders. He was responsible for organizing the Board of Trade in 1695 and served as a commissioner of the Board until 1700.

Locke is generally considered a major figure in the history of political thought and political theory because his ideas paved the way for the ascendancy of political liberalism, and modern representative government. However, the realization of self-interest as the motivating force of conduct, which is inherent in his entire political philosophy, also played a profound role in the breakdown of state regulation of economic life and the development of modern economic doctrine. The decline of state intervention in the economy went hand-in-hand with the erosion of the monopolistic interests of MERCANTILISM and the GROWTH of competition.

In the history of economic thought, the labor theory of property that Locke developed in his masterpiece *Two Treatises* provided a philosophical foundation for the classical labor theory of value, as well as more generally for the conditions of the new economy. Interestingly, by anchoring property in labor but upholding unlimited accumulation, Locke's theory of property appealed not only to the rising capitalist class of his time, but to socialists of a later age as well. He made some of his most notable contributions to monetary theory with *Some Consideration of the Consequences of the Lowering of Interest and Raising the Value of Money* (1692) and *Further Considerations concerning Raising the Value of Money* (1695).

Whereas 17th-century writers had usually addressed themselves exclusively to practical questions and policy proposals, Locke attempted to formulate the general principles of value and price. This very modern approach to economic questions, that had significant implications for the development of contemporary thought, provides an interesting and stark contrast to his defense of mercantilism and failure to recognize its underlying fallacy.

During Locke's time, the field of economics had no name or position of its own among scientific disciplines, but there did exist a substantial literature, and it has been estimated that his own library contained at least 115 titles on economics, including William Petty's *Treatise of Taxes and Contributions*. After Lord Ashley was appointed chancellor of the Exchequer, Locke first offered his views about interest and monetary policy in a memorandum in 1668. The memorandum was eventually published in revised and expanded form more than 20 years later as *Considerations* when the issue of a reduction in the legal maximum interest rate again came under debate.

Locke's position was that any statute contrary to natural law was inappropriate, and so natural law, not laws made by humans, should determine interest rates and monetary value. Moreover, he argued that interest-rate legislation would be evaded by individuals unwilling to give up the opportunity for gain. This process would drive the effective rate of interest higher than the market-determined rate, cause shortages of loanable funds, hamper trade, and redistribute wealth in unmerited ways. Though written to address the specific ideas suggested by the title, the pamphlet dealt with broader issues such as the nature and function of money and a derivation of the implications of the quantity theory of money as a special case of the demand and supply theory of price determination. Though Locke's arguments failed to convince Parliament to defeat the bill to lower the legal rate of interest from 6 percent to 4 percent, his first economic essay did become a classic work in the development of monetary thought.

Locke applied the theory of price determination that he developed in the *Considerations* to all exchangeable GOODS, including MONEY, although he regarded money as a special good. The model, though primitive by today's standards, was innovative for his own time and was reasonably accurate in predicting qualitative effects on price in response to various types of change. Locke also demonstrated that quantity demanded was negatively related to price and quantity supplied was positively related to price. He formulated the concept of an EQUILIBRIUM price, and in fact used the term equilibrium in certain contexts consistent with modern usage.

Locke recognized two functions of money: as a measure of value and as a claim to goods. He believed that the latter function required gold and silver, at least for international transactions, because of the generally agreed-upon intrinsic value of precious metals. His monetary economics generally focused on the ratio of a country's monetary stock to its volume of trade. Locke argued that comparisons of this ratio between countries determined international price levels. Contrary to the typical mercantilist preference for low prices as a stimulus to exports, Locke warned of the danger of prices at home falling below those abroad.

Consequently, his views concerning monetary requirements for international purposes represented the extreme mercantilist position that a favorable balance of trade was necessary to avoid the dire effects on trade, agriculture, employment, wages, terms of trade, and population movements that a relative drop in money stock would cause. He is credited, along with Petty, with the introduction of the concept of velocity of circulation to what is now called the quantity theory of money. His formulation of the theory was much more refined than it had been previously, even though it led him to the fallacious and inconsistent conclusion concerning the continuous inflow of specie. The fact that one of the best minds of the 17th century failed to see that a country is unable to accumulate treasure indefinitely may be due to his belief that the world's money stock had risen significantly and, as a consequence, home prices had fallen substantially below that of other countries. Eventually Locke's argument concerning specie flows and the role of trade was rebutted by David HUME's description of the automatic specie-flow mechanism.

Locke's justification of private property originated in the natural-rights doctrine. His fundamental premise was that each person is endowed at birth with property in his/her person. As such, the person is entitled to the product of his/her labor, and by applying that labor to the earth, the yield of the earth becomes the individual's property as well. In Locke's view, virtually the whole value of the products of the soil were due to labor, the remainder being a gift from nature. Implicitly, there was also the view that man has a duty to be industrious, and industry, in turn, would produce private property. However, even though in a state of nature, limits to accumulation existed, and the introduction of commodities of greater and greater durability, and ultimately, the introduction of money made the unlimited accumulation of property possible.

The same introduction of money which provided a store of value to prevent waste, also made greater and greater inequality possible. Locke did not resolve the issue of wealth inequality with the equal rights given by nature. Moreover, he avoided a direct admission that a conflict could exist between the law of nature and what humankind arranged by consent. He may have had in mind that the government should moderate such inequality, but he did not make that explicit. Locke's defense of private property was not intended to be a deliberate attack on landed interests, but taken as part of his entire philosophy, the effect was to undermine the claim of landowners to special status. This perspective later helped establish acceptance of private property as an institution of capitalism.

Later writers relied upon a utilitarian-based argument to justify private property rather than the labor theory-based argument developed by Locke. However, Locke's conception of the guarantee of liberty in society, secured by the requirement that government be established by the consent of the people, and designed for the good of the people, had an important impact on the development of later economic thought, particularly through the influences of Adam SMITH and Francois QUESNAY.

Locke did not specify what constituted the good of the people, and so did not tie his political philosophy to an economic structure. Had he done so, his ideas likely would not have such long-lasting significance since his own general acceptance of mercantilist economic views certainly formed a clear contrast with the LAISSEZ-FAIRE position of Smith. To Smith, Locke's natural liberty with statements about the rights of individuals against government and his own concept of laissez-faire were inseparable. He constructed his *Wealth of Nations* on the premise that the pursuit of self-interest guided by the invisible hand of competition would produce the good of the people, whereas government intervention in the economic arena would inhibit it.

The equal right of all to pursue self-interest, but not to infringe upon the rights of others incorporated by Smith throughout the *Wealth of Nations* was very similar to Locke's conception. Moreover, since government alone could strip persons of their property, the sanctity of private property became yet another argument in favor of laissez-faire economic policy. Hence, the virtues of Locke's natural law were transformed into the requisites of capitalism.

BIBLIOGRAPHY. W.E. Kuhn, *The Evolution of Economic Thought* (South-Western, 1953); Ingrid H. Rima, *Development of Economic Analysis* (Routledge, 2001); Eric Roll, *A History of Economic Thought* (1973, fourth edition); Joseph A. Schumpeter, *History of Economic Analysis* (Oxford University Press, 1954); Henry William Spiegel, *The Growth of Economic Thought* (Duke University Press, 1991); Karen I. Vaughn, *John Locke: Economist and Social Scientist* (University of Chicago Press, 1980).

ELEANOR T. VON ENDE, PH.D.
TEXAS TECH UNIVERSITY

Lucas, Robert E., Jr. (1937–)

AT ROBERT LUCAS' Nobel Prize ceremony in October 1995, the honors committee praised his advancement of the field of world economy. "He is the economist who has had the greatest influence on microeconomic research since 1970," read the citation issued by the Swedish Academy of Sciences. The Nobel award honored, chiefly, his work in developing and applying the hypothesis of rational expectations, thus transforming MICROECONOMIC analysis and deepening the world's understanding of economic policy.

This rational-expectation hypothesis formulated by Lucas earlier in his career is the assumption that people make use of the best available information about government policy when making their decisions, rather than committing the systematic errors assumed by earlier theories.

The eldest child born to Robert Emerson and Jane Templeton Lucas, he enjoyed a quiet childhood in Yakima, Washington. Lucas spent his earliest years helping out in his parents' business, a popular ice cream shop near the center of town. The shop failed in the 1938–39 economic downturn and the Lucases relocated to Seattle where both parents took up new occupations.

To keep his family fed, Lucas' father grabbed whatever job he could find. A man of high principles, ambition, and intelligence, he eventually became president of the Lewis Refrigeration Company, where he began only a few years earlier as a mechanic. "I remember many technical and managerial discussions with him," Lucas recalls of his father. "When I took calculus in high school he enlisted my help on a refrigeration design problem . . . and actually used my calculations. It was my first taste of real applied mathematics."

In 1955, Lucas' excellent high school grades earned him a scholarship to the University of Chicago. He graduated with a degree in history, intent to pursue his studies on a graduate level. But, after receiving a Woodrow Wilson Doctoral Fellowship that took him to the University of California to study classical history, he soon became aware of, and eager to learn more of the history of economics. Ancient Greeks and Romans put aside, Lucas pursued a graduate degree in an entirely new career.

Returning to Chicago, he immersed himself in economics, mathematics, and calculus. By 1963, Lucas' post-graduate work caught the attention of Pittsburgh's Carnegie Mellon Institute, which offered him a faculty position. It was at Carnegie that Lucas became interested in dynamics and the formation of expectations. He focused his attention on modern general equilibrium, functional analysis, and the probability theory. During the following years, as he returned to his academic roots in Chicago, he authored a number of academic writings explaining his findings and theories.

In 1980, Lucas was named the John Dewey Distinguished Service Professor at the University of Chicago.

BIBLIOGRAPHY. Robert E. Lucas, Jr., *Lectures on Economic Growth* (Harvard University Press, 2002); Robert E. Lucas, Jr., *Studies in Business Cycle Theory* (MIT Press, 1981); Robert E. Lucas, Jr., Autobiography, www.nobel.se; "Economic-Expectations Pioneers Earns Nobel Prize," *The Boston Globe* (October 11, 1995); E.C. Witt, "Interview with Robert Lucas" (University of Chicago, October 7, 1997).

JOSEPH GERINGER
SYED B. HUSSAIN, PH.D.
UNIVERSITY OF WISCONSIN, OSHKOSH

Luxembourg

A TINY COUNTRY (less than 1,000 square miles) with its roots in the Middle Ages, Luxemburg's history is closely tied up with that of the neighboring Low Countries. In 1830, the duchy became officially part of the newly formed country of BELGIUM until an 1839 international conference declared it to be an independent, and perpetually neutral nation in its own right.

Despite its independence, Luxemburg did share in the Belgian economic boom of the 19th century and was among the first European countries to participate in the INDUSTRIAL REVOLUTION, building a steel industry on the basis of considerable coal reserves discovered in 1850. Luxembourg joined the Prussian Zollverein and was able to make use of rapidly expanding railway systems throughout central Europe. Most of its steel exports were handled by a single company, ARBED (Acieries Réunies de Burbach-Eich-Dudelange), which is still the largest employer in the country.

Because of its small size but wide economic interests, Luxemburg has been active in working toward European unification. In 1921, it worked with Belgium and the NETHERLANDS to form the economic union Benelux. Luxembourg was a founding member of the European Coal and Steel Community, a precursor to the EUROPEAN UNION (EU), which was headquartered in Luxemburg's capital. Many important institutions of the EU are, as of 2003, located in Luxemburg, including the European Investment Bank, the European Court of Justice, the European Court of Auditors, the Nuclear Safety Administration, and the General Secretariat of the European Parliament.

Since the 1950s, the government has been actively courting new businesses by providing tax and other incentives for companies willing to relocate there. There has been moderate success, especially in the satellite and hydro-electric fields. Despite these efforts to promote industry, however, the modern economy of Luxemburg is shifting toward the service sector. For example, the country is home to over 220 banks and 1,300 investment funds and provides a host of ancillary investment services. With a population of nearly a half-million people, Luxembourg had a GROSS DOMESTIC PRODUCT (GDP) of $20 billion in 2002.

BIBLIOGRAPHY. E.H. Kossman, *The Low Countries 1780-1940* (Oxford University Press, 1978); Franz Lang and Renate Ohr, eds., *International Economic Integration* (Springer Verlag, 1995); Luxemburg in Figures, www.statec.lu; *CIA World Factbook* (2002).

LAURA CRUZ
WESTERN CAROLINA UNIVERSITY

Luxemburg, Rosa (1871–1919)

A POLISH-BORN COMMUNIST THEORIST and revolutionary, Rosa Luxemburg was born the youngest child of a lower middle-class Jewish family in Russian-occupied POLAND. She became involved in activism against the Russian Empire while still in her teens; in 1889 she was forced to flee RUSSIA at the age of 18 for fear of imprisonment for her revolutionary activities. As did many of her contemporaries, she fled abroad, joining a number of other notable exiles committed to revolutionary change in Russia.

She went first to Zurich, Switzerland, where she studied politics and law, receiving her doctorate in 1898 with a dissertation on the industrial development of Poland. There she also became involved in the international socialist movement, coming to know Russian radical intellectuals such as Georgi Plekhanov. In Zurich, the basic form of her later theoretical work began to take shape, as she argued for an internationalist form of SOCIALISM, charging that the nationalism favored by many

Russian and Polish radicals remained mired in harmful bourgeois attitudes. With a group of like-minded socialists she founded the Polish Social Democratic Party (later the foundation of the Polish Communist Party).

Luxemburg married a German in 1898 to gain German citizenship, and moved to Berlin, the center of European socialist politics at the time. She entered into the divisive debates then raging within the German Social Democratic Party (SPD), championing Marxist orthodoxy alongside Karl Kautsky against the revisionist challenge mounted by Eduard Bernstein. Kautsky and Luxemburg held that revisionist socialism (working within the parliamentary system to affect change) was ineffectual and only true proletarian revolution could achieve the transformation of society from capitalist to socialist.

The outbreak of the Russian revolution of 1905 convinced her that advanced industrial countries like GERMANY were no longer the only possible locations for the beginning of a proletarian revolution, and that the relatively undeveloped Russian Empire was ripe for change. She went to Poland to agitate for revolution, but was jailed in the Tsar's successful crackdown. While imprisoned, she drew upon her experience to refine her theoretical approach, stressing the value of the mass strike as the main weapon of the proletariat. She returned to Berlin after her release in 1906 and taught at SPD schools until the outbreak of WORLD WAR I in 1914.

When the SPD cast its lot with the German government at the start of the war, the anti-militarist, internationalist Luxemburg openly split with the party. With Karl Liebknecht, she founded an opposition group in 1916, calling for an end to the war through revolution and the establishment of a proletarian state in the aftermath. The organization was named the Spartakusbund after the Roman slave who broke his chains and led an insurrection for freedom. This Spartacus League did not achieve much success during the war and Luxemburg once again was imprisoned.

Upon her release in November 1918, during the chaos of the German revolutionary movements, she quickly sought to mobilize the workers of Berlin to create a leftist government for Germany. With Liebknecht, she formed the German Communist Party shortly thereafter. On January 15, 1919, both Luxemburg and Liebknecht were arrested. While the exact details of what followed remain unknown, Liebknecht and Luxemburg were shot sometime shortly thereafter by troops of the paramilitary Freikorps and dumped into the Spree river.

Luxemburg's principal works include *Reform or Revolution* (1889), a staunch defense of orthodox Marxism; *The Mass Strike, the Political Party, and Trade Unions* (1906), her statement of the crucial place of mass strikes in political action; *The Accumulation of Capital* (1913), her major theoretical work on the failures of capitalism; *The Crisis in German Social Democracy* (1916), a statement of principles for what became the Spartacus League; and *The Russian Revolution* (1917), a work highly critical of the nationalist and dictatorial tendencies she saw in the Bolshevik Revolution in Russia.

BIBLIOGRAPHY. J.P. Nettl, *Rosa Luxemburg* (Oxford University Press, 1966); Jacob Mathilde, *Rosa Luxemburg: an Intimate Portrait* (Lawrence and Weishart, 2000); Donald E. Shepardson, *Rosa Luxemburg and the Noble Dream* (P. Lang, 1996); Elzbieta Ettinger, *Rosa Luxemburg: a Life* (Beacon, 1986).

CHARLES ROBINSON, PH.D.
BRANDEIS UNIVERSITY

M

MacArthur, Douglas (1880–1964)

SON OF U.S. ARMY GENERAL Arthur MacArthur, Douglas MacArthur grew up on military posts around the world. Both his father's success and his mother's ambition sent him to the U.S. Military Academy at West Point, where he graduated in 1903 at the top of his class and began a career that would span half a century.

His combat experience in WORLD WAR I earned him recognition for his bravery and leadership, and his postwar revitalization of the near-moribund academy established his administrative competence. He served as chief of staff under both Herbert HOOVER and Franklin ROOSEVELT, becoming quite controversial for his decision to destroy the shantytown housing of the Bonus Expeditionary Force. Veterans of World War I were camped in Washington, D.C., attempting to get a promised bonus early and MacArthur had them rousted. He survived the controversy, moving on to become military advisor to the Philippine Commonwealth before retiring in 1937.

After Pearl Harbor, MacArthur returned to active duty, escaping the Philippines before they fell, then leading troops in the slow drive across the southwest Pacific to Japan. At war's end he presided over the Japanese surrender ceremonies aboard the battleship *Missouri* in Tokyo Bay.

With the war ended, MacArthur headed the occupation force that rebuilt Japan. Already a legend with over 30 years' service, MacArthur made probably his most lasting contribution to history during his five-and-a-half years as Supreme Commander of the Allied Powers in Japan, when he oversaw the development of capitalism in the conquered nation.

Japan's surrender was unconditional, leaving the Japanese in no position to negotiate their reconstruction. MacArthur was charismatic and willing to rule by fiat. Although theoretically subordinate to the allied command, MacArthur ran Japan pretty much as he chose. It was a one-of-a-kind, not-to-be-repeated episode in which MacArthur's power was likened to an American Caesar, as some historians noted later.

Planning for the occupation began as early as the immediate aftermath of the Japanese attacks of December 1941. The Potsdam Proclamation of July 1945, spelled out general objectives to demilitarize and democratize Japan, but it left the details to the on-scene commander, MacArthur. And MacArthur delegated to his extensive staff. He largely rejected the experts on Japan, preferring his own people, and much of the work that those people did rested on their earlier experience in the NEW DEAL environment. Land reform did away with tenancy, labor was organized, and the constitution outlawing war also provided quite progressive civil rights, some of which went beyond those enjoyed in the United States. MacArthur's staff reorganized the schools, rewrote the textbooks, and rewrote the laws.

Making this happen was a staff of 5,000–6,000 people, moving in and out as tours began and ended. Mostly, they worked in Tokyo, but there were offices throughout Japan. Tens of thousands of bilingual Japanese served in support functions. And there was the backdrop of a military presence, more than 100,000 men. And, above all, MacArthur's radical remaking of Japan rested on the revival of Japanese prewar traditions of democracy and the continuance of the Japanese bureaucracy from the central ministries to the village administrators. Consistently, the defeated either tolerated or actively accepted MacArthur's vision and made it happen.

During MacArthur's remaking of Japan, his authority rivaled, and in some instances exceeded, that of the emperor. He certainly had stronger authority in Japan than the governments he represented and the government of the defeated enemy. Through his staff, he implemented policies and processes that brought devastated Japan from the ashes to a leading position in the world's economy. He designed and his staff wrote the constitution that brought democratic government to Japan. He preserved the emperor, sheltered him from the war crimes trials, and defined the nature of Japan's democracy. He made Japan a demilitarized, non-aggressive, non-threat to its neighbors.

MacArthur went on to command the UNITED NATIONS forces in South KOREA, to challenge President Harry TRUMAN's limits on that war, and to get fired in 1951 for insubordination. MacArthur returned to America a hero and presidential contender or at least pretender. The Korean War dragged-on until the inconclusive armistice of 1953.

A brilliant soldier and administrator, MacArthur was also vainglorious, arrogant, self-serving, and intolerant of criticism. All of those characteristics combined to make him one of the most remarkable individuals of a remarkable century.

BIBLIOGRAPHY. John Dower, *Embracing Defeat: Japan in the Wake of World War II* (W.W. Norton, 2000); David Fromkin, *In the Time of the Americans: FDR, Truman, Eisenhower, Marshall, MacArthur: the Generation That Changed America's Role in the World* (Knopf, 1995).

JOHN H. BARNHILL, PH.D.
INDEPENDENT SCHOLAR

Machiavelli, Niccolo (1469–1527)

RENAISSANCE FLORENTINE diplomat, politician, and scholar, author of treatises, satires, and plays, Niccolo Machiavelli is most well known for his authorship of *The Prince*. Employed by the republican government of Florence on numerous diplomatic missions, Machiavelli sought to enhance the reputation of Florence and elevate it above other Italian city-states. When the Florentine republic collapsed to be succeeded by a Medici dictatorship, however, he was barred from public life. *The Prince* is dedicated to the Medici prince, Lorenzo the Magnificent (1492–1519), in hopes of paving the way for Machiavelli's return to public service in Florence.

The Prince is written in the form of an advice manual to the would-be sovereign on how to attain and retain the greatest amount of power in the most efficient and effective way. Machiavelli conceptualizes humans as actors caught between the randomness of circumstance (*fortuna*), that cannot be controlled, and prowess or

skill (*virtù*, literally manliness), defined as the human capability to act creatively in the face of fortune. Thus, the successful prince must be both skilled in his choices and benefit from a certain amount of good luck, but his skill is decisive. This balance can best be achieved by appearing to be acting in good faith, according to moral and religious principle, while all the while being willing to act solely in one's own interest, without regard to the moral consequences of such action.

Machiavelli takes as his model Cesare Borgia (1476–1507), whom he met at an embassy in 1502. Cesare was the duke of Romagna and ultimately, ill-fated son of Pope Alexander VI (Rodrigo Borgia) who managed to unite the Papal States and viciously trick his own mercenaries into obedience before his fortunes crumbled after the death of his father. In the end, Machiavelli turns to a diagnosis of the problems of Italy, arguing that Italian princes have lost their states due to their inability to inspire the loyalty of their nobles or the good will of their subjects, or foster sufficient military strength. The whims of chance can never be a sufficient explanation for the failure of a prince, he argues, for the decisive quality of a leader is his ability to deal successfully with circumstance.

The Prince was typically understood by contemporaries as disgusting, immoral manual of *Realpolitik*, and was condemned by Pope Clement VII and placed on the *Index of Prohibited Books* in 1559. It was rumored to be a favorite book of Otto von BISMARCK, and served to justify the reason of state politics throughout the 19th century.

If read solely on the basis of *The Prince*, Machiavelli's politics can be seen to advise directly that the only basis for successful political action can be the ground of optimized political expediency. Machiavelli recommends that the prince be cruel, that he manipulate his subjects, and that he never admit his true thoughts; he also notes that the true prince is only hampered by immutable moral or political allegiances. Still, Machiavelli is merely formalizing and legitimizing a strategy of political behavior that is as old as humanity; as Leo Strauss noted, his contribution was the attempt to make such behavior politically defensible.

It would be simplistic, however, to assume that the surface meaning of the text so objectionable both to contemporaries and moderns is the only or primary interpretation to be observed, for rhetorical playfulness was the hallmark of the Renaissance philosopher, and Machiavelli was the author of several satires and dramatic works. Particularly his extended praise of the failed Cesare Borgia was read by some contemporaries as sarcastic; on the other hand, many commentators have read the praise of Cesare as serious and interpreted the conclusion of the text as a call for the unification of Italy. Moreover, a letter of Machiavelli's admits to his hopes of currying favor with Lorenzo, which casts further doubt on the sincerity of the content. Modern interpreters have drawn multiple conclusions from this very pliable text; for instance, the sort of behavior recommended to Machiavelli's prince can be viewed along with Thomas Hobbes' politics as the basis for non-cooperative game theory, and Machiavelli's thought also had a substantial influence on the writings of Benedict Spinoza.

In the later 20th century, Machiavelli's thinking spawned a rash of business books that promulgated and popularized the literal interpretation of *The Prince* as a basis for effective leadership and decision-making. A fuller picture of Machiavelli's thought can be gained from reading his other works, in particular *Discourses on the First Ten Books of Titus Livy,* which argues for virtue as the basis of successful democracy.

BIBLIOGRAPHY. Sebastian de Grazia, *Machiavelli in Hell* (Princeton University Press, 1989); Niccolo Machiavelli, *The Prince,* George Bull, trans. (Penguin, 1999); Friedrich Meinicke, *Machiavellism: The Doctrine of raison d'état and its place in modern history* (Transaction Publishers, 1998); Garrett Mattingly, "Machiavelli's Prince: Political Science or Political Satire" *The American Scholar* (v.27, 1958).

SUSAN R. BOETTCHER, PH.D.
UNIVERSITY OF TEXAS, AUSTIN

macroeconomics

PART OF ECONOMICS that studies aggregate behavior of the economy, macroeconomics especially relates to the determination of national income, interest rates and the price level, long-run growth and business cycles and government fiscal and monetary policies.

Macroeconomics is widely believed to have originated with the work of John Maynard KEYNES, although Keynes never used the exact term. The approach he took in his famous *General Theory of Employment, Interest and Money* (1936), however, definitely inspired macroeconomics as a discipline.

In the 1930s, the capitalist world experienced the worst DEPRESSION in its history, with output and income falling 30–40 percent and unemployment reaching 25 percent of the workforce. The SOVIET UNION, in the meantime, seemed to be achieving spectacular rates of economic growth especially in its industrial sector, while Adolf Hitler and his allies threatened democracy and political stability from the extreme right. It is not perhaps surprising that, under those circumstances, even staunch believers in economic freedom and the efficiency of markets were taking an increasingly pessimistic view about the chances of a system based on economic freedom to survive.

Prior to Keynes, economics was focused mostly on the determination of prices that would make SUPPLY automatically meet DEMAND. In particular, the price mechanism was supposed to lead to equilibrium in the labor market that would guarantee full employment. At the time when this prediction seemed to be completely failing, Keynes claimed that employment was a function of total output, which was determined by forces outside of the price mechanism, and that previous theory was useful only in understanding how total output was allocated among different uses and distributed among different factors of production, not how much of output is produced in the first place. Total output (income) was governed instead by quantity relationships, including consumption and saving as a function of income, on the one hand, and "animal spirits" of investors and liquidity-preference determination of the interest rate governing the volume of investment, on the other hand. In Keynes' view, the level of total output (income) determined thereby need not correspond to the total output level needed to maintain full employment. His claim was that economic theory before him had been dealing with a special case in which these two levels happened to coincide, while his was a more general theory (hence, the title of his book). Keynes also proposed policy measures, such as increased government spending that could be implemented by a proactive government in order to deal with economic disasters like the Great Depression, thereby breaking away from a century-old tradition of the economic profession to advocate LAISSEZ-FAIRE (unfettered play of competitive supply and demand) in economic policy.

Post–World War II years and neoclassical synthesis (the IS-LM model). Keynesian views won over the economic profession and government policy-makers in an amazingly short period of time. To a large extent this was due to a skillful presentation of his theory by others, most prominently by John HICKS and Paul SAMUELSON. Hicks' article, "Mr. Keynes and the Classics," introduced the basic ideas of the IS-LM interpretation of Keynes which became orthodoxy in macroeconomics for decades, while Paul Samuelson, working in the same spirit, completed the neoclassical synthesis, that is, a synthesis of Keynesian quantity relationships with the neoclassical equilibrium analysis.

The key ingredients of the IS-LM (neoclassical synthesis) model of macroeconomics were the consumption function, the investment function and the money-demand function.

According to the IS-LM theory of total-income determination, a stable relationship links consumption and saving (as the difference between income and consumption) to income. When income changes, people tend to change their consumption in the same direction, but the changes are less than one-to-one with the corresponding changes in income. Investment is determined through the investment function, which is obtained by equalizing the return on investment ("the marginal efficiency of capital," in Keynes' terminology) to the interest rate.

The main difference with the neoclassical theory is that saving is not a function of the interest rate, so that the interest rate does not act to equalize desired savings to desired investment. Instead, once investment demand is determined from the investment function, the volumes of consumption and of saving adjust through total income changes, bringing savings equal to investment. Hence, to each interest rate determining the amount to be invested corresponds a unique income level that generates the amount of savings equal to investment. Since investment demand goes down when the interest rate goes up, a higher interest rate would generate excess saving as compared to investment. Hence, total income has to go down in response to a higher interest rate. This is reflected in the downward sloping shape of the IS (investment-saving) curve.

The INTEREST RATE is determined in the market for money. The supply of money is given exogenously (by the decision of the CENTRAL BANK), while its demand depends positively on income (because more income means more demand for money as a means of servicing real transactions) and negatively on the interest rate (because higher interest rate increases the opportunity cost of holding money, and not investing it in bonds or other interest-bearing instruments). A given quantity of money can be allocated between two alternative uses (transaction demand and liquidity preference) only by having higher income (increasing the transaction demand) correspond to a higher interest rate (reducing liquidity preference). This is reflected in the upward sloping shape of the LM (liquidity-money) curve.

The intersection point of these two curves uniquely determines the equilibrium level of the interest rate and output (aggregate income). The level of output could not be above the full employment level (because that would be unfeasible and produce only inflation without any increase in real output) but it could well be below the full employment level. The policy implications are that whenever equilibrium output does fall below full employment level, government needs to intervene by increasing its spending (which would shift the IS curve to the right in the diagram below) or by increasing money supply (which would shift the LM curve to the right). In theory, both ways would lead to the restoration of full employment; in practice, it was argued, government-spending programs are more effective because they affect effective demand directly while increasing money supply works only indirectly through the effect of lower interest rates on liquidity preference. In particular, in deep recessions liquidity preference may be so high that

the economy would fall into the "liquidity trap," a situation in which increasing money supply does not lead to lower interest rates and is thus completely ineffective in increasing effective demand and output level.

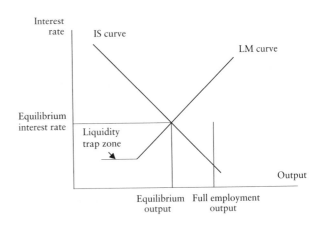

Stagflation of the 1970s and the monetarist counterrevolution. By the late 1960s, it seemed that Keynesian macroeconomics had completely won over the profession, both intellectually and in terms of policy. Samuelson in his famous introductory economics textbook claimed that with the advent of macroeconomics, the government, using a proper mix of fiscal and monetary policies, could completely eliminate the kind of depressions that capitalism had suffered earlier in its history. Despite this and other similar claims, it was precisely around that time that the neoclassical synthesis macroeconomics started breaking down as a policy guide, and also became increasingly challenged theoretically.

A popular artifact of Keynesian macroeconomics was the PHILLIPS CURVE. This curve first made its appearance in 1958 when a British economist, A.W. Phillips found a negative statistical relationship between the rate of changes in money wages and unemployment in Britain. Keynesian economics transformed the wage-unemployment relationship into inflation-unemployment relationship and developed the notion of a trade-off between price stability and full employment. If the government wanted to promote full employment, it had to pay the price of higher inflation and vice versa.

The 1970s brought about a situation that had never been observed before and that was certainly not consistent with the IS-LM macroeconomics and with the Phillips Curve: a combination of a RECESSION and high INFLATION. Under such conditions, orthodox macroeconomic policy of the time became completely paralyzed: fighting recession and UNEMPLOYMENT called for expansionary fiscal and monetary policies, but that would exacerbate inflation, and vice versa.

One more negative effect of macroeconomic intervention by means of increasing government spending that became increasingly realized at that time was the increasing share of government spending in most market economies (for example, in the United States from less than 20 percent of the GROSS DOMESTIC PRODUCT in the 1940s to 28 percent in the 1960s). This increase in expenditure and in the tax burden (and/or government deficits) was blamed for diluted incentives for hard work and private investment.

With the IS-LM macroeconomics, and policies based on it, seriously compromised, a different trend in macroeconomic theory represented by monetarism and supply-side economics rapidly gained popularity. According to MONETARISM, the liquidity preference theory of the demand for money is flawed because it does not take enough account of the choice of holding wealth in the form of commodities and capital goods, rather than only in the form of bonds and other financial assets or money. Monetarism also places emphasis on the role of expectations, in particular, inflationary expectations in shaping the macroeconomic equilibrium. The leading monetarist Milton FRIEDMAN argued that the negatively sloped Phillips Curve was only true for a short period of time (from several months to two years), while in the long run the curve was actually a vertical line passing through the point of the "natural rate of unemployment," determined by non-monetary factors (institutional and other aspects of the labor market itself).

If the government tried to increase employment beyond that natural rate by injecting more money, the trade-off between inflation and unemployment would be recreated at ever-increasing levels of both inflation and unemployment. What is worse, after a while the public will learn to adjust its expectations much faster and the overall disruption to the monetary exchange can actually even make inflation and unemployment positively related to each other.

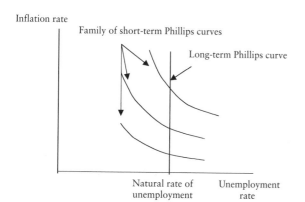

Supply-side economics complemented monetarism by focusing on negative effects of government expenditure. If borrowing covers the increase in government spending, this leads to higher interest rates, and it "crowds out" private investment and also consumption. If it is covered by higher taxes, it dilutes incentives to work and to invest in technological innovation. Supply-side economists favored reducing the government sector and the tax burden, especially on corporations and on high-income people to help rebuild fundamental strength of the market economy.

Dynamic disequilibrium approach to macroeconomics. Another challenge to the orthodox version of macroeconomics came from a minority of Keynesian economists strongly opposed to the neoclassical synthesis from the point of view completely different from monetarists and supply-side economists. In the view of this group of macroeconomists (sometimes called "the new Keynesians"), macroeconomics is essentially about the capitalist economy being constantly in a situation of dynamic disequilibrium rather than neoclassical EQUILIBRIUM.

A neoclassical equilibrium model basically assumes that the market acts as an impersonal auctioneer that constantly adjusts prices so that demand always equals supply, and that no transactions take place at wrong (that is, non-market-clearing) prices. This view is shared by the neoclassical synthesis version of Keynesian economics with the only difference being the possibility of some price rigidities, especially in the labor market and/or the liquidity trap.

The dynamic disequilibrium perspective rejects this whole approach and replaces it with the notion that since business conditions (and expectations thereof) are constantly changing, market transactions inevitably have to be carried out under non-market-clearing prices. In this view of the economic world, discrepancies between supply and demand decisions are omnipresent and universal. Whenever demand is less than supply or vice versa, the actual volume of transactions is "rationed" by the smaller of the two, leaving some consumers or some suppliers with unsatisfied demand or unsold supplies. The general guiding principle is that "money buys goods but goods do not buy money," so that income and effective demand depend on monetary factors and liquidity preference. Some ideas from this dynamic disequilibrium approach (although recast in equilibrium terms) have been since absorbed into modern macroeconomics in the form of cash-in-advance models and models incorporating concepts from search theory.

Modern (new classical) macroeconomics. Although monetarism and supply-side economics may no longer exist as independent schools of thought, modern macroeconomics has definitely absorbed them and has moved away decisively from the Keynesian quantity-adjustment-liquidity-preference theory. Economic models of modern macroeconomists are very similar to those used by microeconomists, and they consist of descriptions of consumers and firms, their objectives and constraints, and analyze those models and try to fit them to data using methods very similar to microeconomics. The focus, however, is on issues like long-run growth and business cycles rather than the explanation of relative prices. It is this difference in focus, rather than in method that still distinguishes macroeconomics from microeconomics. In other words, macroeconomics remains a separate field within the broad discipline of economics in that it deals with the overall effects on economies of the choices made by all economic agents, rather than with the choices of individual consumers or firms.

The key concept of the new classical macroeconomics is that of rational expectations. Rational expectations is an assumption according to which all information that is available in the market gets built into agents' expectations, so that no predictable change in economic parameters can have any, even short-term effects on the outcomes. In particular, no predictable change in government expenditure or money supply can affect the real economy. Hence, stabilization policies are meaningless in principle.

For example, agents with rational expectations will anticipate that an increase in government expenditure, even if it is covered by borrowing, will lead to an increase in future taxes and will save to provide for that anticipated rainy day (the Ricardian equivalence). It is only by complete surprise that changes in government policies can affect the real economy, and since government policies are closely monitored and analyzed by the market, such surprises are very unlikely to succeed. Moreover, even if surprises were possible and the government could, in principle, conduct macroeconomic policies aimed at stabilizing the economy, the value of such stabilization, it is argued, would be very limited and the government resources would be better spent elsewhere.

Instead of effective demand management, the largest part of modern macroeconomics concentrates on the study of factors affecting long-run growth, such as the accumulation of capital (including human capital) and changes in total factor productivity caused by technological progress, institutional changes and the like. This branch of modern macroeconomics is not only quite distinct from Keynesian macroeconomics in its method of analysis; it is actually its complete antipode since Keynesian macroeconomics was explicitly focused on a very short period during which the capital stock was assumed to be fixed.

The theory of long-run growth starts from the basic assumptions about utility maximization by the representative consumer (either assumed to be infinitely lived or representing a certain generation in the overlapping generation model) and it then goes on to analyze the consumption-investment decision, the accumulation of capital, technological change, and so on. The interest rate is determined by the rate of return on the capital good (real investment) and the portfolio choice of a representative agent allocating savings among various assets, financial and tangible. The neoclassical theory of growth is currently becoming more and more prominent as the leading form of macroeconomics of the 21st century.

Another branch of macroeconomics, the theory of the real BUSINESS CYCLE is more related to Keynesian macroeconomics in that at least it also focuses on the same time horizon. However since it builds the theory from micro-principles and assumes that supply equals demand in all markets, including the labor market, the method of analysis and the conclusions are completely different. In particular, unemployment, which was caused by not enough effective demand in the Keynesian system, is explained in terms of job search and other structural factors related to the labor market itself. More generally, the business cycle in its modern interpretation has a real, not monetary character in that it is generated by various exogenous and unanticipated shocks. Those shocks, through a complex mechanism of interactions produce cycle-type repercussions in investment, interest, and unemployment rates. Modern theory of the business cycle thus shares with the growth theory its skeptical attitude to government stabilization policies.

BIBLIOGRAPHY. John Maynard Keynes, *The General Theory of Employment, Interest and Money* (Macmillan, 1936); Mark Blaug, *Economic Theory in Retrospect* (Cambridge University Press, 1996); Robert Barro and Xavier Sala-i-Martin, *Economic Growth.* (McGraw-Hill, 1995); Stephen D. Williamson, *Macroeconomics* (Addison-Wesley, 2002); Andrew Abel and Ben Bernanke, *Macroeconomics* (Addison-Wesley, 2001).

SERGUEY BRAGUINSKY
STATE UNIVERSITY OF NEW YORK, BUFFALO

Madison, James (1751–1835)

THE FOURTH PRESIDENT of the UNITED STATES, James Madison, was born into a wealthy Virginia planter family, and graduated from the New Jersey College at Princeton in 1771.

At that time, issues over British control of America were reaching the boiling point. Madison joined the patriot cause, serving on the local Committee of Safety. In 1776, he participated in the Virginia Convention that declared independence and drafted a state constitution. Madison was elected to the Governor's Council in

1777, where he served under Governors Patrick Henry and Thomas JEFFERSON.

In 1780, Madison became a delegate to the Continental Congress, operating under the Articles of Confederation. He was quickly frustrated with its inability to accomplish anything substantial, and became a leading proponent for more powerful government. After four years, Madison returned to the Virginia Legislature, where he supported Jefferson's Bill for Religious Freedom and other reforms.

By 1787, Madison was a leading advocate for a convention to reform the Articles. When a convention was called in Philadelphia, Madison arrived with a draft that formed the basis for the new U.S. Constitution. Almost as important, Madison encouraged a reluctant George WASHINGTON to attend. Without Washington's prestige, the Convention's work probably would not have been ratified. Madison took detailed notes at the Convention, which, published after his death, are the best record of the debates.

Opposition to the proposed Constitution was widespread. Opponents objected to the powers given to the central government. Madison worked with Alexander HAMILTON and John Jay to draft a series of articles that would become known as the Federalist Papers to push New York's ratification. Madison's debates against Patrick Henry at the Virginia Ratifying Convention were critical to that State's ratification.

Although Madison succeeded with ratification, he lost his subsequent effort to become a U.S. Senator. Instead, he was elected to the House of Representatives, and only won that election (defeating James MONROE) by promising to enact a Bill of Rights—something he had opposed during ratification. Madison proposed 19 Constitutional Amendments. Twelve were sent to the states for ratification. Ten became the Bill of Rights, while another was eventually approved centuries later as the 27th Amendment in 1992.

For years, Madison had been an advocate of stronger federal government. However, as a Congressman, he began opposing measures to strengthen government. Two of his main adversaries were his coauthors of the Federalist Papers. He vehemently opposed Hamilton's plan to assume state debts from the Revolution, toning down his opposition only after Jefferson brokered a deal between them. Madison opposed the Jay Treaty involving trade, which he saw as favoring Great Britain.

Madison also opposed the creation of the Bank of the United States, which he argued was unconstitutional, and was against creating a large standing army or navy. He allied himself with Secretary of State Jefferson, and the two fought Hamilton's influence over Washington's presidency.

When John ADAMS became president, Madison discouraged Vice President Jefferson from cooperating with the administration, arguing that he should be a voice of opposition. He also anonymously wrote the Virginia Resolutions, arguing that a state could nullify unconstitutional federal actions.

Upon Jefferson's election in 1800, Madison became U.S. Secretary of State. During this time, Britain and FRANCE were at war giving Madison the opportunity to negotiate the Louisiana Purchase, doubling the size of the nation. The war, however, also proved costly to the United States. Both Britain and France seized American ships with impunity, often forcing American sailors to fight on foreign naval vessels. Because the United States had no navy of significance, it could not resist these actions. Madison proposed an embargo, simply ending all trade with both countries in the hope that this would force them to compromise. Instead, most of the harm fell on New England, which depended heavily on such trade. By the end of Jefferson's second term, some New Englanders were threatening secession. Congress eventually voted to end the embargo over Madison's objections.

Despite the controversy over the embargo, Madison won the 1808 presidential election overwhelmingly, winning most states outside of the New England coastline. However, British outrages on the high seas continued. By 1812, Madison urged Congress to declare war. Madison hoped to capture CANADA and force Britain off the continent forever. However, the small U.S. armies, made up primarily of militiamen, were not up to the task. The British invaded all along the coastline, including a raid on Washington, D.C. Madison attempted to direct defenses, escaping only just ahead of British troops who burned the White House.

The only, early victories came from the small U.S. Navy that Madison had opposed for so many years. The Navy captured or destroyed several British vessels in the Great Lakes and in the Atlantic, but their small numbers assured that Britain would continue to dominate the seas. The Americans successfully repulsed an invasion into New York State, and the biggest victory ironically came in 1815, when Andrew JACKSON defeated the British in the Battle of New Orleans, not having heard that the Treaty of Ghent had ended the war a few weeks earlier.

With the war over, Madison focused on a domestic program that repudiated many of his earlier positions on small government. Thus, he supported a stronger professional army and navy, a re-chartering of the Bank of the United States (which he had allowed to lapse in his first term), a tariff to protect U.S. industries, and using federal money to build roads and canals to bind the nation together.

Madison left office in 1817 after the election of his Secretary of State James Monroe. As a private citizen, he continued to support the tariff and the Bank of the

United States. He also repudiated his earlier views on state nullification. In 1829, he came out of retirement to support reforms at the Virginia Constitutional Convention. Madison died in 1835, the last survivor of the Constitutional Convention.

BIBLIOGRAPHY. Hamilton, Madison and Jay, *The Federalist Papers* (Mentor Books, 1999); James Madison, *Notes of Debates in the Federal Convention* (W.W. Norton, 1987); Ralph Ketcham, *James Madison: A Biography* (University Press of Virginia, 1990); Robert A. Rutland, *The Presidency of James Madison* (University Press of Kansas, 1990); Gary Wills, *James Madison* (Times Books, 2002).

MICHAEL J. TROY, J.D.
THOMAS D. JEITSCHKO, PH.D.
MICHIGAN STATE UNIVERSITY

Malaysia

LOCATED IN SOUTHEAST Asia, Malaysia consists of two non-contiguous regions. Occupying most of the Malay Peninsula, Peninsular Malaysia or West Malaysia, borders Thailand in the north and is across from SINGAPORE in the south. Approximately 400 miles east across the South China Sea from Peninsular Malaysia, East Malaysia occupies most of the northwestern coastal part of Borneo. East Malaysia shares Borneo with the sultanate of Brunei and with the Kalimantan region of Indonesia.

Malaysia's population is approximately 23.8 million (2001), with the vast majority living in Peninsular Malaysia. There is great ethnic, religious, cultural, and linguistic diversity among the population. This diversity is the result of centuries of immigration and trade, particularly with INDIA, CHINA, and Arab nations. Furthermore, there was very little homogenization of cultures, the result being that each culture has remained basically intact.

The majority of Malaysians live in *kampongs* (a village or community of houses) that consist of dwellings on stilts. The four main forms of settlements are fishing villages, paddy or wet-rice villages, mixed-crop villages, and cash-crop villages. The other forms of rural settlements are primarily associated with those who settled in Malaysia since the early 19th century. The introduction by the British of the plantation system, and the subsequent cultivation of rubber and palm oil, changed the face of rural Peninsular Malaysia and led to the development of large towns and cities centered around the tin and rubber belt along the peninsula's west side.

The early history of Malaysia is scarce. What is known is that there was early contact with China and with Hindu influences from India. Politically, Malaysia was subdivided into small kingdoms and chiefdoms. Be-

ginning in the 18th century, Great Britain became active in the area and, by the early 19th century, had gained control of Peninsular Malaysia and most of northern Borneo. As more and more people immigrated to Malaysia a pluralistic society developed.

The occupation of Malaysia by Japan during WORLD WAR II caused economic disruption and exacerbated communal tensions. After the war, some local self-government was introduced, which led to the creation in 1948 of the Federation of Malaya (which occupied what is now West Malaysia) and in 1957 culminated in the Federation of Malaya achieving its independence from Great Britain. In 1961, Malaya's first prime minister, Tunku Abdul Rahman, proposed a federation consisting of Malaya, Singapore, Sarawak, Sabah, and Brunei. All but Brunei joined in 1963. In 1965, due to economic and political disputes, Singapore exited the federation.

Since independence, Malaysian politics have been marred by numerous ethnic disputes. However, these disputes have not prevented Malaysia from experiencing rapid economic growth. Since the early 1970s, Malaysia has transformed itself from a producer of raw materials into one of the fastest-growing economies in Southeast Asia, and has led economists to include the country among Asia's "newly industrialized economies" (NIEs). While primary production is important (Malaysia is the largest producer of rubber and palm oil), Malaysia has focused on export-oriented manufacturing (particularly electronics) to drive its economic growth. This emphasis on manufacturing has led to the development of a variety of heavy industries, including steel-making and automobile assembly. Peninsular Malaysia accounts for the majority of the country's manufacturing output.

Since the early 1970s, the Malaysian government has implemented a social and economic restructuring plan, initially known as the New Economic Policy (NEP), which attempts to strike a balance between the goals of economic growth and the redistribution of wealth. The government has also encouraged the private sector to take a greater role in restructuring, leading to the privatization of many public-sector activities, including the national railway, airline, and telecommunications company.

Malaysia's economic growth has created a demand for labor, which has tended to increase wages. However, despite economic incentives, there has been a limited flow of workers from East to Peninsular Malaysia, thus prompting an interest in recruiting foreign workers.

BIBLIOGRAPHY. Ooi Jin-Bee, *Peninsular Malaysia* (Longman Publishing Group, 1976); Barbara Watson Andaya and Leonard Y. Andaya, *A History of Malaysia* (St. Martins Press, 1984); *CIA World Factbook* (2002).

S.J. RUBEL, J.D.
INDEPENDENT SCHOLAR

Malta

THE REPUBLIC OF MALTA is an independent republic of the Commonwealth of Nations, a small group of islands consisting of Malta, Gozo, Kemmuna, Kemmunett, and Filfla. The Maltese archipelago is located in the Mediterranean Sea, south of Sicily.

The Republic of Malta consists of the islands of Malta and Gozo and has a combined area of approximately 199 square miles, with a population of 391,700 in 2002. Located on the island of Malta is the capital, Valletta.

Valletta is the leading port of the country. Manufacturing for export, ship construction and repair, and tourism are Malta's chief industries. Shipping-related industries are vital to Malta's economy, including repair facilities and transport centers.

Malta's $1.2 million trade deficit each year makes the island highly dependent on foreign markets and services. Primary purchasers of Maltese products are FRANCE, UNITED STATES, GERMANY, SINGAPORE, and the UNITED KINGDOM. Principal exports include clothing, basic manufactures, and machinery. Principal imports are machinery, textiles, chemicals, raw materials, food, and fuels. Leading sources for imports are Italy, France, United Kingdom, Germany, and the United States.

In 1964, a new constitution, substantially amended in 1974, has brought the Maltese government to a parliamentary democracy. Malta is among the candidate countries set to join the EUROPEAN UNION (EU) in 2004.

BIBLIOGRAPHY. Neil Wilson, *Lonely Planet: Malta* (Lonely Planet, 2000); Shirley Jackewicz Johnson, et al., *The Spenders of Malta* (Rizzoli, 2001); *CIA World Factbook* (2002).

CHRIS HOWELL
RED ROCKS COLLEGE

Malthus, Thomas Robert (1766–1834)

ALTHOUGH SOMEWHAT controversial, Thomas Robert Malthus was an important figure in the development of classical economic thought. He addressed several topics in political economy, but is most widely remembered for his treatments of population growth and the potential inadequacy of aggregate demand.

The growth of population was the topic of his *Essay on the Principle of Population* that first appeared in 1798 and established his enduring fame. His most significant other volume was *Principles of Political Economy*, published more than 20 years later. Only since the 1930s, when aggregate demand again was recognized as constituting a central problem in economics did John Maynard KEYNES and others recognize Malthus as a forerunner of modern thought.

Malthus was the son of Daniel Malthus, a distinguished English scholar who prided himself on his advanced ideas and friendships with such leading intellectuals of the period as David HUME and Jean-Jacques Rousseau. Malthus grew up during the Enlightenment, was 10 years old at the onset of the American Revolution, graduated from Jesus College, Cambridge, in 1788 and was ordained a minister of the Church of England that same year. However, the Reign of Terror that followed in the wake of the FRENCH REVOLUTION stimulated discussions between the younger Malthus and his father concerning the possibility in human affairs of the extensive diffusion of liberty and happiness.

The father subscribed to an optimistic belief in the perfectibility of humankind and society that had been in popular esteem. Robert Malthus was far more pessimistic, and attributed the vices and misery that plagued society to the prolific fertility of the human race, rather than to evil institutions. Malthus' theory asserted that population, when left unchecked increases geometrically, while subsistence increases (at best) only arithmetically. By emphasizing the strict dependence of population growth on the food supply and by explaining poverty in terms of a simple race between population and the means of subsistence, the Malthusian theory of population growth became an integral part of classical economics and a point of departure for virtually every discussion of population problems. (This also earned economics the appellation of the "dismal science.")

In his *Principles*, Malthus examined the causes of economic growth and perceived that there could be difficulties in maintaining full employment. His concerns stemmed from the view that the while the process of saving leads to a reduction in the demand for consumer goods, the process of investment leads to an increase in the production of consumer goods. He concluded that because there was insufficient effective demand from the laborers and the capitalists, the difference had to be filled primarily by landowners since they consumed goods, but did not add to production.

BIBLIOGRAPHY. Mark Blaug, *Economic Theory in Retrospect* (Cambridge University Press, 1978); Thomas Robert Malthus, *An Essay on the Principle of Population* (Cambridge University Press, 1976); Henry William Spiegel, *The Growth of Economic Thought* (Duke University Press, 1991).

ELEANOR T. VON ENDE, PH.D.
TEXAS TECH UNIVERSITY

manifest destiny

MANY AMERICANS in the 19th century thought they had a special, God-given mission to eventually take over all of North America; this belief was known as manifest destiny. The expansionist impulse had been pulsing for a while; right from the founding of the nation, Americans had pursued new lands and expressed a confidence in the republic's distinct calling. President James MONROE acquired new territory in Florida, and in 1823 issued a statement of policy that asserted the nation's prominence in North America. Beyond declaring American neutrality from foreign conflicts, the Monroe Doctrine affirmed that the UNITED STATES would oppose any further colonization of the western hemisphere by European nations, and would view any incursion into the continent as a threat.

The idea that the United States had a special role to fulfill in North America would take on new significance in the late Jacksonian period. Democrats saw land as key to the very survival of republican government: new territories would provide room for the growth of settlement, and preserve the agrarian character of the nation. In 1845, New York journalist John O'Sullivan used the phrase "manifest destiny" to refer to the notion that Americans were providentially ordained to settle the entire continent. O'Sullivan believed that readily available land would ensure that America did not suffer some of the negative consequences of industrialization that were plaguing nations like Britain, including overcrowding and class unrest. Although the notion of manifest destiny was initially applied to the lands west of the Mississippi, the concept would eventually be broadened as a rationale for American expansion abroad.

Manifest destiny proclaimed Americans were providentially ordained to settle the continent west to the Pacific Ocean.

In 1843, President John TYLER opened secret negotiations with Texas for admission to the Union, but faced opposition from Northern abolitionists, worried about the expansion of slavery, and moderates, fearful of war with Mexico. The issue was revived by the 1845 election of Democrat James K. POLK, an outspoken expansionist. Polk hoped to acquire for the United States not only Texas but Oregon, and the territories which make up present-day New Mexico, Arizona, and California. A deal was struck with Great Britain to secure Oregon, but tensions with Mexico reached a breaking point in 1846. When Mexican troops crossed the Rio Grande to meet American soldiers led by Zachary TAYLOR, Congress declared war. U.S. forces invaded northern Mexico and eventually took New Mexico and California. A weakened Mexico agreed to cede all claims to Texas in the Treaty of Guadalupe Hidalgo, and established the Rio Grande as the United States's southern border; the size of the nation grew by 20 percent.

Belief in manifest destiny also implied a conviction of the superiority of the white race. American Anglo-Saxons, in this view, had a mission to bring the forces of progress and democracy to those already inhabiting the land. Journalists and politicians argued that the American people were obligated to extend their democratic principles from the Atlantic to the Pacific. In practice, however, much of this process of expansion was anything but democratic. Native Americans were driven relentlessly from territories desired by whites. In the southwest, Mexican settlers were dismissed as shiftless and undeserving of the land they inhabited. Both natives and Mexicans were depicted as inferior races unable to properly make use of the land. These racial beliefs helped to justify the aggressive efforts by white Anglo-Saxons to remove all other groups from disputed territories. Some expressed doubts that either natives or Mexicans could ever be fully integrated into the United States as citizens, and should instead be treated as colonial subjects.

The spirit of manifest destiny waned somewhat in the years after the Mexican-American War. While the acquisition of vast new lands seemed a triumph for the expansionist cause, dispute over the status of slavery in these territories would intensify sectional conflict within the United States, and contribute to the outbreak of the AMERICAN CIVIL WAR.

During the 1850s, many Southerners were attracted by the idea of acquiring Cuba. President Franklin PIERCE asked his secretary of state and three diplomats to recommend a course of action. The Ostend Manifesto, produced in 1854, suggested that America pursue purchase of Cuba from Spain, and asserted that if Spain refused to sell, the United States would be justified in seizing the territory. Reaction both at home and abroad was decidedly negative, and Pierce had to abandon the scheme as

Northerners accused him of trying to acquire another slave territory to appease the South.

By 1860, the larger, continentalist dimension of manifest destiny no longer seemed practical. Few suggested that America should push to acquire either British North America (which would involve going to war with Great Britain) or Mexico (where a racially mixed population raised uncomfortable questions about the inclusiveness of American democracy).

But the expansionist impulse would not remain dormant. In 1867, America negotiated the purchase of Alaska from Russia. By the last years of the 19th century, Americans expressed concern that there was nowhere left on the continent where they could expand. Historian Frederick Jackson Turner declared that the American frontier was officially closed, as white settlement had moved westward to the Pacific. The nation would need to find new outlets for its growth. Presidents Benjamin HARRISON and Grover CLEVELAND aggressively courted Latin America. Business leaders actively pursued foreign markets for goods, and identified certain lands as strategically desirable. Hawaii, with its sugar production and strategic location as a stepping-stone to Asia, was annexed in 1893 after the removal of nationalist Queen Liliuokalani. Samoa was the next possibility for American expansionist tendencies.

The most dramatic example of this new, international expression of manifest destiny would be in Cuba, where nationalists hoping to achieve independence from Spain were asking for American assistance. The United States remained neutral until after the election of William MCKINLEY, despite the efforts of sympathetic journalists to whip up public support for the Cubans. The explosion of the battleship *Maine* in 1898 in Havana Harbor propelled the United States into the war, and after ten weeks the fighting was over. America easily defeated the Spanish forces.

America's quick and relatively painless victory would set off a national debate about the future of the newly acquired territories of Guam, Puerto Rico, and the Philippines. Cuba was granted independence by Spain, but these other colonial possessions were judged unprepared for self-government. Critics charged that the United States had repudiated its own history by becoming an imperial power. A movement led by Emilio Aguinaldo hoped that the United States would recognize the independence of the Philippines, and waged guerrilla warfare against American authorities.

Yet business interests as well as many other groups including religious missionaries insisted that America should take an active role in shaping the future of these territories. By the early 20th century, America took on a new role as overseer of colonial territories.

Manifest destiny was an idea that emboldened Americans over a span of decades to actively pursue a strategy of territorial expansion. These initiatives were, at times, the subject of heated debate, and could have negative consequences for other groups who did not necessarily agree with America's sense of mission. Throughout the 19th century, this impulse to expand persisted—a peculiarly American combination of optimism, ambition, self-confidence, and capitalism. And once the possibilities for expansion within the continent were exhausted, a similar impulse drove American expansion around the globe, not only in the acquisition of new lands but also in the pursuit of new markets.

BIBLIOGRAPHY. Norman A. Graebner, ed., *Manifest Destiny* (Bobbs-Merrill, 1968); Thomas R. Hietala, *Manifest Design: Anxious Aggrandizement in Late Jacksonian America* (Cornell University Press, 1985); Reginald Horsman, *Race and Manifest Destiny: The Origins of American Racial Anglo-Saxonism* (Harvard University Press, 1981); Frederick Merk, *Manifest Destiny and Mission in American History: A Reinterpretation* (Alfred A. Knopf, 1963); Anders Stephanson, *Manifest Destiny: American Expansionism and the Empire of Right* (Hill and Wang, 1995).

SARAH ELVINS
UNIVERSITY OF NOTRE DAME

Marcuse, Herbert (1898–1979)

A MAJOR 20TH-CENTURY political philosopher, Herbert Marcuse applied a combination of Marxist theory and Freudian analysis to the study of modern Western politics, culture, and society. His focus on individual liberty and the deconstruction of modern society's repressive cultural institutions helped make him an icon of radicalism and an important intellectual influence on the New Left in 1960s and 1970s Europe and North America. He was born on July 19, 1898, in Berlin, GERMANY and died on July 29, 1979, in Starnberg, West Germany.

After serving in the German army during WORLD WAR I, Marcuse began university studies in Heidelberg where he also became an active member of the Social Democratic Party. He took his doctorate in literature in 1922 and after a short career selling books, he returned to Heidelberg in 1928 to study under one of the major philosophers of the time, Martin Heidegger. Marcuse remained there until 1933 when he accepted a position with the Institute for Social Research (the Frankfurt School), a Marxist think tank based in Frankfurt (but that later opened branches in Geneva and then New York). As a Jew and a political activist, Marcuse fled Germany soon after the rise of the Nazis to power, going first to Geneva in 1933 and then in 1934 to the UNITED STATES.

Marcuse settled in New York City, where he continued his intellectual work with the Frankfurt School. After the United States entered WORLD WAR II, Marcuse served his adopted country in the Office of Strategic Services and within the U.S. State Department, a role he continued into the 1950s. He then returned to academia, accepting professorships at Columbia and Harvard (1951–54), Brandeis University (1954–65), and the University of California, La Jolla (1965–76). From within the American academy, Marcuse launched a series of articles, books, and lectures in which he refined his Marxist-Freudian inquiry into reflections on capitalism and modern society's effects on the individual.

His trenchant critiques brought him to the height of his popularity and influence in the 1960s and 1970s. His major works included *Eros and Civilization* (1955), *One-Dimensional Man* (1964), *An Essay on Liberation* (1969), and *Counterrevolution and Revolt* (1972).

BIBLIOGRAPHY. Douglas Kellner, *Herbert Marcuse and the Crisis of Marxism* (University of California Press, 1984); John Bokina and Timothy J. Lukes, eds., *Marcuse: New Perspectives* (University of Kansas Press, 1994); Charles Reitz, *Art, Alienation, and the Humanities: A Critical Engagement with Herbert Marcuse* (State University of New York Press, 2000); Robert W. Marks, *The Meaning of Marcuse* (Ballantine, 1970).

CHARLES ROBINSON, PH.D.
BRANDEIS UNIVERSITY

marginal analysis

MANY, IF NOT MOST, economic decisions can be viewed as choosing the magnitude of a variable associated with both costs and benefits. For example, each month households must choose how much of their disposable income to save. SAVING brings benefits in increased consumption possibilities in the future, but at a cost that can be reckoned in foregone consumption today. Similarly, firms must choose how much to produce. Extra production brings the possibility of increased revenue, but will typically require increased input employment and, therefore, increased production costs.

Marginal analysis is a particular method for making this type of choice. Specifically, marginal analysis involves considering the relative merits of a given choice, by asking whether a net improvement could be achieved by making a slightly larger (or smaller) choice. So, for instance, we ask whether saving a little bit more of today's disposable income would be better, rather than jumping directly to the question of what amount of saving is best.

The answer to the question depends upon whether the benefits made available by increasing (or decreasing) the size of the choice variable by a small amount exceeds the extra costs incurred. If the benefit exceeds the extra cost, the original choice under consideration cannot be optimal, in which case the decision-maker can eliminate it from consideration and move on to consider the relative merits of a slightly larger (or smaller) choice. Continuing in this way, the decision-maker will eventually be led to the optimal size of the variable under consideration.

The label "marginal analysis" comes from terminology economists have developed to distinguish the incremental effect of a change in a choice variable on associated benefits or costs from the level of total benefits or total costs. Economists call the extra benefit associated with a small increase in the size of the choice variable, the marginal benefit. If one additional dollar's worth of saving today enables one to consume an extra $1.10 worth of goods tomorrow, the marginal benefit of saving (measured in dollars of tomorrow's consumption) is $1.10. Similarly, the extra COST incurred when a choice variable is increased by a small amount is called the marginal cost.

In short, then, marginal analysis can be defined as comparing the marginal benefit and marginal cost of a small change in the magnitude of a choice variable for the purpose of determining whether such a change would result in a net improvement.

For most economic problems, marginal benefits tend to decrease as the choice variable becomes large, while the marginal cost begins to rise. As long as that pattern holds, marginal analysis suggests a simple rule that decision-makers should always follow, which is sometimes called the equimarginal principle, as explained by economist Steven Landsburg: Select the choice variable size that equates marginal benefit with marginal cost.

Provided that marginal benefits are declining in the size of the choice variable (or at least not rising) and marginal costs are rising (or at least not declining), and provided that the value of the choice variable at which marginal benefit equals marginal cost is among the available options, the optimal size for the choice variable will be the size at which the equimarginal principle is satisfied.

This follows from the fact that the equimarginal principle is no more than the first-order condition for maximization of the net benefit function, where net benefit is defined as total benefit less total cost. Hence, as long as the choice variable is continuous and total benefit and total cost are both continuous, the equimarginal principle will identify any inflection points of the net benefit. Decreasing marginal benefits and increasing marginal cost will ensure that the inflection point is unique and a local maximum rather than a local minimum.

One of the most surprising and frequently cited implications of marginal analysis is that the price and production quantity that maximize a firm's profit will be unaffected by changes in certain types of costs. Specifically, fixed costs (costs that are independent of the amount of output produced) will have no impact on a firm's optimal price and production quantity. For example, if the amount of property TAX a firm pays each year rises, a profit-maximizing firm will not adjust the price at which it sells its output or the amount it produces.

This follows immediately from the equimarginal principle. At the profit-maximizing production level, the marginal cost of production will just equal the extra revenue that selling another unit of output would provide. While an increase in property taxes would affect the total cost of production, it would not affect the marginal cost. Since the property taxes would have to be paid regardless of the amount the firm produces, the extra cost of producing another unit of output is independent of the size of the tax.

BIBLIOGRAPHY. William J. Baumol and Alan S. Blinder, *Economics Principles and Policy* (The Dryden Press, 2000); Alpha C. Chiang, *Fundamental Methods of Mathematical Economics* (McGraw-Hill, 1984); Steven Landsburg, *Price Theory and Applications* (South-Western, 2001).

JOEL D. CARTON, PH.D.
TEXAS TECH UNIVERSITY

market

MARKETS ARE SITES where economic exchange occurs: physical locations, such as farmer's markets, malls, or downtown shopping areas or virtual sites, such as the internet or the postal system. People go to markets to find commodities that meet their needs or to find customers whose needs can be met with products they own and are willing to sell. Either way, people go to the market to engage in exchange or, at the least, to pursue the possibility of such an exchange. The exchanges that define sites as markets can be commodity for commodity exchanges, otherwise known as BARTER, or commodity for money exchanges.

Barter and local exchange trading systems. Barter exchange continues to be a significant process in many communities, although it has ceased to be the prevalent mode of exchange in virtually all communities. In contemporary societies, barter may sometimes provide traders with a means for evading tax authorities. For example, a plumber may agree to fix a faulty pipe for an auto mechanic in exchange for the auto mechanic repairing a busted exhaust system on the plumber's automobile. The exchange of good for good is not accounted for in any records, and does not result in an increase in the identifiable taxable income or sales for either of these two parties. However, tax evasion is not the only, or the most important, reason for the persistence of barter exchange.

Barter continues to play a role in exchange relationships in many rural communities, as well as in impoverished urban areas, because it provides a means for trade to take place without the need for money as the medium of the exchange. By definition, impoverished communities suffer from a relative scarcity of currency. However, the lack of money does not mean that these communities lack tradeable skills or resources. Barter markets can, under certain conditions, provide the mechanism for a community to realize hidden wealth.

Nevertheless, barter has, over time, given way to exchanges involving goods trading for money. These monetized exchanges make it much easier to carry out trades. It eliminates the famous necessity of a coincidence of needs, where party A must simultaneously have what party B wants and need what party B has. An elementary form of a monetized market results from a local exchange trading system (LETS). LETS allows economic agents in local communities to exchange with each other without the need of a national currency as medium of exchange. The first LETS was developed in Canada in 1983 as an adaptation of a barter exchange system. LETS reveals the importance of money to the growth of market transactions. It is simply too difficult to meet all local needs and tap local talents with barter alone.

LETS aside, monetized exchanges employing national (or multinational) currencies also facilitate long-distance transactions, since state-sponsored currencies are typically very portable. This allows for the expansion of market transactions across larger geographical spaces and, more recently, into cyberspace.

Global markets. Indeed, in the contemporary world exchanges for money increasingly take place across national boundaries and often involve multiple currencies. Money can change hands via electronic transmission, although goods continue, at least for the foreseeable future, to require more traditional means of transport. It is possible for a telecommunications firm in Kuala Lumpur to purchase equipment from a firm in Kansas City by mail, telephone, or, increasingly, the internet. The market for telecom equipment is, therefore, global. And this is made possible by a wide range of technological inventions and innovations, both in terms of hard technology and changes in how the institutions are organized. For example, the money transfers required to conduct long-distance trade are typically facilitated by computerized systems of accounting for currency flows across national borders. The banks and other financial institutions that manage these monetary flows are increasingly transnational and supported by nation-based central banks that keep reserves of many national currencies and act as intranational and international clearing institutions. Thus, while barter exchange is one end of the market spectrum in terms of complexity, international market exchanges are on the opposite end.

The complications to market expansion posed by multiple national currencies have been reduced, in part, by a tendency toward trade in a small number of hard currencies. The U.S. DOLLAR, the Japanese YEN, and the EURO are examples of such hard currencies. The reasons that certain national currencies have been internationalized in this way are similar, in many ways, to the reasons for the rise of monetized exchange as a substitute for barter exchange. If a national currency, like the U.S. dollar, becomes widely accepted in exchanges in many nations, then the utility of the dollar as a medium of exchange is greatly enhanced. The greater the utility of the dollar, the greater its value vis-à-vis other currencies. The reverse also holds. Thus, the ascendance of a currency to the status of hard currency creates a virtuous cycle. This virtuous cycle benefits both the nation issuing the hard currency and those nations that use it. To the extent the U.S. dollar achieves hard-currency status, the greater the global demand for the dollar in currency markets.

The stronger the dollar the more attractive U.S. financial and other asset markets become, because U.S. assets are not only denominated in dollars but generate future cash flow in this hard currency. And the hard currency status of the dollar would also benefit markets within and between other nations. For example, if the U.S. dollar is accepted in both countries A and B, but their domestic currencies have more local acceptance, then it may be easier to make exchange agreements between firms in the two countries if the monetary terms are denominated in U.S. dollars. Thus, the rise of hard currencies has the side effect of generating increased international transactions and more globalized markets.

Indeed, the U.S. dollar was, from its inception, a catalyst for the development of both local and cross-border markets, helping to forge a single market among the constituent states of the UNITED STATES, replacing the British pound, one of the world's first truly hard currencies, which had played a similar role in the American colonies. Today the euro is playing a similar role in uniting the economies of the EUROPEAN UNION (EU). Because the euro is readily accepted in exchange within the EU and the EU represents, collectively, one of the world's largest economies, the euro was born as a hard currency.

Markets in cyberspace. The growth of markets in cyberspace is speeding up the globalization of market exchange and creating increased pressures on political and economic authorities to lower impediments to such exchange. Financial markets, in particular, have been significantly extended within cyberspace. A side effect of the growth of financial market transactions within cyberspace has been to pressure financial institutions to provide 24-hour services to their cyberspace clients. It has become commonplace for brokerages, for example, to offer "after hours" trading, and for banks to make it possible for their customers to pay bills, transfer funds, and carry out other financial transactions outside of normal banking hours. Thus, the market has grown not only in spatial terms, but in temporal terms, as well.

Labor markets are also being transformed and extended within cyberspace. The buying and selling of the potential to perform specialized labor is the defining characteristic of capitalism. As it becomes possible to link buyers and sellers of laboring potential across larger geographic distances, due to internet-based labor markets, the difficulties of matching DEMAND and SUPPLY in the labor market should be significantly reduced. In addition, pressures to reduce, though not necessarily eliminate, some of the differentials between same-skill wages across geographic regions increase. Over time, the ability to lower these market differentials will depend critically upon both the ability of workers to relocate and their willingness to do so. The expansion of labor markets across international borders remains particularly problematic as multilateral trade agreements have not, in general, included free-labor mobility alongside free-capital mobility as an important condition.

Markets and political boundaries. The impediments to the growth of international labor markets points out the fact that the presence of monetized exchange is not a sufficient condition for expanding markets across the political boundaries separating nation states. Other barriers to international markets include TARIFFS (taxes imposed on imports) and QUOTAS (quantitative restrictions on imports), administrative rules, monopolized merchant systems, poor infrastructure for the transport of goods and the transmission of data, and discriminatory exchange-rate systems. These impediments to expanded markets can only be eliminated by the signing and enforcement of agreements between national governments.

Since the end of WORLD WAR II, there has been a trend toward such agreements, both bilateral and multilateral, to reduce and, in some cases, completely eliminate barriers to international markets. The multilateral agreements have been particularly important in reshaping global exchange relationships and domestic/national market conditions. The first such major multilateral agreement was the GENERAL AGREEMENT ON TARIFFS AND

TRADE (GATT). More recently, this movement toward globalized markets was reinforced and moved forward by creation of the WORLD TRADE ORGANIZATION (WTO).

Hard currencies, technological changes that facilitate the rapid electronic transmission of data, the development of international laws governing contracts, GATT and WTO, and other such institutional developments have all worked to facilitate expanded, more globalized exchange processes. Have there been benefits from these expanded markets? The expansion of markets across international boundaries makes it possible for producers in country X to respond not only to demand in country X, but also in countries Y and Z. The enlarged market for producers in country X creates the potential for expanded production, more employment, and higher national income in that country. And what about costs of expanded markets? Certainly expansion in global markets has hurt specific industries in certain countries as firms in these industries found it difficult to compete with similar firms with lower cost structures in other nations.

In capitalist economies, market competition can often lead to bankruptcies of firms, including widespread collapse of entire industries, and employment problems for workers with skills linked to those firms and industries. The pressures to compete in the global marketplace may push national governments to implement public policies that reduce the costs of doing business in certain industries, or for business as a whole, in order to make domestic firms more competitive, and to avoid the ill effects of bankruptcies and layoffs. This may, however, result in a shift in public policy priorities away from such issues as environmental protection, worker health and safety, and/or income redistribution, even if a majority of the domestic population favors such policies. In this sense, globalized markets may conflict with democratically determined political priorities.

The nexus between markets and the larger society. Markets do not exist in isolation from other social processes. Markets are always important determinants of other social processes, including political processes, and vice versa. For example, labor markets influence the way school schedules are arranged and, more generally, our perception of time and space, or popular opinions about appropriate dress and behavior. Markets for consumable goods influence architecture, transportation systems, and the language we use. And, in turn, markets are necessarily shaped, directly or indirectly, by a wide range of political, cultural, environmental, and other economic processes. For example, the environmental movement has spawned new markets in biodegradable products, natural clothing, and organic foods.

Indeed, it is this interaction of the market with other social processes that makes it such an important catalyst

for economic growth and development. Because the market exists as a series of transactions between unique economic agents, it becomes a mechanism for signaling and mediating differences of perception. If economic agents are dissatisfied with an existing array of products, they can signal this displeasure through their market activities. Other economic agents, picking up on these signals, can respond by offering alternative products. This can result in new invention and innovation, as part of the response to these signals. Similarly, economic agents may respond favorably to the lower cost and/or higher quality of products generated by new, experimental technologies, resulting in the more widespread adoption of such technologies.

Thus, the market can motivate economic agents to take actions that have benefits for the larger society, stimulating higher productivity, better quality products, more rapid economic growth, and the sort of transformation in underlying technology that is described in the economics literature as economic development.

But the signals that markets send are not always positive or even benign. Because the market is nothing more than the collection of transactions of real human beings, then markets can only signal certain of the innermost desires of those human beings who engage in trading, with some human beings having access to more resources with which to signal their desires than others. This, in and of itself, indicates that markets are not innately fair. But it also indicates that market transactions reproduce the prejudices of those economic agents who are in a position to act as traders. If traders are prejudiced against the French, for example, then they may be unwilling to buy French products no matter how high the quality or how low the price. Their actions signal that French products are less desirable, perhaps resulting in a drop in French production, regardless of whether or not these products are better than the favored alternatives. There may be no way to know, by observing the market, if the prejudices are shaped by perceptions of differences in quality or prejudices based on more irrational factors. The market cannot tell us this.

Similarly, if economic agents are addicted to nicotine, their purchase of cigarettes may be a relatively involuntary response to their addiction, rather than a signal that cigarettes are a desirable product. Nevertheless, the demand for cigarettes may generate a higher production of a good that has significant negative social impact.

And because markets bring together unique human beings, or groupings of human beings, to engage in transactions, there is never a market within which the two parties are equal. By definition, in the real world, there will be differences in knowledge, social connections, MARKET POWER, and other relevant factors that will influence the transaction at hand.

Markets in theory and practice. This opens up the question of the difference between the markets we encounter in the real world and the markets that are postulated within economic theory. Theorizing the way markets work, and the role of markets in the larger society, have been an important aspect of all the major economic theories of the past three centuries. Dating back to the works of Adam SMITH and David RICARDO, and then elaborated in a new way by Karl MARX, the market-exchange process was seen as the realization in monetary terms of underlying relationships between different kinds of human labor.

The relative social value of the labor was reflected in the relative prices of commodities in the market. Human labor is valued according to the demand for the products of that human labor, and the value of the products are determined by the value of the human labor embodied in them. This is a tautology. The decision to define the value generated in market exchange in this way was a function of the underlying morality of the theorists. Marx, in particular, wanted to argue that the apparent equality of market exchange, as depicted in orthodox theories, was only a surface illusion masking an underlying relationship of exploitation. The wage rate is determined in the market for labor, but it actually reflects the relative powerlessness and lack of CAPITAL of workers. The price of other commodities reflects the real value of this labor, as well as the value of the material inputs consumed in production.

For Smith, Ricardo, and Marx, the market served not only as a means of satisfying needs and allowing producers to realize monetary returns, but was, in some fundamental way, the manifestation in social exchange of more complex social relationships. A key consequence of the approach of Smith, Ricardo, and Marx was to draw attention to the contingent and contested nature of market exchange and production.

Neoclassical ECONOMIC THEORY was developed to counter the Marxian conception of the market, and restore the notion of the market as the real reflection of underlying equality in society. The normative conclusions of neoclassical economic theory depend critically upon this alternative conception of market exchange.

HOMO ECONOMICUS (HM), the economic agents who engage in market transactions in the neoclassical model, are assumed to be relatively simple-minded entities, shaped by a thought process called UTILITY maximization, which is constrained at the level of decision-making by a limited budget. In the strict version of the theory, HM has access to the same information as the other participants in market exchange relationships (symmetric information); is able to correctly assess the effect of market transactions upon his well-being and future budget constraints; does not lie or cheat; is consistent and unemotional in his preference orderings (rational-

ity); and his preferences are uninfluenced by all possible manner of non-market processes (including peer pressure), among other restrictions. It is typically assumed that the transactions between these economic agents result in all the observable prices and quantities in real-world markets.

In other words, the real world is believed to be understandable by reference to the model of the market constructed based on HM. The most utopian version of this model results in PARETO OPTIMALITY: the best of all possible worlds created by market exchanges. It is from this model that the popular conception of the "free market" originates. The neoclassical conception of the market has become an important polemical tool in public policy debates, particularly those involving the role of government in shaping and enforcing rules of market exchange.

The market remains a contested concept. A wide range of heterodox (non-neoclassical) theories have developed alternative conceptions of the market. Often the argument in favor of the alternatives is that they incorporate more real-world characteristics than the neoclassical orthodoxy. This has been the case with behavioral-finance theorists, for instance, who have set themselves the very pragmatic and testable task of making sense of price movements in real-world financial markets. The financial markets represent a wonderful laboratory for the analysis of markets. These markets come as close as any to meeting certain market-condition assumptions of the strict form of the neoclassical model, yet frequently (if not every day) violate many of the conclusions of that model.

The corporate-finance version of neoclassical economic theory, the efficient-market hypothesis, predicts that markets will be fairly valued at any particular moment in trading. However, markets frequently go through significant revaluations that indicate rapidly shifting opinions about fair value. These shifts are not sufficiently explained by shocks external to the market. In other words, the behavioral-finance theorists have come to recognize that the participants in real-world markets are not HM, but emotional and often inconsistent economic agents, highly sensitive not only to non-market processes, including cultural processes (hubris, fear, uncertainty, fads), but are often hypersensitive to the emotional waves of other market participants.

In other words, the traders in the markets hypothesized by behavioral-finance theorists are capable of engaging in irrational trades. The resulting understanding of the market may not be as aesthetic as that in the neoclassical conception or lead to as unambiguously non-interventionist public policies, but behavioral-finance theorists argue that it would likely have more utility in decision-making involving market behavior, such as portfolio-management decisions involving publicly traded securities.

Markets and capitalism. Perhaps one of the reasons for the disagreements over the concept of markets is the important role that markets have played in the rise to prominence of capitalism. Capitalism, as an economic system founded upon the free wage-labor relationship, can only exist if there are markets for the buying and selling of the capacity to perform labor, that is, labor markets. Thus, most immediately, capitalism requires the existence and expansion of such labor markets. In labor markets, this capacity to perform labor is the commodity that is exchanged, typically, for currency. No wage-labor markets, no capitalism.

The existence of labor markets may, in turn, depend upon the existence of widespread markets in consumer goods. Labor markets cannot exist without a significant number of people willing to work for a wage. But it is widely accepted within both orthodox and heterodox economic theories that people work for a wage because the wage embodies a bundle of useful goods, of consumption goods. Thus, the wage may be paid in kind, where the worker directly receives as part of the wage such consumer goods as food, clothing, shelter. If the wage is monetized, then there must be sufficient goods available for purchase in money such that the worker can buy these goods with her wage. The wage is, therefore, only of indirect value to the worker. Perhaps, then, the idea that markets are critical to capitalism is well-grounded. The labor market may be linked by definition to capitalism, but perhaps widespread consumer-goods markets are conditions for the existence of the labor market. Thus, markets and capitalism are closely linked.

On the other hand, it would be a mistake to assume a one-to-one correspondence between markets and capitalism. While capitalism may need markets to exist and growth in markets to expand, this does not mean that markets need capitalism. Indeed, non-capitalist economic systems have often been highly dependent upon market exchange. Markets have been, under certain circumstances, conditions for the existence of self-employment, SLAVERY, and FEUDALISM. Slavery in the United States, for example, was a particularly market-oriented system of production, with most slave plantations producing goods for export outside of the local region, and many plantations exporting to foreign markets. It would, therefore, be problematic to see the rise in market exchange as necessarily leading to the rise in capitalism. These are two different sets of social conditions.

BIBLIOGRAPHY. Robert Heilbroner, *The Worldly Philosophers* (Simon & Schuster, 1953); Donald Katzner, *Walrasian Microeconomics: An Introduction to the Economic Theory of Market Behavior* (University of Michigan Press, 1988); Douglass North, "Markets and Other Allocation Systems in History: The Challenge of Karl Polanyi," *European Economic History Review* (v.6, 1977); Adam Smith, *An Inquiry into the Nature and Causes of the Wealth of Nations* (1776, Modern Library, 1994); Richard H. Thaler, *Advances in Behavioral Finance* (Russell Sage Foundation, 1993); Richard D. Wolff and Stephen A. Resnick, *Economics: Marxian versus Neoclassical* (Johns Hopkins University Press, 1987).

SATYA J. GABRIEL
MOUNT HOLYOKE COLLEGE

market efficiency

THE NOTION THAT THE prices of financial assets reflect all the available information on those assets is referred to as MARKET efficiency. In an informationally efficient market, the PRICE of an asset exactly reflects the value of the asset based on available information. Therefore, any change in price will only occur following the arrival of new information. Since such new information is not predictable, movements in stock prices cannot be predicted on the basis of current information. Thus, except for the normal increase necessary to induce investors to bear the risk inherent in holding stock, stock prices in an efficient market will follow a "random walk." A random walk is a process in which stock returns in successive periods are independent and identically distributed. This would imply that stock returns should follow no particular trend and would therefore have zero serial correlation.

The Efficient Markets Hypothesis (EMH) refers to the proposition that stock markets are informationally efficient. There are three versions of the hypothesis. The weak form of the EMH states that stock prices reflect all historical information pertaining to the prices and trading volumes. Under this hypothesis, any attempt to discern and exploit patterns in stock price movements is unlikely to be profitable.

Technical analysis refers to the practice of identifying specific patterns in past stock price data that may be used to generate buy and sell recommendations. Technical analysts use a variety of techniques to identify such features in stock prices as momentum and reversal.

Momentum refers to the property for stock prices to continue to move in the same direction as in the recent past, while reversal refers to the tendency of stock prices to "correct" the past trend and move in the opposite direction. One way to test for the presence of such properties in stock prices is to examine the serial correlation of stock returns. Momentum implies that today's returns would be positively correlated with yesterday's returns, while reversal implies a negative correlation. Studies indicate that stock returns display mild momentum over short and intermediate horizons ranging from a week to several months. Accordingly, market participants have developed several trading strategies to exploit these properties.

One such strategy uses the filter rule, that prescribes buying stocks whose prices have increased by a fixed percentage in the recent past, and selling those whose prices have decreased. Stock returns also appear to follow strong trend reversals over periods of several years, leading to the development of the contrarian strategy of investing, which involves buying stocks which have performed poorly in the past few years and selling those that have done well.

Under the weak form of the EMH, trading strategies such as those based on filter rules and the contrarian strategy will not be profitable. Since past price information is available to all market participants, any such patterns would also be observed by the rest of the market, precluding their use as signals to beat the market. Studies in foreign currency and stock markets appear to indicate that relatively simple trading rules based on past prices, such as the moving-average rule might produce abnormally high returns (i.e., beat the market). The moving-average rule involves buying those stocks whose current prices are below the average price over a certain fixed period in the past, such as the previous 100 days, and selling those whose prices are above the moving average.

If markets systematically tend to overreact, then such a strategy would identify those stocks whose prices have been pushed too high or low in reaction to past events. One common problem with such studies is that the risk inherent in these strategies is not easily measured. Therefore, it is not possible to confirm whether any returns to these strategies are over and above the level necessary to compensate for their risk.

The semi-strong form of the EMH states that stock prices incorporate all publicly available information, which includes past price information as well as non-price information such as the status of the company. Fundamental Analysis refers to the practice of studying the financial statements and market prospects of a company in order to make a judgment as to its attractiveness as an investment. In deciding whether to invest in a stock, analysts look at several financial indicators such as the P/E ratio which is the ratio of the price of the company's stock to its earnings per share (EPS), the Dividend Yield, which is ratio of the dividends per share to the share price and the book-to-market ratio, which is the ratio of the book value of a share to its market value. According to the semi-strong form of the EMH, none of these indicators is likely to yield a profitable investment strategy, since all of them are based on publicly available information. Studies have shown that several indicators such as the firm size, book-to-market ratio, dividend yield, earnings yield and the P/E

ratio have predictive power for stock returns, implying that they may be usable in trading strategies to generate abnormal returns. These results are referred to as anomalies in the market. However, alternative explanations have been suggested for these results that do not rely on market inefficiency.

The strong form of the EMH suggests that all information including insider information is incorporated in stock prices. Under this version, even insider information would not be useful as a trading tool to beat the market. Studies have indicated a tendency for stock prices to rise after aggressive purchases by insiders and to fall after aggressive insider selling, indicating an ability on the part of insiders to make abnormal profits. However, studies also indicate that attempts to mimic INSIDER TRADING by following the SECURITY AND EXCHANGE COMMISSION's (SEC) "Official Summary of Security Transactions and Holdings" may not be profitable, implying that markets quickly incorporate the information in these reports.

One technique commonly used to test whether markets are efficient is the event study. This method involves isolating the effect of an informational event on the stock price, by studying the trend in stock returns prior to and after the event. Under this method, stock returns are first predicted assuming normal circumstances (i.e., absent the event). If the event had a significant impact on the stock price, then the stock returns post-event would have to be abnormally high or low relative to the predicted returns in the absence of the event. Therefore, the cumulative abnormal return (CAR) over a given post-event period such as week or two weeks would be a measure of the impact of the event.

Event studies have been used to analyze the impact of dividend and earnings announcements by firms. In an informationally efficient market, an announcement of unexpectedly good or bad performance (the event) must be quickly incorporated into the stock price, leading to a sudden change in the stock price around the event. Thus, the stock return should be abnormally high or low immediately following the event, but should not continue to deviate from the predicted value for much longer. In other words, there should be no continued drift in the CARs. However, studies of earnings announcements by firms find such a drift: the CARs continue to grow for up to two months after the announcement, implying a slow reaction on the part of the market to earnings surprises. This appears to indicate some form of market inefficiency.

A direct test of market efficiency is whether it is possible for market participants to make consistently high profits. Studies of mutual fund performance indicate that fund managers do not consistently outperform the market, once risk is appropriately accounted for. For example, while funds that invest only in small stocks will likely yield higher average returns than large stock funds, these higher returns are due to the higher risk inherent in these stocks. Overall, it appears that markets are largely efficient.

BIBLIOGRAPHY. Rolf Banz, "The Relationship Between Return and Market Value of Common Stocks," *Journal of Financial Economics* (v.19, 1981); Zvi Bodie, Alex Kane and Alan J. Marcus, *Investments* (McGraw-Hill); John Y. Campbell and Robert Shiller, "Stock Prices, Earnings and Expected Dividends," *Journal of Finance* (v.43, 1988); Jennifer Conrad and Gautam Kaul, "Time-Variation in Expected Returns," *Journal of Business* (v.61, 1988): Werner F. M. DeBondt and Richard Thaler, "Does the Stock Market Overreact?" *Journal of Finance* (v.40, 1985): Eugene F. Fama and Marshall Blume, "Filter Rules and Stock Market Trading Profits," *Journal of Business* (Supplement, January, 1966); Eugene F. Fama and Kenneth R. French, "Permanent and Temporary Components of Stock Prices," *Journal of Political Economy* (v.96, 1988); Eugene F. Fama and Kenneth R. French, "Dividend Yields and Expected Stock Returns," *Journal of Financial Economics* (v.22, 1988).

NARAYANAN SUBRAMANIAN, PH.D.
BRANDEIS UNIVERSITY

market power

MARKET POWER REFERS to the ability of MARKET participants to substantially affect prices to their own benefit. While one usually thinks of sellers possessing market power, the definition also applies to situations in which a buyer has the ability to substantively affect the prices paid for a good or service. This is often the case when the government is the sole purchaser of a good, for example, or when a large company is dealing with small suppliers for certain inputs.

Market power thus contrasts with perfectly competitive markets, in which market forces determine prices and individual buyers and sellers have little or no power to affect them. The most extreme form of market power is usually associated with MONOPOLY.

Market power is of concern when it is directed against consumers in final goods and services markets. Indeed, it is a major indication of unfair, and possibly illegal, trade practices. Hence, it is important to have guidelines that establish how market power can be detected. There are two competing formalizations of market power. Both rely on comparisons between the cost of producing something and the price that the firm is charging.

The marginal cost approach to market power. The first formalization is conceptually quite sophisticated, and considers mark-ups of prices above marginal costs. Marginal costs are the costs that are incurred when producing the final unit of a good or service. These include all the material and labor costs that go into producing that unit, but usually do not account for overhead expenses, as these costs are incurred even if units were not produced. Economists generally prefer this method because in price negotiations, the only cost considerations that matter to the firm are marginal costs, as all other costs will be incurred regardless of the sale under consideration.

The average- or unit-cost approach. The second formalization relies on average (unit) costs, and attempts to measure the degree by which prices exceed the unit cost (a cost measure that accounts for all the costs incurred in production). Due to its simplicity, policy-makers and administrators usually prefer this formalization. The main drawback to this approach, however, is that many costs are subject to accounting interpretations and can be very subjective.

Both concepts may be hard to apply to many cases of interest, though, particularly if marginal costs are extremely low compared to unit costs. Consequently, other proxies are often used to determine the presence of market power. To illustrate, briefly consider two industries: computer operating systems, where market power was purported to be detected via market share; and airline travel, where market power was detected by price comparisons in different markets.

In 2000, the Antitrust Division of the United States Justice Department brought a suit against MICROSOFT, alleging—among other things—that Microsoft had established a monopoly in computer-operating systems. The Microsoft operating system, Windows, is used in approximately 80 percent of computers worldwide. Such a high market share was presumed to indicate significant market power. While Microsoft did not contest this figure, it strongly disputed its significance, claiming that despite having a virtual monopoly, it did not have any market power. In particular, Microsoft argued that it faced effective competition from four sources that limited its market power:

1. Competition from other (small) providers that were currently in the market

2. Potential new entrants who would immediately enter the market if Microsoft were to charge a high price

3. If Microsoft were to increase their prices, people would simply remain with the previous (and now slightly outdated) version of the operating system

4. The possibility existed to pirate their software if it were priced too high.

In addition, Microsoft presented evidence that the monopoly price for their operating system would be somewhere between $900 and $2000 (in contrast to the approximate $100 they were charging). While this may be somewhat compelling evidence, it appears clear-cut that Microsoft used its dominant position in order to gain advantages for its other products. Ultimately, the Justice Department and Microsoft settled out of court in November 2001.

In AIRLINE travel, the traditional measures of market power are also hard to assess. If a plane is to fly a given route, then the marginal cost of letting one more passenger on board may be negligible, yet no one would expect airline tickets to be sold for next to nothing. However, the unit cost may also be hard to assess, given varying fleet utilization rates and other complicating factors. Finally, the complicated fares and schedules that most airlines offer make it hard to determine the relevant price. However, in 1993, a government investigation found that airfares out of airports that were served by a single airline were almost a third higher than in those served by several airlines. By the early 2000s, between the terrorist attacks, war news, disease alerts, and the resulting drop in air travel, airlines' market power became more a matter of survival, as shocks to the airline industry often resulted in large losses to airlines (and sometimes lead to bankruptcies).

BIBLIOGRAPHY. Luís M.B. Cabral, *Introduction to Industrial Organization* (MIT Press, 2000); Alan B. Krueger, ed., "Symposium on The Microsoft Case," *The Journal of Economic Perspectives* (v.15/2, 2001); W. Kip Viscusi, John M. Vernon, and Joseph E. Harrington, Jr., *Economics of Regulation and Antitrust* (MIT Press, 2000).

THOMAS D. JEITSCHKO, PH.D.
MICHIGAN STATE UNIVERSITY

marketing

RESEARCH ABOUT MARKETING is at the intersection of three disciplines: economics, social psychology, and communication studies. Usual definitions of marketing often include standard formulations such as "marketing is a process that identifies, anticipates and satisfies customer requirements profitably." This means in order to maximize sales and profits, producers of goods and services must simply try to give the customer what she wants. In order to reach this goal (and to know exactly what the customer really wants), marketing experts can use different methods to understand how the consumer would be fully satisfied and adjust production plans accordingly. Different approaches are possible: surveys, laboratory tests, consumer satisfaction services, focus groups, and comparisons with other labels and trademarks, among other tools.

Opposing concepts. Although it is an important part of every organization's strategy and PLANNING, in order to succeed marketing's aims and methods cannot be reduced to just a simple formula, such as "The right product, at the right time, in the right place, at the right price." Endless competition among manufacturers (and as well among retailers) creates distortions between producers, consumers, and intermediaries, all along the production chain. Moreover, this idealistic conception of a fluid producer-consumer relationship with constant feedback is sometimes challenged by the down-to-earth facts of day-to-day reality. This explains why marketing can be conceived in two opposite ways. Is marketing a responding attitude toward the customer's real needs or, on the other hand, an active attempt to suggest new products to a potential consumer, who wasn't aware of those needs, or not even looking for anything in particular to buy?

This second definition corresponds to the other side of marketing, which is, now and then, presented as a kind of invisible method of creating new desires, and therefore new needs for new consumers. According to this contested approach, marketing would make you want something you don't absolutely need (or something you can't really afford). Vance Packard wrote, in 1957, an alarming and famous book about the hidden potential powers of marketing, *The Hidden Persuaders: What Makes Us Buy, Believe—and even Vote—the Way We Do.*

Even if Packard's book was a huge success that sold more than a million copies, these arguments and demonstrations are to be taken with moderate doubts, knowing that mass psychology and behavioral studies have evolved in recent decades. Nevertheless, we have to admit that many products that are sold almost everywhere are not the best, or the more valuable ones in their respective field. The adequacy between quality, availability, and convenience is not automatic, and changes from one to another. For instance, fast-food restaurants are to be found everywhere, but fine-cuisine restaurants, or meals made with only natural products, are available only in specialized outlets.

On the other hand, we know that consumers do not necessarily compare all different products every time they go shopping. According to where they live and the stores they shop, some of these consumers do not always have access to all labels and specific products because of product DISTRIBUTION. Marketing is not just a method for reaching the customer in more than one way, it is also about how to create and sustain a hopefully durable relationship between the seller and the buyer.

Serving clients is a dedicated procedure. Gaining confidence and new customers is essential for a company to grow. This means either making people aware of what you have to offer in order to make them use it, or even attracting customers from your competitors by offering them something else, something more, i.e., better treatment or optimal conditions. But changing a CONSUMER's habits, even for the better, can be a complicated mission for a marketing agent. Client retention becomes the next challenge for marketing experts; satisfying a customer's requests and never taking her for granted.

This is why marketing is not simply a strategy to reach new customers, but also a way to get a broader market share, by convincing commercial partners to give a better visibility to one's products (in stores, in displays, in show cases, in promotions, in general advertisement). This preference over other labels can either be given, negotiated, traded, paid for (in cash, bonuses, or by sharing profits on a preferred scale). Consequently, this also means that a product's qualities are not always enough to reach the largest market share. According to aggressive marketing theorists, special arrangements, exclusive rights, and trade agreements are proven to be more efficient methods. Consumer behavior studies have proven that many people just choose what is easily within reach, without much questioning. They naturally rely on store managers' judgments to do the right pre-selection of products that are offered, no matter on what real grounds these choices are effectively based and made.

History of marketing. Strategies for reaching new customers are even depicted in the Bible, but the systematic study of marketing is quite recent in universities and business schools. According to Morgen Witzel, the author of an 8-volume reference on marketing, "It was only in the early 20th century that marketing began to emerge as a coherent business discipline." Many theoretical reflections about the constant need to reach newer markets were written in the 19th century by Karl MARX and Adam SMITH.

Consumer relations have profoundly changed in a few centuries. We can easily imagine the figure of an old, hardworking craftsman from previous centuries, who built in his workshop either precise violins or tailored clothes for specific customers. When he was too busy or had too many orders at the same time, he just refused new customers. Today, mass-production often precedes sales, and builders do not always know who will buy the products at the time they are being made. The craftsman always knew for whom he was working. We now just have a general portrait of groups of customers, which are identified as "markets" that need appropriate packaging and labeling.

Strategies of persuasion. Advertising is a key element in marketing. We have to remember that one century ago,

A marketing team must deliver more than the right product at the right time, place, and price.

people said "propaganda" instead of "advertising," knowing the fact that there is, in every advertisement, a dose of persuasion. A message is not just informative; it can also try to promote and persuade potential customers. Professional publicists will often say that they don't sell a product but rather an image, a way of living, a selected position in social hierarchy. As French sociologist Pierre Bourdieu has explained, public taste can be analyzed according to social status, education, or salary. This explains why some marketing strategies choose to target precise groups (elder, ethnic groups, linguistic minorities) when they promote a specific product, not because it is only made for a small portion of the public, but because a particular group responds better to corresponding arguments and motivations

Some multinational corporations can have many different advertisements for a single product in the same country. For example in CANADA, advertisements and commercial spots in French, that used to be dubbed translations of an English message in many media (magazines, television) until a few years ago, are more and more produced locally by firms that are more aware of the local valued habits, fashions, and common tastes. In the UNITED STATES, some retailers project different images of their customers in advertisement spots and catalogs (for instance, by including more visible minorities, or using some overweight models), as they also try to target African American or Spanish-speaking customers with a specific approach.

In an era of GLOBALIZATION, new markets are not necessarily abroad and far away; organizations tend to identify and target the many specificities among a nation's various groups.

Ethics and commercial aims. Ethical issues have been raised about marketing strategies. Is there a limit to the search for new customers and larger market shares? For example, should a company offer imported sparkling water beverages in poor regions of the world, where populations can hardly afford them, and would rather need to drink milk or natural fruit juices? Should companies advertise beer and alcohol in the media (on television, in magazines, and newspapers), knowing the fact that a good portion of the population has to fight with a drinking problem? Should advertising about cigarettes and tobacco be controlled by the state? Should television stations be allowed to broadcast advertisements for toys on Saturday mornings, during programs scheduled for kids? Many countries have created rules and limits for certain advertising practices.

Offering a product can sometimes create a desire, but the desire is not always a response to a genuine need. One of the contemporary missions of some marketing strategists has been to provoke, to increase the artificial needs of consumers, in order to sell more, following the logic that says corporations have to fight and compete in order to get their competitor's customers. This can partly explain the appearance of consumer studies and the many consumers-advocate associations.

People are more aware about the possible creation of waste inherent to consuming; they care more about re-using, recycling, and protecting resources and environment. As author Andrew Crane explains, marketing and morality have to consider issues about pollution in the way they present new products.

Keep the customer satisfied. A successful marketing plan is often presented as a strategy to give more than what is asked for by the client. For instance, we hear that "McDonald's isn't really selling food but rather offering entertainment." This means the consumer will probably find something to eat through a privileged relationship, bound to be long-term, with the people she will interact with. It also means that a successful approach must consider marketing services rather than just selling products. To be fully successful, all employees must be aware of this vision. The need for a dedicated attitude of customer service adds a challenging mission to internet retailers, who have to create new ways of conviviality in virtual exchanges.

For some reason, some people never go to stores, never watch television, never go to bookstores, never check film listings in newspapers when they want to choose which movie to watch. There have to be special approaches to reach, in more different ways, these unusual customers who nonetheless are willing to buy products they are being offered. Book clubs, mail-order services from catalogs, internet retailer websites, and CD subscriptions are all examples of alternate strategies that can offer a relatively wide range of products to specific potential customers who cannot always compare brands, labels, or even prizes.

Some customers are not particular in their tastes and choices. They could say on some occasions: "I need a book to read during my next trip," or "We need some music for the party." They won't say: "I absolutely need the new boxed set of the Rolling Stones." Their respective requirements and criteria are, in some cases, simple: something to use (or read or listen to) that is not bad and not too expensive. Sometimes, consumers will just look at the bestsellers in each category of product to make their choice more rapidly.

Supply and demand. The adequacy between needs and availability, SUPPLY and DEMAND, is not always in perfect balance. There seem to be many more products and services available than ever before. In order to reach more customers and to offer more and more of what could be bought, companies try to occupy the largest area of space in stores. Knowing that, there are still products that are more difficult to find in any country: imports. Imported products usually occupy a domain where no equivalent exists. Imported products (food, wine, music) are supported by different advertising strategies, through alternate networks. But alternate artifacts sometimes become the new fashion, the new wave. One country's mass culture can be seen as alternate in another country: In 2003, Céline Dion's songs in French are a huge success in Canada and FRANCE; but these CDs have to be specially imported into the United States and can't be found everywhere.

What cannot be marketed. There are certain products and services that cannot be advertised as ordinary merchandise, such as legal and medical services. For example, it is not possible to offer a company's stock shares in an advertisement (with some exceptions such as Initial Public Offerings through a financial agent). Some drugs and vaccines cannot be advertised directly to the public, but personal representations and advice may be given by a drug company's representative to a dentist or a doctor who meet privately for this purpose.

In these cases, marketing strategies are conceived accordingly and include statistics, data, previous studies, and recent articles in scientific or medical journals. Physicians are solicited by different companies that compete with each other; they get samples of new products that sometimes guide their future medical choices. Many companies also try to influence (or convince) hospital leaders, professors in universities and institutions, professionals in research centers to reach certain agreements and exclusive partnerships. Marketing pharmaceutical services is a distinct universe as well, with its own rules.

Some legal services are also offered and made in appropriate methods. Some professional corporations (lawyers, engineers) try to set bounds to advertisement made by their members, because all of them are supposed to be equally competent and reliable.

The marketing of the president. Because there are non-profit applications of marketing concepts, most marketing strategies work not only for products and services, but as well for persons, political parties, or nonprofit organizations to promote their ideas, candidates, and representatives. Motivations can range from elections at any level, raising funds for a charity, campaign finance, or any other "good cause." (Promoters say they always defend and advocate "good causes.")

Oddly, marketing methods for persons operate about the same as for objects; one has to state the person's qualities, advantages, but also his or her charisma, his or her image. These elements are usually constructed and packaged; they are selected according to the perceived preoccupations and expectations of the general public. For example, the construction of a public image (for a poster, on television, in public appearances) is used in order to show how the candidate already succeeds in what he or she promises, proving to combine essential qualities such as dignity, honesty, reliability, and popularity. Since a person always has an image (almost by default) when appearing in the media, people who prepare public relations prefer to impose the positive image they have planned, instead of having to change an unwanted, contested, controversial reputation. One has to only look at the packaging of presidential candidates in the United States during an election year to see the forces of marketing at work.

Institutional advertising and marketing. Some important marketing strategies are made for organizations that have nothing to sell or promote. Public services such as nuclear plants, police stations, non-profit associations, and charities sometimes pay for advertisements that only show their support to another cause. We say they promote their image, as some companies who take space in the media just to say they care about something, or just to wish a "Happy Holidays!" to everyone. The goal of most of these marketing campaigns is to win a positive sentiment over public opinion, or to improve an image and visibility. Nonetheless, these strategies have to be planned and targeted.

Institutions, public services, and governments at all levels often use what they call information campaigns or publicity campaigns to communicate and promote ideas, decisions, projects, new laws, and policies for the good of the population. Governments need to communicate

with citizens who have the right to be informed. Basically, these messages are not harmful, but nor are they harmless. They project simple, elementary rules to control important issues and matters in a society where people have to live together and share a resources: Drive carefully; don't waste water when reserves are low; don't spit on the floor; please don't smoke.

More complex messages also exist, in order to change habits or to make people accept rules, such as neighborhood crime-watch organizations and "don't drink and drive" campaigns. Public sectors use these marketing approaches because they are efficient and can target specific audiences.

Marketing entertainment, media, and culture. Books, music, movies, and television programs often need to be marketed to specific audiences. The marketing of motion pictures is a good example to understand strategies behind cultural industries. In newspapers, movies ads often carry a few approving quotes, even the newest ones, saying nice comments, such as "A masterpiece; the best film of the year," and "One of the most moving pictures I have seen." These authoritative approvals are important; they testify to the value of the movie being promoted. But the quoted critic may be on the other side of the world. There is always one critic, somewhere, at some point, who will be moved or charmed by any film, and the marketers compile these critics' quotes to select only the very few words that glorify their film.

The same logic applies to publishing and book critics, who receive free review copies of recent (or forthcoming) books from publishers (or distributors). Since only the biggest firms can afford to give away so many free copies for promotion purposes, only those among the most important can obtain the main reviews. And since books that have received the most reviews usually attract more attention, critics just amplify the visibility of already successful works and authors. In fact, very few critics are doing research to locate alternate but valuable works to give them the appropriate attention and coverage.

New economy and new technologies. Since the early 1990s, branches of the new economy have modified the limits of what can be marketed. Consultants now sell business solutions, special advice and training for people and enterprises. Change, in itself, has become a motive and a goal; uninspired managers sometimes feel satisfied only if they have made frequent changes, no matter if they were justified or not. There are people who buy useless goods; in the same way that others ask for useless services and command useless changes. Marketing couldn't survive without the word "New."

Record companies have borne the brunt of marketing in the new economy. In 2003, many had to think of new strategies because of weak demand and poor sales, sometimes attributed to illegal music copying off the internet. In order to avoid piracy among CD users and buyers, some companies even offered free movie tickets to people who bought selected new CDs, instead of downloading music or copying a friend's CD.

With the progress of technology, scholars have made original theoretical developments and interdisciplinary links between marketing and cultural studies. In a collective book, British sociologists Paul du Gay, Stuart Hall, and others have observed how the famous Sony Walkman was conceived and perceived as a way of life for users, and not just as a useful portable machine to play music. The authors are also aware of what they call "the culture of production," presented as "an integral part of the company way of life, that informs the perceptions of outside observers."

Marketing is not just about goods and services; it is more and more about the lifestyles, images, consumer-related actions and behaviors of those who live in highly developed capitalist societies. Often, there seems to be an endless antagonism against much-criticized marketing studies and a seemingly more respectful conception enabled by consumer studies. In the end, ironically, it may be that marketing has to justify itself and market its own image and social pertinence.

BIBLIOGRAPHY. Pierre Bourdieu, *Distinction: A Social Critique of the Judgment of Taste* (Harvard University Press, 1990); Pierre Bourdieu, *Acts of Resistance: Against the Tyranny of the Market* (New Press, 1999); Andrew Crane, *Marketing, Morality and the Natural Environment* (Routledge, 2003); Harvey Daniels, *Literature Circles: Voice and Choice in Book Clubs and Reading Groups* (Stenhouse Publishers, 2001); Paul du Gay, Stuart Hall, Linda Janes, Hugh Mackay and Keith Negus, *Doing Cultural Studies: The Story of the Sony Walkman* (Sage, 1997); Bruce I. Newman, *The Mass Marketing of Politics: Democracy in an Age of Manufactured Images* (Sage, 1999); Bruce I. Newman, *The Marketing of the President: Political Marketing as Campaign Strategy* (Sage, 1993); Vance Packard, *The Hidden Persuaders* (Random House, 1957); Carl Shapiro, Hal R. Varian, *Information Rules: A Strategic Guide to the Network Economy* (Harvard Business School, 1998); Morgen Witzel, ed., *Marketing: Early Theories of Business and Management* (University of Chicago Press, 2000).

YVES LABERGE, PH.D.
INSTITUT QUÉBÉCOIS DES
HAUTES ÉTUDES INTERNATIONALES

Markowitz, Harry (1927–)

AWARDED THE 1990 Nobel Prize in Economics with William SHARPE and Merton MILLER, Harry Markowitz was recognized for his theories on evaluating stock-market risk and reward and on valuing corporate stocks and bonds. Markowitz used statistical techniques to identify optimal portfolios or portfolios that diversify assets to maximize return while minimizing investment risk.

These portfolios could then be combined with a risk-free asset and graphed on the Capital Allocation Line which shows the trade off of risk versus expected rate of return. Markowitz's work laid the foundations for the Capital Asset Pricing Model, which was developed by William Sharpe, John Lintner, and Jan Mossin in the mid-1960s.

Markowitz was born in Chicago, the only child of Morris and Mildred Markowitz who owned a small grocery store. Growing up in Chicago, he had a wide range of interests from playing the baseball and violin to reading popular accounts of astronomy, physics, and philosophy. Markowitz enrolled at the University of Chicago where he obtained a Bachelor of Philosophy in 1947, a M.S. in 1950, and a Ph.D. in 1954. During his time at Chicago he studied under Milton FRIEDMAN, Jacob Marschak, Leonard Savage, and Tjalling KOOPMAN.

In 1952, Markowitz left Chicago and joined the RAND Corporation where he met Sharpe with whom he would share the Nobel Prize. At RAND, Markowitz worked on industry-wide and multi-industry activity analysis models of industrial capabilities with Alan S. Manne, Tibor Fabian, Thomas Marschak, Alan J. Rowe and others.

After leaving RAND, he held positions with Consolidated Analysis Centers, Inc. (1963–68); the University of California, Los Angeles (1968-69); Arbitrage Management Company (1969–72); and IBM's T.J. Watson Research Center (1974–83). He became a professor of finance at Baruch College of the City University of New York in 1982. In 1989, Markowitz was awarded the Von Neumann Prize in Operations Research Theory by the Operations Research Society of America and the Institute of Management Sciences for his works in the areas of portfolio theory, sparse matrix techniques and his development of the SIMSCRIPT programming language. He is also the co-founder, with Herb Karr, of CACI, a computer software company which supports SIMSCRIPT, a language used to write economic-analysis programs.

BIBLIOGRAPHY. Zvi Bodie, Alex Kane, and Alan Marcus, *Investments* (McGraw-Hill, 2002); Harry Markowitz, "Portfolio Selection," *Journal of Finance* (March. 1952); Nobel Museum, "Autobiography of Harry M. Markowitz," www.nobel.se/economics.

KIRBY R. CUNDIFF, PH.D.
HILLSDALE COLLEGE

Marshall Plan

ON JUNE 5, 1947, U.S. Secretary of State George C. Marshall addressed the graduating class at Harvard University after the commencement ceremonies. What he announced was a plan that would ultimately lay the foundation of Western Europe's unprecedented economic ascent after WORLD WAR II, and would also hasten the descent of the "iron curtain" separating the Communist Eastern from the democratic Western states of Europe.

The unconditional surrender of the German forces in May 1945, marked the cessation of armed conflict in Europe. The devastation in human and economic terms was truly catastrophic, and even after military action had stopped, misery and devastation continued as armies of refugees were displaced across Europe. The European economies seemed on track toward recovery through most of 1946, but then progress came to a standstill as key supplies proved lacking. Food was limited and there was a widespread shortage of coal—the main form of energy used in production and for heating.

The crisis deepened in early 1947. The winter had turned out to be unusually cold and long, increasing the demand for coal. At the same time heavy snowfalls seriously hampered the mining industry in England, further reducing the amount of coal available. Coupled with these shortages were also severe currency crises that threatened to devalue European currencies.

As a result of the economic hardship, communist parties gained considerable popular support and political strength especially in ITALY and FRANCE, and also elsewhere in Western Europe. There was a very real concern among U.S. officials that communism would take hold in the democracies of Western Europe and that these would subsequently align themselves with the SOVIET UNION.

In response to this situation the UNITED STATES already had a string of ad hoc bilateral agreements in place. However, it was becoming clear that these would not suffice to solve the problems due to their limited scale and scope. Moreover, what was needed were not stopgap measures and mere temporary relief, but a long-term strategy to secure economic and political stability.

When Marshall traveled to Harvard University to accept an honorary degree, he gave his speech in which he first summarized the gravity of the situation, and then made what he called "a suggestion":

Aside from the demoralizing effect on the world at large and the possibilities of disturbances arising as a result of the desperation of the people concerned, the consequences to the economy of the United States should be apparent to all. It is logical that the United States should do whatever it is able to do to assist in the return of normal economic health in the world, without which there can be no political stability and no assured peace. Our policy is directed not against any country or doctrine but against hunger, poverty, desperation and chaos. Its purpose should be the revival of a working economy in the world so as to permit the emergence of political and social conditions in which free institutions can exist. Such assistance, I am convinced, must not be on a piecemeal basis as various crises develop. Any assistance that this Government may render in the future should provide a cure rather than a mere palliative. [. . .]

It is already evident that, before the United States government can proceed much further in its efforts to alleviate the situation and help start the European world on its way to recovery, there must be some agreement among the countries of Europe as to the requirements of the situation and the part those countries themselves will take in order to give proper effect to whatever action might be undertaken by this government. It would be neither fitting nor efficacious for this government to undertake to draw up unilaterally a program designed to place Europe on its feet economically. This is the business of the Europeans. The initiative, I think, must come from Europe. The role of this country should consist of friendly aid in the drafting of a European program and of later support of such a program so far as it may be practical for us to do so. The program should be a joint one, agreed to by a number, if not all European nations.

The plan thus had two key features: First, to provide a coordinated effort that should be designed to restore confidence and lay the foundation for long-term growth. And second, the particulars of the plan should be drawn up in Europe with the idea of coordinating economic help across borders, and, if possible, with all European nations involved. Moreover, it was hoped that economic cooperation between European countries would remain in place well after the initial plan was implemented.

The reception of the Marshall Plan in Europe was very positive. The first meeting of foreign ministers took place in Paris. At this meeting, however, the Soviet foreign minister, V.M. Molotov, declined participation denouncing the plan as an imperialistic U.S. scheme. Eastern European countries were also pressured to decline participation. POLAND and Czechoslovakia, who had previously indicated their desire to participate, withdrew as well. Consequently, the Committee for European Economic Cooperation (CEEC) that was set up and began work on coordinating economic strategies, operated without Eastern participation.

Ultimately, this rift also solidified the division of GERMANY as West Germany moved ahead with a currency reform as part of its economic stabilization efforts that finalized the economic division of the two Germanys.

The Soviet response was not unanticipated, given that the plan was in part conceived in order to stabilize democratic forces in Western Europe and required economic cooperation, and thus economic disclosure, from the Soviet Union and its satellites. However, there is not nearly enough evidence to support the notion that the plan was specifically designed to lead to this kind of breach between East and West.

Europe was not the only place that Marshall's suggestion had to overcome opposition. In order to establish the Marshall Plan, Congress had to pass the Economic Cooperation Act (ECA) that established the European Recovery Program (the official name of the Marshall Plan). At the outset there was substantial Congressional skepticism concerning the costs and the effectiveness of the proposal. There was also political opposition to providing money to a country that had been an enemy only a few years earlier. However, in addition to working closely with legislators, Marshall lobbied the American people directly in a fashion that has been likened to a presidential campaign. In the end the ECA passed overwhelmingly, its fate having been decided largely by tremendous popular support.

During the years 1948 to 1952, the total amount of financial support to the 14 European recipients of Marshall Plan monies exceeded $13 billion. In the wake of the transfer of these funds and due to the cooperation across Western Europe, some of the most impressive economic growth in history took hold. Indeed, in West Germany the post-war recovery became known as the Economic Miracle. Another effect of the Marshall Plan was to forge strong economic and political ties between Western Europe and North America.

In 1953, Marshall was awarded the Nobel Peace Prize, which he graciously accepted as a representative of the American people.

BIBLIOGRAPHY. William L. Clayton, "GATT, The Marshall Plan, and OECD," *Political Science Quarterly* (v.78/4, 1963); William C. Cromwell, "The Marshall Non-Plan, Congress and the Soviet Union," *The Western Political Quarterly* (v.32/4, 1979); Heinrich E. Friedlaender and Jacob Oser, *Economic History of Modern Europe* (1953); Harold L. Hitchens, "Influences on the Congressional Decision to Pass the Marshall Plan," *The Western Political Quarterly* (v.21/1, 1968); Scott Jackson: "Prologue to the Marshall Plan: The Origins of the American Commitment for a European Recovery Program," *Journal of American History* (v.65/4, 1979); www.marshallfoundation.org.

MICHAEL J. TROY, J.D.
THOMAS D. JEITSCHKO, PH.D.
MICHIGAN STATE UNIVERSITY

Marshall, Alfred (1842–1924)

ALFRED MARSHALL INHABITS a very peculiar place in the history of modern economic thought as it pertains to capitalism. He was well known in his own day as a professor of economics at Cambridge University in England, where he helped increase the academic prestige of economics, and authored the classic *Principles of Economics* (1890). Today he is less read or discussed. To a large extent that is because Marshall's world—the late Victorian era in British history—and its views of capitalism seem remarkably distant from our own.

But in certain ways Marshall belonged to our modern world. His life was framed by a youthful period of religious doubt and the influence of Charles Darwin. Marshall showed how the precise application of mathematics (a subject he studied intensely before turning to philosophy, then finally economics) could help economic study become more objective (think today of economists' diagrams and mathematical formulas; these are the concepts Marshall helped pioneer). At the same time, Marshall believed economics should not be divorced from ethics or history. Indeed, as one author sympathetic to his thoughts, Gertrude Himmelfarb, put it, Marshall believed "economics was a species of moral philosophy."

Marshall tried to provide a moral justification for industrial modern capitalism—the sort that marked England's history during his life. For example, Marshall did not simply stress the economic function of a diligent work ethic but argued for its moral necessity. He explained that "as human nature is constituted, man rapidly degenerates unless he has some hard work to do." Following this line of argument, he became famous for condemning alcohol abuse among the working class. Such abuse not only damaged individuals, Marshall maintained, it kept them oblivious to the actual state of their affairs and the gradual improvement of life via free-market economics and industrial ingenuity.

Indeed, progress was central to Marshall's social thought. He was known for introducing the idea of time into modern economics, and arguing against prior economic thought that worked from "statical" assumptions (his word). He believed increased technological efficiency nurtured "the steady progress of the working classes during the 19th century," since work would become less brutal. Everywhere he looked, Marshall saw industrialism's abundance and wealth helping to alleviate poverty.

Of course, Marshall knew full well that his arguments faced challenges from social critics and political activists. While Marshall was lecturing and writing, Marxists had grown more popular with their critique of capitalist exploitation and the increasing misery of the working classes. Marshall knew that any argument on behalf of modern capitalism needed to recognize its critics.

He also believed that capitalism had to be defended against the legacy of classical political economy. He argued against two of the most important predecessors in economic thought: Thomas MALTHUS and David RICARDO. Malthus argued that population growth foreordained an exhaustion of resources, while Ricardo believed workers' wages would stagnate as greedy landlords grew richer. Both visions struck Marshall as too pessimistic, too contrary to his own hopeful views on political economy. As his biographer, Peter Growenewegen, put it, Marshall "wished to jettison the pessimistic conclusions of classical economics" and hoped to "substitute a law of progress which included belief in the possibilities for improving human nature itself."

Marshall also developed a more complex theory of PRICE while working in the traditional framework of supply and demand. Some economic thinkers had believed that cost of production determined price while others stressed the utility of goods to consumers. Marshall combined both views into one. Each factor played a role, and more importantly each factor changed over time. With all of the different issues Marshall discusses in *Principles of Economics*, readers come away with a very complex understanding of market capitalism. Though complex, Marshall's views were extremely optimistic, believing everything would work out in the end.

Though an optimist, Marshall also believed capitalism needed to be reformed. He worked with the Charity Organization Society and supported self-help initiatives among workers trying to improve the quality of their lives. He hoped chivalry would correct the grosser abuses known to industrial capitalism. In these initiatives and ideas we can glimpse Marshall's deeply moral understanding of modern capitalism—an understanding that often feels quite foreign to our own.

BIBLIOGRAPHY. Peter Groenewegen, *A Soaring Eagle: Alfred Marshall, 1842–1924* (Edward Elgar Publishing, 1995); Robert Heilbroner, *The Worldly Philosophers*, 5th Edition (Simon & Schuster, 1980); Gertrude Himmelfarb, *Poverty and Compassion: The Moral Imagination of the Late Victorians* (Alfred A. Knopf, 1991); John Maynard Keynes, ed., "Alfred Marshall," *Memorials of Alfred Marshall* (August M. Kelley Publishers, 1966). Alfred Marshall, *Principles of Economics* (Macmillan, 1961).

KEVIN MATTSON, PH.D.
OHIO STATE UNIVERSITY

Marx, Karl (1818–83)

A PHILOSOPHER, AN ECONOMIST, and a sociologist, but perhaps most of all renowned as the founder of so-called scientific socialism and as a prophet of Marxism, Karl Marx was born in Trier, GERMANY, and died in London, England, in 1883, the year when, incidentally, two other great economists who wrote on the broad subjects of capitalism, Joseph SCHUMPETER and John Maynard KEYNES were born. Marx's two greatest contributions to the intellectual life of his time, and beyond it, were the *Communist Manifesto* written together with Friedrich ENGELS in 1848, and a three-volume treatise on the political economy of capitalism, *Capital* (1867–95).

Life and work. After school, Marx first entered Bonn University to study law but he soon transferred to Berlin University where he became interested in philosophy. He received his doctoral degree in 1841 in Greek philosophy. By that time, he was already deeply involved in radical political movement. In 1842, he became editor of a radical liberal newspaper, *The Rhenish Gazette*, which was banned by the authorities in 1843. In that year, Marx also got married and moved to Paris. It was in Paris that Marx met his lifetime friend and ally, Engels, and became a communist, based on his experience of mixing with workers' groups. In 1848, he and Engels wrote the *Communist Manifesto* that became the political credo of the communist movement.

Marx settled in London in 1849, where he spent most of the time in the reading room of the British Museum studying and developing his economic and political theories. He suffered from extreme poverty and was helped out by Engels, and other friends, and supporters who sent him money. He was a very hard worker but toward the end of his life his health failed him reducing his creativity and forcing him to leave *Capital*, his lifework unfinished. He died at the age of 64.

Despite the fact that for most of his life Marx was an academic scholar, his motto was "all previous philosophers only tried to explain the world, while the true task is to change it." He has certainly had a profound influence on changes in the world after him although we will never know if that was indeed the kind of changes that he would have approved of.

Economic interpretation of history. Although Marx is most well known as a prophet of communism, this aspect of his work is really important only to communists. We will come to it, but start with Marx's contributions that go beyond the political message of communism, and that continue to live on in modern-day social sciences.

The biggest such contribution is the economic interpretation of history, which in the words of Schumpeter was one of the greatest achievements in sociology of all times. The economic interpretation of history does not mean that people are motivated only or primarily by economic motives in their behavior. The true meaning of

Marx's message, in this regard, was that religions, philosophical concepts, schools of art, ethical ideas, and political movements are shaped by the economic conditions of their times and that changes in the economic conditions account for their rise and fall. Those changes (the "development of the productive forces" of a society) can be influenced by non-economic factors, but in the end the needs coming from the economic side will meld political and other institutions in a way that is required for their continued development.

At least part of Marx's vision is still alive today in works by economists and political scientists who have absolutely no sympathy for the political message of Communism (for example, in economics it is related to theories accounting for the formation of preferences and social institutions, as in the works of the Nobel Prize-winners Gary S. BECKER and George AKERLOF).

The theory of class struggle and the Communist Manifesto.

The economic interpretation of history is closely related (although, by no means, identical) to Marx's theory of social classes and his understanding of the historic process as inherently driven by class struggle. Classes are defined in their relationship to material means of production (OWNERSHIP of factors of production, in modern terminology). The development of productive forces gradually changes the relative importance of factors of production and that is translated into relative changes in their power. As the ascending class fights against the declining class, the social order and the whole political and ideological landscape undergo drastic changes, often by means of a violent revolution. This logic is applied to past human history in the *Communist Manifesto* and it is extended to predict the future, in which the takeover by the ascending class under the bourgeois system, the proletariat, will eventually result in a classless society, and an unlimited potential for economic development.

Although the theory of class struggle is not accepted in its Marxist form by modern social sciences, many of its insights, including the role that competition for political influence plays in shaping institutions and government policies still live on. Also, although the prediction of an imminent collapse of the capitalist system and the proletarian revolution has not materialized, some of the most forceful passages in the *Communist Manifesto* actually refer to the greatest achievements of the "bourgeoisie" class, and to complete changes in the ways human history has been made after its ascendance to power (that is, after the advent of capitalism).

Marx can thus be credited with being one of the first thinkers to recognize the fact (widely accepted today) that the capitalist (free market) system represented one of the biggest breakthroughs in human history, since the dawn of civilization.

The theory of surplus value and exploitation.

Marx begins the exposition of his labor theory of value (which is rooted in David RICARDO's labor theory of value) in *Capital* by asking a question, what it is that makes commodities comparable in terms of values. His answer is that it is the general fact that they are all products of labor. He does mention that a commodity must have value in use as a precondition to having any value at all, but he does not seem to be aware of the implications of this.

More precisely, when postulating that the value of commodities is governed by the number of hours of labor "socially necessary" to produce them, Marx refers to some standard, commonly prevailing production technology, apparently without noticing that one needs to know values (equilibrium of relative prices), before it can be determined what makes a production technology commonly prevailing in the first place. Modern theory of value (largely developed after Marx's death) explains relative prices by the interaction of "social necessity" (human wants) and the quantity of scarce resources (labor among them) used in their production, so that from a scientific point of view, the labor theory of value, including Marx's version, is side-stepped.

Modern economists point out the labor theory of value alone is not enough to purport Marx's political message that the proletariat (workers) are being exploited by the bourgeoisie (capitalists). Under the labor theory of value, it is still true that all producers get paid according to the number of labor hours embodied in their product, so there seems to be no room for extra profit (surplus value) accruing to capitalists. To get around this difficulty, Marx makes labor a special commodity. What hired workers (in contrast to self-employed artisans) sell in the market is labor force, not the product of their labor. The value of labor force is determined by whatever labor is "socially necessary" to produce it, that is, the value of food, clothing, housing, and other components of the "reproduction of labor force," according to Marx.

This socially necessary value of reproduction of labor force is always less than the value of the product of labor (Marx never explains why), so when capitalists hire labor they derive value from owning the product of labor, which is in excess of what they pay for the labor force.

Marx uses the theory of surplus value and exploitation to derive various laws governing the evolution of capitalism and to predict its eventual self-destruction. As the capitalistic way of production spreads, exploitation of the proletariat becomes a bigger and bigger fact of social life. At the same time, the accumulation of capital reduces the rate of surplus value (which is generated only by current labor, not by capital goods). In the end, private ownership of capital has to be abolished and the proletariat takes over the production process, eradicating exploitation.

Marx and Marxism. Marx's theory of surplus value was rooted in the empirical facts of his era, when labor was indeed paid very meagerly, while owners of capital enjoyed very high profit rates. Although Marx's theory was true, it only meant that a large part of the labor force was still employed in the pre-modern sector where their income was confined basically to subsistence level, and made possible the divergence between the "value of labor force" and the "value of its product." Only in the presence of a vast "reserve army of labor" could the determination of the wage rate be treated as exogenous to the capitalist production and its markets.

The very logic of capitalistic development, that Marx so well understood (as shown, in particular, by the *Communist Manifesto*), was pointing strongly toward changes making the theory of exploitation problematic. The spread of manufacturing and the retreat of traditional agriculture and artisanship brought the determination of the "value of labor force" into the realm of supply and demand in the capitalist sector. The accumulation of capital also led to the development of capital markets and to overcoming institutional barriers between workers and capitalists. Marx's predictions about the historical trend of capitalist development apparently failed to materialize.

This did not lead, however, to the demise of Marx's political message. Although radical followers of Marx hardly understood the depth of his theory, they were quick to seize its slogans. Some of the most repressive and intolerant regimes in human history were created in the 20th century in the name of "Marx," although Marx's original message was neither anti-democratic nor against individual freedom. The horrors of Josef Stalin's communism in the SOVIET UNION are no more, and no less, rooted in Marx than the horrors of the Medieval inquisition in Spain are rooted in the teaching of Jesus. Marx's message ended up being used by social reactionary forces; the locomotive of progress bypassed his vision, leading to the development of productive forces that Marx thought were only possible with the rise of proletariat and communism, in a completely different fashion.

BIBLIOGRAPHY. Karl Marx and Friedrich Engels, *Manifesto of the Communist Party* (International Publishers, 1948); Karl Marx, Friedrich Engels, ed., *Capital: A Critique of Political Economy* (International Publishers, 1967); Joseph A. Schumpeter, *Capitalism, Socialism, and Democracy* (Harper, 1950); Joseph A. Schumpeter, *History of Economic Analysis* (Allen & Unwin, 1954); Mark Blaug, *Economic Theory in Retrospect* (Cambridge University Press, 1996); David Riazanov (Golden-dach), *Karl Marx and Friedrich Engels* (International Publishers, 1927).

ZELJAN SCHUSTER, PH.D.
UNIVERSITY OF NEW HAVEN

Matsushita Electrical Works

MATSUSHITA ELECTRIC, headquartered in Osaka, JAPAN, was founded in 1918, when 23-year-old Konosuke Matsushita started a small workshop with only two employees (his wife and brother-in-law) to design, make, and market an improved attachment plug.

Since then, the Matsushita group of companies has become a comprehensive, worldwide electronic-product manufacturer whose products range from digital components to consumer electronic products, home appliances, factory automation equipment, information and communications equipment, and housing-construction products. Ranked as the 45th-largest company in the world in 2002, Matsushita had nearly $55 billion in sales. Spanning a wide variety of fields, it serves residential housing, office complexes, commercial facilities, factories and assortments of public-utility structures.

Matsushita faces changes caused by an information-technology (IT) revolution, environmental concerns, and marked shifts in social demographics. As a result, the company has initiated four new business areas that are targeted to help solidify its customer base. These include: IT-related products and services; elderly care and support care products; stock renovation solutions for residential, commercial and public arenas; and "Green and Clean" environmentally sound products.

BIBLIOGRAPHY. "Global 500: The World's Largest Companies," *Fortune* (July, 2002); Matsushita, www.matsushita.jp; John Knotter, *Matsushita Leadership* (Free Press, 1997).

JOSEPH GERINGER
SYED B. HUSSAIN, PH.D.
UNIVERSITY OF WISCONSIN, OSHKOSH

McFadden, Daniel L. (1937–)

WINNER OF THE 2000 Nobel Prize in Economics (with James J. HECKMAN), Daniel McFadden is known for his theoretical and methodological research into the economic behavior of individuals and households. Chief among McFadden's contributions to capitalist economics is his development of theory and methodology to analyze consumers' choices among a finite set of alternatives. Such discrete choice analysis is used to examine many practical phenomena, including a commuter's choice of travel mode (car, bus, train, etc.) or a household's choice of telephone service plan.

McFadden was raised on a remote farm in North Carolina. He attended public schools until his suspension from high school in his junior year for circulating a petition. Entering the University of Minnesota by examination at age 16, he graduated with a B.S. in physics three years later. He began graduate study in physics, also at Minnesota. However, McFadden's interests in the study of human behavior shortly led him to enter the Behavioral Science Training Program at Minnesota, from which he earned his doctoral degree (with emphasis in economics) in 1962.

After a short post-doctoral position at the University of Pittsburgh, McFadden began his professorial career in the economics department at the University of California, Berkeley. In 1977, he moved to the Massachusetts Institute of Technology's (MIT) economics department, and from 1986 to 1991 directed the Statistics Research Center at MIT. In 1991, McFadden returned to Berkeley, where he established the Econometrics Laboratory (with computers named after his first grandchild, Emily) and remained a chaired professor of economics. In his non-academic life, McFadden owned a small farm in the Napa Valley, producing grapes, figs, wine, and olive oil.

While purely statistical methods for analyzing discrete choices were available before McFadden's work, his important contribution was to link the econometric models to an underlying theory of rational consumer choice. In this approach, an individual is assumed to evaluate the characteristics of the available choices and choose the alternative that yields the highest satisfaction, or "utility." Since the empirical researcher does not observe all the factors that the individual considers when making his choice, there is an unobserved (to the econometrician) component in the analysis.

McFadden showed that when the unobserved component has an extreme value probability distribution, then the resulting probability that the individual chooses a given alternative takes a particularly simple form. This econometric model is known as the conditional (or multinomial) logit model, and the consumer choice theory generating it is called a random utility model.

In subsequent work, McFadden and others generalized both the random utility model and the resulting empirical models. In the nested logit, generalized extreme value, and mixed logit models, less restrictive assumptions are imposed on the individual's choice problem. McFadden also developed the method of simulated moments, a statistical and numerical method that made the

multinomial probit discrete choice model (developed by others) feasible to implement. With these advances, empirical researchers now have a panoply of econometric models from which to choose to analyze discrete choice problems.

Using these discrete choice models, McFadden has investigated urban transportation demand, demand for telephone and electricity service, and the elderly population's demand for housing. Other researchers have used tools provided by McFadden to examine a host of economic problems, including demand for recreational alternatives, choice among brands of consumer products and services as disparate as ready-to-eat breakfast cereals and airline travel, and even sociological phenomena such as occupational choice, marriage, and childbearing.

McFadden has made many other contributions to economic theory and methodology. He introduced duality theory (which shows that the cost and profit functions are alternative descriptions of a firm's technology, and that the expenditure and indirect utility functions are alternative descriptions of a consumer's preferences) to applied econometrics. He also developed methodology to quantify welfare losses from environmental damage, and used it to assess the value of the Alaskan environmental damage resulting from the Exxon *Valdez* oil spill.

BIBLIOGRAPHY. The Royal Swedish Academy of Sciences, *The Scientific Contributions of James Heckman and Daniel McFadden* (2002); Daniel McFadden, "Conditional Logit Analysis of Qualitative Choice Behavior," *Frontiers of Econometrics* (1974); Daniel McFadden, "Econometric Analysis of Qualitative Response Models," *Handbook of Econometrics* (v.2, 1984).

JAMES PRIEGER, PH.D.
UNIVERSITY OF CALIFORNIA, DAVIS

McKesson Corporation

A LEADING PROVIDER of healthcare supplies, information, and care-management products and services, McKesson Corporation traces its roots back to 1833, when John McKesson and Charles Olcott opened a small drug import and wholesale shop in New York City's financial district. The Olcott & McKesson business thrived, providing clients botanical drugs—herbs, roots, leaves, bark, and vegetable extracts. Early on, they brought Daniel Robbins on board and in 1853, after Olcott died, the company was renamed McKesson & Robbins.

By the turn of the century McKesson & Robbins persuaded many of the nation's largest wholesale drug distributors to become its subsidiaries. The result: a nationwide McKesson & Robbins network that rivaled the huge drug chains that were spreading across the country. For decades a pharmaceuticals wholesaler, McKesson increasingly looked to expand and meet demands of complex healthcare-delivery systems across the world.

McKesson's products are inclusive of the healthcare industry and include a vast array of products, from pills to surgical masks. Its pharmaceutical and supply distribution system reaches all parts of the healthcare-delivery system, from druggists to nurses to home-care providers. The company ranked as the 57th largest company in the world in 2002 with sales of $50 billion.

BIBLIOGRAPHY. "Global 500: The World's Largest Companies," *Fortune* (July, 2002); "Clinical Reference Systems" www.medformation.com; McKesson History, www.mckesson.com.

JOSEPH GERINGER
SYED B. HUSSAIN, PH.D.
UNIVERSITY OF WISCONSIN, PSHKOSH

McKinley, William (1843–1901)

THE 25TH PRESIDENT of the UNITED STATES, William McKinley was born in Niles, Ohio. In 1860, he enrolled in Allegheny College, but poor health and finances caused him to leave after one term. When the AMERICAN CIVIL WAR began, McKinley enlisted in the Ohio Infantry Regiment commanded by another future resident, Rutherford B. HAYES. Commended for his heroism at the Battle of Antietam, McKinley received a commission as a second lieutenant. By the end of the war he had become a brevet major.

After the war, McKinley briefly attended Albany Law School, but left after a year without graduating. He returned to Ohio and established a legal practice in Canton.

After a brief political career in Ohio, McKinley was elected to the U.S. House of Representatives in 1876. McKinley became chairman of the House Ways and Means Committee in 1889 where he sponsored the McKinley Tariff of 1890, drastically increasing tariffs. The public backlash of these increases resulted in a landslide Democratic victory in the 1892 Congressional elections, with McKinley losing his seat. The following year, however, he was elected governor of Ohio.

McKinley had been considered for the Republican nomination for president during the 1888 convention, but Benjamin HARRISON was ultimately nominated. In 1892, McKinley challenged the incumbent President Harrison, but lost the challenge and Harrison subsequently lost to Democrat Grover CLEVELAND. By 1896, McKinley was the leading choice for the Republican nomination.

The 1896 election focused on economics. At the time the country was going through one of its worst DEPRESSIONS. Democrats blamed, among other things, McKinley's 1890 Tariff. However, the main debate was one over monetary policy, as the country was experiencing strong deflation, with agricultural products hardest hit. Democrat William Jennings Bryan advocated replacing the GOLD STANDARD with a system in which silver (in addition to gold) was used to back dollars. Such a policy would most likely have resulted in INFLATION that would benefit debtors primarily in the south and west.

McKinley argued that a protectionist tariff was more important. The campaign also strongly advocated a hard-line gold standard that would create the financial stability necessary for a good economy. The Republicans argued that the depression, which occurred during a Democratic presidency, was the result of bad fiscal policies supporting silver.

McKinley had a major money advantage, raising about $16 million for his campaign, compared to $500,000 for Bryan. This contributed to the largest Republican victory since President Ulysses GRANT's. Nevertheless, economists now look upon Bryan's economic arguments during the campaign more favorably than those of McKinley.

Upon election, McKinley called Congress into special session to enact the Dingley Tariff, raising rates to the highest level they had ever been. It wasn't until shortly before the next presidential election that he delivered his promised Gold Standard Act of 1900.

Foreign affairs soon took center stage. Tensions between SPAIN and the United States had been rising for several years when, in 1898, the battleship *Maine* mysteriously exploded during a visit to Havana, Cuba (now believed an accident). A reluctant McKinley accepted Congress' declaration of war. The United States quickly captured CUBA, Puerto Rico, Guam, and the PHILIPPINES. A peace treaty granted independence to Cuba and gave the rest of the captured territories to the United States. Shortly thereafter, the United States also annexed Hawaii, and occupied Wake Island and part of the Samoan Islands.

With America's newly acquired Pacific territories, interest turned to CHINA. All major world powers (RUSSIA, UNITED KINGDOM, GERMANY, FRANCE, and JAPAN) were interested in China. Rather than fight for colonial control, Secretary of State John Hay established an "Open Door" policy where all the major powers would be entitled to equal trading rights. Many Chinese, however, did not accept the policy and tried to expel all foreigners in the Boxer Rebellion of 1900. McKinley sent in U.S. troops to crush the rebellion.

After his re-election, McKinley seemed poised to continue American expansion, focusing on building a canal to connect the Atlantic and Pacific Oceans. His plans, however, were cut short when an anarchist shot and killed him in September 1901, at the Pan-American Exposition in Buffalo, New York.

Ironically, the McKinley administration's expansion of the American dominion led to increased Republican opposition to tariffs, as they interfered with increasing foreign trade.

BIBLIOGRAPHY. John M. Dobson, *Reticent Expansionism* (Duquesne University Press, 1988); Rebecca Edwards, "1896 Presidential Campaign," iberia.vassar.edul; Paul W. Glad, *McKinley, Bryan, and the People* (Ivan R. Dee, 1964); Lewis L. Gould, *The Presidency of William McKinley* (University Press of Kansas, 1981).

MICHAEL J. TROY, J.D.
THOMAS D. JEITSCHKO, PH.D.
MICHIGAN STATE UNIVERSITY

Medici, Cosimo de' (1389–1464)

COSIMO "THE ELDER" de' Medici was the personification of the new class of noble: the merchant prince. By monopolizing both finance and government in Florence, he generated a fortune that he used in the service of his family, his city, and the rising tide of commercial activity that was shaping European institutions.

De' Medici grew up in the city of Florence that had become wealthy through the production, trade, and finance of the cloth industry for some two centuries. His family produced the famous red Florentine cloth, and had banking operations throughout Europe in which they developed many of the financial tools still in use today. In addition, the Medici had held several high positions in Florentine government and were thus both economically and politically influential. De' Medici was, therefore, well placed to straddle the worlds of commerce, finance, and government, and did indeed pioneer the issue of bonds for consolidating public debt.

When his father Giovanni died, de' Medici inherited profitable interests in cloth, agriculture, banking, and a political legacy that had popular appeal. This popular appeal is generally attributed to two characteristics: First, to his relatively amiable and humble public demeanor, and second, to a restructuring of the Florentine tax system that shifted the burden from commoners to the wealthy, including himself.

De' Medici was able to project himself as an advocate of democracy, while restricting the eligibility of candidates for public office to his clique. This power enabled him, working behind the scenes, to adjust the tax levy on his actual or potential enemies, to either bankrupt them, or to bring them under his direct control by extending loans to them. This monopolization of finance was leveraged to keep Florence, a city of 100,000 people without any defensive walls, safe and prosperous in the middle of a regional power struggle pitting Venice, Milan, the Pope, SPAIN, FRANCE, and assorted mercenaries.

Although not an intellectual, he had been educated in the style of the noble merchants of Florence. He was introduced to classical literature, had traveled extensively, and became acquainted with the emerging humanists of the era. He compensated for his unscrupulous methods of acquiring wealth by funding artists to refurbish and decorate the churches and monasteries of Florence. He was also the sponsor of numerous intellectuals and classical scholars, including bringing the greatest Greek sages, along with their libraries, from the Byzantine Empire to Florence. These initiatives challenged the medieval Christian perception of human nature with regard to wealth acquisition. While only part of a long and broad set of transformations ushering in the modern era, de' Medici was certainly paradigmatic in becoming a publicly involved businessman, not unlike the leaders of most capitalistic economies to this day.

BIBLIOGRAPHY. James Cleugh, *The Medici: A Tale of Fifteen Generations* (Doubleday, 1993); L. Collison-Morley, *The Early Medici* (University of London, 1936).

HARRY KYPRAIOS, PH.D.
ROLLINS COLLEGE

Mellon, Andrew (1855–1937)

ONE OF THE WORLD'S greatest bankers, industrialists, and philanthropists, Andrew Mellon was born in Pittsburgh, Pennsylvania, the son of an Irish-immigrant judge and banker, Thomas Mellon, and Sarah Jane Negley. He attended Western University of Pennsylvania (now the University of Pittsburgh), but left college to go into the lumber business with his brother, Richard.

In 1874, he entered the family's banking firm established in 1870. The brothers Mellon assumed control of the bank, T. Mellon and Sons, upon their father's retirement in 1886. By 1889, Andrew was head of the bank. He married Nora McMullen, in 1900, and they had two children. Nora Mellon disliked Pittsburgh and spent most of her time in her native Britain with their children. The Mellons eventually divorced.

Mellon has been called a financial genius, skilled in choosing growth industries for diversification and investment, thus enabling his family to continue to prosper in the face of downturns in any segment of the economy and even during widespread depressions. He expanded Mellon holdings with the founding of Union Trust Company and Union Savings Bank, and invested heavily in steel, iron, coal, oil, insurance, public utilities, public transportation, and construction. He was also instrumental in establishing Pittsburgh Coal Company, Gulf Oil Company, Koppers Gas and Coke Company, American Locomotive Company, Union Steel Company, and the Aluminum Company of America, and built the steel mill town of Donora, Pennsylvania. Unassuming, frail, and soft-spoken, he was known for his business integrity and for allegedly being the second richest man in the world behind John D. ROCKEFELLER.

Mellon became politically active during the debate over American participation in the League of Nations. Along with close friend Henry C. FRICK, he financed a "war chest" for the anti-League forces. His banks would also underwrite $1,500,000 of the Republican Party's 1920 campaign debt.

Mellon resigned as president of Mellon National Bank in 1921 when President Warren G. HARDING, who admired men of wealth and appreciated his support during the campaign, appointed Mellon, whom he called "the ubiquitous financier of the universe," secretary of the Treasury. The president predicted that he would be the greatest Treasury secretary since Alexander HAMILTON. Once in office, Mellon demonstrated independence, and in contrast to the many corruptions of the Harding administration, he protected his department from the spoils system and only hired officials based on merit.

On offering his resignation to President Calvin COOLIDGE on Harding's sudden death in 1923, Coolidge told Mellon to "forget it." Mellon soon developed a close working relationship with the new president, becoming Coolidge's most trusted cabinet member. A private line was even installed between their desks, and Mellon became a key figure in Coolidge's efforts to restore trust in government following exposure of the many scandals of Harding's presidency.

Mellon came to admire the honest, hardworking, and frugal Coolidge and his debt-reducing, tax-cutting, pro-business, small-government policies, policies Mellon helped to influence and forge. Together they dramatically cut income and corporate taxes and the national debt. Both were widely credited with the great prosperity of the 1920s; yet Democratic critics accused Mellon of favoring the rich.

As chairman of the World War Debts Commission, Mellon created a plan mandating full repayment of the foreign debts resulting from World War I, but worked to prevent oppressive repayment terms, and negotiated understandings with 13 debtor countries. After failing to convince Coolidge to run for another term in 1928, he continued as secretary of the treasury under President Herbert HOOVER until resigning after the Republican defeat of 1931. With the advent of the Great DEPRESSION many blamed him for the economic catastrophe, but some recent historians have looked more favorably upon his 11-year stewardship of the Treasury. Before returning to private life, Hoover appointed him ambassador to Great Britain. He briefly served in that post from 1932 to 1933 before returning to Pittsburgh.

In 1913, Mellon and his brother Richard founded the Mellon Institute of Industrial Research at Pittsburgh in memory of their father. In 1967, the institute merged with the Carnegie Institute of Technology, forming Carnegie-Mellon University.

During a "Grant Tour" of Europe and its museums with Frick in 1880, a right of passage for wealthy young Americans during the Gilded Age, Mellon began acquiring paintings. His collection would become one of the world's largest collections of masterpieces. Inspired by London's National Gallery, in later life he determined to give his collection to the American people and build a gallery for it. Therefore, through his A.W. Mellon Educational and Charitable Trust, he founded the National Gallery of Art in Washington, D.C., after stipulating that the institution not be named after him, and searched the globe for additional works to donate. For example, from 1930-31, he purchased 21 paintings from the Hermitage Museum in Russia and, in 1936, acquired another 42 masterworks of art. The gallery would become Mellon's greatest philanthropic legacy among many.

BIBLIOGRAPHY. David Finley, *A Standard of Excellence* (Smithsonian Institution Press, 1975); David Koskoff, *The Mellons* (Crowell, 1978); Andrew Mellon, *Taxation: The People's Business* (Macmillan, 1924); Harvey O'Connor, *Mellon's Millions* (John Day, 1933).

RUSSELL FOWLER, J.D.
UNIVERSITY OF TENNESSEE, CHATTANOOGA

Menger, Carl (1840–1921)

FOUNDER OF the AUSTRIAN SCHOOL of economics, Carl Menger published his groundbreaking *Principles of Economics* in 1871. Born in Nowy Sacz, a city in southern POLAND that at the time was a part of the Austro-Hungarian Empire, Menger was one of three sons from a prosperous family. His brothers Anton, a scholar of law and SOCIALISM, and the author of *The Right to the*

Whole Produce of Labour (1886), and Max, a member of the Austrian parliament, were well known in late 19th-century Vienna. Menger studied at the Universities of Vienna (1859–60) and Prague (1860–63) and earned his doctorate in law from the University of Krakow in 1867. He began his career in journalism, covering economic issues for newspapers in Lemberg, now the Ukrainian city of Lviv, and Vienna.

The publication of the *Principles of Economics* earned Menger a position as a lecturer at the University of Vienna in 1871 and as a professor in 1873. He developed a reputation as a popular lecturer and, in 1876, was asked to tutor the 17-year-old Archduke Rudolf, the crown prince of AUSTRIA and heir to the throne. The lectures were based on Adam SMITH's *Wealth of Nations*, and Rudolf's extensive notes, with Menger's corrections, were eventually discovered and published in 1994. Emperor Franz Josef approved Menger's appointment as chair of law and political economy at the University of Vienna in 1879. Menger retired from his position at the university in 1903.

Menger's greatest contribution to capitalist economics was the development of the marginal-utility theory of value. Along with two contemporaries who worked independently, William Stanley JEVONS and Leon WALRAS, Menger created the so-called marginal revolution by introducing a subjective approach to economics. The classical economists who preceded him considered the cost of production as the main determinant of value, a view that led to obvious contradictions.

Consider someone whose labor has clearly created nothing of value, a person digging a hole and then filling it in, for example. The classical view implies that the value of the hole is equal to the value of the labor used to create it. Menger resolved this apparent contradiction by explaining that the value of a good is not objective, but instead is subjective because it depends on the utility that human beings receive from it.

Menger also recognized that the value of a good depended not on its overall utility, but on the utility of an extra, or marginal, unit of the good. That insight, that marginal utility determines value, allowed Menger to explain paradoxes of classical economics such as the fact that diamonds, which had virtually no productive uses at the time, were valuable, while water, which was extremely useful, was almost worthless. Menger noted that the difference in value between the two goods is due to the abundance of water and the scarcity of diamonds. As long as large quantities of water are readily available, the value of receiving an extra unit of water is low. Diamonds, on the other hand, are quite rare so that the value from an extra unit is high. Thus, even though water is far more useful than diamonds, the latter are more valuable because their marginal utility is higher.

In addition to the direct impact of his work, Menger influenced the field of economics through the work of other distinguished members of the Austrian school of economics. His best-known students were Friedrich von Wieser and Eugen BÖHM-BAWERK. Wieser, who succeeded Menger at the University of Vienna when he retired in 1903, wrote *Social Economics* (1927) and is credited with inventing the term MARGINAL UTILITY. Böhm-Bawerk, who published *Capital and Interest* (1884) and *The Positive Theory of Capital* (1891), developed Menger's ideas in the areas of economic growth and capital theory. Later members of the Austrian school included Ludwig von MISES and Friedrich von HAYEK, both of whom credited Menger for the substantial achievements of the Austrian School of economics. The Nobel-laureate Hayek, for example, wrote of the Austrian School that "its fundamental ideas belong fully and wholly to Carl Menger."

Though economic historians debate the extent to which their achievements represent a revolution, there is no doubt that Menger, and his contemporaries Walras and Jevons, made an enormous contribution to the study of economics. Today, the field has thoroughly appropriated marginal-utility theory and most sophisticated economic models explicitly incorporate the subjective utility introduced by Menger.

BIBLIOGRAPHY. Blaug, Mark, ed., *Carl Menger* (Edward Elgar, 1992); Bruce J. Caldwell, ed., *Carl Menger and His Legacy in Economics* (Duke University Press, 1990); Carl Menger, *Principles of Economics* (New York University Press, 1871); Erich Streissler, ed., *Carl Menger's Lectures to Crown Prince Rudolf of Austria* (Edward Elgar, 1994).

JEFFREY R. GERLACH
COLLEGE OF WILLIAM AND MARY

mercantilism

IN THE 15TH CENTURY, the monarchs of Europe began consolidating their territories. They brought more money to their coffers by overturning medieval trade restrictions that had created tolls at virtually every city or river crossing.

Having consolidated at home, they began attempting to extend their power into the world at the expense of their rivals. PORTUGAL and SPAIN, first to consolidate, were first to venture forth. Portugal explored around Africa to INDIA and CHINA and got a Papal gift, BRAZIL. Spain built an empire from the Philippines to the Americas. Spain had a larger population, and its New World possessions were rich in gold and silver, so Portugal faded over time while Spain persisted in imperialism through the 19th century. Spanish gold and silver aided other rising powers, the NETHERLANDS, FRANCE, the UNITED KINGDOM, as they built empires of their own.

But there was never enough bullion, and the states began to emphasize commerce: Buy little, sell much, and bank the difference. In the 17th and 18th centuries, Europe went through what Adam SMITH, in retrospect, would call mercantilism.

Mercantilism was a closed system in which each participant attempted to acquire as much tangible wealth, gold and silver, as possible. To do so, mercantilists discouraged unfavorable balances of trade, emphasized home self-sufficiency supplemented by colonial possessions that provided material the home could not make for itself and also provided guaranteed markets for home goods. The system required high tariffs on competing goods, low tariffs on colonial output needed at home. It also generated an activist government willing to impose navigation restrictions and tight, central controls over quality and types of goods produced. And colonial trade meant strong merchant fleets, usually armed, for both practical and symbolic reasons. The spread of the flag also made large populations desirable, both to produce at home and to populate abroad. Thrift was a mercantile virtue, given the finite stock of wealth. Applied mercantilism proved more difficult.

Spanish mercantilism. The rest of Europe had colonies throughout the world. Spain had the New World's gold and silver. All trade came through Seville, every ounce of Bolivian and Mexican silver. Spanish ship tonnage rose from 10,000 tons in 1540 to more than 40,000 tons in 1608; thereafter it declined. Silver imports rising sevenfold through the period allowed Spain a mighty military and an aggressive foreign policy, but Spain's failure to develop beyond agriculture meant Spanish silver also went into rival coffers, as Spain bought foreign finished goods (violating one of the tenets of mercantilism). Genoa, Italy, the Netherlands, England—all used Spanish wealth to expand trade into Scandinavia and other regions with small demand for the products of these countries.

England wasn't content to wait for Spanish silver to trickle through porous mercantilism. English pirates attacked Spanish ships from the 1530s, and by 1560, Sir John Hawkins and other "sea dogs" made a career bringing Spanish wealth to England. Queen Elizabeth I backed Sir Francis Drake's 1577–78 voyage through the Strait of Magellan, up west America, by the Spice Islands, through the Cape of Good Hope, thence to England. This voyage brought Elizabeth 264,000 pounds sterling. Investors realized a 4,000 percent profit. Drake became a knight.

Despite its flaws, the Spanish system lasted centuries. The new world had more than metal. The *encomienda,* or plantation system, gave ambitious Castilian nobles an opportunity to amass large estates. The land was good for agriculture and stock raising, and the in-digenous peoples could be made to work. The system had a drawback, bureaucracy, but that was in Spain, and the colonials were far away.

Spanish America always had a population problem, failing another tenet of mercantilism, the large overseas population. As early as 1503, the indigenous population was insufficient for labor needs, so Spain began the *asiento,* contracting the slave trade to variously Spanish, Flemish, English, Portuguese, Dutch, French, and Genoese contractors. Attempts to control the trade below demand led to widespread smuggling, another leak in the system. Spanish Asia also employed the *encomienda* system, but the indigenous peoples provided enough labor that slavery was not required.

Manila, the Philippines, was the entrepot for trade between Mexico and China that lasted from the 16th through the 19th centuries—silver for silk and porcelain. Spanish mercantilism was hardly beneficent. It entailed exploitation of colonists and indigenous populations, brought inflation to Spain and much of Europe, and added little economic benefit to the masses of Spaniards. Still, it worked through the 19th century.

When the easy money disappeared and the mercantilist nations began debasing their coin and the easy expansion to Asia ended, the result was an economic crisis. A new approach was needed, and the Netherlands took the lead.

The Netherlands. Dutch merchants took over trade, introduced new banking and shipping methods and tools, cut costs, and dominated the older mercantilists, still state-driven. The Dutch controlled European commerce from 1648–72. They ran the Baltic trade, had a good share of the American and Asian, and dominated re-exports. Antwerp and Hamburg and Amsterdam were dominant trading cities because of their aggressiveness, innovation, and abilities to economize. They did not arm their vessels, they did establish joint-stock companies drawing large numbers of investors with small sums of capital. By the 1670s, the Dutch merchant fleet was larger than the combined fleets of England, France, Spain, Portugal, and Germany.

The Dutch turned the old Baltic trade's bullion drain into a positive trade balance. Dutch bankers also provided credit to other Europeans, bringing in additional wealth. The Dutch successes led to jealousy and a series of wars with the English in the 17th century. The Dutch lacked the military resources and strong leadership they needed, so their dominance faded, but their Asian empire would remain through much of the 20th century.

France. The French fought the Dutch using routine mercantilist tools: higher tariffs and port fees; a crackdown on smuggling; state sponsored companies to rival the Dutch East and West Indies Companies; and as a last resort a war. French mercantilism was the brainchild of Jean Baptiste COLBERT, chief minister to Louis XIV from 1661 to 1683. Colbert established strong central regulation, but he made sure that the middle-class prospered. He banned export of money, set tariffs high on foreign goods, and subsidized French shipping generously.

Colbert spread the French empire from the West Indies into Canada, Louisiana, Africa, and Asia. He made the French empire a closed system with French merchants buying from the colonies or home-sources only. He built a fleet of 300 ships, discouraged the taking of holy orders, and provided bounties for large families. Between 1715 and 1771, French trade increased eight times, almost catching the English level. Colbert made the decisions in France; in England central control was weaker.

England. The English effort began in the 1660s under the Stuarts. Finally, there came to be an emphasis on planning, maximizing industrial capacity, and the intricacies of international rivalries and diplomatic jousting. Despite the late start and the weaker central-policing, mercantilism did boost England out of its rural patterns; at its peak, the economic expansion was unlike any that had gone before.

English mercantilism took its most familiar form in the series of Navigation Acts. Sharing the assumption that colonies were to take home finished products and give raw materials and excess income, England promoted colonies for its own benefit, not the benefit of the colonies.

England, like the other mercantilist empires, attempted to control trade through navigation acts. And like the others, English success was mixed. England regulated shipping as early as the time of Richard II in the 14th century, but it was sporadic; as late as 1642 the Long Parliament was exempting American goods from import and export fees. Under Oliver CROMWELL, England enacted its first mercantile-era navigation act. This act restricted imports from America, Asia, and Africa to British ships only. Imports from Europe were restricted to ships of England or the producing country. This act was directed primarily at the Dutch, with little consideration given to its impact on the colonies.

The Navigation Act of 1660 tightened controls, restating the rules of the first act and also enumerating items that colonials could ship only to England or English territory. Because they competed with England's home manufacture, finished goods from the northern colonies suffered more greatly than raw materials from the southern ones. As time passed, though, England enumerated raw materials as well. The Corn Law of 1666 protected English grains at the expense of American ones, leading to a shift in New England to manufacturing. In 1672, another act enumerated items in inter-colonial trade. And import fees grew as well. Increasingly, England's protection of its home industries appeared to be damaging colonial interests. However, enforcement was lax, and smuggling was widespread among northern traders to the non-English West Indies. Also, at least some of the time, England defined colonial manufactures as equal to domestic ones, so colonials and home manufactures alike enjoyed the protection of England's protective tariff walls against European competition.

The Molasses Act of 1733 was extremely damaging. Directed against the French West Indies, this act set extremely high tariffs on sugar and molasses. It had the potential to destroy the New England export of flour, fish, lumber and livestock; these items were barred from England due to the Corn Laws, so there was no other market than the West Indies.

The English established a Board of Trade and Plantations in 1696, but it failed to control the colonies. Conniving customs officials and weak governors either abetted or ignored widespread smuggling, in the colonies as at home. And juries in admiralty court generally refused to convict smugglers. Colonial contempt of Parliament grew over time as it became increasingly obvious that the body had no ability to enforce its laws.

Although navigation acts sometimes benefited nascent colonial industries or providers of otherwise scarce and expensive raw materials such as ships' stores, overall the restrictions were highly lucrative for England. The New England balance sheet for 1759 showed £38,000 worth of exports against imports of £600,000. Cash flow was a colonial problem, but the illegal trade with the West Indies helped.

World. Mercantilism appeared to be an effective system: Tobacco, rice, coffee, sugar, and rice went to European cities such as Lisbon, Cadiz, Bordeaux, London and Liverpool, which re-exported unfinished products and shipped finished items to the colonial plantations. Some cities also grew wealthy as shippers of slaves.

Slave ports included Liverpool and Lisbon as well as those on the west coast of Africa. Cheap finished goods bought valuable live bodies that slavers packed tightly for the trip to the Americas, replacing them with cotton, tobacco, and other plantation crops from the Caribbean, American South, and Brazil. Over time, mercantile controls weakened. Growing populations and increased inter-colonial trade led to increasing autonomy, less willingness to heed the needs of the mercantile home.

In Asia, the mercantile approach was marginally successful. Initially, Europeans had less to offer than they wanted to buy, so they relied on new-world bullion to make up the difference. This violated the mercantilist tenets of preserving a favorable balance of payments and promoting home-manufacture while minimizing dependence on others. Over time however, Europe abandoned mercantilism in favor of free trade, and European manufactured goods, plus a dominating European presence, established much of Asia as subordinate to Europe economically as well as politically.

In India, where the BRITISH EAST INDIA COMPANY had a presence from 1608, the initial effort succeeded due to divided indigenous governors willing to grant favorable terms of trade. Also significant was company military superiority. Once in control, the company became rapacious, and eventually it required military assistance from England to preserve its position. In 1773, the British government took over control of India from the company, which remained until 1858.

Conclusion. Mercantilist practices varied, as did degrees of success, but all attempted to use the same rules to attain the same goals. As wealth consisted mostly of bullion, the goal was to maximize the amount in the state's control. To do that, countries either acquired colonies or worked toward favorable balances of trade with their rivals. The governments aggressively promoted economic development, restricted colonies to provision of raw materials and markets, and tried to keep the system closed through navigation acts and other laws to control competition. As long as economic theorists assumed that the supply of wealth was finite, limited to the world supply of gold and silver, mercantilism was logical. In 1776, Adam Smith published *An Inquiry Into the Nature and Causes of the Wealth of Nations*, and suddenly wealth equated to productivity, not metal. There were no limits. Free trade replaced mercantilism as the dominating practice. Of course, by this time, England had established its industrial prowess and did not need the protective tariffs. Instead, English industry needed free trade to establish its hegemony.

BIBLIOGRAPHY. Thomas A. Brady Jr., Heiko O. Oberman, and James D. Tracy, eds., *Handbook of European History, 1400–1600: Late Middle Ages, Renaissance and Reformation, Vol. I: Structures and Assertions* (Brill Academic, 1994); Robert B. Ekelund, Jr. and Robert D. Tollison, *Politicized Economies; Monarchy, Monopoly, and Mercantilism* (Texas A&M, 1997); Peter J. Hugill, *World Trade Since 1431: Geography, Technology, and Capitalism* (Johns Hopkins University Press, 1993); John J. McCusker, *Mercantilism and the Economic History of the Early Modern Atlantic World* (University of North Carolina Press, 2001); Dietmar Rothermund, *Asian Trade and European Expansion in the Age of Mercantilism* (South Asia Books, 1981); James Tracy, ed., *The Rise of Merchant Empires: Long-Distance Trade in the Early Modern World, 1350–1750* (Cambridge University Press, 1990).

JOHN H. BARNHILL, PH.D.
INDEPENDENT SCHOLAR

Merck & Company

A PHARMACEUTICAL company headquartered in Whitestation, New Jersey, Merck reported approximately $40 billion in sales in 2000. Like most drug companies, Merck invests heavily in RESEARCH AND DEVELOPMENT (R&D), allocating $2.6 billion in 2001, and having spent some $15 billion in R&D over the preceding 10 years. Such investment has produced various vaccines and medicines that treat cardiovascular, gastrointestinal and infection diseases, and glaucoma and arthritis. More recently, Merck developed a drug that treats HIV infection called Crixivan.

Merck produces both human and animal health products including Zocor, Mevacor, Vasotec, and Pepcid. These are some of the best-selling prescription and nonprescription medications in the world. Merck employs over 78,000 people in 120 countries and owns 21 factories worldwide.

Merck's history began in Darmstadt, Germany, in 1668 when Frederic Jacob Merck, an apothecary, used his knowledge of chemistry to found a fine-chemicals firm. In 1891, succeeding generations of Mercks relocated the business to New York City. By the 1930s, the company was specializing in the research and production of pharmaceuticals. After a merger in 1953, Merck expanded the organization internationally.

BIBLIOGRAPHY. www.activemedia-guide.com; www.merck.com.

ARTHUR HOLST, PH.D.
WIDENER UNIVERSITY

Merrill Lynch

ONE OF THE MOST recognized, leading financial management and advisory companies in the world, Merrill Lynch does business in 36 countries, and its total client assets are currently approximated at $1.3 trillion. As an investment bank, Merrill Lynch is the global underwriter of debt and equity securities and strategic advisor to global corporations, governments, institutions and individuals.

In the words of CHIEF EXECUTIVE OFFICER (CEO) Stanley C. O'Neal, "We are building a new kind of company—a growth company, diversified and disciplined, agile and accountable; a company that lives by the proposition that the only sustainable advantage is to find ways of adding real value to clients in the markets we serve."

Throughout 2002, Merrill Lynch focused on restructuring mandated by a market of ups and downs, terrorist attacks, war, and a wobbly economy. The company has honed controlled expenses, diversified revenues, and liberated resources—all in a state of reserve for the future. Resizing, reshaping, a new Merrill Lynch is, according to its public relations, "a portfolio of diversified businesses (armed) to deliver superior client service and shareholder value across economic cycles."

Full-year net earnings (2002) were $2.5 billion, or $2.63 per diluted share—the third-best operating performance in the company's history, despite a decline in net revenues due to a tougher operating environment. Simultaneously, the firm exceeded its profitability target with a pre-tax profit margin increasing to 20.2 percent. At the end of its 2002 fiscal year, with a bolstered balance sheet, its capital base was stronger and larger, and with liquidity position better than in many years.

Succinctly, three customized businesses have emerged in the company's restructuring: Global Markets and Investment Banking (GMI); Global Private Client (GPC); and Merrill Lynch Investment Managers (MLIM).

GMI serves corporations, financial institutions and governments with comprehensive investment-banking and strategic-advisory services—including debt and equity trading, underwriting and origination, and mergers and acquisitions.

GPC is the world's premier provider of wealth management services, with more than $1 trillion in client assets. For individual investors, GPC ensures high-quality service through a segmented offering that meets clients' needs. Through Merrill Lynch's new cash-management platform, "Beyond Banking," clients can manage their everyday financial transactions separately from, but linked to, their investment holdings.

MLIM is a huge money manager with $462 billion under management, serving a diverse, global base of mutual-fund investors, high-net-worth individuals, pension funds, corporations, governments and other assorted institutions.

"Merrill Lynch was founded on the idea that the world is full of opportunity," states the company's chairman, David H. Komansky. "While some people question the very concept of globalization, (we) remain convinced that open, free and fair markets are the surest way to global prosperity." Reporting total revenues of almost $39 billion in 2002, Merrill Lynch was ranked as the 95th largest company in the world.

BIBLIOGRAPHY. "Global 500: World's Largest Companies," *Fortune* (July 2002); Merrill Lynch, www.plan.ml.com; *Hoover's Handbook of American Business* (Hoover's Inc., 2003).

JOSEPH GERINGER
SYED B. HUSSAIN, PH.D.
UNIVERSITY OF WISCONSIN, OSKKOSH

Merton, Robert C. (1944–)

CO-WINNER, ALONG WITH Myron SCHOLES, of the 1997 Nobel Prize in Economics, Robert C. Merton begins his autobiography, "I was born in New York, NY on 31 July 1944, the middle child between two sisters, Stephanie and Vanessa." Merton's father was a leading sociologist on the faculty of Columbia University. "My father introduced me to baseball, poker, magic, and the stock market (only magic didn't take root)." Financial practice intrigued Merton from an early age. "As early as 8 or 9 years of age, I developed an interest in money and finance, even at play. I created fictitious banks such as the RCM Savings of Dollars and Cents Company. I gladly balanced my mother's check book."

As Merton explained, "I was a good student but not at the top of my class." He studied applied and pure mathematics in Columbia's Engineering School. Entering the California Institute of Technology's Ph.D. program in applied mathematics, Merton left after only a year to study economics at the Massachusetts Institute of Technology. "My decision to leave applied mathematics for economics was in part tied to the widely-held popular belief in the 1960s that macroeconomics had made fundamental inroads into controlling business cycles and stopping dysfunctional unemployment and inflation. Thus, I felt that working in economics could 'really matter' and that potentially one could affect millions of people."

Merton explains: "I see my research interests as fitting into three regimes of roughly equal lengths across time: 1968 to 1977, 1977 to 1987, and 1988 to the present, with a reflective year 1986-88. Thee first period was my most productive one for basic research, in terms of both the number of papers produced and originality and significance of contribution. The central modeling theme was continuous-time stochastic processes with continuous-decision-making by agents. Locating this modeling approach within mathematical economics, I see my models falling in the middle range between simple models (e.g., one or two-periods with a representative agent) designed to give insights (associated by some with the MIT school) and full general equilibrium models on a grand scale involving an arbitrary number of agents with general preferences and production technologies (often associated with the Berkeley school)."

Merton recounts, "in 1987, I took my first-ever sabbatical year. . . This reflective year was a watershed, both for my research and for where it would take place. In effect, *Continuous-Time Finance* was the crowning synthesis of my earlier work. Its Chapter 14 on intermediation and institutions, however, represented a bridge to a new direction of my research. From that time until the present, I have focused on understanding the financial system with special emphasis on the dynamics of institutional change. In particular, I am studying the role of financial technology and innovation in driving changes in financial institution and market design, the management of financial-service firms, and the regulatory and the accounting systems."

Along with Myron Scholes' derivative-security research, Merton was cited by the Nobel Committee for "a new method to determine the value of derivatives." This method, the Black-Merton-Scholes stock option pricing formula, by facilitating economic valuation in many areas, has proven useful in the finance industry and the study of economics.

BIBLIOGRAPHY. Robert C. Merton, "Lifetime Portfolio Selection under Uncertainty: The Continuous-Time Case," *The Review of Economics & Statistics* (v.51/3, 1969); Robert C. Merton, "Optimum Consumption and Portfolio Rules in a Continuous-time Model," *Working Papers* (MIT, 1970); Robert C. Merton, "Financial Innovation and the Management and Regulation of Financial Institutions," NBER Working Papers 5096 (National Bureau of Economic Research, 1995); Robert C. Merton, "Applications of Option-Pricing Theory: Twenty-Five Years Later," *American Economic Review* (v.88/3, 1998); Zvi Bodie and Robert C. Merton, *Finance* (Prentice Hall, 2000).

ELIZABETH BISHOP, PH.D.
AMERICAN UNIVERSITY

Metro

RANKED AS THE 72nd largest company in the world by *Fortune* magazine, Metro AG is the German management holding for a group of retail and wholesale chains. The company was formed in 1996 from the merger of several other German retailers, based on the Kaufhof Group, created by legendary German entrepreneur Otto Beisheim.

With 2,310 retail locations in 26 countries, Metro achieved net sales of €51.5 billion (2002) and profits of €412.0 million (2001), with assets of more than €20 billion and 234,000 employees worldwide. With 46.3 percent of its revenue achieved outside Germany, Metro has a significant international presence on the European and Asian continents, the countries last entered having been Vietnam and Japan. The optimization of the store portfolio, judicious internationalization, and effective logistics are regarded the cornerstones of the company's rapid growth.

Metro AG is divided into four strategic business units: cash and carry markets, food retailing, non-food specialists, and department stores, and trades under the brands Metro Cash & Carry, Real, Extra, Media Markt, Saturn, Praktiker, and Kaufhof. With a share of more than 45 percent of total corporate revenue, the cash and carry outlets have become global leaders in the self-service wholesale segment. With 416 stores in 24 countries and up to 17,000 food products and 30,000 non-food products carried, Metro cash and carry pursues a different strategy than WAL-MART's Sam's Clubs, that carry about 4,000 products. Metro stock (Meog.de) trades on German stock exchanges (DAX).

BIBLIOGRAPHY. Annual Reports and Quarterly Reports, www.metrogroup.de; "Global 500: World's Largest Companies," *Fortune* (July, 2002).

WOLFGANG GRASSL, PH.D.
HILLSDALE COLLEGE

Mexico

A FEDERAL REPUBLIC of more than one million square miles, Mexico borders the UNITED STATES to the north, the Gulf of Mexico and the Caribbean Sea to the east, Belize and Guatemala to the southeast, and the Pacific Ocean to the south and west. It has an ethnically diverse population of 98 million, with a significant presence of numerous indigenous groups primarily concentrated in the south and southeast. Despite more than a century of modernization efforts, Mexico remains a nation of contrasts. Vast sectors of the population are inserted into the global economy through trade and the use of modern technology, but a significant amount of people still live in isolated communities as their ancestors did hundreds of years ago. This divide is one of the most salient issues facing Mexico in the 21st century.

In the early 1500s, SPAIN inaugurated 300 years of colonial administration over the *Virreinato de la Nueva España*, much of which would become Mexico. The conquest and early colonial period was not only brutal for the vanquished Aztecs, but war, disease, forced labor and migration largely decimated other indigenous populations in Mesoamerica. Spanish conquest was aimed primarily at the extraction of mineral wealth, and, secondarily, at the conversion of souls to Christianity, goals that occasionally clashed. Vast amounts of silver flowed from central Mexico in Spanish ships, oiling the wheels of European commerce during the early stages of capitalist development.

Although the independence movement was born from the discontent of *criollos* (Mexico-born Spanish elites) over Spanish rule as in the rest of Latin America, in Mexico it rapidly received the widespread support of the indigenous and *mestizo* peasantry. Independence was declared on September 16, 1821, at the crest of popular rebellion and following a decade of bloody conflict with Spain. A fragmented political elite and strong regional leaders throughout the country resulted in a period dominated by civil war. In a quick war with the United States in 1847, Mexico lost a good deal of its northern territory.

Internal convulsion between conservatives and liberals ensued, resulting in a second foreign occupation, this time by the French with their imposition of Maximilian of Hapsburg as emperor (1863–67). His defeat at the hands of Benito Juárez inaugurated a long period of economic liberalism and political stability. In particular, the rise of Porfirio Díaz to power resulted in massive inflows of foreign capital, primarily for the extraction of minerals and other raw materials for export to the United States.

The vast wealth generated under the Porfiriato (Díaz regime) concentrated in few hands, blocking the aspirations of a nascent middle class of professionals, and creating ample resentment among the peasantry and fledgling working class. Demands for elections free of fraud went unheeded, and following electoral fraud in the presidential elections of 1910, Francisco I. Madero called for open rebellion, inaugurating the Mexican Revolution. Although the more radical factions of the revolution were defeated, the armed upheaval of a peasantry allied to Emiliano Zapata, and ranch hands loyal to Francisco Villa, left its imprint in the Constitution of 1917, where a balance was struck between a salient role for the state and the prerogatives of the private sector.

The more radical provisions of the 1917 Constitution were not fully implemented until Lázaro Cárdenas (1932–38) made bold use of Article 27 to redistribute 44 million acres of land to communes or *ejidos*. He also used this constitutional article to expropriate foreign oil companies during their stand-off with oil workers in

Hotels and resorts along Mexico's Pacific coast draw tourism dollars into the country's gross domestic product.

1938, establishing *Petróleos Mexicanos* as a state monopoly. The Cárdenas administration created the framework for a stronger state role in the economy, and provided the political foundation for the creation of the *Partido Revolucionario Institucional* (PRI) during the administration of Miguel Alemán (1946–52).

The PRI established a corporatist political structure based on three sectors. The peasantry represented by *Confederación Nacional Campesina*, the working class represented by the *Confederación de Trabajadores Mexicanos*, and the middle class, grouped in the *Confederación Nacional de Organizaciones Populares*. Using material rewards for organizations supporting the party, issuing stiff punishments for detractors and the opposition, and most likely making use of some electoral fraud, the PRI was able to remain in control of the presidency until 2000. During the 1950s and 1960s, the country underwent what has been termed the Mexican miracle, a long period of high economic-growth rates and low inflation characterized by an active state, but with ample room for the private sector.

By the 1960s, growing inequality had generated discontent. As social tensions rose, guerrilla activity made an appearance in Guerrero, and protests in Mexico City resulted in the 1968 Massacre of Tlatelolco, where an undisclosed number of students were killed by security forces.

Luis Echeverría (1970–76) attempted to diffuse social tensions with redistributive policies including the largest reallocation of land since the Cárdenas administration. His statist orientation placed business leaders in a heightened state of alert, starting a slow but steady movement of business support away from the PRI. Echeverria's successor, José López Portillo (1976–82), took office as vast oil reserves were discovered in the Gulf of Mexico. The quadrupling of oil prices in 1973–74 had sparked interest in exploration, and this was followed by large investments in oil extraction. Convinced that Mexico had found the road to riches, the administration of López Portillo borrowed heavily from international commercial banks, bringing the foreign debt of the country to $80 billion in 1982.

In August 1982, Mexico gave the opening salvo in what came to be known as the Latin American debt crisis. A recession engineered by the Ronald REAGAN administration to reduce inflation in the United States resulted in the sharp increase in international interest rates, and a significant drop in the price of oil, by then Mexico's main export. Unable to make payments on its foreign debt, Mexico declared a moratorium.

The INTERNATIONAL MONETARY FUND (IMF) stepped in with financial resources to make payments on condition of the implementation of austerity measures and the liberalization of the economy. The administration of Miguel de la Madrid (1982–88) struggled to revive the domestic economy while implementing IMF policies. In 1986, Mexico joined the GENERAL AGREEMENT ON TARIFFS AND TRADE (GATT) and 743 state enterprises were privatized or shut down between 1982 and 1988. Nevertheless, de la Madrid was unable to control inflation until the implementation of the *Pacto de Solidaridad* in 1987, freezing wages and prices in an attempt to stave off inflation without further economic contraction.

Carlos Salinas de Gortari (1988–94) was elected the following year amid allegations of widespread fraud. He rapidly moved to consolidate his power with high-profile political maneuvers such as the arrest of Joaquin "La Quina" Hernandez Galicia, an influential union leader with the petroleum workers union. Once firmly in control, Salinas deepened the neoliberal reforms of his predecessor. Changes to Article 27 of the Constitution in 1992 put an end to land reform and threatened existing *ejidos*. His proposal to negotiate a North American Free Trade Agreement (NAFTA) led to its signature in late 1993 and inauguration on January 1, 1994. The end of land reform and the opening of trade in agriculture under NAFTA were interpreted by many Mexicans as a violation of the spirit of the Mexican Revolution and the letter of the Constitution of 1917. A group of Mayan peasants staged an armed rebellion on the day NAFTA went into effect, catapulting their enigmatic leader, Subcomandante Marcos, to instant celebrity status in Mexico and around the world.

The same year, fissures within the PRI itself resulted in two high-profile assassinations, including the party's presidential candidate. Political uncertainty was followed by investors' anxiety, resulting in the reduction of capital flows to Mexico, higher costs of borrowing and the shortening of its maturity. When Ernesto Zedillo (1994–2000) took office in December, foreign-exchange reserves had been driven down trying to defend the value of the peso. Within days of the inauguration, investors ran from the peso leading to its sharp devaluation and a balance of payments crisis that required a $40 billion bailout by the IMF and the U.S. Treasury Department, launching a series of financial crises in emerging market economies.

Zedillo's presidency focused on re-establishing growth and solidifying the pro-market reforms of his predecessor. The political patronage system based on the corporatist organization of the PRI had been in crisis since the mid-1980s. Zedillo's technocratic approach and further reforms to the political system weakened the party even further. Vicente Fox (2000–06) of the *Partido de Acción Nacional*, won the 2000 presidential election, breaking 71 years of one-party rule. A former executive of Coca-Cola in Mexico, Fox pursued even closer relations with the United States, going as far as proposing the integration of the labor markets of the two countries. His initiatives were soon disregarded in the United States and the

George W. Bush administration became preoccupied with national security issues and the Middle East.

Although the economy recovered rapidly from the 1995 crisis, growth has remained sluggish and highly dependent on the U.S. economy, which, in 2003, absorbed 90 percent of Mexico's exports. Under NAFTA, Mexican manufactures have gained unrestricted access to U.S. markets, boosting the economies of Mexico's northern region where the infrastructure and semi-skilled labor necessary for industrial production is concentrated. However, NAFTA has also brought rising concerns regarding the fate of hundreds of thousands of peasants, primarily in the central and southern regions, whose survival is endangered by rising imports of subsidized U.S. corn. The intended beneficiaries of proposed infrastructure development in these regions (i.e., Plan Puebla-Panama), many of them indigenous people, are deeply rooted in their lands. Attempts to integrate them as wage laborers into a modern, export-oriented economy are likely to meet resistance as this represents a threat to their millenary cultures.

BIBLIOGRAPHY. Alan Knight, *The Mexican Revolution* (Cambridge University Press, 1986); Nora Hamilton, *The Limits of State Autonomy: Post-Revolutionary Mexico* (Princeton University Press, 1982); Nora Lustig, *Mexico: The Remaking of an Economy* (The Brookings Institution, 1992); David Barkin, *Distorted Development: Mexico in the World Economy* (Westview, 1990); Roderic Camp, *Politics in Mexico* (Oxford University Press, 1996); Roger Hansen, *The Politics of Mexican Development* (Johns Hopkins University Press, 1973); Judith Teichman, *Privatization and Political Change in Mexico* (Pittsburgh University Press, 1995).

LEOPOLDO RODRÍGUEZ-BOETSCH
PORTLAND STATE UNIVERSITY

microeconomics

THE BRANCH OF ECONOMICS that deals with the behavior of, and the interaction between, individual economic units, such as consumers or firms, is called microeconomics. As a positive science, microeconomics explains social and economic phenomena as the result of rational individual behavior. As a normative science, microeconomics offers techniques to judge the value of different economic and social policies or institutions. Its methods can thus be used to predict how well alternative policies achieve certain goals set forth by the investigator.

Individual behavior. One aim of microeconomics is to examine individual choices and decisions, based on two fundamental premises: That all economic agents possess certain well-defined objectives (preferences), and that they act according to these objectives in an optimal and coherent way. For example, it is commonly assumed that the objective of a firm's management is to maximize profits, and that it chooses among its possible actions the one that best achieves this objective. Combined, these two assumptions comprise the principle of rationality, on which most of economic science is grounded.

While microeconomics often regards agents as purely self-motivated, its approach is general enough to accommodate a wide range of preferences, including a concern for the well being of others (altruism). In choosing the best course of action, economic agents are usually constrained: A consumer can only buy as much as can be afforded with a certain income, while a firm can only sell as many products as the market can bear. Microeconomics thus tries to understand all individual behavior as the solution to a constrained optimization problem. The microeconomic tools for examining such problems extend to dynamic choice (decisions must be made over time with varying constraints), and choice under uncertainty (not all decision-relevant variables are known).

Interaction and aggregate behavior. The scope of microeconomics reaches beyond the analysis and prediction of individual behavior. Economic agents typically engage in *interaction* with one another, and many variables of economic interest are determined through interaction only. The second aim of microeconomics is thus to understand the nature and outcome of such interaction. The following example illustrates the ways this question can be approached.

Consider the market for a certain good. How much someone buys or sells of this good depends on its price. In a market equilibrium, a price will obtain at which aggregate supply is just enough to satisfy aggregate demand (the price is said to clear the market). The price of a good is hence the outcome of the sum of all demand and supply decisions. The very fact that goods have prices through which their value can be determined in a meaningful way, is the consequence of individuals interacting as buyers and sellers in markets.

In markets with many consumers and many firms, each single participant has only a small influence on the price. If the number of market participants is large enough so that each agent can neglect the influence of her actions on aggregate variables, then microeconomists speak of perfect competition. In a relatively small group of individuals, on the other hand, one must account for the fact that each person's actions directly affect the choices of others (imperfect competition). In a market with only two competing firms (duopoly), for

example, the output decision of one firm can be expected to have a direct affect on the output decision of the other firm. Those situations are called strategic, and microeconomists use the tools of GAME THEORY to examine them.

Microeconomics as a normative science. The market example also highlights the normative aspects of microeconomics. The exchange of goods between agents creates value for all involved participants, by which one can judge the success of alternative market designs and competitive regulations. A desirable market outcome should be efficient, in the sense that it leads to an allocation of economic resources that cannot be changed for mutual advantage. Thus, inefficient markets do not exhaust all gains from trade. Microeconomics also offers methods to quantify the overall value that is generated by various forms of market institutions, by deriving measures of social surplus, or welfare.

Not all things can be traded among individuals, however. Groups often have to make choices for themselves that affect their members in different ways. For example, a country must choose a single labor standard, but its citizens typically have differing opinions on what it should be. For welfare statements to be meaningful in this context, individual preferences must be aggregated into a social counterpart. As a sub-branch of microeconomics, social choice theory can identify circumstances under which a society at large can adhere to the same rationality principle as its members.

Microeconomics vs. macroeconomics. Microeconomics shares with MACROECONOMICS the fact that it can make predictions about aggregate variables. While no clear-cut borderline between these two branches of economics exists, several differences and similarities can still be found.

One difference is contextual: Typically, the questions that are addressed using macroeconomics are motivated by and associated with issues of national economic interest; such as how INFLATION, UNEMPLOYMENT, or output, depend on each other. It has become customary to refer to economic inquiry that is concerned with these variables as macroeconomics, while questions concerning consumers, firms, or single markets, have been associated with microeconomics. A second difference is methodological: Macroeconomic analysis often assumes relationships between variables that, in principle, are the outcome of microeconomic interaction, but are not being treated as such. For example, to address a particular question, a macroeconomist may assume that interest rates and savings are positively correlated. A microeconomist, on the other hand, would try to explain this relationship by examining how individual savings decisions in a bond market determine the interest rate.

Economic issues can be very complex to analyze, as typically a large number of variables affect situations of interest. Both microeconomists and macroeconomists deal with these complexities by using economic models: Formal (i.e., mathematical) representations of the real world that are based on a few key assumptions, while neglecting other aspects of the problem. Since economic models are necessarily abstract, the hope is that the insights that they offer are general enough to be applicable to a wide range of specific issues. As a consequence of economics using models, its results require careful interpretation, because they can change when previously neglected features are accounted for. Often, however, a model's validity can (and should) be tested empirically, using ECONOMETRICS.

The extending scope of microeconomics. Many social issues related to disciplines other than economics can be addressed by microeconomic methods. Doing so, one assumes that people adhere to the rationality principle even when making "non-economic" choices. Then individuals' decisions whether to commit crime, whom to vote for, or whether to smoke, have been successfully analyzed by microeconomists. Similarly, microeconomic models of interaction among agents have been used to study the "marriage market" or outcomes of political elections. This research has resulted in many interesting new insights. It is needless to say that many of those areas, while not traditionally associated with economics, are of profound importance for the economic well being of individuals, groups, and nations.

BIBLIOGRAPHY. N. Gregory Mankiw, *Principles of Microeconomics* (South-Western, 2000); Edgar K. Browning and Mark A. Zupan, *Microeconomic Theory and Applications* (John Wiley & Sons, 2003).

TILMAN KLUMPP, PH.D.
INDIANA UNIVERSITY, BLOOMINGTON

Microsoft

THE LARGEST PRODUCER of consumer-level computer software in the world, Microsoft products include the most successful operating system (the various incarnations of Windows), the most successful internet browser (Internet Explorer), and the most successful productivity suite (Office), each of which are considered the industry standard. Microsoft ultimately has been credited with turning computers away from a mere toy of hobbyists and toward mass, popular acceptance, but the company has also been accused of bullying the industry and operating as a MONOPOLY.

Microsoft was formed in 1975 by Bill GATES and Paul Allen, two childhood friends and, later, both Harvard University dropouts. Upon discovering the Altair 8080 (the first computer designed for home use, available as a assembly-required kit), the two wrote a BASIC programming language program for the machine and began selling it to computer companies such as Radio Shack and Texas Instruments. Gates and Allen moved their company from Albuquerque, New Mexico, to Washington State in 1979 and proceeded to produce a wide variety of programming-language software programs. At a time when computer companies primarily focused on hardware and proprietary software, Microsoft only sold software that was compatible with a wide variety of hardware. Microsoft also licensed its software to hardware manufacturers at low rates, hoping to grow via a high quantity of business rather than high profit margins.

Microsoft made the move into operating systems after being approached by IBM in 1980 for input on a new computer line. When asked to supply an operating system for this new system, Microsoft bought an existing program from a local company, modified it, changed the name to MS-DOS (short for Microsoft Data Operating System), and released the product in 1981. Microsoft licensed MS-DOS not only to IBM but to many other manufacturers, thus making IBM-compatible machines easy for companies to build as long as they upheld MS-DOS (and Microsoft by extension) as the de facto software standard.

After an abortive attempt at designing their next generation operating system in conjunction with IBM, Microsoft moved to a graphical interface, where the user operates the computer by manipulating on-screen images, as opposed to MS-DOS, which requires typed-in commands. Graphical user-interfaces had existed since the late 1970s at Xerox's research lab, and commercially since 1984 with the release of the Apple Macintosh. Microsoft's first serious graphical operating system, Windows 3.0, was released in 1990 (earlier, fairly inefficient versions existed as far back as 1984). Industry critics often commented on similarities between Windows and Apple Macintosh's operating system; Apple also thought the two systems were too alike and filed a copyright lawsuit (which it lost) against Microsoft in 1991.

Microsoft grew enormously in the 1990s. One of the company highlights in this decade was the release of the productivity suite Office, which combined spreadsheet, word-processing, and (among others) presentation software; rather than simply bundling software together, Office attempted to integrate the component programs by having them look and operate in similar fashions and by making data easy to move from one program to another. Office was originally designed and sold for the Macintosh in 1989 (other than Apple itself, Microsoft is the world's largest producer of Macintosh software) and released in a Windows-compatible edition in 1990.

Microsoft also increased its share of the operating system market with the release of Windows 95, a complete overhaul of Windows 3.0. Windows 95 was wildly successful, selling over 1 million copies in its first four days of release. Because Windows 95 included a link to the company's fledgling internet service Microsoft Network, America Online accused Microsoft of unethically using its position as producer of the leading operating system in an attempt to dominate the internet market. When Microsoft bundled its Internet Explorer web browser with its next operating system update (Windows 98), the U.S. Justice Department (prompted by web browser rival Netscape) investigated Microsoft and declared the company a monopoly in 2002.

Since its early acquisition of the MS-DOS forerunner, buying and altering existing products has been a regular business practice for Microsoft. Instead of just modifying existing products, however, Microsoft has also bought entire companies in order to acquire a particular program; when Microsoft wanted to enter the web-page design software market in 1995, they bought Vermeer Technologies in order to take over their FrontPage program. These acquisitions have sometimes proven ruthless; when talking to America Online about a possible merger, Bill Gates told AOL executives, "I can buy 20 percent of you or I can buy all of you, or I can go into this business myself and bury you."

As of 2003, Microsoft continues to push computer software as the core of their business. They are also making substantial pushes into the portable electronics market (with Windows CE-run handheld devices) and into home gaming (the X-Box). Microsoft is also developing home automation software to spread its Windows brand further into people's lives.

BIBLIOGRAPHY. Randall E. Stross, *The Microsoft Way: The Real Story of How the Company Outsmarts Its Competition* (Addison-Wesley, 1996); *Inside Out: Microsoft, In Our Own Words* (Warner Books, 2000); Jennifer Edsrom and Marlin Eller, *Barbarians Led By Bill Gates: Microsoft from the Inside: How the World's Richest Corporation Wields Its Power* (Henry Holt, 1998); Cheryl D. Tsang, *Microsoft First Generation: The Success Secrets of the Visionaries Who Launched a Technology Empire* (John Wiley & Sons, 2000).

MIKE S. DUBOSE
BOWLING GREEN STATE UNIVERSITY

Mill, John Stuart (1806–73)

A GIFTED 19TH-CENTURY thinker, John Stuart Mill made important contributions not only to economics but also to political science and philosophy. He was the eldest son of James Mill, a close friend of Jeremy BENTHAM and mentor to David RICARDO. As a key figure of the philosophical radical movement, James Mill wanted his son to be a recipient of the intellectual traditions of both Bentham and Ricardo. Accordingly, John Stuart Mill became the target of a highly rigorous intellectual training that his father considered necessary for his proper development.

The story of John Stuart Mill's education has been told in his *Autobiography*, published shortly after his death. He began to learn Greek and arithmetic at age three; Latin, at age eight; followed by mathematics, chemistry and physics. During early adolescence, his training in philosophy and political economy began. His formal training in economics started with a thorough reading of Ricardo's *Principles of Political Economy and Taxation* followed by an equally intensive study of Adam SMITH. He was still a teenager when he edited the five volumes of Bentham's *Rationale of Evidence*. When Mill was 17, his father was appointed to the India Office, and in turn obtained a clerkship for his son with the British EAST INDIA COMPANY. His formal career with the East India Company lasted for 35 years, terminating with his retirement when the company was liquidated in 1858.

The psychological costs of his remarkably intense education were manifested in a mental crisis at the age of 20, but after a period of depression, Mill recovered to become one of the leading intellectuals of his time. He frequently wrote articles on literary and philosophical topics. His first major work *A System of Logic*, published in 1843, was favorably received and widely read. A few years later, he ventured into economics with *Some Unsettled Questions in Political Economy*, somewhat of a prelude to his main work. His great summary of classical economics *Principles of Political Economy, with Some of Their Applications to Social Philosophy*, published in 1848 (the same year as *The Communist Manifesto* by Karl MARX and Friedrich ENGELS) was the leading textbook in its field for more than 40 years. It was written in less than two years during a time when Mill was also working full time at the India Office

The structure of this work intentionally resembled *The Wealth of Nations* rather than Ricardo's *Principles* because Mill wanted to address wider concerns than those associated with pure political economy. Mill's *Principles* is divided into five books: Production; Distribution; Exchange; Influence of the Progress of Society on Production and Distribution; and Of the Influence of Government.

Other publications, including *On Liberty* (1859), *Considerations of Representative Government* (1861), *Utilitarianism* (1863) *Auguste Comte and Positivism* (1865), and *The Subjection of Women* (1869), demonstrate the breadth of his scholarship. In the latter publication, Mill addressed the benefits for men of equal rights for women.

Mill was an exceptional person, not only intellectually ahead of his own generation, but also a rebel, both against his father's disregard of emotional factors in his philosophy of life and against some of the doctrines his father applied to the social sciences. He was a champion of individual liberty, but an active social reformer. He sought new influences to widen his perspective, among them Samuel Taylor Coleridge, Thomas Carlyle, Johann Wolfgang von Goethe, and Auguste Comte. It was Comte's attempt to interpret history as the progressive development of the human intellect that likely stimulated Mill's own search for a philosophy of history. Yet among those prominent names, Mill himself believed that the greatest intellectual and emotional influence was his friendship and subsequent marriage to Harriet Taylor. She apparently taught Mill to be receptive to the humanistic socialist ideas of the time, and he credited her with convincing him of the importance of the distinction between laws of production and laws of distribution.

Mill believed that in a competitive economic framework, individual and social interests were generally compatible with one another, but he also noted many of the popular exceptions to LAISSEZ-FAIRE that have now become a part of modern capitalism. He adhered to the classical position that social policy could not modify production functions. However, to counter Ricardian predictions of a dreaded stationary state at which wages would be at a subsistence level, he recommended exceptions to pure laissez-faire principles. These reforms would encourage individuals in society to act in a more humane way, resulting in a more equitable distribution of income.

Mill advocated high rates of taxation on inheritances, rather than a progressive income tax that could create disincentive effects. He also favored the formation of producer cooperatives. Not only would workers acquire financial benefits from receiving a share of profits and interest from the cooperative, but society would also benefit from the potential productivity increases that such incentives would generate. He emphasized the importance of worker education, with respect to the practice of birth control, in order to dampen the effects of diminishing returns in agriculture, and regarded unions as a means to improve the position of the working class.

In retrospect, Mill probably held too rigid a view of the unchangeable nature of the laws of production. After all, technological development constantly changes production relationships. That does not, however, diminish the real message of the distinction: most important to Mill was the fact that society could affect the distribution of income initially produced by the economic machine,

and that it was a central role of government to establish policies that promoted equality of opportunity.

To Mill, the conflict between the interests of landowners and those of the rest of society was obvious, but he rejected the socialist condemnation of private property and competition. Moreover, though Mill did not dispute the Ricardian prediction of falling rates of profit and the inevitability of the stationary state, he argued that it could be highly desirable to society. He believed that when the pace of economic activity slowed, less attention would be focused on increasing the quantity of material goods produced and more attention could be directed toward improvements in the quality of life.

Mill's *Principles* was clearly intended to summarize and synthesize all economic knowledge to date, but it also made important original contributions to economic theory. Even though Mill was inclined to emphasize his connection to classical economics, his advances also signaled the transition to neoclassical economics. He formulated, using purely verbal analysis, a description of static equilibrium price formation that is consistent with modern treatments, and developed a theory of jointly supplied goods. These contributions demonstrate the ability of a great mind to derive by means of verbal thought processes the insights equivalent to those later established mathematically.

Historians of economic analysis also credit Mill for his important contributions to the theory of international trade. Ricardo's comparative-advantage analysis had strengthened Smith's arguments concerning the benefits of unregulated international trade. The Ricardian model demonstrated that where comparative advantages existed, international trade could increase world output and benefit all trading nations. However, Ricardo did not specify the terms of trade that would emerge (and hence the distribution of gain between the trading partners), but rather suggested that the international price would likely be about halfway between the two domestic prices.

Mill, using his concept of reciprocal demand, concluded that the terms of trade would depend on the relative strengths of demands for the imported products by the trading countries. Though he did not employ formal mathematics to derive this conclusion, it was surprisingly correct, and later economists such as Alfred MAR-SHALL and Francis Edgeworth, who added the graphical analysis, praised his analysis. His other contributions to trade theory included an analysis of tariffs on the terms of trade and the effects of transportation costs on the trading outcome.

Though for much of his career Mill accepted the wages fund doctrine, an integral piece of classical economic theory, he also supported the formation of labor unions. Unions and strikes seemed to be appropriate tools to counter the bargaining power of the employing firm, and to Mill, far from being restrictions of competition, were actually necessary for a free market. Historically, the wages fund concept was derived from the view, suggested by both Smith and the PHYSIOCRATS, that it was necessary for the employer to "advance" wage goods or their monetary equivalents to workers during the production process.

However, opponents of labor-union formation had used the wages-fund doctrine to demonstrate that attempts by labor to increase wages would necessarily be unsuccessful. Finally in 1869, Mill recanted the wages-fund theory, without changing his position about the need for population control and without amending his presentation of the theory in the seventh edition of his *Principles.* Accordingly, Mill also concluded that arguments concerning the inability of union activities to raise wages were invalid. His decision not to revise the treatment of the wages fund theory in his text may have been practical or philosophical: such a revision would have required major reconstruction of much of his theory, but it would have also implied a sharp break from the classical framework that he learned as a child.

Another important conclusion generally accepted by classical economists was SAY'S LAW, often summarized as "supply creates its own demand." Mill offered a logical (and new) defense of this position to the critics, by developing a theory of BUSINESS CYCLES. He said that in an economy with credit money, the possibility of a general oversupply existed, not in the Malthusian sense of general gluts, but because of changing expectations in the business community. He generalized that such an oversupply would be of short duration, but noted the importance of business confidence.

Mill committed his intellect to an elegant synthesis and improvement of economic knowledge at a time when classical economics was being criticized on all sides. Though always an independent thinker, he listened and attempted to address many of the concerns that were levied against classical economic theory from many different perspectives. He made significant theoretical modifications to the existing Ricardian model, and made several important original contributions that have often been overlooked or obscured. Perhaps more importantly, he insisted that political economy should contribute to human welfare and help establish intelligent policy. His eclecticism makes it difficult to unequivocally classify his ideology, but his dedication to social reform was undeniable.

BIBLIOGRAPHY. Robert B. Ekelund, Jr. and Robert F. Hebert, *A History of Economic Theory and Method* (McGraw-Hill, 1997); Harry Landreth and David C. Colander, *History of Economic Thought* (Houghton Mifflin, 1993); John Stuart Mill, *Autobiography of John Stuart Mill* (Penguin, 1924); Takashi Negishi, *History of Economic Theory* (North Holland, 1989); Henry W. Spiegel, *The Growth of Economic Thought* (Duke University Press, 1991).

ELEANOR T. VON ENDE, PH.D.
TEXAS TECH UNIVERSITY

Miller, Merton H. (1923–2000)

MERTON MILLER RECEIVED the Nobel Prize in Economics in 1990 with Harry MARKOWITZ and William SHARPE for his contributions in the field of corporate finance. Miller clarified which factors determine share prices and capital cost of firms. He laid, along with Frances MODIGLIANI, what are now considered the foundations of corporate financial theory.

The Modigliani-Miller irrelevance theorem states that under the conditions of no brokerage costs, no taxes, no bankruptcy costs, only one interest rate, and perfect information transfer it does not matter how a firm structures itself. While these assumptions are unrealistic, they were a starting point from which researchers could add more variable complications and determine optimal debt-to-equity ratios for firms.

Miller was born in Boston, Massachusetts, the only child of Joel and Sylvia Miller. His father, an attorney, was a Harvard University graduate, and Miller attended Boston Latin School and then entered Harvard in 1940 where one of his classmates was Robert M. SOLOW. He completed his study of economics in only three years and graduated in 1943.

During WORLD WAR II he worked as an economist first in the Division of Tax Research of the U.S. Treasury Department and subsequently in the Division of Research and Statistics of the Board of Governors of the Federal Reserve System. In 1949, he returned to graduate school at Johns Hopkins University in Baltimore.

Miller's first academic appointment after receiving his Ph.D. from Hopkins in 1952 was visiting assistant lecturer at the London School of Economics in 1952–53. From there he went to the Carnegie Institute of Technology (now Carnegie-Mellon University). At Carnegie his colleagues included Herbert SIMON and Modigliani. Modigliani and Miller published their first joint "M&M" paper on corporation financial theory in 1958 and collaborated on several subsequent papers until well into the mid-1960s.

In 1961, Miller left Carnegie for the Graduate School of Business at the University of Chicago where he stayed until his death except for a one-year visiting professorship at the University of Louvain in Belgium during 1966–67. His graduate students at Chicago included

Eugene Fama, founder of the efficient market theory, and Myron SCHOLES. At Chicago, where he was Robert R. McCormick Distinguished Service Professor, most of his work continued to be focused on corporate finance until the early 1980s when he became a public director of the Chicago Board of Trade.

Miller then became interested in the economic and regulatory problems of the financial services industry, and especially of the securities and options exchanges. Miller also served as a public director of the Chicago Mercantile Exchange where he had served earlier as chairman of its special academic panel to study the stock-market crash of October 19–20, 1987. Miller and fellow Chicago Nobel-Prize laureates, Milton FRIEDMAN (1976), Theodore SCHULTZ (1979) and George STIGLER (1982) are extremely strong supporters of free-market solutions to economic problems.

Miller's first wife Eleanor died in 1969 leaving him with three young daughters. He later married his second wife Katherine. Miller died in his long-time home in Hyde Park, Chicago. He was the author of eight books, including *Merton Miller on Derivatives* (1997), *Financial Innovations and Market Volatility* (1991), and *Macroeconomics: A Neoclassical Introduction* (1974, with Charles Upton).

Eugene Fama, the Robert R. McCormick Distinguished Service Professor of Finance, Miller's first Ph.D. student at Chicago and a 37-year colleague, says, "All who knew him at Chicago and elsewhere recognize him as a path-breaking, world-class scholar, a dedicated teacher who mentored many of the most famous contributors to finance and a graceful and insightful colleague who enhanced the research of all around him."

BIBLIOGRAPHY. Eugene F. Brigham and Joel F. Houston, *Fundamentals of Financial Management* (HBJ College, 1999); Nobel e.Museum, "Autobiography of Merton Miller," www.nobel.se/economics; The University of Chicago News Office, "Merton Miller, Nobel Laureate," (2000).

KIRBY R. CUNDIFF, PH.D.
HILLSDALE COLLEGE

mining

ONE OF HUMANKIND'S oldest economic activities, mining is the act of digging mineral substances from the earth. Indeed, eras of human progress, the Stone Age, Bronze Age, Iron Age, etc., are defined by the ability of civilizations to collect and process different minerals and ores. Globally, mining directly accounted for $361 billion in gross world product in 1998 and employed 13 million workers. These figures represent only 0.9 per-

Merton H. Miller, along with his Chicago School colleagues, supported free-market solutions to economic problems.

cent and 0.5 percent of global income and employment respectively, but mining directly affects nearly every other sector of the economy. While iron ore production is a "mere" $25 billion per year business worldwide, it is the primary input into the $200 billion steel industry. Similarly sand, gravel, and cement are the lifeblood of the multi-trillion dollar global construction industry.

Taxonomy. The mining industry is generally broken up into three major sectors. The first is fuels, which includes the fossil fuels of petroleum, natural gas, and coal as well as uranium. These ENERGY commodities are generally separated from the rest of the mining industry. The metals sector is defined on the basis of an element's position on the Periodic Table and includes iron, copper, gold, aluminum, lead, and other commercially important ores. Iron is the most widely mined metal in the world with annual production exceeding one billion metric tons valued at $25 billion in 2000. While other metals are mined in much lower quantities, their relatively higher values per kilogram make them nearly as economically significant.

In 2000, worldwide production of copper was 12.7 million metric tons at a value of $22.3 billion, zinc production was 0.8 million metric tons at a value of $10.7

billion, gold production was 2,550 metric tons at a value of $22.9 billion, and the production of platinum-group metals was 365 metric tons at a value of $8.0 billion. Total worldwide raw metal production was roughly $125 billion in 2000. Metal ores typically require significant processing in order to produce high-grade metals, and therefore the value of the finished materials may be substantially higher than value of the ore itself.

For example, the production of aluminum from bauxite ore is highly energy-intensive, and thus the cost, in 2000, of the ore required to produce one ton of aluminum was just over $100 while the value of the finished crude aluminum was roughly $1,750. Ores containing only trace amounts of the metal may be economically viable to mine so that the total quantity of ore mined in the copper, gold, and iron industries is of a comparable magnitude despite, the huge differences in the production of the finished metals. Metal-ore mining tends to be concentrated in specific geographical locations. For example, 35 percent of world copper ore production takes place in CHILE, and 53 percent of platinum comes from mines in SOUTH AFRICA. The UNITED STATES, a large country with a diverse mining industry, produces nearly one-third of the world's molybdenum while depending on foreign sources for all of its nickel, tin, and tungsten.

The final mining sector is industrial minerals. This sector includes construction materials such as sand, gravel, crushed and cut stone, and cement; minerals for use in industrial processes such as phosphate, soda ash, and lime; and minerals for direct consumption such as gemstones, salt, and clay. Production of industrial minerals exceeds that of metal ores both in physical quantities and economic value.

World cement production alone in 2000 of cement was 1.6 billion metric tons with a value of $117 billion, and annual world production exceeds $1 billion in sand and gravel, crushed and cut stone, phosphate rock, salt, soda ash, boron, and clay. In the United States, roughly three-quarters of $40 billion in GROSS DOMESTIC PRODUCT (GDP) accounted for by the non-fuels mining industry is a result of industrial minerals. As opposed to metal ores, the production of industrial minerals, particularly construction materials, tends to be more evenly distributed geographically, due to the relatively high transportation costs in comparison to the value of the materials. The exception to this general rule is gemstones, which are, of course, expensive and lightweight. For example, three-quarters of world diamond production comes from just three countries: AUSTRALIA, the Democratic Republic of Congo (Zaire), and RUSSIA.

Mining itself comes in two basic forms, surface or open-pit mining and underground mining. Surface min-ing involves the collection of minerals at or near the surface of the land. Strip mining is a type of surface mining where a relatively thin covering layer of soil, or overburden, is removed to expose minerals just beneath the surface. Quarries are surface mines where cut or crushed stone is extracted. Open-pit mining is frequently used for coal and both metal and industrial minerals with essentially all sand, gravel and stone collected in this fashion. The nature of surface mining allows for massive economies of scale with the largest mines covering several square miles.

Underground mining involves digging tunnels to access minerals found below the immediate surface. Shaft mines are dug vertically to allow access to veins of ore deep underground through the use of elevators. Drift mines enter into the sides of hills or mountains using horizontal tunnels, and slope mines use inclined tunnels to get at deposits relatively near the surface. A significant portion of coal is mined using underground mining as well as large quantities of metal and gemstones.

Scarcity. Economics is defined as the study of the allocation of scarce resources among competing users, and therefore it is no surprise that economists have long studied the issue of resource SCARCITY. The most significant early economist in the field is Thomas MALTHUS (1766–1834), an English clergyman whose 1798 work, *An Essay on the Principle of Population*, examined population growth and agricultural output. Malthus theorized that since populations grow geometrically while the amount of arable land was essentially fixed, population growth would eventually outstrip food production leading to widespread famine and poverty. Malthus' concepts are easily adopted to the mining industry where stocks of minerals can be seen as fixed in supply and exploited by an ever-growing population.

Standard measures of mineral scarcity such as the Static Reserve Index, calculated by taking the currently known deposits of a resource and dividing by the current annual usage, point to very limited time periods before various minerals are exhausted. Modern scholars who expand upon Malthus' ideas, such as Paul Ehrlich and Donella Meadows, are known as Doomsday theorists or Neo-Malthusians, and they suggest that the world is doomed to run out of critical, depletable resources, such as minerals, within a generation.

On the other side of the issue, the so-called technological optimists such as Julian SIMON point out that Malthus' dire predictions have failed to come true in the two centuries since they were first proclaimed. Malthus, they say, did not properly account for advances in technology that allowed population growth to slow and agricultural production to rise. Similarly, the optimists believe that apocalyptic predictions about running out of basic minerals fail to account for the possibility that new sources will be discovered, substitutes will be developed, and consumption will fall as prices rise in the face of scarcity.

The case of copper is instructive. In 1950, the U.S. Geological Survey estimated worldwide proven reserves of 90 million tons. At the then annual rate of consumption of 2.2 million tons, the Static Reserve Index indicated a 40-year supply of the metal. Fifty years later, after an additional 250 million tons of copper had been mined, estimated reserves had risen to 340 million tons due to new discoveries of deposits, and the development of technologies that allowed production of metal from lower grade ore. Further reducing the consumption of copper and extending the "life expectancy" of this valuable resource was the development of fiber optic cable, which reduced the use of copper wire in transmitting data. Indeed, in 1998, the market price of copper, adjusted for general inflation, stood at its lowest level in history at roughly a quarter of its peak price in the 1960s. Economists would infer from these low prices that despite the fact that consumption of this finite resource has increased, copper has actually become less scarce over the past 50 years.

Mining, labor history, and government regulation. The difficult and dangerous nature of mining, particularly coal-mining, made the industry a natural target for union organizers. Many of the most significant and violent moments in labor history were directly related to the coal- and hard-rock mining industry. The 1876 execution of 10 members of the "Molly Maguires," the largest mass execution in U.S. history, came directly from the violent conflict between Irish coal-miners and the Philadelphia and Reading Coal and Iron Company. In the 1897 Lattimer Massacre, police opened fire on Pennsylvania coal-miners who were participating in a post-Labor Day rally, killing 19 marchers. The infamous 1914 Ludlow Massacre occurred when 20 people, including 15 women and children, were killed by members of the Colorado National Guard and Colorado Fuel and Iron Company gunmen attempting to break a months-long coal-miners' strike.

The United Mine Worker Association (UMWA), the largest and most historically significant miners union, was formed in 1890 by the merger of two smaller local unions in Columbus, Ohio. The formation of the new union was due in part to the efforts of William Wilson who later went on to serve as the nation's first secretary of labor under Woodrow WILSON in 1913. Other notable figures in the mining labor movement included John L. Lewis, president of the UWMA from 1920–60 and a leader in the formation of the Congress of Industrial Organizations (CIO), Bill Green, Treasurer of the UWMA and later a president of the American Federation of Labor, and Mother Jones, a prominent union organizer.

Unionization led to the establishment of the shorter workday in 1898 and collective bargaining rights in 1933.

The federal government increased regulation of mining in the early 20th century. The U.S. Bureau of Mines was formed in 1910 and established the nation's first mine-safety research program, the first national program to collect data on mine accidents, and the first trained mine-rescue teams. The Federal Coal Mine Health and Safety Act of 1969 regulated increased mine safety and provided the first standards to prevent black lung disease. The law was extended to the metal and nonmetal mining sector in 1977.

In 1907, the worst year on record for mining fatalities, 3,242 coal-miners died in job accidents out of 680,000 workers, for a fatality rate of nearly 1 in every 200 laborers, an astonishing number. Complete figures on metal and industrial mineral fatalities were not kept until the 1930s, but typical fatality rates were roughly half that of the coal industry. By the year 2000, total U.S. mining fatalities had fallen to less than 100 in an industry with 350,000 employees. Still, despite huge improvements in mine safety thanks to improved technology and government regulation, mining remains the country's most dangerous industry based on fatalities, with a death rate roughly twice that of police officers.

Mining and economic development. Many geographical areas can trace their early economic development directly to nearby mineral deposits: San Francisco, California, and the Sutter's Creek gold rush of 1849, Denver, Colorado, and the gold and silver boom of 1859, and Johannesburg, South Africa and the gold discoveries of 1886. While mining towns often exhibit a boom and bust cycle, with bustling cities left as ghost towns once mineral deposits are exhausted, in some cases, nearby transportation centers continued to flourish after mining interest subsided.

Unlike the petroleum industry, which created the vast wealth of the oil barons, the miners and mining companies themselves rarely "struck it rich." The reasons for this are both geological and economic. First, the rich veins of ore tended to be modest in size unlike the huge pools of oil that lay under western Pennsylvania and the American southwest. Second, the start-up costs for operating a small mining operation were low in comparison to the costs of drilling for oil, and therefore, the mining industry attracted vast numbers of fortune-seekers whose sheer numbers dissipated any economic profits. The theory of perfect COMPETITION suggests that free entry leads to zero economic profits.

Finally, many of the richest mining discoveries were in remote and inaccessible areas such as the rugged Colorado Rockies and the bitter-cold Yukon Territories.

The high costs of basic supplies significantly reduced potential profits. Indeed, the majority of the fortunes generated by mining booms were by shippers and suppliers such as Charles Crocker, Collis P. Huntington, and Mark Hopkins, merchants during the California Gold Rush who later formed the Central Pacific Railroad.

A few great fortunes were made, of course. The Big Four of the Comstock Lode, John Mackey, James Fair, James Flood, and William O'Brien, made their fortune on the massive silver deposits discovered in western Nevada and later through investments in banks, utilities, and hotels throughout the west. William Randolph Hearst, who built the great publishing empire, inherited his fortune from his father, George Hearst, the primary investor in the Homestake Mine in the Black Hills of South Dakota. The "unsinkable" Molly Brown, who later gained fame as a survivor of the Titanic, was married to J.J. Brown who made his fortune in the Little Jonny gold strike in Leadville, Colorado in the 1890s.

Mining and developing nations. Mining has had a substantial impact on the economies of developing nations as well. The production of basic metals and minerals in poor countries fit squarely within the traditional colonial economic model (mercantilism) where colonies would supply raw materials in exchange for finished goods manufactured in the home country. The criticism of the colonial model of economic growth takes several forms.

Aside from the basic human-rights issue that proposes that citizens of a region should have the right to self-determination, others have argued that the colonial model condemns primary materials producers to low levels of economic growth. First, basic commodities are subject to wild swings in prices that cause general economic instability in mineral-producing regions. Second, if the model of technological improvements and substi-

tution effects suggested by the technological optimists is correct, basic commodity prices will tend to fall over time as metals and minerals become relatively less scarce. In fact, the real price of most metals has fallen over the past half-century.

As pointed out by economist Jagdish Bhagwati, in cases where a country produces a significant portion of the world's total output of a particular commodity, attempts to increase economic output through expanding production may lead to world prices that are lowered to the point where the country experiences the paradoxical case of "immiserizing growth."

Finally, unlike manufacturing economies where production can easily change from one product to another, countries that specialize in mining production do not tend to be able to transform the productive capacity of the economy to other uses when the mineral resources are exhausted.

Mining and the environment. Mining came under increasing criticism in the later years of the 20th century due to its impact on the environment. Metals mining alone produces over 5 billion tons of tailings waste each year. Mining operations also release significant pollutants due to the processes used to extract the pure metal from the ores. For example, most smelting operations release significant quantities of SO_2, a gas responsible for acid rain, and CO_2, the primary greenhouse gas. Similarly, the chemical process used to leach gold from ore uses cyanide as the main ingredient.

BIBIOGRAPHY. Payal Sampat, "Scrapping Mineral Dependence," *State of the World 2003* (Worldwatch Institute, 2003); U.S. Geological Survey, *Minerals Yearbook* (2002); Tom Tietenberg, *Environmental and Natural Resource Economics* (Addison-Wesley, 2000); Julian Simon and Herman Kahn, *The Resourceful Earth: A Response to Global 2000* (Blackwell, 1984); Donella Meadows, *Beyond the Limits: Confronting Global Collapse, Envisioning a Sustainable Future* (Chelsea Green Publishing, 1992); U.S. Mine Safety and Health Administration Department, www.msha.gov.

VICTOR MATHESON, PH.D.
WILLIAMS COLLEGE

Open-pit mining collects sand, gravel, and stone for industrial production in the United States.

Minsky, Hyman P. (1919–96)

ADEPT AT EXPLAINING HOW lending patterns and mood swings can push an economy into speculative booms or serious declines, Hyman Philip Minsky is one of the more celebrated economists of our time. He argued that these swings are inevitable in a free-market society unless the government exercises control via regulation.

Often described as a radical, his tireless research into the world of economical fluctuations drew respect even from some of his more mainstream foes. In fact, Minsky's theories, centering on the instability of the financial system in a capitalist society, served as a genesis of the Wall Street paradigm. He showed Wall Street how financial markets could easily slip into excess.

"A fundamental characteristic of our economy is that the financial system swings between robustness and fragility," he once wrote. "These swings are an integral part of the process that generates business cycles."

A native of Chicago, Minsky earned a bachelor of science degree in mathematics from the University of Chicago in 1941. While a postgraduate student, however, he switched fields of study to economics and finance after being greatly influenced by Henry Simons, a professor and noted economist of the day. After serving with the U.S. Army overseas during WORLD WAR II, he achieved a master's degree in public administration in 1947, then moved on to Harvard University where he received his doctorate in finance.

Minsky was an adherent of the Keynesian school of economics—that is, a follower of John Maynard KEYNES whose lifelong reflections centered on the causes perpetrating an unstable market system. But, it wasn't until Minsky's diagnoses of the monetary problems that a logical explanation came forth. As the *New York Times* wrote in his obituary, "Minsky found that in prosperous times, when corporate cash flow rises beyond what is needed to pay off debt, a speculative euphoria develops and soon lending gets beyond what the borrowers can pay off from incoming revenues."

Throughout the 1950s, Minsky's research broke new ground. During his own time, his views struck revolutionary chords with conservatives—hypotheses on financial fragility, fiscal policies, financial retrenchments, and recessions. "But, in the last 15 years," says economist Steven Fazzari, "there has been an outpouring of new research, both theoretical and empirical, that rediscovers and validates [Minsky's] views."

Most of Minsky's teaching career was spent at Washington University in St. Louis, Missouri, where he taught economics from 1965 until his retirement 25 years later in 1990. Prior to that, he served in the department of economics at the University of California, Berkeley, and the Carnegie Institute of Technology.

BIBLIOGRAPHY. Hyman Minsky, "Financial Instability Hypothesis," *Thames Papers on Political Economy* (1978); Hyman P. Minsky Obituary, *New York Times* (1996); University of Connecticut, Department of Economics, www.ideas.recep.org.

JOSEPH GERINGER
SYED B. HUSSAIN, PH.D.
UNIVERSITY OF WISCONSIN, OSHKOSH

Mirrlees, James A. (1936–)

JAMES A. MIRRLEES WAS born in 1936 in Scotland and studied mathematics and economics in Edinburgh and later at Cambridge University, England, where he obtained his Ph.D. in 1963. After holding a professorship at Oxford University, he returned to Cambridge in 1995 as a professor of political economy. In 1996, Mirrlees was awarded the Nobel Prize in Economics, jointly with William VICKREY, for his work in the fields of public economics and economic development.

Mirrlees is most prominent for his work on optimal income taxation. He considers the classic utilitarian government whose objective it is to redistribute income from those in society with the greatest abilities to those with the fewest abilities. The problem the government faces, however, is that it cannot determine the innate abilities of members of society. Instead, the government only observes the income of individuals. This yields the classic problem of a utilitarian government: if taxes are levied on the basis of income (which is known to the government), instead of on someone's actual earning ability (which the government does not know), then taxing high-income individuals to redistribute income to those with low incomes creates disincentives to work. Mirrlees devised taxation schemes that account for the disincentives that the scheme itself creates, and thus derived tax schemes that are optimal in light of the informational asymmetry the government faces regarding peoples' abilities.

His work has since been extended to analyze all types of situations in which the relevant information, on which to base decisions, is not observed such that straightforward approaches create disincentives that may be very costly to society and, indeed, counterproductive. In particular, Mirrlees has extended his analysis to study the optimal design of hierarchies in organizations.

BIBLIOGRAPHY. Robin Boadway, "The Mirrlees Approach to the Theory of Economic Policy," *International Tax and Public Finance* (v.5, 1998); James A. Mirrlees, "An Exploration in the Theory of Optimum Income Taxation," *Review of Economic Studies* (v.38, 1971); Agnar Sandmo, "Asymmetric Information and Public Economics: The Mirrlees-Vickrey Nobel Prize," *Journal of Economic Perspectives* (v.13/1, 1999).

THOMAS D. JEITSCHKO, PH.D.
MICHIGAN STATE UNIVERSITY

Mises, Ludwig von (1881–1973)

ACKNOWLEDGED AS ONE of the great economists of the 20th century and a champion of individual rights, Ludwig von Mises was born in Lemberg, then part of the Austro-Hungarian Empire, and now the city of Lviv in the UKRAINE. The oldest son of a prosperous engineer, Mises received his doctorate from the University of Vienna in 1906. In 1909, he became an advisor to the Austrian Chamber of Commerce, a post he held until 1934 when he emigrated from AUSTRIA.

In 1912, Mises published his first great work, *The Theory of Money and Credit*, in which he explained the role of money in an economy using microeconomic principles. At the time of the book's publication, the prevailing view among economists was that money was "neutral," meaning changes in the money supply affect only prices. Mises, though, pointed out that increasing the money supply lowers the purchasing power of money, but also changes relative prices and incomes. When the money supply expands, early receivers of the money, like the government itself, benefit more than those who receive the new influx later.

As a result, monetary inflation is a redistribution of wealth to the government and some favored groups from the rest of the population. Mises concluded that any supply of money is optimal and that every change in the money supply has pernicious effects.

Despite its important contributions, *The Theory of Money and Credit* received little attention in the English-speaking world. John Maynard KEYNES reviewed the book in the prestigious Cambridge *Economic Journal* in 1914 and concluded that it was neither "constructive" nor "original." More than a decade later, those surprising conclusions became more understandable when Keynes wrote that his knowledge of German was poor so that "new ideas are apt to be veiled from me by the difficulties of the language." Economist Friedrich von HAYEK noted, "the world might have been saved much suffering if Lord Keynes's German had been a little better."

In 1920, Mises published his second great work, *Socialism*, in which he explained why central-planning could not succeed. Mises realized that the market does not measure value directly, but only indirectly using prices. Without markets and prices, the central plan could not allocate resources efficiently because it could not calculate the values of goods and services directly. *Socialism* had an enormous influence in the 1920s and 1930s, not only by raising questions about central-planning, but also by converting many of its socialist readers into advocates of free-market capitalism. Commenting on its importance to members of his generation, Hayek stated, "To none of us young men who read the book when it appeared was the world ever the same again."

Mises left Vienna in 1934 to avoid the increasing threat to Austria from the Nazi regime in GERMANY. He worked first at the University of Geneva and then fled to the UNITED STATES, where he became a professor at New York University, a position he held until he retired at the age of 87. In 1949, he published his third great work, *Human Action*, a major economic treatise in which he based the study of economics on the choices of individuals as they seek to achieve their most valued goals.

Mises's importance is measured not only in his own work, but also in the work of the many economists he influenced. A partial list of those who participated in his renowned seminars in Vienna includes Hayek, Fritz Machlup, Oskar Morgenstern, and Lionel Robbins. Vernon L. SMITH, winner of the 2002 Nobel Prize in Economics, argues that even today the value of Mises's work has not diminished: "Reading Mises after 50 years, I am impressed with how stimulating, relevant, and crisp *Human Action* is for the state of economics at the end of the second millennium. It has endured well because many of its major themes—property rights, liability rules, the efficacy of markets, the futility of interventionism, the primacy of the individual—have become important elements in microeconomic theory and policy."

BIBLIOGRAPHY. Israel M. Kirzner, *Ludwig von Mises: The Man and His Economics* (Intercollegiate Studies, 2001); Ludwig von Mises, *Human Action* (Yale University Press, 1949); Ludwig von Mises, *Socialism* (Jonathan Cape, 1936); Ludwig von Mises, *The Theory of Money and Credit* (Jonathan Cape, 1934); Margrit von Mises, *My Years With Ludwig von Mises* (Arlington House, 1976); Murray N. Rothbard, *Ludwig von Mises: Scholar, Creator, Hero* (Mises Institute, 1988); Vernon L. Smith, "Reflections on *Human Action* After 50 Years," *Cato Journal* (1999).

JEFFREY R. GERLACH
COLLEGE OF WILLIAM & MARY

Mitsubishi Motors Corporation

HEADQUARTERED IN TOKYO, this worldwide manufacturer of autos and other vehicles is one of the fastest-growing corporations and the fourth-largest automaker in JAPAN. Mitsubishi Motors Corporation (MMC) "mixes the diversity of talent and resources needed to compete in a global industry," says its public relations literature. But the company's record of success and longevity lends credence to the realization that their public relations boast is not idle. Mitsubishi Motors has been producing automobiles, buses, automotive parts, and powertrains across the world since 1917, virtually nonstop.

What financial shortcomings Mitsubishi has been experiencing in the early 2000s, due to competition and a slowdown in the buying market, has been ameliorated by DaimlerChrysler coming to its aid, acquiring a 34 percent stake in the company and lending its expertise.

Mitsubishi four-wheel-drive vehicles are sold on six continents—Asia, Africa, Europe, South America, Australia, North America, and also in the Middle East. Models vary from continent to continent and include passenger cars such as the sedans Diamante, Galant, Colt and Aspire; mini-hatchbacks like the ek-Wagon and ek-Sport; and light commercial vehicles Delica Van, Delica Truck, SpaceStar, L200 and Lancer Cargo.

One of the keys to Mitsubishi's high reputation is its ability to meet local demands. Specifications vary from model to model, depending upon the location where they are sold. Customization, then, is Mitsubishi's salute to customer satisfaction. North America has been a productive business partner since the early 1970s, selling Mitsubishi products under the Chrysler trademark. Mitsubishi Motors of North America, Inc. manufactures, finances, distributes and markets cars and SUVs through nearly 700 dealerships spread throughout the UNITED STATES, CANADA and MEXICO. A major manufacturing facility in downstate Illinois, which began its assembly line in 1988, has turned out more than 2 million vehicles.

Mitsubishi ranked in 2002 as the 12th largest company in the world, reporting almost $106 billion in sales.

BIBLIOGRAPHY. Mitsubishi Motors Corporation, www.mistubishimotors.com; *Hoover's Handbook of Business* (2003); "Global 500: World's Largest Companies," *Fortune* (July 2002).

JOSEPH GERINGER
SYED B. HUSSAIN, PH.D.
UNIVERSITY OF WISCONSIN, OSKKOSH

Mitsui & Company, Ltd.

FOR MANY YEARS, Mitsui of JAPAN has provided an unparalleled breadth of products and technical services to virtually all industries, assisting its vast and diverse line of customers to meet their business goals and objectives head on—whether tomorrow or next year. The functions and capabilities offered are as strategic and disparate as the industries it serves. Mitsui has enjoyed a reputation of nimbly responding not only to its customer base, but to its own quality-driven self-image, flexible in the face of economic and social trends in order to keep constant its successes year after year.

The company's products and services cover the needs of a global environment. Divided into five groups, each group is dedicated to supplying the demands of a specific industry and/or medium: the Metal & Minerals Group (steel and iron products); the Machinery, Electronics & Information Group (i.e., telecommunications and motor vehicles); the Chemical Group (including petroleum and plastics); the Energy Group; and the Consumer Products and Services Group.

Dictated by Mitsui's Five Initiatives, the company aims to offer a full range of capabilities, services along the value chain, service across industries, global services, and creative disposition of its automation.

Reporting more than $101 billion in revenue in 2002, Mitsui ranked as the 13th largest company in the world.

BIBLIOGRAPHY. "Global 500: The World's Largest Companies," *Fortune* (July 2002); Mitsui's, www.mitsui.co.jp; *Hoover's Handbook of Business*, www.hoovers.com.

JOSEPH GERINGER
SYED B. HUSSAIN, PH.D.
UNIVERSITY OF WISCONSIN, OSHKOSH

Mizuho Holdings

TOKYO-BASED MIZUHO HOLDINGS is the holding company for Mizuho Financial Group, including the integrated operations and assets of the Dai-ichi Kangyo Bank, the Fuji Bank, and the Industrial Bank of Japan. The first-of-its-kind merger and integration, which was completed on April 1, 2002, it was the penultimate example of consolidation among Japanese banks, leaving Mizuho Holdings as the world's largest bank, with a trillion dollars in assets. Although the Japanese word *mizuho* means "golden ears of corn," it's more than corn that Mizuho holds.

"We have established the framework of the Mizuho Business Model," explains Terunobu Maeda, Mizuho Holdings' CHIEF EXECUTIVE OFFICER (CEO). "Our group companies (can now) offer a comprehensive range of value-added financial services (to) meet the needs of customers more quickly and appropriately."

More practically, what the consolidation really means is that Mizuho Holdings now leads JAPAN's financial industry in the 21st century. Its mechanism is based on five basic principles: the bank wants to offer a wide range of the highest-quality service to customers; maximize shareholder value and, thus, gain the trust of the society; offer rewarding job opportunities; maximize the benefits of the consolidation to effect cost reductions; and create a new corporate climate.

BIBLIOGRAPHY. "Global 500: The World's Largest Companies," *Fortune* (July 2002); Mizuho, www.mizuho-fg.co.jp; *Hoover's Handbook of Business* (Hoovers, Inc., 2003) www.hoovers.com.

JOSEPH GERINGER
SYED B. HUSSAIN, PH.D.
UNIVERSITY OF WISCONSIN, OSHKOSH

modernization theory

MODERNIZATION THEORY attempts to develop a general theoretical model of development of capitalism in areas with non-capitalist societies. The object of analysis of modernization theorists are the countries that were formerly the colonies of European countries, or whose historical development was heavily influenced by them. Modernization theory is also being applied to understand and help the transition of the former SOVIET UNION-bloc countries to capitalist societies.

Modernization theory took shape slowly in the late 1940s and 1950s as a result of the accumulation of empirical and analytical contributions made by a number of U.S. academics sponsored by the U.S. government to help it understand the social conditions in newly independent countries of the Third World. Undertaken in the background of the developing Cold War, this effort had an immediate, practical end: that is to quickly "modernize" willing Third World countries with the help of U.S. financial, managerial, technical, and military assistance so that these countries would remain a part of the capitalist "free world."

Two streams of literature have informed the foundational principles of modernization theory: First, the 19th-century liberal belief in social progress—evolutionary economic development, democratization, and secularization of society—and that this is a universally unilinear process; and second, the structural-functionalist theoretical stream spawned by the writings of Talcott Parsons in early 1950s.

The theory's logical structure is constructed around positing a duality of traditional and modern societies. The concept of modern society is an abstraction of Western liberal capitalist societies. This abstraction is referred to as Industria by some seminal writers in this tradition. The opposite of Industria is the concept of Agraria. Agraria is then defined as a society that lacks the characteristics of Industria or liberal democratic capitalist societies. In the real world, the entire third world was classified as traditional by modernization writers. It was a general belief among them, based on their philosophical principles, that all traditional societies are on their way to becoming modern, just as the current modern societies previously completed this journey (this belief is called unilinearity).

Traditional societies were seen by this theory to have to go through the modernizing process in all their major social subsystems: economic (from subsistence production to market economy); social (from traditional/religious behavior to secularism); political (development/strengthening of the institutions of the state); familial (giving up extended family for nuclear family); and individual-psychological (community orientation of behavior to self-interested behavior).

The process of acquisition of modern characteristics by traditional societies was termed development. Further, that the process of development could be speeded-up by providing key capital, technical, and military inputs to developing countries' governments by the UNITED STATES. The acceptance of these ideas by the majority of scholars, consultants, research foundations, and government officials in the United States led to the creation of official foreign-aid programs. Additionally, multilateral financial institutions were given the role of channeling resources to developing countries.

This modernization model was applied to all "free-world" developing countries during the 1950s and 1960s. However, after two decades of development these countries had little to show in terms of economic or social development. Additionally, it was not a coincidence that anti-democratic regimes took hold in almost all of them as modernization theorists and practitioners generally held the view that democracy would either have to wait until economic development was achieved, or it would follow automatically.

Modernization theory came under severe criticism in late 1960s, especially from proponents of the DEPENDENCY THEORY who criticized it for being ahistorical, ignoring external economic and political factors, ethnocentricity, unilinearity (all countries will follow the same stages of development as Western capitalist countries), and accused it for being a tautology based on its concepts of traditional and modern. Others criticized it for assuming traditional values and social behaviors to be inherently irrational and obstacles to development. In response, modernization theory was modified and developed by writers in this tradition especially after the 1970s.

The new modernization theorists preserved their basic approach in terms of upholding:

1. the national level as the unit of analysis

2. the focus on key internal variables of social values and institutions

3. the key concepts of traditional and modern

4. the key value-belief that modernization is beneficial and desirable.

They also modified the theory in important ways. The major modifications made to the theory were:

1. it was accepted that traditional values are not necessarily obstacles to development

2. that attention had to be given to the historical circumstances of the country under study

3. the possibility of different paths to development was accepted

4. the role of external obstacles/factors facing developing countries were incorporated into analytical framework.

These modifications greatly expanded the theory's scope of applicability and strengthened its robustness. The modifications spawned new studies that included (but were not limited to) the role of religion in the economic and social development of traditional countries, and the role of extended family structure in propelling business enterprise.

Clearly, the new modernization theory has a great potential for development and expansion not only in terms of the logic of the theory, but more importantly in the explanation of the multifaceted and dynamic social reality in the developing world. It also faces some clear challenges, not the least of which are the various ways in which it could possibly (and potentially) collapse into an upgraded classical liberalism.

BIBLIOGRAPHY. Alvin Y. So, *Social Change and Development: Modernization, Dependency and World-system Theories* (Sage Publications, 1990); B.C. Smith, *Understanding Third World Politics: Theories of Political Change and Development* (Indiana University Press, 1996); M. Shamsul Hague, *Restructuring Development Theories and Policies: A Critical Study* (State University of New York Press, 1999).

AURANGZEB SYED, PH.D.
NORTHERN MICHIGAN UNIVERSITY

Modigliani, Franco (1918–)

ITALIAN-BORN, AMERICAN economist awarded the 1985 Nobel Prize in Economics, Franco Modigliani was cited for the development of his life-cycle theory of household saving and his work on capital costs. He also contributed to rational-expectations theory.

After studying law in Italy, Modigliani emigrated to America in 1939 and became an American citizen. In economics, he worked to correct and extend the theories of British economist John Maynard KEYNES, arguably the most influential economist of the 20th century. Modigliani received his Ph.D. in economics from the New School for Social Research in 1944, where he taught until 1949. After that, he taught at the University of Chicago and the Carnegie Institute of Technology (now Carnegie-Mellon University) before settling at the Massachusetts Institute of Technology in 1962, where he remained for the rest of his career.

One of Keynes' central insights, called the consumption function, stated that when people make more money, they increase their consumption by less than the increase

in their income. As a result, they save a greater portion of their income than they did before. This implied that in periods of economic growth, the ratio of saving to income should increase. Simon KUZNETS (1901–85) found that national income data did not support Keynes's view. Economists began searching for ways to make the consumption function fit the data.

Milton FRIEDMAN (1912–) argued that people based consumption and saving decisions on their expected permanent income, not just on having more income at the moment. About the same time, Modigliani argued that each person's consumption/saving ratio depended on his/her stage of life. Under his view, young people saved little, middle-aged people saved a lot for retirement, and older people spent their savings. Modigliani's most controversial assumption is that people save only for their own consumption, not for their heirs.

In 1958, Modigliani and Merton MILLER argued for the Modigliani-Miller theorem, showing that (under certain assumptions) a corporation's value was unaffected by the amount or structure of its debts. This was significant not merely because of what it proved, but because prior to their work, there had been very little theoretical analysis of corporate finance.

Throughout his career, even into his eighties, Modigliani remained influential among economists and was engaged in the political economies of America and Europe.

BIBLIOGRAPHY. J.M. Keynes, *The General Theory of Employment, Interest, and Money* (Prometheus Books, 1936); Simon Kuznets, *National Product Since 1869* (Ayer, 1946); Milton Friedman, *A Theory of the Consumption Function* (Princeton University Press, 1957); Franco Modigliani and Albert Ando, "The 'Life Cycle' Hypothesis of Saving: Aggregate Implications and Tests," *American Economic Review* (March, 1963); Franco Modigliani and Merton Miller, "The Cost of Capital, Corporation Finance and the Theory of Investment," *American Economic Review* (June, 1958).

SCOTT PALMER, PH.D.
RGMS ECONOMICS

Monaco

MONACO OR AS IT IS commonly called, Monte Carlo, is a small, exclusive enclave on the French Mediterranean coast. It is the home of international jet-setters who enjoy the mild winters and warm summers in southern FRANCE. With a population of 35,000 in two square kilometers of territory, wealth is a requirement. Because of its status as a tax haven, data on Monaco is problematic.

Monaco was formed by the ruling Grimaldi family in 1297 and was re-established in 1814 after the French Revolution. From the start, Monaco was a haven for wealthy royalty who felt they were unfairly persecuted by emerging tax systems of growing mercantile cities and states during the Renaissance. After the emergence of capitalism as an economic system in Western Europe, Monaco began to attract heads of business and finance as well, for the same reasons it originally attracted royalty and nobility.

Today, French is the official language with English, Monagasque, and Italian widely spoken. The GROSS DOMESTIC PRODUCT (GDP) per capita is estimated at $27,000, and unemployment is at 0.1 percent. Its ethnicity is really the wealthy from all over the globe, but especially business leaders and nobility in Europe.

Surprisingly, despite its reputation as a tax haven for the rich and famous, Monaco has a diverse economy based on 300,000 tourists a year (25 percent of GDP), conventions, banking, and insurance. It also has a small industrial sector (33 percent of GDP). Gambling revenues account for over 4 percent of the state income annually and value-added taxes (VATs) for 55 percent. The state has more than 4 percent GDP growth, with a heavy dependence on imports from France.

Recently, Monaco has been criticized for poor tax records and is now seeing increased influence from France and the EUROPEAN UNION. The royal Grimaldi family tolerates such influence so long as the limelight is cast away from further tax issues in Monaco.

BIBLIOGRAPHY. A. Decaux, *Monaco and its Princes: Seven Centuries of History* (Perrin, 1989); S. Jackson, *Inside Monte Carlo* (Stein and Day, 1975); *Monaco Investment and Business Guide* (International Business Publications, 2002).

CHRIS HOWELL
RED ROCKS COLLEGE

monetarism

A LINE OF ECONOMIC thought pioneered by Milton FRIEDMAN at the University of Chicago, monetarism criticizes macroeconomic stabilization policies based on Keynesian MACROECONOMICS. Based on the quantity theory of money, and rooted in the neoclassical tradition, monetarism was propagated intellectually by Friedman in the 1950s and 1960s, and it came to be increasingly accepted as a policy guide following the resurgence of neo-conservatism in the late 1970s to the early 1980s. Monetarism, from a theoretical point of view, has since then been absorbed into new classical economics (also sometimes referred to as Monetarism Mark II), the chief proponents of which are Robert E. LUCAS Jr. at the University of Chicago, Thomas Sargent at New York University, and Robert J. Barro at Harvard University.

Neoclassical quantity theory of money. In the neoclassical approach, money, first and foremost, serves as a medium of exchange. Although historically speaking, useful commodities such as gold or silver served the role of money, it was primarily not their value in use, but their value as a medium of exchange that determined the price of money (its purchasing power in terms of other goods and services). This has become even more apparent when commodity-based money was replaced by fiat money, non-redeemable banknotes issued by central banks; and deposit money was guaranteed only by the creditworthiness of the banks with which it was deposited. The value of money (especially fiat money) as a medium of exchange, however, cannot be determined without knowing how much of it is available to mediate "real" exchange transactions. In other words, money derives value from people using it in exchange for commodities, but this value cannot be determined without knowing what basket of commodities could be exchanged for a given quantity of money.

To resolve this problem, the quantity theory of money makes an important assumption that there is a certain given volume of "real" transactions that does not depend on the quantity of money available. Moreover, the speed of circulation of money (the rate at which it changes hands) is also determined largely by the degree of development of the banking system, the technological progress in the financial sphere, and so on, that is, by forces not related to the quantity of money itself. In the words of one of the most prominent neoclassical advocates of the quantity theory, Irving FISHER: "An inflation of the currency cannot increase the product of farms and factories, nor the speed of freight trains or ships. The stream of business depends on natural resources and technical conditions, not on the quantity of money."

This idea is compactly expressed in the famous quantity equation, $MV=PT$, where M is the quantity of money, V is its velocity (speed of circulation), P is the general price level and T is the volume of real transactions. If T is given by real economic forces and V also does not change, M and P will be related one-to-one. In particular, if the quantity of money is determined by the central bank, then P will be governed by this decision. For example, a decision by the central bank to increase the quantity of money will lead to a corresponding increase in the price level (inflation) and will not have any effect on real economic activity.

Keynesian macroeconomics and liquidity preference. One possible objection to the quantity theory of money, that was raised within the neoclassical school, is the possibility of an endogenous supply of money (the real-bills doctrine). If the quantity of money is not entirely determined by the CENTRAL BANK, but is instead at least partly determined by real economic forces (working through extending or shrinking credit lines), the quantity theory clearly does not work. This line of criticism was never incorporated fully into the mainstream economics, however. Instead, both Keynesian (that is, anti-monetarist) and monetarist lines of thought equally accepted the idea that supply of money is governed by an exogenous policy decision.

Instead of targeting the assumptions about the supply of money, Keynesian macroeconomic theory targeted for criticism the demand for money assumed in the neoclassical quantity theory. According to the liquidity-preference theory, which came to be one of the cornerstones of macroeconomic orthodoxy from the 1950s through the 1970s, money is being demanded not only for the purpose of servicing transactions but also as an asset. The latter, in the words of John Maynard KEYNES, amounted to "the speculative motive . . . i.e., the object of securing profit from knowing better than the market what the future will bring forth."

Later Keynesians added to this a precautionary motive (desire to hold part of wealth in money form at times of increased uncertainty) to conclude that the demand for money is inherently unstable. The quantity theory, which assumed a stable demand function for money in terms of real transactions, was thus considered to be a poor guide for practical policy. The liquidity preference theory of money demand was used to deny the one-to-one relationship between the quantity of money and the general price level and to make the demand and supply of money an essential part of the determination of the real output and real interest rate in the framework of IS-LM (investment-saving, liquidity-money) analysis.

Friedman's restatement of the quantity theory. It should be noted that the approach to money as an asset had not been unfamiliar prior to Keynes. In fact, it formed the basis of the "Cambridge version" of the quantity theory originating with Alfred MARSHALL. In this version, the quantity equation was written not as MV=PT but rather in the form of M=kPY, where M and P denote the same things as in MV=PT while Y denotes real income and k represents the share of wealth that individuals decide to hold in the form of money. Assuming that real income is independent of the quantity of money and k (which is the inverse of the velocity of circulation V in the Fisherian equation) is also chosen by individuals independently of M, the same one-to-one relationship between M and P continues to hold. When, in 1956, Friedman wrote his famous paper, "The Quantity Theory of Money: a Restatement," arguing against Keynesian theory of liquidity preference, he appealed to the Cambridge rather than the Fisher version of the quantity theory to restate the argument.

In contrast to Keynesian liquidity preference theory which considers only the choice between money and financial assets (BONDS), Friedman argued that the demand for money should be considered as being determined by a whole array of rates of return on various assets, including commodities and physical capital. Friedman also included the expectations about the rate of change in the price level (INFLATION) as an important determinant of the demand for money, and he later forcefully presented this point in policy recommendations centered around the thesis that government stabilization efforts, in fact, have de-stabilizing effects through confounding expectations. Friedman also advocated the view (which to him was more of an empirical fact rather than a theoretical construction), that since the linkages connecting money to spending are numerous, the link between money and the price level is strong and relatively stable.

Phillips Curve controversy and the natural rate of unemployment. A popular artifact of Keynesian macroeconomics is the PHILLIPS CURVE. This curve first made its appearance in 1958 when a British economist, A.W. Phillips found a negative statistical relationship between the rate of changes in money wages and unemployment in Britain. Keynesian economics transformed the wage-unemployment relationship into an inflation-unemployment relationship, and developed the notion of a trade-off between price stability and full employment. If the government wanted to promote full employment, it had to pay the price of higher inflation and vice versa.

In the 1970s, however, a completely new situation emerged in which a deep RECESSION was accompanied not by falling but by rising inflation. Under such conditions, orthodox macroeconomic policy of the time became completely paralyzed. Fighting recession and unemployment called for expansionary fiscal and monetary policies, but that would exacerbate inflation and vice versa.

Friedman and the monetarists had an explanation, the role played by expectations. Since the demand for money depends, in particular, on the expected rate of inflation, a surprise increase in the supply of money, not built into those expectations, can indeed lead people to spend more and to supply more labor. This happens because of the money illusion. People see that their money balances are increasing (or that nominal wages are rising) but they do not yet perceive that this is happening throughout the economy so that the general price level is rising, and reducing the purchasing power of money balances and nominal wages.

When this latter fact becomes common knowledge, however, expectations are adjusted and real spending and labor supply return to their original levels, leaving only a higher inflation rate as an eventual outcome. The negatively sloped Phillips Curve, Friedman argued, was only true for a short period of time (from several months to two years), while in the long run the curve is a vertical line passing through the point of the "natural rate of unemployment" determined by non-monetary factors.

If the government tried to increase employment beyond that natural rate by injecting more money, the trade-off between inflation and unemployment would be recreated at ever increasing levels of both inflation and unemployment. What is worse, after a while the public will learn to adjust its expectations much faster and the overall disruption to the monetary exchange can actually even make inflation and unemployment positively related to each other.

The natural rate of unemployment (which is the monetarist counterpart to the concept of full employment) is the statistical unemployment rate governed by the balance of job-separation and job-acceptance rates. The idea is that the functioning of an even perfect market mechanism is never frictionless, so that some people are constantly separated from their jobs and start searching for a new job, while others who have been unemployed for some time finish their search and accept a new job. As long as the process of the job search takes time, some fraction of the work force will be constantly unemployed (although, of course, they will not be the same people).

The length of the job-search process is governed by various factors, including institutional factors such as the level of unemployment benefits and the degree of unionization, but it does not depend on monetary factors and, moreover, since unemployment is basically voluntary, it does not require any effective demand management. If the government wants to reduce the unemployment rate, the monetarist argument goes, it should concentrate on improving the institutional structure of the labor market (in particular countering monopolies by which trade unions are meant) and not try to attain that goal through macroeconomic policies.

The monetarist counterrevolution. The policy implications of this expectations-augmented view of inflation and the natural rate of unemployment vision were aptly called the monetarist counterrevolution. Contrary to previous beliefs that governments should engage in proactive, effective demand management to secure full employment, the monetarists' view of the world was that such stabilization policy would have only short-term effects at best, while in the long run it will produce nothing but inflation. From the monetarist perspective, in the long run "money does not matter," in the sense that changes in the quantity of money only lead to corresponding changes in the price level. Disruptions to the monetary mechanism, however, do matter in that they confuse expectations and create the environment of instability and uncertainty, the welfare costs of which can be very high. In terms of practical policies, Friedman recommended a stable, credible commitment on the part of the central bank that would announce an increase in money supply by a certain number of percentage points each year (roughly equal to the potential real growth rate of the economy), and stick to that rule regardless of short-term business conditions. Such a rule would produce a zero average inflation rate over the long run and would have positive effects on the real economy by making the monetary sphere predictable and stable.

In the wake of stagflation in the 1970s, monetarist prescriptions were tried in practice in the UNITED STATES, UNITED KINGDOM, and JAPAN, among other countries. Central banks in those countries, under strong political leadership from neo-conservative governments decisively shifted the focus of their policies to combating inflation rather than promoting employment and growth. Tightening money supply initially produced deep recessions, but that was something that Friedman had predicted would have to be endured for a period of time needed for inflationary expectations to be adjusted. In the long run, however, according to Friedman and monetarists, expectations would adjust and full employment (equal to the natural rate of unemployment) would prevail with zero or no inflation. Neo-conservative governments also turned very heavily against the trade unions, the most famous episode being Britain's Margaret THATCHER's confrontation with the miners' union, which changed the nature of the British labor movement for good.

Monetarists' predictions generally turned out to be true. By the second half of the 1980s, inflation largely became a thing of the past in most industrialized countries, while growth rates and employment did not appear to have suffered any long-term setbacks as compared to previous decades (or had even improved, notably in Britain). Although targeting money supply as the goal of macroeconomic policy was implemented only briefly in the early 1980s, the emphasis on controlling inflation is omnipresent in contemporary central banking in industrialized countries. It is also inherent in policy recommendations that are given by international financial institutions to developing countries, reflecting the long-lasting intellectual impact of monetarism.

Rational expectations and modern monetarism. Monetarism by itself may no longer exist as a distinct school of macroeconomic thought; it has been incorporated into the new classical school of macroeconomics under the name of "rational expectations" (sometimes also called "monetarism mark-II"). New classical macroeconomics shares with Friedman's early approach the emphasis on microfoundations of macroeconomic models, that is, the insistence that money demand, in particular, should be derived from some basic principles of utility maximization. The important difference with early monetarism and the work by Friedman is that the new classical macroeconomists are even less willing to compromise with Keynesian views. In particular, they have replaced Friedman's view of slowly adjusting expectations by the concept of rational expectations.

Rational expectations is an assumption according to which all information that is available in principle gets built into agents' expectations, so that no predictable change in economic parameters can have any, even short-term, effects on the outcomes of actions already taking account of all the existing information. It is thus only by "complete surprise" that changes in money supply can affect the demand for money, and since government policies are closely monitored and analyzed by the market, such surprises are very unlikely to succeed. Moreover, even if surprises were possible and the government could, in principle, conduct macroeconomic policies aimed at stabilizing the economy, the value of such stabilization, it is argued, will be very limited and the government resources are better spent elsewhere. Friedman certainly approves of this view.

BIBLIOGRAPHY. Irving Fisher, *Of Money, Its Determination and Relation to Credit, Interest, and Crises* (Macmillan, 1912); Milton Friedman, *Studies in the Quantity Theory of Money* (University of Chicago Press, 1956); Milton Friedman and Anna Schwartz, *The Monetary History of the United States* (Princeton University Press, 1963); Alfred Marshall, *Money, Credit and Commerce* (Macmillan, 1924); Mark Blaug, *Economic Theory in Retrospect* (Cambridge University Press, 1996).

SERGUEY BRAGUINSKY
STATE UNIVERSITY OF NEW YORK, BUFFALO

monetary policy

IN THE UNITED STATES, monetary policy is conducted by the FEDERAL RESERVE, which is the country's central bank. Generally speaking, monetary policy involves changes in the money supply. However, it is common to speak of INTEREST RATES when discussing monetary policy. This is because most central banks in developed countries now target the interest rate as a short-term instrument instead of the money supply.

Regardless of the specific target, however, the role of monetary policy and the actions of a central bank are important elements in the economy as both the money supply and money demand play a central role in economic fluctuations. In particular, the Federal Reserve plays a key role in MACROECONOMIC policymaking. The Federal Reserve influences the money supply and may even respond to money demand shocks. A shock to money demand simply means that the demand for real balances has changed suddenly and unexpectedly.

Of course, in the absence of a monetary policy response this implies that interest rates in the economy will change. Accordingly, when interest rates change, spending and thus real output may change. To the extent that the Federal Reserve responds to money demand shocks, then the Federal Reserve may be an important player in the business cycle. Additionally, the Federal Reserve may set into motion a chain of events that will lead to an increase or decrease in the nation's money supply. Doing so affects interest rates and thus spending and output.

A monetary system specifies how people pay each other when they conduct transactions. Thus, money serves as a means of payment. Moreover, the monetary system places some meaning on the prices of goods and services so that money acts as a unit of account. In the United States, for example, the unit of currency known as the DOLLAR performs these functions. As stated above, monetary policy involves changes in the money supply instituted by the central bank. The nominal money supply, in a narrow sense, is defined as the amount of currency (i.e., paper money issued by the government) plus the amount of deposits held by people and businesses at banks. This definition of the money supply reflects those assets (e.g., cash and checking accounts) that can be used immediately for transaction purposes.

Technically, the narrow definition of money supply known as M1 includes other very liquid assets, for example, traveler's checks. The Federal Reserve is the issuer of currency in the United States and therefore has direct control over that component of the money supply. However, the amount of funds that people and businesses place in their checking accounts (i.e., deposits) is not controlled by the Federal Reserve. It should be apparent that the Federal Reserve cannot control the money supply in the strictest sense, but that it may influence it.

The monetary base. The monetary base is directly controlled by the Federal Reserve, however. Known as high-powered money, the monetary base is defined as the sum of currency and reserves held by banks at the Federal Reserve. By law, the Federal Reserve has the power to require member banks to maintain minimum levels of reserves. These levels are determined as a percent of customer deposits. In fact, the required reserve ratio is the percent of customer deposits that banks must hold in the form of reserves. While banks may hold more than the minimum required amount, they are not allowed to hold less than that amount. As private sector banks typically are in business to increase shareholder wealth or firm value, they will not want to hold too much of their customers deposits in the form of what is called excess reserves. This is because banks may earn (expected) profit on these excess returns if they produce loans with these funds instead of simply holding onto them. Making loans is risky, though, as there is always the possibility of default. As such, some banks, for a variety of reasons, may actually decide to hold excess reserves, though typically this amount is not very large. Competition and the pursuit of profit tend to eliminate excess reserves.

If banks do not hold the required amount of reserves then they are in violation of Federal Reserve policy and face the possibility of being reprimanded, fined, or even closed. Of course, no bank would want that to happen and so it is rarely the case that banks fall below the required amount of reserves.

It is the case that banks may find themselves in need of funds in order to maintain the desired reserves amount. This may happen if there is an unusually large amount of withdrawals, for example. In this situation, a bank may look to borrow funds from another bank so that they would maintain the level of reserves required or desired, if they would like to hold more than the minimum. There exists a very well organized market for such loans. The market is for very short, in fact, overnight loans from one bank to another bank. Since all banks are presumably in business to increase shareholder wealth (or some measure of value), we would not expect one bank to loan another bank (which is also most likely a competitor) the use of some funds overnight for free.

Instead, banks charge each other interest just as they charge interest to any of their other customers. The interest rate that is charged in this overnight interbank market for loans is called the federal funds rate. The federal funds rate actually plays a critical role in the conduct of monetary policy.

In order to understand the role that the federal funds rate plays in monetary policy, however, it is beneficial to step back and look at the interaction that the private sector and the public sector have through the financial system. To do so, consider the balance sheets of four market participants: private nonfinancials (i.e., nonbank businesses and households), private banks (i.e., financial institutions), the Federal Reserve, and the government (i.e., Congress, Administration and Treasury).

A balance sheet simply records an entity's assets and liabilities. Assets are things of value that an entity owns while liabilities are what an entity owes others. An accounting identity exists in which liabilities plus net worth must equal assets. Note that this implies that if one pays off all of one's liabilities (presumably by liqui-

dating some or all of one's assets) then whatever is left over is net worth.

Assets and liabilities. Consider now four forms of assets and liabilities: currency, BONDS, deposits, and reserves. In this context, the government borrows funds by issuing bonds and thus bonds are a liability for the government. Whoever holds or owns the bonds has an asset. Holders of bonds include private nonfinancials, banks, and the Federal Reserve. The Federal Reserve issues currency and thus currency is a liability for the central bank. Nonfinancials and banks hold currency as an asset, while nonfinancials place some of their funds in banks as deposits.

Thus, deposits are a liability for banks and an asset for nonfinancials. However, banks are required by the Federal Reserve to hold a certain percentage of their deposits in the form of reserves at the Federal Reserve. Reserves are an asset for banks but a liability for the central bank. Finally, banks make loans to nonfinancials and so are carried as an asset on bank balance sheets and are a liability for nonfinancials who must repay the loan. This brief description highlights how these different entities are linked through the financial system and paves the way for the conduct of monetary policy to work.

The Federal Reserve changes the money supply via open-market operations which are the buying and selling of previously issued government bonds. The market actually operates in New York City. An open-market purchase of government bonds from the public (i.e., the nonfinancials and private banks) injects new money into the economic system and will therefore increase the money supply. If the opportunity cost of money is the interest rate, then an increase in the money supply tends to push down the interest rate. An open market sale of government bonds will involve money being removed from the system as nonfinancials and private banks effectively pay the Federal Reserve for these assets. An open-market sale reduces the money supply and tends to raise the interest rate. Note that the Federal Reserve directly controls the monetary base and by using open-market operations can add to or subtract from the monetary base. Moreover, there is a direct relationship between the monetary base and the money supply.

The relationship between the money supply and the monetary base is due to two factors. The first is the required-reserve ratio, which implies that reserves will equal the amount of deposits times the required reserve ratio. The second is the currency-to-deposit ratio, which is the amount of currency people hold as a ratio of their checking deposits. Given the definitions of money supply, monetary base, required reserve ratio and currency to deposit ratio, an algebraic expression exists in which the money supply equals the money multiplier times the monetary base. The construction of the money multiplier is given by the ratio of 1 plus the currency-to-deposit ratio to the sum of the currency-to-deposit ratio and the required-reserve ratio.

Thus, the central bank can estimate how much a given dollar-change in the monetary base will change the money supply. Knowing the answer allows the Federal Reserve to determine how much a particular open market operation will change the interest rate. The interest rate that the Federal Reserve focuses on is the federal funds rate. In fact, the Federal Reserve now selects a target for the federal funds rate and performs open-market operations so that the actual federal funds rate is maintained within some desired band around this target. Generally speaking, the Federal Reserve is quite good at accurately hitting the target they have chosen.

Other tools. There are, however, other policy tools available to the Federal Reserve. As mentioned, the required-reserve ratio may alter the amount of reserves and thus the money supply. Additionally, banks may borrow directly from the Federal Reserve at the interest rate known as the discount rate. The amount of borrowing is affected by how costly it is to borrow from the Federal Reserve and, for example, a higher discount rate will reduce the amount of borrowed reserves and thus reduce the money supply.

Actual monetary policy decisions in the United States are determined by the Federal Open Market Committee (FOMC). The FOMC consists of the seven members of the Board of Governors of the Federal Reserve System and five of the 12 presidents of the Federal Reserve district banks. Historically, the FOMC set the growth rate of the money supply in the 1970s and early 1980s. Once set, the bond traders at the New York Federal Reserve Bank would make the appropriate open market operations to achieve the desired growth rate.

Since the mid 1980s, however, the monetary policy in the United States has focused on setting and maintaining a short-term interest rate (i.e., the federal funds rate). Again, open-market operations are used to achieve this goal.

BIBLIOGRAPHY. J.M. Barron, M. Lowenstein, and G.J. Lynch, *Macroeconomics* (Addison-Wesley, 1989); B. Bernanke and A. Blinder, "The Federal Funds Rate and the Channels of Monetary Policy," *American Economic Review*, (v. 82, 1992); D. Romer, *Advanced Macroeconomics*, (McGraw-Hill, 1996).

BRADLEY T. EWING, PH.D.
TEXAS TECH UNIVERSITY

money

MONEY IS ANYTHING that is generally accepted as a means of payment. Without money, market or capitalist economies could hardly have developed and its invention is among the most important of all economic factors. Money has three useful functions: unit of account, store of value, and medium of exchange. The latter is the most pertinent, although money as a store of value plays a crucial role in MACROECONOMICS. One of the most important issues in the theory of money concerns its quantity and its relation to the general price level.

Money as unit of account reduces the problem of relative prices because money serves as the *numéraire* in which the prices of all goods can be expressed. This role is the least important and does not give money its distinct character for any good can serve as a *numéraire*. Money also serves as an asset that people can use to store value. It is like other financial assets in this regard, except that it generally does not earn interest. Money's most important function, medium of exchange, reduces the transaction costs of trade. The institution of money as a facilitator of trade and its ability to reduce transaction costs makes it among the most celebrated and studied topics in economic theory. No one will deny that the pursuit of money, that is, its purchasing power, is a prime economic incentive.

Money evolved through an invisible-hand process much the same way as natural selection in biology. Carl MENGER (1892) was among the first to recognize that money was invented in the sense that the state or some set of individuals agreed to create the institution of money. The first form of money was a commodity. Some commodities are more acceptable than others as a form of exchange in a barter economy. In order to avoid the double coincidence of wants, some commodities will come to be exchanged more often than others.

Some commodities possess more of the characteristics that a superior money must have: portability, divisibility, scarcity, identity, etc. Those that possessed these qualities came more and more to be traded and used as a medium of exchange rather than as a commodity. Economist R.A. Radford (1945) discusses how cigarettes evolved as money, through a natural-selection process, in a prisoner-of-war camp. It is plausible, therefore, that money evolved through a similar process. The role of the state, however, is not to be denied in this process.

The evolution of money theories. In early economics, the mercantilists believed that bullion was wealth or at least that its accumulation was good for the economy. The first sound thinking on money surfaced in the period after the influx of gold and silver from the New World but it was not until the 18th century that economists began to form accurate theories of money. David HUME's (1752) specie-flow mechanism clearly illustrated the relation of money to the general price level, and the differences between real and nominal values. Adam SMITH (1776), of course, devotes a chapter to this topic and sets the course of monetary theory for the next century.

Henry Thronton (1802) is the early exception to this quantity theory of money, although he did not deny its validity. Thornton begins a tradition of money of integrating the rate of interest and a mechanism by which changes in the quantity of money affect the price level. In his classic presentation, the BANK OF ENGLAND as a CENTRAL BANK, with all or almost all the modern functions of such a bank, came to play a vital role in the credit process and therefore in the money creation or destruction process. The bank rate thus performs the role of equating the demand and supply of funds (that is to say, credit and the quantity of money). Thornton was among the first to establish the conditions for monetary equilibrium by considering the rate of interest as the adjusting mechanism.

Knut Wicksell (1898) continued in the same vein as Thornton, albeit one via David RICARDO rather than Thornton, and firmly established the Swedish School as one of the foremost in monetary theory. Wicksell's innovation was to clearly spell out the transmission mechanism of monetary disturbances. Wicksell pioneered the saving-investment approach to money. Whenever the natural rate differs from the money or bank rate, the cumulative process is set into motion. When the bank rate falls below the natural rate, there is an excess demand for funds that creates the fuel for an excess demand for goods and puts in action the upward pressure on prices. The resulting inflation will halt only once the bank rate is adjusted to the natural rate of interest.

Saving had already been integrated into the quantity theory of money, but in another form: the controversial SAY'S LAW. Say's Law is simple: In a specialized economy, economic agents supply products because they wish to earn an income with which to spend in the economy. That is to say, earned income will be spent; purchasing power is automatically created when income is received. Any income received in money that is not spent or saved does represent non-spending, but really it is potential spending that will one day be actualized. The actualizing is hastened by the fall in prices that accompanies a fall in aggregate demand. That is to say, excess money balances, savings will be spent when prices fall sufficiently. Writers in the 19th century employing Say's Law did recognize unequivocally saving in their monetary analysis but failed to see its connection to investment spending.

The theories and models were almost as varied as their number. All had one thing in common, however, a central focus on the rate of interest in their analyses. All also were concerned with showing what happens when the economy is in disequilibrium because of the interest rate and the adjustment process bringing the economy back to EQUILIBRIUM.

D.H. Roberston (1925) made one of the earliest contributions in Wicksellsian monetary economics with a rather complex model that explicitly took into account saving and investment in a temporal setting. One of his more colorful insights involved forced saving, which he called automatic stinting or imposed lacking. When the economy is in full employment and the bank rate falls below the natural rate of interest, investment increases. The resources for increased investment come at the expense of consumption. If households expected to save a certain amount in a forthcoming period and end up saving more than expected, this is forced saving. Robertson, without explicitly stating it, had discovered *ex ante, ex post* analysis. This analysis would receive explicit attention and central focus in Gunnar MYRDAL's (1939) examination of the temporal nature of the saving-investment process. For the first time, expectations had figured prominently in monetary theory.

Monetary equilibrium became rigorously defined by Myrdal and the concept developed into the notion of neutral money. The addition of expectations to the monetary model was an enormous supplement to the saving-investment approach. The key to understanding the role of money in the business cycle is the divergence of expectation among the different classes of economic agents and individuals themselves. Households, as savers and spenders, could make a set of decisions that are not synchronized with firms, as both sellers of output and buyers of inputs, especially labor input. A central factor in their decisions concerns the interest rate, a variable that can diverge from its natural rate because of monetary influences. (Differing views on the expected rate of inflation would have to wait decades from when Wicksellian monetary economics reigned supreme, in the 1920s to 1936).

R.G. Hawtrey took Wicksellian analysis in yet another direction. He observed that credit was often unstable and therefore a central bank is necessary to cope with banks and business that either made credit too tight or too ample. Hawtrey's innovation was to add inventory adjustments to changes in credit and money that work through the interest rate. When credit becomes tight, spending also becomes stringent and inventories accumulate. The opposite occurs when credit becomes abundant and the interest rate low. Thus Hawtrey anticipates John Maynard KEYNES's analysis.

One of the most controversial Wicksellian strains was contributed by Friedrich von HAYEK (1931) in his work, *Prices and Production*. Hayek attempted to wed Austrian capital theory and Wicksell's theory of money to construct a theory of cycles. His theory showed that money via the interest rate can influence capital structure by temporarily altering the period of production but with semi-permanent repercussions on the mix of capital goods and consumer goods and therefore employment and capital returns.

The Keynesian revolution and beyond. Monetary theory took a dramatic turn in 1936 with Keynes's *General Theory of Employment, Interest and Money.* Keynes departed with his earlier monetary theory and this may have been a step backward as many economists were later to appreciate. His liquidity preference theory of the interest, where the supply and demand for money determine the interest rate—saving and investment determine income and not interest—is a sharp break with the Wicksellian mold. One saving grace of the liquidity preference theory is the emphasis on the role of money as an asset. Keynes, after all, underscored the function of money as a store of value.

The demand for money would become a crowning achievement of Keynes's monetary analysis in the *General Theory.* Keynes's three motives for holding money, transaction, precautionary, and the speculative, would become imprinted into the literature on monetary economics.

Money as an asset that people wish to hold is the idea behind Keynes's speculative demand. James Tobin (1958), a follower of Keynes, extended Keynes's analysis to the inclusion of holding money along with other assets, an option Keynes did not allow for. Starting with the assumption of risk aversion, Tobin showed that people would want to hold money as part of their portfolio, even when money has a zero rate of return, because of its low level of risk. Money becomes part of a diversified portfolio of assets.

The 1950s saw several major advancements in the theory of money and money demand. Foremost of these was the resurrection of the quantity theory of money by Milton FRIEDMAN (1956). The quantity theory of money is one of the most important in economics. And it is based on an identity:

$$MV = PY$$

where M is the quantity of money, V the velocity of circulation, P the price level and Y the level of real output. The equation simply shows that what is spent must necessarily equal what is sold. This equation is due to Simon Newcomb and Irving FISHER in another variation. (The original form considered the transactions of quantities of goods traded for money rather than the output.) The equation, however, can be used to form a relation among the variables if it is considered as function. The causal relation among the variables is from left to right. The right hand side, PY, is nominal income and it is determined by the quantity of money and its velocity. (M and P are considered at points in time, while V and Y are specified over periods of time or per unit of time.)

A useful equation in monetary theory is the transformation of the equation of exchange from its static form as stated above into a dynamic form using percent changes or growth rates:

$$\text{percent}\Delta M + \text{percent}\Delta V \approx \text{percent}\Delta P + \text{percent}\Delta Y$$

where percentΔM is the growth rate of the money supply, percentΔV is the rate of change of velocity, percentΔP is the rate of inflation and percentΔY is the rate of growth of real output. The equation is useful because it shows that if velocity is constant, then the rate of growth of the money supply determines the rate of growth of nominal GDP (PY) and if Y is determined by non-monetary factors, the rate of inflation is equal to the rate of growth of money supply.

In the quantity theory of money, it is usually accepted that money is important in the short run but not in the long run (unless it is accelerating inflation and especially hyperinflation). Money affects real factors in the short run but usually does not affect real variables in the long run. Changes in the supply of money have been identified with creating the business cycle, major RECESSIONs, and even the Great DEPRESSION (although it is unlikely that changes in the money supply created the Great Depression, it certainly aggravated the situation).

The Cambridge version of the quantity theory turns the equation of exchange in demand for money. The equation:

$$M = kPY$$

where k is now equal to 1/V and is simply the fraction of nominal income that people wish to hold as money balances. The condition for equilibrium is now:

$$M_S = M_D = kPY,$$

where M_S is the supply of money and M_D is the demand for money. Missing from the equation is the rate of interest. But using $M_D = f(Y, r)$, the dynamics of money supply adjustment is easy to explain as money is one asset in a portfolio and all others that are interest bearing. When $M_D > M_S$, people attempt to restore their money balances by selling assets driving the interest rate down until balance is restored and when $M_S > M_D$, people use their excess money balances to buy assets and thereby drive the interest rate up again until balance is restored. One of the keys to this approach is that it considers money as one of many assets, albeit the most liquid of all.

The interest rate approach, at least in considering the transaction motive, would come into its own in the 1950s with the work of William Baumol (1952) and James Tobin (1956). Baumol and Tobin showed that the transaction demand for money is an inverse function of the rate of interest. Like any other good or asset, money has an opportunity cost, and that is the rate of interest.

Phillips Curve. The PHILLIPS CURVE is an important addition to Keynesian monetary theory. A.W. Phillips (1958) observed that in the United Kingdom there existed what seemed like a stable relationship between the rate of change of money wages and the rate of unemployment. When the rate of money-wage rate inflation was high, unemployment was low and vice versa. This tradeoff between unemployment and inflation (as later reformulated by Paul SAMUELSON and Robert SOLOW) quickly became known as the Phillips Curve. The Phillips Curve is really another form of the aggregate demand curve. When aggregate demand is high, the general price level rises and is usually accompanied by a lag in money wages. This means that real wage rates fall and the demand for labor increases. This results in lower unemployment. However, as Friedman once remarked, sustained inflation is always a monetary phenomenon and the Phillips Curve, over long periods, must be related to the money supply.

The correction to the Phillips Curve that takes into account the fall in real wages that accompanies high, or rather, as we will see, increasing, rates of inflation is the addition of expectations. The expectations-augmented Phillips Curve became the breakthrough that allowed a new variety of quantity theorists to supplant the primacy of the then-Keynesian approach to monetary economics. The natural rate of interest would give way to the natural rate of unemployment. The natural rate of unemployment can be thought of to exist when the economy is in monetary equilibrium in the sense that the expectations of economic agents are correct and identical. Any rate of growth of the money supply, and therefore inflation, is consistent with the natural rate of UNEMPLOYMENT. The tradeoff between unemployment and inflation is nonexistent in the long run. A concept related to the natural rate of unemployment is NAIRU, the nonaccelerating inflation rate of unemployment became a popular policy variable in 1980s and 1990s. This is the rate at which there is no tendency for inflation to either increase or decrease (monetary equilibrium).

Quantity theorists had taken matters one step further in 1970s with an article that had been written by John Muth in 1961. (By the 1960s it became apparent to many scholars on the subject of money that the key to understanding the money supply's effects lay in expectations.) The theory of rational expectations had seized economists' line of thought so that it became *the* theory of money by 1990s. The idea behind rational expectations is quite simple. People form their expectations of variables by devising optimal forecasts, that is, predictions that take all information into account. An optimal forecast includes an expectation of the variable that takes in all information and a stochastic component. Thus for inflation, Π:

$$\Pi^o = \Pi^e + \varepsilon.$$

Since the expectation of $\varepsilon = 0$, a rational expectation of inflation, Π^e, is equal to the optimal forecast. The po-

tency of rational expectations comes into play in policy matters, where it asserts that the supply of money can only affect real economic variables through purely random changes.

BIBLIOGRAPHY. W.J. Baumol, "The Transactions Demand for Cash: An Inventory Theoretic Approach," *Quarterly Journal of Economics* (1952); M. Friedman, "The Quantity theory of Money—A Restatement," *Studies in the Quantity theory of Money* (University of Chicago Press, 1956); R.G. Hawtrey, *Good and Bad Trade: An Inquiry into the Causes of Trade Fluctuations* (Constable, 1913); R.G. Hawtrey, *Currency and Credit* (Longmans, Green, 1919); F.A. Hayek, *Prices and Production* (Routledge, 1931); J. Hicks, *Value and Capital* (Clarendon Press); D. Hume,Of Interest; Of Money"*Essays, Moral, Political and Literary* (1752); J. Muth, "Rational Expectations and the Theory of Price Movements," *Econometrica* (1961); R.A. Radford, "The Economic Organization of a P.O.W. Camp," *Economica* (1945); J. Tobin, "The Interest-Elasticity of Transactions for Cash," *Review of Economics and Statistics* (1956); J. Tobin, "Liquidity Preference as Behavior Towards Risk," *Review of Economic Studies* (1958); K. Wicksell, *Interest and Prices* (Augustus M. Kelley, 1936).

ZELJAN SCHUSTER, PH.D.
UNIVERSITY OF NEW HAVEN

monopoly

A MONOPOLY IS DEFINED as a market structure in which there is one single provider of a good or service present in the market: the monopolist. The implication of this particular form of MARKET structure is that the prices for these goods and services are then determined by the objectives of the monopolist, and are limited only by the buyers' willingness to pay for the good or service. This is precisely because there are no other providers, so the monopolist is not constrained by any rival firms.

The polar opposite of a monopoly is a market structure characterized as perfectly competitive—usually considered as a market with many firms that compete against each other. However, regardless of the actual number of firms, a market is perfectly competitive if each firm can essentially only charge the going market price, or otherwise risk losing all of its customers to competing firms.

Profit-maximization, perfectly competitive markets. Economists usually assume that the objective of a privately run firm is to maximize the PROFIT it makes, where profit is measured as the total revenue earned by the firm minus the total costs incurred in producing the good or service. This profit motivation is assumed to be the same regardless of the type of market structure that the firm operates in. It is instructive to contrast how this profit motive plays out in both a monopoly and in the polar opposite, a perfectly competitive market, as this will reveal how a monopolist maximizes profit and what is necessary for it to do so.

One of the defining features of a perfectly competitive market is that firms can freely enter (or exit) the market. If firms are pricing above the COST of the product that is sold, firms will be able to make a profit. However, firms outside the industry are also looking to make profits, and given that they are free to enter the market, they will enter and charge a slightly lower price than the incumbent firms, but will still stay above costs. Such an adjustment on the supply side of the market increases the number of firms in the market and lowers prices—competition is fiercer now than before. Provided that profit opportunities still exist in the market, firms will continue to enter; again, resulting in more competition, i.e., lower prices. This adjustment process goes on, until prices are so low that they are at or near the cost of producing the product, so that it is no longer profitable for new firms to compete in the market.

Thus, a desirable feature of the perfectly competitive market is that although firms maximize profits, the end result of free entry is that goods and services are actually sold at (or near) cost, that is, with little or no mark-up.

It is now clear how a monopolist can make a profit above the profit that firms in perfectly competitive markets make: there is no other firm in the market that could undercut the monopolist's price and steal its customers. Hence, the monopolist can maintain prices substantially above the cost of production, limited only by its customers' willingness to pay. It is also clear now what is necessary to sustain a monopoly. New firms must somehow be prevented from entering the monopolist's market. That is, there must be some barriers to entry so that high profits are not bid away.

Barriers to entry. There are several common barriers to entry that may preserve a monopolist's position as the lone seller in a market. One of the most commonly observed is a legal barrier to entry. For instance, the government may have issued an exclusive license to a firm to supply a market. This is the case when a PATENT is granted that effectively lets a firm monopolize a particular market for a certain period of time, as in the pharmaceutical industry, for example.

Second, there may be barriers to entry that stem from specialized know-how (for example, management expertise) that gives the monopolist an absolute cost advantage. This can be the case if only a single firm possesses the particular expertise on how to produce something at low enough costs to supply the market.

A third factor that may prevent firms from entering a market is that they do not have access to critical resources. Thus, as an example, the aluminum company Alcoa managed to purchase the mining rights to most readily available bauxite. As bauxite is a principal mineral in the production of aluminum, potential competitors in the aluminum market were denied access to a key scarce resource.

A fourth reason that additional firms may not enter a market has to do with the particular technology used to produce the good or service in conjunction with the market size that is being supplied. For instance, a small municipality may not have enough residents to cover the large overhead costs associated with the provision of a sewer system for more than one company. Such instances are referred to as "natural monopolies" (see below), because it may be the case that no second firm would ever want to enter the market to begin with (since if they did enter, they would make a loss).

Costs associated with monopolies. Monopolists are often accused of imposing unnecessary costs on society. The fact that the monopolist's customers must pay a higher price may be the source of much concern over the existence of monopolists. However, economists do not consider this higher price to be a cost on society per se. When a customer pays a higher price for a good or service, then the customer will have less surplus (money), and the monopolist more. However, the monopolist (i.e., the owner of the firm) is also a member of society. Thus, this transfer of money reflects a shifting of money from one member of society (the customer) to another (the owner of the monopoly firm). This may raise questions of equity or fairness, but not questions of efficiency. And it is the latter, namely efficiency, that determines what constitutes cost to society overall.

Nevertheless, an implication of the higher prices charged by monopolists, is a reduction in the supply of the good or service sold, as some costumers will be priced out of the market. And this does raise issues of efficiency. In particular, if the monopolist is charging a price above the cost of production and as a result, some people will no longer purchase the good or service, even though they would have been willing to pay for all the costs of producing it, then the fact that these transactions do not take place is a cost to society.

Hence, what is inefficient, and thus costly to society, is not that some transactions take place at higher prices, but rather that some transactions that would be worthwhile, do not take place at all because some people are priced out of the market.

Once the distinction between equity (fairness) and inefficiency (waste) is drawn, the above costs of monopoly may be easy to see; yet there are also more subtle costs associated with the presence of monopoly. One such cost is closely related to the amount of profit that a monopolist can make in a market. Recall that the monopolist's ability to make profit crucially depends on the fact that there are no other firms in the market. If an unlimited number of other firms were able to freely enter the market, profits could easily erode to zero. Consequently, the monopolist may engage in activities to protect its position in the market. Many of these activities can be socially wasteful. Similarly, if firms see the potential to create a monopoly in a particular market, they may also engage in activities that are designed to secure a monopoly position. Again, these activities designed to create and secure the monopoly from entry may very well be socially wasteful.

Since the monopolist's profits are considered "rents," this socially wasteful behavior is referred to as rent-seeking or rent-protecting activity. An example of this type of cost to society is the lobbying of legislators to grant or protect exclusive licenses. The lobbying activity is exclusively designed to secure monopoly rents, so lobbying itself does not add anything of value to society, yet resources (time and money) are used up in the process of lobbying legislators or regulators.

Another type of cost or inefficiency associated with monopoly is related to the fact that the monopolist does not face any competitors that put pressure on the firm to perform well. This type of inefficiency—referred to as X-inefficiency—may to some degree contradict profit-maximizing behavior, but it is easy to see that a firm that is not facing any competition may very well slack a little and provide a substandard service, even if this results in lower profits.

Finally, it has frequently been argued that monopolies are slow to innovate, at least when compared to competitive markets. This is because for a perfectly competitive firm to "get ahead," it must outperform its competitors. By coming up with cheaper ways of providing the same goods and services or by finding ways to provide higher quality goods and services, a firm in a perfectly competitive market may—at least for a while—be able to make profit. A monopolist on the other hand already makes a profit and improvements to its product-line may not be worth the effort, even if it does allow for a slight increase in sales.

Purported benefits associated with monopolies. There are some who see advantages to monopolies. Ironically, one example sometimes cited is the exact opposite of the final cost associated with monopoly listed above, i.e. less innovation. That is, some claim that monopolists are more efficient at innovation than other firms are. The logic here is that in order to finance the enormous amounts that RESEARCH AND DEVELOPMENT (R&D) of new products and production techniques cost, a firm must have a lot of money. Since monopolists make the most profit, they have the most money available for R&D.

However, two things must be pointed out here. The first is that just because a monopoly makes a lot of money, does not mean that it is used for R&D, it might just as well be spent elsewhere. Moreover, if any firm has a really innovative idea, it stands to reason that the firm may be able to arrange for venture capital to finance R&D even if it does not have its own funds available.

Nevertheless, there are two important points about innovation and benefits associated with monopoly. The first is that monopolies are sometimes created in order to protect innovation, and thereby create innovations. This is the case where a PATENT is granted. The idea here is that only if a firm's innovations are protected from immediate copying will the firm reap some benefit from its R&D. Thus, patenting new research makes R&D more profitable, and hence leads to more innovation. But this just says that (temporary) monopolies that are created through patents are beneficial to innovation, even if the monopoly itself has little incentive to further innovate.

The other important point about innovation and beneficial monopoly is that some firms may evolve into monopolists merely by being much better at providing goods and services to customers than the potential rival firms. In this case, having a monopoly might also not be such a bad thing, as it can only exist because its products are so much better and/or less expensive than any other firms' would be.

Monopolies in the real world. In part due to the costs to society associated with some monopolies, the state has an interest in prohibiting business practices intended to establish monopolies. This poses some real-world issues for government agencies that are in charge of prosecuting monopolists, e.g., the U.S. Justice Department's Antitrust Division.

First, as monopoly is defined as a market structure, it is important to identify the relevant boundaries of the market in question. Indeed, in most anti-monopoly cases, defining the relevant boundaries is the most contentious issue and takes up the most time. There are at least two dimensions in which this can pose a problem, first in terms of the geographic location, and second in terms of the product in question.

Geographic location is important because buyers are able to travel to get to other firms or shop over the internet or phone. Hence, even if there is only one firm in a particular area, it may not be a monopolist. Indeed, the relevant geographic market may be local, national, international or even global (for example, this was argued in the civil aircraft industry when the Boeing–McDonnell Douglas merger took place). As far as defining the product in question is concerned, consider, say, the market for bread. Is the relevant market so narrow as to include only sliced white bread, or is it as broad as to include all possible different types of loafs of bread, rolls, buns, muffins, pita bread, nan bread, pumpernickel, tortillas, and so on? The answers to these questions usually lie in CONSUMER BEHAVIOR. Principally, whether consumers seem to consider different products as substitutable for each other. One way of measuring this is to see how demand for one good is affected by price changes in the other good.

The second difficulty faced in identifying monopolies is that true monopolies rarely exist. In the "real world" what is of actual concern is usually that a single firm dominates a market, even though this firm may face some smaller competitors. Examples of such firms, in the early 2000s, were Intel in the market for computer chip production, Microsoft in operating systems, Kodak in photographic products or Gillette in the market for wet-shaving products. However, much of what is said about monopolies may apply equally well to dominating firms.

Finally, the purpose of taking legal action must be considered carefully. Thus, is it truly in the best interest of society to go against a monopoly, or is it only in the interest of potential rival firms? For instance, if a firm is identified to be a monopolist, but it has attained this position because it simply produces a much better and cheaper product than anyone else, it may be that society is best off without interference with the firm. Indeed, many economists worry that courts are more concerned with the existence of monopoly power rather than the causes for it.

Government-run monopolies. While one usually thinks of monopolists as profit-maximizing, privately operated firms that do not have any competitors, sometimes it is the government that has a monopoly on a particular good or service. There are four different types of government-run monopolies.

Historically, the most important reason for a government to run a monopoly was to raise revenue. Because of the profitability of monopolies, many different types of goods and services have, in the past, been exclusively available through a government-run or a government-licensed operation. Examples include Royal licenses granted for the sale of spices, tobacco products, playing cards, or matches in Europe and state-run or licensed ferry transport services in some areas of the United States. Contemporary examples of the government's desire to raise revenue through monopolies are government-run GAMBLING AND LOTTERIES.

In some cases, governments manage monopolies for some goods and services not necessarily in order to gain revenue, but in order to exert greater control over the distribution of the goods and services in question. This is, for instance, the case for the state-run distribution systems for alcoholic beverages in some states.

The third common occurrence of government monopolies is found due to historical lock-ins and vested interests, when it comes to goods and services provided to the government through the government itself. Thus, in many municipalities, there may exist certain services that the government could buy on the open market. But instead, a separate government agency may be set up that exclusively provides the service. For instance, the servicing of publicly owned vehicles or landscaping of public areas in a community is rarely contracted for with private companies, but instead a separate government agency is established to provide the service. As these agencies do not have to compete for the service they provide in terms of better prices or quality, these types of monopolies are heavily criticized as being expensive to maintain, thus costing the taxpayer unnecessarily. Nevertheless, these types of monopolies on services provided are very widespread due to the vested interests and political power of those employed in the agencies.

Natural monopolies and regulation. Finally, governments often operate what are called natural monopolies, an industry in which it is more efficient to have one single firm provide the good or service. Thus, utilities are often cheaper to provide if there is only a single provider. This is because it may cost a lot to set up the necessary infrastructure to deliver the utility, but once it is in place, it is relatively cheap to provide the service. In such cases, it can be socially wasteful to have several firms incur the large overhead costs necessary to provide the good or service. These markets are therefore often referred to as natural monopolies, and instead of competition, the government either provides the service itself, or licenses another firm to (exclusively) do so (usually subject to some regulatory restrictions). Examples are provision of water, gas, sewers, electricity, phone and cable lines, and railroads.

However, in very large markets, the costs associated with a lack of competition and/or regulation are often greater than the savings experienced by limiting the number of providers, so such markets are increasingly deregulated and opened up to varying degrees of competition. An exception to this trend of deregulation and increased competition is found in extreme cases of high overheads coupled with low costs of providing additional services. For instance, the provisions of national defense, law enforcement, and the court system are very costly, but the level of service provided remains nearly unaffected as additional citizens benefit from the service. These extreme cases of natural monopolies are examples of what are called public goods. They will presumably largely remain government monopolies.

BIBLIOGRAPHY. Luís M.B. Cabral, *Introduction to Industrial Organization* (MIT Press, 2000); Harvey Leibenstein,

"Allocative Efficiency vs. 'X-Efficiency,'" *The American Economic Review* (v.56/3, 1966); Richard A. Posner, "The Social Costs of Monopoly and Regulation," *Journal of Political Economy* (v.83, 1975); Kip Viscusi, John M. Vernon, and Joseph E. Harrington, jr., *Economics of Regulation and Anti-Trust* (MIT Press, 2000).

THOMAS D. JEITSCHKO, PH.D.
MICHIGAN STATE UNIVERSITY

Monroe, James (1758–1831)

THE FIFTH PRESIDENT of the UNITED STATES, James Monroe was born in Westmoreland County, Virginia. At age 16, he entered the College of William and Mary. Two years later, in 1776, he left college to join the Continental Army during the AMERICAN REVOLUTION. Monroe received a lieutenant's commission and was commended for bravery in combat. Seriously wounded during a daring charge at the Battle of Trenton, Monroe was promoted to captain and eventually attained the rank of colonel.

After failing to gain a field command, Monroe resigned his commission and returned to Virginia, where he was appointed state military commissioner. He also pursued a legal career by studying law with a prominent lawyer, Thomas JEFFERSON, who would become his mentor and political patron.

In 1782, Monroe won election to the Virginia Assembly and then to the Continental Congress. During this time, he began working and corresponding with James MADISON, who came from the same part of Virginia and shared a sense that the Continental Congress needed to be strengthened.

Their relationship became strained when Monroe opposed ratification of the U.S. Constitution in 1787. He objected to the powers of direct taxation and to the power given to the Senate. At Patrick Henry's request, Monroe ran for U.S. Congress against Madison but lost. Two years later he went to Washington, D.C., as a senator, where he joined Jefferson and Madison in opposition to Alexander HAMILTON's attempts to increase the size and power of the federal government.

In 1794, President George WASHINGTON assigned Monroe to a diplomatic post in post-revolutionary FRANCE. His pro-French views, however, led him to be recalled two years later. Monroe returned to Virginia where he was elected and served as governor from 1799 until 1802.

President Jefferson called on Monroe, in 1803, to travel to France as a special envoy to purchase a port along the Mississippi River. Napoleon instead offered either to sell all of Louisiana or nothing. Although the constitutionality of such a purchase was in question and it was clearly beyond the scope of his appointment, Monroe began the negotiations, working with Secretary of State Madison to secure the Louisiana Purchase.

Monroe spent four more years in Europe as minister to Britain. During this time Britain was at war with France and was blocking all U.S. trade. Monroe secured a treaty to relax these restrictions, but Jefferson refused to submit the treaty for ratification because it did not prevent Britain from boarding American ships and kidnapping American seamen for service in the British Navy.

Monroe, believing he had secured the best terms possible, fell into disagreement with the administration. In 1808, he further estranged himself from Madison by running against him for president. With Madison's election, Monroe returned to state politics and served another year as governor.

In 1811, Madison looked beyond their personal rivalry and asked Monroe to return to the federal government as secretary of state. In 1814, Madison also assumed the duties of secretary of war.

Upon Madison's retirement in 1816, Monroe easily won election as president. In 1820, Monroe was so popular that he ran uncontested for re-election, losing only one electoral vote nationwide.

Despite such unity, the issue that would divide the nation for the next half century rose on the horizon: As Missouri sought admission to the Union, members of Congress sought to condition admission on a ban of slavery. Monroe, a slave-owner himself, believed the federal government had no right to tell a state whether it could legalize slavery. He compromised, however, to accept the agreement to admit Missouri as a slave state and Maine as a free state (thus keeping balance in the U.S. Senate) and, at the same time, limiting future slave states to Southern territories.

Throughout his career, Monroe consistently fought to keep power diffused and government small. He was the only president to have taken a significant role in opposing the ratification of the Constitution. While he supported projects to improve coastal defenses, when Congress sent him a bill to build canals and make other internal national improvements, Monroe vetoed the bill. Even though Madison had signed similar laws, Monroe held that the federal government had no such authority.

During his eight years in office, federal spending decreased from $30 million per year to $20 million. Federal debt shrank from $123 million to $84 million, despite a financial panic in 1819 that significantly decreased federal revenues.

Monroe is best known for foreign affairs. He pressured SPAIN into ceding Florida in 1819. He also announced a new policy, drafted by his Secretary of State John Quincy ADAMS, that the United States would oppose any European intervention in the Western Hemisphere. Although the United States did not have the military might to enforce this policy at the time, the Monroe Doctrine became a cornerstone of U.S. foreign policy.

Monroe left office in 1825, heavily in debt. He spent years trying to recover expenses owed by the government for his years of service. In 1829, he presided over Virginia's Constitutional Convention.

BIBLIOGRAPHY. Harry Ammon, *James Monroe: The Quest for National Identity,* (Bookthrift, 1990); Stewart Brown, ed., *The Autobiography of James Monroe* (1959); Noble E. Cunningham, Jr., *The Presidency of James Monroe* (University Press of Kansas, 1996); George Dangerfield, *The Era of Good Feelings* (Ivan R. Dee, 1952).

MICHAEL J. TROY, J.D.
THOMAS D. JEITSCHKO, PH.D.
MICHIGAN STATE UNIVERSITY

Montesquieu, Charles de (1689–1755)

FRENCH NOBLEMAN, LAWYER, and Enlightenment political thinker, Charles de Montesquieu is most well known for his works *Persian Letters* (1721), a thinly veiled critique of 18th century French laws, customs and mores, and *On the Spirit of the Laws* (1748), a central treatise of Western thought that describes government and its workings.

Though Montesquieu defended monarchy as the ideal form of government and nobility as the best safeguard of liberty, in particular his articulation of the idea of separation of powers, a concept that stretched back to the Roman historian Polybius, was influential in subsequent political and constitutional thought. Montesquieu's ideas about economics and commerce appear ambivalent from the modern perspective; they bear a strong resemblance in many respects to those of Alexis de Tocqueville, who was simultaneously attracted and repelled by the merchant orientation of American democracy a century later.

Montesquieu claimed that commerce made nations flourish, increased the population, and fostered peace between trading partners. He praised the people of commercial cities like Marseilles and nations like England as disciplined, hard working, moderate, and frugal. While supporting status differences between people of the same country, a situation supported by commerce and luxury, he feared the effects of too much luxury and consumption as corrupting to the classes who enjoyed them. Particularly in private correspondence and diaries, he re-marked that commerce was beneath the notice of a great nation and that the avarice of the Dutch (the most successful trading people of the period) was repellent.

He felt that too intensive pursuit of commerce had destroyed both Greece and Carthage, saving ultimate respect for the Romans, whom he did not view as a commercial power. In the *Spirit of the Laws*, he stated that commerce can only exist with democracy as long as it promotes virtue; when too much luxury is achieved, society will become corrupt. Still, his writing is an important component of a body of literature developing in the century before Adam SMITH's *Wealth of Nations* that emphasized the sweetness that commerce and trade brought to human association, ideas emphasized by other thinkers such as John Miller and James Steuart.

According to such arguments, commerce and trade forced those inclined to behave badly to be civilized out of interest; hence, according to Albert Hirschmann, the most influential interpreter of this literature, commerce led to the victory of interest over passion. For example, in "How Commerce Emerged in Europe from Barbarism," Montesquieu suggests that violence against the Jews persisted until they conceived of the bill of exchange (an early financial instrument for currency exchange and long-distance money transfer), which simultaneously made their wealth invisible and forced rulers to behave fairly. Montesquieu's participation in this strand of thinking separated him from mercantilists, who emphasized the competitive aspects of trade and ideas of economics as a zero-sum game. At the same time he opposed the creation of public debt as too likely to lead to overweening government power.

Montesquieu should be read as a supporter of expanded trade and commerce, but not a capitalist thinker along the lines of Smith.

BIBLIOGRAPHY. Roger Boesche, "Fearing Monarchs and Merchants: Montesquieu's Two Theories of Despotism," *Western Political Quarterly* (v.43, 1990): Albert O. Hirschmann, *The Passions and the Interests: Political Arguments for Capitalism before its Triumph* (Princeton University Press, 1997); Alan MacFarlane, *The Riddle of the Modern World: Of Liberty, Wealth and Equality* (Palgrave, 2000); Charles de Montesquieu, *The Spirit of the Laws*, Anne M. Cohler, et al., eds. (Cambridge University Press, 1989).

SUSAN R. BOETTCHER, PH.D.
UNIVERSITY OF TEXAS, AUSTIN

moral hazard

THE CONCEPT OF moral hazard traces its origins to the specialized jargon of the INSURANCE industry. In that context, the concept is typically illustrated as a difficulty that arises in the design of insurance contracts. The causes for the difficulty lie in the insurance provider's inability to monitor and prescribe the future behavior of the insured individual.

Consider for example, a HEALTH-insurance contract whereby an individual pays a premium to the insurance company every month in exchange for the promise that the insurance company will reimburse all medical costs incurred by the insured in the event of an illness. In order to determine what would be a suitable premium, the insurance company will need to consider the likelihood of illness for its prospective customer and the magnitude of the resulting medical care costs.

But the likelihood of illness depends in part at least on the conduct of the individual, specifically on his or her exercise of precaution, dietary habits, and so on. Whereas an uninsured individual may take these precautions in order to reduce the likelihood of bearing the medical costs associated with illness, an insured individual may fail to take them, or in any event, take fewer precautions given that their effects in the form of lower medical care expenses would benefit only the insurance company.

Moral hazard arises when behavioral changes induced by the purchase of an insurance contract increase the likelihood of the insured event. Conversely, it could be argued that the problem of moral hazard would be resolved if these behavioral changes could be prevented by contract agreement between the insurance company and its customer. The prevalence of moral hazard in insurance markets follows then from the fact that it is virtually impossible for the two parties to agree to an enforceable contract that suppresses altogether the hazard of behavioral changes by the insured party.

The main consequences of moral hazard problems for the characteristics of insurance contracts are the use of coinsurance and deductibles. Under coinsurance, the insurance company does not provide full coverage for the costs incurred by the customer when the insured event occurs. Continuing with the example used above, the contract may state that only 80 percent of the medical care costs will be reimbursed. The effect of coinsurance is that the benefits of reduced medical bills are now shared between the insurance company and the insured individual. In this way, coinsurance restores, partially, the insured individual's incentives to take precautions against the risk of illness. The purpose of deductibles in insurance contracts is similar, since they establish that during the insurance period only costs or losses incurred above a fixed amount, the deductible, will be reimbursed by the insurance company. Rather than sharing every dollar of costs or losses as under coinsurance, the insured individual bears 100 percent of the costs up to the deductible and 0 percent of costs in excess of it.

According to modern economic theory, the problem of moral hazard in insurance contracts is an example of a broader class of problems arising from the existence of asymmetric information between the parties to a contract or other exchange relationship. Accordingly, economists state that the interaction between two parties is beset by a potential moral-hazard problem when the economic outcome from the interaction for at least one party depends on actions chosen by the other party that cannot be specified in advance because they are not observable.

This characterization explains why economists refer to moral hazard problems as problems of hidden action, and why moral-hazard-like phenomena are reckoned to be at work in a large variety of economic contexts.

For example, consider an agency relationship whereby one individual (the principal) hires another (the agent) to perform a set of tasks. While the agent's effort while performing these tasks determines the principal's economic payoff from the agency relationship, the agent's choice of effort cannot be prescribed in advance because it would be unobservable. This creates a moral-hazard problem because the agent will choose its own effort without giving any consideration to the benefits of greater effort that would accrue to the principal.

As illustrated by the example of the insurance contract, solutions to moral hazard problems take the form of adaptations in the terms of the relationship between the principal and the agent that align the goals of the agent's choice of action with the interests of the principal. Thus, for example, sales agents whose effort cannot be monitored by their principal may be compensated with commissions on actual sales, and top corporate executives whose decisions the shareholders cannot specify in advance may receive their compensation in the forms of shares or stock options.

As is more generally the case for asymmetric information conditions, moral-hazard problems may be the source of economic inefficiencies when the adaptations in the terms of contracts required by the desire to alleviate the effects of moral hazard, prevent the parties from reaching other goals.

Consider again the case of medical insurance presented above. The main goal of an insurance contract is to transfer the risk of medical expenses due to illness from the insured individual to the insurance company. While coinsurance and deductible terms alleviate the moral hazard problem, they do so by forcing the insured individual to bear part of the risk.

BIBLIOGRAPHY. Hal R. Varian, *Intermediate Microeconomics: A Modern Approach* (Norton, 1999); David E.M. Sappington, "Incentives in Principal-Agent Relationships," *Journal of Economic Perspectives* (v.5/2, 1991); Mark V.

Pauly, "The Economics of Moral Hazard: Comment," *American Economic Review* (v.58/3, 1968).

ROBERTO MAZZOLENI, PH.D.
HOFSTRA UNIVERSITY

Morgan Stanley

A WALL STREET investment-banking company, Morgan Stanley is also the largest U.S.-based securities firm in terms of total capital, common equity, and net income. It underwrites stocks and bonds and is one of the 10 largest asset managers in the world. Morgan Stanley's client list has included such "blue chip" companies as DuPont, U.S. STEEL, AMERICAN TELEPHONE & TELEGRAPH (AT&T), Mobil, and GENERAL MOTORS. Notoriously conservative for most of its history, the firm became more aggressive in the 1970s and pioneered the first hostile corporate takeover.

Morgan Stanley began in New York in 1935 as a branch of the mighty J.P. Morgan & Company. Created because the Glass-Steagall Act forced J.P. MORGAN to erect a high wall between commercial-banking and investment-banking, Morgan Stanley expected to merge into J.P. Morgan & Company when the political climate changed. Whenever possible, the two Morgan firms would cooperate. While Morgan provided financing for the new company, utility bond expert Harold Stanley acted as president. In 1941, the companies dissolved their formal link.

Chiefly an issuer of "blue-chip" bonds, Morgan Stanley would go to any length to serve a client. Partners stepped in to serve as chairmen of companies in difficulty, as happened with the bankrupt farm-equipment manufacturer J.I. Case in 1961. Morgan Stanley's greatest accomplishment came in the 1940s when it promoted the newly formed WORLD BANK. Besides offering publicity in the form of booklets, Morgan Stanley organized huge syndicates of underwriters to help the World Bank provide development assistance to the poorest people on the planet. This account marked the summit of the firm's success. Its monopoly of much of America's industry made it reluctant to explore foreign markets.

By the 1960s, the firm had developed a reputation as a distinguished but stodgy company where employees had to possess elite lineage, brains, and money. The firm managed securities issues alone or not at all. The only advertising that it undertook came in the form of large "tombstone" advertisements that listed the members of an underwriting syndicate.

A changing business climate forced Morgan Stanley to become more innovative to survive. It began real advertising in the 1970s. In 1971, it opened a sales and trading operation, a lowly but profitable line that Morgan Stanley had traditionally subcontracted to other firms. To attract traders, Morgan Stanley introduced production-oriented compensation that eroded collegiality. Clients pushed the company to engage in aggressive takeovers and it opened the first mergers and acquisitions department on Wall Street. It conducted the first hostile raid in 1974.

By 1989, the firm had become one of the sharks of Wall Street. It raided other firms for analysts and conducted corporate raids for clients. It sold junk BONDS and leveraged buyouts. It 1997, it merged with another very aggressive bank to become Morgan Stanley Dean Witter.

Morgan Stanley served as the chief investment banker to American industry while the United States rose to global economic dominance. Besides fueling this growth, the company pioneered business practices that destroyed the conservatism of investment-banking.

BIBLIOGRAPHY. Ron Chernow, *The House of Morgan: An American Banking Dynasty and the Rise of Modern Finance* (Atlantic Monthly Press, 1990); Charles R. Geisst, *The Last Partnership: Inside the Great Wall Street Dynasties* (McGraw-Hill, 2001); Frank Partnoy, *FIASCO: Blood in the Water on Wall Street* (W.W. Norton, 1997).

CARYN E. NEUMANN, PH.D.
OHIO STATE UNIVERSITY

Morgan, John Pierpont (1837–1913)

AN INVESTMENT BANKER who became the most powerful financial leader of the Progressive era, J.P. Morgan was born in Hartford, Connecticut, and died in Rome, Italy, en route to the UNITED STATES.

Best known for preventing the 1895 collapse of the U.S. Treasury during a run on gold, Morgan is also credited for developing the industrial might of the United States by organizing financing for RAILROAD, steel, and agricultural machinery firms. As head of the Northern Securities Company, Morgan also became the first victim of the Sherman Antitrust Act when the Supreme Court ruled against him in 1904. At the time of his death, he headed the largest private bank in the world.

The son of Junius Morgan, a merchant banker, and Juliet Pierpont, the daughter of a Unitarian minister, J.P. Morgan was educated at public schools in Hartford and Boston. He entered the Institution Sillig at Vevey in Switzerland in 1854 and spent two years at Germany's Göttingen University. In 1857, Junius arranged for the

New York City merchant bank of Duncan, Sherman & Company to give his son a job. With only weak state controls of the banking system, banks often took substantial risks and could easily fail in financial panics. Morgan helped the bank through its near-collapse in the panic of 1857 and then struck out on his own in 1861. Morgan's experiences with Duncan, Sherman taught him to avoid speculation, and the bank that he built would become known for its conservatism as well as its profitability. J.P. Morgan & Company was a New York City-based private wholesale bank that put together syndicates to share the risk of underwriting new issues of bonds or stock. Underwriting contracts committed the bank to sell securities at a minimum price. The bank only made money if it could sell the stocks and bonds above the contract price. Morgan normally acted as a lead banker, taking as much as 50 percent of an issue and placing the rest with other banking houses. He then tendered these shares to retail stockbrokers, commercial banks, and wealthy individuals who were clients of the house.

Morgan's banking skills fueled American expansion by providing funds necessary for the country's growth. The United States simply lacked the financial wherewithal to fund its developing industries, while European nations had capital surpluses that could be tapped to pay for massive American projects such as railroad expansion. Morgan pried loose European money by reducing the risk associated with investment in American securities.

To get investors, Morgan sought to guarantee that American companies would pay timely dividends on stocks and bonds. He hoped the securities would appreciate in time, thereby providing him with a profit. This made Morgan into the opposite of Gilded Age railroad-stock manipulators such as Jay GOULD and Jim FISK who benefited from collusive agreements to fix rates and fares. Morgan skirmished with Gould and Fisk but ultimately won the railroad war. In 1885, Morgan brought together various railroad barons associated with the New York Central and Pennsylvania Railroads on board his yacht, the *Corsair*, and used the threat of no more financing to arrange an end to their destructive rate wars. The Corsair compact caused a rise in the share-value of eastern railroads and greatly increased Morgan's prestige.

Besides a lack of dividends, the other major risk to investors involved currency exchange. After 1873, the United States fixed the value of its dollar according to the price of gold. Farmers and others in the Populist movement preferred a silver standard because the fluctuating rate would reduce the amount of interest they paid. Morgan worked to keep the United States on the gold standard because it minimized the risk of foreign-investor losses through adverse currency exchange rates. Morgan's stands helped to maintain the inflow of European funds that were so necessary to American expansion, but made him enemies among farmers.

Morgan's dependence on gold led him to prop up the U.S. Treasury. In 1895, the government appeared to be ready to abandon the gold standard in the face of political pressures and a major DEPRESSION that had caused a run on the precious metal. Morgan rushed to offer aid to President Grover CLEVELAND. The private pact formed at the White House provided for the purchase of more than $62 million in gold for the U.S. Treasury and saw Morgan guarantee the Treasury against gold withdrawals from February through the end of September 1895.

Morgan's enormous financial power frightened many Americans and, partly in response to concerns about the might of the banker, the Sherman Antitrust Act passed in 1890. The aim of the new law was to forbid combinations in restraint of trade, and Morgan became the first to be ensnared by it. In railroad reorganizations, Morgan had typically maintained control through selecting company presidents and by placing his men on the boards of directors. A hard-fought war with railroad barons over the Northern Pacific forced Morgan, in 1901, into a new strategy of forming a holding company, Northern Securities, to control railroad stock. The state of Minnesota brought suit and President Theodore ROOSEVELT ordered his attorney general to enter the case in an effort to curb the excesses of big business. In 1904, the U.S. Supreme Court ruled the Northern Securities Company in violation of the Sherman Antitrust Act and forced its dissolution. Morgan formed another trust, U.S. STEEL in 1901, but kept prices high enough to foster competition. When the government attempted to shut down U.S. Steel, Morgan's competitors came to his defense.

Morgan's financial wizardry created a safe environment for investors. By means of stabilizing the flow of money, he created a foundation for the growth of the United States.

BIBLIOGRAPHY. Vincent P. Carosso, *The Morgans: Private International Bankers 1854-1913* (Harvard University Press, 1987); Ron Chernow, *The House of Morgan: An American Banking Dynasty* (Atlantic Monthly Press, 1990); Herbert L. Satterlee, *J. Pierpont Morgan* (Ayer, 1939); Andrew Sinclair, *Corsair: The Life of J. Pierpont Morgan* (Little, Brown, 1981); Jean Strouse, *Morgan: American Financier* (Random House, 1999).

CARYN E. NEUMANN, PH.D.
OHIO STATE UNIVERSITY

Morocco

THE KINGDOM OF MOROCCO borders Algeria to the east and southeast, the western Sahara desert to the south, the Atlantic Ocean to the west, and the Mediterranean Sea to the north. Casablanca is the largest city and economic hub; Rabat is the capital.

The population of Morocco is approximately 31.1 million. Arabic is the official language. Berber and French are also spoken, with French often used for business, government, and diplomatic purposes. The population is almost equally divided among urban and rural dwellers.

In 682, Arabs took control of Morocco, ending Byzantine rule. In the 1400s, Europeans set their sites on conquering the country. In the early 1900s, France and Spain divided Morocco. In 1956, Morocco gained independence from France and Spain and in 1961, King Hassan II took power and ruled until his death in 1999. Hassan's foreign policy often diverged from other Arab nations, and generally sided with the UNITED STATES and Western European nations. Greater liberalization and an increased sense of freedom characterized the 1990s, culminating with the creation of a bicameral legislature.

Industry accounts for about one-third of Morocco's GROSS DOMESTIC PRODUCT (GDP), services about half, and agriculture about 15 percent. Morocco's industrial sector includes the processing of raw materials for export and the manufacture of consumer goods for domestic purposes. Since the 1980s, the government has focused on privatizing operations and attracting private investment. Morocco's manufacturing sector is comprised predominantly of smaller enterprises and includes the production of textiles, wine, refined petroleum, footwear, and construction materials.

Morocco's currency is the dirham and its central bank, the Banque al-Maghrib, issues currency, regulates the credit supply, maintains the foreign currency reserves, oversees the government's specialized lending organizations, and regulates the commercial banking sector.

In 2002, Morocco's exports were valued at approximately $8.2 billion annually and its imports at $12.4 billion. Its leading exports are phosphates and fertilizers, foodstuffs, and minerals. Morocco's leading imports are semi-processed goods, machinery and equipment, consumer goods, fuel, and food. Its export/import partners include FRANCE, SPAIN, GERMANY, ITALY, the UNITED KINGDOM, INDIA, and the United States. In the 1990s, Morocco negotiated a formal association with the EUROPEAN UNION (EU), which calls for the establishment of a Euro-Mediterranean free-trade zone. Morocco has entered into other trade agreements to minimize its dependence on Europe.

Morocco continues its efforts to restrain government spending while enhancing private activity and foreign trade. Economists point out Morocco faces the challenges of managing its external debt and enabling freer trade with the EU.

BIBLIOGRAPHY. Abdellah Hammoudi, *Master and Disciple: The Cultural Foundations of Moroccan Authoritarianism* (University of Chicago Press, 1997); Rahma Bourquia and Susan Gilson Miller, ed., *In the Shadow of the Sultan: Culture, Power, and Politics in Morocco* (Harvard University Press, 1999); CIA *World Factbook* (2002).

S.J. RUBEL, J.D.
INDEPENDENT SCHOLAR

Mundell, Robert (1932–)

WINNER OF THE 1999 Nobel Prize in Economics, Robert A. Mundell attended the University of British Columbia and the University of Washington. He received his Ph.D. from the Massachusetts Institute of Technology in 1956 with a thesis on international capital movements.

The movement back and forth from floating to fixed EXCHANGE RATES of his native Canada was probably the reason that led Mundell to do his seminal work on the effects of monetary and fiscal policies in a the presence of free-capital mobility. This became known as the Mundell-Fleming model, which can be summarized as follows: If a country had a fixed exchange-rate system, monetary policy (i.e., changes in money supply in an economy) was completely ineffective, while fiscal policy (i.e., changes in the taxation system, government expenditures, and transfer payments) was effective at raising GROSS DOMESTIC PRODUCT and income. The results were reversed in the case of a floating exchange-rate regime.

Later, Mundell would postulate that any country could only have two of the following three variables: Free-capital mobility, fixed exchange-rate, and effective monetary policy. For instance, a country that decides to allow the inflow and outflow of capital and to stabilize its currency, loses its ability to adjust interest rates to fight inflation or recession.

Mundell's latest contribution is in the field of "optimum currency area." Under what circumstances should a country give up its currency and adopt another one? Mundell emphasized that an essential feature of an optimum currency area would be the high internal mobility of workers; that is the willingness and ability of labor to move from areas lacking jobs to regions where labor was in demand. This research is especially timely considering the adoption of the EURO currency in the EUROPEAN UNION and its inherent effects on worker mobility.

BIBLIOGRAPHY. Robert Mundell, *International Economics* (Macmillan, 1968); Rudiger Dornbusch, "Nobel Laureate Robert A. Mundell," www.mit.edu.

ARSÈNE A. AKA, PH.D.
CATHOLIC UNIVERSITY OF AMERICA

Munich Re

FOUNDED IN 1880 BY German entrepreneur Carl Thieme, Münchener Rückversicherungs-Gesellschaft AG (Munich Re) is now one of the largest worldwide players in the reinsurance business. Headquartered in Munich and represented by offices in 33 countries, the company holds investments of €162 billion (2001), with €36.1 billion of gross premiums written (2001) and a profit of €250 million (2000). In 2002, it ranked 79th on the Fortune Global 500 index. In 1889, Thieme also founded ALLIANZ AG, the large property and life insurer, and through crossholdings the two companies have retained close links until the present day.

Munich Re started to trade on the stock exchange only eight years after its foundation. It also started global activities in its first years. The company has been a pioneer in shaping particularly the nature of reinsurance business. Over time, it has ventured into other types of business such as asset management, export-credit insurance and, together with primary insurers, into agricultural and workers-compensation insurance.

The shares of Munich Re trade mainly in the German stock market's Xetra system. About 43 percent of stock is held by investors from the financial sector, the free float amounting to 57 percent.

BIBLIOGRAPHY. Annual Reports and Quarterly Reports, www.munichre.com; "Global 500: World's Largest Companies," *Fortune* (July 2002).

WOLFGANG GRASSL, PH.D.
HILLSDALE COLLEGE

Myrdal, Gunnar (1898–1987)

ONE OF THE DARKEST days for the reputation of the Nobel Prize in Economics came in 1974, when the Nobel Committee announced that the prize would be shared by Gunnar Myrdal and Friedrich von HAYEK. There was no doubt that each, individually, was worthy, but their political and economic views were at opposite poles, and the Nobel Prize that year solemnly memorialized the deep ideological rifts in the discipline. Myrdal championed an activist state while von Hayek wrote against big government.

Myrdal's early work on *Monetary Equilibrium*, that synthesized the oral tradition of Knut Wicksell with Myrdal's own contributions, created the distinction between *ex ante* and *ex post* that is now in every economics textbook. He criticized John Maynard KEYNES for "the attractive Anglo-Saxon kind of unnecessary originality," because the English economists didn't know German (*Monetary Equilibrium* was published in Swedish in 1931, in German in 1933, but English only in 1939—after Keynes' *General Theory* had swept the discipline).

Later, Myrdal studied the interactions of politics and economics in developed and developing countries. As an elected representative to the Swedish Senate, a board member of the Bank of Sweden, and executive secretary of the UNITED NATIONS Economic Commission for Europe, Myrdal was active in attempting to put his ideas into action. In 1944, he wrote a perceptive book on the great American problem of race: *An American Dilemma: The Negro Problem and Modern Democracy*. This applied Wicksell's business-cycle models of cumulative processes to social and political dynamics, bringing him closer to a new institutionalist position.

Myrdal's Nobel Prize lecture made a plea for the moral duty of Western democracies to assist developing countries, not just by simple income transfers but by facilitating basic reforms to reduce the inequalities in poor countries. Myrdal believed that an economist inevitably starts from certain valuations that colored any later analysis; therefore analysis should begin with an explicit statement of the value premises.

BIBLIOGRAPHY. Gunnar Myrdal, *An American Dilemma: The Negro Problem and Modern Democracy* (HarperCollins, 1962); Gunnar Myrdal, *Monetary Equilibrium* (Augustus Kelley, 1939); Gunnar Myrdal, Nobel Prize Lecture, www.nobel.se.

KEVIN R FOSTER, PH.D.
CITY COLLEGE OF NEW YORK

N

NAFTA

THE NORTH AMERICAN Free Trade Agreement (NAFTA) is a treaty between the UNITED STATES, MEXICO, and CANADA to facilitate commerce between the partner countries by eliminating or reducing tariffs and other non-tariff barriers to trade and investment. The treaty is seen as the nucleus from which to build hemispheric free trade in a Free Trade Area of the Americas (FTAA). Together with the EUROPEAN UNION (EU), it is the most prominent example of the regionalization of international trade, which is often seen as being at odds with global liberalization under the auspices of the WORLD TRADE ORGANIZATION (WTO).

History. NAFTA was signed by the governments—and subsequently ratified by the legislatures—of the United States, Mexico and Canada on December 17, 1992. It was preceded by a free trade agreement of 1989 between Canada and the United States. The treaty is a highly specific and voluminous document, implementation of which began on January 1, 1994. Side agreements were worked out to correct perceived abuses in labor and the environment in Mexico. On the basis of the successful conclusion of the treaty in December 1994, heads of state of 34 American countries (all except Cuba) agreed in principle at the Hemispheric Summit in Miami that negotiations for a Free-Trade Area of the Americas (FTAA) will be completed no later than 2005. The choice between these two alternatives was deliberately left open in order to achieve unanimity. One alternative, favored by the United States, would be the accession of all other American countries to NAFTA; the second route, supported by Brazil and other Latin American countries, proposes the foundation of a free trade area by keeping intact subregional arrangements.

Treaty provisions. NAFTA provides for elimination of all tariffs on industrial products traded between the signatories within a period of 10 or 15 years. Tariffs on half of the import categories were eliminated immediately while all agricultural provisions will be implemented by the year 2008. In addition, NAFTA eliminated or reduced non-tariff trade barriers (such as quotas or sanitary measures) and added free trade in other important sectors such as investment; trade in services, intellectual property, COMPETITION, the cross-border movement of business persons, and government procurement.

Air transport, telephone and basic telecommunication services, and government services are explicitly excluded from liberalization. The treaty also makes concessions to special national interests, for example with an exemption protecting Canadian cultural industries or by U.S.-sponsored patent regimes in pharmaceuticals. It also created new institutions charged with executing or supervising the treaty: the Free Trade Commission, the Commission for Labor Cooperation, the North American Commission for Environmental Cooperation, the North American Development Bank, and a dispute settlement mechanism which may utilize the services of other international arbitration panels. With the exception of the last-mentioned, these institutions have very limited power and resources.

Trade law. The NAFTA treaty creates regional trade law and institutions to implement it. In addition to material norms relating to the freedom of commerce, the treaty also instituted procedural guarantees, particularly recourse to international arbitration panels (one of which is the International Center for the Settlement of Investment Disputes—ICSID) the rulings of which cannot be appealed in any national courts.

One of the disputed legal issues is that of the direct effects of NAFTA in domestic law. Mexican and U.S. constitutional law permit treaties to have such effect, the Canadian constitution precludes it. However, the United States has expressly legislated against direct applicability in domestic courts (Article 102 NAFTA Implementation Act).

Another disputed issue is the investor-to-state dispute settlement mechanism of Chapter 11 of NAFTA. In *The Loewen Group, Inc. v. United States* (ICSID Case No. ARB(AF)/98/3), the claimant, a Canadian operator of funeral homes, alleged violations of three provisions of NAFTA—the anti-discrimination (or equal protection) principles set forth in Article 1102, the minimum standard of treatment (or due process) required under Article 1105, and the prohibition against uncompensated expropriation set forth in Article 1110. In effect, the claimant held the United States liable for a highly controversial judgment by a Mississippi state court under Article 105 of NAFTA, which makes federal states responsible for actions of its constituent units, and under Article 1105, which gives investors "full protection and security."

The United States objected to the jurisdiction and competence of the ICSID tribunal. In a decision issued on January 9, 2001, the tribunal rejected one of the United States' objections to jurisdiction, and decided to hear the other objections with the merits of the case. The United States continues to reject the tribunal's jurisdiction over the claims and denies that any of the alleged measures violated the NAFTA.

Canada also seems to have principled objections to the application of Chapter 11. In the United States, particularly the guarantees against expropriation under Article 1110, which have been interpreted to override national law such as zoning ordinances and to give foreign investors rights to compensation against takings by U.S. authorities, have become the focus of a heated debate over national sovereignty versus supranational contractual duties. In a similar lawsuits, a NAFTA tribunal has awarded California waste disposal company Metalclad Corp. damages after the governor of the Mexican state of San Luis Potosí and a town council had refused to allow the company to open a toxic waste site, which the court interpreted as an illegal taking by authorities. It is likely that Chapter 11 of NAFTA will have to be adapted, failing which changes will have to be made to the U.S. tort system.

NAFTA law contains other innovations (and pitfalls) the business community should know about. For example, different from U.S. domestic law (19CFR102 of 1999) which defines a product as originating in the country in which it has undergone a "substantial transformation," Articles 311ff. of NAFTA mark a product as originating from where it was converted from one product classification to another, which leads to the necessity of having to mark products coming from NAFTA and non-NAFTA countries differently.

NAFTA business. During the implementation period to date (2003), trade between the treaty partners has increased significantly, and particularly Mexico has experienced a surge in foreign investment inflow. By 2004, already 99 percent of all products will be traded freely, and liberalization will be completed by 2008. Between 1994 and 2002, U.S. exports to Canada grew by 40.5 percent while imports grew by 64 percent. U.S. exports to Mexico grew by 91.9 percent while imports grew by 172.2 percent. It is often argued that Canada may have gained least from the treaty, since it had already had a free-trade arrangement with the United States, and trades relatively little with Mexico.

NAFTA (390 million consumers and GNP of $9.2 trillion) has created the world's second-largest free market, after the European Economic Area (EEA), the free-trade area of the EU and three EFTA countries (385 million consumers and GNP of $8.6 trillion), which accounts for nearly 50 percent of world trade. With the accession of ten countries to EU membership in 2004, EEA will continue to remain the largest trading bloc and will also lead in GROSS NATIONAL PRODUCT (GNP). However, implementation of FTAA is likely to shift leadership in world output, if not in trade, again to the Americas.

NAFTA has caused many firms to adopt an integrated North American strategy by merging the operations of the three signatory countries. This permits savings in sourcing, production, and management. Also, firms from outside the region increasingly regard NAFTA as one trading region. This has, for example, the effect of European companies setting up production operations in Mexico, where factor costs are comparatively lowest, and selling final products in the United States and Canada, where purchasing power is highest.

Since 1965, Mexico has allowed duty-free imports of machinery, components, and equipment as long as at least 80 percent of final products are exported. NAFTA has further accelerated the development of this industry, within an in-bond free trade zone along the border with the United States. Many U.S. companies have shifted all or part of their production to Mexico. Through Mexico, and also through Canada, third-country businesses also have free access to NAFTA markets subject to local content requirements. For example, Japanese carmaker HONDA produces minivans in Ontario, Canada, for export to the United States and Europe.

Policy. NAFTA has had its advocates and opponents since the inception of negotiations. While most business interests have supported the trade agreement, many labor groups and environmentalists have opposed it. Opponents include also economic nationalists and isolationists as well as determined free-trade activists objecting to any inter-governmental (and particularly multilateral) agreements on liberalization, which they would rather see negotiated bilaterally, or regard as dispensable if countries liberalize their markets unilaterally. In the United States, opposition to NAFTA has lessened in recent years but is still vocal on occasion, as it was in 2002 during the debates on presidential "fast track" authority to negotiate further trade agreements.

One of the most frequently advanced arguments has been that NAFTA would shift less-qualified jobs from the United States to Mexico, particularly to businesses along the border—the "giant sucking sound" argument, after a phrase coined by 1992 presidential candidate Ross Perot. In actuality, employment effects have been relatively small while the increase in trade has been enormous. The growth of exports and imports between the United States and Mexico rose more than twice as much as trade with the rest of the world, producing significant regional gains as predicted by the theory of comparative advantage.

Economic integration of free trade areas is restricted to the exchange of goods and services and the opening of capital markets, which is regarded as incidental to open products markets. Common external tariffs, which are the hallmark of customs unions, or free markets for factors of production, which are the hallmark of economic unions, have never been intended under NAFTA. However, policy questions arise as to what exactly open-product markets imply. Sale of personally delivered (or "embodied") services across borders finds its limitation with immigration restrictions, required training standards, or national professional licensing rules. For example, under the treaty, the United States was required in 2001 to open its borders to Mexican trucking, whose cost is substantially lower than that of the American trucking industry. Political lobbying by the latter regarding safety considerations has prevented the opening of transport markets for Mexican operators, and the case has become a matter of litigation between the two governments. Though there has been some movement toward permitting Mexican trucks to operate in the United States, final resolution of the issue is still pending (2003).

The next major development in western-hemisphere trade will be the completion of FTAA. In parallel, Mexico concluded a free trade agreement with the European Union in 2000 while Canada signed an agreement with the Andean Group in 1999. In the discussion about FTAA, arguments about gains from trade clearly predominate. Currently, U.S. exports to NAFTA partners are about four times as great as exports to the rest of the hemisphere, and imports from NAFTA partners are five-and-a-half times as great. However, there are still several contentious issues, particularly agriculture, investment, and government procurement. Also, there are hardly any constituencies in the United States for an extension of NAFTA or FTAA beyond a free-trade zone, while many other countries in the Americas would also like to see a liberalization of factor movements, particularly of U.S. immigration rules.

Occasionally, plans for a more ambitious regional integration are proposed, such as the creation of a North American Union modeled after the successful example of the European Union. The president of Mexico, Vicente Fox Quesada, has boldly made this proposal. However, at the moment it seems that in the United States there is not sufficient support for any deeper integration than a free-trade area, while even the path to FTAA is still wrought with political difficulties. In addition, there are arguments critical of further regional integration if this imperils the success of a worldwide liberalization of markets as pursued under the WTO.

BIBLIOGRAPHY. Jeffery D. Abbott and Robert T. Moran, *Uniting North American Business: NAFTA Best Practices* (Butterworth-Heinemann, 2002); Maxwell A. Cameron, *The Making of NAFTA: How the Deal Was Done* (Cornell University Press, 2000); Peter Hakim, Robert E. Litan and Strobe Talbott, eds., *The Future of North American Integration: Beyond NAFTA* (Brookings Institution, 2002); Frederick W. Mayer, *Interpreting NAFTA* (Columbia University Press, 1998); Robert A. Pastor, *Toward a North American Community: Lessons from the Old World for the New* (Institute for International Economics, 2001); Jerry M. Rosenberg, ed., *Encyclopedia of the North American Free Trade Agreement, the New American Community, and Latin-American Trade* (Greenwood, 1995); Willem Thorbecke and Christian Eigen-Zucchi, "Did NAFTA Cause a 'Giant Sucking Sound'?," *Journal of Labor Research* (v.23, 2002); NAFTA Secretariat, www.NAFTA-sec-alena.org; Free Trade Area of the Americas, www.ftaa-alca.org.

WOLFGANG GRASSL
HILLSDALE COLLEGE

NASDAQ

THE NATIONAL ASSOCIATION of Securities Dealers Automated Quotation (NASDAQ) is the world's largest electronic stock market. Unlike traditional markets, which trade at one central location, NASDAQ trades are conducted over an innovative computer network, thus enabling real-time market data to be sent to users worldwide. NASDAQ's unique open floor allows an unlimited number of participants to trade—estimated at more than 1.3 million users in 83 countries.

One of NASDAQ's greatest strengths is the role the market plays in helping young companies transition to public ownership. As a result, NASDAQ is comprised of innovative technology companies that have, for the most part, remained loyal to the electronic stock market as they have matured. For that reason, NASDAQ's top companies, such as Microsoft, Intel, and Oracle, were once considered high risks, but now dominate the market.

Formation of a new trading system. NASDAQ formally began operations on February 5, 1971, though planning for such a system had begun in the 1960s. NASDAQ used computers to centralize information—at a then-whopping cost of $25 million—thus ensuring that traders had the best information available as they bought and sold stocks.

Prior to the arrival of NASDAQ, companies that went public through the Initial Public Offering (IPO) process traded via telephone via the Over the Counter (OTC) Bulletin Board. As these companies grew and matured, they eventually joined the AMERICAN STOCK EXCHANGE (AMEX), and then graduated to the big leagues of the NEW YORK STOCK EXCHANGE (NYSE).

Once on the NYSE, a single trade specialist on the floor of the exchange determined the company's trading price. Many observers believed that this was a tyrannical system, particularly irksome after the stock market's numerous corrections and collapses. The process of graduating from IPO to NYSE was hierarchical and though steeped in history, somewhat archaic in the 20th century. A young company, however, had no viable alternative if it planned to have its stock widely traded.

Gordon Macklin served as National Association of Securities Dealers (NASD) president and forged the way for the NASDAQ. Rather than rely on a single stock exchange specialist, Macklin foresaw a trading system that linked buyers and sellers electronically, thus opening the bidding process to people on computer terminals across the globe. The traders would use computers to guarantee efficient pricing, thus eliminating the need for traders to be in the same room or debate sales over the phone. Initially, more than 800 securities dealers subscribed to NASDAQ, which presented information on 2,400 unlisted securities.

A core group of more than 500 financial firms, called market makers, make up the core of NASDAQ's market infrastructure. These firms trade on NASDAQ and thus act as distributors. They put their own money to listed securities, and then distribute the shares to buyers. A key to this system is that the market makers are required to list their bid and ask prices at all times, therefore giving participants access to the necessary information to make an informed decision. Since they put their own money into NASDAQ, the market makers guarantee that trades are made quickly and that enough buyers and sellers are trading.

Within a year, NASDAQ traded an average of 8 million shares a day, already besting the volume of the American Stock Exchange (AMEX). Taking full advantage of the burgeoning computer industry, NASDAQ used technology to improve the information flow between traders. By 1984, the market capitalization of the largest 1,000 NASDAQ companies reached $174 billion.

1987 stock market crash. Joseph Hardiman, Macklin's successor as head of the NASD, had an inauspicious beginning to his tenure—the October, 1987 stock market crash, in which NASDAQ fell 11.4 percent and the Dow dropped 508 points in one day. "Black Monday" revealed NASDAQ weaknesses. Hardiman quickly moved to address the challenges.

Hardiman worked to solidify and strengthen the exchange, particularly for large companies. Hardiman wanted to eliminate the second-class status that enveloped NASDAQ and the other smaller exchanges, all of whom stood in the shadow of the larger and more powerful NYSE. In an effort to elevate the prestige for companies listed on NASDAQ, Hardiman enacted tougher entrance standards and made it more difficult for under-performing companies to remain on NASDAQ. The weak penny stocks that symbolized fragility were removed from the board.

The fact that the market rebounded so quickly after the 1987 chaos has played an important psychological role for many investors. Because the general recovery started so soon, they believe that the market always recovers. This phenomenon has been seen in investment trends on NASDAQ the past several years. For example, when the composite dropped 5 percent in July 2000, U.S. investors responded by sinking more than $17 billion into stocks, up 40 percent from the same time the previous year.

Growth of NASDAQ. Hardiman's reforms solidified NASDAQ and enabled the market to experience phenomenal growth. Taking on a kind of renegade or upstart public persona, NASDAQ became the primary vehicle for companies to stage IPOs. For instance, in the first nine months of 1994, 425 companies went public via NASDAQ, while only 50 did the same on the NYSE and a mere 11 on AMEX.

Despite the steps Hardiman took to make the NASDAQ exchange more reputable and viable, the NYSE still ruled Wall Street. Market cap of the NASDAQ 1,000 skyrocketed to $624 billion in 1994, but lagged far behind the NYSE, which boasted a total market cap of $4.5 trillion.

The NASD president could, however, take pleasure in the speed that NASDAQ companies hit important financial milestones. In the mid-1990s, there were more than 125 companies listed on the exchange with valuations of more than $1 billion. Many of the business world's most exciting and innovative enterprises were listed on NASDAQ, including Microsoft, Cisco Systems, Intel, and Oracle.

When NASDAQ celebrated its 25-year anniversary on February 8, 1996, 543 million shares were traded, more than 60 times the shares traded daily in 1971. More impressive was that in that quarter-century span investors were rewarded with an 11-fold return.

Because NASDAQ relied on technological innovation and was IPO-friendly, companies that had similar ideas about technology gravitated to it. Many young tech companies needed a certain amount of nurturing. NASDAQ gave them access to capital and buyers willing to bet on the future. By 1996, technology companies comprised nearly 20 percent of NASDAQ and 40 percent of its $1.2 trillion market capitalization.

Not all observers were enamored with NASDAQ's success. In the mid-1990s, then-SEC (SECURITIES AND EXCHANGE COMMISSION) Chairman Arthur Levitt Jr. criticized the exchange because its traders, in his view, made too much money and charged too much for individual investors to participate. Levitt thought that NASDAQ should operate more like the other markets and become less of a freewheeling environment.

Levitt and the U.S. Antitrust Division also launched an investigation when an academic analysis of NASDAQ charged that its dealers were involved in a widespread price-fixing effort. Although economists challenged the report, it set off a number of lawsuits and intensified President Bill CLINTON's administration's efforts to reform the exchange. The SEC hoped to regulate NASDAQ trading, thus increasing investor power and introducing price stability.

These regulatory efforts attracted media attention, but did not slow the masses of investors (large and small) flocking to the upstart market. In 1995, the NASDAQ composite index shot up almost 40 percent, while share volume surpassed 100 billion. That same year, NASDAQ also upgraded its infrastructure to accommodate the increased activity. By sinking $170 million into its computer systems, the market ensured that it could handle one-day volume of 1 billion shares.

In 1997, Hardiman retired and turned over the reigns to Frank G. Zarb, the former CEO of consulting firm Alexander & Alexander Services and investment firm Smith Barney. Zarb recognized the power of the "new economy" of the late 1990s and pushed for further technological innovations that would prepare NASDAQ for the rush to trade online. He also continued the efforts at establishing a global trading center.

The dot-com boom and bust. In 1999, benefiting from the boom in internet stocks, NASDAQ became the largest stock market in the United States by dollar volume. Its domestic strength bolstered an aggressive expansion program into markets around the world. One such agreement set up a subsidiary in JAPAN, while other efforts were directed at European markets.

In early 2000, the organization signed deals with the London, Québec, and Frankfurt stock exchanges to create joint ventures using the NASDAQ brand. The creation of a 24-hours-a-day exchange took a step closer to reality.

Internally, NASDAQ changed significantly during the dot-com boom—the heyday of the "new economy." NASD members voted to restructure the organization in 2000. As a result, NASDAQ was spun-off into a shareholder-owned, for-profit company. Leading business observers and pundits viewed the electronic market to be the most important mechanism for pumping money into the economy, in turn leading to countless jobs and new companies being created. For example, the NASDAQ reached the 2,500 milestone in late January, 1999. At the end of the same year, the figure jumped to 4,000.

Between 1997 and 2000, nearly 1,700 companies were taken public. These offerings raised $316.5 billion. On March 10, 2000, NASDAQ closed at 5,048, its 16th record high of the year, after a total gain of 86 percent in 1999.

Unfortunately, the tremendous amount of money being pumped into NASDAQ had a dark side as well. The almost daily euphoria of IPOs made NASDAQ a haven for get-rich-quick schemes and investors looking to cash in on the mania. Day-traders entered the market en masse, jumping in and out of stocks at an alarming pace, and attempting to profit on fluctuations in the market. They specialized in cashing out—or having a zero balance—at the end of each trading day.

Ordinary people, who would be considered fiscally conservative in any other circumstances, viewed NASDAQ as a national hobby, rather than a complicated market. Millions of people that had little business in the market began opening online accounts. With little knowledge of market fundamentals, these people fed a speculative bubble that soon burst.

In early March 2001, NASDAQ fell below the 2,000 mark for the first time in 27 months. In one day, NASDAQ dropped 6 percent (192.39 points), marking a yearlong fall that reduced the market by 60 percent.

The dot-com bubble burst with alarming efficiency. Within 10 weeks of hitting its all-time high, the NASDAQ market fell 37 percent, eliminating $2.3 trillion in market value. Internet stalwarts saw their stock prices drop 90 percent or more in a matter of months. Amazon.com, the online bookseller and marketplace, had its stock reach $105 in late 1999, despite having never posted a profit. After the market fell, the stock traded around $10 a share. Yahoo!, the ubiquitous online directory, dropped 93 percent from its peak price of $237.50 a share in early 2000.

NASDAQ companies lost trillions of dollars during the dot-com catastrophe, but those that survived were fortunate. Thousands of others went bankrupt, leading to devastating effects for individual investors, who were often left holding the bag.

The dot-com collapse seriously weakened the national economy at a time when many people assumed that the stock market would continue to rise indefinitely. The United States fell into a RECESSION, though many economists and observers refused to label it as such. As a result of the faltering economy, millions of people were laid-off in the early years of the 21st century. Only record-low interest rates and increased consumer-credit debt propped up the economy and averted the possibility of a worldwide depression.

The terrorist attacks on the World Trade Center complex and the Pentagon in September, 2001 and subsequent military actions in Afghanistan and Iraq further undermined efforts at strengthening the economy. At the same time, millions of traders fled NASDAQ and anything that hinted of technology or the internet.

Rather than being considered the new masters of the universe, technology leaders faced public ridicule for not realizing that they were riding a bubble soon to burst. Investment bankers such as Mary Meeker and Frank Quattrone, who fueled so much NASDAQ trading with their optimistic statements about the strength of internet companies, went into virtual seclusion.

The present and future NASDAQ. NASDAQ has capitalized on the technology introduced by its member companies to increase its own visibility. The market's Web site (www.nasdaq.com) is one of the most popular financial sites on the internet, averaging about 7 million page views per day. In addition, NASDAQ opened MarketSite Tower in the heart of New York City's Times Square. The Tower is seven-stories high and holds the largest video screen in the world. The dazzling site and broadcast studio provides the perfect backdrop for news stations CNBC, CNNfn, Bloomberg, and CBS Market-Watch to televise from on trading days, ensuring great publicity for the market and its companies.

On May 12, 2003, Robert Greifeld was elected president and chief executive officer of NASDAQ, replacing Hardwick (Wick) Simmons, who had been named CEO in early 2001. Greifeld joined the market from SunGard Data Systems, a global Information Technology provider. Simmons' tenure was tumultuous, including the September 11 terrorist attacks and a series of corporate accounting scandals (such as ENRON, Global Crossing, Tyco and WORLDCOM) that rocked people's faith in the stock market.

Despite the furor over the rise and fall of the dot-coms, NASDAQ has matured and gained a solid foothold in its ongoing battle with the NYSE. In little more than three decades, NASDAQ has grown from a far-fetched idea into one of America's great economic success stories.

BIBLIOGRAPHY. John Cassidy, *Dot.con: The Greatest Story Ever Sold* (HarperCollins, 2002); Robert J. Flaherty and Benjamin R. Kaplan, "Twenty-Five Candles," *Equities* (v.44/3, 1994); John Steele Gordon, *The Great Game: The Emergence of Wall Street as a World Power 1653-2000* (Scribner, 1999); Mark Ingebretsen, *Nasdaq: A History of the Market That Changed the World* (Prima, 2002).

BOB BATCHELOR
INDEPENDENT SCHOLAR

Nash, John (1928–)

AMERICAN MATHEMATICIAN and 1994 Nobel laureate, John Forbes Nash, Jr., was born in Bluefield, West Virginia. He graduated from Carnegie Mellon University in 1948 with B.S. and M.S. degrees in mathematics, and from Princeton University in 1950 with a Ph.D. degree in mathematics. His 27-page dissertation, "Non-Cooperative Games," became the foundation of the modern analysis of strategic interaction, or GAME THEORY.

After obtaining his Ph.D., Nash held instructor positions at Princeton University and later at the Massachusetts Institute of Technology (MIT), where he was tenured in 1958 at the age of only 29. During these years, he also held various summer positions at the RAND Corporation in Santa Monica, California, the U.S Air Force's think tank concerned with strategic issues. At the time, RAND officials were eager to apply Nash's ideas to the military and diplomatic challenges of the Cold War.

In 1957, Nash married Alicia Larde, one of his former graduate students at MIT. Around the end of the 1950s, he was diagnosed with paranoid schizophrenia. Nash's illness interrupted his personal and academic life. After resigning from MIT, Nash traveled through several European countries before returning to Princeton, New Jersey, where he lived a quiet life, spending his time hanging around the university campus. Although he was not holding an academic position, he privately continued working on mathematical problems.

In the early 1990s, Nash experienced a rare remission or recovery from his illness. By then, his work on non-cooperative games, which he undertook as a graduate student, had transformed much of modern social science. Game theory was now a striving field within economics. Borne out of the ideas contained in Nash's doctoral thesis, a host of new results and methods has been developed and successfully applied to innumerable strategic problems. For his seminal work on non-cooperative game theory, Nash was awarded the Bank of

Sweden Prize in Economic Sciences in Memory of Alfred Nobel in 1994. He shared the prize with John HARSANYI of Hungary and Reinhard SELTEN of Germany.

Game theory and Nash Equilibrium. Nash encountered game theory as a graduate student at Princeton. A popular book by John von Neumann and Oskar Morgenstern, *Theory of Games and Economic Behavior,* contained the first formalization of a general theory suitable for the study of conflict of interest between individuals, countries, or organizations. As a metaphor for a real-life strategic situation, a game can be either cooperative or non-cooperative. In a cooperative game, binding agreements between individuals (players) are always possible, while a non-cooperative game excludes this possibility unless explicitly modeled.

Nash is credited with having been the first to introduce a clear formal distinction between cooperative and non-cooperative games. However, von Neumann and Morgenstern's book already contained a treatment of a special class of non-cooperative games, two-person zero-sum games. These are games with two players whose interests are diametrically opposed. Many real-life strategic situations are in the realm of non-cooperative games, yet involve more than two players and some common interest among them. At the time Nash entered graduate school, game theory was silent as to how such games should be approached.

In his thesis, Nash defined an equilibrium point in a general, non-cooperative game as a profile of strategies taken by the players that is self-enforcing, in the sense that no player wants to change her strategy if all others adhere to their equilibrium strategies. This construct is now called a Nash Equilibrium. In it, all players' expectations are fulfilled and their chosen strategies are optimal. If one assumes that games are played by rational players, then prediction of the outcome of any game is basically a search for a Nash Equilibrium.

Nash Equilibrium may involve the use of mixed strategies, through which players select randomly among their available actions with certain probabilities. For instance, the pitcher in a baseball game delivers the ball with various speeds and various spins, as predictability would be to this player's disadvantage. In his famous existence proof, Nash showed that if one allows for the possibility of such mixed strategies, an equilibrium point exists in all games with a finite number of players and strategies.

Historically, it is interesting to note that the early economists Cournot, Stackelberg, and Bertrand anticipated Nash's Equilibrium concept in their well-known oligopoly models. Nevertheless, these works remained special to their particular contexts, and did not attempt a generalization of their results to the theory of non-cooperative games the way Nash did.

Nash wrote many other highly acclaimed papers in economics and mathematics. Within the theory of cooperative games, he introduced a fundamental and widely applied solution for bargaining problems, the Nash Bargaining Solution. He further led an effort to base cooperative game theory on results from non-cooperative game theory, a project later called the Nash Program.

BIBLIOGRAPHY. S. Nasar, *A Beautiful Mind* (Touchstone, 1998); J.F. Nash, "Equilibrium Points in N-Person Games," *Proceedings of the National Academy of Sciences* (v.36, 1950); J.F. Nash, "The Bargaining Problem," *Econometrica* (v.18, 1950); J.F. Nash, (1951), "Non-Cooperative Games," *Annals of Mathematics* (v.54, 1951); J.F. Nash, "Autobiographical Essay," (The Nobel Foundation, 1994); J. von Neumann and O. Morgenstern, *Theory of Games and Economic Behavior* (Princeton University Press, 1944).

TILMAN KLUMPP, PH.D.
INDIANA UNIVERSITY, BLOOMINGTON

nationalization

THE ASSUMPTION OF PRIVATE assets by a government or an entity controlled by a government is referred to as nationalization. It differs from confiscation. When property or assets are confiscated, former owners receive no compensation. However, when a government nationalizes assets, former owners do receive compensation. The level of compensation usually does not reflect the assets' market value and is either predetermined by the government or negotiated with the former owners.

Nationalization also differs from eminent domain. Although the process is similar, the purpose differs. Governments use eminent domain to seize property for a specific purpose and compensate former owners. For example, a government might use eminent domain to acquire land to build a road or public building, rather than seizing an entire industry or business sector as is done through nationalization.

Nationalization is often politically motivated. A national government may decide that ownership of some or all of industry within the country is controlled by too few people and use nationalization to protect the nation from the power of a select few.

Nationalization may also be motivated by national security. To protect assets, business sectors, and industries vital to a nation's survival, a national government assumes their ownership and management. This often occurs during a period of war or when the independence of the nation is threatened. Governments may also use nationalization as a vehicle to protect against foreign ownership that might jeopardize the sovereignty of the country.

Nationalization is often associated with the politics of SOCIALISM. In socialism and the related political system of communism, the country's assets are held in common by the government to avoid the rise in power and influence of the middle-class business community.

Newly established nations also use nationalization after they gain independence from their former colonial rulers. The newly formed governments use nationalization to exert control over the nation, guide the growth of business and industry, restrict the power of the former colonial nation, and establish sovereignty.

Nationalization in the 20th century was used for political and economic reasons. The RUSSIAN REVOLUTION of 1917 brought a communist government to power and created the SOVIET UNION. The Soviet leader, Vladimir LENIN, established a mixed economy in which large businesses were nationalized along with the companies that developed the nation's natural resources, while small businesses remained in private hands. The Soviets used nationalization to eliminate foreign influence, to gain the maximum benefit out of consolidated business operations, and to eliminate the Russian business class, possible opponents of the new government.

The Mexican Revolution of 1917 and subsequent nationalization of industry in MEXICO in 1938 set an example for other countries in the 20th century. The most vital foreign investments nationalized by Mexico were American petroleum investments. The United States government recognized the right of Mexico to nationalize, but Secretary of State Cordell Hull declared that "No government is entitled to expropriate private property, for whatever purpose, without provision for prompt, adequate, and effective payment." Hull's statement of principle guided the U.S. government's actions whenever Americans' assets were nationalized

The 1929 stock-market crash and subsequent worldwide Great DEPRESSION brought a wave of nationalization in Europe as a way to deal with the economic crisis. Many European countries nationalized banks and insurance companies to maintain the nations' financial structure and protect themselves against total financial collapse. The United States' response to the Great Depression under President Franklin D. ROOSEVELT'S NEW DEAL programs did not include nationalization. When confronted with the closing of American banks in 1933, Roosevelt used the power of the government to assist private banks but did not nationalize them.

During WORLD WAR II, any nations seized control of business and industry to direct their wartime economy. Great Britain nationalized industries to control production and direct industrial output to the war effort. The United States created war production boards and worked in cooperation with industry to achieve wartime production goals instead of nationalizing assets.

After World War II, the number of nations nationalizing their economies expanded. Eastern European nations, starting with Czechoslovakia, nationalized industries in 1945 and 1946. As Eastern European countries adopted communist governments, they copied the Soviet Union's pattern of nationalization. In Western Europe, nationalization was a response to the decline of economic importance and a way to preserve a measure of control. FRANCE and Great Britain nationalized natural resource operations like coal- and iron-ore-mining as well as the steel and food-processing industries. Rebuilding European economies from the devastation caused by World War II required greater control and coordination. Consolidation of unprofitable operations also saved jobs.

Nationalization became synonymous with the socialization of European economies in the second half of the 20th century. SWEDEN became the prime example of a socialized democracy and used nationalization to create a mixed economy. France and Great Britain extended nationalization to service industries including broadcasting, banking, and telecommunications.

Former colonies nationalized industry during this period. In the 1950s, EGYPT nationalized the SUEZ COMPANY, provoking France and Great Britain to send military forces to the area. In 1951, the Iranian government nationalized the Anglo-Iranian Oil Company. Throughout Africa and South America, governments nationalized foreign and domestic investments to consolidate power and to foster competition with stronger economies. New Asian governments like the People's Republic of CHINA, Democratic Republic of VIETNAM, and Republic of INDIA used nationalization to further their political goals.

In the late 1970s, deregulation gained momentum in Western economics as the process of nationalization lost favor. Most nationalized firms lost money and failed to innovate. Consequently, they were unable to compete in the global marketplace. In the last two decades of the 20th century, PRIVATIZATION replaced nationalization, taking assets previously nationalized and selling them to private interests either in whole or as components. Funds raised through the sale of these assets were returned to national treasuries. With the election of a Conservative Party in Britain in 1979, under the leadership of Prime Minister Margaret THATCHER, the British government began aggressively privatizing. The privatization movement started with state-owned enterprises like British Steel and British Airways and moved on to firms like British Telecom and electric and water utilities. The privatization movement spread from Britain to the European continent as many European members of the EUROPEAN UNION (Common Market) prepared for increased competition from an open market.

The collapse of the communist governments of Eastern Europe and the demise of the Soviet Union in the late

1980s and early 1990s also brought a wave of privatization. New non-communist governments experimented with voucher programs to return some of the value in formerly nationalized firms to their citizens. Some governments resorted to direct sale of assets to foreign investors as a means of strengthening national governments and protecting employment through foreign infusions of capital and innovation.

In the 21st century there are still calls for nationalization as a way to preserve some industries from total collapse but nationalization as a widely accepted economic process has fallen out of favor.

BIBLIOGRAPHY. Cary W. Blankenship, "Dissertation Nationalization of Industry in Czechoslovakia in 1945: Impact on the United States, Britain, France and the Soviet Union" (unpublished, 2002); Martin Chick, *Industrial Policy in Britain, 1945–1951: Economic Planning, Nationalisation and the Labour Government* (Cambridge University Press, 1998); Robert Gilpin, *The Political Economy of International Relations* (Princeton University Press, 1987); Robert L. Heilbroner, *The Nature and Logic of Capitalism* (W.W. Norton & Company, 1985); G. L. Reid and K. Allen, *Nationalized Industries* (Penguin., 1973); Tony Prosser, *Nationalized Industries* (Clarendon Press, 1986); Samuel L. Sharp, *Nationalization of Key Industries in Eastern Europe* (Foundation for Foreign Relations, 1946).

CARY W. BLANKENSHIP, PH.D.
TENNESSEE STATE UNIVERSITY

NEC

NEC PLAYED AN IMPORTANT role in attracting foreign capital and technology to facilitate JAPAN's early 20th-century industrialization. Nippon Electric Company was founded in 1899 as a joint venture with the American firm Western Electric. The company specialized in telephones and switching systems during its first two decades. In 1925, NEC imported Western Electric broadcasting equipment for Radio Tokyo (later NHK) and began its own electron tube development program.

As Japan's overseas empire grew in the 1930s, NEC was a leading provider of communications infrastructure. The company supplied China Xinjing Station with 100kW radio broadcasting equipment in 1934. It assisted the Ministry of Communications with long-distance telephone line carrier equipment in 1937. NEC successfully tested microwave multiplex communications for the first time in Japan in 1944.

After Japan's defeat in WORLD WAR II, NEC was a leader in the country's economic and technological recovery. In 1950, NEC began development of transistor technology. With the outbreak of the KOREAN WAR, NEC signed an export contract for radio-broadcasting equipment with Korea. In 1954, NEC began its research on computers and introduced its first all-transistor computer in 1959.

During Japan's 1960s rapid economic growth, NEC cooperated closely with the Japanese government to develop the computer industry. The government provided low-interest loans and other SUBSIDIES. Japanese firms were also pressured to buy domestic computers whenever possible. In this protected environment, NEC began its integrated circuit research in 1960, entered a technology-sharing agreement with Honeywell in 1962, and provided ground equipment for the trans-Pacific broadcast of the 1964 Tokyo Olympics Games.

At the same time, NEC expanded its overseas operations. Nippon Electric New York was incorporated in 1963. In the late 1960s and early 1970s, NEC sold communications equipment in South America, Europe, and CHINA. In the early 1980s, NEC acquired American high-tech companies and began producing semiconductors and computers in the United States. In the face of increased competition, many American firms complained that Japanese government support gave NEC an unfair advantage. This criticism subsided somewhat with the 1990s Japanese RECESSION and American information-technology boom.

NEC is a worldwide manufacturer and distributor of semiconductors, computers, mobile telephones, network equipment, and internet services. Net sales for 2002 were $38.3 billion, ranking NEC as the 85th largest company in the world.

BIBLIOGRAPHY. Marie Anchordoguy, *Computers Inc.* (Harvard University Press, 1989); NEC, Annual Report, History, www.nec.com; Clyde Prestowitz, *Trading Places* (Tuttle, 1988); "Global 500: World's Largest Companies," *Fortune* (July 2002).

JOHN SAGERS, PH.D.
LINFIELD COLLEGE

Nestlé

NESTLÉ WAS FOUNDED by Henri Nestlé in 1867 in Vevey, SWITZERLAND, where the company headquarters remains in the 2000s. Henri Nestlé, a trained pharmacist, was searching for an alternative to breast milk for infants who were premature or whose mothers could not breast-feed. Thus, Nestlé began life as a producer of infant formula/cereal.

Since then, Nestlé has become the largest food company in the world, via internal growth and aggressive external acquisitions. Particularly since WORLD WAR II, Nestlé has expanded beyond its primary "milk-coffee-chocolate" focus to encompass a far broader food product range, although products using either coffee or cocoa as the primary input still account for approximately 40 percent of group profits. Nestlé is also one of the world's oldest multinational enterprises, having first expanded beyond its national borders to produce in the UNITED KINGDOM and GERMANY by 1874, an early strategic necessity given the small market size of the Swiss market.

Nestlé is currently the world leader in mineral water (acquiring Vittel in 1969, Perrier in 1992, and San Pellegrino in 1997), instant coffee (having developed the first soluble coffee in 1938) with a 56 percent global market share, powdered and condensed milk with a 40 percent global market share, and confectionery (acquiring Rowntree and Perugina in 1988). Nestlé also has a commanding market presence in pet food (acquiring Spillers in 1998, and Ralston Purina in 2001). Nestlé's most important global brands include Carnation, Kit Kat, Buitoni (pasta), Friskies (cat food), Stouffers (ready-made meals), Nescafé, and Perrier, as well as a myriad of local and national brands. Finally, Nestlé is present in cosmetics (obtaining a 26 percent stake in the French firm, L'Oréal, in 1974) and pharmaceuticals (acquiring Alcon Laboratories, a leading ophthalmic company in 1977).

In 2002, overall group sales were $50.1 billion, an increase of 19.5 percent since 1998. Of total group sales, Nestlé's revenues (by percentage) across business segments were as follows: beverages (26.2 percent), milk products (26.2 percent), prepared dishes (17.7 percent), confectionery (12.1 percent), pet food (12 percent), and pharmaceuticals (5.8 percent), with a net profit margin of 8.5 percent. Worldwide, Nestlé has approximately 250,000 employees, of whom 41 percent are located in Europe and 34 percent in the Americas, and operates more than 500 factories in 85 countries around the world, as well as 17 research and development facilities.

Within the food and beverage industry, competition is intensifying, mainly due to falling trade barriers (with the implementation of the Single European Market or emerging opportunities in Asia and Latin America, for example), the increasing market share of private-label manufacturers, and the increasing consolidation of the retail industry by firms such as WAL-MART and Aldi (Germany). Amid these structural changes, Nestlé believes that it is crucial to be close to the consumer in terms of branding and product customization, as tastes are mostly based on local culture. With respect to production, logistics and supply chain management, however, decision-making is more centralized, to take advantage of any possible economies of scale.

BIBLIOGRAPHY. "Nestlé and the 21st Century" (Harvard Business School, 1995); S. Wetlaufer, "The Business Case against Revolution: an interview with Nestlé's Peter Brabeck," *Harvard Business Review* (February 2001); www.nestle.com; "Global 500: World's Largest Companies," *Fortune* (July 2002).

CATHERINE MATRAVES
ALBION COLLEGE

Netherlands, the

DURING THE MIDDLE AGES, the tiny northwestern corner of Europe was largely overlooked by contemporaries, not without some justification. The Dutch were overshadowed by their neighbors to the south in Flanders, which was a major center of industrial production and trade. The residents in the north subsisted from fishing or pastoral agriculture. In the 15th century, the herring industry increased when herring schools shifted their routes to cross the North Sea, and the area began to prosper, especially with the help of continual technical improvements.

The soil conditions in the Netherlands were not conducive to supporting a large population, so from a very early date, towns, such as Amsterdam, started importing grain from eastern Europe. The influx of grain reduced food prices and encouraged Dutch farmers to switch to specialty goods, including industrial crops like hemp and flax, which they could produce more efficiently and at a greater profit. This complex division of labor has led some historians to call the Netherlands the first modern economy.

The increased prosperity coincided with the Dutch Revolt against Spanish rule. During the Middle Ages, the towns of the Netherlands had negotiated independent taxation policies with their foreign rulers. Through a series on innovations, often referred to as a financial revolution, the towns of Holland became creditworthy corporations and the Dutch, in general, learned to handle money very well. When a new Spanish king, Philip II, threatened that financial independence, it triggered a revolt that was fueled by religious differences. The Spanish held on to the southern provinces of the Low Countries, but were unsuccessful in their attempts to retake the north. Protestant sympathizers in the southern provinces were forced out and thousands emigrated to the northern provinces. They brought with them CAPITAL, advanced skills, and the desire to succeed in a new LAND. Seemingly overnight, the thriving industries of the south, including textile production and printing, were transplanted to the north and Amsterdam became the central clearinghouse for nearly all European international trade.

The 1590s were a time of great famines in ITALY and the Dutch used the dire circumstances as an excuse to infiltrate Mediterranean trade, which brought much needed cheap grain from the Baltic. Once the Dutch delivered the grain, however, they did not leave. They took over shipping in the area and established valuable trading links with Iberia and the Middle East. They didn't stop there. Despite a Portuguese monopoly, a number of small Dutch partnerships organized expeditions to Asia. In 1602, the Dutch government forced the competing firms to consolidate because they believed that a large unified firm could better battle the other national interests. The new corporation was called the United (Dutch) East India Company, commonly referred to by its initials, VOC.

Though it was chartered by the state, it was a privately owned corporation and the largest single commercial enterprise the world had ever seen. The company had over 2,000 investors, but with the long time lag (a single round-trip voyage took as long as 3 years) and the costs of establishing a headquarters in Asia, there was concern about how to distribute profits. This predicament led to the creation of first modern corporation, in which the company's life is independent of individual ownership and the investors have limited liability. VOC stocks were the first stocks sold in an open market and formed the genesis of the stock market in Amsterdam.

The Dutch used their knowledge of inter-Asian trade, gathered from the headquarters in modern day Jakarta, to dominate the trade between Europe and Asia, which was almost absurdly profitable. For the next 50 years, the VOC returned an average of 27 percent per year return to its investors. They attempted to do something similar in the Americas and founded the West India Company in 1621. By 1674, the company was completely bankrupt and despite briefly holding a portion of BRAZIL, the company never succeeded in establishing a colonial empire. The Dutch retained a few islands in the Caribbean and plantations along the wild coast of Suriname. The Asian colonies would continue to be profitable, though on a more modest scale, until their independence following WORLD WAR II.

The Dutch had the most advanced economy in the 17th century, but they lost that status by the 18th. The expense of nearly continual warfare, combined with hostile economic policies in neighboring countries, exhausted their financial reserves and the country built up considerable debt. With relatively high taxation and wages, Dutch industries became less competitive and many withered away altogether. In the 18th and 19th centuries, the Netherlands had ceased to be a vigorously prosperous nation, though it remained quite wealthy. The wealth was derived from large-scale investment, especially in foreign enterprises and nations, including the new UNITED STATES.

The Dutch economic base, though it was considered modern in the 16th century, was obsolete at the beginning of the 20th. It was the last European country to industrialize, and never adopted the technologies of the first INDUSTRIAL REVOLUTION, which were not well suited to its rich, well-educated population. Instead, they became leaders in the science-based technologies of the second industrial revolution, and two of the firms founded at that time, Philips (electronics) and ROYAL DUTCH SHELL GROUP (petrochemicals) remain world leaders.

In 2002, the Netherlands had a population of more than 16 million, and a GROSS DOMESTIC PRODUCT (GDP) of $434 billion, yielding a GDP per capita of $26,900, one of the highest in the world.

BIBLIOGRAPHY. Violet Barbour, *Capitalism in Amsterdam in the 17th Century* (1963); Jonathan Israel, *The Dutch Republic: Its Rise, Greatness, and Fall 1477–1806* (Clarendon Press, 1995); E.H. Kossman, *The Low Countries, 1780–1940* (Oxford University Press, 1978); Jan de Vries and Ad van der Woude, *The First Modern Economy: Success, Failure, and Perseverance of the Dutch Economy, 1500–1815* (Cambridge University Press, 1997); J.L. van Zanden, *The Rise and Decline of Holland's Economy* (Manchester University Press, 1993); "The Netherlands," *CIA World Factbook* (2002).

LAURA CRUZ
WESTERN CAROLINA UNIVERSITY

New Deal

FRANKLIN D. ROOSEVELT (FDR), in his presidential nomination acceptance speech to the 1932 Democratic Party Convention, provided the nation with a biting critique of the Republican Party and the way the Herbert HOOVER administration had dealt with the Great DEPRESSION. FDR described programs that he would push to relieve the effects of the greatest economic crisis in American history. In conclusion Roosevelt declared, "I pledge you, I pledge myself, to a new deal for the American people."

The NEW DEAL, Roosevelt's agenda to deal with Depression, included legislation to assist the average American suffering from high UNEMPLOYMENT and deflation of the economy. In addition, Roosevelt tried to enact progressive reforms to restore confidence in the American economy and government. The New Deal ushered in a new era in activist government as an agent of change. Conservative forces criticized the New Deal as an attempt to bring socialism to the UNITED STATES. Liberal activists believed that the New Deal did not go far enough to change the structure of America's economy and society.

Most historians concur that the New Deal did not cure the Great Depression but did rebuild confidence in America and created the modern regulatory environment.

Roosevelt used a cautious approach to solving America's economic problems.

For example, during the 1933 banking crisis he used the government to support the banking system without fully nationalizing the system as many European nations did. FDR also tried to maintain a balanced budget while funding the New Deal, raising taxes on the wealthy and cutting government spending in areas like the military. The new regulatory restrictions on business and increased taxes on the rich earned Roosevelt the label "traitor to his own class" since he was part of the wealthy class, but sided with the less fortunate.

Historians divide the New Deal into three main phases, the first 100 days, the first New Deal, and the second New Deal.

The first 100 days. By the time Roosevelt took office in March 1933, after a resounding victory in November 1932, the American economy had deteriorated. The unemployment rate exceeded 25 percent, with 13 million people not working. Banks in 38 states had closed. On March 4, FDR's inauguration day, the banking centers in New York and Illinois closed, bringing the nation's financial system to complete standstill. The day after Roosevelt's inauguration, he issued an executive order closing all banks, asked Congress to meet in emergency session, and proposed new banking legislation. By March 10, both houses of Congress had passed FDR's banking legislation, initiating government supervision of and assistance to private banks. On March 13 the largest and strongest U.S. banks reopened and saw more deposits than withdrawals on that day.

During the first 100 days of the Roosevelt administration more legislation was passed than during any other period in American history. In contrast to the previous administration that tried to stimulate investment and production, the New Deal used the power of the federal government to encourage consumption, influencing factories to produce more goods and hire more people. Central to the New Deal was the National Recovery Administration (NRA) that tried to bring a measure of government planning to the industrial sector. The NRA imposed restrictions on prices and wages along with controls on production levels. Another of the NRA's aims was to bring peace between management and labor. This legislation was declared unconstitutional by the Supreme Court in 1935, which led Roosevelt to attempt to limit the power of the federal court.

The Civilian Conservation Corps (CCC) was another piece of legislation passed in the first 100 days. Aiming to reduce youth unemployment and provide financial support for families, the CCC allowed men between the ages of 18 and 25 to work on environmental projects like building roads and paths in national parks. Workers were provided food and shelter and paid $30 monthly, of which they had to send home $25.

Another early piece of legislation created the Federal Emergency Relief Administration (FERA) to provide cash payments to needy families, support charitable relief organizations like church-run soup kitchens, and offer work to destitute families. Eventually FERA's work programs were offered through the Works Progress Administration and cash payments to the unemployed became unemployment insurance under the Social Security Act.

One of the weakest sectors in the American economy was the agricultural sector, since it had not prospered during the 1920s when the industrial sector had expanded at an unprecedented rate. During the Depression farmers suffered from surplus production and low prices. To assist them, Congress passed the Agricultural Adjustment Act (AAA) that paid farmers subsidies to leave some of their acreage fallow. Roosevelt hoped that reduced production would support higher prices and therefore stabilize farm income. Unfortunately, large farms used the program but small farms could not make the program work. In 1936 the Supreme Court ruled the price regulatory elements of the AAA unconstitutional and Congress reworked those provisions. Although the reworked AAA ceased after World War II, it became the philosophical basis for future farm-subsidy programs.

In addition to Roosevelt's early efforts to save the American banking system from collapse, the administration proposed and Congress enacted two pieces of legislation that altered the financial sector. The 1933 Glass-Steagall Act banned commercial banks from selling stock or participating in corporate underwriting. Glass-Steagall created two distinct and separate banking groups, commercial/retail banking and investment banking. Glass-Steagall also created another organization that is part of the American banking structure, the Federal Deposit Insurance Corporation (FDIC), to insure bank deposits. Insured banks paid a fee to the FDIC that created a fund to protect depositors against loss. Initially deposits were insured up to $2,500; the amount today is $100,000.

The New Deal tried to stimulate the American economy through federal spending. Two programs enacted in the first 100 days are clear examples. Recognizing that the South was the poorest region in the country, the administration proposed the creation of a regional planning and development agency, the Tennessee Valley Authority (TVA). TVA's purpose was to construct hydroelectric dams on rivers in the mid-south to control flooding and produce cheap electricity. Dam construction would create construction jobs and allow TVA to offer inexpensive electricity to industry willing to locate in the area. In addition, inexpensive electricity would now be affordable to rural southerners.

The other program enacted in the first 100 days to stimulate employment was the Public Works Administration (PWA). During PWA's existence from 1933–39, 6 billion federal dollars financed federal and nonfederal construction projects including roads, public buildings such as post offices and federal courthouses, and the first federal public housing. In addition to TVA and PWA, the New Deal created the Civil Works Administration specifically to provide emergency relief during the harsh winter of 1933–34.

The early New Deal combined relief and reform programs to attack the desperate problems of the Great Depression. Roosevelt understood that his biggest task was to restore confidence to the American people. In his first inaugural speech in March 1933, he said the now famous words, "First of all, let me assert my firm belief that the only thing we have to fear is fear itself—nameless, unreasoning, unjustified terror." Roosevelt tried to reassure the American people, through his words and actions, that the federal government would do everything within its power to solve the problems. As the New Deal matured from the first 100 days into the first New Deal, the main emphasis shifted from relief to reform.

The first New Deal. Once major American relief efforts of the first 100 days became part of the program to combat the Great Depression, the Roosevelt administration drafted new legislation to regulate and stimulate the American economy. In 1934, three pieces of New Deal legislation became law, creating the FCC, FHA, and SEC.

The Federal Communications Act created the Federal Communications Commission (FCC) to regulate the new wireless and wired communications industry. Its main focus was the emergent radio industry in America. The FCC issued broadcast licenses, regulated broadcast content for community standards, and encouraged new technologies. Eventually, the FCC also regulated the television industry.

The Great Depression severely depressed home ownership in the 1930s. In 1934, the administration proposed creating the Federal Housing Administration (FHA), which provided mortgage guarantees to reduce the down payment for a mortgage from 30 percent of the purchase price to 10 percent. The new FHA guarantee extended the standard mortgage loan from 20 to 30 years, lowering monthly payments and therefore making homes more affordable to middle-income families. The FHA enacted new building standards and codes such as for electrical wiring and plumbing, helping standardize construction practices. The Federal Housing Administration remains an active participant in the home-mortgage industry today.

One of the most significant pieces of legislation passed in 1934 as part of Roosevelt's efforts to rebuild public confidence in the economy and the business community was the Securities and Exchange Act, which established the SECURITIES AND EXCHNAGE COMMISSION (SEC). The stock market crash of October 1929 had destroyed confidence in the various stock exchanges and in the business community. The SEC was given the responsibility to oversee American stock exchanges and the activities of publicly held firms. Roosevelt turned to one of America's best-known stock traders, Joseph P. KENNEDY, as the SEC's first commissioner. The SEC required publicly traded firms to submit quarterly reports, audited for accuracy, to stockholders and the general public. Companies wishing to sell stock would submit a series of reports; all the transactions would be open to the public. This access to corporate information gave rise to modern stockbrokerage houses and stock analysts. The SEC remains a vital part of the federal government's efforts to maintain openness and responsibility in stocks and equities.

In 1935, the administration continued to send Congress legislation to reform business and provide relief to the unemployed. However, the Supreme Court declared the National Recovery Act unconstitutional, creating a new obstacle for Roosevelt. In spite of this setback, Congress passed the Wagner Act that formed the National Labor Relations Board (NLRB). The NLRB ushered in a new era in labor-management relations, requiring collective bargaining and giving the president new powers to impose binding arbitration when the nation's economic security was in danger. The Wagner Act and the NLRB, though modified since, continue to provide the legal structure for labor-management relations in the United States.

Building on earlier New Deal programs, the Roosevelt administration pushed through new legislation in 1935 such as the Works Progress Administration (WPA), the Rural Electrification Administration (REA), and the National Youth Administration (NYA). The WPA expanded the scope of the PWA through new funding for construction projects and also provided funding for professional fields still suffering from the Great Depression. Actors, writers, painters, historians, photographers, dancers, and musicians benefited. This newly expanded program became controversial when WPA-funded plays and art works were criticized for their content or themes.

The REA brought electricity to rural America. Most private electric utility companies did not want to make the substantial investment to extend electricity to non-urban areas of America. The return on investment would be low because of declining rural population and a dependence of rural America on falling farm income. Low-cost electricity created by hydroelectric dams of the

TVA became available to the rural south through the REA. Other regions of the country also benefited, most notably the west, where new hydroelectric dams were funded.

The NYA went beyond the CCC and its basic efforts to remedy youth unemployment. The National Youth Administration supported education and training by giving young people grants to stay in school. This program supported two million students in high school and college and kept them out of the work force, reducing the pool of eligible workers. Once the United States entered World War II, the program was discontinued but the idea surfaced again in the education provisions of the GI Bill.

The most significant and long-lasting New Deal program, Social Security, also came into existence in 1935. Characterized as an old-age pension program, Social Security became the primary federal program to assist the elderly, those unemployed, dependent mothers and children, the handicapped, and Americans in need of public-health programs. It was designed as a payroll deduction program for federally guaranteed retirement payments. The American public was told that an account would be set up at Social Security and that payroll deductions would be paid into the fund. However, in reality the payments went into a central fund and underwrote payments made to the present generation of claimants. Those working would pay for those retired through regular paycheck deductions. Folded into the legislation was an unemployment insurance program that both the employer and employee paid into a central fund to provide. Individuals who had paid into the fund and lost their jobs would be eligible for a specified number of monthly payments. Since the originally enacted legislation became law, a number of other programs have become apart of the system, including Medicare. Social Security is considered the most successful New Deal program and has been credited with the transformation of the elderly from the poorest segment of the American population into the wealthiest.

Roosevelt took the Supreme Court's 1935 ruling that the National Recovery Act was unconstitutional as an attack by conservative forces to end his efforts to revive the American economy. FDR took his case to the American people when he ran for a second term in 1936 and won a landslide victory. This greatest margin of victory in modern electoral history encouraged Roosevelt to take on the Supreme Court in his second term. FDR's second term as president is considered the second New Deal.

The second New Deal. The second round of New Deal legislation was less ambitious and in many respects an attempt to protect the legislation passed during the first 100 days and the first New Deal. Roosevelt proposed legislation to Congress to put more justices on the Supreme Court to enable him to appoint new justices to the court. He justified the legislation because the court was behind in its work; new justices would allow it to catch up. The court presented a convincing argument that it was up-to-date on its work and did not need any new justices. Roosevelt failed to get this legislation, often called the court-packing bill, passed by Congress, but the Supreme Court did start to favor New Deal legislation with its approval of the Wagner Act and Social Security.

The major piece of legislation proposed by the Roosevelt administration in 1937 was the Farm Security Administration (FSA). The FSA built on the earlier Agricultural Adjustment Act, part of which had been declared unconstitutional. The aim of the FSA was to provide federal aid to small and tenant farmers.

From the beginning of FDR's efforts to deal with the Great Depression in 1933 until the summer of 1937, the American economy improved each year and considerable progress was achieved in reducing unemployment. However, in the summer of 1937 the American economy went into a deep recession, caused by a dramatic drop in consumption. In order to maintain a balanced federal budget while funding new programs like Social Security, Roosevelt had reduced funding to older programs like WPA, which provided income to many people. So, when people were dropped from the program they restricted their spending.

In 1938, the last of the major New Deal legislation became law with the passage of the Fair Labor Standards Act. This law set a minimum wage of 40 cents an hour and a 40-hour work week for any company engaged in interstate commerce.

The nation and the world shifted focus in 1938 from the economic problems on the home front to the growing clouds of war worldwide. After 1938, the Roosevelt administration focused on maintaining existing programs and keeping a watchful eye on international events.

The New Deal is not considered a success in economic terms, not because of what was done but because the programs did not go far enough. Roosevelt acted in a conservative manner; much higher federal spending to stimulate consumption would have been needed to end the Depression. In fact, higher federal spending on the military during World War II did end the Depression. In the terms of solidifying the federal government's relationship with the average citizen, however, the New Deal was a great success because it set basic standards for living in America and the federal government became a guarantor of those standards.

BIBLIOGRAPHY. Roger Biles, *A New Deal for the American People* (Northern Illinois University Press, 1991); Kenneth Davis, *FDR: The New Deal Years, 1933–1937* (Random

House, 1986); David M. Kennedy, *Freedom From Fear: The America People in Depression and War, 1929–1945* (Oxford University Press, 1999); William Leuchtenburg, *Franklin D. Roosevelt and the New Deal* (Harper Collins, 1963); Robert A. McElvaine, *The Great Depression: America, 1929–1941* (Crown Publishing Group, 1984); Arthur M. Schlesinger, Jr., *The Age of Roosevelt*, 3 vols. (Houghton Mifflin, 1957–60); Dixon Wechter, *The Age of the Great Depression* (Macmillan, 1948); newdeal.feri.org.

CARY W. BLANKENSHIP, PH.D.
TENNESSEE STATE UNIVERSITY

New York Stock Exchange

CAPITALISM IS BASED on surplus, and stock exchanges create capital surplus financing by investor purchase of securities. It also allows the investor a vehicle with which to indirectly affect market change, sometimes for a profit. The New York Stock Exchange (NYSE) prides itself on being the main center of capitalism in New York City, and indeed, the NYSE has spearheaded the emergence of capitalism from its beginnings.

The original Dutch exchange. Originally inhabited by Native American Indian groups who traded with Dutch seafarers in the early 1600s, Manhattan, protected from the open sea by Long Island, was an excellent natural port for the emerging global trade of mercantilist economies. The Dutch establishment of New Amsterdam as trading port and settlement saw native goods like tobacco, fur, timber, fish, and foodstuffs flow out of native lands in exchange for finished European goods and products from around the globe.

From the start, New Amsterdam was a global community of traders, who often moved goods by Dutch ships and were financed by Dutch banks and credit houses. The Dutch role as middlemen in the emerging global trade gave them ideas on how to participate in the mercantilist system. The Protestant Dutch had been fighting a war of rebellion against the Spanish Empire in the 1500s and 1600s. Their small population and small land mass was balanced by their masterful seafaring skills and ships, and their ability to function as middlemen, private-company founders, and financiers for the mercantile markets around the globe. Eventually the Dutch mastered a model of international trade, port cities, shipping, financing, and trade that became the basis for modern capitalism. One can see the Dutch imprint on New York City and its famous stock exchange to this day.

During the Dutch revolt against Spanish rule, the small Dutch states developed a capitalist style stock system to fund its defeat of the Spanish mercantile economy. SPAIN had a large colonial empire, with excellent Portuguese seafaring ships, the best land army in Europe, and silver from its American colonies. However all of its products had to be bought from Europe due to small Spanish production. To combat this, the Dutch developed trade companies, finance banks, and credit houses to fund and control the Spanish economy. Spanish silver fleets crashed the European money markets when they arrived, or crashed the Spanish economy when hurricanes or Dutch and English piracy delayed them. The Dutch banking houses, feigning neutrality, offered open loans and credit to the Spanish crown and to its arms manufacturers.

Dutch trade companies, producing real profits in global trade, sold stock to raise funds that supported the bank and credit houses. Spain became dependent on this finance system and went bankrupt five times between 1518–44, when it was at the height of its power. The system worked so well, that when London burned in the 1660s it was completely remade on the Dutch model and became the hub of international trade and capitalism.

This Dutch model of security exchange was transferred to the settlement of New Amsterdam and led to the rise of the New York Stock Exchange. Geographically, a 1653 stockade or wall of wood was laid across lower Manhattan as a defense for the trading community.

Early Wall Street. In 1685, as the British took control of the Dutch settlement, Wall Street itself was laid out along the stockade route. Hence the name "wall" street. In 1790, the newly independent UNITED STATES issued $80 million in bonds to help finance its revolutionary war debt. These war bonds, as they came to be called, were the first major publicly traded securities and marked the arrival of a pure U.S. investment market. Often overlooked, the war bonds had multiple impacts on the economy beyond the obvious. They financed necessary defensive and offensive positions of a nation or state in foreign affairs, thus impacting foreign trade and exchange rates as well as stability of the market. Second, they also established a permanent link between the military and the arms industry both in peace and in war, a link that often directly impacts a capitalist economy. If such bonds are used to fund offensive war efforts such as the war with Mexico in 1848 (MEXICAN-AMERICAN WAR), then the dividends can be even greater. The acquisition of territory and resources provides more fuel for a capitalist-style economy.

In 1792, the historic Buttonwood Agreement was reached between 24 significant merchants and brokers. The agreement was signed by all 24 members on Wall Street and marked the official emergence of a U.S.-derived, New York securities exchange. The Bank of New

York became the first corporate stock traded and the first listed company on the NYSE. This pattern was remarkably similar to the Dutch model of finance of the previous century.

In 1825, the Erie Canal was opened to connect the Great Lakes with the eastern seaboard port of New York City. New York State bonds were used to finance the canal and were actively traded on the exchange. While the canal was never profitable as a private enterprise for the state, the trend of publicly financed and traded bonds for the building of civilization infrastructure was established.

With the NYSE firmly established as the new nation's center for trade, not even the great fire of 1837 could derail it. The NYSE's original home at a rented room on 40 Wall Street was eventually abandoned. The market panic of 1857 saw market value decline 45 percent during the year. The collapse of the Ohio Life Insurance & Trust Company led to an 8 percent drop in a single session during the year. The market did re-establish itself but only with the AMERICAN CIVIL WAR of 1861–65. Trading securities of seceding states was suspended and along with war bonds, this move helped doom the Southern economy during the war. The name of the New York Stock Exchange (NYSE) became official in 1863, replacing the cumbersome New York Stock & Exchange Board (NYS&B).

The victory of the Northern, industrial, capitalist economy over the Southern, agrarian economy was part of the war effort by the North. A number of NYSE members including business and finance leaders, were advisors for President Abraham LINCOLN during the war. At Lincoln's assassination in 1865 the NYSE closed for a week. It eventually moved to its first permanent home, a five-story building on 10-12 Broad Street that opened

The famous "controlled chaos" of the floor of the New York Stock Exchange lies at the core of capitalism in America.

at the end of the war in 1865, and served as the center of the NYSE until 1903. The intersection of Wall and Broad Streets became the center of securities trading in the United States.

In 1868, membership in the NYSE could be sold as a property right. This ominous sign that everything in the country could be bought or speculated upon, eventually culminated in the financial panic of 1873 during the administration of President Ulysses S. GRANT, The NYSE closed for 10 days after Jay Cooke & Company, a Philadelphia bank firm, failed due to speculation on railroad stocks. The financial panic that gripped the nation exposed corruption throughout the Grant presidency and carried on into future presidential administrations. Many of Grant's appointees were involved in schemes to bilk investors of money in securities fraud. The Grant presidency established the linkage between the economic welfare of the nation and the perceived effect the presidency could have on the economy with foreign policy, legislation, and appointees.

Late 19th century. Increasingly in the last third of the 19th century, big-business interests played a stronger role in both politics and Wall Street as the NYSE area was then known. National news companies like the Hearst empire were quick to establish this link in the eyes of the American public and Wall Street became a common phrase.

Industrial leaders such as Andrew CARNEGIE, and financiers such as J.P. MORGAN who bought out Carnegie, became the most powerful and wealthiest men in America, and perhaps the world. Morgan controlled the largest company in the world, U.S. STEEL, one of six major railroads in the United States, and floated the bond that backed the gold reserve to stabilize the American economy after the panic of 1893. The use of the NYSE as a financial and securities tool for private gain and public control was clearly involved with the terrible fluctuations in market value during the last third of the 19th century. Progressive reform under President Theodore ROOSEVELT would move toward government control of the banking system, and better regulation of the use of the NYSE.

In 1907, rumors of New York bank collapses triggered a run on city banks. J.P. Morgan stepped in again to stabilize the crises with a massive infusion of cash into the banks. The stock market stabilized and the complex, sometimes contentious relationship between big business, finance, the government, and the stock market was realized.

In 1914, WORLD WAR I forced the shutdown of security exchanges around the globe due to falling prices. The NYSE shut down for more than four months. However the final result of war saw the permanent establishment of U.S. industry as the world's largest producer of industrial goods, and the United States as the creditor nation for debt-ridden, rebuilding Europe. Wall Street supplanted London as the world investment capital as foreign issues became common at 18 Broad Street.

Black Thursday and beyond. The Roaring Twenties followed and funded the addition of a massive, 23-story building on 11 Wall Street in 1922. The "garage" section of the trading floor was also added at this time. However, the postwar boom was followed by a global DEPRESSION in the 1930s. On October 24, 1929, "Black Thursday," stock prices fell 13 million shares. Five days later the market crashed on volume of close to 20 million shares. During the Depression, the first salaried president of the NYSE, William McChesney Martin, Jr., was appointed in 1938.

The start of WORLD WAR II (1939–45) marks the entry of women onto the stock floor. The post-war boom saw the market recover and a push to include more middle-class Americans in stock investing. In 1955, President Dwight D. EISENHOWER had a heart attack, prompting large sell-offs at the NYSE. In 1956, the postwar boom and Cold War environment provided impetus to add another addition to the NYSE at 20 Broad Street.

The assassination of President John. F. KENNEDY in 1963 forced the closing of the NYSE to avoid massive sell-offs. In 1967, Muriel Siebert became the first female member of the exchange just as the traditional paperwork of the NYSE caused a crisis, forcing increased automation of the exchange. In 1969, a third trading room, the Blue Room, was added. In 1970, Joseph L. Searles III became the first African-American member, and in 1971 the NYSE became a not-for-profit corporation, as ironic as it may seem. A board of directors with 10 public members was given control to increase public perception of participation in 1972. Further changes included the first non-U.S. member, Bruno Des Forges in 1976.

The 1970s saw the NYSE affected by the Richard NIXON presidency scandal, the end of the Vietnam War, and the Jimmy CARTER presidency's economic recession. The 1980s looked like an era of recovery as stock values soared only to be burst by the October 19, 1987, DOW JONES Industrial Average drop of 508 points, the largest in history. Two days of unprecedented volume followed with a total of over 608 million shares traded.

The 1990s saw the collapse of the Cold War and further meteoric rise of market values on the NYSE. But on October 27, 1997, the Dow Jones plunged again 554 points. The 3-D Trading Floor (3DTF) was added in 1999 to accommodate the increasing role of technology in securities exchange. This marked the fourth trading room of the NYSE. Another record high was achieved by the Dow on January 14, 2000, at 11,722,98 and was followed by the largest single day gain of almost 500 points on March 16, 2000.

Global stocks and technology companies played a major role in the traditional NYSE but their overvalue at the turn of the millennium led to stock values plummeting on April 14, 2000, by 617 points. The fifth and final trading room was added in 2000 at 30 Broad Street. Its construction was directly related to the huge economic boom associated with technology stocks

The terrorist attacks on the World Trade Center in New York City led to a four-day closure of the NYSE. When it reopened on September 17, 2001, a record 2.37 billion shares exchanged hands. The NYSE has survived bull and bear markets for over 200 years as the center of American, and now global, securities exchange. A sixth trading floor is planned to open in the near future.

BIBLIOGRAPHY. E. Chancellor, *Devil Take the Hindmost: A History of Financial Speculation* (Farrar Straus & Giroux, 1999); D. Colbert, *Eyewitness to Wall Street: 400 Years of Dreamers, Schemers, Busts, and Booms* (Broadway Books, 2001); R. Davies, *A Comparative Chronology of Money from Ancient Times to Present Day* (University of Wales Press, 2002); J. Galbraith, *The Great Crash of 1929* (Mariner Books, 1997); J. Galbraith, *A Short History of Financial Euphoria* (Penguin Books, 1994); C. Giesst, *Wall Street: A History* (Oxford University Press, 1997); C. Geisst, and R. Grasso, *100 Years of Wall Street* (McGraw-Hill, 1999); J.R. Gordon, *The Great Game: The Emergence of Wall Street As a World Power, 1653–2000* (Scribner, 1999); C. Kindleberger, *Manias, Panics, and Crashes: A History of Financial Crises* (John Wiley & Sons, 2000); D. Scott, *How Wall Street Works* (McGraw-Hill, 1999); R. Sobel and B. Mitchell, *The Big Board: A History of the New York Stock Exchange* (Beard Group, 2000).

CHRIS HOWELL
RED ROCKS COLLEGE

New Zealand

AN ISLAND NATION in the south Pacific Ocean, New Zealand is southeast of AUSTRALIA and comprises two main islands—North and South Islands—and many smaller islands. It is a member of the British Commonwealth of Nations.

The population of New Zealand is 3.9 million. Approximately three-quarters are of European descent, 10 percent Maori, 4 percent Polynesian, with Asians and others making up the rest. English is the predominant language, but Maori and Samoan are also spoken. Nearly three-quarters of the population lives on the North Island and while New Zealand has a strong rural sector, the majority of its people live in cities. Since WORLD WAR II, the annual rate of immigration has generally surpassed that of emigration. Recently Asians and Pacific Islanders have become the predominant immigrant groups.

Around 800 C.E., New Zealand was settled by Polynesian Maoris and remained isolated until the mid-1600s when European explorers arrived. In 1840, the British proclaimed their sovereignty over the country. In 1907, New Zealand became an independent dominion. With the beginning of World War II, New Zealand's economy was mobilized for the war effort, including the enactment of wage and price controls. In 1973, New Zealand and Australia pledged increased cooperation, which was a response to the loss of trade caused by Britain's entry into the European Economic Community (EEC). In 1984, the government instituted sweeping policy reversals, called Restructuring, that were geared toward changing the role of the state in New Zealand's economy, and toward transforming the economy from an agrarian basis dependent on concessionary British market access, to a more industrialized, free market structure that could compete globally. The government also banned nuclear-powered and nuclear-armed vessels from its ports. This decision strained relations with the UNITED STATES and led to the United States suspending its defense obligations.

New Zealand's labor force is more than 1.9 million, with about two-thirds engaged in services, one quarter in industry, and about 10 percent in agriculture. Since the introduction of the Employment Contracts Act in 1991, which gave workers the right to decide whether to belong to an employee organization or not, union membership has significantly declined.

New Zealand's currency is the New Zealand dollar. New Zealand's banking system consists of several commercial and trustee saving banks and one central bank, the Reserve Bank of New Zealand, which has the sole power of issue of currency. Since the 1980s, New Zealand's capital markets have become extremely competitive, with many specialty institutions emerging. In 1985, the government freed transactions in foreign exchange, and, for the first time, the exchange rate was floated in a competitive market.

New Zealand's exports are valued at approximately $14.2 billion annually and its imports at approximately $12.5 billion. It is the leading exporter of dairy products in the world and second only to Australia as an exporter of wool. New Zealand's major imports are petroleum, iron, steel, textiles, and heavy machinery. Most manufactured goods are imported free of duty. Since the importance of trade with Britain has been reduced, there is now greater importance placed on trade with the Middle East, JAPAN, and the United States.

Though New Zealand's per capita incomes have been rising, they remain below the level of the EUROPEAN UNION's four largest economies. Since New Zealand is still heavily dependent on trade to drive growth, it has been affected by the global economic slowdown and the slump in commodity prices in the early 2000s.

BIBLIOGRAPHY. W.H. Oliver and B.R. Williams, ed., *The Oxford History of New Zealand* (Oxford University Press, 1983); Colin James, *The Quiet Revolution: Turbulence and Transition in Contemporary New Zealand* (Allen and Unwin, 1986); Keith Sinclair, ed., *The Oxford Illustrated History of New Zealand* (Oxford University Press, 1998); R.C. Mascarenhas, *Government and the Economy in Australia and New Zealand: The Politics of Economic Policy Making* (Austin & Winfield Publishers, 2002); "New Zealand," *CIA World Factbook* (2002).

S.J. RUBEL, J.D.
INDEPENDENT SCHOLAR

Nicaragua

NICARAGUA IS THE SECOND poorest country in the western hemisphere after Haiti, and the poorest in Central America. After decades under a brutal dictatorship, Nicaragua experienced a popular uprising in 1979, and the Sandinista National Liberation Front, a group of leftist rebels fighting the government for almost two decades, took power. The Sandinistas nationalized part of the industrial sector, confiscated land from the dictator Anastasio Somoza, and implemented land reform. Large estates were turned into state farms; other land was redistributed to agricultural cooperatives or later to individual peasant families.

Although the Sandinista leadership operated a mixed economy with a sizeable private sector, the Ronald REAGAN administration opposed it on anti-communist grounds. The United States imposed an embargo on Nicaragua in 1985, and funded and assisted the "contra" forces, led by ousted government officials and based in Honduras and Costa Rica. The contras attacked Nicaraguan troops and civilians, especially agricultural cooperatives and government health and education workers.

In the 1980s, Nicaragua received massive material aid and volunteer assistance from many countries. But military spending and a collapse of tax revenues led the government to resort to printing money, generating inflation over 30,000 percent at its peak.

In 1990, the Sandinistas lost in national elections and became an opposition party. A drastic stabilization and structural adjustment program brought inflation down to below 10 percent, but exacerbated unemployment and poverty. Nicaragua still suffers deep poverty and an enormous external-debt burden. Recently, flood, drought, and economic hardship have driven hundreds of thousands of Nicaraguans to migrate to Costa Rica to find employment.

BIBLIOGRAPHY. Joseph Collins and Paul Rice, *Nicaragua: What Difference Could a Revolution Make?* (Grove Press, 1986); Institute for Food and Development Policy, Rose Spalding, ed., *The Political Economy of Revolutionary Nicaragua* (Allen & Unwin, 1987).

MEHRENE LARUDEE, PH.D.
UNIVERSITY OF KANSAS

Nigeria

THE FEDERAL REPUBLIC of Nigeria covers 923,768 square kilometers in western Africa and encompasses 36 internal states. Nigeria is a country of diversity. Its climate ranges from equatorial in the south to tropical in the center and arid in the north. Over 25 ethnic groups make up its population, often creating disagreements over how the economy of the country should be managed.

As a British colony, Nigeria's abundant resources were often exploited, but the British moved the nation forward with public roads, railroads, and increased export trade. Nigeria won its independence from Great Britain in 1960; and after 16 years of military rule, a new constitution was ratified in 1999, establishing a three-branch government, including a president, a bicameral legislature and a supreme court. A major goal of the new government has been to establish economic reforms.

Economically, Nigeria has suffered from exploitation, corruption, and mismanagement. Its dependence on oil and oil-related products resulted in an economic collapse in the late 1970s and early 1980s. While almost 31 percent of Nigeria is arable land, agricultural workers continue to live at subsistence levels, partially because of frequent drought and flooding. In 2000, 45 percent of the nation's residents lived below the poverty line, while most of the wealth remained in the hands of the top 10 percent of the population. Nigeria's human resources are potentially strong as the country is the most populous in Africa (130 million in 2002), but have been drained by the low life-expectancy rate of 50.6 years, a high incidence of deaths from AIDS (250,000 estimated in 1999), and a high infant-mortality rate of 72.49 deaths per 1,000 live births.

In 1989, the WORLD BANK declared Nigeria qualified to receive funds from the International Development Association (IDA), and in 2000, Nigeria received a debt-restructuring grant from the INTERNATIONAL MONETARY

FUND (IMF) and the Paris Club to help them institute economic reforms.

Nigeria's abundant natural resources include natural gas, petroleum, tin, columbite, iron ore, coal, limestone, lead, iron, and zinc. While its major exports continue to be petroleum and petroleum products, cocoa, and rubber, the government has encouraged the growth of industries such as crude oil, coal, tin, columbite, palm oil, wood, animal hides, textiles, cement and other construction products, food products, footwear, chemical fertilizer, ceramics, and seeds, in order to develop a diverse economy. Nigeria continues to import machinery, chemicals, transport equipment, manufactured goods, food, and live animals even though its agricultural products includes cocoa, peanuts, palm oil, corn, rice, sorghum, millet, tapioca, yams, rubber, cattle, sheep, goats, pigs, timber, and fish.

BIBLIOGRAPHY. Martin P. Mathews, *Nigeria: Current Issues and Historical Background* (Nova Science, 2002). Helen Chapin Metz, *Nigeria: A Country Study* (Library of Congress, 1992); Harold D. Nelson, *Nigeria: A Country Study* (U.S. G.P.O., 1982); "Nigeria," *CIA World Factbook* (2002).

ELIZABETH PURDY, PH.D.
INDEPENDENT SCHOLAR

Nikkei

THE LONGEST RUNNING stock price index in JAPAN's history, the Nikkei Stock Average (Nikkei) has been calculated continuously since September 7, 1950, when the newly reopened Tokyo Stock Exchange (TSE) began using the DOW JONES method to calculate the stock-price average. This is the method still in use today and the Nikkei has grown to become Japan's leading and most widely quoted index of stock market activity. Similar to the Dow Jones Industrial Average, the Nikkei is used to calculate the average stock price of 225 leading stock issues traded in the first section of the TSE (medium to large capitalization stocks).

Like the Dow Jones, the Nikkei is a price-weighted index in which the movement of each stock is weighted equally regardless of its market capitalization. Calculated as the arithmetic mean of the stock prices of 225 stocks selected from the approximately 1,400 in the TSE, it therefore does not fully represent the real average price of the stock market. Listed on the Nikkei are some of the worlds most widely known companies: TOYOTA, SONY, HONDA, Fuji Photo Film, and NEC.

The Nikkei is calculated to accurately reflect the performance of stocks on the Japanese stock market at any given time, and the mixture of stocks in the index can be altered to reflect trends in the current market. In its original format the Nikkei's component stocks were changed only because of special circumstances such as liquidations and mergers; throughout the 1980s there were only eight changes. Now however, while the 225 stocks are selected to represent the overall performance of the market, emphasis is placed on maintaining the index's historical continuity while keeping the index composed of stocks with a high market liquidity. A maximum of 3 percent of the average's component stocks, or 6 out of the 225, may be removed each year if they have relatively low market liquidity. However, while it is true to say that the Nikkei is the average price of 225 stocks traded on the first section of the TSE, it is different from a simple average in that the divisor is adjusted to maintain continuity and reduce the effect of external factors not directly related to the market. These 225 stocks represent 36 industry classifications at the heart of Japan's economy.

It was not until the postwar occupation of Japan that a recognizable share-exchange evolved, primarily as a means of destroying the economic power of the Zaibatsu—large, family-owned companies who controlled Japan's pre-war economy. A formal structure for the TSE was established when the Japanese parliament passed the Securities and Exchange Law in 1948.

While the name Nikkei Stock Average only came into being in May 1985, there has been a continuous TSE price average since 1950. Originally known as the Tokyo Stock Exchange Adjusted Stock Price Average, in July 1971, Nihon Short-wave Broadcasting (NSB) took over responsibility and began calculating and announcing what was now the NSB 225 Adjusted Average. On May 1, 1975, Dow Jones & Co granted exclusive rights to the name and Dow calculation method for the new Nikkei Dow Jones Stock Price Average. In May 1985, the Nikkei Dow Jones Stock Price Average became the Nikkei Stock Average and at the same time the Nikkei Dow Jones 500 Stock Average became the Nikkei 500 Stock Average.

Since 1971, the Nikkei has been calculated by Nihon Keizai Shimbun, Inc. (NKS) the leading Japanese financial information services company, therefore any addition or removal of stocks is at the discretion of NKS. Because of the method of calculation, the composition of the selected stock, and the historical continuity of the Nikkei, most market reports quote the Nikkei when they talk about the Japanese stock market.

The Nikkei has continued to develop and expand. On January 4, 1982, the Nikkei Dow-Jones 500 Stock Average was introduced, covering an adjusted average for 500 stocks. Since October 1, 1985, the index has been calculated every minute during trading hours. In September 1991, Nikkei took the major step and started calculating and announcing the market value-weighted

All Stock Index for all stocks listed on Japan's eight stock exchanges, this was aimed at producing an accurate reflection of the Japanese stock market. Since October 1991, components have been checked every year, and those of relatively low liquidity have been replaced by issues of high liquidity. Therefore, the index corresponds to changes in the market environment while maintaining consistency. In October 1993, the Nikkei Stock Average of 300 Selected Issues (Nikkei 300) was introduced. This was a weighted average of 300 selected stocks, aimed at giving a stock-price average more representative of the market as a whole.

The Nikkei has developed into more than the simple arithmetic mean of the stock prices of 225 selected stocks. It is now used as a base for futures-trading worldwide. Nikkei Stock Average Futures are traded on the Singapore International Monetary Exchange, Osaka Securities Exchange, and the Chicago Mercantile Exchange. International futures-trading on the Nikkei 300 began in February 1984.

In April 2000, in a major revision aimed at bridging the widening gap between the Nikkei (which was based on traditional industries) and the growth in the Japanese stock market of information technology companies. The shares that were removed were mainly mining, textiles, and chemicals and were replaced with others from growth sectors such as telecommunications, in an attempt to make the Nikkei more representative. In a further change, the share used to calculate the average will be reviewed every year.

The Nikkei Stock Average continues to provide a range of functions within the Japanese financial markets, when necessary adapting to new market trends and developments, and introducing new services to meet changes in demand.

BIBLIOGRAPHY. Robert Zielinski and Nigel Holloway, *Unequal Equities—Power and Risk in Japan's Stock Market* (Kodansha International, 1991); Nikkei, www.nikkei.co.jp; www.harrisdirect.com; Jason Singer and Craig Karmin, "East Meets West? Nikkei Index May Slide to Close Once-Vast Gap with Blue Chips," *The Wall Street Journal* (September, 2001).

DEREK RUTHERFORD YOUNG, PH.D.
UNIVERSITY OF DUNDEE, SCOTLAND

Nippon Life Insurance

OF THE THREE MAJOR life insurance companies in JAPAN—Nippon Life Insurance, DAI-ICHI MUTUAL LIFE and Sumitomo Life—the former leads the way. Nippon is, in fact, one of the world's largest insurers in total assets and policies in force. The company's strategic plans involve cutting through the competition by being the comprehensive total-insurance company of the new century.

Equipped with what Hoover's business reference describes as a "door-to-door sales corps," Nippon sells its specialized packages of life and group insurance, as well as annuity products. Nippon continues to expand and grow. Throughout the Orient and the world, Nippon participates in an assortment of activities including real-estate development and management, and a variety of educational-based and philanthropic projects. Recent deregulation has given Nippon the green light to move into the expanding areas of corporate and residential lending. Still, it is pushing further to expand in both life and non-life insurance products.

Headquartered in Osaka, Japan, Nippon owns many overseas holdings that focus on providing insurance to Japanese companies and to citizens abroad. American offices are located in New York City, Chicago, and Los Angeles. In January 2003, Nippon became the first Japanese life insurer to market policies in China on a full-scale basis, partnering with SVA Information Industry Company.

In 2002, Nippon ranked as the 33rd largest company in the world according to *Fortune* magazine, with nearly $64 billion in revenue.

BIBLIOGRAPHY. "Global 500: The World's Largest Companies," *Fortune* (July 2002); Hoover's Online, www.hoovers.com; *The Japan Times*, www.japantimes.co.jp.

JOSEPH GERINGER
SYED B. HUSSAIN, PH.D.
UNIVERSITY OF WISCONSIN, OSHKOSH

Nippon Telegraph & Telephone Corporation

OVERCOMING THE COMPETITIVE thrusts of companies such as American Telephone & Telegraph (AT&T), Nippon Telegraph & Telephone (NTT) stood, in early 2003, as the world's largest telecommunications company. On top of systems and solutions that benefit its huge customer base, Nippon boasts of having installed more than 25 million subscriber telephone lines, as well as millions of high-speed internet lines.

Nippon, with headquarters in Tokyo, JAPAN, is a holding company for regional local phone companies NTT East and NTT West, a long-distance carrier called NTT Communications, and several research-and-development entities. It operates a major internet service provider, as well, and owns 64 percent of Japan's leading cellular phone company. At the turn of the 20th century, NTT had branched out internationally, in the UNITED STATES and in the Pacific arena.

Established recently, in 1985, its continual success is largely founded on two factors—ability and know-how. Business analysts say the company possesses an innate talent to effectively and quickly serve the customer, and it has a savvy for reorganization, putting the most efficient technologies behind the steering wheel.

RESEARCH AND DEVELOPMENT (R&D) are the elemental drivers. While the holding company performs fundamental research, its "regionals" conduct specialized research. Simultaneously, Nippon's R&D departments—NTT Comware, NTT Facilities, and NTT-ME—apply important technology such as software development and implementation, and telecommunications security, thresholds to what NTT calls, the new millenium's "Information Sharing Society." In 2002, NTT ranked as the 16th largest company in the world with sales of nearly $94 billion.

BIBLIOGRAPHY. "Global 500: The World's Largest Corporations," *Fortune* (July 2002); Nippon Telegraph and Telephone, www.ntt.co.jp; Hoover's, www.hoovers.com.

JOSEPH GERINGER
SYED B. HUSSAIN, PH.D.
UNIVERSITY OF WISCONSIN, OSHKOSH

Nissan Motor Car Company

NISSAN MOTOR is JAPAN's second-largest automobile manufacturer, behind TOYOTA and ahead of HONDA. Its cars are world famous and include the Sentra, Altima, Infiniti, among others. Besides sedans, Nissan's vast output includes a sports car, the 350Z, as well as the Frontier pickup truck, Pathfinder SUV, not to mention satellites and pleasure boats.

Based in Tokyo, Nissan owns several plants in Japan and Europe (including FRANCE, GERMANY and the UNITED KINGDOM), and also in MEXICO and the UNITED STATES. The Nissan Technical Center of North America, located near Detroit, Michigan, boasts high-skill engineering capabilities and serves as the design-enhancement center for all autos manufactured for American and Canadian consumption.

Formed from the merger of two companies in 1925, Nissan adopted its present name in 1934. Interrupted by WORLD WAR II, production slowed to a whisper afterward and did not return to full output until 1955. Sales accelerated in the early 1960s when Nissan went global.

During the 1990s, the company suffered a sharp decline in profits, a result of fierce competition among worldwide auto manufacturers. In 1999, however, a strategic partnership between Nissan and French-car-maker, Renault, sparked a revival. Renault, also hurting from the sting of hard times, bought 37 percent of Nissan in an attempt to rejuvenate both companies. The collaboration worked, thanks not only to an adoption of a no-loopholes quality plan, but also to a new chairman, Renault's Carlo Ghosn, who took over Nissan's chair. Chief Executive Officer Ghosn's expense-slashing, penny-pinching form of management quickly—and respectfully—earned him the nickname, "Le Cost Cutter" when the red ink on the ledgers suddenly changed to black.

Since April 2002, Nissan has been adhering to its blueprint for future security. The plan, called Nissan 180, is a comprehensive operational business thrust ensuring continued growth, increased profits, and zero debt. *Fortune* magazine reported Nissan had sales of nearly $50 billion in 2002 and ranked as the 58th largest company in the world.

BIBLIOGRAPHY. "Global 500: The World's Largest Companies," *Fortune* (July 2002); Nissan Motor Car Company, www.nissan.co.jp; Hoover's, www.hoovers.com.

JOSEPH GERINGER
SYED B. HUSSAIN, PH.D.
UNIVERSITY OF WISCONSIN, OSHKOSH

Nissho Iwai

A JAPANESE GENERAL TRADING company specializing in risk management in international transactions, Nissho Iwai traces its roots to JAPAN's late 19th- and early 20th-century industrial revolution when two general trading companies formed to conduct transactions across cultural barriers. In 1901, Bunsuke Iwai created Iwai & Company to market products from Japan's fledgling steel industry in Western countries. The next year, Iwajiro Suzuki founded Suzuki & Company and established a global network of offices to trade sugar.

Suzuki soon expanded into sugar-refining, flour-milling, tobacco-marketing, beer production, insurance, shipping, and ship-building. Suzuki grew rapidly in response to Allied demand for war materials and shipping services during WORLD WAR I. In the postwar recession, however, the company could not sustain its excess capacity and bankruptcy forced Suzuki's 1928 reorganization as the Nissho Company.

The Iwai group meanwhile grew to include Daicel Chemical Industries, Nisshin Steel, Kansai Paint, and Fuji Photo & Film. In 1968, complementary business lines led to Nissho and Iwai's merger. In the 1970s, Nissho Iwai managed international urban-planning and construction projects in newly developing countries. The advertisement, "If Rome had to be built in a day, Nissho-Iwai would most likely get the job" reflected the company's ambition in these new ventures.

In the year ending in March 2002, Nissho Iwai's employees at 30 domestic Japanese and 131 overseas offices conducted transactions worth $43 billion in its principle businesses of steel, chemicals, foodstuffs, construction, and urban development. It ranked as the 74th largest company in the world in 2002.

BIBLIOGRAPHY. Kiyoshi Kojima and Terutomo Ozawa, *Japan's General Trading Companies* (OECD, 1984), Nissho Iwai, "Annual Report" and "Corporate Info," www.nisshoiwai.co.jp (2003); "Global 500: World Largest Companies," *Fortune* (July 2002).

JOHN SAGERS, PH.D.
LINFIELD COLLEGE

Nixon, Richard M. (1913–94)

RICHARD NIXON WAS born in Yorba Linda, California, in 1913, the year before World War I broke out in Europe. By 1941, the world was again at war, and Nixon joined the U.S. Navy after receiving a law degree from Duke University. In 1946, Nixon successfully ran for the House of Representatives, where he served for four years. He had become a U.S. Senator by the time Republican presidential candidate Dwight EISENHOWER chose him as his vice-president. Nixon ran for president in 1960 but lost to John KENNEDY with the closest popular vote in American history (49.7 percent to 49.5 percent). He used the intervening years to good advantage and became president in 1968 with 43.4 percent to Hubert Humphrey's 42.7 percent.

Richard Nixon inherited a country already suffering from INFLATION (a decrease in purchasing power) brought on by the VIETNAM WAR and stagflation (a slowing economy accompanied by rising prices). Nixon's expertise was in foreign policy, and he was unprepared for economic crises. Based on the advice of his economic advisors, Nixon sent his first budget to Congress with a $4 billion cut. Most of the cuts were aimed at social programs, such as subsidized lunches. Nixon was haunted by the memory of three recessions under Eisenhower for which the Republicans had suffered. Contrary to his preferences, Nixon approved congressional tax cuts in 1969 that placed a minimum tax on the wealthy and removed some individuals below the poverty line from the tax rolls. However, he alienated Congress by impounding funds appropriated for specific programs.

Despite a Republican tendency to let business alone, Nixon blocked acquisitions by large corporations and outraged foreign investors with his economic policies. He interfered in strikes by invoking the Taft-Hartley Act. In September 1969, he placed a freeze on federal construction programs and encouraged states to do the same. Nixon followed the advice of George Shultz, the secretary of labor, and devised a full-employment budget, planning as if the employment level were no more than 4 percent, expanding the money supply faster than the FEDERAL RESERVE was inclined to do, and holding down prices and wages. In June 1970, Nixon established a Government Procurement and Regulatory Review Board and announced that the COUNCIL OF ECONOMIC ADVISORS (CEA) would deliver inflation alerts. In the Economic Stabilization Act of 1970, Congress gave the president the right to regulate prices, rents, wages and salaries; however, no one really thought a Republican president would do so. Nixon's 1971 budget ran a deficit calculated at $11.6 billion, and the value of the U.S. dollar dropped precipitously.

On August 15, 1971, Nixon announced a new economic policy on national television, providing for a 90-day wage-and-price freeze, reviving Kennedy's investment tax, adding additional TARIFFs on imports, setting forth new spending cuts, lifting the excise tax on automobiles to encourage sales, agreeing to postpone welfare reform, and calling for increased revenue sharing (federal money distributed to state and local governments). Initial reaction from the business world was positive, and the public grew hopeful. Then gas prices soared. Nixon instituted a 15 percent cutback on gasoline, closed gas stations on Sundays, and even had gasoline-ration stamps printed, although they were never used.

Since the wage-and-price freeze was only in effect until November 13, Nixon instituted the second phase of his economic policy by establishing the Citizens' Price Commission to restrain prices and the Citizens' Pay Board to oversee wages and stop them from rising to inflationary levels. Also, by 1971, U.S. gold reserves had declined by $10 billion due to trade imbalance and overspending. Nixon decided to de-link the dollar from the gold standard, thus ending the BRETTON WOODS agreement.

Nixon won re-election in 1972 with a comfortable margin (60.7 percent to George McGovern's 37.5). But when the third phase of Nixon's economic plan proved unsuccessful, stock-market prices dropped and prices rose. In March, Nixon ordered a limit on the price of beef, pork, and lamb. The public was aghast when national television showed baby chicks being slaughtered because farmers could not afford to raise them. The fourth stage of the economic plan continued a price freeze until August 12 when food prices rose by 60 percent. Inflation was now at 14.5 percent. The economic situation was serious, but the political climate overwhelmed economics as Nixon was named an "unindicted co-conspirator" in the Watergate scandal, leading to the U.S. Congress preparing impeachment proceedings. On August 8, 1974, Nixon became the only president in United States history to resign from office.

BIBLIOGRAPHY. Rowland Evans, Jr. and Robert D. Novak, *Nixon in the White House: The Frustration of Power* (Random House, 1971); Allen J. Matusow, *Nixon's Economy: Booms, Busts, Dollars and Votes* (University Press of Kansas, 1998); "Public Papers of Richard Nixon," www.nixonfoundation.org; Paul A. Samuelson, *Economics* (McGraw-Hill, 1973); Arthur M. Schlessinger, Jr., *The Imperial Presidency*, (Houghton-Mifflin, 1973); Melvin Small, *The Presidency of Richard Nixon* (University Press of Kansas, 1999).

ELIZABETH PURDY, PH.D.
INDEPENDENT SCHOLAR

non-alignment

SIMPLY PUT, NON-ALIGNMENT refers to the policy of those countries that had remained neutral in the Cold War competition between the UNITED STATES and the SOVIET UNION, between the North Atlantic Treaty Organization (NATO) and Warsaw Pact, though not necessarily between SOCIALISM and capitalism.

In terms of world system theory, one could state that ever since the end of WORLD WAR II, each sector of the world system, the core, the semi-periphery and the periphery, has had an ideology of its own. For the core countries, it was capitalism (or liberal democracy), for the semi-periphery it was socialism, and for the peripheral countries it was non-alignment. Though in many Third World countries national ideology was characterized by different blends of capitalism, nationalism, regionalism, socialism, and ethnic and religious self-identification, the same was true of the core and semi-periphery countries as well, as evidenced by Euro-communism, democratic socialism, Irish nationalism, Polish Catholicism, and Slavic parochialism. Each sector, nonetheless, had its dominant ideology and non-alignment was the dominant ideology of the Third World, i.e., of the countries located at the margin of the world system.

Contrary to popular perceptions, non-alignment was an ideologically conceived proposal for alignment, and a successful one. Under a self-evasive label, this ideology served to create the largest 20th-century alliance in the world. Though formed as a non-military alliance, the non-aligned movement had more members than both the NATO and Warsaw Pact groups. Also, contrary to conventional wisdom, and even contrary to INDIA's Jawaharlal Nehru's moralist claims, non-alignment was not the middle path but a competing strategy aimed at making the Third World a partner in the global distribution of power and resources. It was hoped that non-alignment would also forge, to use EGYPT's Gamal Abdel-Nasser's words, a "community of thought" and a "friendship of struggle" which will "awaken" and "bind together" people of Asia and Africa.

The term and the concept. John Kenneth GALBRAITH has chronicled that President John KENNEDY had "mused that with so many countries opting for a neutralist policy, maybe the United States should be neutral too. I suggested . . . that the term was meaningless. Countries were, indeed, communist or non-communist."

While Europeans, at least in the beginning, called this stance neutralism, its founders preferred to call it non-alignment; a term reportedly coined by Indian Defense Minister Krishna Mennon.

"Mennon must have perceived the advantages perceived by the arcane word, which follows the noble traditions of other such words as non-violence, non-resistance, and non-attachment, words that defy accurate definition but vaguely uplift the human spirit and inspires it to build ideologies and philosophies around it," Galbraith wrote. In response to a reporter's insistent questioning, Mennon is known to have said: "Yes, in a sense non-alignment is an ugly word; it is a negative word but when you use it the way we do, it becomes positive." A number of scholars have attempted to link it to India's history, religious ethos, and national temperament. For instance, Michael Brecher has suggested: "The central message of India's philosophical tradition dating back from the Buddha has revolved around the rejection of the absolutes and extreme positions. On the contrary, it has stressed philosophical relativity, intellectual Catholicism and tolerance of opposites."

Rudolphs have summed up their observations in one sentence: "The most striking feature of Indian politics is its persistent centrism." Others see a parallel between non-alignment and the social separation of castes in India. Nehru has said: "I have not originated non-alignment; it is a policy inherent in the circumstances of India . . . and inherent in the very circumstances of the world today."

This mode of analysis, however, fails to take into account that:

1. Non-alignment was not created by India alone, at least four other nations and their leaders had played an equally important role in the formation of this coalition and movement

2. Even if we were to analyze only India's role in the process, non-alignment was more a reflection of the imperatives of the Indian state than Indian culture, though the two are not totally unrelated

3. It does not catalog consequences of non-aligned movement in terms of power politics by depoliticizing and defocusing the analytical project.

In a policy speech before the World Affairs Council in Los Angeles on April 21, 1961, President Ahmad Sukarno of the Republic of INDONESIA explained:

> We call our foreign policy independent and active. Others call us neutralist. Others call us uncommitted. Who can be neutral in this world today when the very nature of mankind is threatened? Who can be uncommitted when colonialism and imperialism still flourish and are still aggressive in the world? Who can be uncommitted when international social justice and international democracy is still just a dream and a vision?
>
> We are not neutral, and we will never be neutral so long as colonialism and imperialism continue to exist anywhere and in any manifestation anywhere in this world of ours. We will not be uncommitted so long as certain states are unwilling to accept demand for international social justice and international democracy.

A clear definition of non-alignment was enveloped in the criteria for inviting countries to the non-aligned conference adopted at the preparatory meeting held in Cairo, Egypt, in June 1961. "The country should have adopted an independent policy based on the coexistence of States with different political and social systems." Thus peaceful coexistence of "states with different social or political systems" and "supporting the movements for national independence" became two key elements of the definition of non-alignment.

The founders. The non-aligned movement was founded by five individuals: Nasser of Egypt, Jawaharlal Nehru of India, Joseph Tito of Yugoslavia, Sukarno of Indonesia, and Kwame Nkrumah of Ghana. These individuals shared common views about imperialism, colonization, decolonization, and sustainable independence of Third-World countries. They represented local and regional aspirations for sovereignty, independence, freedom, equality, peace, and progress. Their first goal was to expedite the process of decolonization and limit the reach of neo-colonialism. Their second goal was to maintain their independence and sovereignty. And their third goal was to seek democratization of the world order. At its roots, it was essentially a coalition of the dissident leaders of the semi-periphery (the socialist camp) and the main leaders of the periphery (the third world). Its original members represented the largest Muslim state (Indonesia), the largest Arab state (Egypt), the largest South Asian state (India), the most independent socialist state (Yugoslavia), and at that time the most politicized African state (Ghana).

Three of these five men were leaders of regional movements: Nasser of Pan Arabism, Kwame Nkrumah of pan-Africanism, and Tito of anti-Stalinism within the European communist community; in a way forerunner of Euro-communism. All of them were third world internationalists with varying degrees of sympathy for socialism, though each of them interpreted socialism very differently. Most of them were cognizant that receding colonialism will be replaced by emerging modes of neo-colonialism and thus imperialist exploitation of third world countries by Europe will continue under a different guise. Non-alignment was to be a defense against both colonialism and neocolonialism. As an expression of this unity against colonial occupation, Israel was never allowed to become a member of the non-aligned movement.

The subsequent leaders of the non-aligned movement include many historic figures such as Fidel Castro of Cuba and Nelson Mandela of South Africa.

Primary motivations. The primary motivations of this movement were to maintain newly gained independence; to ensure territorial integrity of newly decolonized states; to inculcate peaceful co-existence among states professing different social, political and economic systems; to build an environment of mutual trust and mutual benefit; and most importantly not to get embroiled in the Cold War. In effect, it was a third world response to the Cold War shaped by history of struggles against imperialism and colonialism. Its vision was eloquently formulated by one of its leaders: "We believe that peace and freedom are indivisible, and denial of freedom anywhere must endanger freedom elsewhere and lead to conflict and war. We are particularly interested in the emancipation of colonial and dependent countries and peoples, and in equal opportunity for all races."

Although the participating African and Asian countries shared a colonial past, their forms of government were not the same. Therefore the leaders of these countries decided to come together for the common purpose of maintaining peace and mutual cooperation.

To the extent that all politics is local, each leader had calculated a set of local advantage in co-authoring of the vision underlying the Cold War.

Nehru: a tryst with destiny. While these leader held many ideas and ideals in common, they differed in their secondary motivations and aspirations. For Nehru, the non-aligned movement was, *inter alia*, an embodiment of the Indian dream. On December 4, 1947, Nehru had written:

"We will not attach ourselves to any particular group. That has nothing to do with passivity or anything else. . . . We are not to going to join a war if we can help it; and we are going to join the side which is to our interest when the time comes to make the choice. There the matter ends."

Nehru felt that "the initiative comes to our people now and we shall make the history of our choice." Later, Nehru was even more candid: "We are asked to collect the smaller nations of the world around us . . . I think it is, if you like, opportunist in the long run—this policy that we have so far pursued before we became the government, and to some extent after we became the government . . ."

Nehru visualized fulfillment of six major goals through the establishment of the non-aligned movement:

1. Projection of India's interests at a global scale

2. Containment (or counter-containment) of its arch rival Pakistan

3. A major and lasting alliance with the Arab/Muslim world (which turned out to be a masterpiece of Indian diplomacy

4. Pressing a subtle advantage of neutrality over China

5. Establishing and lead a voting bloc at the UN

6. Enhancing India's bargaining position vis-à-vis both camps.

Nasser: seeking strategic partnership and strategic depth. Speaking to a large gathering at Rosetta, Egypt on September 19, 1959 Nasser said:

We have responsibilities toward our own country and toward the whole world. We are a small country and a small people but we have a role to play in the world, in world politics and in the world community. . . . By setting an example we can prove that there are in the world spiritual powers more powerful than the methods which they used in the Medieval times when they came here to occupy our land. Conscious of our responsibility towards the world, we announced our policy of positive neutrality. This policy of course got us into trouble, for positive neutrality means that we are subject to no influence from either camp but follow a policy of complete independence and prevent any attempt into our affairs.

For Nasser, non-alignment meant five things:

1. Further consolidation of the power of nationalists in Egypt vis-à-vis the Muslim Brotherhood, the communists and the army

2. Building a global coalition against Zionist occupation of Arab lands

3. Preventing what happened to the duly elected Iranian Prime Minister Dr. Mohammad Mussadegh from happening to other leaders in the region

4. Forging greater unity between Africa and Asia reflective of Egypt's dual Arab and African identity

5. Enunciating a contemporary Egyptian ethos enabling it to play a meaningful role in world affairs.

Tito: innovation in the service of liberation. Marshal Tito once told Nasser and Nehru: "I have seven complicated problems. I have *one* state that uses *two* alphabets, the Latin and the Slav; which speaks *three* languages, Serb, Croat, Slovenian-Macedonian; has *four* religions, Islam, Orthodox, Catholic, and Judaism; *five* nationalities, Slovenes, Croats, Serbians, Montenegrans, and Macedonians; *six* republics; and we have *seven* neighbors."

For Tito non-alignment was a resource for:

1. Maintaining Yugoslavia's unique identity within and without the socialist bloc

2. Legitimation and consolidation of his own power in Yugoslavia

3. Reducing Soviet control and domination over Yugoslavia without (direct) reliance on the West

4. Experimenting with new, non-communist and non-capitalist modes of development

5. Forging close links of mutual understanding and support between East European dissidents and third world nationalists.

Sukarno: wider aims of revolution. "To be released in all its strength and glory" Sukarno told his audience in the United States, "a nation also needs a vision, an ideal, a philosophy. For us in Indonesia, that philosophy is summed up in what we call our Pantja Sila, and, if I may say so, Pantja Sila holds for us an importance comparable to that in which your Declaration of Independence was held by the founding fathers of the United States. However, Pantja Sila was defined and accepted by our nation before we declared our independence and during the years of revolutionary struggle, when sometimes the outlook seemed grim and black, that clear definition of our national aims supported us and gave us strength." Pantja Sila, the Five Pillars, consists of: belief in God, nationalism, internationalism, democracy, and social justice.

For Sukarno, non-alignment had several advantages:

1. Strengthening Indonesian position vis-à-vis the Dutch

2. Instituting a modernist approach to nation-building and state formation

3. Projecting and applying at least three of the five principles, internationalism, democracy, and social justice, at the international level.

Nkrumah: a continental approach. Nkrumah, who in his vision and aspiration was as much a leader of Africa as of Ghana, wholeheartedly believed "The greatest contribution that Africa can make to the peace of the world is to avoid all the dangers inherent in disunity, by creating a political union which will also by its success, stand as an example to a divided world. A Union of African states will project more effectively the African personality. It will command respect from a world that has regard only for size and influence."

For him "continent" was the primary unit of thought and organization. He believed that "Under a major political union of Africa there could emerge a United Africa, great and powerful, in which the territorial boundaries which are the relics of colonialism will become obsolete and superfluous, working for the complete and total mobilization of the economic planning organization under a unified political direction. The forces that unite us are far greater than the difficulties that divide us at present, and our goal must be the establishment of Africa's dignity, progress and prosperity."

For Nkrumah, non-alignment had several local advantages, which included:

1. Consolidation of his power vis-à-vis the feudals and feudalist parties

2. Expansion, legitimation, and consolidation of pan-Africanism

3. A means of limiting the encroachment of neocolonialism

4. Generating goodwill and collaboration not only among nations but also among various regions of the world.

Brief history. Though the movement traces its origin to the Bandung (Indonesia) Conference of 1955, which was co-sponsored by Pakistan, India, Sri Lanka, Burma, and Indonesia, perhaps, the first foundational stone was laid by the leaders of Peoples Republic of China, who had articulated five principles of peaceful co-existence, which were later incorporated into Sino-Indian pact of 1954 over Tibet. These five principles (popularly known as Panch Sheel) are: mutual respect for each other's territorial integrity; non-aggression; non-interference in each other's affairs; equality and mutual benefit; and peaceful co-existence. Though the movement started off with only 25 countries, its present membership includes 144 countries, which means many UN members.

The milestones in the evolution of the non-aligned movement include the following: Sino-Indian Treaty of

1954, Bandung (Indonesia) Conference, 1955, First Summit at Belgrade 1961, the Second Summit at Cairo 1964, Third Summit at Lusaka, 1970, the Fourth Summit at Algiers, 1973; the Fifth Summit at Colombo, 1976; the Sixth Summit at Havana, 1979; the Seventh Summit at New Delhi, 1983; Eighth Summit at Harare, 1986; Ninth Summit at Belgrade, 1989; Tenth Summit at Jakarta, 1992; Eleventh Summit at Cartagena de Indias, 1995; Twelfth Summit at Durban, 1998; Thirteenth Summit at Kuala Lumpur, 2003.

Its increasing importance can be gauged by the increasingly larger number of countries, including European and North Americans, who attend its summits as observers and guests. For example, Brazil, China, Croatia, Kazakhstan, Kyrgyzstan, Mexico, Ukraine, and Uruguay attended its 13th Summit in 2003 Summit as observers. Moreover, the following countries attended this summit as guests: Australia, Bosnia-Herzegovina, Canada, Finland, France, Germany, Greece, Hungary, Ireland, Italy, Japan, Netherlands, New Zealand, Poland, Republic of Korea, Romania, Russian Federation, Slovak Republic, Slovenia, Switzerland, United Kingdom of Great Britain, and the United States.

Objectives. The objectives of the Non Aligned Movement have evolved over the last half-century, but its original goals included: granting freedom to people under colonial and alien domination; establishment of a just international economic order; elimination of the causes and horrors of war and, especially elimination of nuclear weapons; promotion of human rights; condemnation of all forms of racial discrimination; protection of the environment; abolition of imperialism, colonialism and neo-colonialism; peaceful co-existence and amiable settlement of international disputes; and strengthening the role and effectiveness of the UN.

Membership of the non-aligned movement was based on a five point criteria:

1. Independent policy based on non-alignment and co-existence of states with different social and political systems

2. Consistent support for national independence movements

3. Not a member of a multilateral military alliance concluded in the context of great power conflicts

4. If a country has a bilateral military agreement with a great power, or is a member of a regional defense pact, it should not be concluded in the context of great power conflicts

5. If it has conceded military bases to a foreign power, the concession should not have been in the context of great power conflicts.

Role in world politics during the Cold War. The overall role of the non-alignment movement during the Cold War can be classified into ten categories:

1. Prevent reemergence of colonialism and intensification of neocolonialism

2. Balance the world order

3. Help regulate competition between East and West

4. Ease North-South tensions

5. Promote nuclear disarmament

6. Create an effective system for overall security

7. Institutionalize decision-making and consensus-building mechanisms among the non-aligned nations

8. Strengthen international law and international institutions such as the UN

9. Prevent war, build peace, and conduct itself as "the largest peace movement in history"

10. Seek to lessen the gap of power and wealth among "have" and "have-not" nations.

Nuclear disarmament was one of the main planks of the non-alignment movement during the Cold War period, more so during the early phase than the later. In the later phase, several non-aligned countries including India and Pakistan had, contrary to their earlier assertions and public pronouncements, joined the nuclear race and became nuclear powers.

In the diplomatic field, there was a far greater convergence of interest between the second world (socialist) and third world countries than between the first and third world countries. In terms of its voting patterns during the Cold War, the third world was closer to the socialist camp than the capitalist camp.

Role in world politics during the post-Cold War period. Now that the Cold War has ended, is the non-aligned movement still relevant and still needed? The answer given by former UN Secretary General Boutros Bourtros-Ghali is an emphatic yes. Speaking at the 35th anniversary of the non-aligned movement, the former secretary general pointed out that despite the fold up of colonialism and Cold War, the "underlying philosophy" of non-alignment remains relevant and of immense enduring value for all nations. Its continued relevance is premised on the following principles: "rejection of power and military might as the basis of international order; assertion of independence and sovereign equality as the organizing principles of international relations; recognition of the universal need for development, and the link between disarmament and development; commitment to multilateral decision-making on global issues through the Unites Nations; and belief in solidarity that transcends—yet draws strength—from diversity."

Its original message for self-determination, freedom, independence, and sovereignty has been complemented with calls for North-South and South-South cooperation, on the one hand, and for democracy among the nations on the other. Today the scope of the non-aligned movement has been expanded to include political as well as economic cooperation with focus on development, industrialization, population control, debt relief, education, health care, and poverty alleviation. Its action agenda for the 21st century includes development, peacemaking, rule of international law, creation of an international culture of democracy among nations, ecology, resource preservation, and knowledge and technology transfer.

"The sovereign equality of nations has always implied a common stake in, and responsibility for, the survival and betterment of humanity." Close cooperation among the members of the non-aligned movement and similar cooperation between members of the non-aligned movement and countries of Eastern and Western Europe is being necessitated by the emergence of a unipolar world order. Pressing need for both balancing and stabilizing the unipolar world order necessitates such cooperation. In recent years, ecology, education, and human development have been added to this list. Its new leaders are calling for a renaissance of the non-aligned movement.

BIBLIOGRAPHY. Mohamed Hassanein Heikal, *The Cairo Documents* (Doubleday, 1973); Ahmed Sukarno, *For Liberty and Justice* (Department of Information, Republic of Indonesia, 1961); Kwame Nkrumah, *Consciencism: Philosophy and Ideology of De-Colonization* (Monthly Review Press, 1990); Jawaharlal Nehru, *India's Foreign Policy: Selected Speeches, September 1946–April 1961* (Government of India, 1983); *President Gamal Abdel Nasser's Speeches and Press Interviews* (U.A.R. Information Department, 1961); Rikhi Jaipal, *Non-Alignment: Origins, Growth and Potential for World Peace* (Allied Publishers Private Limited, 1987); J. L. Black, *Origins, Evolution and Nature of the Cold War* (ABC-CLIO, 1086); Andre Fontaine, *History of the Cold War: From the Korean War to the Present* (Pantheon Books, 1968).

AGHA SAEED, PH.D.
UNIVERSITY OF CALIFORNIA, BERKELEY

nonprofit organizations

NONPROFIT ORGANIZATIONS play an integral role in a capitalist economy. No longer is the establishment of a nonprofit organization merely an exercise in obtaining tax-exempt status for wealth protection, but rather, it is about acquiring social benefits of every variety, including the advancement of ideas, the promotion and safeguarding of cultures and religions, and the protection of valuable resources.

Within the profit sector, firms are motivated to be streamlined and efficient so that profits can be distributed to their owners/investors. The nonprofit, however, has other motives, and that is to exist for charitable or educational purposes, and to devote its funds and resources to the maximization of ends that its members and donors desire to attain, on a no-profit, no-loss basis. A nonprofit organization gets tax-exempt status with the Internal Revenue Service (IRS) because its trustees or shareholders do not benefit financially from any profits.

Nonprofit, of course, is not equated with losses, but instead is based on a breakeven concept so that those who run the organization can concentrate on carrying out the organization's stated goals without having to supply financial gain to those who fund the organization.

The separation of "for-profit" and "nonprofit" sectors is an admirable notion, for it has to do with people who are out to earn a return on investment, and those who want to invest in doing charitable works and producing desired outcomes. After all, certain goods and services cannot be profitable and therefore need the voluntary, financial support of interested individuals, as well as tax breaks from the IRS.

Society reaps substantial, non-monetary benefits from the operation of nonprofits, including what we derive from scholarly think tanks, educational institutions, health organizations, family and religious organizations, cultural-ethnic societies, historical preservation societies, and those organizations that assist people with disabilities or place homeless pets into good homes. These non-monetary gains are essential for the "good life" enjoyed by those living under a free-trade, capitalist system. Without the advantages derived therein, the individuals who benefit from charitable nonprofits would have less freedom because of government subsidies and welfare arrangements.

The nonprofit sector consists of voluntary coalitions and/or partnerships of individuals that have decided to take up a worthy cause, and hence, this replaces what otherwise could be public sector advancement into that particular area. After all, certain goods and services are necessary within a capitalist society, and if the production of these goods/services is not taken up voluntarily by individuals, the government will step in and tax the private sector in order to fund these goods/services for the public sector. In that case, political lobbying, partisan interests, career focus, and other unpleasant exploits are much more likely to have a negative influence on the goals and operations of an organization.

In addition, interested private parties typically exude a great passion for the cause and voluntarily invest their time, effort, or money. The satisfaction of deeds well done or the achievement of objectives is unquestionably a motivating factor for humans that strive to meet philanthropic ideals. An aspect of the social benefits received by way of a nonprofit organization is that no one individual is forced to pay for an outcome or benefit that he does not approve of. People who do not approve of a nonprofit's activities need not interact with them.

However, the characteristics of nonprofit economy are such that government both encourages and discourages nonprofits through subsidies and restrictions, while both proclaiming their virtues and conveying skepticism. In a truly capitalist economy, the government would have no bearing on the formation, mission, or social outcome of any organization, whether profit or nonprofit. However, in a mixed economy such as the UNITED STATES, opportunistic and political behavior still manage to play a large role within the nonprofit sector of the economy.

Simply because nonprofit organizations reside in a "hidden" sector of our economy, where scant attention is sometimes paid, doesn't mean that there is little interest in this part of the economy. Indeed, all of our lives are touched in some way by an array of nonprofit organizations working toward serving public interests in voluntary, non-coercive ways. In view of that, the nonprofit form of enterprise is essential to both beneficiary individuals and society as a whole.

BIBLIOGRAPHY. Morton Backer, *Modern Accounting Theory* (International Thomson, 1966); Randall G. Holcombe, *Writing Off Ideas: Taxation, Foundations, and Philanthropy in America* (Transactions Publishers, 2000); Burton A. Weisbrod, *The Nonprofit Economy* (Harvard University Press, 1988).

KAREN DE COSTER
WALSH COLLEGE

North, Douglass (1920–)

WINNER OF THE 1993 Nobel Prize in Economics (jointly with Robert FOGEL), Douglass North was cited for having "renewed" research in economic history by rigorously "applying economic theory and quantitative methods in order to explain economic and institutional change." North helped usher in the cliometric revolution in economic history and later played a key role in redirecting economic historians away from excessive dependence on theories emphasizing optimization, instead focusing attention on institutions and their role in economic evolution.

As student at the University of California, Berkeley, North triple-majored in political science, philosophy, and economics. Upon graduation, he entered the U.S. Merchant Marines, became a skilled navigator, and used his considerable free time to read widely. Following World War II, he enrolled in Berkeley's graduate economics program, completing a dissertation in 1952 that examined the history of the life insurance industry.

After joining the faculty of the University of Washington in Seattle, North published a series of well-regarded articles on American economic history. In 1960, he was named coeditor of the *Journal of Economic History*, where, despite objections by many more traditional economic historians, he used his position to open the journal to the new cliometric work of young scholars, such as Robert Fogel. Cliometrics takes its name by adding the suffix "metrics" (to measure) to "Clio" (the Greek muse of history). The essence of cliometrics is to unite economic theory with measurement to explain history.

North's first book, *The Economic Growth of the United States, 1790–1860* (1961), is regarded as a landmark in the transformation of economic history. Backed by a host of quantitative evidence, it argued that the three regions of the American economy were initially separated by high transportation costs. As steamboats, ocean-shipping, and canals linked these regions in the decades before the AMERICAN CIVIL WAR, each progressively specialized in its own comparative advantage. The South exported sugar, rice, tobacco, and increasingly cotton; the North became a financial, commercial and manufacturing center; and the West dedicated its resources to food and animal production. Trade allowed them to complement each other, spurring economic growth. The book's central contribution showed how economic theory and measurement could explain the broader contours of history. During this period, North became a veritable apostle for the new cliometric approach, as exemplified by his brief textbook, *Growth and Welfare in the American Past* (1966), which challenged many conventional views on important topics in American economic history, using basic economic theory and quantitative evidence.

In the mid-1960s, North turned his attention to European economic history, and became convinced that standard economic theory was incapable of explaining longer-term economic change. His subsequent research sought to go beyond economic growth's proximate causes (such as technological change and investment) to its ultimate causes. This task required an understanding of institutions, property rights, and governance.

The first major product of this new approach was *Institutional Change and American Economic Growth*

(1971), written with Lance Davis. It developed a model in which individuals and organized groups modified institutions (such as laws, regulations, and property rights) when they believed that changing existing institutional rules would generate benefits greater than the costs of innovation. North and Davis used their model to examine institutional changes in land policies, finance, transportation, manufacturing, service industries, and labor markets.

Next, North joined Robert Paul Thomas in writing *The Rise of the Western World* (1973), which, in a mere 158 pages, aimed to explain the fundamental factors of Western Europe's economic development between 900 and 1800. It argued that changes in population and technology altered relative prices and induced new institutional arrangements, especially the decline of feudalism and the rise of the market economy.

North was not completely satisfied with these books' central ideas, however. In *Structure and Change in Economic History* (1981) he discarded the assumption of efficient institutions and began explaining why inefficient rules would tend to exist and persist. North's overarching model was built on new theories of property rights, the state, and ideology. This exceptionally ambitious book was recognized as a treasury of bold generalizations and provocative insights. However, critics warned that North had overstated, oversimplified, and disregarded conflicting evidence, and questioned the usefulness of such grand theorizing. Similar reactions greeted *Institutions, Institutional Change, and Economic Performance* (1990). North had clearly moved beyond his cliometric roots—there is not a single table in either book.

North continued teaching at the University of Washington until 1983, when he moved to Washington University in St. Louis. There he established the Center in Political Economy, and began advising governments, including Russia, the Czech Republic, Argentina and Peru, on how to create institutions beneficial to economic growth.

BIBLIOGRAPHY. Claudia Goldin, "Cliometrics and the Nobel," *Journal of Economic Perspectives* (1995); Donald N. McCloskey, "Fogel and North: Statics and Dynamics in Historical Economics," *Scandinavian Journal of Economics* (1994); Johan Myhrman and Barry Weingast, "Douglass C. North's Contributions in Economics and Economic History," *Scandinavian Journal of Economics* (1994); Roger Ransom, Richard Sutch, and Gary Walton, eds., *Explorations in the New Economic History: Essays in Honor of Douglass C. North* (Academic Press, 1982).

ROBERT WHAPLES, PH.D.
WAKE FOREST UNIVERSITY

Norway

THE KINGDOM OF NORWAY is a constitutional monarchy with a population of approximately 4.5 million people (2002). It covers approximately 125,181 square miles in northern Europe and occupies the western part of the Scandinavian Peninsula. Norway shares a border with SWEDEN in the east, FINLAND and RUSSIA in the northeast. The capital, Oslo, is the largest city in the country. Norway also has territories in the Arctic Ocean, south Atlantic, and in Antarctica.

During WORLD WAR II, the Norwegian merchant fleet provided aid to the Allies during the war. Even though half of the Norwegian merchant fleet was sunk during the war, Norway quickly recovered its commercial position. Norway's postwar economic policy included a mixture of SOCIALISM and measures such as controls over prices, interest, and dividends.

Approximately 75 percent of Norway's land is nonproductive. Less than 4 percent is cultivated and the country has to import over 50 percent of its food. There are pasture lands in the mountains that are used for cattle and sheep; to the north, the pastures are used for raising domesticated caribou, reindeer. One-fourth of the land is forested, and as such Norway's timber is the chief natural resource and one of the main industries. Tourists are attracted by the fantastic fjords and the midnight sun. Fishing is very important and Norway exports cod, herring, and mackerel as fresh, canned, or salted product to the entire world.

Petroleum was first discovered in Norway in the Ekofisk field in 1969 and is now vital to the nation's economy, becoming, along with natural-gas production, the country's chief industry. While this industry brings increased employment, it also ties Norway to the fluctuating world petroleum market that can cause increased inflation. Norway has other mineral resources that are heavily mined: pyrites, copper, titanium, iron ore, coal, zinc, and lead. Norway also produces nickel, aluminum, ferro alloys and semi-finished steel. Food manufacturing, pulp and paper, electrochemical, electrometallurgical, and shipbuilding industries are also important to the economy.

Norway trades mainly with the UNITED KINGDOM, GERMANY, Sweden, the NETHERLANDS, DENMARK, and the UNITED STATES. In 1972 and 1994, Norwegian voters rejected membership in the EUROPEAN UNION.

BIBLIOGRAPHY. F. Hodne, *The Norwegian Economy: 1920–1980* (Palgrave Macmillan, 1983); J.W. Moses, *Open States in the Global Economy* (Palgrave Macmillan, 2000); Royal Norwegian Embassy, www.norway.org.

L. BARNHILL
RED ROCKS COLLEGE

O

occupation

WHEN WE ASK SOMEONE "What do you do?" we expect to hear about that person's job, or perhaps that she is unemployed. We might add "for a living," and that in itself is telling as well. It has become second nature to us. Working for a salary or professional fees, usually bound by a contract (i.e., having an occupation), has been for many decades the main way to become an effective member of modern societies for a huge majority of citizens. Most people pay for their food, their housing and everything else with the money they get in exchange for the tasks they do for others, usually employers. The very origin of the word "salary" shows the historical depth of working life: Roman soldiers got their pay in salt, hence salarium.

We should remind ourselves, however, that it has not always been like that. Hunter-gatherers or feudal peasants either consumed their own products or the goods they bartered for them. They worked for their lords some days of the week, but got only protection (often from their own lords' punishment) as a payment. Only medieval artisans, organized into guilds, can be counted as forerunners of the modern notion of occupation. Among other things, guilds set up a credential system, so that a rigid hierarchy of apprentices, journeymen, and masters was established, and guildsmen successfully excluded non-affiliated outsiders. Only when one of his products was voted a masterpiece by the masters of the guild was the journeyman admitted. There were merchant and craft guilds, such as goldsmiths, cobblers, stone masons (whose secret association gave birth to the freemasons, who still have the squares and compasses used in stone buildings as their symbols), or carpenters.

But in the first stages of industrial society, paid work was associated with poverty and poor health, it was a de-meaning activity (except for the very upper crust of professionals), and it was not usually meant to be a steady source of income. The putting-out system, for instance, very common in the textile business, meant that merchants arranged with workers for production to be carried out in their own homes, but no commitment was in principle made to maintain that arrangement from year to year, or even order to order. Occupations, considered as stable, legally bound arrangements with productive concerns, often related to educational degrees and/or vocational training, and around which foreseeable and acceptable life courses could be organized, are something of an innovation. Just consider that, only in 1938, the Fair Labor Standards Act managed to ban oppressive child labor, reduced the maximum workweek to 44 hours, and set the minimum hourly wage at 25 cents. And that regulation covered only a lucky fifth of the American working population.

In fact, it can be said that occupations with some degree of legal protection are part and parcel of a wider social compact, championed by progressive politicians, manufacturers and trade UNIONS in the first decades of the 20th century. For instance, Henry FORD famously changed the rules of an industry bent on paying as little as possible to, and getting as much working time (both in weekdays and in daily hours) as possible from, its labor force. He stated that "the people who consume the bulk of goods are the people who make them. That is a fact we must never forget—that is the secret of our prosperity." This placed the regulation of occupations, in terms of leisure time, stability and benefits, at the heart of management concerns. Planned production, heavy investment in machinery and assembly lines and around-the-clock shifts required a loyal and dependable workforce, "scientifically organized" by management pioneers such as Frederick Winslow Taylor into carefully defined occupational categories.

Occupation as identity. Today, we all know that a person's "place" (status, prestige, welfare, even leisure options or lifestyle) in society is, to a great extent, a function of her job and its conditions. We are all aware of what it means to have a blue- or a white-collar job, and even though all workers may take pride in their identity, life chances are unevenly distributed. Systematic sociological classifications such as the Goldthorpe Classes are easy to identify with our own map of social structure. From the upper-service class (from administrators to higher-grade professionals) to the unskilled workers, the routine non-manual or the petty bourgeoisie (composed of small proprietors, among others), our job has a lot to do with what our life prospects are. Health, political participation, or newspaper readership are a few examples from the host of traits associated with people's location in the occupational structure.

It is true that to a (classical) Marxist the great cleavage in capitalistic societies runs along the owners of the means of production (the employers or large shareholders) and those who only own themselves (i.e., their ability to work for the former). That is the source of class conflict, and the engine of history in Marxist terms. But it seems obvious that there is a great deal of difference, at least in life conditions as experienced day-to-day, between corporate managers, neurologists, web designers, longshoremen, and garbage collectors. Inequality studies have accordingly placed the distribution of occupations at the core of their view of society. Now, try to picture how occupations (and the social positions attached) are distributed in American society. Most survey respondents would answer that the resulting image is a pyramid, with a tiny tip of super-rich and a wide base of low-wage manual workers; or more commonly they suggest something like a diamond, with few people on top and at the bottom, and a wide middle class of reasonably well-to-do workers.

Social structure researchers have argued that American society could be instead depicted as a double diamond, with a small one comprising a privileged class of around 20 percent of Americans, where we find the superclass (1–2 percent of large shareholders, investors, and proprietors) and credentialed professionals, all highly educated and highly paid, such as engineers, executives in large firms, etc. This diamond of the privileged is set on top of another diamond four times as big. The area in which they contact would be the comfort class, where we find skilled blue-collar workers (say, a successful carpenter or plumber) or many types of professionals (such as nurses or teachers). But this comfort class comprises less than 10 percent of the population, 50 percent of whom would be really in the thick part of the lower diamond, or the contingent class. The lower tip of the big diamond corresponds to the excluded class

of people who work only every now and then, perhaps no more than 10 percent of Americans.

One of the main points here is that your place in the occupational structure is related not only or directly to your educational success, but to several other types of capitals. For instance, whom you know, and the people whom these people in turn know (i.e., your social CAPITAL), are crucial to getting the information and influence required to improve your job prospects. Another aspect of inequality linked to occupational status is that of the uncertainty surrounding the contingent class. Workers are always at risk; even when they have relatively well-paying jobs, illness or lay-offs may very quickly wreck their lives, as they live paycheck to paycheck.

Occupation, education, and skill. Occupations are closely linked to education, to transferable skills or human capital. The more specialized your skills, and the harder to acquire them, the better you can bargain for your rewards in the labor market. The opposite also holds, and it has been said that the gap between those able to command good conditions and high compensation and low-wage workers increased markedly in the last quarter of the 20th century, by at least 30 percent in terms of income.

Many researchers attribute this growth in inequality to a combination of factors, among which the demand for ever more skilled labor stands out, together with the shift from industry into services (which also hurts non-college educated workers) and institutional factors, such as the decline in unionization rates.

Technological change and the universal improvement in education have certainly been the factors behind the growth in total human capital present in the economy. A good way to realize the size of this transformation is to compare the fraction of total hours worked in the private business sector that were carried out by people with different levels of education in different periods. Let's start with 1948. Men with less than 4 years of schooling pitched in 8.3 percent of all worked hours, whereas those with 5 to 8 years of education worked 35.6 percent. The share of the best-educated workers, with 16 or more years of schooling, was 6.0 percent. However, by 1999, men with less than 4 years of schooling worked less than 1 percent of all hours that year, and the share of those with 5 to 8 years of schooling had decreased to 3.4 percent. But the figures for the best educated, college and postgraduate with more than 16 years of formal education, were now over 28 percent.

This sea-change summarizes the extraordinary historical transformation in what occupations are like, and therefore what American workers' life is about. Capitalism is, most of all, a dynamic system, in which firms are prodded by the carrot of profit and the stick of bankruptcy towards ever-changing production and consumption structures. The Austrian economist Joseph SCHUM-PETER famously called this a process of "creative destruction." Occupations, the forms in which human work participates in this system, have accordingly a history of their own. There are jobs that do not exist anymore in practice (just think of horseshoe-hammering blacksmiths), and other occupations have declined enormously in the number of people involved (all kinds of agricultural workers). Still others have sprouted along the route of industrial and human service innovation. Information-technology activities, for instance, have witnessed a tremendous growth in recent decades.

Along those years, it was often the case that some jobs could not be given a category or a title by the employers. We could mention, as arcane as occupations go, ISO specialists (who aid in checking the compliance of firms and products to the Industrial Standard Organization norms such as the ISO 9002), or dialysis reuse technicians (that, as all other health-related occupations, have experienced a boost linked to an aging population). But in fact, many new or emerging occupations are little less esoteric or glamorous (think of aerobic coaches, or schoolbus aides).

Quality of life. It is crystal clear that the quality of a person's life is closely related to her occupation. If a society is to be considered fair, it should then be possible within it to move toward better jobs in one lifetime (career mobility) or for the next generation to move up the occupation ladder (intergenerational mobility), whether its shape is a double or single diamond. Taken to the extreme, this is the familiar "rags to riches" story, but a milder version of "making it in the land of opportunity" is widely believed to be part of the American outlook on society. But, is it true? Do low-wage Americans have a greater chance than other citizens of advanced societies to "make it," or see their children "make it"? Although no easy answers are available, it seems that mobility is not greater in the UNITED STATES when we compare it to other countries, and it could be getting even worse. The only outstanding difference is the degree of inequality, which can be measured for example by the result of dividing the income of the top 20 percent of the working population by that of the bottom 20 percent. With data from the late 1990s, U.S. credentialed workers earned nine times as much as those in the lowest part of the contingent class and the excluded. Compare that to GERMANY (less than five times) or to CANADA (a little over five), not to mention the egalitarian Nordic welfare states, where the best-paid workers earned only 3.5 times as much as their less-qualified fellow countrymen. Just to give a glimpse of the growth of income inequality among executive positions and low-pay ones in the last decades, it has been claimed that CHIEF EXECUTIVE OFFICERS (CEOs) now earn 419 times the pay of the average workers in their firm, up from 326 times in 1997 and 42 times in 1980.

What can we expect occupations to be in the near future? Even after the internet bust, technological change will probably continue pushing for greater returns to investment in education, and greater inequality in the same measure. But apart from these trends, changes in occupations are bound to affect our own identity; they will probably be less capable of telling us who we are. It has been noted that, as an average, a college-educated American will probably change jobs more than 12 times through a lifetime. Information technology and new forms of corporate organization, based on flexibility and short-term projects, mean that strong ties to people and firms may not develop as they did in the past. Trust, loyalty, and a sense of one's own bearings have to do with a certain continuity in place and time. The story we tell about ourselves may become difficult to weave, because of the instability that modern capitalistic practices increasingly build into our everyday life.

BIBLIOGRAPHY. Margaret M. Blair and Thomas A. Kochan, eds., *The New Relationship: Human Capital in the American Corporation* (Brookings Institution Press, 2000); Richard Freeman, *The New Inequality: Creating Solutions for Poor America* (Beacon Press, 1998); Al Gini, *My Job, My Self: Work and the Creation of the Modern Individual* (Routledge, 2000); Eric Greene, Laurie, Julie and Bruce Arnesen, eds., *Labor Histories: Class, Politics, and the Working-Class Experience* (University of Illinois Press, 1998); Robert Perrucci, *The New Class* (Rowman and Littlefield, 1999); Robert B. Reich, *The Work of Nations* (Random House, 1994); Richard Sennet, *The Corrosion of Character* (W.W. Norton, 1998); Studs Terkel, *Working: People Talk About What They Do All Day and How They Feel About What They Do* (Pantheon, 1974); Amy S. Wharton, ed., *Working in America: Continuity, Conflict & Change* (McGraw-Hill, 1998).

EMILIO LUQUE, PH.D.
UNED UNIVERSITY, SPAIN

Ohlin, Bertil (1899-1979)

AWARDED THE 1977 Nobel Prize in Economics, Bertil Ohlin was a Swedish economist and leader of a political party. He is credited, in conjunction with Eli HECKSHER, with introducing one of the most influential economic theories of the 20th century.

Ohlin's education started at the University of Lund in SWEDEN, where he studied mathematics, statistics, and economics. He then went on to study under Hecksher at the Stockholm School of Business. Ohlin then moved to the Stockholm University, where he would learn under some of the most prominent Swedish economists of his time, Gustav Cassel, Knut Wicksell, David Davidson and others. In 1924, he presented his thesis on international trade theory. This lead to his seminal work titled "Interregional and International Trade" in 1933.

Ohlin acknowledges the immense influence Hecksher's writings had on his trade theory and particularly Hecksher's paper in 1919 titled "The Influence of Foreign Trade on the Distribution of Income."

The trade theory came to be known as the Hecksher-Ohlin Factor Endowment Theory. The main question posed by this theory was how nations trade with each other. The earlier trade theories had focused on the Absolute Advantage (Adam SMITH) and Comparative Advantage (David RICARDO). There was no discussion of how the countries got the advantage; hence, the factor endowment theory proposed that the trade pattern should stem from the availability of resources within a country. Factor abundance and factor intensity formed the building blocks of this new theory proposed by Hecksher and Ohlin.

The trade pattern between countries would take place under the following principle: A country will export a commodity that uses its abundant factor inten-

sively. A labor-abundant country would produce a commodity that uses labor intensively and a capital-abundant country would produce a commodity that uses capital intensively.

For this work, Ohlin was awarded the Nobel Prize jointly with James MEADE. In recognizing his work, the Nobel committee praised Ohlin's work on patterns of international trade, resource allocation, intra-national trade, and the international division of labor.

After submitting his thesis, Ohlin spent two years traveling to England and the United States. He studied both at Cambridge and then at Harvard universities, and Ohlin credited these experiences as immensely useful and influential in his future writings. His academic career ranged from being selected as a chair of the economics department at the University of Copenhagen, to the chair of the Stockholm School of Business, to lecturer at various universities in Europe and the United States.

Ohlin was also very active in Sweden's political arena. He was elected leader of the Liberal Party in Sweden, holding the position from 1944–67 during which time the liberal party was the government's main opposition.

During his entire career, Ohlin had published over 1,200 articles both in academic journals and several newspapers. His writings resulted in major academic works written in the area of regional growth, international trade, and factor prices.

BIBLIOGRAPHY. "Bertil Ohlin Autobiography" www.nobel.se/economics; Robert Carbaugh, *International Economics* (South Western, 8th Edition); Beth Yarbrough and Robert Yarbrough, *The World Economy: Trade and Finance* (Dryden, 1997); Michael Todaro and Stephen Smith, *Economic Development* (Addison-Wesley, 2002); History of Economic Thought, cepa.newschool.edu.

JAISHANKAR RAMAN, PH.D.
VALPARAISO UNIVERSITY

Swedish economist Bertil Ohlin proposed new theories on international trade and resource allocation.

oil

ALTHOUGH OIL WAS of little importance as a source of ENERGY before the 20th century, humans have used petroleum for thousands of years. Ancient Sumerians, Assyrians, and Babylonians used crude oil collected from seeps near the Euphrates River. Egyptians used it for medicinal purposes, while Persians used oil to soak incendiary arrows. In the late 19th century, petroleum was mainly used for illumination in kerosene lamps as whale oil became scarcer.

By the early 20th century, oil joined coal, wind, wood, and muscle power as one of the world's main sources of energy. The century saw a dramatic increase in overall world energy production and consumption, and oil was the key. Indeed, it soon replaced coal as the world's main fossil fuel. First steam ships and railroads, then automobiles and airplanes utilized oil, making it the main fuel used in transportation by about 1930. Oil would also be used extensively for heating. Furthermore, petroleum became important in the production of plastics, synthetic fibers, and many other chemical products. Oil deposits, however, are scattered unevenly around the world. This fact requires large international corporations to extract, transport, process, and deliver oil. These oil companies maintain a worldwide network of wells, pipelines, tankers, and refineries.

In addition, in the 20th and into the 21st century, oil played an important role in international relations. A country's petroleum reserves have significant economic and political consequences. Oil's importance as a global issue is intensified due to the fact that most of the world's petroleum deposits are found in a few large fields.

Most oil fields are small and insignificant, but perhaps half of the world's original oil reserves are located in fields known as supergiants, which contain more than five billion barrels. There have been fewer than 40 supergiants discovered since exploration began in the mid-19th century, and less than 5 percent of the world's known fields have produced about 95 percent of all of oil. Most of these large fields are located in the Persian Gulf region of the Middle East, making the area a flashpoint in international political and economic relations.

Early oil booms in the United States and Russia. The first significant oil boom in the world took place in Pennsylvania when hard-rock drilling began in 1859. For the first time, inexpensive oil was available for widespread use. By late 1860, there were some 75 wells producing oil in a part of the state known as the Oil Regions. There were also at least 15 refineries in the area and more in nearby Pittsburgh. The region produced 450,000 barrels in 1860. Production increased with the discovery of the first flowing well in 1861 and by 1862, output was 3 million barrels. Stories of instant wealth attracted many who sought to make their fortune. However, the early oil industry already demonstrated a tendency to be subject to great price fluctuations. Thus, while prices had reached $10 per barrel in January 1861, by the end of the same year prices had declined to a mere 10 cents per barrel.

The AMERICAN CIVIL WAR played a major role in the Pennsylvania oil industry. Traditionally, the North had imported turpentine from the South in order to produce camphene, a cheap illuminating oil. However, when the war broke out, Northerners turned to Pennsylvania oil for lighting. Furthermore, because the North no longer benefited from revenue generated by Southern cotton exports, Northerners began to export more oil in order to recoup the lost revenue. In addition, after the war, many veterans flocked to the oil regions, contributing to a great speculative boom that saw prices reach nearly $14 per barrel. Investors formed hundreds of new oil companies all along the East Coast in cities such as New York and Washington, D.C. However, there soon followed a period of depression, leading to low prices in 1866–67. Among the companies that came out of this initial oil boom was John D. ROCKEFELLER's STANDARD OIL COMPANY, which he established in 1870 and which soon came to dominate the industry.

The Pennsylvania oil boom was soon followed by one in Russia, making the country the world's leading producer by the turn of the century. In the 1860s, Russia imported most of its kerosene from the United States. Soon, however, Russia became a major oil producer itself when oil was found near Baku on the Aspheron Peninsula, an outgrowth of the Caucasus Mountains on the Caspian Sea. There had been a primitive oil industry in the early 19th century that the government controlled. The Russian government then opened up the industry to competitive private enterprise in the 1870s, leading to the expansion of drilling and the construction of refineries. Foreign interests soon played a key role, such as the Swedish Nobel family and the French Rothschilds.

For example, Ludwig Nobel developed some the first oil tankers, leading to a revolution in the oil transportation industry. In the 1880s, a railroad was completed from the oil fields and refineries to the Black Sea, which opened up world markets to Russian oil. Soon, Russian petroleum was competing with U.S. kerosene in Europe. By 1888, Russia was producing more than 20 million barrels of oil. Living and working conditions in the oil fields were poor, which led to much worker agitation, and in 1903, a work stoppage in the oil fields set off a strike wave in the country. Then, during the 1905 revolution, the flow of Russian oil diminished greatly due to further worker struggles. With little new investment in the early 20th century, the Russian oil industry soon declined. After the creation of the SOVIET UNION in 1917, the Russians tapped the oil reserves in Siberia and largely ignored Baku (now in the country of Azerbaijan), leaving polluted water and abandoned oil derricks.

The oil booms in Pennsylvania and Russia both paled in comparison with what would soon occur in Texas. Oil production on a small scale began in Texas in the 1890s. Then in 1900, drilling began on the coastal plain near Beaumont, Texas, on a hill known as Spindletop. Using rotary-drilling techniques borrowed from water-well drilling, in January 1901, a well on Spindletop known as Lucas I began flowing at 75,000 barrels per day. This gusher started the Texas oil boom and within months more than 100 companies operated more than 200 wells.

A number of major oil companies were involved in Texas oil production, which allowed them to erode much of the traditional power of Standard Oil Company.

For example, Shell (ROYAL DUTCH SHELL GROUP) sought to diversify from its Russian production and also strengthen its position against Standard. Shell was among the companies that took advantage of Texas petroleum being especially good for use as fuel oil. Soon, the oil industry was transformed, as petroleum was now used increasingly for fuel in ships and railroads rather than for illumination. The Sun Oil Company also played a significant role in Texas, not only in production but also in the storage, transportation, and marketing aspects of the industry. Sun acquired storage facilities in Texas and also built a refinery near Philadelphia to receive Texas crude oil by boat. Finally, the early Texas oil boom saw the birth of Texaco, which started in 1902 as the Texas Company. After becoming Texaco in 1906, this company (now CHEVRON TEXACO) was among the leaders in producing and selling gasoline. Soon, oil production spread to other parts of Texas and to neighboring states such as Louisiana and Oklahoma.

An even bigger oil boom in Texas began in 1930. The East Texas reservoir, known as the Black Giant, was the biggest oil deposit in the United States discovered to date. Within a year, there were more than 1,000 wells pumping out 1 million barrels per day. This vast new supply, however, led to lower prices. For example, in 1926, the price of oil in Texas was $1.85 per barrel. By May 1931, the price had fallen to 15 cents. Much of the production during the East Texas boom was controlled by small, independent producers, not by the big oil companies. The Texas Railroad Commission, which had certain control over the oil industry, sought to limit production by these many small producers in order to restore higher prices. The commission was unsuccessful at first, leading the governor to send in the National Guard and the Texas Rangers to shut down production. Prices rose again in 1932. The governor granted the Texas Railroad Commission the power to issue pro-rationing orders, thus allowing the commission to set quotas on oil production. Nevertheless, authorities had only limited success in limiting production. First, they set quotas too high and production still outstripped demand. Second, there was much production of so-called "hot oil" illegally produced above the quotas. Federal government intervention would be required to more successfully deal with the supply and demand issues in Texas during the 1930s.

Petroleum in Latin America: Oil booms in Mexico and Venezuela.
In the early 20th century, there was significant exploration and production of petroleum in MEXICO. Exploration efforts found oil in the rainforests of Veracruz along the Gulf Coast and drilling began in earnest in 1906. Two foreign-owned companies dominated the early Mexican oil industry, Pan American Petroleum and Mexican Eagle. Major discoveries in the country began in 1910 with the Potero del Llano 4 well, said to be the biggest "strike" in the world at the time. With these major strikes centered near Tampcio, Mexican Eagle became one of the world's leading oil companies and Mexico became a major producer. Mexican oil supplies were especially important to the United States market. Mexico was a critical source of oil during WORLD WAR I and, by 1920, 20 percent of the U.S. market was supplied by Mexico. By 1921, Mexico had become the second-largest producer in the world.

Although many in Mexico saw oil as a way to achieve economic success, the petroleum industry encountered a number of problems. Oil companies viewed the rainforest and indigenous populations in the area as obstacles, and there would be great environmental and human costs. In addition, saltwater seeped into the Mexican oil fields, making production more difficult. Foreign competition from the United States and VENEZUELA also harmed Mexico's position as a leading producer. Eventually, the Mexican oil industry also became a battleground for the major oil companies and the country's government. The Mexican Revolution, which began in 1910, sought national ownership of mineral resources such as oil. The 1917 constitution established government ownership of the subsoil. Along with many new regulations and taxes, the stipulations of the new constitution led foreign companies to begin to withdraw investment from Mexico and the country began to decline as a major producer.

In 1937, there was a dispute between U.S. and British oil companies and the oil workers' labor unions. The conflict led to a strike and subsequent legal battles. Then, the companies refused to honor a wage increase ordered by an arbitration tribunal. In response, Mexican president Lázaro Cárdenas ordered the expropriation all foreign oil companies. Cárdenas then created a national oil company known as *Petróleos Mexicanos* (PEMEX). Cárdenas' actions led to sanctions by the United States and Great Britain. Nevertheless, the oil nationalization was a major victory for Mexican nationalists and was largely supported by all sectors of Mexican society.

Then, in the late 1970s, Mexico discovered large deposits of oil and gas on its eastern coast. By 1980, the country had estimated reserves of 200 billion barrels. These vast deposits provided a great deal of hope for the Mexican government, but would also contribute to a major economic crisis. With world oil prices up due to events in the Middle East, the Mexican government counted on oil revenue for its foreign exchange in order to further expand petroleum production and thus create jobs. To this end, the government began to import equipment and technology, relying on foreign loans. This situation led to a rise in Mexico's trade deficit, which in turn caused high inflation. When oil prices fell significantly in 1981, projected government earnings also shrank dramatically. In turn, there was a flight of dollars and a government devaluation of the Mexican peso. Mexico became mired in a RECESSION marked by high UNEMPLOYMENT. In danger of defaulting on its foreign loans, Mexico accepted IMF loans and austerity programs.

The political changes in Mexico that eventually paved the way for NATIONALIZATION led the oil companies to look elsewhere for new wells. The companies expected that world petroleum demand would grow and that there was the potential for shortages. Furthermore, the experiences of World War I showed the strategic importance of oil. That, combined with the great profits that could be made, led the companies to seek oil in countries such as Venezuela in the 1920s. Venezuela under the dictator Juan Vicente Gómez, who came to power in 1908, offered a favorable climate for foreign oil-investment, in contrast to Mexico. In the early 1900s, the country was still relatively poor, under-populated, and agricultural. Gómez saw oil as a way to both develop his country and make himself rich at the same time. To this end, Gómez ended the nationalistic policies of his predecessor Cipriano Castro and sought to promote foreign investment.

Oil exploration and production in Venezuela was difficult at first, as the country was not well mapped, there were few roads, and diseases were widespread. Nevertheless, by 1913, Royal Dutch Shell was already involved in Venezuela and would soon be joined by Standard of New Jersey. The 1922 Petroleum Law set the terms for concessions, taxes, and royalties. Then in December 1922, the Barroso well in the La Rosa Field in the Maracaibo Basin, which belonged to Shell, starting spewing 100,000 barrels per day, which marked the start of the oil boom in Venezuela. Soon, hundreds of foreign oil interests flocked to Venezuela. Gomez sold off concessions to his friends and family, who then resold them at great profit to the foreign oil companies.

The Venezuelan oil boom transformed the country's economy and society. In 1921, Venezuela produced 1.7 million barrels of oil. By 1929, the country produced 137 million barrels, making it second only to the United States. Oil accounted for 76 percent of the country's export earnings and about half of all government revenue. Venezuelan petroleum also made the foreign oil companies wealthy. Shell, Standard of New Jersey, and Gulf controlled nearly 90 percent of Venezuelan oil, so the country still remained dependent on foreign investment. The Venezuelan population also changed as many foreign workers came to work in the oil fields, especially Caribbean blacks.

Gómez died in 1935 and the Venezuelan oil industry he built soon began to change. By the late 1930s, the

The production of refined oil and petrochemicals remains the world's major energy industry, despite alternative resources.

country was more dependent on oil than ever before, as petroleum made up 90 percent of exports. Gomez's successors sought to reform the industry. At the same time, foreign companies and governments wanted to avoid nationalization, as Venezuela was an important source of cheap oil, especially during WORLD WAR II. In March 1943, a new petroleum law called for equal sharing of profits between the Venezuelan government and the oil companies. In exchange for solidifying and extending concessions and allowing for new exploration, the Venezuelan government received the same amount of revenue as the foreign oil companies.

In the 1970s, the Venezuelan government nationalized the country's oil industry. In 1971, the government announced that when oil concessions began to expire in 1983, they would revert to the STATE. Furthermore, no new concessions would be granted. In response, companies lowered their investments in Venezuela, leading to decreased production. Increases in world oil prices in 1973 led to heightened demand for nationalization. Thus, in 1975, President Carlos Andrés Pérez announced that nationalization would take place on January 1, 1976. The nationalization process went relatively smoothly. The government compensated foreign oil firms with $1 billion, while creating a national oil company known as *Petróleos de Venezuela* (PDVSA). The Venezuelan government signed service contracts with foreign companies to obtain technology and personnel. They also made marketing agreements with the companies in order to sell Venezuelan oil on the world market. While PDVSA did become a major force in the world oil industry, Venezuela remained largely dependent on oil exports for its economic well-being.

Oil in the Middle East. By the 1920s, the Middle East surpassed Latin America as a major oil-producing region and became a key to world politics and economics due to its vast petroleum reserves. In the years after World War I, oil in the Middle East became an important international issue and the world's major petroleum companies sought to find the richest deposits in the region. After the war, the Ottoman Empire disintegrated and the British and the French divided the region into protectorates. Both European countries were interested in potential oil deposits in the Middle East, particularly in Iraq. The oil industry in the region came to be dominated by the Turkish Petroleum Company (TPC). BRITISH PETROLEUM (BP) controlled about half of the company, while Shell and French interests each owned roughly one-fourth of the shares. Initially, the TPC sought to keep U.S. companies out of the region. However, U.S. government pressure soon led to the participation of U.S. companies and many of the world's major oil firms signed the Red Line Agreement, in which none of the parties would seek concessions in the Middle East except through the TPC. The agreement included all of the Middle East except Iran and Kuwait.

The boom in Middle Eastern oil began in Bahrain, a group of islands off the coast of the Arabian Peninsula that was a British protectorate in the inter-war period. The British firm BP was not interested in developing BAHRAIN, however, and the oil concession there passed first to Gulf and then to Socal. Socal struck oil in 1931 and by 1933 had begun exporting oil from Bahrain.

Bahrain served as the stepping-stone to SAUDI ARABIA. King Ibn Saud was looking for potential sources of revenue and in 1933 signed an agreement with Socal. The company gained the right to drill for oil in the desert nation in exchange for an annual rent and substantial loans to the Saudi government. In 1936, Texaco joined Socal in exploring Saudi Arabia and production began in 1939. A decade later, in 1949, the Trans-Arabian Pipeline took Saudi oil across SYRIA and LEBANON to the Mediterranean Sea, where tankers could then send it to Europe. Thus, King Ibn Saud succeeded in transforming himself from a desert warrior into a major world political figure.

Oil companies also found substantial deposits in KUWAIT. Intially BP and Gulf struggled for control of oil rights in this small Middle Eastern country. Then in 1934, both companies signed a joint agreement with the ruling skeikh. By 1938, they had discovered major petroleum reserves.

Oil and World War II. Oil played a major factor in the outbreak of World War II, especially in the Pacific Theater. By the early 20th century, JAPAN had emerged as a major world military and economic power. The Great DEPRESSION, however, hit Japan very hard, heightening the island country's sense of vulnerability as it lacked most of its necessary raw materials. As the Japanese

government played an increasingly larger role in politics in the 1930s, it sought to build up the country's military and industrial strength in the case of war. However, such preparations were difficult due to Japan's almost complete lack of oil reserves. By the late 1930s, Japan produced only about seven percent of its own petroleum. About 80 percent of its imports came from the United States and another ten percent came from the Dutch East Indies. Therefore, any war against the United States would be extremely harmful to Japan. This situation led the Japanese to implement new restrictive oil policies in order to reduce the role of foreign oil companies in Japan, and to prepare for any potential military conflicts. The official outbreak of war with CHINA in 1937 did lead the government to seek to improve its relationship with the foreign oil firms. The government also devised an ambitious but ultimately unrealistic plan to develop synthetic fuels.

Japanese territorial expansion in Asia meant a potential oil embargo by the United States. At the same time, the outbreak of war in Europe meant that many colonial possessions in Asia were vulnerable to Japanese attack. These conditions influenced the Japanese to attack Pearl Harbor in order to take out the Unites States, and allow Japan to expand. Leading up to the Pearl Harbor attack, U.S. President Franklin ROOSEVELT was reluctant to completely shut off oil supplies to Japan, but by August 1941, U.S. policy virtually ended oil exports as Japanese assets had been frozen. Soon the British and Dutch East Indies also cut off the flow of oil to Japan. Last-ditch attempts at negotiation failed, leading the Japanese to launch an attack on Pearl Harbor to protect its eastern flank, especially to make tanker routes from Sumatra and Borneo safer. The United States did not, however, simply allow Japanese expansion in Asia. With its greater industrial capacity, including vast oil reserves coming from domestic sources as well as Latin American allies, the United States was able to defeat Japan in 1945.

OPEC and oil shocks. In September, 1960, five of the world's leading oil producers created the ORGANIZATION OF PETROLEUM EXPORTING COUNTRIES (OPEC). The founding members—Saudi Arabia, Venezuela, Kuwait, Iraq, and Iran—founded the cartel in order to defend the price of oil. Together, they controlled more than 80 percent of the world's total exports. Other oil-exporting countries in Asia, Africa, and Latin America joined OPEC later. Yet at first, international oil companies and the Western industrial countries paid little attention to OPEC. Several factors limited the effectiveness of OPEC during the 1960s. In most producing countries, the major oil reserves still belonged to the international oil companies. Furthermore, there was a significant petroleum surplus on the world market. Also, members often did not wish to challenge the United States and others industrial powers.

For example, King Faisal in Saudi Arabia took a relatively pro-West stance and the democratic government of Venezuela was friendly to the John F. KENNEDY Administration. Political rivalries such as those between Iraq and Kuwait also limited the effectiveness of OPEC. To make matters worse, the cartel's two founding fathers—Abdullah Tariki of Saudi Arabia and Juan Pablo Pérez Alfonso in Venezuela—withdrew from politics. Finally, throughout the 1960s, new oil reserves around the world added to the existing surplus. For example, significant reserves were found in ALGERIA and LIBYA. Thus, there was now more new petroleum seeking markets that there was demand. After correcting for inflation, oil prices dropped by some 40 percent in the decade.

This situation changed in the 1970s. Unhappy with low oil prices that had contributed to much of the world's postwar economic boom, OPEC members decided to cooperate in order to raise prices. In protest of Western favoritism toward Israel, after the fourth Arab-Israeli conflict known as the Yom Kippur War in October 1973, Arab OPEC members decided to halt oil shipments to the West. Within a year, world oil prices had quadrupled, leading to an "oil shock" in many developed countries. Countries such as Japan, which imported 99 percent of its oil, and those in Western Europe, which imported 96 percent of their oil, were especially hard hit. Even the United States, the country closest to being oil self-sufficient, felt the effects. The economic consequences were the worst since the 1930s, marked by high inflation, lower living standards, and high unemployment, which hit 13 percent in Western Europe. Thus, the oil shock contributed to the end of the post–World War II economic boom. There was some recovery by 1976. However, the fundamentalist Islamic Revolution in Iran led to higher prices again in 1979. By 1982, however, oil prices began to decline due to efforts of the industrialized nations to reduce their dependence on OPEC oil. Furthermore, unity among the OPEC countries faltered, especially with the outbreak of the Iran-Iraq War in 1980.

The actions of OPEC and higher oil prices in the 1970s had a number of important consequences. Governments in the OPEC countries now took in much larger revenues, which they could spend developing their own countries or invest abroad. They invested some of the oil dollars in the industrialized world, but also provided aid to developing countries through mechanisms such as the OPEC Fund for International Development. In part, this aid was necessary due to the fact that non-oil producing countries in the developing world were hit especially hard by rising oil prices.

The initial success of OPEC policies inspired hope among many in the Third World. Nationalists in developing nations applauded the transfer of wealth from the rich industrial countries to those of the developing world. They believed that this might mark the shift of world economic inequalities. In the end, however, OPEC had to adjust its prices due to declining demand. Nevertheless, the importance of the Middle East on the world political stage had increased dramatically. The region could no longer be ignored by the world powers. This increased importance can be seen in the 1991 Persian Gulf War and the invasion of Iraq by the United States and Great Britain in 2003.

There were also important changes in the developed countries. Seeking to reduce their dependence on OPEC oil, Western nations sought to locate and exploit more of their own oil deposits. Notable were significant reserves in Alaska and the North Sea. Developed countries also increasingly turned to non-OPEC oil exporters, such as Mexico and the Soviet Union. Conservation efforts increased in many countries, as many were forced to rethink the consumerism illustrated by high energy use. In addition, many industrialized countries explored and developed alternative sources of energy, such as nuclear power. Nevertheless, as prices steadily decreased after the oil shock, the world still depended a great deal on oil as the main source of energy.

BIBLIOGRAPHY. Anthony Sampson, *The Seven Sisters: The Great Oil Companies and the World They Made* (Viking Penguin, 1975); Michael Economides, et al., *The Color of Oil: The History, the Money and the Politics of the World's Biggest Business* (Round Oak Publishing, 2000); Roger Olien, *Oil in Texas: The Gusher Age, 1895–1945* (University of Texas Press, 2002); Steven Topik and Allen Wells, *The Second Conquest of Latin America* (University of Texas Press, 1998); John Wirth, ed., *Latin American Oil Companies and the Politics of Energy* (University of Texas Press, 1986); Daniel Yergin, *The Prize: The Epic Quest for Oil, Money, and Power* (Simon & Schuster, 1991).

RONALD YOUNG
GEORGIA SOUTHERN UNIVERSITY

Okun's Law

TO THOSE WHO WORRIED about the micro-distortions caused by macro-stabilization policies, James TOBIN riposted, "It takes a heap of Harberger Triangles to fill an Okun Gap."

The gap between potential and actual GROSS DOMESTIC PRODUCT (GDP) is known as the Okun Gap; Harberger Triangles are the deadweight loss wedges caused by taxes, familiar to most economics students. Okun's Law translates the output gap to unemployment statistics ("Potential GNP: Its Measurement and Significance").

Clearly, there is a political aim as the original article admitted, "If programs to lower unemployment from 5.5 to 4 percent of the labor are viewed as attempts to raise the economy's 'grade' from 94.5 to 96, the case for them may not seem compelling. Focus on the 'gap' helps to remind policymakers of the large reward associated with such an improvement."

Okun's Law was intended as a mere rule of thumb. For every percentage point that unemployment was from its long-run value, gross domestic product (GDP) was about three percentage points away from its potential. So if the long-run unemployment rate were 4 percent, an unemployment rate of 5 percent meant that GDP was 3 percentage points away from potential. The exact coefficient has been mooted ever since (usually to be revised downward). It is sometimes reformed into a dynamic relation, linking a change in unemployment to GDP growth rather than level.

Such a large relationship is not due only to employment. If we consider an aggregate production function Y=f(K,L), then it would surely be surprising that an increase of one percent in L would increase Y by such a great deal more. The additional leverage comes from the fact that, as labor utilization approaches capacity, firms work their inputs harder: additional hours per worker, greater labor force participation, and greater productivity per worker. Okun's original paper estimated that just over half of the increase came from increased person-hours, with increased labor productivity making up the remainder.

BIBLIOGRAPHY. Arthur M. Okun, "Potential GNP: Its Measurement and Significance," Proceedings of the Business and Economic Statistics Section, American Statistical Association (ASA, 1962); J. Tobin, "How Dead is Keynes?" *Essays in Economics: Theory and Policy* (MIT Press, 1982).

KEVIN R. FOSTER, PH.D.
CITY COLLEGE OF NEW YORK

oligopoly

DESCRIBING A MARKET or industry, an oligopoly exists when there are relatively few firms and many buyers. In such a market environment, each buyer takes the market conditions as given but each firm is aware that its actions will have an effect on its rival's action. Most goods and services are provided in oligopoly markets rather than perfectly competitive or monopoly markets, and economists have been concerned with oligopoly theory ever since Augustine Cournot's pioneering work, published in 1838. Even today, the oligopoly question, how prices are determined when there are only a few sellers in the market, is a central area of investigation of the field of INDUSTRIAL ORGANIZATION.

Cournot provided the first formal theory of oligopoly. Realizing that strategic interaction is important if there are only a few sellers in a market, he proposed a solution concept and examined the stability of the solution, studying both the case of substitute goods and the case of complementary goods. Cournot furthermore discussed the possibility of collusion among the sellers and how his oligopoly solution related to the perfectly competitive equilibrium. An essential feature of Cournot's oligopoly model is that the sellers choose production quantities simultaneously and a "neutral auctioneer" sets the market-clearing price for the aggregate quantity.

Cournot's solution to the oligopoly problem shows that there is an inverse relationship between the number of sellers in a market and the deviation of the price from marginal cost (i.e., deviation from the perfectly competitive solution). Cournot's path-breaking work went unnoticed for about 50 years until J. Bertrand reviewed it in 1883. Bertrand criticized Cournot's work by contending that it is more appealing to let the sellers set the prices themselves, without the help of an auctioneer. His proposed modification, sellers setting prices rather than deciding on quantities, resulted in a radically different solution to the oligopoly problem.

According to Bertrand, price will be equal to marginal cost as long as there are two or more firms; the oligopoly solution will be the perfectly competitive outcome no matter how many sellers there are in the market. This result is sometimes referred to as the "Bertrand Paradox" in the oligopoly literature.

F.Y. Edgeworth (1897) solved the Bertrand paradox by introducing capacity constraints. Given that none of the firms in an oligopoly are capable of producing the quantity demanded at a price equal to marginal cost, high price firms face a non-zero residual demand and prices are not equal to marginal cost in equilibrium. Edgeworth went on to show that in the case of capacity constraints, or more generally in the presence of decreasing returns to scale, no solution exists to the oligopoly problem.

Heinrich von Stackelberg (1934) pioneered the role of commitment in oligopoly theory and showed that, while in general oligopoly equilibrium may exist, there are a number of possible market scenarios under which equilibrium fails to emerge. Von Stackelberg also was the first to explicitly introduce asymmetries between oligopoly firms by distinguishing between so-called leaders and followers. One can argue that after Cournot and Bertrand, besides the contributions of Edgeworth and von Stackelberg, the theory of oligopoly largely lay dormant until GAME THEORY imposed itself as a tool for the analysis of strategic interaction, and therefore oligopoly theory.

During the 1960s and thereafter, beginning with M. Shubik and R. Levitan, game theorists and economists rediscovered the works of Cournot and Bertrand and realized that the analysis of oligopoly behavior was a subject well suited for game theoretic analysis.

Today, the various theories of oligopoly behavior can essentially be viewed as a set of different games, representing different market scenarios. The strategic interactions among rival firms in an oligopoly have been analyzed using the theories of static games, finitely and infinitely repeated games, sequential move games, and dynamic games. Using the notion of a static game it can be shown that both the Cournot and Bertrand solution to the oligopoly problem can be viewed as a Nash Equilibrium for a well-specified market game in which firms choose their actions simultaneously.

The difference between the two solutions (Cournot vs. Bertrand) comes from the assumption made regarding the set of actions available to the firms. Cournot's solution is obtained if the set of actions is restricted to the set of quantities while Bertrand's solution is a Nash Equilibrium for a game in which the firms' action are the set of prices. The different welfare implications of the two approaches were also confirmed, i.e., under quite general conditions regarding demand and cost structure, the Bertrand-Nash Equilibrium is more competitive than the Cournot-Nash Equilibrium.

Given these contrasting results, an important question to ask is which scenario is more likely to emerge in a particular market? There are a number of oligopoly models that have endogenized the choice of quantity or price as a strategy variable. Not surprisingly it can be shown that, given a choice, oligopoly firms prefer quantity to price as a strategy variable. However, the static models of oligopoly also show that a serious theory of oligopoly behavior cannot be timeless. George STIGLER (1964) stressed the importance of such factors as the speed with which rival firms learn of price cuts by other firms, the probability that such price cuts are detected by rival firms, as well as the scope of retaliation by other firms in response to price cuts.

Applying the notions of finitely and infinitely repeated games, a great deal of work has been done to investigate the possibility of tacit collusion in oligopoly, taking into account the possibility of defection from the collusive outcome as well as retaliation if defection indeed takes place. In short, tacit collusion cannot arise in finitely repeated games of oligopoly behavior.

Both the so-called backward induction method and the notion of a sub-game perfect equilibrium imply that if oligopoly firms interact a finite number of times, the collusive outcome cannot be an equilibrium outcome for any stage of the game. This picture changes quite drastically if one allows for infinitely repeated interaction in oligopoly markets. Given that rival firms inter-act with each other forever, the collusive outcome can be supported by so-called trigger strategies as an equilibrium outcome at each stage of the game. These trigger strategies take the form of triggering a retaliation response if one or more firms ever deviate from the collusive strategy.

The important point is that tacit collusion may arise as an equilibrium outcome in an oligopoly market. In addition to repeated games, two-stage games applied to the oligopoly model have highlighted the importance of timing, the essential role played by sunk costs and commitments. Employing the concept of sub-game perfection, these models of oligopoly behavior show that commitments at early dates, such as investment in capacity, can influence the outcome of oligopolistic interaction at later dates.

Finally, dynamic games of oligopoly behavior considering price, quantity, investment, and other state variables as strategies have resulted in additional insights into possible outcomes for oligopoly markets. While the application of game theory has resulted in many additional insights into oligopoly behavior and equilibrium in oligopoly markets, it also has shown that the basic notions of oligopoly behavior put forward by Cournot and Bertrand are still the benchmark models of oligopoly theory.

One should not view the set of different models that aim to explain oligopoly behavior as competing models, but rather as models that are relevant for different particular oligopoly markets.

BIBLIOGRAPHY. J. Bertrand, "Review of 'Theorie mathematique de la richesse sociale' and 'Recherches sur les principies mathematiques de la theorie des richesses,'" *Journal des Savants* (1883); Augustine A. Cournot, *Researches into the Mathematical Principles of the Theory of Wealth, English Edition* (Augustus M. Kelly,1960); F.Y. Edgeworth, *The Pure Theory of Monopoly* (Macmillan, 1925); M. Shubik and R. Levitan, *Market Structure and Behavior* (Harvard University Press, 1980); G. Stigler, "A Theory of Oligopoly," *Journal of Political Economy* (1964); X. Vives, *Oligopoly Theory: Old Ideas and New Tools* (MIT Press, 1999); J. Tirole, *The Theory of Industrial Organization* (MIT Press, 1989); H. von Stackelberg, *Marktform und Gleichgewicht* (Springer-Verlag, 1934).

KLAUS G. BECKER, PH.D.
TEXAS TECH UNIVERSITY

OPEC

THE ORGANIZATION OF Petroleum Exporting Countries (OPEC) is a group of oil-exporting countries that have banded together to set uniform output and price goals in the international petroleum market. It consists of 11 countries: ALGERIA, INDONESIA, IRAN, IRAQ, KUWAIT, LYBIA, NIGERIA, Qatar, SAUDI ARABIA, the United Arab Emirates (UAE), and VENEZUELA.

Member countries contain roughly 75 percent of the world's proven crude OIL reserves, and supply about 40 percent of the world's output. Members' share of production within OPEC was, in December 1998: Venezuela 10.98 percent, Algeria 2.89 percent, Indonesia 4.98 percent, Iraq 8.42 percent, Iran 12.99 percent, Kuwait 7.36 percent, Libya 4.94 percent, Nigeria 7.32 percent, Qatar 2.36 percent, Saudi Arabia 29.58 percent, and UAE 8.09 percent.

OPEC was formed at a meeting held September 14, 1960, in Baghdad, Iraq. The founding members were Kuwait, Iran, Iraq, Saudi Arabia and Venezuela. These countries were coordinating their responses to the actions of the major multinational oil companies known as the Seven Sisters. The Seven Sisters were British Petroleum, Chevron, Exxon, Gulf, Mobil, Royal Dutch Shell, and Texaco. For much of the first half of the 20th century, these multinational corporations dominated the world oil market.

The oil-producing countries did not have adequate technology, manpower, or capacity to carry on the production of oil on their own. Under those circumstances, Venezuela first began to share profit with the oil corporations, partly from a revised tax system. Venezuela later encouraged the Arab oil-producing countries to follow suit. Saudi Arabia realized the potential quickly and reformed its tax system.

Though OPEC existed since 1960, it was not until a decade later that its power increased. OPEC's share of world production was 28 percent in 1960 and 41 percent in 1970. The first of the "oil shocks" occurred during and after the 1973 October war between EGYPT and ISRAEL. The Arab members of OPEC aligned with Egypt, demanding an end to UNITED STATES support of Israel.

When the United States refused, the Arab countries imposed an embargo. The first oil shock increased the (nominal) price of oil by almost three times: the price for benchmark Saudi Light increased from $2.59 in September 1973, to $11.65 in March 1974. The world economy soon fell into a recession. The second oil shock occurred in 1979, when the Iranian Revolution caused a drastic reduction in oil exports from Iran. Iran reacted to an American embargo on Iranian oil by prohibiting the exportation of Iranian oil to American firms.

The war between Iran and Iraq in 1980 made the situation worse. The effect of the second oil shock was short-lived, however, as non-OPEC countries significantly increased production. There was an increase in oil price in the early 1990s (the third mini-shock) when Iraq attempted to annex Kuwait. The sudden decrease of the oil exported from Iraq and Kuwait caused the oil price to spike. Increased production by Saudi Arabia moderated the situation.

Whether OPEC is a cartel is subject to debate. A cartel is defined as a group of producers of a product that band together to obtain as much market share as possible, and to adjust output levels and prices to make the most profits. The objective is to function as much like a monopoly (single-seller industry) as possible. The profit-maximizing operation of a cartel occurs when the production quota allocated to each member is determined by the equality of the additional cost of production (member marginal cost) and the additional revenue gotten from that additional unit (cartel marginal revenue).

For example, assume that it were determined that the additional revenue received from the sale of a barrel (bbl) of crude oil were $10. Allocating production would be similar to running an auction for the right to produce each bbl. A producer bidding the lowest would get to produce each additional bbl, until the lowest price any can produce for is $10. Many economists believe that cartels are unstable because members have the incentive to raise their profits by undercutting the set cartel price and stealing customers. Once this cheating is detected by other members, they retaliate by cheating on the others until the cartel falls apart. The longevity of OPEC has proved to be an exception to this theory.

OPEC as a cartel. The degree to which OPEC works as a cartel is an ongoing discussion. The OPEC countries do not all share the same interests. Each has different strategies, so it is often hard to reach consensus. Countries with larger reserves and small populations, like Saudi Arabia, generally desire to increase production. They fear that higher prices will induce technological change and the development of new deposits, which in turn will reduce the price of oil. Countries that have lower reserves, or larger populations, prefer to reduce the supply. The reduced supply would increase the price on the world oil market, if the demand remains unchanged. Negotiations among the oil ministers of the member nations involve reinforcing common goals and reconciling these different interests. If the ideal operation of a cartel, as described above, is not followed, and that is what is meant by "not functioning as a cartel," then OPEC is probably not functioning as a cartel fairly often. However, if the goal of maximizing the size of the profit pie is not enough to keep the cartel together, some members have religious and political ties that seem to provide the glue.

In the contemporary world economy, OPEC has the potential to wield a significant influence due to its large reserves and market share, and the reluctance of many oil-dependent industrialized countries to seriously develop substitutes and to implement serious oil-conservation strategies. Some observers believe, however, that the emergence of non-OPEC competitors in the late 20th century has limited OPEC's ability to influence global oil markets, and the Saudi political alliances forged with the United States adds weight to incentives not to restrict oil output and raise prices.

These growing sources of non-OPEC oil have reduced U.S. dependence on oil from OPEC. Also, like all economic players, OPEC is vulnerable to the ups and downs of global economic activity. For some OPEC countries, oil is the most significant, or the only significant, export commodity. These countries face the challenge of keeping their economies alive when there are economic slowdowns, and especially when the oil reserves run out. If they build infrastructure, invest in communications and computer technology, and diversify their economies to produce goods and services other than oil, their economies might not suffer much in the long run.

BIBLIOGRAPHY. "OPEC: The Oil Cartel," British Broadcasting Corporation, news.bbc.co.uk; Lynne Kiesling, "Non-OPEC Oil Producers Change the Dynamics of Oil Markets," www.rppi.org; Rilwanu Lukman, "OPEC: Past, Present and Future Perspectives," www.opec.org; Saudi Arabian Information Resource, www.saudinf.com; WTRG Economics, www.wtrg.com; Daniel Yergin, *The Prize* (Simon & Shuster, 1991).

JOHN SORRENTINO, PH.D.
MAHBUB RABBANI, M.A.
TEMPLE UNIVERSITY

Opium Wars

THE OPIUM WARS occurred during CHINA's rule by the Manchus, the hunting, fishing, and farming people from central Manchuria who had succeeded the Ming (1644) and maintained a superior standard of living until the 1700s.

The Manchus had expanded the empire, treating non-Chinese as "tributary states," and like the Ming, disdained foreign "barbarians," allowing only government-recognized monopolies to trade with the Spanish, Portuguese, Dutch, and English.

By the 18th century, the British EAST INDIA COMPANY was restricted to trading in a special area of Guangzhou (Canton) during a limited time period, and only with the official merchant guild. As European demands for Chinese tea were added to the existing market for silks and porcelains from the mid-17th century to the beginning of the 18th century, the Manchus benefited from a trade surplus, paid in silver.

As the 18th century progressed and demand for Chinese tea grew, Britain's emergence as a formidable naval power was paralleled by the increasingly disdainful attitude toward China by European philosophers, British merchants, and the British government.

European Enlightenment thinkers had once praised China for its ethics and the lack of church domination; however, they now identified modernity and liberty as essential and pointed to Chinese repressions. European cultural superiority coexisted with demands that China grant the British economic concessions, allowing them to buy tea closer to its source in the Yangzi river provinces, and to abolish the tributary system and interact with other nations through published tariffs, ambassadors, envoys, and commercial treaties.

A formal request by the king's cousin, Lord George Macartney (1793), to the Manchu Emperor Qianlong was first delayed by Macartney's refusal to kowtow (show respect) and then denied when the emperor dismissed Macartney's 600 cases of manufactured items, informing the king in a letter that the Chinese "possess all things" and had "no use for Britain's manufactures."

The Opium Wars were the Western response to Qianlong's refusal to cooperate, rooted in the early recognition by the British East India company that opium's ability to ease emotional and physical pain and its highly addictive properties could be used to solve the balance of payments problem with China. From British India, exports of opium to China rose from 200 chests in 1729, to 4,500 in 1800, shortly after Macartney's visit.

The Chinese responded by banning opium importation and domestic production by 1800 and punishing smoking opium. However, exports rose to 40,000 by 1838. Soon smuggling and criminal gangs allowed the drug to make its way throughout all levels of Chinese society, including the emperor's court, and it became next to impossible for the government to crack down on drug dealers. The crisis was exacerbated when silver began to drain out of China.

In 1839, imperial official Lin Zexu was sent off to Guangzhou to stop foreign traders from importing opium and Chinese from smoking it. Lin was partially successful, closing opium dens, arresting 1,600 Chinese, and executing Chinese dealers; however, neither threats, bribes, trading options, nor the barricading of foreigners in their factories compelled foreigners to turn over their opium stocks.

Prior to the onset of fighting, attempts were made to end the standoff. The British superintendent in Guangzhou, Charles Elliot, turned the merchants' opium over to Lin, who destroyed it, ordering that trade in Guangzhou would be confined only to merchants who would not deal in it. However, in London, the opium trading firm of Jardin, Matheson and Company's lobbying resulted in victory for commercial interests, and by 1840, a British force of 47 ships left India to confront the Chinese.

Lin's purchase of cannons for the fortification of Guangzhou came to naught, as the British bypassed this port, directly attacking Ningbo and Tianjin, pillaging coastal areas, seizing cities, and killing thousands of Chinese. With the 1842 Treaty of Nanjing and 1843 Treaty of Bogue, Great Britain gained Hong Kong, the Manchu were ordered to pay $21 million in Mexican silver, the ports of Guangzhou, Fuzhou, Xiamen, Ningbo and Shanghai would open with consulates, and the British would be granted most-favored-nation status.

Tariffs and customs duties would be fixed only after consultation with the British, whose subjects would henceforth be tried in British consular courts in China. Pursuant to renewed fighting in 1856, China was forced to open 11 more ports, sanction the Christian missionary presence, and legalize opium, in accordance with the Treaty of Tianjin (1858), which represented British, French, Russian, and U.S. interests.

Hostilities ended by 1860; however, the Opium Wars signaled the beginnings of an unequal treaty system that would essentially remain until the communist victory in 1949.

BIBLIOGRAPHY. John K. Fairbank, *Trade and Diplomacy on the China Coast* (Stanford University Press, 1953); Arthur Waley, *The Opium War through Chinese Eyes* (Stanford University Press, 1958); Patricia Buckley Ebrey, *Cambridge Illustrated History of China* (Cambridge University Press, 1996).

CRISTINA ZACCARINI
ADELPHI UNIVERSITY

optimorum of market

OPTIMUM OPTIMORUM (Latin) is equal to saying "the best of the best." The optimorum, as it is often briefly referred to, is the global optimum or the state where a given allocation can no longer be improved. When there are several allocations, each of which may be locally optimal, the optimorum is the best among these. The optimorum is analyzed in the economic theory of distribution, not in PRICE theory. Synonymous terms are bliss point or satiation point.

In a wide sense, the concept of a global optimum is used in many areas of economics (e.g., general EQUILIBRIUM theory and welfare economics, public economics, and international trade theory) and of management science (particularly in those areas that apply mathematical methods such as linear programming and GAME THEORY). The optimorum concept is important in capitalist economies since it expresses the fundamental idea that economic choice re-

lies on trade-offs and that different patterns of consumption or production may lead to efficient solutions among which only one is also globally the best.

The following conditions are held to define the optimal organization of an economy:

1. Factors of production must be used such that the marginal rates of substitution in production are equal for all producers (= efficient factor input)

2. Every factor bundle is to be distributed such that the marginal rates of substitution in consumption are equal for all consumers (= optimal distribution)

3. Production and consumption are to be matched such that the marginal rate of transformation equals the marginal rates of substitution in consumption (= optimal matching between production and consumption).

These conditions define PARETO OPTIMALITY, situations where no change can make one individual better off without making another worse off.

However, such local optima need not be global optima. If a social welfare function is assumed, Pareto-optimality is a necessary yet not sufficient condition for its identification. The optimum optimorum is the best Pareto-optimal point.

The distinction between local and global optima is crucial in analyzing social welfare functions, where the maximorum is the point of maximum social well-being at which it is no longer possible to reorganize an economy such that one individual is better off without simultaneously reducing another individual's utility level. Efficiency, then, is not some unique point toward which society may direct its efforts. Rather, many efficient solutions (in production and distribution) are feasible, and each is different in resource allocation, commodity distribution, and the distribution of overall utility.

Clearly, the challenge of finding an optimal economic organization for a society cannot be resolved by appeals to efficiency alone. This insight has become extremely important for public policy analysis. It has also prompted the development of economic research paradigms such as the theory of second best, which defines policy implications for situations when Pareto-optimal solutions cannot be attained and an optimum optimorum can consequently not be found.

BIBLIOGRAPHY. Paul A. Samuelson, *Foundations of Economic Analysis* (Harvard University Press, 1947); Amartya Sen, *Collective Choice and Social Welfare* (North Holland, 1970); Aimo Törn and Antanas Zilinskas, *Global Optimization* (Springer-Verlag, 1989).

WOLFGANG GRASSL
HILLSDALE COLLEGE

Orientalism and Eurocentrism

THE TERM, ORIENTALISM, is used at least in four senses:

1. Specialized, purportedly objective, often classicist study of Asian and African cultures, languages, and literatures

2. A European artistic approach to depiction of Asia and Africa in paintings, novels, poems, movies, and other genres as primitive, exotic, depraved, bizarre, mysterious, and lascivious

3. A style of thought based upon on ontological and epistemological distinction made between the Orient and (most of the time) the Occident

4. A method of critiquing hegemonic western practices of producing knowledge about non-Europeans as a means of gaining greater power over the lands and lives of the latter; described by some as anti-Orientalism.

In academics, however, Orientalism now primarily connotes two major activities: A western ideological approach to production of knowledge about the Third World, and a systemic critique of such knowledge production.

Orientalism as a western system of producing knowledge about non-Europeans. "It is not the sum of the works of the Western specialists and scholars who have studied non-European societies," notes Samir Amin. Orientalism "refers to the ideological construction of a mythical Orient whose characteristics are treated as immutable traits defined in simple opposition to the characteristics of the Occidental world." In that sense, it is a theme-generating device that provides structure, coherence, depth, and direction to Western narratives about the non-west. This ideological construction can be summarized into six categories: 1) historiography; 2) aesthetics (art, language, literature, and culture); 3) politics; 4) economics; 5) education; and 6) religion.

While historiography deals with institutionalized memory of conflicts, moral and material trajectories of human societies, and the shape of history itself, the Orientalist historiography, like a Hollywood movie, assigns a subordinate role, if not a villain's role, to the Oriental in all these realms. The Orientalist aesthetics, as commented above, having shown the Oriental as primitive, exotic, depraved, bizarre, mysterious, and lascivious, celebrates its own wonderful benevolence, an attitude eloquently conveyed by Joseph Conrad in the novel *Heart of Darkness*: "It gave me the notion of an exotic Immensity ruled by an august Benevolence."

Orientalist attitude toward non-European politics has been crystallized through the image of Oriental despotism, and of the economy through what has been disparagingly called the Asiatic mode of production. Karl Wittfogel, best known for his "hydraulic hypothesis," has argued that vast irrigation needs of Oriental societies including EGYPT, Mesopotamia, INDIA, CHINA and pre-Columbian MEXICO and PERU, had resulted in tight water control through formation of centralized and bureaucratized authoritarian empires deeply hostile to change. On the other hand, being free of such limitations, Europe was able to rise to contemporary technological heights. As far as the Asian mode was concerned, even Karl MARX felt that it was based on "the unchangeableness of Asiatic societies" and "the constant dissolution and refounding of Asiatic states."

Lord Thomas Babington Macaulay's perspective on education of Indians ("We must at present do our best to form a class who may be interpreters between us and the millions whom we govern; a class of persons, Indian in blood and color, but English in taste, in opinions, in morals, and in intellect.") remains the quintessential example of Orientalist philosophy of educating the natives.

The truths of the weak are seen as weak truths in need of replacement by the victor's ethics and religion. It is typified by what Missionary Cram, of the Boston Missionary Society seeking converts among the Senacas, had told a group of their leaders in summer of 1805: "You have never worshipped the Great Spirit in a manner acceptable to him; but have all your lives been in great errors and darkness. To endeavor to remove these errors, and open your eyes, so that you might see clearly, is my business with you." Likewise, Macaulay's rhetorical question: "We are to teach false history, false astronomy, false medicine because we find them in company with a false religion?"

What lies at the heart of these constructions of the Orient is great colonial poet Rudyard Kipling's conception of the Oriental as "half child and half beast," an enduring image that continues to characterize imperial narratives from Kipling and E.M. Forster to Bernard Lewis and Howard Bloom and from Macaulay to Samuel Huntington. Inculcating new relations of force and obligation, these narratives endow the colonizer with, to use Forster's phrase, "the power to do good" to the Orientals, who are treated as nameless and faceless phantoms. This, as historically observed, necessitates civilizing and Christianizing the Oriental who is seen both as barbarian and pagan.

The Orientalist mission is thus characterized by four main goals: to civilize the barbarians, to Christianize the pagans, to create among the Orientals a scientific outlook and a rational attitude, and to recreate the Orient in the Western image in the name of modernity, democracy, progress, advancement, peace, and liberation.

Orientalism as a critical method. This critical evaluation of this Western system of knowledge production about non-Europeans is conducted through analysis of a series of canonical texts including those by Chaucer, Mandeville, Shakespeare, Dryden, Pope, Byron, HUME, Kant, HEGEL, Vico, Gibbon, Marx, Weber, and Dostoyevsky, and many others. In other words, this critical method focuses on writers, thinkers, poets, philosophers, and scholar-administrators who reside at the center of the Western culture and learning, and not those at its margins.

This school of thought has found its ablest exponent in the writings of Edward Said. From Said's point of view: "Taking the late 18th century as a very roughly defined starting point, Orientalism can be discussed and analyzed as the corporate institution for dealing with the Orient—dealing with it by making statements about it, authorizing views about it, describing it, by teaching it, settling it, by ruling over it: in short, Orientalism as a Western style for dominating, restructuring, and having authority over the Orient."

The single most important contribution of Said's theory of Orientalism has been to "place imperialism at the center of the Western civilization" both in terms of its constitutive economic, social, and cultural role as well as its regulative role in shaping and defining the relations of force, commerce, and ideas among the Western and non-Western nations.

Primarily, Said deals with European methods of knowledge production and relates them to issues of knowledge and power. This critical method interrogates operations of power in terms of both "discourse of power and power of discourse" to reveal how and why Western assertions of "power to do good" are repeatedly located in the triple claims of innocence, omniscience, and benevolence.

Said's critical apparatus. Said is concerned with corporate Western discursive practices, their prodigious—or hegemonic—productivity, durability, and strength. It is only through these discursive practices, Said believes, that the West was able to build an enormously systematic discipline "to manage—and even produce—the Orient politically, sociologically, militarily, ideologically, scientifically, and imaginatively during the post-Enlightenment period." Said's project is to study a series of historical encounters, interactions and relationships. Orientalism, writes Eqbal Ahmed, "is about the relationship of knowledge to power, of culture to imperialism, and of civilization to expansion."

It is also about the relationship of COLONIALISM to science and social science, about the complex coalition between soldier, statesman, scholar, and saints of the dominant culture against the subjugated peoples; about European trusteeship over the other races who, as Karl Kautsky has phrased it, "are regarded as children, idiots or beasts of burden;" about triangulation of systems of control through coordination of state, ideology, and culture.

It is not enough, however, to study these ideas and relations in the abstract without reference to distribution of power and prestige among the individual and institutional actors. Ideas, cultures and histories, he argues, cannot be seriously studied without their configuration of power also being studied. Once placed in the matrix of socio-historic power relations, it becomes possible to "show that European Culture gained in strength and identity by setting itself off the Orient as a sort of surrogate and even underground self," Kautsky writes.

It is important to note that, while developing a theoretical framework to explore Orientalism's accumulated capacity to control natives' lives down to the core of their existence, Said also examines the historical trajectories of resistance, recovery, and revival of subjugated cultures and peoples; and further explores how these activities are reported in the Western media, academia, and official discourses.

Said's Orientalism was complemented, refined, and completed by his magnum opus, *Culture and Imperialism*, in which he articulates the notion of the contrapuntal method, which is both a political and an academic technique for critiquing one-sided history, for inserting missing links into the institutionalized memory and forging a polyphonic scholarship that contains a multiperspectival gaze.

Said's critical apparatus can be summarized in terms of eight primary concepts: 1) discursivity, 2) representation, 3) subject positioning, 4) positional superiority, 5) poetics, 6) strategic location, 7) strategic formation, and 8) the contrapuntal method.

The notion of discursivity deals with essential plot lines and themes of a series of 18th-, 19th-, and 20th-century narratives constructed to define self and the inferior other. Said argues that one cannot possibly understand the efficiency and controlling capacity of Orientalism without examining it as a discourse. It is precisely its constitutive rhetorical function that provides with basic information about how "European culture was to manage—and even produce—the orient politically, sociologically, militarily, ideologically, scientifically, and imaginatively during the post-Enlightenment period."

The idea of discursivity is closely tied to the notion of representation. To talk of representation is to talk of how the Orient is signified and given meaning in the Western thought process; how it is placed in the social, moral, and intellectual hierarchies; and who speaks for the Orient, with what authority and for what purpose? Also, who is given or denied a voice in historical texts and, thus, in history itself.

Subject positioning or inculcation of desired structures of belief and attitude in cultural in-groups and out-groups is a strategic part of representation. In the Orientalist discourse, the stipulated subject positioning is, among other things, accomplished through a flexible positional superiority "which puts the Westerner in a whole series of possible relationships without losing him the relative upper hand," Said explains. The Westerner is guaranteed in advance the role of the hero, liberator, discoverer, inventor, and savior in every significant narrative. This positional superiority almost always brings about a happy marriage of power and virtue in the Western hands.

A tool for a certain kind of representation and a certain kind of subject positioning, poetics refers to a complex existential and experiential process of imbuing time and space with meaningful feelings and may range from designating a house as haunted to a continent as dark and a system as evil. "Strategic location is a way of describing the author's position in the text with regard to the Oriental material he writes about. . . . Everyone who writes about the Orient must locate himself vis-à-vis the Orient; translated into his text, this location includes the type of narrative voice he adopts, the type of structure he builds, the kind of images, themes, motifs that circulate in his text—all of which add up to deliberate ways of addressing the reader, containing the Orient, and, finally representing it or speaking in its behalf," Said writes.

This strategic formation is a way of analyzing the relationship between texts and the way in which groups of texts, types of text, even textual genres, acquire mass, density, and referential power among themselves and thereafter in the culture at large. Every writer on the Orient (and this is true even of Homer) assumes some Oriental precedent, some previous knowledge of the Orient, to which he refers and on which he relies. Additionally, each work on the Orient affiliates itself other works, with audiences, with institutions, with the Orient itself.

These textual and inter-textual relations are to be analyzed not to find what may lay hidden in the Orientalist text, but that which is observable in its exteriority. A premeditated representation is the final product of this exteriority. "And these representations," Said continues, "rely upon institutions, traditions, conventions, agreed upon codes of understanding for their effects, not upon a distant and amorphous Orient." In surveying the exteriority, what one should "look for are styles, figures of speech, setting, narrative devices, historical and social circumstances, not the correctness of the representation, nor its fidelity to some great original."

And finally, the contrapuntal method refers to identification and analysis of acts designed to refute subjugating arguments, regain territory, reclaim identity, supply missing links of history and memory, and, in the final analysis, create a multi-perspective understanding of society, history, and human relations.

Eurocentrism. Like any other ethnocentric perspective, Eurocentrism is a worldview with Europe as the ultimate model and criteria of almost everything, and all other regions, peoples and cultures are located, named, and evaluated on the basis of self-reference criteria.

Eurocentrism is, in part, based on claims of "only in the West" as clearly articulated by Max Weber in the following passage: "Only in the West does science exist at the stage of development which we recognize as valid. . . . [The] full development of a systematic theology must be credited to Christianity under the influence of Hellenism, since there were only fragments in Islam and in a few Indian sects." The "only in the West" list includes modern conceptions of capitalism, state, citizenship, labor, art, culture, literature, music, journalism, architecture, organization, and technology. And the European is discoursed as the "inventor of invention."

It is a viewpoint that emphasizes absolute and permanent superiority of the Western civilization over all other civilizations. Europe is portrayed as the embodiment of universal truths that must be emulated by everyone else. This claim to universalism, critics hold, becomes a vehicle for demanding and forcing "a homogenization of aspirations and values." Its primary themes include progress, technology, democracy, modernity, post-modernity, individualism, capitalism, and rationalism, etc. All these themes can be summed up as the quality of European-ness. This "European-ness lies in the form of the original settlement history, . . . a decentralized, aggressive part-pastoral offshoot and variant of western Asian agricultural society, molded by the forest," explains historian J.M. Blaut. These themes are perpetuated in and through humanities, social sciences, art and aesthetics, journalism, religious activities, politics, and even science and technology (to the extent that technology also doubles up as ideology, as some have argued).

Categorizing Eurocentrism as an ideology-dressed-as-theory, Samir Amin describes it as not the sum of the works of the Western specialists and scholars who have studied non-European societies, but a mythic construction of the European self and the non-European other. What distinguishes Eurocentrism from other ethnocentric perspectives or claims is the nature of its self-constituting myth.

This myth, Amin explains, is not "properly speaking, a social theory integrating various elements into a global and coherent vision of society and history. It is rather a prejudice that distorts social theories. It draws from a storehouse of components, retaining one or rejecting another according to the ideological needs of the moment. For example, for a long time the European bourgeoisie was distrustful—even contemptuous—of Christianity and, because of this, amplified the myth of GREECE."

The main attributes of Eurocentrism include: Arbitrary annexation of Greece to Europe; arbitrary annexation of Christianity to Europe, as the principal factor in the maintenance of European cultural unity; construction and depiction of a racist image of the Near East and other more distant Orients; the Eternal West vs. the Eternal East ("The East is East and the West is West, and the twain shall never meet."); imagined continuity of the European learning and progress; false backward projection of the North-South split; total separation of Greece from the Orient, from Egypt and Phoenicia in particular, to justify claims of Aryan purity and superiority.

But more importantly, it introduces the notion of Manichaenism in the conception of self and the other by rejecting any possibility of tracing the origins of the Orient and the Occident to common or shared origins. Cross-pollination of ideas and mutual learning among civilizations and peoples are denied, and so is the human equality of non-European peoples. Critics believe, that this rhetorical move enables Eurocentrics not only to claim moral and intellectual superiority but also an inherent right to use military and political authority over various parts of the Orient, as and when deemed necessary or useful. Its ultimate efficacy lies in creating a right to rule over others; justifying use of violence; legitimizing military occupations; reordering lives; redesigning social, educational, political and economic systems; and forcibly recreating the Orient in the image of the Occident.

Thus, it sets up a task for the European man, who is the embodiment of good, not only to affect the separation of good and evil, but to rule over the darker areas of the world, to bring light and learning to them. To that end, Eurocentrism is a celebration of European power to create and destroy; its increasingly greater sway over nature, time, space and life; and its capacity for seemingly endless progress and pleasure. The European history is seen as the prototype of the world history, in effect, the history of each society. Thus what is good for Europe is emphatically, and at times forcibly, presented as good for the world.

A statement by great humanist writer Fyodor Dostoyevsky about Russia's European role in Asia inadvertently but brilliantly discloses the value content of Eurocentrism. He writes:

> What is the need of the future seizure of Asia? What is our business there? This is necessary because Russia is not only in Europe, but also in Asia; because the Russian is not only a European, but also an Asiatic. Not only that; in our coming destiny, perhaps it is precisely Asia that represents our main way out. . . . In Europe, we are hangers-on and slaves, whereas to Asia we shall go as masters. In Europe, we were Asiatics, whereas in Asia we, too, are Europeans. Our civilizing mission in Asia will bribe our spirit and drive us thither.

Since the end of the Cold War, Eurocentrism has found its eloquent and theoretically compact expression in Samuel Huntington's formulation about the clash of civilizations. In his much-discussed essay "The Clash of Civilizations?" Huntington writes: "Western concepts differ fundamentally from those prevalent in other civilizations. Western ideas of individualism, liberalism, constitutionalism, human rights, equality, liberty, the rule of law, democracy, free markets, the separation of church and state, often have little resonance in Islamic, Confucian, Japanese, Hindu, Buddhist, or Orthodox cultures."

This line of reasoning reveals a deep-seated contradiction between Western claims of universality and uniqueness. While the West seeks to recreate the Third World in its own image, it also continues to imply and assert that the Oriental lacks the potential to become the Occidental. A subtler form of recent Eurocentrism has been put forward by scholar-administrator Anthony Lake. In his policy speech titled "From Containment to Enlargement," Lake notes:

> Democracy and market economies are ascendant in this new era, but they are not everywhere triumphant. There remain vast areas in Asia, Africa, the Middle East, and elsewhere where democracy and market economics are at best new arrivals—most likely unfamiliar, sometimes vilified, often fragile.
>
> But it is wrong to assume these ideas will be embraced only by West and rejected by the rest. Culture does shape politics and economics. But the idea of freedom has universal appeal. Thus, we have arrived at neither the end of history nor the clash of civilizations, but a moment of immense democratic and entrepreneurial opportunity. We must not waste it.

These concepts were further clarified and put into operation by President George W. BUSH in his State of the Union Address on January 29, 2002:

> No nation owns these aspirations, and no nation is exempt from them. We have no intention of imposing our culture. But America will always stand firm for the non-negotiable demands of human dignity: the rule of law; limits on the power of the state; respect for women; private property; free speech; equal justice; and religious tolerance. America will take the side of brave men and women who advocate these values around the world, including the Islamic world, because we have a greater objective than eliminating threats and containing resentment. We seek a just and peaceful world beyond the war on terror.

While "no nation owns these ideals,"the United States, and by implication the West, continues to possess trusteeship over these non-negotiable ideals, as well as the right to enforce them by necessary means.

Orientalism and Eurocentrism. While Eurocentrism is a construction of the European self (individual, group, race, nation, state, civilization, etc.) as superior, moral, rational, and Godly, Orientalism is a construction of the Oriental other (individual, group, race, nation, state, civilization, etc.) as inferior, infantile, dangerous, beastly, and evil. Eurocentrism and Orientalism are two halves of the same unified concept and each part presupposes the existence of the other and remains incomplete without it.

Eurocentrism has gained a new significance in the context of 21st century globalization. At least for the foreseeable future, it has become its official ideology.

BIBLIOGRAPHY. Edward Said, *Orientalism* (Pantheon Books, 1978); Anouar Abdel-Malek, "Orientalism in Crisis" (UNESCO, 1963); Wilfred Cantwell Smith, "The Place of Oriental Studies in a University," *Diogenes* (v.16); Edward Said, *Culture and Imperialism* (Vintage Books, 2000); Anouar Abdel-Malek, "Civilization and Social Theory," *Social Dialectics* (Macmillan, 1981); Samir Amin, *Eurocentrism* (Monthly Review Press, 1989); Immanuel Wallerstein, "Eurocentrism and its Avatars: The Dilemmas of Social Science" (Keynote Address at International Sociological Association East Asian Regional Colloquium, 1996); Eqbal Ahmed, *Confronting Empire* (South End Press, 2000); Samuel Huntington, "The Clash of Civilizations?" *Foreign Affairs* (1993); Anthony Lake, *From Containment to Enlargement* (John Hopkins University, 1993); J. M. Blaut, *Eight Eurocentric Historians* (The Guilford Press, 2000); Max Weber, *The Protestant Ethics and the Spirit of Capitalism* (Charles Scribner's Sons, 1976); Victor Kiernan, *The Lords of Human Kind: European Attitudes to Other Cultures in the Imperial Age* (Serif, 1996); Karl Wittfogel, *Oriental Despotism: A Comparative Study of Total Power* (Knopf Publishing Group, 1981); Karl Marx, *Capital* (International Publishers, 1977).

AGHA SAEED, PH.D.
UNIVERSITY OF CALIFORNIA, BERKELEY

ownership

THE POWER TO EXERCISE control over an asset or resource is regarded as ownership. Often defined also as the residual rights of control, meaning that ownership confers on the owner the right to exercise control over the resource only within certain limits determined by the legal system and/or contractual obligations. The most important components of the bundle of rights that define ownership are exclusivity and alienability. Exclusivity refers to the right to determine who may (and who may not) use the resource in a particular way. Alienability refers to the right to reassign ownership to someone else, including the right to offer for sale at any price.

Why ownership? This is a basic question that has existed throughout human history. The development of the economic science has furnished us with an answer. When resources are scarce, assignment of ownership (property) rights becomes essential to avoid wasteful fight over those resources. Consider a simple example of a person who is given a certain amount of resources (budget) and chooses a bundle of consumption goods and services that maximize his or her UTILITY (satisfaction) within that budget. What if the person could attempt to "improve" the budget constraint by stealing from others? That is, what would happen if ownership were not fully protected?

First of all, if A can steal from B, it means that B can also steal from A. If both steal equal amount from each other, A will end up with exactly the same budget as before. But the problem is actually much worse. If stealing becomes a norm, it means that a lot of time and effort has to be spent on trying to steal from others and also on protecting oneself from becoming a victim of stealing by others. This time and effort will result in actual reduction in the budget constraint and satisfaction from consumption. For example, whenever someone buys a bicycle, she also has to buy a heavy and expensive lock. Unlike other parts of the bicycle, the lock is not needed to enjoy the ride, however. It is a necessary addition to the bicycle because the bicycle might be stolen (because ownership is not perfectly protected in practice). Such socially wasteful expenditure on various protective devices and activities is very widespread even in most law-abiding societies, but in societies that have failed to assign and/or protect ownership they can and do make life really miserable.

The assignment of ownership (property rights) becomes even more important when we think of the production process. Scarce goods are not like "manna from heaven." They must be produced by allocating resources to the production process. Imagine that a farmer plants corn, cultivates it, etc., but his neighbor reaps and sells it. "After some such experiences the cultivation of land will be abandoned," explains Richard Posner in *The Economic Analysis of the Law*. In the presence of scarce resources, absence of ownership rights would kill any investment in improving the productivity of the society.

Private or collective ownership? This question has given rise to hot debates and has been a subject of controversy, including political rivalry between believers in individual freedom and private ownership, on the one hand,

and socialists, on the other hand. First of all, the nature of controversy has to be clarified. Neither pure private nor pure collective ownership have ever existed in any human society. In a society whose economic system is based on private ownership, collective ownership is very widespread. The most important form of it is, of course, ownership within a family (household). Housing, cars, televisions, children's toys, and many other items are usually in collective, not private ownership in any family, and many of the most important economic decisions about how to allocate resources within the family are often made collectively. Public goods, such as national defense, security, roads and bridges, fire service, etc., are also owned and exploited collectively despite the fact that they are scarce and valuable.

On the other hand, most societies based on collective ownership do also admit private ownership, at least in personal consumption. Thieves stealing goods from other people were prosecuted under a collectivist SOVIET UNION regime not less strictly than under a regime based on private ownership. Hence, the real debate between advocates of private ownership and advocates of socialism is limited to an argument about whether productive resources should be owned privately or collectively.

Efficient execution of collective ownership requires a high degree of altruism of co-owners toward each other or a well-functioning system of bureaucratic execution, or both. But while altruism is quite efficient within a family (or, more generally, within a well-defined small group of people repeatedly interacting with each other), it becomes quite inefficient when extended to the marketplace. There is no alternative to bureaucratic execution of collective ownership over some public goods, such as national defense, but the bureaucracy becomes progressively ineffective when it attempts to expand the sphere of its control over a large and complex economy.

Most countries that have achieved sustained economic progress and high standards of living of population have done so based on private, not collective ownership of most productive resources. The Soviet Union and its allies after WORLD WAR II had achieved some moderate economic success based on state ownership, but the success was short-lived and all those countries are currently in the transition to private ownership. Moreover, state ownership over production resources in the former Soviet Union was not at all collective in the real sense. Whenever it was enforced, it was, by and large, private ownership by the top-ranking communist officials.

Ownership and economic efficiency. Private ownership has arisen from scarcity of resources and its institution is vital to provide the society with an environment in which economic development can take place. A separate question is whether the identity of a particular owner matters for efficiency, or whether it is important just to have a well-delineated assignment of ownership rights, no matter who the owners are.

On a very high level of abstraction, it can be shown that it is the institution of private ownership that matters while the identity of the owner does not matter for resource allocation. A famous example (Ronald COASE, *The Firm, the Market, and the Law*) discusses this issue in the context of interaction between ranching and farming. In the example, stray cattle grazed by the rancher damage crops in the neighboring plot of land cultivated by the farmer. If the rancher and farmer can negotiate, there will be a socially efficient amount of crop damage from straying cattle regardless of who owns the land (or which party is legally liable for the damage). If the land is owned by the rancher, the farmer will have to pay him to limit the size of the herd, and the farmer will be willing to pay up to the amount at which the value of an additional ton of crops is exactly equal to the value of the last steer removed from the herd. If, on the other hand, the land is owned by the farmer, then it will be the rancher who will offer the farmer to compensate him for the damage in exchange for allowing to graze the herd. Once again, the rancher will be willing to pay up to the amount at which the value of the last steer added to the herd is exactly equal to the value of the last ton of crops destroyed. It is clear that the size of the herd and the amount of damage to crops will be the same in both cases, the only difference being that the rancher's income will be higher and the farmer's income lower in the former case while the opposite will be true in the latter case.

The above argument, under the name of the Coase Theorem, became a standard part of modern economic theory but also a subject of much controversy. In particular, Coase himself strongly opposed what he perceived to be a misuse of his example intended only as an illustration of what might happen if negotiations and market transactions were costless. Coase argues that his real point was that the assignment of ownership does matter in practice, because in the real-world negotiations, contracts and market transactions are not costless. In the presence of transaction costs, the identity of the owner can be very important.

Among transaction costs that make the identity of the owner especially important are the costs associated with possible dilution of surplus from investment. In order to make the production process really efficient, one or more parties involved often have to commit in advance to making a certain investment that would lose much of its value, should the transaction subsequently fall through. For example, an engineer can design and allocate capital equipment and also invest a lot in training workers to work with this specific capital equipment. If the ownership of the capital equipment is not assigned, however, workers may later "hold up" the engineer demanding that they are given a lion's share of profits, and threatening to quit and take the equipment with them. If such behavior is possible, a forward-looking engineer will have to think twice before investing her time and effort in a costly design and workers' training.

As a result, innovative activity, the engine of economic growth, might be severely hampered. If the engineer is given ownership over the firm, however (which means that she can exclude any single worker or all of them together from using the capital equipment), the workers cannot hold her up any more, and economic efficiency will be restored. If the society decides that for some reason workers are entitled to a better compensation than the wage offered by the owner, it is always possible, theoretically at least, to attain the socially desirable distribution of income through a tax system, not tampering with private ownership of productive resources and economic efficiency.

Truncation of ownership and the agency problem. In practice, taxation does restrict private ownership and does have consequences for economic efficiency. It is just one instance of the truncation of ownership rights by various legal constraints and regulations that are part of our everyday life. The exercise of ownership rights is also effectively constrained by the time the owner can allocate to actually executing the control rights bestowed on him.

Truncation of ownership by taxation and regulation is implemented by the society for both economic and non-economic reasons. An example of the former would be government regulation of automobile emissions. Air pollution caused by any single automobile passing along a road cannot possibly be the subject of negotiations and market-based transactions between the owner of the automobile and passers-by who suffer from inhaling exhaust fumes. Transaction costs are clearly too high for the Coase Theorem to work in such a context. Hence, the government steps in, sets and enforces certain guidelines, effectively reducing the degree of freedom with which automobile owners can exercise their private ownership.

An example of a non-economic constraint on ownership would be the legal prohibition of slavery. This law prohibits not only slave ownership, but it also prohibits an individual from selling himself into slavery of his own free will. Thus, we can say that even an individual's right of ownership of himself is not complete in the modern society (remember that the definition of full ownership includes the right to sell at any price). Military conscription is another example of a legal constraint on an individual's right to exercise ownership with respect to his own human capital.

Just as with the case of high transaction costs making the identity of owners matter, truncation of ownership rights also results in changed incentives. For example, a high income-tax leads to less incentives to work, and also to less incentives to invest in education and training. A

minimum wage in the presence of a tendency for some employers to discriminate against minorities will hurt the employment prospects of minorities (because they will not be able to offer to be hired at a lower wage to induce discriminating employers to hire them). Enforcement of seat belts and airbags can lead to people driving more recklessly (because they feel more protected in their automobiles) and threaten the safety of pedestrians. The general lesson is that questions of imposing limits on the exercise of ownership rights should be analyzed from various angles and especially from the point of view of how they affect economic incentives. It should also be not forgotten that the extension of a private right of action often (always?) curtails another private right of action.

One of the biggest limitations on the exercise of ownership stems from the fact that the time and effort owners can allocate to controlling valuable resources in their ownership is limited. This problem clearly manifested itself in socialist economies based on state or collective ownership. As the economy grew large, it became simply impossible to coordinate and control the use of all productive resources from one command center. But the problem of control also persists in capitalist societies based on private ownership because the desires of owners must be translated into cooperative action by employees (the agency problem), and because it is often optimal to increase the size of the firm to the extent that exceeds the capabilities of a single private owner. A joint stock company has to be formed and the problem of diffuse ownership arises.

The agency problem requires incentive schemes (such as performance bonuses and other profit-sharing schemes, stock options, threat of takeovers, etc.) for employers or hired managers to act in the interests of owners. Also, since control becomes weaker both when ownership is too diffused and when it is too concentrated (the latter because one individual has to oversee too many firms), absolutely equal and a very unequal distribution of wealth both lead to weak exercise of property rights. A certain, but not too large, degree of wealth inequality seems to be exactly what is required for private ownership to be executed effectively.

BIBLIOGRAPHY. Gary S. Becker, *A Treatise on the Family* (Harvard University Press, 1991); Serguey Braguinsky and Grigory Yavlinsky, *Incentives and Institutions: The Transition to a Market Economy in Russia* (Princeton University Press, 2000); Ronald Coase, *The Firm, the Market, and the Law* (University of Chicago Press, 1988); Harold Demsetz, *Ownership, Control, and the Firm* (Blackwell, 1988); Richard Posner, *The Economic Analysis of Law* (Little Brown, 1972); Oliver Williamson, *The Economic Institutions of Capitalism* (Free Press, 1985).

SERGUEY BRAGUINSKY
STATE UNIVERSITY OF NEW YORK, BUFFALO

P

Pakistan

THE ISLAMIC REPUBLIC OF PAKISTAN in southwest Asia borders INDIA (east), IRAN (west), AFGHANISTAN and CHINA (north), and the Arabian Sea (south). The northerly Himalayan Mountains have summer rains and winter snows that drain south across the hot Punjab and Sindh plains into the Arabian Sea via the Indus River drainage.

Pakistan was founded as a Muslim state when the subcontinent became independent from the British Empire in 1947. There are 145 million people, of which 36 percent are urban. Urdu is the national language, but English is spoken as the medium of official business. The rupee is the official currency. GROSS DOMESTIC PRODUCT (GDP) per capita is about $500 or an equivalent of purchasing power parity of about $2000. The GDP growth rate is 4.8 percent (2002).

Unemployment is around 6 percent, inflation less than 4 percent, and foreign debt is at $31 billion. The current (2003) semi-civilian regime of General Pervez Musharraf was installed after the elections in October 2002. Military replacement of civilian rule is common in times of strife and accounts for Pakistan's strong ties with military suppliers from the West, and for its debt. A nuclear arms contest between India and Pakistan has further exacerbated Pakistan's debt.

Musharraf has had difficulty in ending endemic, economic corruption but has been successful in attracting renewed economic aid by fighting terrorism. However, disputes with Pakistan's largest independent power producer HubCo, the INTERNATIONAL MONETARY FUND (IMF), and sanctions for nuclear tests have hurt the flow of investment. Additionally, a tax system overhaul failed to collect $1.6 billion of the anticipated $7 billion in taxes, and led to a general strike by the All Pakistan Organization of Small Traders and Cottage Industries in May 2000.

Poverty, healthcare, education and basic infrastructure problems plague 40 percent of the population. Agriculture employs about half of the 38 million workers, producing cotton, rice, wheat, and sugar cane. Textiles are a key export in a trade deficit of about $1 billion. Pakistan, in the 1960s, was officially considered by the United Nations as a model developing country with growth strides in social and economic indicators. But the historic dispute with India over the status of the Kashmir region led to increasing responsibility by the military in Pakistani society. The resulting political instability proved to be the Achille's heel of the developing country.

However, consistent import-export trade with the UNITED STATES, JAPAN, GERMANY, and the UNITED KINGDOM indicates Pakistan can participate in the global market if it is stable and capable of producing exportable surplus.

BIBLIOGRAPHY. I. Husain, Pakistan: The Economy of an Elitist State (Oxford University Press, 1999); S.R. Khan, ed., Fifty Years of Pakistan's Economy: Traditional Topics and Contemporary Concerns (Oxford University Press, 1999). J. Saeed, Islam and Modernization: A Comparative Analysis of Pakistan, Egypt, and Turkey (Praeger, 1994); S.A. Zaidi, Issues in Pakistan's Economy (Oxford University Press, 1999).

CHRIS HOWELL
RED ROCKS COLLEGE

Palestine

PALESTINE REFERS TO A REGION approximated by the combined areas of present-day Israel, the West Bank and Gaza. Following 400 years under Ottoman rule it was placed under British mandate in 1919, after the Balfour Declaration of 1917 stated British support for "the establishment in Palestine of a national home for the Jewish people . . . [provided that] nothing shall be done which may prejudice the civil and religious rights of existing non-Jewish communities."

Rapid immigration brought Jews to 31 percent of Palestine's population by 1947, when the UNITED NATIONS proposed dividing it into a Jewish state with 500,000 Jews and 500,000 Arabs, an Arab state with mostly Arabs, and an international enclave of Jerusalem and Bethlehem. Zionists accepted this, but Arabs rejected it.

In 1948–49, Jewish military attacks on Arab villages led to the flight of about 700,000 Arabs. In May 1948, the British mandate ended and the state of ISRAEL was declared. By 1949 Israel had about 700,000 Jews and 100,000 Arabs; Jordan got the West Bank and EGYPT the Gaza Strip. But in 1967 Israel occupied these lands militarily.

Today, over 3 million Palestinians live under Israeli occupation. In 2001, and even more severely in 2002, Israeli military measures in Palestinian Authority areas have resulted in the destruction of much capital plant and administrative structure, widespread business closures, and a sharp drop in GROSS DOMESTIC PRODUCT (GDP), which stood at $1.7 billion (per capita $800) in 2002.

BIBLIOGRAPHY. Charles D. Smith, *Palestine and the Arab-Israeli Conflict* (St. Martin's Press, 2001); Sara Roy, *The Gaza Strip: The Political Economy of De-Development* (Institute for Palestine Studies, 2001).

MEHRENE LARUDEE, PH.D.
UNIVERSITY OF KANSAS

Panama Canal

THE ISTHMUS OF PANAMA IS ONLY about 50 miles wide, by far a shorter route between the Atlantic and Pacific oceans than the 8,000-mile trip around South America. But it is a difficult 50 miles, through jungles and across the Continental Divide.

Initially, the Spanish built a road across the isthmus, and the first interest in an isthmian canal came only a few years after the Spanish took possession. The Camino Real, the treasure road linking the oceans, was slow and difficult, so surveys in the 1520s and 1530s tested the feasibility of building a canal. Philip II (1556–98) abandoned the idea, arguing that if God had intended an isthmian canal, He would have built it. Spain retained Panama for the next three centuries, and the canal idea languished.

Panama became independent in 1821, joined in the short-lived Gran Colombia, then became a province of Colombia. European and American interest in the isthmus was strong, for it was the shortest route between the Pacific and Atlantic oceans. In 1846, the UNITED STATES won the right to build a trans-isthmian railroad, invaluable during the western gold rush. When finished, the 47.5-mile railroad was the first transcontinental railway in the world. But a canal seemed more practical. Americans explored other options, but the isthmus was the best.

In the last quarter of the 19th century, with European imperial competition heating, interest in a canal became especially strong. In 1876, France's Ferdinand de Lesseps sent Navy Lieutenant Lucien N.B. Wyse to the isthmus. When Wyse returned, De Lesseps rejected his ideas because they entailed construction of tunnels and locks. Wyse went back to Panama, checked two potential routes, and opted for a route closely paralleling the railroad; this route seemed practical although it would require construction of a 23,160-foot tunnel at Culebra. Wyse negotiated the concession with Colombia in 1878, winning exclusive construction rights for his company and a 99-year lease. De Lesseps was on hand for the ceremonial first cut in 1880. In 1881 the first worker died of yellow fever. Already more than a thousand workers were engaged, but the Culebra cut was delayed due to general disorganization of the company's operations. The company spent more than $25 million buying the railroad. In 1882, the company established hospitals on each side of the isthmus, and by 1883 the company had 10,000 workers. In 1884 the labor force was 19,000, primarily West Indian.

In October 1884, Philippe Bunau-Varilla became a division engineer at Culebra, overseeing both dry and wet excavation. Soon, he became director general of the canal project. He had no success in overcoming the landslides that plagued the sea-level canal. And yellow fever became a constant killer of workers. Bunau-Varilla fell victim, but he survived, recovering in France. Back in Panama in 1887, Bunau-Varilla abandoned the sea-level canal and began a high-level lock canal, with a series of pools connected by locks. The canal at its maximum height would be 170 feet. Work resumed, but in 1889 the money ran out. The company dissolved, the work slowed, then halted. By 1894, liquidation was complete. Wyse renewed the concession for the company, but the company was rocked by scandal.

The canal had cost $287 million and only 11 miles had been dug. It had cost the lives of 20,000 men to move 50 million cubic meters of earth and rock. Thousands of investors lost their money, and some cried fraud. Both Ferdinand de Lesseps and his son, Charles, were among those indicted and found guilty.

The work continued, however, and in 1898 the company set a new canal plan in place. The new plan called for two high-level lakes to raise ships over the Continental Divide; eight sets of locks would gradually lift ships. The subsequent American plan would appropriate much of this one. For the French, it was too late; by 1898 the company had only half its original capital. It could abandon the project or sell it. Negotiations took five years, but finally in 1904 the United States bought the rights for $40 million. Construction began shortly after, and the 10-year project ended-up costing about $387 million.

The final American plan was developed by John F. Stevens, chief engineer of the U.S. Isthmian Canal Commission, in 1906. The canal opened for business on August 15, 1914, allowing ships to move from the Atlantic to the Pacific easily, a trip of 51 miles being much safer and easier, not to mention faster, than an 8,000-mile trip around Cape Horn.

The United States operated the canal through the 20th century. Increasingly, Panamians and other South Americans protested the continuing American presence. In 1977, President Jimmy CARTER and General Omar Torrijos signed a treaty phasing out American control and transferring American military bases on December 31,1999. Despite strong opposition from the U.S. public and Senate, Carter narrowly won approval of the treaty. Under the terms of the treaty of September 7, 1977, a transition Panama Canal Commission took over the canal and zone in 1979, and a Panamanian Panama Canal Authority assumed responsibility in 1999. The canal, by treaty, became neutral, and Panama took over former U.S. military facilities.

In 2002, Hong Kong-based Hutchison-Whampoa operated the canal ports. The canal employed 14,000 people, only 4,000 of whom were Panamanian.

The principal business of the canal is trade between the United States East Coast and Asia, anticipated to grow as China-U.S. trade increases. The canal also carries trade between Europe, the United States West Coast, and Canada, and increasingly, North-South American trade. The canal has a capability to handle about 50 ships a day, with its record day being 65. Passage averaged 24 hours per ship. In fiscal 2001, canal traffic averaged 33 ships per day for a total of 12,197; this was a decline of the 34-per-day average of the previous year. Size was a problem, with the 50,000-ton Panamax class ships being the largest the canal could handle.

To some, the canal at century's end seemed obsolete. It accommodated ships carrying up to 65,000 tons, but modern ships could carry as much as 300,000 tons. This disparity raised interest in building a new canal, perhaps through Colombia, Mexico, or Nicaragua. A canal through either of the first two would be sea level, as attempted at first in Panama. A Nicaraguan canal would require locks, as did the completed Panama Canal. Another proposal was to dredge 765 million cubic me-

ters of earth and rock and convert the Panama Canal to sea level, one 1960s proposal suggested the use of nuclear explosives.

The canal commission committed to a $1 billion modernization in 1996, widening the narrow eight-mile long Gaillard Cut that allowed access only for a single Panamax-class vessel. Completed in 2002, this expansion allowed two Panamax ships to pass simultaneously. Modernization of canal technology and tugboats were other investments by which the commission hoped to increase traffic by 20 percent.

BIBLIOGRAPHY. David McCullough, *Path Between the Seas: the Creation of the Panama Canal, 1870-1914* (Touchstone Books, 1999); U.S. Energy Information Administration, www.eia.doe.gov; Panama Canal Commission, www.pancanal.com; Jeremy Snapp, *Destiny by Design: The Construction of the Panama Canal* (Pacific Heritage Press, 2000).

JOHN H. BARNHILL, PH.D.
INDEPENDENT SCHOLAR

Pareto optimality

ONE MAJOR CRITERION with which the value of an economic outcome can be evaluated is Pareto optimality. Under the condition of Pareto optimality, an outcome is suboptimal if one can make a Pareto improvement in the allocation of production and consumption between individuals. A strict Pareto improvement makes all individuals better off. A weak Pareto improvement makes at least one individual better off without making any individual worse off. The Pareto optimality criterion is often used in social welfare, management and political economy since a Pareto improvement is universally beneficial (or at least not harmful). Therefore, in an efficient market all individuals should be in favor of a Pareto improvement, and in an election, since no one is harmed, all voters should be in favor of a Pareto-improving resolution.

Born in 1848, Vilfredo Pareto was an Italian economist and sociologist. Pareto's early training was in engineering at the University of Turin where, in 1870, he completed his thesis on "The Fundamental Principles of Equilibrium in Solid Bodies." After completing his degree he worked as an engineer, but also began applying his mathematical training to economic problems. In 1893, he followed Léon WALRAS as the chair of political economy at the University of Lausanne, Switzerland. His mathematical analysis of economic outcomes had far-reaching implications.

Vilfredo Pareto's well-known contributions, other than Pareto optimality (1906), are the ideas that income distributions throughout society are stable through time and the theory of the "circulation of elites." The latter theory states that while some individuals are born into higher social strata, these strata rotate as today's elite is overthrown by lower classes who become the new elite. Pareto died in 1923 in Geneva.

Pareto optimality is an important concept in welfare economics since it provides an objective criterion. If a Pareto improvement does not harm anyone, then there should be no opposition. The competitive equilibrium in a perfect market is one example of a Pareto optimal solution. If there were Pareto improvements to be made, then that would imply gains to trade, and the economy would move to the Pareto optimal equilibrium.

Consider a simplified example of a Pareto improvement. Two individuals are riding a train. One person is trying to read her newspaper to research business trends for an important meeting, the other person is talking loudly on his cellular phone transacting business with his office. In this situation, we can see that this may not be the best allocation. The person trying to read the paper cannot concentrate with the loud conversation, and the person talking on the phone is getting distracted by mean stares and eye-rolling. What often happens in this type of situation is that enough people complain and cell phones get banned from the train. Taking a look at the value of work being done, there may be a Pareto improving solution:

	Reader	Talker
Value of Work done with Talking	$250	$500
Value of Work done without Talking	$400	$50

If cell phones are banned, a total of $450 of work gets done between the two individuals. Letting them talk, however, generates a total of $750. The higher total indicates that a reallocation can be made to make both better off than with the regulation. For instance, if the Talker is allowed to use the phone, yet is required to pay his seatmate $150, a Pareto improvement is made. The Reader only does $250 worth of work, but plus $150 brings her to the $400 she could have made without the talking. The Talker earns $500 less the $150 payment, leaving $350 which is more than the $50 she would have if legally restrained from talking on the cell phone.

As seen in the above example, some Pareto improvements seem awkward since we do not usually see cash payments made on the train, and many Pareto improvements are left undone. A competitive equilibrium in a perfect market will achieve the Pareto optimum, but there are cases of market breakdown where the outcome is sub-optimal. Information asymmetry can cause a mar-

ket breakdown. If it cannot be verified that the Pareto improving transfer has been completed before one must take action, then a common result is that individuals do not honor agreements.

Another information problem is accurately calculating the transfer. If you ask the Reader how much her work is worth, what is keeping her from saying $500 or $550? This is why information asymmetries often end up with a second-best outcome (or third or fourth-best) rather than the Pareto optimal solution.

BIBLIOGRAPHY. Vilfredo Pareto, *Manual of Political Economy* (Augustus M. Kelley, 1969); Joseph Schumpeter, *History of Economic Analysis* (George Allen and Unwin, 1954); Dominick Salvatore, *Microeconomics: Theory and Applications* (Oxford University Press, 2003).

DERRICK REAGLE, PH.D.
FORDHAM UNIVERSITY

partnership

THE GENERAL USAGE of the term partnership in the business world could simply mean a joint venture or a strategic alliance that is based on common interests between two or more business entities. Partnership, in a formal sense, however, is a legal term that refers to a type of business organization when two or more persons form a voluntary association for the purpose of doing business.

The most basic form of partnership assumes each partner has equal executive power over the business and takes an equal share of profits or losses. Any partner can act on behalf of the partnership. By and large, a partnership is a business that is based on a private personal agreement. Government regulations on partnerships are therefore minimal. Besides a simple registration with the local authorities for the application of a business license, there is no legal material that one has to submit to the government to establish a partnership. A business partnership can exist once a personal agreement, usually in written form, has been reached between two or more persons.

There are three types of partnerships in the United States: the general partnership, the limited partnership, and the limited liability partnership. A general partnership is a partnership that carries the typical features of a partnership, such as the sharing of management and profit. Each partner is equally liable for the debts and obligations of the firm in full scale, regardless of which partner incurred it. A general partnership resembles a personal agreement between the involved parties. Since all responsibilities are on a personal basis, there is no need to file any paper work with the state.

The second type of partnership is the limited partnership, or the abbreviation LP. Different from the general partnership, it involves two kinds of partners, the general partner and the limited partner. The limited partner, or the "sleeping partner," does not need to have full liability of the debts and obligations in this partnership. The liability is only limited to the amount invested in the limited partnership. To gain legal recognition for this special partnership arrangement, the business has to have at least one general partner, who will eventually be fully responsible for the partnership, and has to file with the secretary of state to receive a Certificate of Limited Partnership.

A variant of the limited partnership is the family-limited partnership, or FLP. A family-limited partnership is a limited partnership in which ownership is restricted to the family members. FLP differs from other types of partnership and corporate forms because the transfer of interest is restricted and is not publicly traded. It is organized as a way to keep control of a family business among the family members. The younger generation of the family usually will be limited partners who own part of the business but do not have the right to participate in the daily management of it. The senior generation will be the general partner who has the right to manage it but also shares an unlimited liability on the business. The business will eventually be transferred to the family members of the younger generation when the time becomes desirable.

The last type of partnership is the limited-liability partnership, or the abbreviation LLP. It is the same as a general partnership with all of the same characteristics except with regard to the liability of its partners. A new legal organizational form that has been recognized by the U.S. government since 2001, limited-liability partnership is a hybrid between a limited company and a partnership. It is an option for a general partnership whose partners want to retain the basic features of a partnership but at the same time want to have the privilege of limited liability. It is a form that is supposed to be attractive for firms that are organized under a professional partnership, such as attorneys and accountants. In fact, in California for example, this form is only available to attorneys and accountants. Even with the attribute of limited liability, LLP is still treated as a partnership for tax returns.

Partnership has been used as a form of business for centuries. An early form of limited partnership can be traced back to the medieval period and is believed to have an Islamic origin. This business innovation later spread out to other parts of the world and became almost a universal practice in both Europe and Asia. The limited-liability partnership, on the other hand, is a very new design that has been practiced only in the last few years.

From an organizational point of view, there are two other common business organizational forms in history besides partnerships: the sole proprietorship and the corporation. A sole proprietorship is a business run by a single individual. It is the oldest and most common form of business organization. The individual, as the owner, controls the whole business and will be held personally liable for all the debts and obligations of the business. A sole proprietorship of a business is not regarded as a separate business entity and tax returns will be determined by the individual's personal income tax rate. Except for an application for a business license, sole proprietorship is not subjected to any federal or state regulation.

A corporation is a form of business organization that is organized by dividing the company's capital into shares. Modern corporations represent an aggregate ownership where a group of shareholders owns, but does not usually run the enterprise. It is recognized by the government, through registration according to the company law, as a corporate entity that has an independent legal personality. As an organization with legal personality, its property and liabilities can be separated from those of its members. It can therefore hold property, can make contracts, and can sue and be sued. The life of the company as an independent entity can also extend beyond that of the participants and can be independent from any changes to the composition of the shareholders.

A partnership is something in between a sole proprietorship and a corporation. It has more than one owner, but the owners are not like the shareholders of a corporation. It is often simply regarded as an aggregation of persons doing business together. There is no separation of ownership and control within a partnership, similar to the sole proprietorship but different from a corporation. A partner can be the owner and the manager simultaneously.

A partnership does not carry a legal personality from its owners, unlike a corporation. Profits of the business are supposed to pass through from the business to the partners, and each of them will report their profits from the partnership as a personal income, which will be taxed at that time. Therefore it is considered as a "pass-through entity" where the partnership itself does not pay any tax on profits.

Each of these organizational forms has advantages and disadvantages. Sole proprietorship is simple and with almost no government intervention. It only involves very small amount of licensing fees. The owner also has all the control, both on how to run the business and how to utilize the profits. However, the high control of the business by the owner at the time means that the source of capital will be limited to the owner. The owner of a sole proprietorship is also responsible for unlimited liability, which is always a potential risk.

A corporation, on the other hand, can raise capital by selling shares to the public. Unlike the owner of the sole proprietorship, the owner of the shares of a corporation, or the shareholders, could easily transfer the ownership through the stock market. Shareholders are also protected under limited liability. There is, of course, a price for all these advantages. It is relatively costly in terms of legal fees to file for incorporation. The organization of the corporation is also governed by the company law and therefore must fulfill numerous legal requirements accordingly.

A partnership is an arrangement that could solve the problem of capital by pooling resources from more than one partner. Compared with a corporation, it has far less legal restrictions and, therefore, the owners could retain a higher level of control on the operation of the business. The trade-off is that there could be disagreements between partners that could jeopardize the business, and all the partners are responsible for a unlimited liability, whatever the consequence. In a worst-case scenario, a partner has to be responsible for any wrongdoing of the other partner on behalf of the partnership. Because of the risk of being involved in personal liability, a partnership is supposed to be formed among people who are close and personally trust each other. Also, while it is a better option than a sole proprietorship in raising capital, with few exceptions, it is still not a form of business organization that could allow the business to grow to a very large size.

Another disadvantage of partnership is that when one partner does not want to continue to be involved, the partnership has to be dissolved first before any new arrangement can be made. The partners must first fulfill any remaining business obligations, pay off all debts, and divide any assets and profits among themselves. If one of the partners still wants to continue the business, he or she will have to buy-out the part of the business that used to belong to the other partner, and either turn the business into a sole proprietorship, or find a new partner to continue the business.

The alternative forms of partnership that are available allow some degree of flexibility and could overcome some of the disadvantages of a simple form of partnership. A limited partnership allows those who want to have more control of the business, but do not want to form a corporation, to have an alternative source of capital through the recruitment of limited partners. A limited partner can have the chance to invest in a business that is less restricted in terms of government intervention and can enjoy limited liability at the same time.

A limited-liability partnership also carries some attractive advantages. The key advantage is that all members of the partnership could carry limited liability, that is, all partners are limited partners. In the past, this could be achieved only by setting up a company. However, any business that is organized as a corporation will be under double taxation, which means that the profit of the corporation is subject to corporate tax, and any dividend the shareholders received would be taxed as income.

An LLP is taxed differently, in a way that profits made from the business are taxed as personal income just like a general partnership. Because of privilege of the limited liability, the business, even though it is a partnership, has to produce and publish ACCOUNTING information to the Registrar of Companies each year.

BIBLIOGRAPHY. Murat Çizakça, *A Comparative Evolution of Business Partnership* (Brill Academic, 1996); Jack R. Fay, "What Form of Ownership Is Best?" *The CPA Journal* (v.68/8, 1998); J. Dennis Hynes, *Agency, Partnership, and the LLC in a Nutshell* (West Wadsworth, 2001); James R. MacCrate and James B. McEvoy. "Family Limited Partnerships, Corporations, and Valuation Issues," *Appraisal Journal* (v.68/3, 2000); John E. Moye, *The Law of Business Organizations* (Delmar Learning, 1982); Dan Sitarz, *Partnerships: Laws of the United States* (Nova Publishing, 1999); G. Fred Streuling et al., *Federal Taxation of Partners and Partnerships* (Research Institute of America, 1992).

WAI-KEUNG CHUNG
UNIVERSITY OF WASHINGTON

patents

THE SOCIAL VALUE OF INVENTIONS and creative work has long been recognized—and their authors rewarded. As long ago as 1474, the Senate of the Republic of Venice decreed that inventors of "new and ingenious devices" be granted monopoly rights for a term of 10 years, thus establishing what is generally recognized as the first formal patent system.

About three centuries later, the drafters of the UNITED STATES Constitution granted Congress the power "to promote the progress of science and useful arts, by securing for limited times to authors and inventors the exclusive right to their respective writings and discoveries."

In 1790, the U.S. Congress exercised this power by passing into law the first patent statute, stipulating that the author of a "sufficiently useful and important" invention would receive patent rights for a duration of 14 years. Over the following century, patent systems were set up in the majority of industrializing countries. By the end of the 20th century, more than 130 countries had a patent system in place, although the details of patent protection granted to inventors differ across national systems.

In general terms, a patent represents a legal right to exclude others from making, using, or selling an invention or products made by an invented process that is granted to an inventor for a limited term. Accordingly, a patent creates a MONOPOLY over the use of an invention until the expiration of the patent term. The defining characteristics of the regime of patent protection are the duration of the patent rights, the breadth or scope of patent protection, the definition of patentable subject matter (that is, of the kinds of inventions for which patent protection is admissible), and the criteria of patentability that a specific invention has to satisfy.

In the United States, the duration of patent rights is currently set at 25 years from the date when the inventor files a patent application with the Patent and Trademark Office. The continuing validity of a patent is subject to the payment of modest maintenance fees. When a patent is issued, its content is published and a description of the invention becomes available for public scrutiny. The text of the patent includes a description of the invention and a number of claims defining the intellectual property for which the patent right is granted. The holding of a patent can be the source of a legal action by the holder against a third party accused of infringing on the patent. Typically, the accused infringer in a patent suit defends himself or herself by arguing that the patent in question is invalid, or that in fact his or her own actions are not infringing. Notice that the scope or breadth of the patent is decided in the context of litigation, as the courts determine the precise boundaries of the original patent rights. This is an important aspect of patent protection, since the economic value of a patent depends on how easy it is for others to "invent around" an existing patent. Accordingly, a broad scope of protection makes it harder to invent around a patent, whereas a narrow scope makes it easier.

General restrictions on the kinds of inventions that can be patented are common in every national legal system. The U.S. Patent Statute establishes that patents may be granted for the invention or discovery of any "new and useful process, machine, manufacture or composition of matter or any new useful improvement thereof." The term process refers to any "process, art or method and includes a new use of a known process, machine, manufacture, composition of matter or material." The vagueness of the language in the Statute has left the task of interpreting which inventions and discoveries are excluded to the courts. Over the last 20 years, court rulings have considerably expanded the definition of patentable subject matter. Accordingly, classes of inventions that would have likely been considered non-patentable in earlier times are now protected with patents. Notable among these are genetically modified living organisms, gene fragments, software programs, and business methods. These changes in legal doctrine have been quite significant in light of the rapid pace of technological advances in the relevant fields and have generated considerable controversy.

Criteria for a patent. Provided that the invention constitutes patentable subject matter, the decision as to whether to grant a patent hinges on three criteria: the invention must be useful, novel, and non-obvious. An invention is useful if it serves a specific purpose and is beneficial rather than harmful to society. Determining the usefulness of an invention is not always straightforward, particularly in those situations where an inventor rushes to file a patent application without conclusively demonstrating that the invention can serve the claimed purpose. Furthermore, the stated purposes for an invention may be too generic or vague for the invention to deserve patent protection. Along these lines, considerable controversy accompanied the filing of patent applications on gene fragments (Express Sequence Tags, or ESTs) whose utility could only be described as being valuable research tools for mapping complete genes.

The novelty requirement quite simply restricts the award of a patent to inventions that are new, a condition that is not as easy to verify as it may appear at first. Problems with the novelty requirement arise because it is a rare circumstance when the proposed invention is known to the public in the same exact form. More typically, the novelty of an invention has to be assessed by determining how new it is relative to any similar invention previously known or demonstrated, a determination that incidentally may relate to the scope of patent protection on earlier inventions.

Even if useful and novel, an invention may not receive a patent for failing to pass the non-obviousness test. This test asks whether or not the invention demonstrates a sufficient improvement on the prior art to deserve the award of a patent. The implicit assumption is that on the basis of the prior art in a specific area of technology, certain minimal improvements are obvious to any person skilled in the art, and consequently they are denied patent protection. Thus, the non-obviousness requirement defines the minimum inventive step required for the patentability of an invention.

The legal characteristics of patents described above are of considerable significance for the economic analysis of patents. Features like duration and scope of protection, or the inventive step implicit in the non-obviousness requirement, have the potential to play an important role in defining the economic effects of the legal monopoly over ideas created by patents. Specifically, they are likely to affect the performance of the markets for innovative products, as well as the extent of competition among firms in the pursuit of technological innovations. Considering that they may facilitate the formation of market monopolies—an inefficient form of industrial organization by most economists' own reckoning—why have societies throughout history been so keen on awarding patents to inventors?

Early advocates of patents. A variety of legal philosophies have been invoked over time to provide justification for the creation of a patent system. One of the main theses adopted by 19th-century commentators regarded the award of patents as a matter of justice dictated by either a man's natural right to his own property, including property in ideas, or by society's ethical duty to compensate or reward inventors for what they contributed. This emphasis on the just reward for inventive activity appears to be the basis for Adam SMITH's views on the matter in his *Wealth of Nations*. Even though he held a negative opinion of monopolies in general, Smith appears to consider the granting of a temporary monopoly to be the easiest and most natural way to reward the inventor of a machine for the risk and expense incurred.

Other supporters of the patent system charged, on pragmatic grounds, that patents were a bait for inventors to pursue the progress of science and the useful arts, thus benefiting society. The exceptional character of the monopoly created by the award of a patent is articulated clearly by John Stuart MILL, whose analysis anticipates the essential elements of modern economic thought on the role of patents:

> The condemnation of monopolies ought not to extend to patents, by which the originator of an improved process is allowed to enjoy, for a limited period, the exclusive privilege of using his own improvement. . . . That he ought to be both compensated and rewarded for it, will not be denied, and also that if all were at once allowed to avail themselves of his ingenuity, without having shared the labors or the expenses which he had to incur in bringing his idea into a practical shape, either such expenses and labors would be undergone by nobody except very opulent and very public-spirited persons, or the state must put a value on the service rendered by an inventor, and make him a pecuniary grant.

Critics of the patent system often disputed the need for an incentive to promote the inventive work that many considered to be a natural manifestation of human curiosity. In a different guise, a similar point was made by mid-20th-century critics who considered the declining economic role of the lone inventor in favor of the corporation to undermine the justification for awarding patents. This position reflected the belief that the social usefulness of the underlying invention bore no clear relation to the earnings generated by a patent, and furthermore that corporate investment in inventive activity did not depend on the prospect of a patent.

In this regard, an alternative viewpoint supporting the award of patents considers them to be society's consideration for the inventors' willingness to disclose their ideas or discoveries to the public. Under this view, it is recognized that the incentive of a patent award is not necessary to stimulate inventive activity. However, it is believed that inventors would keep their findings secret, or in any event, they would not disseminate their ideas as widely as it would be desirable in light of society's commitment to promoting the progress of science and the useful arts. The award of a patent is seen as a reward for the disclosure of information by the inventors. Note that for the inventors who intended to profit from their discovery by keeping it secret, the patent becomes a substitute means for profiting from the invention. As for other inventors, patents may offer a sought-after symbolic recognition of their creative work and induce them to disclose their inventions.

The social interest in disclosing information about inventions highlights dynamic aspects of the progress of science and the useful arts that other theories pay only scant attention to. In fact, the public disclosure of existing inventions may serve the dual purpose of forestalling duplicative research and experiments aimed at identical discoveries, and of contributing to the body of society's knowledge and ideas that constitutes an important factor for future inventive efforts.

Each of the views about the social function of patents described above, justifies the creation of a monopoly in the use of an invention as a necessary evil that society has to tolerate and endure in order to promote the achievement of a greater good, the progress of science and the useful arts. Building upon this general framework for examining the patent system, many fascinating economic models investigate how changes in the duration and scope of patents or in the criteria for patentability would affect social welfare and the pace of technical advance. It is important to realize that the implications of these theoretical models for the design of the patent system and other policy issues depend on the validity of the general framework they adopt.

Bluntly, an empirical assessment of the context of inventive activity is necessary to determine whether patents induce a significant increase in inventive activity, whether patents induce a significant increase in the disclosure of inventions, and more generally if they perform in the way the theory assumes them to do.

Consider, then, the proposition that patents are necessary as an incentive for inventive activity. The premise for this proposition is that invention is a costly activity and that inventive activity will be forthcoming under the stimulus of a financial reward. Absent a legal property right preventing others from copying, imitating, and using the knowledge underlying an invention, the inventor will not be able to profit from it either directly or by licensing its exploitation to a third party. The patent system's net social benefits should be determined by weighing the social value of the change in inventive activity that the system induces, against the social costs of the monopolistic conditions whose appearance in the relevant product markets the system facilitates. In principle, the changes in inventive activity may be trivial if inventive activity would occur in response to other stimuli, or if the granting of broad and long-lived patents deters firms from performing research in the neighborhood, or from undertaking the kind of follow-up inventive activity that could otherwise improve on the original invention.

Patents in research and development. Whether or not and in which contexts, patents provide a crucial incentive to inventive activity has been the focus of a considerable amount of empirical work. Beginning in the 1960s and as late as the early 1990s, surveys of RESEARCH AND DEVELOPMENT (R&D) managers have been conducted in order to draw a map of the technology areas for which firms consider the prospect of a patent to be a necessary inducement for their R&D investments. The conclusions of these studies have been remarkably consistent and suggest that with the exception of firms in the pharmaceutical industry, firms do not consider patents as a very effective means of protecting their inventions. On the contrary, many survey respondents from firms in the high-tech sectors of the economy indicated that being first to market, learning effects, or sales and service efforts are more important for them to profit from innovation. And in several industries, firms reported that secrecy is an effective means for profiting from innovation in TECHNOLOGY, particularly with respect to inventions focused on new production methods.

A caveat to the validity of these findings is in order, since these surveys have typically focused on large firms with an established R&D department. Patents may play a more important role for other classes of inventors, namely small firms or inventors that pursue a patent with the intention of licensing to other firms the development of any commercial application. These inventors may depend more heavily on patents to protect their invention, either because they cannot rely upon a head start vis-à-vis their competitors due to their small size, or because they facilitate licensing transactions.

It is customarily held that innovation differs from invention because of the development activities that need to be undertaken before an invention can be implemented in a commercial product or a production line. This distinction can be of great economic significance. For example, in the pharmaceutical industry costs incurred after the invention has been made can

easily exceed $100 million and account for a sizeable share of overall drug-development costs. Furthermore, the uncertainty about the outcome of an innovative project is not eliminated at the stage of invention, when the technical feasibility of a concept, or a prototype, has been demonstrated.

The costs and uncertainty of development activities have been invoked to argue that holding a patent on an invention is necessary for a firm to commit financial resources to its development. The holding of a patent on the invention secures the prospective market for the innovating firm. By reducing the threat that a competitor may race to market and spoil the inventing firm's profits, the patent induces it to develop and commercialize the invention. Likewise, when the inventive work and the development work are carried out by different organizations, a patent on the inventive work may be necessary together with an exclusive license in order to induce a firm to engage in the development work. In either case, the primary function of patents is not so much to provide incentives for inventive work, but rather to provide incentives for the development work that will follow.

The distinction is particularly important in those contexts where the inventive work would occur even in the absence of a patent. This is the case when the funding for the inventive activity is not dependent on the profit motive, as it is often the case when the relevant research funds are provided by the public or non-profit sectors of the economy. Indeed, the motivation for these forms of support of research activity is to promote inventions and discoveries that are intended to benefit the public at large. Until some time ago, such public purpose was served by placing the inventions and discoveries achieved in this way in the public domain, thus making them available at no cost. Since the 1960s, critics of this practice in the United States advanced the proposition that publicly funded research at universities and other research institutions had failed to induce innovations, and thus to generate public benefits because the results were routinely assigned to the public domain.

Absent a patent and an exclusive license, it was argued, hardly any firm would be willing to invest R&D dollars in such development work. In spite of the weak empirical evidence supporting it, this proposition became the primary stimulus for sweeping reforms in U.S. government patent policies.

This reform, initiated by the Bayh-Dole Act of 1980, granted universities and other private organizations the right to apply for patent protection on the results of publicly funded research. The widespread exercising of this has wrought considerable changes in the way in which research universities contribute to the national R&D effort. The resulting encroachment of patent rights on what used to be the domain of public science is only one aspect of broader changes in the U.S. patent systems, including the drastic expansion of the definition of patentable subject matter promoted by recent judicial opinions, that have taken place since the 1980s.

These events suggest that even though the findings of empirical research in economics are bearish or inconclusive about the social value of patents, policy decisions have been increasingly animated by a firm belief in the social value of stronger patent protection. Lately, this trend has expanded beyond the boundaries of the United States. The spurious association between the changes in patent policy and the rapid pace of U.S. economic growth during the 1990s has prompted other advanced industrial nations to follow suit, at least in part. Furthermore, while less developed countries have historically benefited from unfettered access to scientific and technological knowledge originating from the advanced economies, the TRIPS (Trade Related Aspects of Intellectual Property) agreement that accompanied the creation of the WORLD TRADE ORGANIZATION mandates a time-table for countries around the world to institute a system of patent protection or to strengthen the protection afforded to domestic and foreign inventors.

Although the immediate effect of these institutional reforms is likely to be negative for many developing countries, their supporters argue that in the long run, these countries will benefit as a result of the induced increases in domestic inventive activity and in their participation in technology transfer agreements.

BIBLIOGRAPHY. Robert P. Merges, *Patent Law and Policy: Cases and Materials* (Lexis Law Publishing, 1997); Kenneth J. Arrow, "Economic Welfare and the Allocation of Resources for Invention," in R.R. Nelson, *The Rate and Direction of Inventive Activity: Economic and Social Factors*, National Bureau of Economic Research (Princeton University Press, 1962); Fritz Machlup, *An Economic Review of the Patent System* (Government Printing Office, 1958); Roberto Mazzoleni and Richard R. Nelson, "Economic Theories About the Benefits and Costs of Patents," *Journal of Economic Issues* (v.32/4, 1998); Nancy T. Gallini, "The Economics of Patents: Lessons from Recent U.S. Patent Reform," *Journal of Economic Perspectives* (v.16/2, 2002); Suzanne Scotchmer, "Standing on the Shoulders of Giants: Cumulative Research and the Patent Law," *Journal of Economic Perspectives* (v.15/1, 1991).

ROBERTO MAZZOLENI, PH.D.
HOFSTRA UNIVERSITY

also enjoys a state MONOPOLY over natural-gas extraction, but greater private competition in drilling and distribution. In 2002, Pemex exported nearly half of its daily output of 3.6 million barrels. The same year Mexico's proven oil reserves were 12.6 billion barrels, mostly located offshore in the Gulf of Mexico.

In 1938, foreign oil companies disregarded a Mexican Supreme Court ruling in favor of oil workers. Using this as a rationale, and citing Article 27 of the Mexican Constitution of 1917, which declared the resources in the subsoil to be property of the state, President Lázaro Cárdenas nationalized all foreign oil companies, establishing Pemex as a state monopoly. Although compensation to the former owners defused tensions with the UNITED STATES, a prolonged boycott of Mexican oil by the United States and an embargo by U.S. oil equipment producers ensued. The confrontation made Pemex an important symbol of Mexican nationalism.

Pemex rapidly changed the focus of the industry from exports to the provision of subsidized oil to the domestic market with the goal to assist the country's industrialization. For a few years in the early 1970s, Mexico became a net importer of oil, but the sharp increase in world oil prices in 1973 sparked interest in exploration and raising production, returning Mexico to self-sufficiency in 1974. During the presidency of José López Portillo (1976–82), Pemex undertook extensive exploration resulting in the discovery of vast reserves. Subsequently, Mexico has become the third-largest supplier of oil to the United States with 1.5 million barrels delivered per day in 2002. Nearly 90 percent of Pemex's exports are to the United States.

Pro-market reforms since the early 1990s have brought forward discussion of the potential PRIVATIZATION of Pemex. President Vicente Fox (2000–06) initially supported its privatization. However, Pemex generates around a third of state revenue and privatization is strongly opposed by vast sectors of the population, so the idea has been shelved and exchanged for modernization of the state enterprise, implying greater engagement with private enterprises.

BIBLIOGRAPHY. Jonathan Brown and Alan Knight, eds., *The Mexican Petroleum Industry in the Twentieth Century* (University of Texas Press, 1992); Pemex, www.pemex.com; U.S. Energy Information Administration, www.eia.doe.gov.

LEOPOLDO RODRÍGUEZ-BOETSCH
PORTLAND STATE UNIVERSITY

Pemex

PETRÓLEOS MEXICANOS (PEMEX) is the world's fifth-largest oil producer. As a vertically integrated state enterprise it enjoys exclusive rights to the exploration, extraction, refining, and retailing of oil in MEXICO. It

Persian Gulf War

IN EARLY 1991, a two-month war between IRAQ and a United Nations (UN) coalition of 32 countries led by the United States entered the history books as the Persian Gulf War. Formed in response to the 1990 Iraqi invasion of KUWAIT, the coalition included forces from the United Kingdom, France, Egypt, Saudi Arabia, and Syria.

Initial hostilities stemmed from the desire of Iraqi leader, Saddam Hussein, to annex the neighboring state of Kuwait as an historic province of Iraq. Iraqi intentions to seize Kuwait had been voiced as early as the 19th century, but became more pronounced after 1961 when Kuwait achieved its independence from Britain. With the third-largest oil deposits in the world and far better port facilities than Iraq, Kuwait made an attractive target. In the months leading up to the outbreak of hostilities, Iraq accused Kuwait of illegally pumping oil from Iraqi oilfields at Rumalla, of intentionally overproducing oil to drive down the price and hurt Iraq's economy, and of failing to forgive war debts incurred by Iraq in its eight-year war with IRAN that had ended in 1988. Seeking to resolve the situation by force, Hussein sent approximately 100,000 Iraqi troops into Kuwait on August 2, 1990, formally annexing the country six days later.

The United Nations responded by demanding a full Iraqi withdrawal from Kuwait on August 3, and then on August 6 calling for a global trade embargo on Iraq. Acting quickly to presumably defend Saudi Arabian oilfields, U.S. President George H.W. BUSH dispatched American soldiers to the region on August 7. Further U.S. deployment in the region followed (Operation Desert Shield) through the end of 1990, with support from military contingents from North Atlantic Treaty Organization (NATO) allies and a number of Arab states.

UN forces, under the U.S. general Norman Schwarzkopf, reached approximately 700,000 by January 1991, with 540,000 of those U.S. personnel, while about 300,000 Iraqi troops occupied Kuwait. Meanwhile the UN Security Council had, on November 29, set a final deadline of January 15, 1991, as the date by which Iraqi forces would have to withdraw or face military reprisal "by all means necessary."

The war began in the early morning of January 17th with a massive Allied air campaign (Operation Desert Storm) designed to eradicate Iraqi aircraft, air defenses, and missile installations. Iraq retaliated by firing medium-range missiles toward ISRAEL and Saudi Arabia, hoping to widen the conflict and disrupt the UN coalition. The Allied air offensive, launched from bases in nearby Saudi Arabia and TURKEY, as well as from as far away as Europe, the Indian Ocean, and the United States, continued throughout the conflict. With an overwhelming advantage in air power, Allied air superiority was quickly achieved and Allied targets soon shifted from Iraqi air defenses to its oil refineries, arms facto-ries, communication infrastructure, and government buildings. As the war progressed, the UN air campaign moved to strike Iraqi forces on the ground in Kuwait and southern Iraq in preparation for an Allied ground assault.

The Allied land invasion (Operation Desert Sabre) began on February 24, following two primary invasion routes. The first struck directly northeast from Saudi territory into Kuwait. Within three days, Kuwait City had been retaken as Iraqi defenses in that region disintegrated or surrendered in the path of U.S. and Arab ground troops. A second avenue of attack was launched across the desert, where a major U.S. armored force outflanked Iraqi defenses on the Saudi border and attacked the rear of the Iraqi lines. The move was a great success and Iraqi defenses crumbled. Bush declared a cease-fire on February 28.

After the cessation of hostilities, Iraq accepted a set of UN resolutions on April 7, 1991. Hussein, however, remained in power and took severe measures to quell rebellions among Iraq's sizeable Shiite and Kurdish minorities. Estimates of the physical destruction wrought by the conflict vary widely. Both Kuwait and Iraq suffered devastating property damage. Estimates of Iraqi casualties range from about 10,000 to more than 100,000. Allied forces lost 343. Kuwait suffered about 5,000 casualties.

After the withdrawal of Iraq from Kuwait, many issues remained unresolved. Faced with Hussein's ongoing intransigence, UN sanctions continued in force and tensions between Iraq and the United States remained high, which portended prospects for the future United States-Iraq conflict in 2003.

BIBLIOGRAPHY. Clayton R. Newell, *Historical Dictionary of the Persian Gulf War 1990–1991* (Scarecrow Press, 1998); Frontline: "The Gulf War: An In-depth Examination of the 1990–1991 Persian Gulf Crisis," www.pbs.org; Micah L. Saffry and Christopher Cerf, eds., *Gulf War Reader* (Random House, 1991); Rick Atkinson, *Crusade: the Untold Story of the Persian Gulf War* (Houghton-Mifflin, 1993); Abbas Alnasrawi, *The Economy of Iraq: Oil, Wars, Destruction of Development and Prospects, 1950-2010* (Greenwood Press, 1994).

CHARLES ROBINSON
BRANDEIS UNIVERSITY

Peru

THE REPUBLIC OF PERU BORDERS Ecuador to the northwest, Bolivia to the southwest, CHILE to the south, COLOMBIA to the northeast, BRAZIL to the east, and the Pacific Ocean to the west. Peru's southern area runs across the high Andes, while its northern tip almost reaches the Equator. Lima is its capital city.

Peru's population is almost 30 million. Approximately 45 percent are Native Americans, about one-third of mixed European and Native American background (*mestizos*), approximately 15 percent unmixed white, and the remainder of African, Chinese, or Japanese descent. Spanish is Peru's predominant language, but Quechua is also an official language. Also spoken are English and Aymara. Since WORLD WAR II the population has rapidly increased and become predominantly urban.

Ancient Peru was the seat of several Andean civilizations. SPAIN conquered Peru in 1533. In 1821, Peru's independence was declared but the country was in constant turmoil until 1845 when Ramon Castilla seized the presidency. Castilla's most important contribution may have been his exploitation of Peru's guano and nitrate deposits. For several decades, taxation of this industry was the government's principal source of revenue. During Augusto Leguia y Salcedo's second term (1919–1930), costly public works projects were begun, financed by loans from U.S. banks, and the rights to the La Brea-Parinas oil fields were given to the International Petroleum Company, a U.S. company.

In the 1950s, Peru began a program geared toward encouraging the growth of domestic industries and limiting the outflow of dollars. By 1960, the economy was much stronger and Peru was receiving foreign capital in the form of loans and development contracts. That year, the government gained approval for the gradual nationalization of the majority of Peruvian oil production facilities.

In 1968, the government seized control over the International Petroleum Company's holdings and, in 1969, a program of economic nationalization began, including the expropriation of foreign-owned ranchlands, the institution of price controls, and a sweeping land-reform law. In 1973, the fish-meal industry was nationalized. These programs affected $600 million in U.S. capital investments.

In the early 1980s, the government attempted to reorganize the economy with reduced government involvement and increased private enterprise. However, the new economic policies failed to lessen the growing economic crisis. The rise in the guerilla movement also exacerbated the economic problems. In 1985, the regime announced that it would pay no more than 10 percent of its export earnings toward its nearly $14 billion in foreign debt. In response, the INTERNATIONAL MONETARY FUND (IMF) declared Peru ineligible for future loans and credits until it adopted a more traditional approach to the economy and debt repayment. In 1987, as Peru's economy continued to slide downward, the government moved to nationalize the banks.

In 1990, the government instituted an austerity program. The program eliminated inflation but caused immediate hardships, most notably among the poor. In 1992 a program of neo-liberal economic policies was begun, including the privatization of state-owned mines and utility companies. In 1993, the United States and other nations resumed loans to Peru.

The large state-owned banks control credit, currency regulation, bank regulation, and foreign exchange. The Banco Central de Reserva del Peru is the CENTRAL BANK and bank of issue. Peru's exports are valued at approximately $7.3 billion and its imports at approximately $7.4 billion. Peru's exports are more diversified than most South American countries and include petroleum, fish meal, cotton, sugar, coffee, copper, and lead. Peru's major imports are pharmaceuticals, transport equipment, petroleum, chemicals, consumer goods, and foodstuffs. Its export/import partners include the UNITED STATES, BRITAIN, BRAZIL, SWITZERLAND, CHINA, JAPAN, CHILE, and GERMANY. Peru is a member of the Latin American Integration Association (LAIA) and the Andean Group. Both organizations work to integrate the economies of Latin and South America.

In 1998, El Niño's impact on agriculture, the ASIAN FINANCIAL CRISIS, and the Brazilian market's instability contributed to a curtailment of Peru's economic growth. Factor in political instability and global economic travails and Peru's economic growth has further been suppressed. The government is working to reinvigorate the economy and reduce unemployment but, for the early 2000s, economic growth is expected to be no more than 3 to 3.5 percent.

BIBLIOGRAPHY. Alfred C. Stepan, *The State and Society: Peru in Comparative Perspective* (Princeton University Press, 1978); Stephen Gorman, ed., *Post-Revolutionary Peru: The Politics of Transformation* (Westview Press, 1982); David Scott Palmer, ed., *The Shining Path of Peru* (Palgrave Macmillan, 1994); Steve J. Stern, ed., *Shining and Other Paths: War and Society in Peru, 1980–1995* (Duke University Press, 1998); *CIA World Factbook* (2002).

S.J. RUBEL, J.D.
INDEPENDENT SCHOLAR

Peugeot Citroën

OVERCOMING COMPETITOR RENAULT to produce FRANCE's best-selling automobile, Peugeot Citroën holds the significant status of being the second-best selling car company in Europe, just behind VOLKSWAGEN.

Peugeot manufactures cars, light commercial vehicles, motorcycles, scooters and light-armored vehicles under the Peugeot and Citroën brands. As well, it produces specialized automotive parts (which sell through Faurecia retailer outlets), transportation and logistics equipment (via an association with the global supply house, Gefco) and offers financial-service arrangements (handled by Banque PSA France).

The group, with its 200,000 employees, has been focused on a three-year rollout to produce 25 new models between 2001 and 2004. It is an expeditious schedule compared to the past; only nine new models were introduced between 1997 and 2001. But, the corporate plan is to deliver to its customers the kind of vehicles they want and expect which leads to a wide variety of choice. Besides changes in design aesthetics, Peugeot designers foresee the cars of the new millennium as environmentally conscious, ultra-safe, and offering interface between the car and outside world.

Environmental priorities include reducing harmful emissions, improving air quality, and increasing the number of cars operable on low-fuel consumption. As for safety, Peugeot's newest models feature a structural front-end resistance three times higher than the norm.

A relatively new scope for Peugeot, and for the auto manufacturing industry as a whole, is the incorporation of the "connected village" approach into vehicles. Upcoming Peugeots will include such systems as assisted navigation, built-in mobile phones, message reception, and transmission services capabilities.

This all leads to the company's objective to boost annual sales volume to 3.5 million cars, 800,000 of which would be sold outside Europe. And that is why Peugeot is investing in two new large facilities—a manufacturing plant in the Czech Republic (opening date 2005) capable of producing 200,000 Peugeot Citroën cars per year; and an assembly plant in central Europe (2006) with an annual capacity of 300,000 units.

Full-year financial statements (2001) show revenues of $46 billion, making Peugeot Citroën the 95th largest company in the world.

BIBLIOGRAPHY. Hoover's, www.hoovers.com; Peugeot Citroën, www.psa.peugeot-citroen.com; "Global 500: World's Largest Companies," *Fortune* (July 2002).

JOSEPH GERINGER
SYED B. HUSSAIN, PH.D.
UNIVERSITY OF WISCONSIN, OSHKOSH

Philippines, the

AN ARCHIPELAGO IN SOUTHEASTERN Asia, between the Philippine Sea and the South China Sea, east

of VIETNAM, the Philippines were ceded by Spain to the UNITED STATES in 1898 following the SPANISH-AMERICAN WAR. The islands attained their independence in 1946 after Japanese occupation in WORLD WAR II.

In the late 1990s, the Philippine economy—a mixture of agriculture, industry, and services—deteriorated as a result of effects from both the ASIAN FINANCIAL CRISIS and extremely poor weather conditions. The Philippines' poverty level reached 40 percent of the population, but one encouraging sign was that the island's active labor force rose slightly from 30 million people in 1999 to 32 million in 2003.

Of the islands' industries, AGRICULTURE (farming, forestry, and fishing) employs approximately 40 percent of the laboring trades to constitute about 17 percent of the economy. Manufacturing, construction, and mining add 16 percent while services make up the remainder.

Major industrial products are textiles, pharmaceuticals, chemicals, wood products and electronic gear. The Philippines is rich in mineral resources, there are major deposits of gold in northern and southern Luzon, iron ore in northern Mindanao, copper in central Luzon, and high-grade chromium ore in both the west-central and southern parts of the island.

At the beginning of the new millennium, the Philippine government continued economic reforms to help its people try to match the pace of development in the newly industrialized countries of east Asia. The strategy included further deregulation and privatization of the economy, and increasing trade integration.

The GROSS DOMESTIC PRODUCT (GDP) per capita was $4,000 in 2001. The future of the Philippines' economy is highly dependent on the economic prospects of its two major trading partners, the United States and JAPAN.

BIBLIOGRAPHY. Alasdair Bowie and Daniel Unger, *The Politics of Open Economies: Indonesia, Malaysia, the Philippines, and Thailand* (Cambridge University Press, 1997); *The New International Atlas* (Rand McNally, 2001); *CIA World Factbook: The Philippines* (2002).

JOSEPH GERINGER
SYED B. HUSSAIN, PH.D.
UNIVERSITY OF WISCONSIN, OSHKOSH

Phillips Curve

THE PHILLIPS CURVE PLOTS the relationship between the rate of inflation and the unemployment rate and it is very common to view the Phillips Curve in a graphical format. Usually, this is done by placing the rate of inflation on the vertical axis and the unemployment rate on the horizontal axis. Doing so, A.W. Phillips first noted the inverse empirical relationship by using wage inflation and unemployment for the British economy.

This original study looked at a 100-year time period, ending in 1957. Modern variations of the Phillips Curve typically replace the wage inflation rate with the inflation rate for consumer prices. In the UNITED STATES, as well as in many other countries, this is measured by the percentage change in the Consumer Price Index or CPI. Moreover, the modern Phillips Curve is often augmented with a term that represents inflationary expectations and is, therefore, referred to as the expectations-augmented Phillips Curve.

First developed by Phillips, the inflation-unemployment rate relationship was later modified by Milton FRIEDMAN and Edmund Phelps. Today, the standard expectations-augmented Phillips Curve relationship is expressed as:

$$\pi = \pi^e - k(u - u^*)$$

In this equation the inflation rate is denoted by π, the expected inflation rate is denoted by π^e, the unemployment rate is denoted by u, and u^* is called the natural rate of unemployment. The latter can essentially be thought of as the unemployment rate that prevails in normal times. Thus, u^* is an equilibrium unemployment rate that the economy naturally gravitates toward over time. In any particular time period, however, the natural rate of unemployment may be greater than, less than, or equal to the actual unemployment rate. Note that the natural rate of unemployment is typically greater than zero as it takes into account such phenomena as frictional and structural UNEMPLOYMENT. The parameter k is greater than zero and indicates the extent to which the inflation rate is associated with the deviation of the actual unemployment rate from the natural rate of unemployment.

In practice, the parameter k is a coefficient that must be estimated. Once estimated, the magnitude of k reveals information about how responsive the current inflation rate is to a deviation of the current unemployment rate from the natural rate of unemployment. Larger values of k indicate more responsiveness while a smaller value of k would indicate less responsiveness. Thus, whenever the unemployment rate is unusually high, which would be the case when $u > u^*$, there is pressure on prices in the economy to rise.

On the other hand, if the unemployment is unusually low, there is a tendency for prices to fall or, at least for the inflation rate to become smaller. It is in this sense that one often hears of the Phillips Curve as illustrating the trade-off that exists between inflation and unemployment. Higher unemployment rates are associated with lower inflation rates while lower unemployment rates are associated with higher rates of inflation.

The expected inflation term picks up the idea that there is inflationary momentum in the economy. That is, if people form their expectations about current inflation from what the inflation rate has actually been in the immediate past, then there is a built-in source of inflation pressure.

For example, if inflation has been high the last couple of periods, it is likely that business owners and workers will expect it to be high in the current period. Thus, they will set their prices and wages in accord with this expectation. Since inflation is the actual percentage change in prices, then to the extent that people raise their prices in anticipation of inflation they are, in fact, placing pressure on prices to rise. It is in this sense that the idea of inflationary expectations leads to inflationary momentum. Thus, according to the Phillips Curve, one source of inflationary pressure is inflationary momentum.

Moreover, the short-run Phillips Curve suggests a trade-off between unemployment and unexpected inflation. Only if expected inflation changes will the short-run Phillips Curve shift. In this context, the shifting of the Phillips Curve reflects the notion that people may have different expectations about inflation, but given these new expectations, there still remains an inverse relationship between unemployment and inflation.

Consequently, any observed relationship between unemployment and actual inflation will change over time as expected inflation changes. Thus we may observe actual inflation being high even when unemployment is higher than the natural rate. This does not invalidate the Phillips Curve relationship rather it simply highlights the point that the curve may shift and the economy may have changed in some way. Indeed, with regard to unemployment, it is unexpected inflation that is relevant, not its level.

Rearranging the expression of inflation one can express the unemployment rate as a function of the natural rate of unemployment and unexpected inflation. Doing so one obtains:

$$u = u^* - (1/k)(\pi - \pi^e)$$

In the long run, if people and business owners have rational expectations of price changes then inflation will equal expected inflation on average. Thus according to the expectations-augmented Phillips Curve, the actual unemployment rate will coincide with the natural rate in the long run and the long-run Phillips Curve is vertical. This implies that changes in the nominal money supply, which affect interest rates and aggregated demand, cannot affect output or unemployment in the long run and therefore money is long-run neutral.

Consequently, the Phillips Curve suggests that policymakers can exploit the trade-off between inflation and unemployment in the short run, but not in the long run.

The result of trying to do so over a long period of time is simply more inflation without any change in the natural rate of unemployment.

In fact, it is typically argued that the ability of the monetary policy authority or central bank (e.g., the FEDERAL RESERVE in the United States) to lower the unemployment rate depends critically on whether or not money is neutral. From a historical perspective, it is interesting to note that during the 1960s, the United States economic policy centered on the ability of a policy-maker to gradually obtain a lower unemployment rate by moderately increasing the inflation rate. However, it was soon recognized that unemployment could not persist below its natural rate without resulting in accelerating inflation.

Economic theory suggests that when output exceeds its potential level, shortages of workers and materials develop resulting in upward pressure on wages and the costs of materials. Note that when the economy is producing an amount of output that is just equal to its potential, the unemployment rate will equal the natural rate of unemployment. As a result of an unusually low unemployment rate and higher than potential amount of output being produced, inflationary pressures begin to build. This is because many firms, in an attempt to keep production levels high, must seek additional workers and/or try to retain current employees who have many good alternative job opportunities. The way to keep and attract workers is to raise wages, compensation, and other benefits. However, these strategies are costly and so firms may find their gross profit margins being squeezed.

As a result, in order to maintain these margins, firms may try to raise prices. Of course, some firms are better able to raise prices than others depending on the market structure in which they operate. Even so, there is pressure on prices to rise and if the overall level of prices does rise, then the economy will experience inflation.

Similarly, when output is below its potential level and the unemployment rate is above the natural rate of unemployment, inflationary pressures begin to subside. In this case, workers' alternative job opportunities are bleak and they may agree to lower wages and compensation in order to keep their jobs. So, when demand has fallen and firms reduce their production levels, they require less workers. The demand for labor has fallen and wages will follow suit. With lower incomes, people will demand less output and prices of goods and services should fall in order to clear markets. Thus, with wages and prices falling, the inflation rate should be lower.

Finally, for convenience purposes, the Phillips Curve is again often re-written replacing the unemployment rate with the deviation of actual output from potential output. Recall that when the actual unemployment rate coincides with the natural rate of unemployment, the economy is said to be producing at potential. Any time the economy's output level deviates from the potential output level then we know that the unemployment rate will differ from the natural rate of unemployment in a predictable manner. This representation using the deviation of output from potential is given by:

$$\pi = \pi^e + g(y - y^*)$$

where y is real gross domestic product, y^* is potential gross domestic product, and the coefficient g measures the responsiveness of inflation to departures of output from potential. Note that if one takes natural logarithms of real output and real potential output, then their difference essentially reflects the percentage by which output deviates from its normal or equilibrium level. In this specification, the parameter $g > 0$ indicates the extent to which the inflation rate is associated with the deviation of gross domestic product from its potential (i.e., the "output gap").

The price adjustment mechanism is succinctly described by the expectations-augmented Phillips Curve. In general, the Phillips Curve shows how inflation depends critically on two components. The first of these components is the degree of inflationary momentum as reflected in the inflation expectations term. The second component is the state of the labor market or, put differently, how the economy is performing relative to some benchmark. This benchmark is either the natural rate of unemployment or potential real output. Policy-makers can use the Phillips Curve to help guide the economy and to maintain the inflation rate at desired levels. Economic forecasters can use the Phillips Curve to make predictions about inflation.

BIBLIOGRAPHY. Milton Friedman, "The Role of Monetary Policy," *American Economic Review* (v. 58, 1968): Edmund S. Phelps, "Phillips Curves, Expectations of Inflation, and Optimal Unemployment over Time," *Economica* (v. 34, August 1967); A.W. Phillips, "The Relation between Unemployment and the Rate of Change of Money Wage Rates in the United Kingdom, 1861-1957," *Economica* (v. 25, November 1958); William Seyfried and Bradley T. Ewing, "Inflation Uncertainty and Unemployment: Some International Evidence," *American Economist* (v. 45, Fall 2001).

BRADLEY T. EWING, PH.D.
TEXAS TECH UNIVERSITY

physiocrats

A FRENCH ECONOMIC movement founded by Francois QUESNAY and a major influence on Adam SMITH and later economists, physiocracy derived its name from the fundamental idea that economic systems should follow the rule ("-cracy") of nature ("physio"). The movement was partly a reaction against two doctrines that dominated the economic life of 18th-century FRANCE and other European nations: MERCANTILISM, the idea that government should promote exports and discourage imports so that the country would accumulate gold; and Colbertism, named after the French commerce minister Jean-Baptiste COLBERT (1619–83), which tried to regulate every aspect of economic life, even to the number of threads in lace. Colbertism also tried to encourage manufacturing at the expense of agriculture.

Quesnay, the founder of physiocracy, came from a farming family in rural France and was orphaned at the age of 13. He educated himself in medicine and became a successful surgeon. His writings included a book titled *On the Circulation of Blood* and two encyclopedia articles about farming. These foreshadowed some of his later ideas about economics.

Quesnay became personal physician to King Louis XV of France in the early 1750s, and did not become interested in economics until a few years later. Shortly thereafter, he met the Marquis Mirabeau, who became Quesnay's first follower. Quesnay's own economic writings tended to be obscure. As Lionel Robbins said in his lectures at the London School of Economics, "I find Quesnay almost intolerably difficult. You need a towel round your head to read Quesnay." Mirabeau, on the other hand, proved adept at popularizing Quesnay's ideas: "The ruminations of one seemingly harmless eccentric physician had now become a School of Thought, a force to be reckoned with."

The main ideas of physiocracy can be seen partly as coming from Quesnay's medical ideas and farming background, and partly as a reaction against the dominant economic doctrines in France at the time. First, the physiocrats thought that only AGRICULTURE and MINING produced new value. They saw manufacturing as a sterile activity that simply rearranged what had already been created by agriculture and mining. As a result, they favored policies to encourage agriculture at the expense of manufacturing, exactly the opposite of the policies favored by Colbertism. They also challenged the mercantilist notion that wealth consisted solely of gold or silver. Instead, the physiocrats saw wealth as coming only from productive activity—agriculture and mining, in particular.

Second, apart from wanting to encourage agriculture, physiocrats advocated LAISSEZ-FAIRE economic policies that would leave each individual free to pursue his or her own interests. Again, these policies were the exact opposite of the heavy regulation favored by Colbertism. The physiocrats' support for laissez-faire also influenced Smith, who was a friend though not a follower of Quesnay.

Third, the physiocrats based their policy recommendations on different grounds from those of Smith, who advocated utilitarian measures to achieve "the greatest good for the greatest number." Instead, physiocrats thought that all policies should simply follow "natural law," by which they meant—rather vaguely—their distinction between productive activity (agriculture and mining) and sterile, unproductive activity (manufacturing).

The centerpiece of the physiocrats' natural-law theory was the *tableau économique* (economic table), a diagram devised by Quesnay that showed how wealth flowed between productive and unproductive sectors of the economy. Mirabeau said that the invention of the tableau was as significant as the invention of writing and money; Smith regarded its distinction between productive and unproductive activity as misguided. Quesnay's flow model of the economy can be seen as an echo of his earlier writings about the circulation of blood.

Quesnay's tableau diagram divided society into three columns: productive laborers (agricultural and mining workers); landlords, who were also productive by virtue of making their land available for cultivation; and unproductive laborers (those in manufacturing and commerce). In the diagram, wealth flows year by year between the productive and unproductive classes. Good economic policy, said the physiocrats, caused enough wealth to flow to the productive classes to maintain and increase their output over time. Bad economic policy allowed wealth to flow away from the productive classes into the hands of the unproductive.

In effect, the physiocrats argued that good economic policy favored agriculture and mining at the expense of manufacturing and commerce, while bad economic policy did the reverse. The implications of this view were not always easy to predict: for example, the physiocrats advocated abolishing all taxes except those on landlords; laborers and businesspeople would pay no tax.

Whatever their errors, the physiocrats are today recognized as the first economists to treat a nation's economy as a system of interacting sectors between which wealth flowed over time. Some of their ideas were anticipated by the Irish economist Richard Cantillon in his "Essay on Commerce" (1755) and extended by the Scottish economist Smith in his famous *The Wealth of Nations* (1776).

BIBLIOGRAPHY. Lionel Robbins, *A History of Economic Thought: The LSE Lectures* (Princeton University Press, 1998); Murray N. Rothbard, *Economic Thought Before Adam Smith*, (Edward Elgar, 1996); Todd G. Buchholz, *New Ideas from Dead Economists* (Penguin Books, 1990); Ronald Meek, *The Economics of Physiocracy: Essays and Translations* (Allen & Unwin, 1962).

SCOTT PALMER, PH.D.
RGMS ECONOMICS

Pierce, Franklin (1804–69)

THE 14TH PRESIDENT of the UNITED STATES, Franklin Pierce was born in Hillsboro, New Hampshire. He graduated from Bowdoin College in Maine in 1824. After studying law, he was admitted to the New Hampshire Bar in 1827; the same year his father became governor.

At age 24, Pierce was elected to the state legislature. In 1833, he was elected to the U.S. House of Representatives, moving to the Senate in 1837 as that body's youngest member. However, he and his wife disliked Washington, and felt they could not live on a senator's pay ($8 per day when in session). In 1842 Pierce resigned and returned to private practice, rejecting several offers to return to politics, including an offer to become James POLK's attorney general.

During the MEXICAN-AMERICAN WAR, Pierce served as brigadier general under General Winfield Scott. Following the war, Pierce rejected the 1848 Democratic nomination for governor but remained active in state party politics.

A deadlock at the 1852 Democratic Convention resulted in Pierce's nomination for president on the 49th ballot. He defeated Scott, his former commander and Whig candidate, in the general election.

Pierce immediately angered Northerners. In his inaugural address he announced support for strict enforcement of the Fugitive Slave Act, which required Northerners to assist in returning escaped slaves to their Southern masters. Later, he also supported the Kansas-Nebraska Act, which allowed the residents of those territories to determine their admission to the Union as slave or free states. This was seen as a betrayal of the Missouri Compromise by permitting Northern territories to become slave states. It resulted in a bloody border war as both sides fought to control Kansas.

Pierce also pursued an aggressive foreign policy to expand slave territories. A secret proposal advocating the taking of Cuba by force, made by James BUCHANAN, the minister to Britain, became public. An embarrassed Pierce had to repudiate the document and forego all attempts to acquire Cuba or any other territories.

Pierce's only successful territorial acquisition was the 1853 Gadsden Purchase, encompassing the southern parts of present-day Arizona and New Mexico. The purpose was to build a transcontinental railroad to facilitate the rapid westward expansion of the still young nation. Pierce expanded U.S. trade in Asia and Latin America, and reduced tariffs with Great Britain.

In 1856 Pierce became the only elected president to lose his own party's re-nomination. They selected James Buchanan instead. Pierce became an outspoken critic of President Abraham LINCOLN and the Emancipation Proclamation, and blamed abolitionist extremism for the AMERICAN CIVIL WAR.

BIBLIOGRAPHY. Larry Gara, *The Presidency of Franklin Pierce* (University Press of Kansas, 1991); Nathan Miller, *Star Spangled Men* (Scribner, 1998); Roy Nichols, *Franklin Pierce, Young Hickory of the Granite Hills* (American Political Biography, 1958).

MICHAEL J. TROY, J.D.
THOMAS D. JEITSCHKO, PH.D.
MICHIGAN STATE UNIVERSITY

planning

THE CONCEPT OF PLANNING in capitalist economics relates to conflict resolutions between the actual and potential as seen by decision agents. It is a conscious activity by decision agents to transform the potential to actual. Planning may also be viewed in terms of conscious intervention to change the actual reality through cognitive designs. Planning is to create a cognitive edifice or structure of change.

Planning relates present perceptions of concrete realities to future possibilities that must be actualized through a rationally continuous process. It is time sequential in that planning consciously links various decision time points to one another and to the initial time thus defining a conscious decision trajectory through the examination of evolving cause-effect chains that are likely to be actualized through current decisions. It may thus be viewed as examining future possibilities and the alternative courses of action, which may be opened to the decision agent. This involves assessing the future contingencies and designing provisions for them.

Planning is conceptually distinguished from decision in that it is simply a conceptual subset of decision space. The general decision space is composed of deliberative and non-deliberative decisions. Planning belongs to the subset of deliberative decisions. Unlike other deliberative decisions, planning is time-points connected on the basis of rational contemplation of the future relative to the present to arrive at a rational cognitive edifice for action over a specified period such as medium-run or long-run, which establishes planning as a dynamic concept.

Planning is different from the plan in that planning is a cognitive creative process that allows the decision agent to think through the desired objectives, and strategies and tactics to effect the objectives given the resource limitations. A plan is the cognitive outcome of the planning that shows things to be implemented and the rules to implement them. All these lead to the defining characteristics of the concept of planning that include conscious continuity, process, present, future, actual, potential and others.

Planning is concerned with present design of future decisions. It involves deliberative cognitive activity of constructing best strategies and tactics for future decision possibilities to bring into being a predetermined desired set of goals as well as to solve future problems of social complexities in a manner that suggests the needed resources for the implementation of the cognitive construct, the plan. This definition and supporting discussions present to us the subject matter of planning.

Rationale and rationality. By examining the definitions of planning, a question arises as to why decision agents should plan. Planning is viewed as a rational process that offers an important way of thinking about the problems of constructive-destructive process where the existing reality is destroyed and a new reality, the potential, is created in its place. Thus embodied in the concept of planning is decision-choice rationality. The rationality involves a systematic and prudent consideration, analysis and evaluation of goals, alternatives, and limitations on these alternatives and the best strategy to realize the goals for which planning is constructed.

The appeal of planning as a guide to behavior in the destructive-constructive process lies in two fundamental ideas:

1. Unconscious and uncoordinated decision activities result in unexpected outcomes and outside human conscious influence thus forcing humans to simply adapt themselves and their organizations to spontaneous changes of their natural and social environment

2. By planning, decision agents do not simply adapt themselves and their organizations to spontaneous changes of their natural and social environment. On the contrary, planning motivates decision makers to take charge of their destiny through a rational construct of decision and choice.

Thus, through planning, decision agents seek, by their own choice, to change and adapt their environment to themselves and to their organizations as "free beings" in order to actualize the potential that they have consciously conceived and willed. In this epistemic thinking, the reasoning basis for planning is derived from the notion that organizational development and its success are victories over odds when they occur. As a victory, the system's successful development does not occur spontaneously by itself. It requires conscious decision intervention where the chance of the actual outcomes of the willed potentials can be raised substantially above all other potential elements by a scientifically designed connected chain of rational decisions and effective information utilization, which constitute the plan.

Rationality is an important defining characteristic of planning. The concept of rationality in planning takes many forms. It may be a simple definition as "the best selection of means to achieve objectives from a system of values acceptable to the evaluator and by which the consequences of the decision can be measured." It may also take other forms as maximization of attainment, relative to the actual knowledge of goals or it may be viewed as deliberative process of decision-making Rationality may also be defined as a process where decision agents follow predesigned selection rules that have been consciously constructed to create a best strategy to realize goals and objectives as willed by decision agents.

By combining the concepts of planning and the notion of rationality a more elaborate definition may be stated. Planning as a mode of rational analysis and decision-making is a cognitive instrument that enables the holder to make choices of strategies and tactics according to certain defined standards of logical consistency. These provide the decision agent with a framework to explain the underlying reasons for the plan and the embodied decision-choice strategies and tactics, and how the facts and judgments are put together to determine the sequence of decision actions into the planning period. The defined standards are the predesigned selection rules. The analysis and design of the rational selection rules constitute the logical structure called the theory of planning that defines the process.

Process. The process of planning may be defined as a set of logical steps that are internally consistent for analyzing decision situations in order to create a plan of choice actions. It is the development of the algorithmic steps that define the content of the plan, which presents a road map for actualizing the potential as conceived. The planning process is established through the theory of planning whose body components are directed to answer the question of: a) What are the logical body components and their parametric boundaries, and b) how are these logical components interrelated to constitute a theoretical unity that establishes the plan and parametric sensitivity for plan implementation?

The theory of planning belongs to the subject matter of prescriptive science rather than an explanatory science. It is about the design of prescriptive rational rules to be followed by the decision practitioner in order to bring into being that which is cognitively conceived. The basic aim of theory of planning conceived in terms of prescriptive science is to improve reality through conscious choice-decision steps of problem solving. The objective is not the explanation of "what there is," but a transformation of "what there is" (the actual) to "what ought to be" (the willed potential). In its skeletal sense it is composed of a) problem definition, b) diagnosis and analysis, c) plan, and d) implementation and evaluation.

The general abstraction of the planning process conceived within the prescriptive science is that the fundamentals of planning conceptually offer us the following cognitive proposition. a) Planning is a future historic map of successful decisions, b) the successful decisions can be duplicated through a scientifically constructed rational decision-making process where a cognitive plan containing optimal prescriptive rules is constructed, and c) the rational plan presents to the decision agent unified sequential rules for implementation toward the realization of the preconceived goals and objectives.

The task of the theory of planning within the ambit of prescriptive science is to establish a set of optimally structural rules of good decision behavior with an efficient use of information and conscious management of the social organism. This requires a logical assembly of a set of optimally prescriptive rules to be followed in order to increase the chance of successful outcomes by actualizing the potential as conceived in the set of all possible goals and objectives. Planning theory seeks to construct a plan to change the organizational state or to actualize the potential inherent in the future states.

The plan. The resulting plan from the planning process as indicated under the theory of planning is constructed with the techniques and methods of logic, mathematics, statistics, systemicity, and other related areas of science. The plan is a model of optimal decision rules that are prescribed to actualize the willed potential. The content of the plan, given the conceived goals, objectives, and constraints include:

1. Optimal decision rules for creating the required conditions for conscious organizational transformations from state to state on the path of potential to actual change

2. A set of optimal rules for interstate and intrastate transformations through an optimally managed process of change in quality and quantity of the key variables including objective setting, constraint identification, and ranking of alternative strategies and organizational states

3. A set of prescriptive rules for an optimal allocation of resources and optimal distribution of output among departmental or institutional sectors

4. A set of optimal decision rules for monitoring the functioning and progress of the system. These monitoring rules will include the recording of outcomes, the deviation from the conceived targets, goals and the derived optimal values under the planning theory

5. A set of optimal rules for collecting, recording, processing, storing, retrieving, distributing and utilizing information about the planned system by decision agents in accordance with the optimal function, control and evolution of the system

6. A set of optimal decision-choice rules for choosing elements in the interstate and intrastate processes.

Testing, evaluation, and implementation. The plan is tested in different ways to see whether it has internally logical consistency as well as whether it is feasible. The logical consistency test is directed to the examination of each alternative optimal solution and strategy relative to the question as to whether the prescriptive optimal rules respond to the goals, objectives and the limitations that resources, broadly defined, place on them. Modification of the plan would be required if the logical consistency test fails.

The plan is also tested to see whether it is feasible. The feasibility test is directed to examine each alternative proposal relative to the question whether the rationally constructed plan can be implemented within the defined constraints given that the logical consistency test has been fulfilled. If the feasibility test fails, the plan would have to be redesigned or resources would have to be found to widen the feasible region of the planning.

Critical evaluation is required when the content of the plan contains multiple optimal solutions or more than one set of optimally prescriptive rules to follow. The evaluation in this case is directed to a question as to which of the set of optimal decision rules must be followed. The answer to this question may require the use of the method of cost-benefit analysis to rank the sets of optimal decision rules for selection and implementation.

The last in the cognitive sequence of the planning process is implementation and continued monitoring of the transformation process. The analysis of the implementation is directed toward the application of the prescriptive optimal rules of decision behavior to affect the outcome of the potential. Monitoring is directed toward the problem of the examination of the system's transformational performance as contained in the plan. The actual performance is then compared to the conceptual ideal or the theoretically conceived target to allow the use of optimal rules of adjustment, plan modification and possible restructuring by examining the initial plan and possible errors of implementation.

Information support. Information is an important central component in planning and the theory of planning. The interconnectedness of information and planning creates a dynamic relationship of decision-information-interactive-processes where planning turns into decision resulting in outcomes which then become information that is fed back into the planning through implementation and adjustment processes.

Every planning process and every plan have an information support. Information has quantitative and qualitative aspects. The quantitative aspects of information is essential to optimize the chances of successful outcome of the planning decision and the plan. The qualitative aspects of information on the other hand is important in exercising subjectively prudent value judgment with deliberative behavior in the planning process, the plan construct and management of the complex and dynamic social system that requires conscious decision-choice behavior in directing its evolution to a desired end.

The information in support of planning may itself be a part of comprehensive planning. In this way, the information system includes the decision agents, the goals and objectives of overall activities of information that include collection, recording, processing and transformation of the information into knowledge that is useful for planning decisions. The knowledge is stored, retrieved and communicated for use in the control decisions required by the prescriptive rules of the plan. The constructed information basis in support of the planning and plan will include past, present and future information. The past is linked to the present and the present to the future through the techniques of forecasting, estimation, prediction, interpolation, and others.

The principal objective for the construction of an information system may be specified as the collection of the relevant and primary data and summarizing it into a form that can serve as a supporting basis for all planning decision. This requires a) the monitoring of the functioning and development of the object under planning where the differences between the actual parametric values and the ideal are recorded; b) collection and storage of the relevant primary information that describes the nature and structure of the plan; c) processing of the primary information, separating relevant from the irrelevant, for the plan; d) distributing the relevant information to appropriate decision units in accord with tasks that they are assigned for implementing the plan; and e) the use of information for the implementation of the optimal decision rules and the management of the function of the plan.

The process and the logic of planning as cognitive activities result in the design of planning models. These planning models assume many different forms depending on the subject, potential and the goal. Generally, three clusters of planning models may be identified. They are substantive, contextual and instrumental models of planning. Any of these models may be comprehensive, strategic or tactical depending on the environment, event, interaction and dynamics of the process of change. Planning models cover areas of human decision-choice activities such as physical and socioeconomic. These classifications may be viewed as cognitive convenience.

Substantive planning model. This model reflects the sectoral activities of the human social system. Such so-

cial activities are imposed by the decisions that are motivated by prevailing divisions of social institution. The nature of substantive planning reflects the organizational nature of the system. It is always partial and driven by sectoral goals and objectives. The set of sectorally induced planning model may conflict with one another where the optimally prescriptive rules in one sector or department may render the optimal decision rules in another sector sub-optimal viewed in a comprehensive sense. The substantive planning models include sub-models of physical planning such as land use, transportation, city, environmental, and many others.

Instrumental planning model. This model relies on planning paradigm where the essential element in the planning process is the partial goal in the sense that it is subsystem-goal oriented. The structure is to plan the instrument required to accomplish the potential. Social instruments such as power or resources are used to influence the planning process and the resulting plan. Instrumental planning models include indicative, allocative, development and social infrastructure models of planning.

Contextual planning model. This model relies on the logic of planning that is guided by ideology and value premises acceptable in the context of social time. The set of contextual planning models includes comprehensive, institutional and socioeconomic planning.

Each of these planning models shape the strategy and tactics of the planning process, the theoretical structure that emerges and the information support that is required to operationalize and implement the prescriptive optimal decision rules embodied in the plan.

Concluding questions. In conclusion, the following epistemically modified questions adopted may be posed.

- How rational are the prescriptive rules derived from the theory of planning?

- Is it conceivable that the optimally prescriptive algorithms and procedures for rational behavior implied in the theory of planning might worsen rather that improve the chances of actualizing the willed potential if such rigid rules of prescription are followed?

- Is it possible to conceive an organizational system that can be rationally controlled in the sense of being engineered, directed to preferred destination and monitored according to human cognition, reason, and will?

- Can such a rational system, if implemented, improve the conditions for the organization and hence the welfare of humans as focused by planning?

These questions are not intended to discredit planning and the theory of planning. They are, however, intended to raise some epistemic concerns about the intelligibility of the prescriptive optimal rules implied in the rational construct of the theory of planning and the uses to which the theory of planning may be put.

BIBLIOGRAPHY. E.R. Alexander, *Approaches to Planning: Introducing Current Planning Theories, Concepts and Issues* (Gordon and Breach, 1992); J. Bognar, *Economic Policy and Planning in Developing Countries* (Akademiai Kiado, 1975); S.I. Cohen, et al., *The Modeling of Socio-Economic Planning Process* (Gower, 1984); K.K. Dompere, "On Epistemology and Decision-Choice Rationality" in *Cybernetics and System Research* (1982); K.K. Dompere, et al., *Epistemics of Development Economics* (Greenwood Press, 1995); F.I. Dretske, *Knowledge and the Flow of Information* (M.I.T. Press, 1981); V.G. Fanasyev, *The Scientific Management of Society* (Progress Publishers, 1971); R. Harrison, ed., *Rational Action: Studies in Philosophy and Social Science* (Cambridge University Press, 1979); R. Hogarth, et al., eds., *Rational Choice: The Contrast Between Economics and Psychology* (University of Chicago Press, 1995); H. Jones, et al., *Forecasting Technology for Planning Decisions* (Petrocelli Books, 1978); L.V. Kantordvich, *Essays in Optimal Planning* (International Arts and Science Press, 1976); T.S. Khachaturov, ed., *Methods of Long Term Planning and Forecasting* (Macmillan, 1976); I.M. Kickert, *Organization of Decision-Making* (North Holland, 1980); J. Kornai, *Mathematical Planning of Structural Decisions* (North Holland, 1975); A. Lewis, "On Assessing a Development Plan," *Economic Bulletin of the Economic Society of Ghana* (May-June, 1959); M.E. Rozen, ed., *Comparative Economic Planning* (Heath, 1967); H.A. Simon, *Models of Thought* (Yale University Press, 1979); T. Sowell, *Knowledge and Decisions* (Basic Books, 1980); G.L. Steiner, *Top Management Planning* (Macmillan, 1969); M. Swain, *Reasons and Knowledge* (Cornell University Press, 1981).

KOFI KISSI DOMPERE
TARESA LAWRENCE
HOWARD UNIVERSITY

Poland

A COUNTRY OF APPROXIMATELY 40 million people in east-central Europe, Poland possesses both fertile agricultural regions as well as valuable mineral assets. Dominated by its powerful neighbors, GERMANY and RUSSIA, for much of its modern history, Poland became Europe's fastest-growing economy in the 1990s after liberating itself from Russian domination.

First recognized as a kingdom in the late 10th century, Poland reached the height of its power on the European continent in the 16th century. Its productive agricultural lands allowed its economy to grow suffi-ciently throughout the period, yet the dominance of the noble class prevented large urban areas with a sizable merchant and trader class from developing. A series of partitions by Poland's neighboring powers, Prussia, Austria (later Austria-Hungary), and Russia beginning in 1772, wiped Poland off the map after 1795. In the 19th century, a series of uprisings, including major rebellions in 1830–31, 1846, 1848, and 1863–64, failed to reunite and free the country from foreign dominance.

In the wake of the January Uprising of 1863–64, a loose set of policies known as Organic Work came to dominate the thinking of Polish nationalists. Admitting the futility of using force against their oppressors, Polish leaders encouraged economic development as the best way to preserve Poland's cultural integrity until independence could be secured. Land reforms that ended feudalism in the Russian Partition in the 1860s also contributed to industrial development by freeing up peasant labor to work in urban areas.

Developed under the managerial expertise of capitalists from Prussia, the city of Lodz in the Russian Partition came to prominence in the mid-19th century as a center of textile production. The city was the most important manufacturing center in the Russian Empire and indeed, the first truly industrial city in the region. On May Day 1892, Lodz witnessed a general strike and insurrection, one of the first in the Russian Empire. The protest, which was brutally suppressed with 46 deaths, involved at least 20,000 workers. In 1905, Lodz was again the site of a general strike, which fueled calls for a revival of the Polish state in defiance of Russian authorities.

Poland enjoyed a period of independence from 1918 until 1939, when Nazi Germany invaded and pursued a set of programs to extract Poland's economic resources while brutalizing its population. At the Yalta Conference in February 1945, Soviet Premier Josef Stalin declared that free elections would take place in Poland after the cessation of the war. It was an empty promise: The Soviets engineered a series of rigged elections, combined with outright repression, which eliminated political opposition to Communist rule. A one-party system under the Polish United Workers' Party (PZPR) governed the state from 1947–89.

With 6 million casualties, over 15 percent of the country's population had perished during WORLD WAR II. Two-fifths of the country's production capacity had been destroyed along with a third of the nation's wealth, and most of its major cities lay in ruins. The Soviet-backed government moved to nationalize production immediately and industrial operations with more than fifty employees came under direct state control in January 1946. The PZPR also started a collectivization program in agriculture; although such efforts in Poland lagged behind other eastern-bloc countries, about one-quarter of the country's land was collectivized by 1955.

In emulation of the SOVIET UNION, Poland implemented its first Six-Year Plan for industrial production in 1950 under PZPR official Hilary Minc. Like the Soviet-style command economy, Poland's blueprint for progress emphasized investment in heavy industries such as steel and iron works over the production of consumer items. The regime's proudest accomplishment was the construction of the massive Lenin Steel Works at Nowa Huta, a planned suburb adjacent to the university and cultural center of Krakow. The site was supposed to bring peasant workers into the industrial age but instead became a symbol of the alienation and inefficiency of a centrally planned economy.

Always the most restive country in the Soviet Bloc, Poland was the first country to oust the Communist Party from office in 1989. Immediately pursuing economic "shock therapy" under the Balcerowicz Plan to privatize the economy, stimulate international trade, and dampen inflation and budget deficits, Poland had the highest growth rate of any European economy by the mid-1990s. Although its heavy industries of iron and steel making, mining, and chemical production remained important, nearly 70 percent of the Polish economy was related to the service sector after 10 years of privatization. Seventy percent of Polish firms had also been transferred from the government to the private sector.

BIBLIOGRAPHY. Jan Adam, *Social Costs of Transformation to a Market Economy in Post-Socialist Countries: The Case of Poland, the Czech Republic, and Hungary* (St. Martin's Press, 1999); Leszek Balcerowicz, *Socialism, Capitalism, Transformation* (CEU Press, 1995); Simon Johnson and Gary W. Loveman, *Starting Over in Eastern Europe: Entrepreneurship and Economic Renewal* (Harvard Business School Press, 1995); Mitchell A. Orenstein, *Out of the Red: Building Capitalism and Democracy in Postcommunist Europe* (University of Michigan Press, 2001).

TIMOTHY G. BORDEN, PH.D.
INDEPENDENT SCHOLAR

Polk, James K. (1795–1849)

THE PRODUCT OF THE SOUTHERN backcountry, James K. Polk emerged from obscurity to become the 11th president of the UNITED STATES. Polk is remembered for his enthusiastic commitment to territorial expansion, specifically during the Mexican War, as well as his support for lower tariffs and an independent treasury.

Strict Presbyterians, the Polks were Scots-Irish immigrants who established themselves as prominent members of the North Carolina elite in the late 18th century. The first of nine children born to Samuel and Jane Knox Polk, James Polk was frequently plagued by bouts of ill health and was forced to undergo a dangerous operation during his teenage years. Though he recovered from the surgery, he would never enjoy the strong physical character required by a planter. Thus, Polk entered the University of North Carolina at Chapel Hill where he excelled and discovered an interest in law. Following his legal training, Polk continued practicing law until beginning his political career with a seat in the lower house of the Tennessee state legislature in 1822.

By 1825, Polk was a member of the U.S. House of Representatives where he served two terms as Speaker of the House. Polk resigned from the House to run for governor of Tennessee, an office he held for just one term. Despite losing his bid for re-election to governor in both 1841 and 1843, as well as a failed bid for the vice-presidential nomination in 1840, the Democratic party nominated Polk for president in 1844. He won the election and was inaugurated on March 4, 1845.

Polk's single term in office was rife with issues, both international and domestic. His program for the economy, which included lower tariffs, an independent treasury system, and federal support for infrastructure projects that dealt only with international commerce or national defense was overshadowed by the country's involvement in the Mexican War, which lasted from 1846–48. The war, incited by the U.S. annexation of Texas, reflected Polk's commitment to MANIFEST DESTINY, or America's divine right to territorial expansion.

Sectional interests largely drove Polk's territorial motivations, and the land gains acquired during his presidency exacerbated the growing tensions between North and South. The competing economic interests of Southern slaveholders and Northern industrial capitalists played out through the western and southwestern land claims. But Polk's ardent belief in manifest destiny and the expansion of America would not be unique to antebellum America; it foreshadowed the imperialism that underscored American foreign policy at the turn of the 20th century.

Polk left office in 1848 and returned to his home state of Tennessee. Always in poor health, he succumbed to a cholera epidemic on June 15, 1849.

BIBLIOGRAPHY. Sam W. Haynes, *James K. Polk and the Expansionist Impulse* (2002); Thomas Leonard, *James K. Polk: A Clear and Unquestionable Destiny* (2001); Paul H. Bergeron, *The Presidency of James K. Polk* (1987); David Williamson, *Presidents of the United States of America* (1989).

LINDSAY SILVER
BRANDEIS UNIVERSITY

Portugal

ONE OF THE SMALLEST EUROPEAN COUNTRIES, Portugal's prospects have improved since joining the EUROPEAN UNION (EU) as one of the economic organization's early members in 1986. With an ongoing policy of privatization, Portugal's GROSS DOMESTIC PRODUCT (GDP) was $182 billion in 2002, reflecting several years of steady growth.

Trade with the EU, and other countries, remains vital to the economy. Agricultural, manufacturing and service sectors all benefit the foreign trade market, 59 percent of Portugal's GDP. On January 1, 2002, Portugal also became part of the European Monetary Union (EMU) and adopted the EURO, signified by the symbol: €. Estimated trade income for Portugal in 2002 was €83 billion.

From the Middle Ages through to the 17th century, Portugal reaped the rich rewards of trade as one of the leading explorers and colonizers of the then-civilized world. Adventurers, exploring the Americas, the Tropics, the Orient and the East Indies—all four directions of the globe—had found great rewards in unexplored corners of the world, and claimed these lands for Portugal, settling BRAZIL and sections of Africa, INDIA, CHINA and JAPAN. Merchant routes to and from Portugal crisscrossed the open seas. The historic names of Vasco de Gama or Prince Henry the Navigator are only a few of the Portuguese entries in the history of world exploration during this period.

Followed by the devastating earthquake of 1755 that destroyed most of the towns along the Algarve coast, including the metropolis of Lisbon, and a losing war with Napoleon in the early 1800s, Portugal lost much of its power. Soon, Portuguese merchants, working out of Brazil were noticing they were being bypassed by the rest of the trading world that dealt directly with the native Brazilian government, leaving the Portuguese merchants by the wayside. Complete Brazilian independence ensued in 1822.

Throughout the latter half of the 1800s, Portugal sank into a maelstrom of people's revolts; hard times followed and the economy crumbled. The 20th century brought more disillusionment as a world war, followed by a series of dictatorships, all but ruined the country. Portugal lost most of its foreign colonies, either through native independence movements or, as some historians have suggested, through colonial mismanagement.

With the overthrow of the last of many dictators in the mid-1970s, the country turned around. "Prior to the 1974 Portuguese revolution, Portugal was one of the poorest and most isolated countries in Western Europe," explains an economic assessment report compiled by the U.S. Department of State. "In the 25 years since, however, the country has undergone fundamental economic and social changes that have resulted in substantial convergence with its wealthier European neighbors."

Now, the Republica Portuguesa is an upcoming economy—capitalist/democratic-based—boasting a per capita GDP purchasing power parity of 75 percent of the four top Western European countries. Portugal continues to maintain a consistent growth, low interest rates, and a steady employment situation.

Portugal's economy is service-based. The parliamentarian government has strategically privatized many state-controlled entities. Over the last decade, except for a brief recession in the 2001–02 season, economic growth has surpassed the EU average.

There are some obstacles, however, looming. One, according to the CIA World Factbook, is a poor educational system that "has been an obstacle to greater productivity and growth." Another is the growing number of central European nations joining the EU, providing more low-cost labor into the EU market.

Agriculture and fishing, once being Portugal's only commodities, now together constitute four percent of the GDP. Industry and services have been booming over the last quarter century and now provide 36 percent and 60 percent, respectively, of the entire GDP. Within the services sector, tourism ranks high. Considered to be a "safe" country, unembroiled by political or religious radicalism, and with low to moderate costs, tourists from around the world continue to discover the unique charms of Portugal.

BIBLIOGRAPHY. "Country Report on Economic Policy and Trade Practices: Portugal," (U.S. State Department, 2001); CIA World Factbook (2002); Library of Congress Country Studies, www.lcweb2.loc.gov; Portugal Live, www.portugal-live.net.

JOSEPH GERINGER
SYED B. HUSSAIN, PH.D.
UNIVERSITY OF WISCONSIN, OSHKOSH

poverty

AN ECONOMIC STATUS, poverty usually ranks lower than some socially accepted minimum standard of living, where each society determines its own definition for the minimum. There are two different poverty concepts: relative poverty and absolute poverty. Relative poverty is defined in terms of relative deprivation, objective or subjective, relative to the mean or median income. Hence, as the level of income and distribution changes, relative poverty changes. Absolute poverty, on the other hand, is a state where the unit of analysis (a person or

Substandard urban housing is only one aspect of poverty for 11.7 percent of people living in the United States.

household or family) does not have the means to afford a certain basket of goods to meet its basic needs.

Among the various different concepts that can be used in defining the so-called poverty threshold line, two stand out: consumption and income. The poverty threshold line based on consumption generally refers to the cost and affordability of meeting basic needs, for example food, shelter, health, and education. The poverty threshold based on income refers to income only, notwithstanding the disagreements as to what kind of income should be used in the estimates. For instance, in the United States, the U.S. Census Bureau calculates the poverty threshold level of income, and thus the poverty line, for different family characteristics. In 2000, it was $17,463 for a family of four with two children. Families falling below this line are considered to be poor. In 2001, the poverty rate, defined as the proportion of the population below poverty line, was 11.7 percent.

In a similar fashion, the WORLD BANK uses $1 and $2 per day, measured in terms of the constant 1994 purchasing power parity (PPP), as the two poverty lines in its international poverty comparisons. In 1999, 2.8 billion people lived below the $2 line and 1.2 billion people below the $1 line in the world. This method of counting people below a given poverty line when divided by the population gives the so-called head-count ratio, a very common measure of poverty. A different measure is the poverty gap ratio, defined as the ratio of the average income required to lift all the poor to the poverty line, divided by the mean income in the economy. The poverty gap ratio not only measures the average income shortfall from the poverty line but also tells us the magnitude of resources we need to eradicate it.

Characteristics of poverty. It is important to know the demographic characteristics of the poor in order to de-

vise policies that would alleviate their poverty. First, women and children constitute a significant majority of the poor. In industrial and in developing countries alike, they experience the worst deprivation. This is specially the case for single women who are heading households with children. Women may not have easy access to gainful employment because they may be forced to stay at home and perform household jobs for which they are not paid. Even women who have access to the labor markets and gainful employment could be more likely to have lower earnings because of economic discrimination in the labor market.

It is not uncommon for women performing tasks similar to those performed by men to be paid less. These lower incomes make it more difficult for their children to have access to adequate health, nutrition, education, sanitation, and other basic needs that contribute to their productive and future earnings capacities. Hence, children born to households headed by women are caught in a poverty trap. Because they are poor, they are more likely to remain poor. The problem is exaggerated if the women are from racial and ethnic minority groups. For instance, in the United States, the overall poverty rate for women in 2001 was 12.9 percent. The poverty rate among households headed by white women was 24.3 percent. The poverty rate for households headed by African-American and Hispanic women was 37.4 and 37.8 percent, respectively.

Poverty is more prominent in large families, especially families with a large number of children. The reason for this is described in terms of the dependency ratio, the number of children under 15 per employed adult. The large dependency ratio in large families contributes to their low per-capita income and poverty.

Typically, poverty is more of an urban problem in industrial countries and a rural problem in developing countries. In industrial countries, the urban poor are often employed in the informal sector as street vendors or in similar occupations. The rural poor, on the other hand, are typically landless peasants at work for large landowners. In both cases, the poor have a lower educational attainment and hence a lower level of human capital. Thus, their defining characteristic is a lack of ownership of physical and human capital. Income is derived from ownership of factors of production and assets. In general, return to labor is less than the return to capital and asset ownership. Within the labor force, the return to unskilled labor is less than the return to skilled labor. Thus, unskilled labor is more likely to be poor than either skilled labor or the owners of capital and assets.

In today's economies, as capital- and technology-intensive production expands, unskilled and semi-skilled labor face eroding incomes and consequently a higher incidence of poverty. Thus, rising inequality in the distribution of income feeds into rising poverty. A related impact of the deteriorating income distribution is that it affects the patterns of consumption and production in the economy. As the incomes of affluent groups rise their consumption increases. The tastes of these groups favor high technology- and capital-intensive production. As production of such goods rises, demand for skilled labor and capital rises, increasing their incomes and affecting the unskilled and semi-skilled labor adversely. Concentration of asset ownership in the high-income groups contributes to the increasing income inequality.

Effects of poverty. The main effect of poverty is that it prevents the poor from accessing the markets in the economy. The poor are excluded from both the labor market and the credit market. The relationship between poverty and the labor market can best be explained in terms of the physical capacity curve. The exclusion of the poor from the labor market is not only the result of a lack of necessary skills, but also due to the lack of necessary nutritional intake to perform even the least skilled tasks. The inability of the poor to afford a necessary minimum calorie requirement leads to malnutrition and under-nutrition. The workers suffer from fatigue and frequent illness and become more susceptible to infection. As a result they cannot hold a job for long periods of time. Their work capacity diminishes, exposing them to higher incidence of poverty. Thus, the poor find themselves in a vicious cycle. Their poverty prevents them from the necessary calorie intake that would improve their work capacity. However, they need a higher work capacity to access gainful employment and to afford the necessary calorie intake. Somehow this cycle needs to be broken.

Access to the credit market is difficult for the poor because of their inability to provide any collateral for credit. Collateral is in fact especially important in the case of the poor because of the high default risk associated with the loans extended to relatively low-income groups. Once again a vicious cycle emerges. To break the spell of poverty the poor need access to the credit markets in order to realize entrepreneurial opportunities that might raise their income and help them accumulate assets. However, the lack of asset ownership limits, if not prohibits, their capacity to borrow.

Policies and poverty. The major policy options to address poverty are concerned with the distribution of income and assets at the macro and micro levels through four different types of measures. One is to eliminate price distortions in the factor markets in order to increase employment of labor. Another is to redistribute assets to the poor to provide them with asset ownership. A third is to redistribute income to reduce income inequality, and a fourth is to publicly provide goods and services to the poor. All four of these measures are to some extent applicable universally, but the first two are less relevant in the industrial world than in developing countries.

The factor price distortion argument maintains that the wage rate paid to labor is relatively high and does not reflect the scarcity cost of labor, leading to relatively capital-intensive production. Because of the presence of strong labor organizations and/or politically inspired legislation that sets the minimum wage artificially high, the actual market wage rate is pushed higher than supply and demand conditions in the labor market would dictate. At the same time, the price of capital, which is the interest rate in, usually, regulated financial markets, is set artificially low because of the political power of the business elite. The discrepancy between these two factor prices favors the use of capital-intensive production. In a typical developing country, this factor intensity is incompatible with its factor endowment. Developing countries are more abundant in labor than in capital, so the price of capital should be relatively higher than the price of labor.

Factor price distortions, however, render labor relatively more expensive leading to capital-intensive production and hence to unemployment. Eliminating the factor price distortions would lead to more gainful employment and therefore to a reduction in inequality and poverty. Hence, the policy recommendation is to liberalize the labor and capital markets along with all the other input markets to allow factor prices to reflect the scarcity costs of the factors of production.

Since inequality in the distribution of assets is a major contributor to income inequality, redistribution of the existing assets and/or creating new assets and channeling them to the poor in the economy is also a policy option. It might be politically undesirable to confiscate in one form or other the existing assets and redistribute them to the poor. In developing countries the assets in question may be land. Transferring the ownership of land by decree to the poor is bound to face severe resistance. An alternative could be to transfer the unused public lands, or to purchase private land at the market price and than transfer its ownership to the poor. Of course, the fiscal resources of the government limit this kind of policy.

In the urban sector, the plight of the poor in terms of asset ownership is more complicated. Since stocks and shares are not realistically the assets they would be holding, property remains one viable option of asset ownership. Hernando DESOTO has extensively written on this issue. His recommendations, adopted in several Latin American countries, revolve around the idea that the economically disadvantaged actually own assets, such as shanty homes that are not recognized officially. He claims that if these informal assets owned by the poor were legalized, the status of the poor would significantly improve. They could then show these assets as collateral and gain access to the credit markets. In addition, the World Bank, recognizing the importance of the OWNERSHIP of assets in fighting poverty, recommended in 1970s the creation of new assets in the economy, which could be channeled to the poor.

Progressive income taxation, theoretically, is another way of redistributing income to reduce poverty and inequality. Taxing the higher income groups in a progressive manner and reducing their disposable income would indeed reduce the income gap between the higher and lower income groups. At the same time, however, it could adversely affect saving and investment in the economy and could reduce total income, rendering the lower-income groups worse-off. Instead, the more effective way of taxing the high-income groups could be by raising indirect taxes, especially levied on the consumption of luxury goods. In our modern world, another source for taxation could be domestic and international financial transactions that are done purely for speculative purposes (a version of the so-called Tobin tax). The implementation of this kind of a tax, however, would be extremely difficult.

Poverty and welfare. Social welfare programs and the provision of public goods (especially consumption goods) and services targeting the poor have been in place for a long period of time in industrial countries in the post-WORLD WAR II period. They come in different forms and have different economic effects. They run a wide spectrum, ranging from consumption subsidies and direct monetary transfers, to the provision of food stamps and school lunches to raise the calorie intake by the poor. Many of these programs have been discontinued on the basis that they take away the incentives to work. Direct-money transfers, especially, are claimed to act as a deterrent to find gainful employment since they reward being unemployed and poor.

A more socially and economically desirable alternative would be to limit the duration of the availability of the free provision of public goods and services and subsidies in order to eliminate the disincentive effects of these policies. If the receiver of such provisions knows that there is a terminal date for them, he would have an incentive to look actively for work. Another viable alternative could be the implementation of workfare programs that would promote cash or in-kind remuneration for work performed by the poor. The work could be in the public sector or elsewhere, but would be directed to the poor and would directly benefit them without reducing their willingness to acquire the human capital and other assets that would provide them the necessary economic opportunities to lift themselves above the poverty line.

Because women and children, regardless of their racial and ethnic background, have a disproportionately high share among the poor, policies directed to them are of utmost importance in lowering poverty. Formal and informal education, and access to other assets are essential to address their poverty. Provision of schooling and nutrition for children, family control to reduce the number of children as well as on-the-job training, and formal education for women are necessary to provide them access to job markets for gainful employment. These kinds of policies would raise the social and economic status of women, and if accompanied by policies that would minimize gender-based discrimination, would help them to participate in economic life as equals with men. Fighting poverty is beneficial for all groups in society in that it not only raises output and income for all, but also minimizes potential social tensions.

BIBLIOGRAPHY. H.M. Chenery, et al., *Redistribution with Growth* (Oxford University Press, 1974); Hernando DeSoto, *The Mystery of Capital: Why Capitalism Triumphs in the West and Fails Everywhere Else* (Basic Books, 2000); Hernando DeSoto, *The Other Path: The Economic Answer to Terrorism* (HarperCollins, 1989); Debraj Ray, *Development Economics* (Princeton University Press, 1998); A.J.M. Hagenaars, "The Definition and Measurement of Poverty," *Economic Inequality and Poverty* (M.E. Sharpe, 1991); L. Osberg, *Economic Inequality and Poverty* (M.E. Sharpe, 1991); P. Ruggles, "Short- and Long-Term Poverty in the United States: Measuring the American Underclass," *Economic Inequality and Poverty* (M.E. Sharpe, 1991); United Nations Development Programme, *Human Development Report* (Oxford University Press, 2002); M. Todaro and S. Stephen, *Economic Development* (Addison- Wesley, 2003); The World Bank, *World Development Report 2003: Sustainable Development in a Dynamic World* (Oxford University Press, 2003); The World Bank, World Development Report 1990: *Poverty* (Oxford University Press, 1990); www.census.gov.

M. ODEKON
SKIDMORE COLLEGE

price

PRICES ARE CRUCIAL FOR THE FUNCTIONING of a free economy. In fact, it is difficult to overestimate their importance. It is no exaggeration to say that prices play a role with regard to the economy similar to the one undertaken by street signs, or maps, as far as our geographical understanding is concerned.

In ancient days, before a territory was captured by an enemy army, the defenders would take down the street signs; in that way, they might slow down the hostile force until help, or a counterattack, could arrive. But they need not have taken them down; merely rearranging them in any haphazard order would have done just as well. The point is, prices do illuminate an economy, but not any old prices will do. Just as only accurate street signs will aid our geographical mobility, so, only market prices can perform this function economically speaking. Price controls are thus, in general, economic arteriosclerosis.

Let us take an example to illustrate this point. A bunch of us decide we are too fat. We want to go on a diet. This means, horrible as it sounds, we will have to eat less cake, ice cream and chocolate, and more rabbit food such as lettuce, tomato and carrots. But right now, before our decision to change our eating habits in this manner, there is no misallocation of resources devoted to these two very different types of foodstuffs. That is, there are not obvious shortages of one of them, and surpluses of the other. If virtually all of us go on this diet, it will be difficult to do unless farmers, grocers, restaurants, change what they offer for sale, in order to accommodate us.

So, what do we do to get them to alter their economic behavior? Sign a petition asking them to grow fewer sugar beets and more carrots, and then send it to individual farmers, or, perhaps, more efficiently, to agricultural organizations? Do we go to our state houses, or to Washington, D.C., demanding that our politicians force growers to do our bidding? Not a bit of it.

In a free society, we simply start to buy more of the "good" foods, and less of those that make life worth living (i.e., taste good). This will have two salutary effects: It will drive up the prices of salad ingredients and reduce the prices of factors of production that go in to making desserts. This, in turn, will lead farmers, not necessarily all of them, remember, we still want some high-calorie foods, but some or many of them depending upon how radically we change our purchasing habits, to plant and harvest a different array of crops. How so? Higher prices for the newly desired foods imply greater profits to be earned in these realms. This will encourage agriculturalists to do the right thing for us dieters. Lower prices for the newly less-desired foods imply decreased profits to be earned from producing them. This will encourage farmers to grow lettuce rather than chocolate or wheat.

When will this process end? These alterations in economic behavior will stop reverberating throughout the economy as soon as prices of the various products are such that once again there are equal profits to be made in growing these two different kinds of foodstuffs.

It is no accident that an economy's investment in chocolate and carrots, at any given time, is a reasonable one, in terms of our desires for these two items. Were it not, prices would change until they were. It is no accident that the amount of wood that goes into baseball bats and hockey sticks is roughly proportionate to con-

sumers' demands for these two athletic implements. Were it not, prices would change until they were.

What economist would appreciate the role that prices play in such allocations of resources? Not one in a thousand. Nor is this really problematic. It is said that fish are not aware of the water they swim in, and we are not aware of the air we breathe (ordinarily speaking, given no emphysema, pollution, etc.). In similar manner, it is the rare person who is even aware of prices, other than to complain they are too high (when buying), or too low (when selling); most participants in the economy are not cognizant of this allocative role that prices play.

But prices do more than merely allocate resources. They also determine relative wealth. Why is it that Michael Jordan and Bill Gates are immeasurably wealthier than most, and that people who ask "Want fries with that?" are at the bottom of the economic pyramid? Again, prices. Were it not that the masses of consumers enjoy far more, and thus are willing to pay higher prices for, the unique things supplied by these individuals, Gates and Jordan would not be enjoying anything like their present standards of living. There might have been two individuals living 100 years ago, before anyone had even heard of computers or basketball, with abilities identical to Jordan's and Gates', and yet they would have contributed relatively little to what others value, and thus would have had far more modest incomes.

Prices also determine how goods are produced. Right now, rowboats are typically made of plastic, wood, or metal. If the price of any of them rises, less of that material will go into these watercraft. It is for this reason that no one builds them out of platinum, even assuming that metal would serve well in a technical maritime capacity. The same thinking applies to the labor market. Whenever one input becomes relatively more

Prices displayed in a market give specific signals to different economic actors in an economy.

expensive, the first thought of the business owner is to substitute for it relatively cheaper factors of production.

When the minimum-wage level stipulated by law rises (wages are the price of renting labor services), the entrepreneur will tend to hire more skilled workers, and fire some of his apprentices. If this law were ever to be rescinded, the typical firm would then be mightily tempted to hire more unskilled employees, and either get rid or, or pay less to, the master craftsmen.

Why is it that the economy of the SOVIET UNION went belly up? On the face of it, this is a surprising occurrence. The Russians are a very intelligent people in many ways. Compared to the rest of the world, they have a disproportionate share of physicists, chemists, biologists, mathematicians, engineers, doctors, etc. They launched Sputnik before the U.S. space program even got off the earth. With but few notable exceptions, virtually all chess grandmasters emanate from that part of the world.

Why, then, was their economy such a shambles? In a word, they lacked accurate prices. Without the free enterprise system, based upon private rights and the unconstrained economic choices of all, their prices could only be arbitrary, set by bureaucrats. It is as if they were blundering around in the wilderness, without street signs, lacking a map, with no Global Positioning System, lacking the rudiments of sonar. Forget about not being able to produce products desired by their citizenry (e.g., butter, toilet paper, vegetables, meat); they couldn't plan their way out of a paper bag to produce in sufficient quantity and quality even the things wanted by the rulers (those groceries plus caviar, guns, rockets, limousines, etc.) In terms of our previous example, they had no way to know not to waste platinum on rowboats.

But not exactly. After all, the Soviet economy did last for 72 years (1917–89). Why were they able to continue, bumbling along, for some seven decades? Well, they did have some accuracy in their prices, although this was no credit to their system. This knowledge stemmed from several sources. For one thing, they had access to the Sears catalog. Why does this rather pedestrian publication have anything to do with so momentous a historical event as the fall of the Soviet Union? Simple; this advertising supplement featured prices of the thousands of items sold by that company. Armed with these, and we use that word purposefully, their economy was able to limp along far longer than otherwise would have been the case. Secondly, the Soviets planted economic spies in Western countries. Yes, economic spies, out after our prices, not our military secrets! For the Sears catalogue and other such publications featured prices of only (well, mainly) consumer goods. More is needed for the functioning of an economy, specifically, labor market prices, capital goods

prices, interest rates, rental prices, the value of one currency in terms of others, etc. Third, there was a black market or illegal market within the Soviet Union itself. Not only did this offer accurate market prices, it directly kept significant numbers of people from starving to death.

It will be easy to see, by this point, that prices convey valuable information. They are almost a language unto themselves. They are very simple: They increase, they decrease, or they stay the same. Each gives very different signals to economic actors. But, whatever they do, we reckon at our peril without the knowledge they convey. The man more responsible than anyone else for promoting the idea that prices are a sort of semaphore, or economic signaling device, was 1974 economics Nobel Prize laureate F.A. HAYEK. For this economist, economic knowledge is widely dispersed throughout society, and prices are the way of amalgamating, or better yet, coordinating this information.

If prices are so important to an economy (and we have only begun to touch the surface in this regard) why are they everywhere and by most people held in such low repute. Why, that is, are there so many laws on the books restricting their free interplay, and their birth in the voluntary decisions of participants in free markets? Let us list just a few of the governmental controls of market prices to get a grasp on the enormity of the problem: rent control, that mandates that prices of rental property, or rents, cannot rise above certain levels; minimum wage laws, that proscribe that the price of labor, wages, cannot fall below certain levels; usury laws, that demand that interest rates, the price for loans, not rise above a stipulated point; socialized medicine, according to which prices for health care services must be held at zero, or at least at very low levels compared to the costs of providing them.

Supports for agricultural products stem from dissatisfaction with market prices for farm goods; they are too low, complain the farmers. In like manner, tariffs on, or quotas against, imports from foreign countries are evidence of dissatisfaction with the rate of exchanges (i.e., prices) either between the two relevant currencies, or are (typically) based upon the view of domestic producers that foreign prices are too low.

One theory locates the source of these unwarranted attacks on freely agreed-upon prices in the widespread ignorance of economics. If people only but knew more about the "dismal science," there would be less acquiescence in the interference with this lifeblood of the economy. Undoubtedly, there is some truth in this; but it cannot constitute the entire explanation, since there are some very knowledgeable people who favor various price control schemes.

Then, there is sheer venality. An often-asked economic question is *"Quo bono?"* (Who benefits?) and nowhere is this more relevant than at present. Rent control is widely thought to benefit tenants (it does not, but that is another question) and thus it should be no mystery as to why renters would favor this policy, and politicians beholden to them scurry to enact such legislation. Minimum-wage laws help highly skilled workers in their competition with their unskilled counterparts; when the latter are bid out of the market and forced into unemployment, the wages of former are more likely to rise. Similarly, domestic producers urge "Buy American!" policies, and cloak them in an aura of patriotism, and job-loss fears, but the last thing they want is for consumers to enjoy lower-priced foreign imports, to their own economic detriment.

Nor are the demands for agricultural prices supports very opaque; an attempt is made to wrap them in motherhood and apple-pie notions of saving the family farm. But the *realpolitik* of votes being concentrated in mid-western states actually accounts for their success. In any case, the lion's share of these payments go to large-scale agribusiness.

There is yet another reason for this attack on prices and concomitantly the debasement of a once free economy: Our high concentration as producers, relative to that as consumers. The average person consumes literally thousands, if not tens of thousands of items in the course of a year, and yet typically produces only one, or at most a few. For example, the music teacher sells only one kind of services, but buys many. Suppose now, that the toothbrush manufacturers come to Washington, D.C., complaining of low toothbrush prices. If they succeed in getting a law passed elevating prices, they will benefit to the tune of millions of dollars.

But how much money does the music teacher spend on toothbrushes in a year? Merely pennies. Will it inure to her interest to bestir herself, and attempt to fight off the toothbrush interests? It will not. It will probably cost her as much as she spends on this product in one year to even get off a single letter (including not only postage and stationary, but time costs as well). And if she does so, will she have an economic interest in opposing the rubber band industry's attempt to suborn prices? No.

Consider, last, a speculative explanation. Most of our time as a race of human beings has been spent in caves, or in forests, living in small groups. There, the only kind of cooperation experienced by us was of the explicit variety. Cave men would hunt together, some would make spears, other gather berries, and then they would share. But prices in the modern day have nothing to do with such explicit assistance. Rather, they are the embodiment of implicit cooperation, as befits a society not with a few dozen members, but with billions.

We have seen how the farmers cooperate with the dieters, even though they don't know them, never met them, and, possibly, might hate them were ever this to

change. Their implicit cooperation is nevertheless achieved through the price system; nothing else (certainly not central planning) could possibly do the job. However, according to this explanation, we are genetically "hard wired," based on millions of years of explicit cooperation as cave people, to recognize only this kind of mutual aid. Hence, the lack of appreciation for the price system. This is why it is so often breached by law, even in the United States, a country devoted to free enterprise and capitalism.

[Editor's Note: Since differential initial endowments of wealth have differential impact on prices, and hence on the menu of choices in the market, one may conclude, ever so grudgingly, a case for intervention premised on equity; such that the market pricing does not exclude entirely those who cannot afford basic necessities such as education and healthcare.]

BIBLIOGRAPHY. Walter Block, "Private Roads, Competition, Automobile Insurance and Price Controls," *Competitiveness Review* (v.8/1, 1998); Walter Block, "Professor Modigliani on price controls: the baleful influence of the perfectly competitive model," *International Journal of Social Economics* (v.22/5, 1995); Gene Callahan, *Economics for Real People* (Mises Institute, 2002); Henry Hazlitt, *Economics in One Lesson* (Arlington House, 1979); Murray N. Rothbard, *Man, Economy and State* (Mises Institute, 1993).

WALTER BLOCK, PH.D.
LOYOLA UNIVERSITY, NEW ORLEANS

price controls

RESTRICTIONS ON MARKET PRICES, such as rent control and minimum-wage laws set by political authorities, are termed price controls. In the absence of price controls, sellers and buyers determine prices by bargaining with each other. Generally, buyers buy more at low prices and sellers sell more at higher ones. If sellers have excess inventories of their products, they must offer lower prices to move this inventory. Lower prices eliminate excess SUPPLY by attracting buyers and repelling sellers.

If buyers, or consumers, cannot buy as much as they want to at current prices, they must offer higher prices. Higher prices eliminate excess DEMAND by repelling buyers and attracting sellers. If at some price, buyers want to buy as much as sellers want to sell then supply equals demand, and the market clears. In this way, competition and bargaining determine market prices.

Authorities can set maximum price controls, or price ceilings, where people cannot trade above a particular price. A price ceiling set below the market price is an effective price ceiling. Effective price ceilings lead to excess demand, or a shortage in a market. By setting prices below market-clearing levels, price ceilings leave markets with too few sellers for buyers to trade with. They can also set minimum price controls, or price floors, where people cannot trade below a particular price. Effective price floors lead to excess supply or a surplus in a market.

Market-clearing prices generally lead to economic efficiency because they result in the greatest number of feasible trades. So long as no one in the market is a monopolist, equilibrium market prices result in consumers getting the products they want at the lowest possible prices, and allow entrepreneurs to earn a normal rate of profit.

Lost trades due to price controls constitute deadweight losses. These dead-weight losses represent feasible, but lost, opportunities for buyers to benefit by consuming goods and sellers to benefit from profit on trading. An example: when minimum-wage laws lead to employers hiring fewer low-productivity workers.

Price controls affect not only the quantity of goods traded in markets, but their quality as well. Since price controls preclude competition over price, it will lead entrepreneurs to compete over the quality of their goods. Many people believe the U.S. airline industry offered better services during the time that the government mandated high airfares. Since airlines could not attract customers with better prices, they did so by offering more comfortable travel. Since airline decontrol, airfares and airline service have both fallen.

Price controls can also reduce product quality. Controls on the rental prices of apartments usually favor renters over landlords; low rents reduce the profitability of owning apartments. Landlords can recapture these lost profits, or reduce their losses, partially by simply spending less on the maintenance of their apartments. People often complain about the living conditions in rent-controlled apartments and blame "slumlords" for failing to properly maintain their property. But, some economists insist we must consider the perverse economic incentives that rent control creates, before we pass judgment on these landlords.

Price controls affect more than just the quantity and quality of goods. Since price ceilings create excess demand for cheap goods, people will have to wait in line for them. While buyers are paying less money for these goods, their waiting costs them more of their time. Market prices ration goods according to the willingness of buyers to spend whatever money they have. Price ceilings ration goods partially according to the willingness of buyers to spend whatever time they have to spend waiting in line. This notion of "rationing by waiting" tells us that price ceilings impose a hidden cost.

Costs and benefits of controls. Apparent money prices of goods remain low, yet individual consumers bear personal costs in terms of extra time spent, beyond normal shopping, in getting the goods that they want. Under these circumstances, buyers find it worthwhile to spend extra time waiting for what they want to buy. However, it would almost certainly be better if they used their time to either work for more pay, or to enjoy some leisure time rather than to waste it standing in line.

There are also real costs to establishing and enforcing price controls. Governments employ officials to set and enforce price controls. The establishment of price controls is not a simple matter, but requires guidance by competent experts, who could be doing some other kind of work. Since price controls prevent some worthwhile trades, some will try to evade them. The enforcement of price controls draws further upon the pool of available labor, leaving less for the production of actual goods.

Though price controls cause many problems, they do benefit specific people. They transfer wealth between consumers and entrepreneurs. Lower (higher) prices benefit consumers (entrepreneurs). If a price control lowers the price of radios by $10, and consumers continue to buy 500 radios per week, then the price control in question transfers $5,000 from entrepreneurs to consumers per week

Consequently, private interests will lobby for price controls. Some entrepreneurs might lobby for price floors, so that they can get higher-than-market prices. But, if they spend large sums of money lobbying for price controls they end up losing part of what they gain. Resources used to transfer existing wealth in this way come at the expense of there being fewer resources to produce new wealth. The losses from enacting and enforcing price controls can easily exceed their dead weight losses.

There is also risk concerning what these transfer benefits will be. When lobbying for rent controls, any potential tenant will have a chance of getting a low-priced apartment. They will also have a chance of not being able to find any apartment. Since some renters will lose out badly, they may all be worse off on average. Thus, the expected payoff to each individual renter from rent control may be less than zero.

The fact that price controls cause dead weight losses, entail costs, and lead to waste, raises questions about why they are so common. Part of the explanation is that officials sometimes commit errors. Price controls are sometimes put into place for the purpose of restraining price inflation. In 3rd-century Rome, devaluation of money caused rampant inflation. In 301, Emperor Diocletian imposed maximum prices in an attempt to stem this inflation. His edict set extensive controls over prices and wages, enforced with the death penalty. His efforts ultimately failed to reign in inflation, despite the extreme penalties imposed on violators.

During WORLD WAR II, President Franklin Delano ROOSEVELT attempted to "hold the line" on the cost of living with price controls. Through the Office of Price Administration, the Roosevelt administration set controls on prices, except for utility rates, fees for services, wages, prices charged by the media, and insurance rates. To enforce compliance, people could sue those who violated these controls for treble damages, seek court injunctions, or even criminal penalties. Many leading figures in guiding early OPA policies were academics, with little real-world experience in markets (among them John Kenneth GALBRAITH). As complaints regarding these OPA policies mounted, the Emergency Price Control Act of 1942 forced these academics out. It did this by requiring a five-year minimum of business experience for all OPA policymakers. The OPA also failed to stop wartime inflation. These price controls ended in 1946, when President TRUMAN vetoed a bill extending them.

Price controls are sometimes put into place in efforts to reduce the costs of government. In 1777, the Legislature of Pennsylvania imposed price ceilings on commodities needed by General George WASHINGTON's Continental Army. Most farmers refused to sell at these prices, and some sold goods to the British instead.

Aside from lobbying and error, some make ethical arguments for price controls. The concept of "the just price" goes back many centuries. It might seem that the term, just price, refers to absolute standards for judging prices. It is, in fact the case, that what people often meant by just prices were simply competitive market prices. However, there are instances where people object to equilibrium market prices as unfair. Emergencies often cause the price of some goods to rise dramatically. During blackouts, increased demand for flashlights and lanterns will cause their market prices to rise. This is often referred to as price gouging or profiteering. Some claim that sellers should not take advantage of emergencies by raising prices on badly needed goods. Laws against price gouging act as temporary price controls during emergencies. Of course, these laws have the same effects as any other such price controls: shortages. However, some economists and policy leaders insist that these measures are necessary for moral reasons.

Some officials also favor price controls to counter monopoly pricing in uncompetitive markets. If some businesses lack competition, they will sell fewer goods at higher prices. Theoretically, some authority could impose price ceilings on monopolists and force them to charge competitive rates. Since officials generally do not know what prices would prevail in competitive markets, direct controls will generate competitive prices only by chance. Because of the difficulty in determining competitive prices outside of experience, it is generally better to consider how one might attain competitive conditions rather than to use price controls in attempts to simulate competitive conditions.

Free markets do not yield perfect results. So, one can always imagine scenarios where price controls yield positive benefits. But, price controls generally have a poor track record in promoting either efficient resource allocation or price level stability. They exist largely due to political considerations, moral assertions, and popular misconceptions. Consequently, many economists are either skeptical of or opposed to their use. Despite these doubts, price controls not only exist, but are a common instrument of public policy in much of the world.

BIBLIOGRAPHY. Yoram Barzel, "A Theory of Rationing by Waiting," *Journal of Law and Economics* (1974); Edgar Olsen and M.A. Walker, *Alternatives in Rent Control: Myths and Realities* (The Fraser Institute, 1981); Steven A. Morrison and Clifford Winston, "Airline Deregulation and Public Policy," *Science* (v.245/4919, 1989); Hugh Rockoff, *Drastic Measures: a History of Wage and Price Controls in the United States* (Edward Elgar, 1984); Raymond de Roover, "The Concept of the Just Price: Theory and Economic Policy," *The Journal of Economic History* (v.18/4, 1958); Robert Schuettinger and Eamon Butler, *Forty Centuries of Wage and Price Controls* (The Heritage Foundation, 1979); Gordon Tullock, "The Welfare Costs of Tariffs, Monopolies, and Theft," *The Western Journal of Economics* (1967).

D.W. MACKENZIE, PH.D.
GEORGE MASON UNIVERSITY

price discrimination

IN A PERFECTLY COMPETITIVE MARKET, all consumers and producers are price takers; no one can affect the market PRICE by varying the amount that they buy or sell. However, in imperfectly competitive markets certain agents may be able to dictate price. For example, a monopolist, as the only seller in a MARKET, and a monopsonist, as the only buyer in the market, have the power to set price. (In this entry, a monopolist will be used to illustrate price discrimination, but the same logic applies to the actions of monopsonists.)

A monopolist may charge a uniform price to all buyers, or if it has information about how willingness to pay varies across customers, it may engage in non-uniform pricing; i.e., it may price discriminate. Price discrimination involves charging a different price to individual consumers or to different groups of consumers. Differing prices resulting solely from differing costs is not price discrimination. For example, if a firm charges a higher price to deliver its goods to customers who live far away because the costs of delivery are higher, that difference in price is not considered to be price discrimination.

There are three requirements for a firm to be able to price discriminate:

1. It must have market power—the ability to set price

2. It must have information about how willingness to pay varies across consumers

3. It must be able to prevent re-sale of its output from those who are charged a low price to those who would be charged a high price (that is, it must prevent ARBITRAGE).

If a monopolist can identify groups of consumers with varying willingness to pay, price discrimination can allow it to greatly increase its profit. Interestingly, it may also lead to lower deadweight loss (i.e., net social loss). A uniform-pricing MONOPOLY produces less output than a competitive market in order to keep prices at the profit-maximizing level; this lower output is the origin of monopoly deadweight loss. However, when a monopolist price discriminates, it can sell additional output without having to lower the price charged to everyone. As a result, the output of a price discriminating monopolist may be higher than that of a uniform-pricing monopolist, resulting in less deadweight loss.

There are three types of price discrimination. First-degree, or perfect price discrimination occurs when the monopolist charges the consumer's exact willingness to pay for each unit of output. As a result, consumer surplus is zero—consumers are paying the absolute most that they are willing to pay and the monopolist captures all of the surplus in the market. The perfect-price-discriminating monopolist will produce the same level of output as produced by a competitive market, and as a result the dead-weight loss of the monopolist is zero. (While there is no efficiency loss associated with a perfect-price-discriminating monopolist, there are issues of equity since the monopolist captures all of the surplus in the market.) For example, car dealers attempt to practice first-degree price discrimination by haggling in order to determine the prospective buyer's reservation price.

Second-degree, or quantity, price discrimination involves charging a different price for large-quantity purchases than for small-quantity purchases. Again, for such pricing to constitute price discrimination, it must not be attributable to cost differences. Block pricing of electricity by utility monopolies is one example of second-degree price discrimination. Users are charged a high price for initial kilowatt-hours of electricity and lower prices for higher usage. This likely reflects that the price elasticity of demand for electricity is inelastic for the first few units and more elastic for additional units.

Two-part tariffs are a special case of quantity price discrimination. The first part of the tariff entitles one to buy the good or service, and the second part of the tariff is the per-unit cost of the good or service. An example of a two-part tariff is the fee structure of an amusement park; the owner might charge a fee for admission to the park plus another fee per ride. In theory, a two-part tariff could be structured such that the per-unit fee is equal to marginal cost and the admission fee is equal to the remaining consumer willingness to pay; such a two-part tariff would capture all of consumer surplus for the monopolist.

Third-degree, or multi-market, price discrimination occurs when monopolists charge different prices to different groups of consumers. As the number of groups of consumers charged a different price approaches the number of consumers in the market, third-degree price discrimination becomes first-degree, perfect, price discrimination. In multi-market price discrimination, the firm acts as a separate uniform-pricing monopolist with respect to each group of consumers. Third-degree price discrimination is probably the most common; examples include senior-citizen discounts on meals and student pricing for movie tickets. [Editor's Note: It is notable that these discounts are marketed as a "favor" to consumers, whereas in reality they are meant to enhance the profitability of the business.]

BIBLIOGRAPHY. R. Schmalensee, "Output and Welfare Implications of Monopolistic Third-Degree Price Discrimination," *American Economic Review* (v.71, 1981); H. Varian, "Price Discrimination and Social Welfare," *American Economic Review* (v.75, (1985); W. Y. Oi, "A Disneyland Dilemma: Two-Part Tariffs for a Mickey Mouse Monopoly," *Quarterly Journal of Economics* (1971).

JOHN CAWLEY, PH.D.
CORNELL UNIVERSITY

prices, floor/ceiling

AS CONTROLS, PRICE FLOORS and price ceilings refer to situations in which prices are predetermined and fixed by a force external to the market (typically a government or central planner).

A price ceiling refers to a case in which prices are set artificially low (i.e., below the market equilibrium price). Buyers and sellers are prohibited, typically by law, from negotiating any price in excess of the ceiling. In other words, a price ceiling stops the market price of a commodity from moving beyond a maximum value much like the ceiling in a room prevents a person from jumping vertically beyond a certain height. A price floor describes a situation in which prices are set artificially high (i.e., above the market equilibrium price).

Buyers and sellers are forbidden to negotiate a price below the floor.

A price floor prevents the market price of a commodity from falling any lower than a particular level in much the same way that a floor in a room stops an individual from tumbling into the room below her. Price floors and ceilings are generally considered to be inefficient by classical economists due to the fact that they interfere with the laws of SUPPLY and DEMAND. They bind the invisible hand and prevent market prices from adjusting to eliminate surpluses and shortages and consequently are completely inconsistent with capitalism.

By establishing artificially high prices, price floors discourage consumers from purchasing as much of a particular commodity as they would have, had prices been allowed to fall. Consumers, in other words, reduce their quantity demanded of the commodity for which the floor has been set. Producers, on the other hand, seek to increase their quantity supplied as higher prices coupled with sticky costs mean higher profit margins. Producers, in other words, choose to generate a greater level of output than they otherwise would have had prices fallen.

In the absence of flexible prices, a surplus would persist until there was a shift in market supply or demand or the price floor was removed, in which case the surplus would put downward pressure on prices until the surplus disappeared. Because they typically generate surpluses, price floors are considered to be inefficient because the resources used to produce the excess quantity supplied could have been used to produce another commodity. Resources in this case are essentially wasted.

One of the most timeless examples of a price floor, and one that is hotly debated as much today as it was in its inception, is the minimum wage. Many economists identify the minimum wage as a leading cause of UNEMPLOYMENT. By preventing wages from falling, the government encourages individuals who might not otherwise seek work to enter the labor force. The quantity supplied of labor rises. Firms, on the other hand, search for cheaper methods of production in the form of machinery and/or foreign labor, thus reducing the number of jobs openings in the United States (i.e., the quantity demanded of labor). The result is a surplus of labor or unemployment. Please note there are many models and sources of unemployment. Even those who feel that the minimum wage may be the root of unemployment acknowledge the fact that the minimum wage is not the sole cause of unemployment.

A government may also choose to mandate artificially low prices in certain situations. The resulting price ceiling encourages consumers to increase their quantity demanded as the income effect makes it possible for consumers to afford more of the commodity with their given budget and the substitution effect persuades individuals to use more of the government-controlled commodity in place of a now relatively more expensive replacement. Producers, on the other hand, respond to the lower prices by reducing their quantity supplied. Lower prices and sticky costs mean lower profit margins making it less appealing for producers to continue to manufacture large levels of output. The result is a shortage that will remain in the market until there is a shift in market supply or demand, or the price ceiling is removed in which case the shortage will put upward pressure on prices until the shortage no longer exists. Since they typically generate shortages, price ceilings are considered to be inefficient because some consumers, despite the fact that they are ready, willing, and able to purchase an item, will be unable to obtain the government-controlled commodity. Consumers will be "forced" to use their money resources to purchase an item that will provide them with less satisfaction per dollar.

A noteworthy example of a price ceiling and one for which a general consensus among policymakers and social critics has yet to be achieved is rent control. Many economists blame the shortage of quality housing in inner cities on rent control. By forcing landlords to keep rental rates artificially low, the government discourages the production of new apartment buildings as well as the upkeep of existing buildings. Potential tenants, on the other hand, flock to rent-controlled tenements leading to a severe shortage of quality apartments.

Arguments in favor of price controls are typically based on issues of equity rather than efficiency. The equilibrium price in a particular market, while it may lead to an efficient outcome, is considered to be unfair to either consumers or producers. In the case of the minimum wage, the equilibrium wage is considered to be "too low" for workers to live on. Consequently, governments enact price floors in labor markets despite the fact that they may contribute to market inefficiencies (i.e., unemployment). The reverse is true in the case of rent control in which the equilibrium price is considered to be "too high" for prospective tenants to afford. Governments, as a result, establish price ceilings in these cases despite the fact that they create a shortage of quality apartments. [Editor's Note: Since price ceilings and floors cause shortages and surpluses, it is therefore necessary that the government provide additional jobs of last resort, as in the case of minimum wage, and be willing to build additional housing units, as in the case of rent control, to enable the markets to clear.]

Price floors, implemented to assist producers and price ceilings, created to aid consumers, distort market incentives and result in inefficient market outcomes. Price ceilings and floors are rare in the United States which has an economic system largely based on the market mechanism.

BIBLIOGRAPHY. William J. Baumol and Alan S. Blinder, *Economics: Principles and Policy* (South-Western, 2002); Don Cole, *Annual Editions: Microeconomics* (McGraw-Hill, 2000/2001); Oren M. Levin-Waldman, *The Case of the Minimum Wage: Competing Policy Models* (SUNY Press, 2001), Arthur O'Sullivan and Steven M. Sheffrin, *Microeconomics: Principles and Tools* (Prentice Hall, 2003); Peter Passell, "Evidence for a Modest Impact from Abolishing Rent Controls," *The New York Times* (May 22, 1997).

KRISTIN KUCSMA, PH.D.
SETON HALL UNIVERSITY

principle of diminishing returns

FIRST FORMULATED BY French baron Anne Robert Jacques Turgot, and later expounded by the classical British economists, the principle (or frequently law) of diminishing returns is today a fundamental element of economic theory. The principle describes how production typically responds to successive increases in the employment of a single input (e.g., LABOR). While initial treatments focused on the case in which labor or capital is added to a fixed amount of land, the principle was eventually extended to apply to any case in which a single input is varied, while all other factors of production are held constant.

According to the principle of diminishing returns, while additional input employment will usually enable increased production, the amount by which production rises with each expansion of input employment will gradually decline as input employment grows. This can be understood as reflecting the fact that production usually works best with a combination of inputs. Fixing all but one input limits the amount that can be produced, and while output can be increased by applying more of the variable input to fixed amounts of the other inputs, the effectiveness of this procedure will diminish as production becomes more and more intensive in that input.

Diminishing returns and the production function. Formally, modern economists usually state the principle as a relationship between the marginal product of an input and the amount of that input being utilized. Let the marginal product of input X be defined as the change in output that occurs when employment of input X is increased by one unit, holding constant the amounts of all other inputs being used. Then the principle can be stated precisely as follows: for each input X used in any production process, the marginal product of X will be a decreasing function of the amount of X employed.

This relationship can be viewed as a statement about the shape of the function that relates output to input employment. Specifically, the principle requires that if (as is usually assumed) the function relating output to input employment is upward sloping throughout, it will also be concave. It is commonly acknowledged that, in many cases, the marginal product of an input will actually rise before it begins to fall. In such instances, the production function is initially convex and only becomes concave once diminishing returns set in.

The debate over Britain's corn laws. While Turgot seems to have been the first to state the principle of diminishing returns clearly, its prominent place in classical political economy can be traced to the early 19th-century debate over Britain's corn laws—legislation that imposed stiff tariffs on imported grain.

Throughout the Napoleonic Wars, Britain had blockaded the European continent in an effort to impose economic hardship on the French. As a result, British grain producers did not have to compete against foreign producers over this period. Grain prices had increased, and previously dormant British lands had been profitably adapted to grain production.

By 1814, the end of the war was in sight. Anticipating that renewed competition against imports would lead to falling prices, British agricultural interests began demanding that protective tariffs be put in place. Accordingly, Parliament appointed a committee to investigate the relationship between agricultural prices and the state of British agriculture, as well as the likely consequences of allowing grain imports to resume.

In 1815, the committee's reports were made public, and within three weeks of their release, David RICARDO, Thomas MALTHUS, Edward West, and Robert Torrens had each independently developed the principle of diminishing returns and applied it to the issue of protectionism. While the authors differed on the question of whether tariffs would be beneficial, all agreed that preserving the wartime advances in British agriculture would require sustaining high prices. Moreover, they claimed, in the absence of sufficient technological progress, population growth and the principle of diminishing returns would lead to still higher grain prices if imports were prohibited.

Diminishing returns and firm supply. For modern economic theory, the importance of the principle of diminishing returns lies in its ability to explain why the short run supply functions of individual producers will be upward sloping.

Let the marginal cost of production be defined as the extra cost incurred when output is raised by one unit. Standard optimization techniques reveal that in order to maximize profit, a perfectly competitive firm must produce the amount of output that makes its marginal cost of production equal to the market-determined price of output. This ensures that a competitive firm's supply function will coincide with the function that relates its marginal cost of production to the amount it produces. Thus, the slope of a firm's supply function will depend upon the slope of its marginal cost function. In particular, upward sloping supply functions will require marginal costs that rise with output.

This is assured, in the short run, by the principle of diminishing returns. Over short-time horizons, all inputs beside labor will be essentially fixed. By the principle of diminishing returns, successive, equal increases in labor employment will raise output in gradually diminishing increments. If so, then a sequence of one unit output expansions can only be accomplished with progressively increasing amounts of extra labor. If labor sells at a fixed per-unit price, then the cost of each successive output expansion will be larger than the last.

BIBLIOGRAPHY. William J. Baumol and Alan S. Blinder, *Economics Principles and Policy, Eighth Edition* (Harcourt College, 2000); Stanley L. Brue, "Retrospectives: The Law of Diminishing Returns," *Journal of Economic Perspectives* (v.7, 1993); John B. Clark, *The Distribution of Wealth: A Theory of Wages, Interest and Profits* (Macmillan, 1908); Edwin Cannan, "The Origin of the Law of Diminishing Returns, 1813-15," *Economic Journal* (v.2, 1892); Anne Robert Jacques Turgot, *Observation sur un Memoire de M. de Saint-Pervay*, ed., Schelle, Gustave, *Oeuvres de Turgot et Documents le Concernant* (Librarie Felix Alcan, 1914, 1767).

JOEL D. CARTON, PH.D.
TEXAS TECH UNIVERSITY

privatization

THE TRANSFER OF the production of goods and provision of services from the public to the private sector is referred to as privatization. Other broader definitions of privatization include any exposure of the public sector to market competition, the outsourcing of public services, vouchers, franchising, and a wide variety of other public-private partnerships. The more restricted, contemporary definition, reflects the kind of privatization that is currently being practiced in industrial and developing countries.

In spite of the fact that privatization is not a new idea and that governments in the past turned frequently to the private sector for provision of goods and services, our contemporary understanding of privatization dates back to the late 1970s and early 1980s. At that time, there was a surge of interest in privatization, in part as a reaction to the 1960s and 1970s policies promoting social welfare, public regulation, and state ownership of economic activ-

ities. In 1979, the Margaret THATCHER administration in the UNITED KINGDOM started an ambitious privatization program. State-owned industries, ranging from airports and rail services to public utilities, were transferred to private ownership over a short period of time. The success of the Thatcher administration with privatization had ripple effects in many other countries, including countries with and without a capitalist economic system.

In the last two decades, privatization has become an important part of government policy in FRANCE, in socialist SPAIN, in AUSTRALIA and New Zealand (both with labor governments), in GERMANY, and in the UNITED STATES. The first significant privatization of the Ronald Reagan administration in the United States was that of Conrail in 1987. Since then, several privatizations took place at the federal, state, and local levels. Examples include the U.S. Postal Service, the energy sector (especially electricity), the Port Authority of New York, and municipal golf courses.

The main ideological argument behind privatization is that the state should not be active in economic life in a free democratic market economy. The ownership of the factors of production should belong to the private sector. The size of the government should be minimized, leading to lower taxes and lower government spending. This paradigm is supported by the neoliberal economic theory, which argues that state-owned economic enterprises are inefficient. According to this theory, publicly owned enterprises lack the profit-maximization orientation and entrepreneurial incentives of private enterprises, and would lead to production decisions dominated by political interests that misallocate scarce resources.

In addition, bureaucratic inefficiencies and the politicization of economic activity would cause a lack of transparency and accountability in the public sector, very often culminating in corruption. The de-emphasis on profitability means that the public sector losses would need to be covered by the state budget, potentially leading to large budget deficits and ultimately to the crowding-out of the private sector in the economy. The neo-liberal argument assumes that private ownership of property rights provides the necessary incentives for maximum efficiency and profitability.

The counter-argument in favor of the presence of the public sector in the economy claims that there are instances when markets do not function efficiently. EXTERNALITIES, lack of perfect information, and increasing returns to scale, for instance, would limit competition, and therefore may prevent markets from optimal functioning. Under these conditions, markets would fail and government intervention in the economy, in the form of either regulation or production, would be justified.

Public choice theory, on the other hand, claims that there is a major fallacy in this last argument. If free markets fail for the reasons mentioned above, there is no guarantee that the public sector would not fail when faced with the same problems, especially given its inefficiency. In this regard and in terms of efficiency gains, a shift from the public to private sector would be more desirable under any circumstance.

In the 1980s, the development policy known as the Washington Consensus moved to the core of the development strategy promoted by the INTERNATIONAL MONETARY FUND (IMF) and the WORLD BANK. This policy emphasizes macroeconomic stability, privatization, domestic economic liberalization, and international openness. It is essentially a pragmatic summary of the economic growth experiences of industrial countries in the post-WORLD WAR II period.

According to this view, price instability in developing countries is the result of their large and persistent budget deficits. These deficits, meanwhile, are driven by the large public sector in the economy because the losses of the inefficient state economic enterprises must be covered by the state budget. The deficits are financed by monetization, that is, the printing of new money, due to the lack of well-developed financial markets. The resulting high inflation leads to higher interest rates, discouraging private investment and hence causing recession and unemployment. An effective way of breaking this vicious cycle is to transfer state economic enterprises to the efficient and profit-oriented private sector.

At the same time, liberalization of the economy by removing all the price and non-price barriers to the free functioning of the market system, would not only stabilize the economy but would reallocate resources in an efficient way and hence would foster growth and development.

Privatization in developing countries has been more problematic than that in industrial countries. The first problem stems from the fact that, unlike in most industrial countries, privatization in developing countries means denationalization of the industries originally nationalized as part of their struggle for national independence. Therefore, state economic enterprise historically has a different "nationalistic" connotation to it. In the industrial world, the role of the state in the economy is simply a matter of public choice. In developing countries, this element of "nationalism" makes privatization more of a political economy issue rather than a pure public choice issue.

In several developing countries, opposition to privatization has been easily mobilized using such nationalistic rhetoric. It needs to be understood that privatization involves not only the transfer of assets but also the transfer of power. Privatization shifts power from the bureaucracy and the politician to the private entrepreneur. Any shift in power invites struggle. It is therefore not surprising that the resistance to privatization in sev-

eral developing countries has come predominantly from the political and bureaucratic elite, condemning privatization as anti-nationalistic.

This has been especially true in cases where privatization involved sales of public assets to multinational companies. The opposition to privatization is actually a coalition of very distinct groups, including not only business groups that economically benefit from the state economic enterprises, but also labor groups adversely affected by public-sector layoffs that accompany privatization.

According to the supporters of privatization, this increase in unemployment, however, is a short-run phenomenon. The more efficient allocation of resources would, in the long run, increase production, creating jobs and absorbing unemployment. Further complications regarding privatization in developing countries involve concerns about increasing economic inequality, and the transfer of public monopoly power to the private sector. The adverse effects of privatization on inequality are summarized by the fact that most public services and infrastructure primarily benefit the economically disadvantaged. For example, public schools, public housing, water, parks, buses, and state healthcare systems are most important for relatively low-income groups, so privatization of such services has a strong effect on their economic well-being. In fact, privatization of public utilities may raise their price to the higher market level limiting availability to disadvantaged groups, and therefore lowering productivity and raising inequality. These problems are aggravated if the publicly owned enterprises are transferred to the private sector as monopolies.

These and related issues are recognized by the World Bank and the International Monetary Fund and are addressed routinely. These financial organizations have not, for instance, made a policy recommendation to transfer a public monopoly directly to the private sector. It has always been assumed that privatization would promote efficiency as a result of increased competition. Breaking up public monopolies before privatization, and creating wide-share ownership rather than bloc sales of shares have been guiding principles.

In fact, it is recommended that privatization schemes emphasize employee participation in ownership arrangements so that the employees become stakeholders in the privatized enterprise. In 2000, the World Bank put into place its Private Sector Development Strategy (PSDS), a detailed overall privatization plan that promotes privatization but recommends measures to lessen its unwanted effects. It proposes subsidies to the economically disadvantaged to afford the social services transferred to the private sector. The plan suggests that privatization would reduce government overload and thus enable the government to focus its attention on the poor and their needs more efficiently. The PSDS also recommends an increasing role for the International Finance Corporation (IFC), a World Bank financial affiliate, in lending to the private sector to finance retraining for the workers laid off to help them gain marketable skills and find jobs.

It is clear that privatization is a more complicated issue in the setting of developing countries than in industrial countries. Political and economic interests are more firmly embedded in the role of the public sector in the economy in the developing world. If, however, the experience of industrial countries provides any lessons for developing countries, the allocative efficiency gains associated with privatization are too high to ignore. In the past, mistakes were made in the implementation of the privatization programs in the developing countries, largely through discounting the short-run adjustment costs necessary for the transition. If privatization is to continue to play an important role in the World Bank and IMF development strategy, lessons need to be learned from these past mistakes, and a fuller appreciation developed of the historical necessity of public enterprises in the first place.

BIBLIOGRAPHY. P. Jenkins, *Mrs. Thatcher's Revolution: The Ending of the Socialist Era* (Harvard University Press, 1988); P. Starr, "The Meaning of Privatization" *Yale Law and Policy Review* (1988); P. Starr, "The New Life of the Liberal State: Privatization and the Restructuring of State-Society Relations" J. Waterbury and E. Suleiman, eds., *Public Enterprise and Privatization* (Westview Press, 1990); D. Welch, and O. Fremond, "The Case-by-Case Approach to Privatization: Techniques and Examples," *World Bank Technical Paper No. 403* (International Bank for Reconstruction and Development and the World Bank (1998); J. Williamson, *Latin American Adjustment: How Much Has Happened?* (Institute for International Economics, 1990); www.privatization.org.

M. ODEKON
SKIDMORE COLLEGE

Procter & Gamble

FORMED BY TWO SMALL SOAP-MAKERS in Cincinnati in 1837, Procter & Gamble (P&G) grew to become one of the largest manufacturing firms in the world, producing not only soap but countless other household items. James Gamble supervised production of tallow candles and soap made of meat scraps and wood ashes, while his partner William Procter managed the office and sales.

The company became a national success in the latter decades of the 19th century. James Norris Gamble, son of one of the founders, developed a new formula for white soap. An accident at the factory led to a vat of

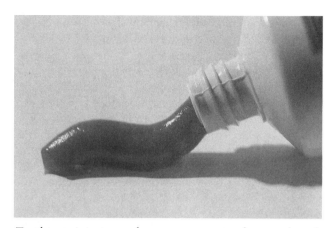

Toothpaste is just one of many consumer products made and marketed by Procter & Gamble.

soap being stirred too long. The result was a bar that floated, a novelty at the time. Ivory soap was advertised as safe for both personal and laundry use. The company's slogans for the product ("It floats" and "99 and 44/100 percent pure") helped to increase sales to 30 million cakes per year by the 1890s. P&G was a pioneer in magazine advertising and promotional efforts, and invested not only in mass-production technology but product development, creating a laboratory at the Ivorydale factory site in Ohio. In labor relations, P&G was also an innovator, adopting a profit-sharing plan in 1887 that rewarded employees with a share of dividends, in an effort to undercut labor unrest sweeping the country at the time.

In the 20th century, P&G continued to introduce products that transformed daily life for American consumers. Crisco vegetable shortening was launched in 1911 with a marketing strategy that combined dealer incentives, free samples, national advertising, and demonstrations. It was a huge success. Tide laundry detergent, launched in 1946, was a marked improvement over others available at the time. Housewives across the country embraced Tide, making it the most popular product in America during the 1950s. Crest toothpaste, first on the market to use sodium fluoride to prevent tooth decay, was another national triumph. In promotion as well, P&G led the way, sponsoring television programs (including the popular "This is Your Life" and "Search for Tomorrow") and using the medium for commercials. The company expanded its operations not just within the United States but globally in the post–WORLD WAR II years.

During the late 1960s and 1970s, P&G came under increasing scrutiny from environmentalists who charged that the chemicals, used in both the production and use of cleaning products, were polluting water supplies and harming animal life. Public pressure forced P&G to find alternatives to phosphate-based detergents. The company also faced lawsuits that linked their Rely tampon brand with potentially fatal toxic shock syndrome. Nevertheless, P&G weathered these crises and continued to grow. By 1980, the company had manufacturing operations in 22 countries, and exported its products to another 100 nations. Today, Procter & Gamble remains a consumer products giant, producing everything from Pampers diapers to Cover Girl Cosmetics to Pringles Potato Chips. And Ivory soap, first developed in the 19th century, remains one of the most highly recognized brands in the world. In 2002, *Fortune* magazine ranked P&G the 93rd largest company in the world with revenues of $39 billion.

BIBLIOGRAPHY. Richard L. Bushman, Claudia L. Bushman, "The Early History of Cleanliness in America," *Journal of American History* (v.74/4, March 1988); Oscar Schisgall, *Eyes on Tomorrow: The Evolution of Procter & Gamble* (J.G. Ferguson Publishing, 1981); Alecia Swasy, *Soap Opera: The Inside Story of Procter & Gamble* (Times Books, 1993); Susan Strasser, *Satisfaction Guaranteed: The Making of the American Mass Market* (Pantheon Books, 1989). Global 500, *Fortune* (July, 2002).

SARAH ELVINS
UNIVERSITY OF NOTRE DAME

producer surplus

AN INDICATOR OF the welfare of the producers in a market, producer surplus is defined as the difference between the price the producers are willing to charge and the price they actually charge for a unit of a product. The market supply schedule is a preference schedule that shows how much the producers are willing to charge in order to produce a given quantity, assuming a constant cost of production. It is a positively sloped schedule, indicating that profit-maximizing producers would be willing to produce more as the unit price of the product increases.

In the graph below, the producers are willing to charge price P_0 for the quantity produced, Q_0. Everything else remaining constant, the producers would be willing to produce a higher output level, Q_1, if they are paid a higher unit price, P_1.

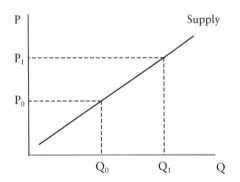

The actual market price of a product that the consumer pays is the result of the interaction between supply and demand. The latter is again a preference schedule that shows the price the satisfaction (utility)-maximizing consumers are willing to pay for a certain quantity consumed, given their level of income. It is negatively sloped, reflecting the inverse relationship between the quantity consumed and the price. Given a fixed income, the consumer would be willing to increase the quantity consumed from Q_0 to Q_1 if the unit price of the product decreases from P_0 to P_1.

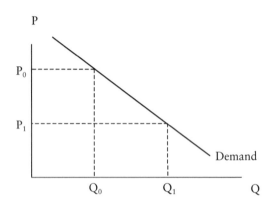

The producers and consumers together determine the market price of the product. The market price is obtained at the point where the quantity demanded is equal to the quantity supplied at that price. In the graph below, the market price at which the producers and the consumers agree to sell and buy the product is represented by the intersection of the demand and supply schedules at the equilibrium point E. In short, the equilibrium price P_e clears the market by setting the quantities produced and demanded, Q_e, equal to each other.

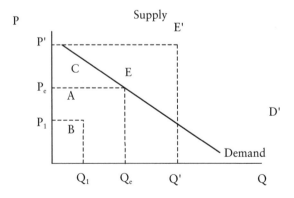

Two important issues concerning the producers should be realized. First, the producers, by agreeing to produce quantity Q_e, actually produce any level of output below it, such as Q_1. Secondly, by charging the equilibrium price P_e they make a profit. They were willing to charge a price P_1 for quantity Q_1 and thereby maximize their profits. Now they are actually charging P_e for Q_1. The difference between the two price levels, P_1 and P_e is the producer surplus for Q_1. In a similar fashion, at every level of production below Q_e, the actual price P_e is higher than the price the producers are willing to charge. Hence, the area below the equilibrium price bordered by the supply schedule and the vertical axis, A + B, is the producer surplus, measured in dollars.

A different way of looking at the producer surplus is that it is the short-run profit of the producer. The supply schedule in a competitive market represents the marginal cost at each level of production. The point Q_1, P_1 is the marginal cost of the producer. The price P_e is the marginal revenue, that is, the revenue associated with the sale of Q_1. Hence, the profit associated with Q_1, the marginal profit, is the difference between P_1 and P_e, which is equal to the producer surplus. The area under the equilibrium price P_e bordered by the supply schedule and the vertical axis, A + B, is the total profit of the producer, which is equal to the producer surplus.

The producer surplus area measures the welfare effects of the changes in the market regarding the producers. If the demand schedule shifts up to D', the equilibrium price moves to P' at E'. Since the supply schedule has not changed, the increase in the actual price the producer is charging raises the difference between the price the producer is willing to charge and is actually charging. The difference between P_1 and P' is greater that that between P_1 and P_e. Accordingly, producer surplus increases by the area C, which is the area between the initial and the new equilibrium prices bordered by the supply schedule and the vertical axis, $P_eP'E'E$. In a similar fashion, this area represents the increase in the profits of the producer because the rise in equilibrium price raises the marginal revenue associated with each unit of sales at the given marginal cost. As a result of the upward shift in the demand schedule, the producer surplus increases and the producers become better off. A downward shift in the demand makes the producers worse off by reducing the producer surplus. [Editor's Note: In the end, it may be noted that producer surplus is the source for profits; and since producer surplus and hence profit increases in response to increasing demand and resultant increasing prices, some theorists consider profits as unearned income and hence exploitive in nature.]

BIBLIOGRAPHY. N. Gregory Mankiw, *Principles of Economics* (South-Western, 2000); Karl Marx, *Theories of Surplus Value* (Prometheus Books, 2000).

M. ODEKON
SKIDMORE COLLEGE

product

A TERM USED BOTH IN MARKETING and in economics, product exists at the microeconomic and the macroeconomic level. In MICROECONOMICS, it refers to the outputs of production, such as goods and services. Thus the marginal revenue product is the extra revenue a firm can obtain from using another unit of an input factor. In MACROECONOMICS, the concept refers to the output, in unit or value terms, of an aggregate such as a state or country (i.e., to the aggregate level of goods and services), as in GROSS DOMESTIC PRODUCT (GDP) or GROSS NATIONAL PRODUCT (GNP).

Economics studies how primary commodities and produced goods and services, including those that are factors of production, become, by virtue of the relative SCARCITY of their supply, economic goods which are traded on markets. The economic literature has few serious—precise, exhaustive and non-circular—definitions either of products or goods. They are usually assumed as primes or, by begging the question, implicitly defined through the concepts of "economic goods" or "normal goods" (versus "inferior" and Giffen goods). This may be due to the simplistic assumption of homogeneous and perfectly substitutable goods under perfect competition.

Carl MENGER claimed four conditions to be necessary for an object to constitute a good:

1. a human want

2. properties of the object in question which render it capable of being brought into a causal connection with the satisfaction of this want

3. knowledge of this causal connection on the part of the person involved

4. command of the thing sufficient to direct it to the satisfaction of the want.

Products as differentiated objects of demand did not start to play an important role before E.H. Chamberlin's *Theory of Monopolistic Competition* (1933). Product is generally used in a broad sense and is defined as follows: "Anything which makes buyers prefer one seller to another, be it personality, reputation, convenient location, or the tone of his shop, differentiates the thing purchased to that degree, for what is bought is really a bundle of utilities, of which these things are a part." Consumer perception, then, determines whether offerings are the same or different products; and the basis for such determination may be "real or fancied," since the satisfaction of wants depends only on what consumers believe will satisfy them.

Generally, product is a term rather used in the business literature and there it usually is understood broadly as "anything that can be offered to a market to satisfy a want or need," as noted by Philip Kotler. This includes physical goods, services, experiences, events, persons, places, properties, organizations, information, and ideas. The logical problem in identifying products exclusively by their want-satisfying powers is that two products (such as two brands of soft drinks or a soft drink and a smoothie) that satisfy the same want or need (say, a desire for a sweet-tasting drink) must, by necessity, be regarded as identical.

It should be observed that "product" as used in macroeconomics is by no means simply an analogue of an individual good. If nominal GDP is expressed as:

$$Y^N = \sum_{j=1}^{n} P_j Q_j, \qquad j = 1, 2, \ldots, n$$

where P and Q are vectors of prices and quantities produced, the dimension of Y is dollars per unit time, and Y may change at constant Q. The usual way of making the underlying utility, which is assumed to be generated by the quantities of goods Q, congruent with Y, is to compute real GDP as:

$$Y^R = Y^N / P$$

However, real GDP does not have the dimensions of a real product, either. It is a derivative measurement, its dimension being base-period dollars (not dollars per unit good) and thus dependent on the price index used. In the ontological sense, then, aggregates of bushels of wheat, BMW automobiles, or haircuts are just as real as the individual products; GDP and GNP as macroeconomic magnitudes expressed in monetary terms are not.

Product classification. Products have been categorized in several ways. By user category, one distinguishes between consumer products and business (or industrial) products, the first being offered to final consumers and the second, as intermediate goods, for consumption by other producers on the business-to-business market. Consumer products in turn are often thought to be either of the following:

1. convenience products, those goods (such as snacks, staples, or newspapers) consumers purchase frequently, immediately, and with a minimum of effort

2. shopping products, goods (such as furniture, appliances, or dental services) which consumers typically seek out and compare on such bases as suitability, quality, style, or price

3. specialty products (such as cars, designer clothes, or artistic performances), which have unique characteristics or brand identification so that consumers are willing to make a special purchasing effort

4. unsought products, which consumers do not normally think of acquiring (such as smoke detectors or life insurance), or which they are not yet aware, requiring support by advertising and personal selling.

By durability, a distinction between durable and nondurable products is common, where some authors regard three years as the appropriate cut-off point. By tangibility, goods are distinguished from services. Furthermore, marketing distinguishes special groups of products on the basis of characteristics of consumption or distribution. Examples for such classification, often on an ad hoc basis, are FMCG (Fast Moving Consumer Goods), investment products (such as mutual funds or equities), packaged products, or bulk products.

Product characteristics. According to one approach, products are seen as reducible to their characteristics—the objective attributes that determine consumers' subjective willingness to pay for them—rather than as "wholes." Consumer demand is actually not directed at products as such, but rather at their characteristics (or properties) such as size, color, shape, texture, or flavor. Consumer theory has thus been reconstructed in terms of property space rather than product space, differences in substitution between goods being understood as actually reflecting differences in the sets of characteristics associated with them. This model underlies the various approaches of functional (or benefit) segmentation and of positioning used in marketing. The market for a product can be segmented by the attributes that are of primary importance to a target group of consumers. Such decomposition of products into their elements constitutes the basis for perceptual maps and attribute-based multivariate methods in market research, for example those used in factor analysis, cluster analysis, and conjoint analysis.

This approach has been criticized from various perspectives. First, it has been argued that consumers seek benefits rather than characteristics, and that benefits are purely subjective expectations that cannot be reduced unequivocally to objective attributes inhering in products. If benefits are located in the minds of consumers and these arbitrarily decide which benefits they impute to a product, in the expectation that these benefits will satisfy their wants, the regularity with which certain products are expected to satisfy certain types of wants becomes inexplicable.

Even more so, different consumers may perceive different characteristics even if they choose between identical goods. Much of the economic literature has suffered from such ontological equivocation between objective features of products and their subjective differentiation and monetary estimation by consumers: "Commodities are differentiated partly by their very nature (without regard to demand), and partly in response to differences in buyers' tastes, preferences, locations, etc., which are as much a part of the order of things within any broad class of product as they are between one class of product and another," Chamberlin explains.

Second, not only are consumers unlikely to have similar marginal rates of substitution between properties, products are also not reducible to simple sets of characteristics independent of each other. Contrary to the characteristics approach, which expresses higher consumer valuation of particular properties strictly as higher willingness to pay, complex products may have interdependent characteristics. Some products may be such, as in the case of shoes without soles or computers without processors, that our willingness to pay for any other characteristic is reduced to zero if one characteristic is found missing or defective. By assuming an atomistic structure of products, the characteristics approach makes unrealistic assumptions. Products are rather, in ontological perspective, complex structures that consist of part-whole relations, necessary and dependent parts, and boundaries.

Structure of products. For consumers, products do not come as undifferentiated wholes, and marketers must decide on the appropriate level of complexity to give a product offering. Ultimately consumers desire core benefits. At this level, however, there will generally be much competition between products. Producers will therefore attempt to gain differentiation by adding further levels of complexity, which may involve services, such as installation, warranty, delivery, or credit.

This strategy of product augmentation increases the degree of uniqueness of a product and may give producers a competitive advantage. Since consumers choose between total product packages rather than between their core constituents alone, it is total products that are of relevance to marketers. Today, most competition takes place at the level of augmented products; in saturated markets, it is there (and not at the level of core benefits) that product offerings can typically gain sufficient differentiation.

Of course, the added benefits of augmented products must be compared to the additional costs of production and marketing in order to decide on the optimum level of product complexity for any market that will allow for maximum profitability. Product complexity may exceed cognitive constraints or may involve irrelevant components, which would suggest that products need to be broken down into modules.

Modularization, as the strategy of developing simpler parts that may be assembled into a more complex whole on behalf of or by consumers, is one of the dominant options in new-product development. Dell Computer, a leading computer manufacturer in 2003, built its business model on consumer-guided product modularization.

Product hierarchy. The question of the optimum complexity of total (or augmented) products is interdependent with that of the levels of demand. From the perspective of consumers, there is a hierarchy of product levels depending on the scope of demand. Consumers' needs or wants are rarely for an individual product that is already known, but more often for meeting certain needs or wants. Using the example of BMW automobiles, the following hierarchy may be distinguished (where for items at each level an alternative at the same level of demand is specified):

Product family: Automobiles

Product category: Passenger cars

Product line: BMW 3 series

Product type: BMW 325i

Product form: BMW 325xi or alternate

Consumer demand is typically for the expected benefits of a need family and gradually becomes more specific as consumers retrieve more information about available alternatives. As consumers make decisions at more specific levels, the number of alternative products competing for the consumer budget decreases. In our example, a BMW 325i would be the product that is ultimately desired, and as a branded product it competes with other items of the same product type and product line. Here, attention must be paid to the logical distinction between type and token or, in marketing, between products (or product types) and their various product forms (such as the cabriolet and coupe variants of the BMW 325i, or different package sizes of a particular brand of cornflakes).

Product differentiation. Economists speak of product differentiation when referring to the production of non-homogeneous goods (i.e., those that are not perfect substitutes for each other). Product differentiation is one of the characteristics of monopolistic competition, a market form under which, given no artificial barriers to entry, many firms sell products differing in physical characteristics, location, service levels, branding, or image. COMPETITION can take the form of price competition or, typical for market situations between monopoly and perfect competition, of product (or non-price) competition, in which advertising plays a major role.

The goal of product differentiation is to reduce the price-elasticity of demand by giving products a higher degree of uniqueness and thus to increase market power and maximize profits. Horizontal product differentiation (as in the case of two brands of toothpaste) occurs if consumer would still rank products differently if they were offered at the same price. Spatial differentiation, such as between restaurants or retail stores, is an example. Products are vertically differentiated if, when offered at the same price, all consumers choose to purchase the same one, that of highest quality. Batteries are, in this sense, differentiated by lifespan.

Consumers generally desire uniqueness and variety in products. The idea that one product can suit everyone looks very outdated in the face of consumers' desire for increasingly unique products that stand out among their competition, and meet individual needs and wants. At the same time, a variety of such products are demanded in most product categories. The economic system of free enterprise has proved singularly efficient in producing this desired variety.

Some manufacturers, however, have been taking product differentiation a step further by customizing products for the individual on a mass scale. Mass customization is currently being achieved with physical products on a fairly superficial level, for example with clip-on changeable phone covers, or modular stereo units, but can also be achieved at a more fundamental level. Online retailers, transaction sites and portals (such as Amazon.com, Ebay or Yahoo!) have adopted the strategy of providing individualized offerings for large numbers of customers.

Product brands. One of the most effective instruments of product differentiation is to brand products. Brands are usually defined in relation to products: "A brand is therefore a product, but one that adds other dimensions that differentiate it in some way from other products to satisfy the same need," Kevin Lane Keller wrote in 2003. The question then arises, what are the addi-

The variety of a baker's daily selection is an example of product differentiation: same flour, but many breads.

tional features of a product that turn it into a brand and account for brand equity—the extra monetary value brands enjoy over non-branded, or less-branded, competing products.

What causes products such as Coca-Cola, Hershey chocolate, or Campbell soup, to be strong brands and to profit from a price premium while other colas, candies, or soups do not? Two answers have generally been given, depending on whether the difference is located in the perceptual space of consumers or in product space itself.

According to the customer-based view, the "power of a brand lies in what resides in the minds of customers," Keller noted. The higher awareness that consumers have of certain products, together with their set of specific brand associations, contributes to brand loyalty, which in turn accounts for brand equity. Marketing management, particularly advertising, can influence higher awareness, and this view indeed holds that all products can in principle be branded.

Brands are thereby reduced to complex symbols that convey different levels of meaning. According to the American Marketing Association, "A brand is a name, term, sign, symbol, or design, or a combination of them, intended to identify the goods or services of one seller or group of sellers and to differentiate them from those of competitors." The realist view of brands regards this definition as relying on a category mistake. It cannot explain, for example, why, regardless of advertising expenditure, certain products lend themselves to branding more than others or why certain brand extensions succeed while others fail.

The realist view emphasizes the nature of brands as branded products and identifies the conditions for successful branding as anchored both in product space and in perceptual space. Products have features that allow for branding to different degrees. Brands, then, are products that are salient within their categories by being demarcated from other less-branded ones by defensible boundaries (drawn by trademark law, control over distribution channels, advertising, etc.). And brand equity is a function of the degree to which brands succeed in occupying niches in product categories afforded by specific combinations of properties of products and how these are evaluated by consumers.

Product management. Companies producing several products usually organize their business around these products, by employing product managers to be responsible for all decisions concerning one product or brand. In companies with a very wide product mix, management at the level of product categories (category management) has recently gained ground.

In addition to branding, product management must decide on:

1. the appropriate complexity of the total product, particularly the mix between tangible and intangible components

2. the product mix, or product portfolio, to be offered

3. the development of new products

4. product life cycle strategies

5. packaging.

The product mix of any company can be analyzed in terms of the width of the assortment, such as the number of product lines offered, and the length of each product line (or the number of distinguishable items).

A product line is a set of closely related products, for example soaps or sports utility vehicles, and the product mix of a company is the set of all product lines and individual products. BMW, for example, has, in its motorcar division, the following product lines, with several product items (models) in each line and several product types (e.g., coupe, convertible, sedan) for many product items: 3 Series; 5 Series; 7 Series; X5; Z8; M Series. The company has other divisions (such as motorcycles, bicycles, the hybrid motorbike-scooter C1, accessories), some of which are again organized along product lines. Excessively long product lines may lead to cannibalization, i.e. some products taking away market share from other, similar ones within the same line because their positioning in consumers' perception is not sufficiently different (and because the difference in price may outweigh any perceived difference in benefits). Typically, companies want to avoid new product introductions that cannibalize their own product offerings. Excessively broad product mixes may lead to brand dilution if an umbrella brand is used; it may then no longer be credible for consumers that one brand stands for product categories which are perceived to be vastly different.

Product proliferation is a term used to describe the current trend of companies to expand the width and depth of their product mixes. Line extensions, or the addition of new products to product lines under an established brand, and brand extensions, or the application of existing brands to new product categories (and often new product lines), are the main instruments of product management that contribute to product proliferation.

Products are, in an analogy with biology, subject to a life cycle. The product life cycle (PLC) shows the path a typical new product takes from its inception to its discontinuation. This model can be applied to specific need families or industries (e.g., transportation), product families (e.g., automobiles), product categories (e.g., passenger cars), product lines (e.g., BMW 3 series), product forms (e.g., station wagons), product items (e.g., BMW 325i), or a particular brand (e.g., BMW).

Mass production gives way to mass customization, as in printing publications per single-reader preferences.

Only a minority of new products being developed turn out to be successes and maintain themselves over a longer period. More rigorous screening and evaluation techniques in the new product-development process are meant to reduce this "flop rate." The vast majority of new products are modifications of existing products (in form, function, or cost), line extensions, brand extensions, or new category entries, while there are only a small number of new-to-the-world products. While line and brand extensions leave the original products in place, product modifications always replace them. New category entries (such as bicycles within the BMW product portfolio) are products that are new to a company but not to the consumer.

New product management thus involves both the management of product development and that of product diffusion. Depending on the nature of the market segment, diffusion patterns can be very different, and it is this difference that determines product life cycles. In spite of the individual nature of product life cycles, four (or five) phases are usually distinguished: 1) introduction; 2) growth; 3) maturity; and 4) decline. At every stage, particular marketing management decisions are most effective to optimize performance. For example, in the introduction phase many products (particularly if demand is highly price-elastic) will be sold through selected distributors at a lower introductory price. Once demand picks up during the growth phase, price will be raised and distribution intensified; during its decline phase, the product may again be available in discount outlets at clearance prices. Advertising and publicity may start before product launch but may no longer be deemed effective toward the end of the maturity stage.

In retailing, the term stock-keeping unit (SKU) is used for any product that is an inventory item and takes up a slot of shelf space. Retailers manage their business primarily at the level of product forms (with an increasing tendency towards category management), since variants of a product including different package sizes are treated as separate SKUs. Manufacturers typically must provide outlets with their own universal product code (UPC), the bar code that is scanned at checkout counters. Because of this, the individual product item now represents a set of products. For example, three television models being shipped to five mass merchandisers would be fifteen products (1 product item ∞ 3 product forms ∞ 5 unique customer UPCs = 15 separate product items to be managed).

BIBLIOGRAPHY. John Beath and Yannis Katsoulacos, *The Economic Theory of Product Differentiation* (Cambridhe University Press, 1991); E.H. Chamberlin, *The Theory of Monopolistic Competition* (Harvard University Press, 1933); E.H. Chamberlin, "The Product as an Economic Variable," *Quarterly Journal of Economics* (v.67, 1953); Wolfgang Grassl, "The Reality of Brands: Toward an Ontology of Marketing," *American Journal of Economics and Sociology* (v.58, 1999); Kevin Lane Keller, *Strategic Brand Management* (Prentice Hall, 2003); Philip Kotler, *Marketing Management* (Prentice Hall, 2003); Kevin J. Lancaster, "A New Approach to Consumer Theory," *Journal of Political Economy* (v.74, 1966); Donald R. Lehmann and Russell S. Winer, *Product Management* (McGraw-Hill, 2002); Carl Menger, *Principles of Economics* (1871, Libertarian Press, 1994); Karl Ulrich and Steven Eppinger, *Product Design and Development* (McGraw-Hill, 2004).

WOLFGANG GRASSL
HILLSDALE COLLEGE

production, individual/social

PRODUCTION IS DEFINED AS human beings making use of available technology to transform raw materials into new products. The natural environment is a condition for the existence of production because it furnishes the basic substance used by human beings in this process of transformation. Motivation to create new goods that are valued either by the direct producer, his kinship unit, or in the larger society, and the skills necessary to carry out the production are other necessary conditions.

Individual production occurs when the production process is carried out by a single, relatively isolated human being. The angler who sets out in his boat to catch fish engages in individual production, as does the farmer who works the land alone. Classical economics grounds many of its analogies in individual production, and uses these parables as examples for generalized theories of human society. Ironically, classical economics also devalues individual production by treating the inan-

imate objects used by direct producers as if they were equal partners in the production process. Land and machinery (CAPITAL) are considered as contributing new value alongside labor in the production process. This treatment of land, labor, and capital as partners in the production process is a major point of disagreement between classical/neoclassical, and Marxian ECONOMIC THEORY. The Marxian economists view human labor as uniquely capable of creating new value. This distinction between the classical/neoclassical point of view and that of Marxian theorists is particularly clear when viewing individual production.

The pursuit of individual production. The simplest example of individual production is a case where the only interaction is between producer and nature. This example is one where individual production occurs outside of human society. The *Robinson Crusoe* story and the film "Castaway" come to mind. These are rare instances where individual production occurs outside society, in complete alienation from other human beings. These examples of castaway, individual production are not likely to be of much use in understanding more typical instances of individual production. And since most economic theories are focused on explaining social relationships there, has not been a great deal of attention paid to such examples.

To a certain extent, individual production is mythologized in popular discourse, as well as in some scientific theories. The myth of individual production is particularly important in the UNITED STATES, where the idea of the relatively autonomous, individual producer is at the core of what has come to be called Jeffersonian democracy. The language of American political discourse has traditionally been rich in direct and indirect references to an independent producer who is conceptualized as engaged in individual production, despite the fact that actual production in the United States has historically been dominated by slave- and wage-labor production, which are not individual in nature. In social science, neoclassical economic theory relies heavily upon a notion of trade between such individual producers, each of whom brings his wares to a perfectly competitive market, and where each producer is devoid of any market power. The neoclassical model has a wage-labor market, which would indicate socialized production, but treats wage laborers analogously to individual producers negotiating contracts with other individual producers in a utopian environment, where no such economic agent has market power or any ability to coerce.

However, individual production outside of the confines of a society is rare. Individual production typically occurs in the context of social relationships formed within a specific society or societies. Thus, it is very likely that the farmer who plows his field alone does so in the context of social relationships with other human beings and institutions that are part of a larger society. The farmer's productive efforts are likely to be motivated by these relationships. In this sense, individual production is not autonomous from the other social relationships in the society. Individual production is shaped by these other social relationships.

For example, markets are social phenomena. They are locations where individuals come together to engage in exchange. It is not uncommon for individual producers to sell their creations in markets. Indeed, the first market economy was not capitalist, but probably one in which individual producers met to exchange their products. The presence of markets where individual producers sell their products acts as a critical motivating force in shaping the quality of those products, the timing of production, and the intensity of the productive efforts. Individual production developed a social patina of workmanship quality as a result of the interaction of market exchange (where public opinion about workmanship was expressed in exchange value) with production techniques.

Other social processes have also played an important role in shaping individual production in concrete societies. Religious institutions and beliefs create motivations in direct producers that influence their productive activity. Certain types of products may be taboo, or religious rules may determine the manner in which production may be carried out. Other products may come into being precisely because of religious beliefs, ceremonies and rituals, or taboos. Similarly, family relationships represent another social influence on individual production. The seamstress who creates clothing in her own relatively isolated workspace may do so to satisfy familial obligations.

Another set of social obligations that, under certain historical conditions, shaped individual production arises in feudal relationships. Feudal relationships exist when a direct producer is obligated to create surplus value, in the form of labor, goods, or money, that is transferred to a feudal lord. The feudal direct-producer, also called a serf, often engaged in individual production. In other words, the serf worked alone, albeit to satisfy a social relationship. This social relationship, based on feudal obligations, motivated the feudal direct-producer to engage in production of a certain type and for a certain duration of time. From these few examples it is clear that, under normal circumstances, individual production is socially determined and often dependent upon social relationships outside of the sphere of production.

Individual production may at times blend with certain types of social production, when more than one human being directly participate and cooperate in the production process. Individual production is typically oriented around a craft and craft skills must be taught. Thus, individual production meets social production in the form of apprenticeships, where new individual producers are gradually created in the teaching and learning process. This context for the socialization of individual production may also be the basis for the exploitation of the apprentice by the master artisan. In that context, FEUDALISM may enter the sphere of individual production, albeit temporarily.

Social production: collectivity. When production occurs directly and unambiguously in the social sphere (involving more than one human being), then it moves beyond individual to social production. The factory is an example of a site of social production, the slave plantation another. In these sites of social production, the workers are transformed from individual producers to a collectivity of producers. The production process becomes a new mechanism for the social connections between individuals. In the economics literature, this transformation of the production process from individual to social production has served as the basis for theories of economic evolution from primitive to more modern forms of economic organization.

Karl MARX considered social production a critical factor in the development of capitalism, an economic system defined by the use of wage labor contracts as the basis for employment of direct producers, and which displaced both the individual production of self-employed artisans and farmers and the social production of feudalism and slavery. He argued that the advanced form of social production, that capitalism brought into being, would create a new type of socialized direct producer. While individual production brought isolation and a sense of alienation from other producers, social production was viewed as bringing a sense of belonging and solidarity. This socialized direct producer would see his interests in the collectivity of workers. The day-to-day practice of social production would teach workers the value of cooperation and this would become the basis for SOCIALISM, a social system that would be grounded in the process of transferring control over the production process from external bosses to the workers themselves.

In Marx's conception of economic evolution, socialism would resolve the contradiction of social production under the command of private capitalists. This conception of social production as creating a new kind of human being, a fully socialized worker, presumes that social production requires a certain type of intellectual transformation in direct producers. In other words, social production is presumed as creating an economic agent with a social consciousness, an active awareness of the value of cooperation and mutual dependence. However, social production may also be conceived as dampening such intellectual awareness. Social production under capitalism has evolved into a system of specialization under a command-and-control form of management.

The command-and-control management structure has fostered a separation between work that requires creative planning and evaluation and manual labor, leaving masses of workers involved to spend their time in work that is not intellectually stimulating. References in literature and film to such modern workplaces as creating drone-like behavior indicates the strength of the view that social production under capitalism is producing a less conscious human being, rather than the revolutionary consciousness that Marx had in mind.

Political economists have even gone so far as to argue that the consciousness created in social production may, in certain societies, foster more alienation, rather than less, as workers develop distrust of other workers competing for the same jobs or promotions. This distrust can be manifested as racism in those societies where concepts of race are part of the public discourse, and play an important part in identity formation (the way workers come to see their own identity and the identity of other human beings). Nationalism or jingoism may also be a more important factor in shaping the consciousness of workers than notions of solidarity or commonality with other workers, particularly those from or in other nations. Thus, social production may bring workers together but it does not guarantee that this togetherness will occur in an environment conducive to the type of community that Marx conceived, where the free flow of communication between workers would be coupled with a high degree of awareness of the value of cooperative enterprise.

The reality is that social production does not occur in a vacuum, but is always part of a larger interplay of political, economic, and cultural influences, many of which are controlled from outside of the workplace.

No matter what the impact of social production upon the culture of direct producers, it is clear that the production techniques that have developed over time have favored such production over individual production. If social production is not a sufficient condition for the development of socialism, it has clearly been a catalyst for technological advance and vice versa. Social production has brought with it a wholesale reorganization of workspaces and of society at large.

Social production is almost always hierarchically organized and grounded in social contracts and/or coercion. The focus on workmanship that epitomized individual production has not been completely lost, but it is typically subsumed to efficiency and low-unit cost considerations. The focus on productivity and low cost has facilitated an enormous expansion in the quantity of products available on markets and the creation of a consumer culture that has, in and of itself, had important feedback effects on social production. The coincidence of social production with the growth of capitalist wage labor relationships and mass production technologies has completely transformed contemporary societies.

BIBLIOGRAPHY. Karl Marx, *Capital: A Critique of Political Economy* (Penguin USA, 1992); Karl Marx, *Grundrisse: Foundations of the Critique of Political Economy* (Penguin USA, 1993); David F. Noble, *Forces of Production: A Social History of Industrial Automation* (Oxford University Press, 1986).

SATYA J. GABRIEL
MOUNT HOLYOKE COLLEGE

production possibilities

WHEN AN ECONOMY'S FACTORS of production and technology are given, production possibilities are the set of the various alternative mixes of output that an economy can produce at a given point in time.

The boundary of the production possibilities set is called the production possibilities frontier, or simply the PPF. Each point in the PPF is defined as follows. Using available resources in the economy to produce some quantity of all possible goods (and services) except one, in the most efficient way, the maximum that can be produced of the last good with the unused resources defines one point in the PPF. A similar exercise can be carried out to determine all other remaining points in the PPF. The PPF describes, therefore, all combinations of goods and services that can be produced in an economy when all of its resources are fully employed, and efficiently so.

Note that, if it were to increase the production of any good, say to produce one more unit of good x, additional resources would have to be allocated for that purpose. However, if the economy were already functioning at its limit, with full employment—that is, if the economy were at its PPF—then resources previously used in alternative activities would have to be displaced and their production levels reduced. This would represent the opportunity COST of the additional unit of x. Hence, the PPF implicitly defines the opportunity cost of producing one more unit of each good in terms of what has to be given up in the production of other goods. It is noteworthy that the opportunity cost of a good need not be constant, and in general it is not. Typically, it will depend on how much of the good in question and of the other goods are being produced; that is, on the specific location at the PPF.

The points in the interior of the production possibilities set, by contrast, involve unemployed resources. It follows that, at those points, the production of any good can be increased without displacing resources used in other activities, and therefore without reducing their production. In fact, at least if all goods are divisible, the production of all goods can be jointly increased until the PPF is reached.

Naturally, the production possibilities set of any economy is not immutable over time. Typically, it changes continuously, although at a very slow pace. Since the available factors of production determine what can be produced in an economy at any point in time (i.e., the production possibilities set), whenever factors of production are added (subtracted) to the economy, its production possibilities expands (contracts). Thus, population growth, due to either demographical aspects or to migration, and investment, for example, are factors that would expand the production possibilities set of an economy.

In fact, the production possibilities set can expand even without changes in the available resources, provided that better technologies, that increase the productivity of the existing factors of production, become available.

Regardless of the cause, growth in the production possibilities set is typically "biased," in the sense that the potential increase in the production of each good may vary depending on the characteristics of the good. For instance, if the growth reflects mainly migration of unskilled labor, then the potential increase in the production of goods that depends heavily on unskilled labor, such as clothing, will be proportionately greater than the potential increase in the production of goods that require little unskilled labor, such as software.

Finally, it is worth noting that the production possibilities set describes only what can be produced in an economy, but it says nothing about what will, or should, be produced. In particular, an economy may operate either at its boundary, the PPF, or at its interior, leaving resources unemployed. That notwithstanding, it is a well known theoretical result that, under certain regularity conditions, a competitive economy without externalities or other market failures will indeed operate at the PPF, fully employing the available resources.

BIBLIOGRAPHY. Avinash Dixit and Victor Norman, *Theory of International Trade* (Cambridge University Press, 1980); Paul R. Krugman and Maurice Obstfeld, *International Economics: Theory and Policy* (Addison-Wesley, 2003); James R. Markusen, et al., *International Trade: Theory and Evidence* (McGraw-Hill, 1994).

EMANUEL ORNELAS, PH.D.
UNIVERSITY OF GEORGIA

productivity

A KEY ECONOMIC STATISTIC IS labor productivity. Productivity is a ratio that measures the output of an input or the output of a multiple of factors. Productivity changes reflect the net saving of inputs per unit of output, and thus the increases in productive efficiency.

LABOR productivity is usually the most important measure of productivity because it constitutes a large share of factor cost in value of most products. The Bureau of Labor Statistics publishes labor productivity data measured by output per hour, output per combined unit of labor and capital input, which is a multifactor productivity measure. For manufacturing industries, output per combined unit of capital, labor, energy, materials, and purchased service inputs are reported. However, aggregate productivity growth is a measure that misses most of the story. If the aggregate productivity growth is broken down to the firms' level one can learn about the rate of growth for continuing and new businesses. For example, the new firms entering the Auto Repair Industry accounted for more than total productivity growth between 1987 and 1992 at 2.7 percent, while exiting firms had a slight loss of 0.3 percent during the period.

Labor productivity growth is essential for achieving higher standards of living. Innovation advances productivity. Productivity growth in manufacturing has averaged 4.4 percent per year since 1993. Global competition has forced many manufacturing businesses to compete more effectively with foreign firms. Japanese automobile industry pioneered "lean" production technique, which compelled U.S. automakers to eliminate waste and improve productivity. Innovation in production technology in steel industry also has increased its productivity.

The upsurge of productivity growth after WORLD WAR II was the result of important policy measures adopted by economically advanced nations. The creation of the WORLD BANK and the INTERNATIONAL MONETARY FUND and of the United Nations encouraged economic relations that became instrumental in advancing productivity.

In addition, multinational firms diffused innovation and managerial and technical skills that helped to advance productivity in developing nations. International licensing of patents also helped diffuse technology. American higher-education trained an increasing number of students from the developing countries. Journals and professional associations diffused knowledge and narrowed the productivity gap between the United States and other industrialized nations.

As other nations approached the U.S. level of productivity per person, the rates and levels of productivity began to converge. The slowdown in productivity in the 1970s was widespread due to the oil shocks in that decade. The economic slow down dampened expenditures for research and development. Other factors such as age and gender mix of the labor force, government regulations to protect the environment and promote health and safety increased the businesses' costs and also exacerbated productivity decline. The decade of 1980s witnessed a reversal of this trend, particularly in the United States. The 1990s decade was marked by a rise in productivity growth. The table below contains a summary of the United States' productivity changes in output per hour for all persons for the business sector for 1960–2000.

*Productivity Changes in Output Per Hour
of All Persons for Business Sector for 1960–2000*

Decade	Business Sector	Nonfarm Business Sector
1960–1970	16.9	16.0
1970–1980	13.4	13.3
1980–1990	14.8	12.2
1990–2000	22.1	21.3

In term of percentages, the decade of 1960s witnessed substantial fluctuations. The highest growth rate for business sector was 4.6 percent in 1962 and the lowest in 1969 at 0.5 percent. For the 1970s the highest rate was 1971 with 4.4 percentage increase and the lowest was –1.7 in 1974. In the 1980s, the highest percentage change was –0.4 for 1982 and the highest was 3.6 in 1983. Productivity increase ranged from a high of 3.9 in 1992 and a low of 0.5 percent in 1993. Except for 1995, for most years of the second half of the decade the rate of increase was above 2 percent. The productivity rate increased to 3.4 percent in 2000.

Diffusion of technological innovations and formation of capital have revolutionized many industries. Support for research and development, reward to inventors, and incentives to promote production efficiency can enhance productivity in the future as well.

Real average labor compensation has increased over the long run at about the same rate as labor productivity. Generally, labor cost per unit of output rises slower than the price level when productivity rises. Productivity gain can thus prevent inflation. When productivity rises, price tends to fall.

Productivity varies across industries. The average annual percentage change for selected three-digit industries for 1987–99 ranged from a maximum gain of 10.2 percent to a minimum of –1.7. Productivity depends on various factors. These factors include the available supply of labor, land, capital and raw materials. Education and skills, the method of production organization and social and psychological and cultural factors also influence productivity.

Productivity also varies among different countries, regions, industries, and among workers. Technological factors and training usually play major roles in raising productivity. The evidence is consistent that job-training programs increase the earning of the disadvantaged adults, particularly those of economically disadvantaged women. Firm-based training becomes more relevant as firms experience rapid technological progress. Training in basic literacy and numeracy, in computer skills, or in teamwork would increase productivity. In the United States, companies invest roughly $60 billion a year on education, training, and upgrading skills. Considering the rapidly changing labor force, this is a modest amount.

Government training programs are primarily aimed at workers who lose their jobs and are disadvantaged. Some are designed for welfare recipients to go to work. These trainings usually include some remedial or vocational education. The Manpower Development Training Act (MPDT) was enacted in 1962 to retain technologically dislocated workers, but the Economic Opportunity Act of 1964 shifted its focus toward disadvantaged workers.

BIBLIOGRAPHY. William J. Baumol and Alan S. Bradford, *Microeconomic Principles and Policy* (Publisher TK, 1994); Economic Report of the President, 2000 & 2001, www.brittanica.com; New Ideas for Measuring Labor Productivity, Census Brief, U.S. Department of Commerce, Economics and Statistics Administration (November, 1998); U.S. Census Bureau, Statistical Abstract of the United States: 2001 U.S. Census, Public New Alert (January 29, 2003).

SIMIN MOZAYENI, PH.D.
STATE UNIVERSITY OF NEW YORK, NEW PALTZ

profit

IN SIMPLE TERMS, PROFIT REPRESENTS the residual return to a firm or entrepreneur, or the difference between the revenue generated by the sale of goods and services and the total costs of production. The total costs include the full opportunity costs of the factors used in production of the output plus the premium charged for the risk taking and the costs of using the owner's CAPITAL. Economists make a distinction between two types of profit.

Normal profit is the minimum amount necessary to induce a firm or entrepreneur to remain in business. Essentially, normal profit equals the opportunity costs of the entrepreneur, which in turn implies a zero level of economic or super-normal profit. Accordingly, super-normal profit or economic profit is any profit over and above normal profit. Basic economic theory contends that economic profit can be earned only in the short-run and originates from MONOPOLY power or innovation.

From the accounting perspective the gross profit is distinguished from net profit. The latter represents the residual after all costs have been deducted, i.e., money costs such as wages, salaries, rent, fuel, and raw materials, interest on loans and non-money expenses such as depreciation. If the unit of observation is a corporation then corporate tax needs to be subtracted from net profits to arrive to the accounting category of net profit after tax; while in the case of sole proprietorship the income tax needs to be deducted from net profit. Gross profit is net profit before depreciation and interest.

Economic profit and accounting profit are the same when all of the factors of production, i.e., land, labor, and capital are credited with their respective full opportunity cost. It is important to note that reported profits of publicly traded companies are not profits from the strictly economic point of view. The principal reason behind that fact is the difference between actual money outlays and full-imputed costs of factors of production.

Having defined profit as a residual sum, it is necessary to explain how a factor of production, namely the entrepreneur, can receive earnings above that which would keep her in a particular business. One way to proceed is to examine the leading theories of profit, which go back to the beginnings of economics as a science. It is useful to divide theories of profit by their appearance in economic theory and by their approach. We have, therefore, the classical, neoclassical, Marxian, Austrian, entrepreneurial or dynamic, and modern school of thought. There is overlap among the many theories and none is entirely exclusive of the others. The modern school is simply a synthesis with a number of distinct elements of former approaches.

Classical profit. The classical theory is best expressed by Adam SMITH, David RICARDO, Nassau SENIOR, and James Mill. For these writers, profit is essentially the reward for capital. Writing before Smith, however, were the PHYSIOCRATS who viewed profit as a surplus for the productive sector of the economy, agriculture. Smith and his followers perceived profit as a reward. Since land received rent, and labor wages, it followed that capital owners received profit. Landowners in classical theory still receive a residual, that which was left over after the reproducible factors of production had been paid. It is sometimes hard to distinguish profit from interest among these writers. It would take a century of work by economists to finally come to view the two as separate categories.

All classical views contain two running themes. The first is that profit, like other categories such as wages and rent, is a distributive share. The second is that profit rates tend toward zero because of competition and accumulation, and, in Mill's view, the onset of the stationary state when capital accumulation comes to halt.

Neoclassical profit. The neoclassical view inherits the central element of the classical view that capital receives profit as a reward. The big difference now, however, is that the prices of all factors of production, including land, are determined at the margin. The level of profit is now the opportunity cost of the owner and perhaps manager of the capital goods he contributes towards his firm. Any supernormal profits are eroded by competition among the capitalists. It becomes apparent in this approach that profit rates may differ among industries as opportunity costs differ.

Rents may now be earned by any factor of production and this leads to Alfred MARSHALL's catch-all term, quasi-rent, as it can be applied to any factor of production. Profit theory in this neoclassical form lies in limbo—it is neither wrong nor an adequate explanation of the essence of profit as business people themselves suppose it to be.

Marxian profit. The Marxian theory of profit relies on the exploitation of labor by the owners of the means of production, the capitalists. The capitalists are forever introducing new machines and technology in order to gain greater productivity and efficiency from the workers—exploitation—and enlarge the size of their profit. They engage in this activity because they are rivals attempting outdo one another in order in increase their profit or simply to stay competitive with another. Exploitation of workers is the byproduct of this race to secure profits by means of machines and technology.

Marx's theory was among the first to regard profit in a dynamic sense. His capitalists are competitive rivals in the true sense, and while profit enters through the backdoor of exploitation, the introduction of new technology and the disturbance of the reigning economic order are the true genesis of the origin of profit. Marx's influence on a later economist, Joseph SCHUMPETER, led to a dynamic view of the role of profit as something that arises out of change. The static classical view and its derivative, the neoclassical, would later be modified into the modern view.

Austrian School profit. The AUSTRIAN SCHOOL focused the economic problem on change and profit; profit as an outcome of change and a disturbance to equilibrium. It is best thought of as the disequilibrium approach. Included in this school is the American economist Frank KNIGHT, whose contribution to profit theory ranks among the most influential. The chief element in the Austrian approach is the, as Friedrich von HAYEK would put it, the problem of knowledge. The fact that knowledge is costly and, in its own right, a certain but peculiar factor of production means it must too receive a reward. That reward is profit. However, knowledge is quite unlike other factors of production and its peculiar nature meant that the essence of knowledge must itself be scrutinized.

Before examining the Austrian approach proper, it is important to examine in some detail Knight's theory. Knight begins his analysis by assuming perfect knowledge. In a world of perfect competition there is no existence of profit. Knight clearly outlines the logic of perfect competition and in so doing makes it necessary to examine life outside of this ideal world. Perfect competition in Knight's analysis is analogous to a world without time. The absence of time implies instantaneous change—a change that is required to adjust any disturbance. Without change everything is predictable. Time cannot be ignored therefore, and neither can change which brings along risk and uncertainty.

Knight then probes into the role of knowledge in economic life. He distinguishes between events that can be predicted with a known probability distribution and those that cannot. Those that can be predicted into certain classes with known probabilities are risks that one can be insured and thus do not present a problem with knowledge. Genuine uncertainty cannot fall into any classified scheme and cannot be accounted for in the decisions of the entrepreneur. Genuine uncertainty, however, is met or undertaken by the entrepreneur and if her instincts—it would be incorrect to call them expectations—are correct, positive profits result.

When dice are rolled, bets can be placed. The winner, however, would never call his earnings profit. In fact, since the probability distribution is known, when the game is played over and over again, there is no uncertainty—the law of large numbers. The problem with uncertainty arises because agents cannot make probability distributions as the events themselves cannot be classed, because they have not occurred enough times, or indeed because the events are themselves unknown. It is the entrepreneur who assumes this uncertainty by creating an organization, the firm, by which he is rewarded for this undertaking. It is an undetermined amount he receives because of the uncertainty of his endeavors. The entrepreneur places at risk his owned assets and organizes these means of production to undertake certain tasks. Organization is one of the primary consequences of his attempt to classify unknowns into knowledge and his reward is profit. The individuals who are ultimately responsible for bearing the uncertainty and risk of the organization are the true entrepreneurs in Knight's theory. A neglected economist, Richard Cantillon, who preceded Smith, elaborated a similar view that entrepreneurs receive profit for bearing risks. But his analysis included thieves as entrepreneurs and is therefore perhaps somewhat inadequate.

While Knight stressed profit as the reward for uncertainty-bearing, Schumpeter, took another tack using the Austrian underpinning of the problem of knowledge. In Schumpeter's scheme the entrepreneur is not a bearer of uncertainty, an organization builder to meet the problems of uncertainty, but rather one who actually creates new knowledge and is responsible for its fruition to market. As the new combinations, as he called innovations, were carried out, profit would arise as a reward. The entrepreneur receives profits because she innovates. She brings to market a new invention, a new method of production, a new product, and is compensated with profit. The financiers of such operations, who bear much of the uncertainty and risk involved are not the entrepreneurs and therefore do nor receive profit. They are paid interest.

Profit as interest. One of the stubborn complications in profit theory concerns the place of interest. Only when economists began to think of interest as the proper reward for capital, whether financial or physical, could a proper theory of profit be constructed. Profit must be a reward for a fourth factor of production. The question is: What is the fourth factor of production and what is its reward? Classical and neoclassical theories of profit are, in many senses, theories of interest.

These two methods of Knight and Schumpeter together with their reliance on time, change, and knowledge form the basis for the entrepreneurial approach. The entrepreneurial explanation of profit is the foundation of the modern theory. We can classify it into four categories according to the origin of profit: 1) uncertainty or risk bearing, 2) innovation, 3) organizational, and (4) arbitrage. Although all of these have change as primary cause of profit, the role of the entrepreneur is different in each. The entrepreneur is, however, a distinct fourth factor of production in the modern theory and his reward, profit, is almost always a residual.

But in the modern theory, it is almost just a matter of degree of entrepreneurial contribution to the output of the firm. For instance, if employees bear part of the risk and uncertainty somehow and perhaps receive bonuses for work well done, they are entrepreneurs. But are they full entrepreneurs although most of their compensation comes in the form of wages? Our view here takes the tack that the entrepreneur is an individual and receives as a reward, profit.

Views of profit. Profit as the reward for innovating is among the more widely accepted explanations for the existence of profit. Entrepreneurs who introduce new products, methods of production, new organizations, etc., are accordingly rewarded. The profit incentive plays a significant role in this process. Schumpeter's theory of economic development is the essence of the entrepreneur *cum* innovator. The entrepreneur, however, does not merely create, but also destroys, displacing less fit characteristics of the economic system with those more viable. The process of creative destruction, initiated and carried out by the entrepreneur is the driving force behind the progress of society. The entrepreneur disrupts a Walrasian equilibrium by changing the order of things. The disequilibrium state is the normal state and profits accrue to the entrepreneur.

The second most widely accepted view of profits is that of uncertainty. It is easy to see the connection between the innovation aspect and the uncertainty view. Both are concerned with change and the introduction of new knowledge. In many respects, these approaches represent different sides of the same coin. The uncertainty approach to profits, however, downplays the role of the entrepreneur in some sense. Uncertainty-bearing is in some respects less active than is innovating. Stockholders in the uncertainty version bear the uncertainty of the corporation but do little more than vote for a board that hires and fires managers. Yet, these stockholders do receive a profit as their reward for bearing uncertainty.

The other prevalent theory, that of arbitrage, sees profit as the compensation for using knowledge and taking risks by bringing distant, in space and time, markets into accordance. When a price discrepancy arises between markets, and it may be temporal in nature, entrepreneurs *cum* as arbitrageurs buy low and sell high and thus earn a profit.

The organizational view concentrates on the ability of an entrepreneur *cum* organizer or manager to shape a firm so that it can better make use of existing resources, including the resources necessary to create knowledge and innovations. The better fit an organization creates, the greater the compensation or profit of its organizer.

BIBLIOGRAPHY. B.S. Keirstead, *Capital, Interest, and Profits* (John Wiley, 1959); F. Knight, *Risk, Uncertainty, and Profit* (Houghton Mifflin, 1921); K. Marx, *Capital, A Critique of Political Economy* (Lawrence and Wisehart, 1969–72); J.S. Mill, *Principles of Political Economy* (Longmans Green, 1909); J.A. Schumpeter, *The Theory of Economic Development* (Harvard University Press, 1934); N. Senior, *An Outline of the Science of Political Economy* (Kelley Reprint, 1965); A. Smith, *The Wealth of Nations* (Modern Library, 1937).

ZELJAN SCHUSTER, PH.D.
UNIVERSITY OF NEW HAVEN

profit maximization

THE MAIN OBJECTIVE OF MOST FIRMS operating within capitalist economic systems is profit maximization. It refers to the situation in which firms choose output levels that provide them with the greatest level of profits possible, where profits are defined as the difference between total revenues and total costs.

Profits are characterized in capitalist systems as the factor payment associated with entrepreneurship, an important part of the production process that includes such non-tangible resources as ideas and the willingness to undertake risk. Profit maximization is the incentive to which most firms respond, and as such is a principal component of capitalism. It is important to note that not all firms choose profit maximization as their main goal. Nonprofit organizations, for example, seek to maximize social welfare by providing as many goods and services to as many people as possible with no emphasis on building up profits.

As the difference between total revenues and total costs, total profit represents that portion of cash inflows that is leftover after all of a firm's expenses have been paid. In its simplest form then, total profit refers to the total amount of cash that a firm's owners will have in their pockets with which they may do whatever they choose. Maximizing profits means more dollars in the hands of business owners and consequently more dollars for new houses, clothes, vacations, etc. That is precisely why profit maximization is the main objective of most firms.

In the case of publicly owned corporations, profit maximization means more dollars that either may be paid out in the form of dividends or plowed back into the company as retained earnings. In either case, shareholder wealth increases. An increase in dividends raises shareholder wealth by increasing cash inflows received by stockholders. Retained earnings indicate that a corporation is using some of its profits to improve the company. Consequently, profits are expected to rise in the future, current stock prices rise and shareholder wealth increases.

Maximizing profits can be achieved in one of two general ways. Firms can maximize profits by increasing total revenues or decreasing total costs. A firm's total revenues will be determined by the selling price of its product and the total amount of output the firm sells.

For example, a firm that sells 100 units of output at $20 per unit will collect total revenues of $2,000. Should the price rise above $20 per unit and/or the amount of output exceed 100 units of output, this firm's total revenues would rise and, assuming fixed or sticky costs, total profits would rise as well. Firms can also maximize profits by decreasing total costs. Total costs can be expected to drop as a result of a decrease in a firm's explicit costs of production (e.g., a drop in wages or a drop in the price of a key input in a firm's production process) or alternatively as a result of an increase in factor productivity.

An increase in factor productivity will boost the level of output a firm can expect to receive from a particular resource and consequently will push down unit costs until the price of the resource rises. Consider, for example, an employee working for $10 per hour who originally produced 5 units of output per hour. Labor costs in this case would be $2/unit. Should the same employee produce 10 units of output one week later, the firm's labor costs would fall to $1/unit.

Profit maximization plays two extremely important roles in capitalist economies. First, it determines which goods and services are produced, and second, profit maximization heavily influences the flow of dollars in financial systems.

Profit maximization is the driving force behind most firms' production decisions. Firms choose to produce more of a particular product when the profit associated with that product rises and choose to produce less of a particular product when the profit associated with that product falls. The more profitable a product, the more resources will be devoted toward its production and vice versa. Because changes in total revenues will change when price or quantity change, consumers can convince firms to produce more or less of a particular product by influencing profits though price. In this respect, profits can be thought of as a principal method of communication between consumers and producers.

By initiating changes in demand, consumers can influence prices and profits, thus encouraging firms to alter their levels of output in a manner that is consistent with consumer desires. A change in total revenue brought about by a change in consumer demand is not the only factor that may determine how profitable or unprofitable a product is, however. The relative profitability of a particular product will also be influenced by changes in the costs of production. Rising costs mean lower profits. Hence, firms typically respond to rising costs by reducing the number of resources purchased consequently reducing production levels as well. Layoffs are a rational response of a profit-maximizing firm facing higher wages particularly when total revenues have been depressed by a drop in demand. How resources are allocated and re-allocated in a market economy is determined largely by changes in profit margins precisely because most firms choose to pursue profit maximization as their primary goal.

In countries like the United States and others that possess highly developed financial systems, profit maximization provides not only the mechanism by which most production decisions are made but also has a significant impact on firms' abilities to raise financial capital. Stock prices reflect the present, discounted value of firms' expected profits and hence determine how easy or difficult it will be for a company to raise cash by issuing securities. A firm that is expected to be extremely profitable in the future can expect the demand for its securities to be high and consequently can expect to raise large sums of money by issuing marketable securities. Higher profits mean more financial capital for firms. Economic growth, employment, and living standards are substantially improved as high levels of CAPITAL ACCUMULATION are made possible.

BIBLIOGRAPHY. William J. Baumol and Alan S. Blinder, *Economics: Principles and Policy* (South-Western, 2002); Marilyn K. Gowing, James Campbell Quick and John D. Kraft, eds., *The New Organizational Reality: Downsizing, Restructuring, and Revitalization* (American Psychological Association, 1997); Leon Levy and Eugene Linden, *The Mind of Wall Street* (PublicAffairs, 2002); Arthur O'Sullivan and Steven M. Sheffrin, *Microeconomics: Principles and Tools* (Prentice Hall, 2003); Patrick Primeaux and John A. Stieber, *Profit Maximization: The Ethical Mandate of Business* (Austin & Winfield, 1995).

KRISTIN KUCSMA, PH.D.
SETON HALL UNIVERSITY

property

See OWNERSHIP.

Protestantism

THE PHRASE "Protestant work ethic" is often quoted ruefully or sarcastically to explain the behavior of the increasing number of people who simply can't seem to stop working, or alternately in reference to the seemingly restless activities of morally upright immigrant forbears. The original uses of the expression, however, were not intended to suggest either that all Protestants work hard or even that only Protestants work hard; the phrase stems from the pen of Max Weber, one of the most influential sociologists of the 20th century, and his now-classic essay of 1904–05, "The Protestant Ethic and the 'Spirit' of Capitalism."

Weber can be said to understand capitalism as a form of profit-oriented enterprise, in which gain is sought through trade, by legal and honest means only, in which the pursuit of business is a career that consists of an orientation to the rational interest of the business at hand, and the search to maximize profit to the greatest extent possible. In his book, Weber argued that the emergence of Protestantism in the 16th century and the theology of Martin Luther and John Calvin had prepared the way for a full-fledged work ethic associated with the Puritans in the 17th century.

In other words, Protestantism did not directly make individuals harder workers; instead, it created the basis for a cultural view, termed "inner-worldly asceticism," that justified work as a moral activity and an end in itself. This view contrasted to pre-modern attitudes toward work (associated with Catholicism) that viewed it as a curse or a necessary evil to be completed in service of the primary goals of human life. Weber uses the example of the uneducated worker facing the transition from agricultural labor to piece work: he must change his orientation from a mentality in which he works only until he has attained sufficient product to meet his needs, to an orientation in which he seeks to fulfill his greatest potential productive capacity.

Capitalism requires not only this new orientation, but also its necessary prerequisites: punctuality, diligence, and willingness to delay gratification. Martin Luther laid the way for this transition by legitimizing secular callings through his doctrine of vocation; Calvin added to it by promulgating the doctrine of double predestination, according to which not all men were saved, but humans could not ascertain who had been justified and who had not. This problem reached its peak in 17th century Puritanism, that Weber argued had equated industry with morality. It made this connection by provoking the believer with a crisis of proof about his prospects for salvation, to which industry and prosperity were proposed as a solution with unintended negative consequences. Ultimately, the only way for Calvinism to surround the doubts created by religious dogma was to seek a perception of the presence of God in the world through the ceaseless pursuit of worldly activity. The final result of the increasing predominance of this Protestant asceticism was a full-fledged pursuit of capitalist ends, an orientation that Weber argued was the worst outcome of the modern world, a so-called "iron cage" of rational control as the predominant mode of thinking, that no longer had need of a religious justification, whose humanistic qualities merely stood in its way.

Thus, his description of the relationship between Protestantism and capitalism is frequently understood as one of the earliest trenchant critiques of emerging modernity. Ironically, the Protestant reformers are read by Weber as having unleashed a process of development that would increasingly secularize the world, for by the 18th century, when Benjamin Franklin was writing, the "Protestant" world-view had become so dominant that it no longer needed its religious underpinnings; everyone, Catholics, Protestants, and even non-Christians, had embraced the Protestant "ethic." Weber's thought stresses a view of capitalism in which concrete administrative and economic developments are subordinated in importance to the philosophical predispositions that permitted them.

A rational orientation toward wage labor is thus more significant on Weber's view than the legal ability of individuals to pursue wage labor won out of the decline of seigneurialism after the end of the 12th century. Weber did not create this view independently; in it, he wove prior work from Georg Jellinek (*The Declaration of the Rights of Man and Citizen*, 1895), Werner Sombart (*The Genesis of Capitalism*, 1901, and Ernst Troeltsch that attempted to relate ascetic Protestantism with modernity and Protestantism in particular with German history. But he was its most intense expositor and defender, and consequently his work has been seminal in sociology of religion, historical theology, and religion.

Criticisms of Weber's ideas emerged as soon as they were published, and he revised and reprinted the essay several times in hope of clarifying fundamental issues. The most troublesome aspects of Weber's ideas relate to his methodology; he relied on a contemporary form of sociology in which, rather than using specific actual examples, he pasted together so-called "ideal types" as proof for his arguments. The consequence of this strategy is that, while the ideas of Protestantism are drawn from theological tracts, no evidence is cited to prove that most individuals of the age actually held these ideas or were motivated by the reasons Weber suggested.

More generally, Weber's work can be read as a response to Karl MARX's conviction that historical development resulted from the motion of cultural ideas in response to economic changes. Weber was trying to suggest in this work that ideas could be just as significant in spurring historical development. Historians have charged that the thesis does not square effectively with reality. Capitalism preceded Protestantism, particularly in Italy, a country that was only marginally tempted by any interest in Protestant theology, where merchant bankers created the financial structures and trade networks fundamental to capitalist development. It developed in parts of the world where Protestantism, and for that matter Christianity, were either unknown or foreign minority religions. Concrete examples of Protestant countries that were not early capitalist successes can be easily cited.

Experts in Calvinist theology have objected that 17th century Calvinism experienced no crisis of proof. They point out that while pastoral literature of the period recommends asceticism in the earthly calling, it also condemns the pursuit of wealth as a pursuit of Satan. Moreover, Calvinism was an international movement; Weber's treatment of it as a monolithic intellectual heritage ignores differences in ideas in France, England, Scotland, Holland and North America. It can also be argued that Weber confused the "works" that Protestant theologians treated (that is to say, the pursuit of good works or meritorious activity) with the worldly activity (industry, diligence, etc.) fundamental to Calvinism; it is precisely the disparagement of good works that separates Protestants from Catholics in the 16th and 17th centuries. Weber also neglects the role and activities of Jews as both rationally oriented in their religion and as mediators and facilitators of capitalist activity. As an alternative to a complete refutation of the accuracy of the thesis, it has also been argued that Weber was correct in his assumption about the relationship of Protestantism to capitalism, but for the wrong reasons. He should have argued that the role of Puritan idealism was rather to push the purification of church government in England, one of the conflicts that precipitated the English Civil War, a conflict seen by some commentators as establishing the fundamental political preconditions for capitalism there.

The multi-causal orientation of Weber's argumentation and the employment of ideal types make it difficult for critics to fully refute Weber's argument despite occasionally contradictory evidence; three generations of sociologists and scholars have attempted unsuccessfully to put the thesis to rest. Weber's ideas were influential in the work of the American sociologists Talcott Parsons and Seymour Martin Lipset. They provide a fundamental orientation for students in the field of Reformation history, and they have won that most affirming of audiences insofar as "Protestant work ethic" is an idea with which almost everyone is familiar.

BIBLIOGRAPHY. Robert W. Green, ed., *Protestantism, Capitalism and Social Science: The Weber Thesis Controversy* (D.C. Heath, 1973); Hartmut Lehmann and Günther Roth, eds., *Weber's Protestant Ethic: Origins, Evidence, Contexts* (Cambridge University Press, 1993); Michael H. Lessnoff, *The Spirit of Capitalism and the Protestant Ethic: An Enquiry into the Weber Thesis* (Edward Elgar, 1994); Gordon Marshall, *In Search of the Spirit of Capitalism: An Essay on Max Weber's Protestant Ethic Thesis* (Hutchinson, 1982); Gianfranco Poggi, *Calvinism and the Capitalist Spirit: Max Weber's "Protestant Ethic"* (Macmillan, 1983); Max Weber, *The Protestant Ethic and the "Spirit" of Capitalism and Other Writings*, Peter Baehr, et al., eds. (Penguin Books, 2002).

SUSAN R. BOETTCHER, PH.D.
UNIVERSITY OF TEXAS, AUSTIN

public

OFTEN COMBINED WITH other words to form such terms as public education, the public sector, public finance, public goods, public policy, and public choice theory, this word generally refers in some way to government (in the American usage). Public finance is the branch of economics concerned with the analysis of government spending and taxing policies. The interplay between free markets and government, or the public sector, has been a significant focus of economic inquiry for centuries, especially since Adam SMITH's famous publication in 1776.

In *The Wealth of Nations*, Smith attempted to convince his readers that adherence to mercantilist principles promoted poor policies. He argued successfully that the wealth of a nation should be judged by the living standards of its people, not the amount of gold accumulated in the national vault, and that mercantilist policies, designed primarily to promote a favorable balance of trade for the nation, did not necessarily promote the well-being of the people of the nation. Proceeding on the assumption that the goal of any policy is to raise the wealth of the nation, Smith developed the famous invisible hand idea, convincing many that given the right conditions, each person's pursuit of their own self-interest would lead to an outcome that was in the best interest of the entire society.

He argued that the result of freedom is not chaos, but harmony, and that in many cases the best public policy is one of LAISSEZ-FAIRE, a French term coined by the Physiocrat Dr. Francois QUESNAY, meaning that government should let things be. Smith envisioned a limited role for government to protect "the society from the violence and invasion of other independent societies" and to protect "as far as possible every member of the society from the injustice or oppression of every other member of it."

Thus, government should guard national security and provide legal protections to the members of society, by passing and enforcing criminal laws, protecting property rights, and enforcing contracts, but government should then step back and allow free markets to determine what to produce, how to produce, and for whom.

Modern views generally allow for a broader range of government functions.

In particular, there are externalities, both negative and positive, that can be corrected by government action to promote a more efficient allocation of resources. Additionally, a modern list of government functions might include the provision of public GOODS, promotion of COMPETITION through ANTITRUST legislation or regulation of business, pursuit of macroeconomic goals, and some intervention intended to make the distribution of income more equitable.

The traditional theory of externalities leads to the conclusion that free-market equilibrium output is inefficiently high in the case of negative externalities, but the famous Coase Theorem questions the implication that government interference is necessary in each case to correct the problem. In the traditional view, some activities lead to costs that spill over to others. For example, the chemical dioxin is released into the environment by paper mills and may have adverse health effects. The market mechanism provides incentives for entrepreneurs to produce paper, but the market mechanism does not ensure the socially optimal level of production if the social costs associated with producing a product exceed the private costs, that sellers take into account because of an environmental cost that is spilling over to others. According to Coase, the problem is an inadequate definition of property rights. The Coase Theorem states that as long as transaction costs are not prohibitive, private agreements will generate efficient outcomes when property rights are clearly defined.

Economists continue to debate government's proper role in environmental policy. Some believe that government should correct negative externalities by regulating or taxing the activity causing the pollution in order to reduce production to the socially efficient level, while others favor having government assign property rights and then letting free markets determine an optimal outcome. Either way, most agree that markets fail in some way when it comes to environmental protection, so some type of action by government is needed.

The theory of externalities can also be applied to situations in which benefits spill over to others. This theory is used to justify government involvement in areas such as education, public transportation, public health, police and fire protection, and supporting the arts. In theory, we could rely completely on free markets to provide, for example, fire protection. In free market equilibrium, consumers could purchase private fire protection until the marginal private benefits equal the marginal costs. This free market equilibrium would be inefficiently low, however, if the social benefits exceed the private benefits. In this example, external benefits accrue to neighbors who enjoy some protection from the spread of fire by virtue of another family's purchase of private protection. These external benefits are part of the social benefits but are not reflected in the determination of free market equilibrium. Thus, government can potentially improve efficiency by finding a way to increase fire protection to the socially optimal level. A similar argument can be applied to other activities that generate external benefits. In the extreme case, a good can generate social or external benefits that are so substantial relative to the private benefits, that it is hard to imagine the market mechanism providing the good in any quantity. This extreme case refers to what are called public goods.

Public goods. A pure public good is defined as one that is non-excludable and non-rival. A good is non-excludable if it is either impossible or too expensive to prevent non-payers from enjoying the benefits of the good once it has been provided. A good is non-rival if one person's enjoyment of the good does not interfere with another person's enjoyment of the good. A classic example of a public good is a lighthouse; once the lighthouse has been built and provided with the equipment and energy needed to produce light, it would be virtually impossible to prevent one ship from enjoying some benefit from the light as it sails close to the lighthouse. Likewise, the fact that one ship has made use of the lighthouse's light does not preclude other ships from doing the same.

National defense is another example of a public good. This theory leads to the conclusion that the market mechanism will be unable to provide public goods since the market mechanism relies on an entrepreneur's expectation of profit to motivate the entrepreneur to provide the good or service in question. With a public good, it is difficult to imagine how one might profitably sell a good that people can enjoy for free, since by their nature public goods are non-excludable. This issue, often referred to as the free-rider problem, prevents reliance on free markets and often necessitates government involvement. Though, in some cases, it is possible to rely on voluntary support, such as for public television, in most cases the only way a public good can be provided is through taxpayer support.

Smith's invisible hand guarantees that resources will be allocated efficiently if the market mechanism is permitted to operate unimpeded, provided markets are competitive and assuming no market failures. In 1892, Congress enacted the Sherman Antitrust Act, recognizing even then that firms do not always operate under perfectly competitive conditions and that the emergence of MONOPOLY power can interfere with the ability of free markets to promote an efficient outcome. Microeconomic analysis demonstrates that the efficient outcome, where marginal benefit equals marginal cost, is achieved under perfectly competitive conditions, but that the equilibrium output under monopoly conditions occurs where marginal benefit exceeds marginal cost and is therefore inefficiently low.

Public policy. Thus, public policy has outlawed the formation of monopoly, except in cases where monopoly power is legally sanctioned, as with patent protection for example. The government has maintained a commitment to fostering competitive markets by carefully scrutinizing proposed mergers that would lessen competition and even forcing firms with too much market power to break up. Government has also attempted to regulate pricing in some instances, particularly where a natural monopoly has been identified. A natural monopolist can effectively service a market at lower cost than could many smaller, competing firms, meaning that a monopolized industry may actually be more efficient than a competitive industry. This phenomenon is generally the result of economies of scale. In some cases, industries that were formerly regarded as natural monopolies and subject to price regulation intended to prevent monopoly abuse have been deregulated, either because technology has altered the situation or because price regulation has not worked satisfactorily. It is possible that the threat of government regulation encourages firms in some industries to keep prices moderate, and there is little question that government keeps a watchful eye on markets to ensure that they work to the benefit of consumers. In the modern era, government is expected to act as a watchdog to make sure individual markets are operating as they should, and also to monitor the entire economy's performance to ensure that macroeconomic goals are achieved.

In the 1930s, a revolution in macroeconomic thinking was brought about by John Maynard KEYNES. The classical school of thought, begun by Smith and continued by such 19th-century scholars as David RICARDO and John Stuart MILL, concluded that the economy is self-regulating and that very little action by government was needed to achieve the macroeconomic goals of full employment, low inflation, and economic growth. The Great DEPRESSION provided a compelling argument that government should play a more active role in managing the economy, and Keynesian thinking soon began to dominate. According to Keynesian theory, short-run fluctuations in output, employment, and prices are the result of changes in aggregate demand.

Specifically, when aggregate demand is weak, output is low and unemployment is high, and government policy can be used to restore the economy to full employment by stimulating aggregate demand with more government spending or lower taxes. Keynes saw the volatility of investment as the main cause of short-term business fluctuations, and showed that relatively small changes in spending can be multiplied into significant changes in aggregate demand because one person's spending is another person's income. That is, if one person lowers his spending, this causes another person's income to fall, which then results in the second person spending less, and the effect continues through the economy and can result in a RECESSION or depression. Keynes convinced many that government has a responsibility to monitor the economy's performance and enact policies to improve the economy when problems develop. He believed that effective policy could stabilize short-term business activity, resulting in an economy that would operate near full employment with stable prices. The Keynesian legacy has greatly enhanced our expectations, causing us to assign responsibility for the economy's overall performance to policymakers.

Policies designed to make the distribution of income more equitable are probably among the most controversial of public policies. Welfare-reform legislation, passed in 1996, was in large part a response to our dissatisfaction with the way government had been pursuing income redistribution since the War on Poverty of the 1960s. Past policies were blamed for creating a welfare trap, which ensnared victims in an endless cycle of dependence from one generation to the next. Presently, government redistributes income to those in poverty within strict guidelines designed to move people from welfare to work with greater emphasis on personal responsibility. The distribution of income that would result from unfettered markets is believed by many to be too unequal and too harsh to those in poverty, but we also recognize that simply taking from the rich to give to the poor may not be the best way to improve the lives of the poor in the long run.

Public sector. There is no question that the size and scope of the public sector has increased dramatically in the United States. After adjusting for inflation, expenditure by the public sector is about 14 times as large today as it was before the Great Depression, government spending per person is almost seven times as high now, and government spending is more than twice as large as a percentage of GROSS DOMESTIC PRODUCT (GDP). Much of the increase in government spending went toward health, income support, and education, due primarily to programs that were implemented in the aftermath of the Great Depression, notably Social Security and Medicare.

Public Choice theory, which focuses on the incentives of politicians, has been very critical of the growth in government. Public choice economists argue that when government identifies a market failure and seeks to develop a public policy to deal with the market failure, it is not motivated to achieve its goal at the lowest possible cost, but to develop a policy that is favored by voters. In an era when government spending reaches into the trillions and government debt into the billions, public policy decisions are no longer the concern of a handful of economists, but of millions of voters. Most of us have very high expectations of what government can accomplish, but we expect politicians to justify the dollars used to accomplish public policy goals.

BIBLIOGRAPHY. Adam Smith, *The Wealth of Nations* (1776, Prometheus Books, 1991); John Maynard Keynes, *The General Theory of Employment, Interest, and Money* (1936, Prometheus Books, 1997); Ronald Coase, "The Problem of Social Cost," *Journal of Law and Economics* (1960); Robert L. Heilbroner, *The Worldly Philosophers: The Lives, Times, and Ideas of the Great Economic Thinkers* (Simon & Schuster, 1992); Harry Landreth and David C. Colander, *History of Economic Thought* (Houghton Mifflin, 1994); Herbert Stein and Murray Foss, *The New Illustrated Guide to the American Economy* (AEI Press,1995); Harvey S. Rosen, *Public Finance* (McGraw-Hill, 2000).

SUSAN DADRES
SOUTHERN METHODIST UNIVERSITY

public goods

IF COMMODITIES USED BY one person do not preclude use by other persons (non-rivalry in consumption), then those commodities are public goods. A second characteristic associated with public goods is that they are non-excludable, meaning that it is not possible to prevent individuals from using the good. A good that is both non-rivalrous and non-excludable is called a pure public good.

Classic examples of pure public goods include good air quality, national defense, or roads: The benefits of these goods can be enjoyed by anyone without lessening the enjoyment by others. At the same time, it is difficult to impossible to exclude someone from using these goods if they are there. Pure private goods, on the other hand, are both rivalrous (depletable) and excludable: A can of soft drink consumed by one person cannot be consumed by another person; furthermore one must pay for the beverage in order to consume it.

In between these two extremes, there are several intermediate cases exhibiting some but not all aspects of public goods. Some goods are non-excludable but still rivalrous, like a free parking spot: Everyone can use it, as long as it is not already occupied. Others are non-rivalrous but still excludable (club goods, below). Finally, the principle of non-rivalry may apply within certain limits only: A highway is a public good unless it is close to being congested, at which point additional users will begin to have a negative impact on the travel time of others.

The free-rider problem. Virtually all economies have a need for goods that are inherently public in nature, such as transportation and communication networks, recreational parks, etc. The availability of these commodities creates economic value, but the extent to which these goods can be provided by private firms is limited. This is due to an extreme form of positive externality, as the provision of a public good by one individual benefits a large number of other people as well. The resulting lack of incentives to produce public goods is known as the free-rider problem, which is best illustrated by the following story.

Consider a group of college students sharing a house. Cleanliness of the house is desirable for the students, but it is also a public good: If one person cleans the house, all roommates can enjoy the benefits. Thus, if they agree to share cleaning chores, each student can easily free-ride on the cleaning performed by her roommates. As a result, their prior agreement to share household responsibilities has no force, and the house is left dirty although everyone would prefer for it to be clean.

In extreme cases, when desirable public goods are not produced at all, we speak of market failure. It becomes a very serious matter when public goods such as national security are concerned. Free-riding and under-provision can be overcome in several different ways, however.

Exclusion and club goods. Many public goods are excludable, meaning that mechanisms exist to prevent use by non-paying consumers. Exclusion makes usage rights of public goods marketable, just as in the private goods case. For example, while a country club's private golf course is a public good (unless it is overcrowded), access is typically restricted to paying members. Once a public good is made

excludable, it is fittingly termed a club good.

An important application of the use of club goods is information—perhaps the most public good of all, as it can be consumed infinitely often without depleting it. Exclusion is necessary to create markets for information. To make people pay for satellite television, for example, operators usually encrypt the signal and provide the necessary keys to subscribers only (technological exclusion). The patent system and copyright laws, on the other hand, are legal institutions designed to prevent individuals from the unauthorized use of knowledge developed by others (albeit only imperfectly).

Government provision. If exclusion is impossible or prohibitively expensive, public goods can be provided by governments and financed through taxation. Large national projects, such as a country's defense apparatus, are often entirely undertaken by the government. For most types of public goods, however, government provision supplements private production. Philanthropic, religious, and other charitable organizations, for example, provide services that often have characteristics of public goods, while depending mostly on private donations. At the same time, these institutions coexist with state-run social programs providing similar goods. A problematic feature of this coexistence is that increased government provision can be accompanied by a decrease in their private production, an effect called crowding out.

To create incentives for the private provision of public goods, governments can subsidize providers, or levy taxes on non-providers. Taxes and subsidies that are being used to internalize public costs and benefits were first proposed by A.C. Pigou (1932), and are called Pigou Taxes accordingly. They are often applied today to promote the use of new environment-friendly technologies that are beneficial to the public, but also costlier than conventional technologies. For instance, when unleaded fuel was first introduced, it was subject to fewer taxes than conventional (i.e., lead-containing) gasoline.

BIBLIOGRAPHY. J. Andreoni, "The Economics of Philantropy," N.J. Smelser and P.B. Baltes, eds., *International Encyclopedia of the Social and Behavioral Sciences* (Elsevier, 2001); B. Lindahl, "Just Taxation: A Positive Solution," R. A. Musgrave and A. T. Peacock, eds., *Classics in the Theory of Public Finance* (Macmillan, 1919); A.C. Pigou, *The Economics of Welfare* (Macmillan, 1932); B. Salanié, *Microeconomics of Market Failures* (MIT Press, 2000).

TILMAN KLUMPP, PH.D.
INDIANA UNIVERSITY, BLOOMINGTON

Q

Quesnay, Francois (1694–1774)

THE ECONOMIC SYSTEM IN FRANCE that eventually became known as the PHYSIOCRATS school was founded and led by Francois Quesnay. The term *physiocracy*, from the French word *physiocrate* meaning "the rule of nature," was not applied to the school until 1776, after Quesnay's death.

This marked the first time in the history of the discipline of economics that a school of thought emerged with a recognized leader, and a group of followers espousing the ideas of the leader. Quesnay appears to have had little formal education, but acquired a knowledge of medicine and began practicing by the time he was 24 years old. Eventually, in 1744, he obtained a degree in medicine.

In 1749, he was appointed as personal physician to Madame de Pompadour, the intelligent and powerful mistress of Louis XV. He resided in the palace at Versailles and became one of the court physicians for the sovereign himself. In 1750, Quesnay met Vincent de Gournay, who is credited with coining the now-famous phrase LAISSEZ FAIRE, and he became more interested in economics than medicine. Quesnay published his first writing on economics in 1756 and 1757, two articles for the *Encyclopedie* in which he advanced the idea that agriculture had a unique capacity to produce a surplus, which he called the *produit net*.

His famous *Tableau économique*, which may well be the most celebrated single page in economics, was originally constructed for the king in 1758. The *Tableau* was a vivid graphic depiction of the interdependence of three interacting sectors of an economy. Most of the later editions of the *Tableau* also emphasized the advantages of compliance with Quesnay's economic views. By the middle of the 1760s, Quesnay had acquired a number of disciples who served to popularize and clarify his views. The intellectual influence of Quesnay and the Physiocrats was quite strong during the decade of the 1760s, but underwent a rapid decline after 1770.

Quesnay's own interests drifted from economics to mathematics, and when Louis XVI ascended to the throne, Quesnay left the palace as a wealthy man, due largely to the patronage of Madame de Pompadour. After being hailed by Adam SMITH, the *Tableau* fell into oblivion and had to be rediscovered by Karl MARX in the middle of the 19th century.

Smith suggested that physiocracy should be understood as a reaction to the extreme mercantilist policies of Jean-Baptiste COLBERT during the reign of Louis XIV. By the early part of the 18th century, agriculture in FRANCE had suffered to such a degree under Colbertism that a backlash against these policies seemed inevitable. The economic setbacks, combined with significant military defeats that deprived France of Canada and Oriental possessions, left the nation a second-level national power in Europe. The preferential treatment given the merchant class, the waste of the nation's resources on the court's extravagances, and the unsuccessful wars all connected Colbertism with corruption and decline in the French mind.

By the 1740s, several articles had been published that contrasted France's economic experience unfavorably with that of England. Consequently by the 1750s, the climate of opinion in France was favorable to the principles put forward by Quesnay, particularly the emphasis on agricultural and tax reform, and the clamor for economic freedom and competition.

The economic order envisioned by Quesnay was a self-regulating one that thrived on the absence of outside restriction. His key postulate was that only the productive class cultivating the land produced a surplus. The sterile or artisan class merely recovered its costs; the proprietary class or landowners served primarily public purposes. Expansion of the economy, therefore, depended on the expansion of the expenditure of the productive class and the consequent expansion of the surplus. To Quesnay, the composition of expenditure was as important to the economy as its growth and stability.

Quesnay and his followers began the tradition of regarding capital as advances for the productive process, and put emphasis on the role of investment in agriculture. He emulated the success of the revolutionary changes that had taken place in the English agricultural system, but the combination of small holdings, traditional methods, and the remnants of feudal obligation made it difficult for France to adopt such improvements. Consequently, Quesnay became an advocate of *grande* agriculture that involved large-scale operations and technologically advanced methods, and that required heavy capital investment.

Tax reform was also part of the physiocratic platform. By highlighting that only the landowners, and specifically the agricultural surplus, could ultimately bear the burden of taxation, Quesnay and his followers drew attention to the principles of tax incidence and shifting. They advocated direct, rather than indirect taxation—in particular, a single tax on land—that would minimize the cost of collection. They maintained the position that a tax on industry merely taxed land in an indirect and therefore uneconomical way. However, the landowners resisted this argument, and ensuing discussions about the policy revealed some of the defects in the *Tableau*.

The issue ultimately became one of the major factors in the decline of the physiocratic influence because Quesnay argued that competition would reduce the value of the product of the sterile class to its costs of production, but could not show why competition in agriculture would not also reduce its surplus to zero. It seems likely that the concept of the *bon prix* or "good price" for agricultural products was essential to maintaining the surplus product in agriculture, but it was not clear how it was to be sustained. Interpreting it as a legal minimum price would be a clear departure from the laissez-faire environment that they supported.

Quesnay did not advocate an attack on the landed interest but it was possible to interpret his ideas that way. Therefore, the long-term practical effect of his teaching and writing was to help remove remaining obstacles for the development of capitalistic industry in France.

BIBLIOGRAPHY. Mark Blaug, *Economic Theory in Retrospect* (Cambridge University Press, 1978); Stanley L. Brue, *The Evolution of Economic Thought* (South-Western, 1994); Philip C. Newman, *Development of Economic Thought* (Princeton University Press, 1952); Ingrid H. Rima, *Development of Economic Analysis* (McGraw-Hill, 2001); Eric Roll, *A History of Economic Thought* (Faber & Faber, 1973).

ELEANOR T. VON ENDE, PH.D.
TEXAS TECH UNIVERSITY

quota

A QUOTA IS ANY QUANTITATIVE restriction, whether a minimum or maximum, applied to economic, political, or administrative procedures. Political and administrative quotas are generally used to guarantee the representation of specific groups in educational or decision-making bodies. For example, some legislatures require that a minimum number of seats be reserved for women in order to ensure their inclusion in party politics.

Economic quotas aim to alter the outcome that would result under market forces. By restricting the quantity of a good or service produced or traded, an economic quota distorts the price of the good or attempts to avoid the price mechanism of allocation altogether. For example, the ORGANIZATION OF PETROLEUM EXPORTING COUNTRIES (OPEC) establishes quotas for each of the member nations in order to limit the amount of oil available in international markets. OPEC quotas restrict oil output in order to generate or maintain higher oil prices.

Quotas are also used in centrally planned economies, where a particular factory or industry must fulfill a minimum level of output, but this minimum is not dictated by price incentives; it is instead decided administratively. To some extent, large corporations also function in this manner regarding production by some of their divisions, but in this case, price information is likely to have significant weight on the administrative decision.

Quotas are pervasive in international trade and the most common forms are non-tariff trade barriers, although this may be changing. Export quotas are used by nations seeking to keep low the domestic price of a good it exports. A country may wish to quantitatively restrict the export of a good in order to reserve a greater amount of it for domestic consumption. Domestic producers, unable to export beyond the quota established by the government, make their output available for domestic consumption, allowing domestic prices to remain below international price levels. Clearly, this is not in the interest of the producers, who would benefit from selling more abroad at a higher price. EGYPT has an export quota on cotton in order to make available cotton-fiber to the domestic textile industry at lower prices.

Import quotas are far more common than export quotas. Import quotas place a maximum on the quantity of a good that can be imported. Beyond-the-quota imports may be forbidden, or, in the case of tariff quotas, they face a high TARIFF rate. By limiting the availability of the foreign-produced good domestically, the quota pushes the domestic price of the good up to levels above the international price. This benefits domestic producers of the good, who respond to higher domestic prices with higher output. Domestic consumers, on the other hand, are negatively affected as they face higher prices for the good.

Import quotas generate a quota rent equivalent to the quantitative restriction times the difference between the domestic and international prices. The implementation of an import quota therefore requires the creation of an administrative system to designate the beneficiary of this quota rent.

One method that generates government revenue is the auction of import licenses equivalent to the quota. Importers will bid for permits to import a fixed amount of the good, with all permits adding up to the total quota. This system splits quota rent between the government receiving the proceeds of the auction, and the importers who win the bids and who will charge a price above the international price that they pay for the good.

Another practice is to grant import licenses according to administrative criteria such as first-come, first-served, or specific requirements that must be met by the importer. This method of allocating the import licenses reserves the entire quota rent for the importers and leaves great latitude to administrative officials, providing a large incentive for lobbying efforts and kickbacks. The importers obtaining the import licenses do not have to pay for them, but they may be willing to spend the equivalent of the economic rent in order to gain timely and privileged access to administrative agencies. Anne Krueger (1974) refers to these efforts to obtain the licenses as rent-seeking activities.

Another option is to enable the foreign producers or exporters of the good to capture the entire quota rent. This system often takes the form of a Voluntary Export Restraint (VER), which means that the nation restricting imports requests the exporting nation to impose quantitative restrictions on the good exported (essentially an export quota but for the protection of the importing nation). The exporting nation must devise a mechanism for the allocation of shares of this quota among exporters. Perhaps the best-known case is their use by the United States against Japanese automobiles during the early 1980s.

Economists consider quotas to have a negative impact on efficiency. Using the concepts of consumer- and producer-surplus, economists determine that the losses to consumers of the good are greater than the gains of the producers plus the quota rent. The difference, called dead-weight losses, is the result of lower overall consumption and higher output of the good. Furthermore, quotas require administrative interference, creating opportunities for graft and corruption, or at least the use of resources aimed at lobbying on the behalf of particular interests, so additional efficiency losses may exist depending on how a quota is administered. In the case of quota auctions, the quota rent may be divided between government revenue and profits to the importing firm, amounting to a redistribution of benefits from consumers to government and the licensed importers, but not a loss in efficiency beyond the dead-weight loss. However, if firms invest resources on lobbying or paybacks to quota administrators up to the entire value of the quota rent may be used in rent-seeking. In this case, the efficiency loss will be the dead-weight losses plus the value of the resources used in rent-seeking activities since these do not generate any benefits to society.

Domestic producers of the protected good prefer quotas over tariffs because quotas place a specific maximum amount on the number of imports, reserving for them the rest of the market. Under a quota, an increase in domestic demand for the good will push the domestic price of the good even higher. With a tariff, an increase in domestic demand will generate larger imports of the good with little or no impact on the domestic price. In a growing economy, the demand for the good is likely to rise over time, so long as the quota is not regularly updated to accommodate rising demand, domestic producers benefit more under quota restrictions on imports than under tariffs.

Import quotas became an increasingly common form of non-tariff barrier during the post-WORLD WAR II years. With efforts at the GENERAL AGREEMENT ON TARIFFS AND TRADE (GATT) focused on the reduction of tariffs, many countries switched to quotas to shelter sectors that they were unwilling to open to international trade. For example, the Multifiber Agreement (MFA), adopted in the 1960s by the United States, imposes quotas on textile products. Quotas are also commonly used by developed nations to protect their agricultural sectors, as is the case with sugar and dairy products in the United States. The American sugar quota results in prices that are double, and occasionally triple, the international price of sugar. Efficiency losses caused by this quota are estimated at $1.5 billion per year.

According to the Uruguay Round of GATT negotiations, all agricultural and textile quotas are to be replaced by tariffs by 2005. The Uruguay Round also called for the elimination of VERs by 1999, but these have re-emerged under new guises. Even within NAFTA (North American Free Trade Agreement), dismantling the U.S. sugar quota for Mexican exports has proved nearly impossible. Quotas, however, are taking a secondary role as a stumbling block for trade liberalization in comparison to the problem presented by agricultural subsidies.

BIBLIOGRAPHY. Steven Berry, et al., "Voluntary Export Restraints on Automobiles: Evaluating a Trade Policy," *American Economic Review* (v.89, 1999); Jagdish Bhagwati, "On the Equivalence of Tariffs and Quotas," *Trade Growth and the Balance of Payments: Essays in Honor of Gottfried Haberler* (Rand McNally, 1965); Anne Krueger, "The Political Economy of the Rent-Seeking Society," *American Economic Review* (v.64/3, 1974).

LEOPOLDO RODRÍGUEZ-BOETSCH
PORTLAND STATE UNIVERSITY

R

railroads

PERHAPS MORE THAN ANY other industry, railroads have traditionally served as emblems of capitalism. The invention of the steam engine and the development of rail-building technology were functions of the INDUSTRIAL REVOLUTION. Railroads then spread that mode of industrial production, and its altered ways of life, across whole countries and continents with incredible rapidity, fundamentally changing the economics of production, distribution, and consumption of most forms of agricultural and industrial enterprises. Once networks had been built, railroads altered the character of national economies, but considerable historiographical debates exist about the relative contribution of railways to capitalism as compared with earlier transport revolutions in, for example, river, canal and road transport. Few, however, dispute the role played by railroads in forging both nations and national consciousness in the 19th century. Historians have also been interested in the roles played by railroads in international relations and in the contribution of colonial railroad development to the particular brand of capitalism that emerged in 19th-century Europe.

The development of railway networks presented tremendous opportunities to entrepreneurs, governments, and individual shareholders, but they also presented colossal risks in the potential losses that investors in railroads might incur. The question of the management of risk has not only applied to the question of financial risk, but right from the inception of railroads, the question of their impact on personal safety has been much debated. (In fact, safety has been debated since the death of Member of Parliament William Huskisson on the day of the first inter-city train journey between Manchester and Liverpool in England in 1830.)

Such debates on safety have always been allied to one of the key economic debates on railways, which concerns the question of who should be responsible for developing railway networks and for operating rail services. Can both of these areas of activity be fulfilled by the private sector, or can one or both of them be entrusted to the state? The different roles played by the state and private capital in the development of railroads in different countries arguably tells us a great deal about the culture of capitalism in those nations. More recent economic debates have concerned privatization, the viability of the extensive rail networks developed in the 19th and early 20th centuries, and the social costs that countries bear when such networks are scaled back. Such debates have looked, in particular, at the place of railroads since the development of alternative forms of mass transportation.

The early railroads. The earliest railroads were developed in Britain at the end of the 18th and the beginning of the 19th centuries (such as the Surrey Iron Railway of 1803 and the Middleton Railway of 1758), with iron rails being developed at broadly the same time as steam engines (the first tracks were used in 1776 at the aptly named Coalbrookdale), while rail cars had antecedents in the wooden wagons that were used to transport goods, such as coal along tracks. The first 20 years of the development of railroads were relatively unspectacular, until the opening of the Stockton-Darlington railroad in 1825, where George Stephenson's locomotive provided the first steam-train service run for the public and freight. Even then, it was not until the 1840s that the so-called Railway Mania began, when 272 separate railroad concessions were granted in a single year. It would seem significant that this sudden expansion of the industry quickly followed the report of the Royal Commission on Gauges, which had instituted a common national standard for track sizes in 1844.

The development of the railroad industry in Britain was of crucial importance to the acceleration of the Industrial Revolution; because of this, many other states followed the British example in the hope of keeping pace with the leading world economic power of the day. The British case quickly showed that the combination of iron rails and steam locomotives had massive potential, introducing efficiencies into the heavy industries that were driving the Industrial Revolution, such as iron and coal. Railways also led to the effective transport of raw materials and finished goods in consumer-oriented industries such as textile production, and, ultimately, in mass passenger transportation. The railway boom was significant not just to the material development of a capitalist economy, but also to the introduction of state regulation in order to guide the development of the rail network. The shift it induced in the popular consciousness recognized the potential gains that could come from investing even small sums of capital in speculative stock ventures.

Who runs the rails? Once the success of railroads was demonstrated in Britain, other industrializing states knew that they too would have to develop rail networks. There then ensued a series of debates concerning the development of rail networks, and the operation of passenger and freight traffic, which are central to the connection between the railways and capitalism.

In a country such as FRANCE, as one case study, the arrangements that were devised for the development of railroads are representative of the particular culture of capitalism, which was to characterize all French development in the 19th century. The French parliament debated such questions at great length between 1834 and the passing of the Railway Acts of 1842, legislating the

The effect of freight railways on the development of the Industrial Revolution is a topic of debate in the history of economics.

creation of a national rail network (which was then developed at an incredible speed). In broad terms, there were two sides of the railway debate: those who believed that the development and operation of railways could only be entrusted to the state, and those who believed that only private enterprise would create an efficient rail network.

Two very different political groupings—socialists and nationalists—put forward the statist case. According to French socialists, railroads were a natural MONOPOLY that could only be effectively operated by the state, for private enterprise could not be trusted because of its potential to exploit its position to generate monopolistic profits, or to develop a rail network which only served major centers, ignoring less profitable routes, or where capital was wasted with rival entrepreneurs duplicating effort by building competing railroads between major cities.

Right-wing nationalists made a similar case, on a different basis, claiming that the state needed to control rail development because of its strategic importance in France's competition with its neighbors. In particular, French nationalists looked at the state-controlled, rational development of railroads in Prussia, and demanded that the French state play a similar role for fear of falling behind the Prussians in industrial and military power (it was believed the Prussian rail lines would allow quick access for massive troop movements into France).

Liberals, on the other hand, opposed state-direction of railroads, arguing that such projects represented a form of double taxation that hit the poorest in society hardest, for it would be the rich who would benefit most from railroads, and who would, comparatively, pay the least for them.

Free-marketeers argued that only entrepreneurs could develop a truly rational and efficient national system of railroads. Such a stance was well articulated by Pierre Larousse when he asked: "In the end, can one expect from the state the same spirit of perfection which drives private interest? Can one expect the same commitment from state functionaries as one would get from officials zealously overseen by their company bosses?"

The synthetic solution of the French state was to build and plan the network as a state-run enterprise, and to then lease operating concessions to a small number of companies who would operate in distinct regions of France. These six companies—Nord, Est, Ouest, Orléans, Lyon, and Midi—might be described as an oligopoly, but the reality of the situation was that each was granted its own local monopoly. This compromise was typical of the French style of capitalist development, and the solution of the question of railway development was described by writers as the dualist theory or the rationalist theory of French development. The negative economic and social consequences of this rational system were overlooked in a mood of general optimism, where politicians from across the political spectrum were keen to be seen as adherents of a cult of progress, and to make grand claims as to the economic gains that such a railway network would bring to France.

Socialist and journalist Pierre-Joseph Proudhon, for instance, claimed that "This transport revolution will eliminate scarcity, allowing producers to bypass intermediaries and to obtain the true value of their goods, creating profits for the worst land, giving work its true value, doubling incomes, and through a fairer distribution of wealth, ensure the end of local famines and depressions."

Rails as revolution. As well as representing important trends in the structuring of capitalist economies, the railroads also inaugurated a series of irreversible social trends, which are an ever-present theme in 19th-century writers' commentaries on the meaning of the railroads, as well as in the works of later critics. Early commentators on railroads, such as Adolph Joanne writing in 1859, identified them as agents of a modernity which would be quickly globalized: "These new tracks, which, in a short time, are destined to cross every surface of the earth (along with the electric telegraph) represent the greatest political, economic, and social revolution in human history." While one might question the hyperbole of Joanne's claim, there is no doubt that railroads changed the character of life in distinct ways across the globe.

Railroads certainly inaugurated new conceptions of time and space, as we know from the many 19th-century novels, poems, and paintings which attempted to describe such changes. Wolfgang Schivelbusch suggests that, "Compared to the ecotechnical space-time relationships, the one created by the railroad appears abstract and disorienting, because the railroad—in realizing Newton's mechanics—negated all that characterized ecotechnical traffic; the railroad did not appear embedded in the space of the landscape the way coach and highway are, but seemed to strike its way through it." In other words, the railway industrialized landscape and experience in a way that had not characterized earlier forms of transport. In doing this, 19th-century writers were attendant to the fact that railroads were not simply connecting people and places, for they were also disconnecting and isolating others (a common theme of novels by writers such as Émile Zola and Guy de Maupassant). As Charles Dunoyer put it in 1840, railways "only serve the points of departure, the way-stations and terminals which are mostly at great distance from each other . . . they are of no use whatsoever for the intervening spaces which they traverse with disdain and provide only with a useless spectacle."

Across the world, optimistic commentators were convinced that railroads would help to create national markets and imbue people with a common, national consciousness. Let us compare, for example, Larousse with J.W. Scott of the American newspaper *Toledo Blade*.

LAROUSSE: Distinctions between agriculture and industry will soon be academic. There will only be one economic sphere in which town and country have ceased to be distinct worlds, ceasing to keep their different morals, cultures, ideas and laws.

SCOTT: To commercial exchanges through the interior, it would give an activity beyond anything witnessed heretofore in inland trade. A face of gladness would animate every department of toil, and new motives be held out for activity in enterprise. Social as well as commercial intercourse of the people of distant states, would break down local prejudices and annihilate sectional misunderstandings. The wages of labor would be improved, and the profits of capital increased beyond the whole cost of these works.

Such blissful optimism was, of course, a common characteristic of the development of 19th-century nationalisms, and reveals to us the central role played by railroads in the construction of an all-encompassing ideology of progress.

Traveling by rail also meant the acceptance of new risks to one's personal safety, especially in a country like France where Larousse noted, in 1878, that there were five times as many deaths caused by railways as there were in England, eight times as many as there were in BELGIUM, and 21 times as many as there were in Prussia. This poor safety record was something of a national scandal, and Larousse was quick to identify the cause of the dangerous quality of rail travel in France, which was the dualist theory of rail management. Larousse and other commentators blamed rail deaths on the companies' rapacious desire for profits, the lack of desire of government to effectively regulate the railroads, the mutual interpenetration of rail companies and government (many deputies and senators sat on the boards of rail companies), and the desire on the part of many safety inspectors to obtain better-paid posts with rail companies. Similar arguments were being replayed 140 years later in Britain in the wake of rail disasters at Southall, Paddington, Hatfield, and Potter's Bar in a privatized rail industry that borrowed the oligopolistic, rational model originated in 19th-century France.

The indispensability of railroads to capitalist development. The question of how indispensable railroads were in the development of capitalist economies has been one of the principal areas of discussion in economic history, particularly since the so-called "Axiom of Indispensability" overstated the importance of railroads to American economic growth. In the name of a "New Economic History of Railroads" these writers took what they saw to be a truism that structured accounts of American history—that America became an industrial power through railroad development—and subjected this claim to historical and economic analysis. In particular, they concerned themselves with the broader economic impact of railroads as compared to the introduction of earlier forms of transport. Carter Goodrich, for instance, notes "Although the early canals were soon supplemented and later overshadowed by the railroads, it must not be forgotten that the initial reduction in costs provided by canal transport, as compared with wagon haulage, was more drastic than any subsequent differential between railroads and canals. The effect of this reduction was decisive for the opening of substantial trade between the east and the west." Robert W. FOGEL moves on from this point to claim that if railways had not existed, then other forms of transport (such as canals and rivers) could have promoted precisely the kinds of growth that eventually came to be seen as being uniquely indebted to the railroads.

While such a claim seems to have a certain logic, and may act as a useful corrective in our thinking about the indispensability of the railroads, much of the evidence marshaled by its advocates seems to give a pretty clear impression of the revolutionary effect of the railways on the American economy. For instance, in 1851–52 boats carried six times as much freight as trains in America, yet as quickly as 1889–90 trains were carrying five times as much freight as boats. And the comparative advantage of trains was not just their cost (for prices kept falling, commodity transport by rail dropped from 1.925 cents per ton mile in 1867 to 0.839 cents in 1895), but the fact that builders directed rail routes in a way that was not possible with river transport, and in doing so a national market was established across the United States, at precisely the time that a unitary political state was being formed.

Just as had been the case in France, the state encouraged the development of rail networks through the granting of concessions, tracts of land, and grants. Such agreements did not, of course, benefit all Americans, and we find a close connection between the colonial expansion westward, the development of railways, and the destruction of Native-American cultures (as has been amply replayed in so many western movies). Fogel also notes that the economic benefits of the new railroads were not shared equally among corporate interests, for large firms, such as STANDARD OIL, were often able to secure especially low freight costs (rebates) as a means of pushing other firms out of the market.

International railroad history. The development of railroad networks in other states revealed different social and economic questions. In RUSSIA, for example, Simon P. Ville suggests "Russian landowners delayed rail development for fear of the social forces it might unleash," cognizant of the twin development of mass politics and transport in countries such as Britain in the 19th century. The Russian case, where railroad development and industrialization developed rather later than in other European states, also revealed distinct economic problems that came from later development, such as the issue of import substitution, and how one could develop a rail network without relying on foreign labor and hardware. The Russian solution to such problems was a program of tariff protection and the offering of privileged concessions to five key firms who were entrusted with the development of a rail network. Such a policy replayed the idea of a state-sanctioned oligopoly that had been developed in France.

An idea which seems to be related to the new economic historians' questioning of the axiom of indispensability is the issue of the huge levels of investment which were made in railroads in the 19th century, and the question of whether such resources might have been more efficiently deployed elsewhere. Such questions may not seem of crucial importance in a country like GERMANY where around 26 percent of GROSS DOMESTIC PRODUCT (GDP) was spent on railroads in the period 1875–79; or Russia, 25–30 percent of GDP in 1896–1900; but they are certainly understandable in the British context where around half of GDP was invested in rail in the 1840s and countries like Spain, where annual GDP devoted to railroads was at times as high as 90 percent.

The Spanish case is particularly interesting because historians have noted that Spanish railroads often did not connect major areas of industrial production, where the greatest economic gains would have come from rail links. Much of the capital deployed in the development of the Spanish railroads came from outside the country, and outside investors often had different priorities than the Spanish state or industrialists. Similar planning problems occurred in France (where too great an emphasis was placed on Paris as the center of the national rail network); Britain (where there was some duplication of routes); and Germany (where states often intentionally failed to connect their lines to those of neighboring states, for reasons of economic and political competition).

The 20th century. While most European railway networks were built in the 19th century, it was not until the early 20th century that extensive railway networks were built across the globe (and even then, there were some geographical areas, such as most of the Arabian peninsula, that were not served by railroads). Of course, the shape and purpose of many non-European rail networks was determined by European colonial powers, whose chief aims tended to be the military control of colonies, and the use of railways as means to exploit raw materials.

Railroads have also been intimately connected to the history of war in the 20th century. A.J.P. Taylor famously claimed that WORLD WAR I had been caused by a coincidence of European railway timetables, while WORLD WAR II will always be remembered not only for the manner in which railroads were used in troop transport, but for their role in the industrialized genocide of the Holocaust.

Technical innovations in rail have been relatively scarce in the past 100 years (diesel, electrification and an increase in speed stand out), especially compared with the dynamic changes that have taken place in road and air transport. In the second half of the 20th century, governments found themselves having to take account of such changes in the way they developed and regulated rail networks.

Where 19th-century governments had to view railroads as the sole providers of modern transport, 20th-century governments had to develop national strategies that encouraged a range of public and private transport. Such decisions were often heavily dependent on the particular political outlook of governments, so that in postwar Britain one finds different governments nationalizing rail (1946), closing much of the rail network (1965), privatizing rail (1994–97), and then effectively re-nationalizing part of the network (2002).

BIBLIOGRAPHY. J.M. Thompson, *Modern Transport Economics* (Penguin, 1974); Robert William Fogel, *Railroads and American Economic Growth* (Johns Hopkins University Press, 1964); Simon P. Ville, *Transport and the Development of the European Economy, 1750–1918* (Palgrave Macmillan, 1990); Patrick O'Brien, *The New Economic History of the Railways* (Palgrave Macmillan, 1977); Philip T. Bagnell, *The Transport Revolution from 1770* (Batsford, 1974); Wolfgang Schivelbusch, *The Railway Journey: The Industrialization of Time and Space in the 19th Century* (University of California Press, 1986); James M. Brophy, *Capitalism, Politics and Railroads in Prussia, 1830–1870* (Ohio State University Press, 1998); Walter Benjamin, *Paris: capitale du XIXe siècle, Le Livre des passages* (1989).

WILLIAM GALLOIS, PH.D.
AMERICAN UNIVERSITY OF SHARJAH

Rand, Ayn (1905–82)

CAPITALISM HAS MANY intellectual defenders, but none as uncompromising as novelist-philosopher Ayn Rand. She escaped from the Soviet Union to the UNITED STATES, just in time to witness her adopted homeland's NEW DEAL rejection of free-market policies. She became famous for her increasingly philosophical novels, culminating with *Atlas Shrugged* in 1957; she then switched exclusively to nonfiction.

Rand's political thought begins by defining capitalism in the strongest possible terms: "When I say 'capitalism,' I mean a full, pure, uncontrolled, unregulated laissez-faire capitalism—with a separation of state and economics, in the same way and for the same reasons as the separation of state and church." She then staunchly embraces capitalism so-defined. Unlike so many pro-capitalist thinkers, Rand does not argue that its economic efficiency outweighs its moral shortcomings. While she hails the wealth-creating power of the free market, her defense of capitalism is a moral one. Laissez-faire is, she believes, the economic system of freedom, justice, and individual rights. The leading moral objections to capitalism, conversely, are unjust and totalitarian.

Even firm proponents of capitalism usually find Rand's position unpalatable. How could anyone treat capitalist outcomes as morally privileged, and deny the good intentions of progressive reformers? Her main moral argument rests on the fact that under capitalism, human relationships are voluntary, based on mutual consent. The consumer and capitalist freely exchange money for products; the capitalist and the worker freely exchange money for time. This is the form of social interaction that Rand sees as uniquely consistent with the rational nature of man:

> In a capitalist society . . . men are free to cooperate or not, to deal with one another or not, as their own individual judgments, convictions, and interests dictate. They can deal with one another only in terms of and by means of reason, i.e., by means of discussion, persuasion, and *contractual* agreement, by voluntary choice to mutual benefit.

Government action, in contrast, is fundamentally involuntary. The taxpayer has to pay his taxes, the businessman obey regulations, whether he agrees with them or not. Rand denies that democracy makes taxes and regulation any less coercive; a genuine contract requires the consent of all participants, not 50 percent plus 1. It is morally wrong, she maintains, to use physical force against a person who is peacefully living his life:

> So long as men desire to live together, no man may *initiate* — do you hear me? No man may *start* the use of physical force against others . . . It is only as retaliation that force may be used and only against the man who starts its use . . . A proper government is only a policeman, acting as an agent of man's self-defense . . .

It follows, from this view, that most of what governments do, from price controls and antitrust laws to public education and conscription, is a violation of human rights. Indeed, taxation itself is morally impermissible; government ought to fund its limited activities solely with user fees and charitable donations.

Rand also defends capitalism on the related ground of merit. Those who succeed under laissez-faire produced every penny of their riches and ought to be lauded for their achievements. Indeed, Rand is arguably the most meritocratic thinker in the history of political philosophy, idolizing the productive genius, and condemning his egalitarian critics:

> It is morally obscene to regard wealth as an anonymous, tribal product and talk about "redistributing" it. . . . Anyone who has ever been an employer or an employee, or has observed men working, or has done an honest day's work himself, knows the crucial role of ability, of intelligence, of a focused, competent mind—in any and all lines of work, from the lowest to the highest. . . . When great industrialists made fortunes on a *free* market . . . they *created* new wealth—they did not take it from those who had *not* created it.

What about those who do poorly under capitalism? Rand would not hesitate to point out that this is typically their own fault; in a system based on merit, the "losers" tend to be lazy, irrational, or otherwise culpably deficient. But even if you are unsuccessful solely through bad luck, that it is no reason to scapegoat the better off.

There is obviously little affinity between Rand's ethical outlook and that of Christianity. An atheist, Rand views anti-capitalism as the natural political expression of Christianity's perverse "altruistic" ethic. Indeed, she deplores the very idea of "unconditional love":

> Love is the expression of one's values, the greatest reward you can earn for the moral qualities you have achieved in your character and person, the emotional price paid by one man for the joy he receives from the virtues of another. Your morality demands that you divorce your love from values and hand it down to any vagrant, not as reward, but as alms, not as payment for virtues, but as a blank check on vices.

In contrast to many defenders of capitalism, then, Rand refused to pragmatically appeal to religious conservatives on their own terms. Anti-capitalist politics follow logically from Christian ethics. Furthermore, Rand observes that for all their so-called radicalism, Marxists and other socialists blithely accept Christian morality. Both Christianity and socialism deny producers the credit they deserve, and proclaim the duty of the able to serve the needy. Could not Karl MARX's slogan "From each, according to his ability; to each, according to his need," just as easily have come from the lips of Jesus?

Rand has a mixed intellectual reaction to free-market economics. She disapproves of its utilitarian moral outlook: "The classical economists attempted a tribal justification of capitalism on the ground that it provides the best 'allocation' of a community's 'resources.'" But she nevertheless relies heavily on economists like Ludwig von MISES to answer practical doubts about capitalism. Monopoly? The "monopolies" to worry about are those that governments create by making competition illegal; on the free market, a firm can only become the sole supplier by being the best. Depressions? They are caused by government manipulation of the money supply, and exacerbated by labor-market regulation that keeps wages above the market-clearing level. Labor unions? They should be legal, but it is folly to give them, rather than rising productivity, credit for workers' increasing living standards.

Her economic history is equally unconventional. She praises the wonders of the Industrial Revolution, blaming government intervention and pre-existing conditions for its ills. As she puts it, "Capitalism did not create poverty—it inherited it." Writing in the 1950s and 1960s, Rand prophetically described the grim economic conditions behind the Iron Curtain. At a time when many experts took official Soviet growth statistics at face value, Rand saw only a Potemkin village of "wretched serfs" hidden behind a facade of Communist propaganda.

Rand's distinctive moral defense of capitalism exerted a powerful influence on 20th-century LIBERTARIAN political thought. It is unlikely that the libertarian movement could have attracted a fraction of its adherents by appealing to economic efficiency or utilitarian cost-benefit analysis. *Atlas Shrugged*, her greatest novel, dared to cast entrepreneurs as oppressed heroes and socialists as neurotic villains. While her artistic decision repelled many, it inspired and influenced a generation of pro-market intellectuals.

BIBLIOGRAPHY. www.aynrand.org; Barbara Branden, *The Passion of Ayn Rand* (Doubleday, 1986); Douglas Den-Uyl and Douglas Rasmussen, *The Philosophic Thought of Ayn Rand* (University of Illinois Press, 1984); Leonard Peikoff, *Objectivism: The Philosophy of Ayn Rand* (Dutton, 1991); Ayn Rand, *Atlas Shrugged* (Random House, 1957); Ayn Rand, *Capitalism: The Unknown Ideal* (Signet, 1967); ChrisSciabarra, *Ayn Rand: The Russian Radical* (Pennsylvania State University Press, 1995).

BRYAN CAPLAN, PH.D.
GEORGE MASON UNIVERSITY

rationing

WHEN GOODS OR SERVICES are allocated without relying on prices, it is termed rationing. In particular, it refers to situations in which the amount that people who would like to buy is greater than the amount available, given the prevailing prices. There are two common instances. The first is in situations of very short supplies of goods and services that cover basic human needs, for example, food-rationing in times of emergencies. The second is in the government provision of goods and services below cost, as is the case in many countries with public health benefits. However, rationing also takes place when there is a fixed amount of supply and prices cannot adjust, for example, sold-out sporting events or concerts. To better understand rationing, it is instructive to see how the price system provides for the (non-rationed) allocation of goods and services.

In a market where sellers and buyers are free to enter into price negotiations, there is no need for rationing. If, at any point in time, there are more people vying to purchase a particular good than there are people willing to sell the good (called excess demand), then prices will be driven up. Due to the higher price, fewer people will want to purchase the good, and more people may be willing to sell the good (as one can make more money by selling it). The price system is said to work if prices increase to the point where just as many goods are being offered for sale as there are people who want to purchase those goods. Rationing is needed if prices cannot freely increase so that the amount of the good that is demanded is not brought into EQUILIBRIUM with the amount supplied.

Rationing is often used in times of crises, when basic necessities for living are in short supply. For example, in times of war, many food items are often in very short supply as production and supply lines become disrupted. The price system could work in these instances, but the consequence would be that as prices rise, some people would no longer be able to provide for the basic needs of their families, and widespread extreme hardship and starvation could result. Consequently, other methods for distributing the scarce food supplies are sought and foods are rationed.

Other common examples where rationing takes place in times of crises are the limitations on how many bottles of drinking water or batteries any individual may purchase in the wake of a hurricane, flood, or earthquake; or how much gasoline one is able to purchase during an oil crisis. Similarly, the rotating stoppage of electricity, called rolling black-outs, in California in the summer of 2002 were a form of rationing in the face of a (man-made) energy crisis.

In some instances, equity considerations lead to government provision of some services, even when there is no immediate crisis. This is, for example, the case in public education. The philosophy is that every member of society should be afforded a minimum level of education, regardless of one's family income. Rationing can become an issue, as within a school district, where all students receive a comparable level of education, even though some would be willing to pay a little more to better the quality of their education.

Similarly, some governments provide universal HEALTH care to all citizens. As medical treatments are near costless in terms of the prices charged to ailing citizens, health care may be demanded to such an extent that rationing becomes necessary.

Whenever the amount demanded of a particular good or service is greater than the amount supplied, the question arises: Who actually ends up getting these scarce goods and services? One method used is that of uniform provision, where everyone (more or less regardless of their specific needs or wants) receives the same amount of the good or service. In the case of public education, all students in a particular school obtain the same educational opportunities—it is generally not possible to pay the school administrator an extra $100 a month in order to receive an extra hour of math instruction every week. In some cases coupons, tokens, stamps, or vouchers (which may not be transferable) may be issued to ensure uniform provision. Similarly, in times of war, households may receive vouchers that they can trade for food.

A second common form of rationing is queuing—the first-come-first-serve method, so to speak. This method is often observed where there are unforeseen shortages, as this method of rationing does not require any particular administrative effort (other than possibly keeping order as people wait in line). Thus, you may observe this form of rationing before rock concerts, when people camp overnight to make sure they will be first in line. However, this method of rationing is also common in the public provision of services, in particular, health care. Thus, countries that provide universal health care usually have longer waits associated with the provision of health services.

Finally, a less common method is random assignment or lotteries. For example, the Immigration and Naturalization Service, faced with an exceptionally large number of applications for green cards from all over the world, also uses lotteries in which some applicants are selected at random to be assigned entry visas.

When prices are not able to adjust in a market in order to equilibrate the quantity demanded and supplied, this does not mean that the laws of economics no longer apply and market forces do not matter. Frequently, where one encounters rationing, a secondary market in which trade takes place simultaneously to the primary (rationed) market will co-exist. For example, people who do not feel that they receive adequate education through the public school system may opt into a secondary market of privately funded schools, or consider home-schooling. Similarly, individuals who are dissatisfied with publicly provided health services may opt for alternative treatments or private care.

In some cases the secondary market is banned, for reasons of professed equity or government control. Nevertheless, secondary markets often appear anyway as BLACK MARKETS, such as ticket scalping before sporting events. Similarly, bribes and outright fraud are often associated with rationing.

Another market response, when the pecuniary price cannot increase, is that the cost of the rationed good increases in other ways. When medical care is dispensed at low prices to assure equal access to treatment regardless of income, waiting in line for treatment is not uncommon. However, other inequities may arise: it may be less costly for, say, an unemployed or retired citizen to wait in the doctor's office than it is for an independent business owner, or someone who has to hold down two jobs just to make ends meet.

[Editor's Note: It may even be noted that price itself serves as a rationing mechanism in a market setting. Those able to afford the price receive the product, those not are turned away empty-handed.]

BIBLIOGRAPHY. Joseph E. Stiglitz, *Economics of the Public Sector* (W.W. Norton, 2000); Roger LeRoy Miller, Daniel K. Benjamin, and Douglas C. North, *The Economics of Public Issues* (Addison-Wesley, 2002).

THOMAS D. JEITSCHKO, PH.D.
MICHIGAN STATE UNIVERSITY

Reagan, Ronald (1911–)

RONALD WILSON REAGAN was the 40th president of the United States. One of the more popular presidents in history, his tenure was marked by the largest military buildup in history, renewed patriotism, record-setting deficits, economic recovery, and scandal. While some critics argue that Reagan's policies brought about the end of the Cold War and restored confidence in the U.S. government, others argue that his administration was enormously corrupt and had mortgaged the future.

Reagan was born in Tampico, Illinois, and moved around before eventually settling in Dixon, Illinois. Reagan's father, Jack Reagan, was an Irish Catholic salesman, renowned raconteur, and alcoholic, and his constant drinking was one of the reasons he drifted from job to job and from town to town. While Reagan did adopt his father's storytelling ability, he strove to avoid his penchant for excess.

For Reagan, a large part of his life centered around the church; he acted with his mother in skits in the church (including temperance skits), he participated in the services, and he dated the preacher's daughter. Reagan was closer to the preacher than he was to his own father, and biographers have credited Reagan's early church experience with instilling a strong sense of morality.

Reagan also had an active life outside of the church. Reagan worked summers as a lifeguard at nearby Lowell Park and reportedly saved 77 people from drowning on his watch. He was also active in high school (competing in drama, football, basketball, and track), and was elected senior class president.

After graduating from high school in 1928, Reagan attended Eureka College and majored in economics and sociology and did fairly well in his studies; while he did not in fact study, he did possess a near-photographic memory, which helped him pass exams. Upon graduating in 1932 in the midst of the Great DEPRESSION, Reagan convinced a Davenport, Iowa, radio station owner to hire him as a temporary, then staff sports-radio announcer. When Reagan was sent to cover the Chicago Cubs spring training in 1937 in California, he used the trip to take a screen test for Warner Bros. studios.

Reagan was offered a contract, and in a movie career that would last until 1964, he acted in more than fifty films in all. Reagan's most acclaimed roles were as George Gipp in *Knute Rockne, All American* (1940) and as Drake McHugh in the 1942 drama *King's Row*; when as president he met Mikhail GORBACHEV, Reagan asked the Soviet leader to tell his staff that not all of Reagan's films were B movies.

Onto the national stage. Politics often intruded on Reagan's life as an actor. Reagan was an active anti-communist. He testified to the Federal Bureau of Investigation (FBI) in September 1941 on communism in Hollywood, became an informant for the agency, and in 1947 testified to the House Un-American Activities Committee.

Reagan was active in industry politics, becoming president of the Screen Actor's Guild in 1947, where he was instrumental in efforts to break the strike of the Committee of Studio Unions (a Hollywood craft union). Reagan was elected Screen Actor's Guild president for five terms, negotiated several union contracts, and used the guild to battle communism in Hollywood. Some biographers claim that it is as union president where Reagan's political values moved from liberal to conservative; Reagan, a Franklin ROOSEVELT Democrat, officially registered as a Republican in 1962.

During the late 1950s, Reagan's film career had begun to slow down. Reagan began to work in television, becoming host and sometimes an actor on *GE Theater* from 1954–62 and *Death Valley Days* from 1964–66, where his contract called for him to deliver motivational speeches at General Electric plants across the country. These speeches were patriotic, pro-business, and anti-communist in nature; over time, however, Reagan started to stress the anti-Washington angle in these increasingly partisan speeches.

It was largely based on the success and effectiveness of these speeches that Reagan was persuaded to enter politics. His first major political act was giving a televised speech in 1964 in support of the presidential campaign of Barry Goldwater, a radical conservative. Reagan ran for governor of California in 1966. Edmund Brown, the incumbent candidate, did not take Reagan seriously, dismissing him as only an actor. Reagan's campaign was heavily managed by a public relations firm rather than politicians, which perfectly fit in with his anti-politician rhetoric. Reagan eventually won the election by a margin of over one million votes by running on a platform of welfare reform and against campus radicals.

Overall, Reagan's governorship yielded mixed results. Although Reagan pledged to lower taxes and shrink the size of the state government, the state budget more than doubled during his tenure. During a time of student protests, his electors identified more with his self-assuredness than his accomplishments, and he served two terms before leaving the governorship.

California as a stepping-stone. Reagan attempted a brief run at the U.S. presidency in 1964 against Richard NIXON, when he announced his candidacy at the Republican convention, but Nixon swiftly defeated his nomination bid. After leaving the governor's office, Reagan planned a more thorough campaign against Gerald FORD for the 1972 Republican nomination, ultimately losing to Ford by a narrow margin. After Ford lost the general election to Jimmy CARTER, Reagan immediately began planning a run for the presidency in 1980.

For his third run for the presidency, Reagan capitalized on an economy that was in tough shape, when double-digit inflation was the norm. Carter had placed an embargo on the sale of grain to the SOVIET UNION in protest of its invasion of Afghanistan, but the embargo was hurting American farmers more than the Soviets. Carter was also particularly vulnerable on foreign policy as the result of his perceived poor handling of the Iran Hostage Crisis. Reagan campaigned on promises of improving the economy and reasserting America's prestige abroad, and easily won the Republican nomination. Along with running-mate George H.W. BUSH, he defeated Carter in the general election.

Throughout his presidency, Reagan adopted the same style of governance he employed in California. He still preferred to have aides work out matters among themselves and then bring a compromise solution to

him for approval. Reagan did experience an almost constant turnover in staff during his presidency, perhaps as a result of his laid-back administration style. Whatever internal turmoil existed paled in comparison to the assassination attempt on Reagan's life just 69 days after the president took office. Despite significant injury, Reagan made a publicly engaging and spirited recovery, rallying his staff, and less than a month after the assassination attempt, he delivered an address to Congress on his economic recovery plan.

Reaganomics. Economic recovery had been at the forefront of Reagan's agenda. The new president had been advised by many experts (including Nixon) to concentrate on domestic policy rather than foreign policy, and for Reagan, this meant fixing the economy. Reagan was a champion of supply-side economics, which entailed jump-starting the economy by putting money into the hands of businesses and business owners, on the theory (called "trickle-down") that they would redistribute their wealth by increasing both expenses and the amount of workers. Reagan's budgets, combined with FEDERAL RESERVE policy, did in fact lead to low INFLATION and sustained economic growth. Reagan, however, was also committed to decreasing taxes while increasing the size of the military budget, and record-setting deficits piled up throughout his presidency.

The remainder of Reagan's domestic policy also met with mixed results. The Reagan administration social programs were often perceived as cruel, including a proposal to eliminate free school-lunch programs for needy children. The administration was also heavily involved with deregulation, and often eliminated environmental regulations that affected businesses.

Capitalism vs. communism. Reagan's first term was marred by the bombing of American marines in a peace-keeping force in Lebanon. Reagan's second term was similarly scarred by the revelation that the administration had been secretly selling weapons to former enemy IRAN and illegally donating the profits to El Salvador anti-communist revolutionaries.

The main focus of Reagan's foreign policy, however, centered on the Soviet Union, and his dealings were mainly powered by his anti-communist inclinations. Reagan initiated the largest military build-up in American history, because he believed the Soviets would destroy their economy trying to keep up.

After leaving Washington, D.C., in 1989 at the end of his presidency, Reagan planned to enjoy retirement at his California ranch. In 1994, Reagan was diagnosed with Alzheimer's disease, a neurological disorder that disintegrates the patient's memory. He subsequently withdrew from public life, and as of the summer of 2003, was cared for by his wife, Nancy.

BIBLIOGRAPHY. Edmund Morris, *Dutch: A Memoir of Ronald Reagan* (Random House, 2000); Gary Wills, *Reagan's America* (Penguin, 2000); Lou Cannon, *President Reagan: The Role of a Lifetime* (PublicAffairs, 2000); Ronald Reagan, *Ronald Reagan: An American Life* (Pocket Books, 1989); Lloyd deMause, *Reagan's America* (Creative Roots, Inc., 1984); Bob Schieffer and Gary Paul Gates, *The Acting President: Ronald Reagan and the Supporting Players Who Helped Him Create the Illusion That Held America Spellbound* (E. P. Dutton, 1989).

MIKE S. DUBOSE
BOWLING GREEN STATE UNIVERSITY

recession

A RECESSION IS A PROLONGED slowdown or contraction in the economy. The national economies of industrialized nations tend to experience BUSINESS CYCLES, periods of expansion and contraction over time. Recession describes the period between a business cycle peak, when economic growth is high and UNEMPLOYMENT is low, and a business cycle trough, when economic growth is low (possibly negative) and unemployment is high. Although the term, business cycle, implies that the changes are regular and periodic, expansions and contractions are irregular in duration and magnitude.

The business media often define an economic recession as two or more consecutive quarters of decline in real GROSS DOMESTIC PRODUCT (GDP, the value of all goods and services produced domestically in a country during a specific period of time). The Business Cycle Dating Committee of the National Bureau of Economic Research has defined recessions in the UNITED STATES since the 1920s using its own standard: "A recession is a significant decline in activity spread across the economy, lasting more than a few months, visible in industrial production, employment, real income, and wholesale-retail sales. A recession begins just after the economy reaches a peak of activity and ends as the economy reaches its trough." A common criterion for a recession is that it is prolonged; for this reason, there is by necessity a delay between when a recession begins and when it is officially declared a recession.

It is not well understood what causes changes in the business cycle. John Maynard KEYNES argued that the psychology of investors was important in determining economic downturns; he referred to entrepreneurialism as "animal spirits," which he defined as: "a spontaneous urge to action rather than inaction, and not as the outcome of a weighted average of quantitative benefits multiplied by quantitative probabilities . . . if the animal spirits are dimmed and the spontaneous optimism falters . . . enterprise will fade and die . . ." Consumer Confidence and Investor Confidence indices are modern measures of optimism or faith in the economy that are collected through surveys, and are used to predict changes in consumer spending and investment, and, therefore, changes in the business cycle. In contrast, Milton FRIEDMAN argued that changes in the business cycle were often caused (sometimes inadvertently) by monetary policy.

Governments often attempt to pull their economies out of recession through expansionary fiscal and monetary policies. Expansionary FISCAL POLICY may take the form of tax cuts or spending increases once a recession begins. It could also take the form of a counter-cyclical spending policy such as unemployment insurance, that injects less into the economy when economic growth is robust, and more into the economy when economic growth is weak. Expansionary monetary policy may take several forms. Reducing the fraction of their assets that banks must keep as reserves allows them to offer additional loans. Lowering the INTEREST RATE that the central bank charges to private banks also facilitates additional private lending. A central bank may also use its own resources to buy government bonds back from the private market; this too injects additional cash into the economy. A double-dip recession occurs when an economy briefly pulls out of recession before plunging quickly back into recession.

A recession is shorter in duration than an economic DEPRESSION, which may last a decade and span several business cycles. President Harry S. TRUMAN made the following distinction: "It's a recession when your neighbor loses his job; it's a depression when you lose yours." Ronald REAGAN, when campaigning against Jimmy CARTER for the U.S. presidency in the midst of an economic malaise in 1980, appended to Truman's quote: "And recovery is when Jimmy Carter loses his."

BIBLIOGRAPHY. "The NBER's Business-Cycle Dating Procedure," Business Cycle Dating Committee (National Bureau of Economic Research, 2002); Milton Friedman and Anna Jacobson Schwartz, *Monetary History of the United States, 1867–1960* (Princeton University Press, 1963); John Maynard Keynes, *The General Theory of Employment, Interest, and Money* (1936, Cambridge University Press, 1978); Arthur F. Burns and Wesley C. Mitchell, *Measuring Business Cycles* (National Bureau of Economic Research, 1946).

JOHN CAWLEY, PH.D.
CORNELL UNIVERSITY

regulation

IN ORDER TO UNDERSTAND the role of government regulation in capitalism, it is necessary to examine the views of major economists. During the 16th and 17th centuries, when the INDUSTRIAL REVOLUTION was changing the way that the world understood economics, the mercantile school of thought was prevalent. The goal of the mercantilists was to make as much money as possible, and they influenced the British government to accomplish their self-interested goals. Consequently, the British government passed regulations that set high TARIFFS to cut down on the import of foreign goods and stimulated export though various subsidies. The 18th-century French PHYSIOCRATS criticized the mercantilists and promoted the idea that government should stop interfering in economics. With the publication of Adam SMITH's *An Inquiry into the Nature and Causes of the Wealth of Nations* in 1776, classical economics became the predominant school of economic thought.

Classical economists, also known as classical liberals, believed the world was capable of producing only a certain amount of resources, and many of their economic ideas dealt with how these limited resources should be divided among various social classes. Classical economists were dedicated to the idea of LAISSEZ-FAIRE, which literally means "allow to do," and in practice means the government should leave the economic system alone. Classical economists endorsed the ideas of John LOCKE (1632–1704), the founder of classical liberalism, who believed that individuals were born with inalienable rights that no government could take away. This belief heavily influenced American politicians who wrote the Declaration of Independence, which promised Americans the rights of life, liberty, and the pursuit of happiness (the right to own property). Locke's endorsement of laissez-faire also influenced the structure of the U.S. Constitution with its commitment to limited government.

Classical liberals accepted only three basic functions of government: protection from foreign invasion, domestic security, and public works (such as building roads and canals). The way to achieve happiness, in the classical liberal view, is for the government to leave individuals alone to become as prosperous as possible. Along with Smith, David RICARDO is credited with founding the classical system of economic thought. Other classical economists include Thomas MALTHUS, who was critical of many aspects of classical economic thought, and John Stuart MILL who synthesized the theories of Smith, Ricardo, and Malthus. Karl MARX used parts of classical theory to develop a socialist economic theory. John Maynard KEYNES, the founder of what has become known as Keynesian economics, stood classical economics on its head. Some modern economists, often known as post-Keynesians, embraced elements of classical economics, while others continued to endorse some aspects of Keynesian thought.

Adam Smith (1723–90). Smith's *The Wealth of Nations* was a direct attack on mercantilist political and economic practices. As a rule, Smith opposed protectionist policies such as tariffs, but he believed tariffs were legitimate in defense industries. Smith did not support monopolies because he thought they interfered with COMPETITION. He was against most government regulations that interfered with competition. Smith favored FREE TRADE whereby each country specialized, producing cheaper products and greater efficiency of resources. He believed that the wealth of a country was derived from the LABOR of the people. Smith distrusted government, believing that no regulations were possible that could increase industrial output beyond what the capitalistic system could maintain. Therefore, the best thing the government could do for the economy, as a rule, was to let it alone. In his opinion, if left alone, the market would reach the point of highest return. Since the well-being of the nation depended on the wealth of the people, Smith did accept a limited amount of government regulation in the area of education and thought government had a responsibility to regulate protections for workers.

Smith contended that political economy should provide ways for workers to support themselves at subsistence levels and was obligated to furnish revenue with which government could fund public works. The latter, of course, called for TAXES. While taxation was definitely a method of government interference, it was necessary to provide the three basic functions of government. Smith was against public debt, but he recognized that the government needed revenue to pay public servants and to maintain an equitable legal system. However, strict restrictions should be placed on the government's right to tax. Taxes should be based on the ability to pay, should never be arbitrary, and should not require a huge administrative force. Smith agreed with Thomas Jefferson (1743–1826) that "the least government was the best government."

David Ricardo (1772–1823). Overall, Ricardo agreed with Smith about government regulation. In 1817, in *The Principles of Political Economy*, Ricardo introduced what became known as the "iron law of wages," which advocated the belief that natural cycles resulted in subsistence wages. Even if workers were unable to survive, the government should never interfere. Like most classical liberals, Ricardo believed that resources were scarce. If government regulation interfered in the natural allocation of resources, the result might be worse than before. Like Smith, Ricardo advocated free trade both domestically and internationally. Specialization, he thought, allowed each country to consume more goods, which benefited everyone. Ricardo proposed that a National Board, under the oversight of Parliament, be appointed to issue bank notes. He also wanted Parliament to tax wealthy capitalists to pay off the national debt.

Thomas Robert Malthus (1776–1834). Of all the classical economists, Malthus was most concerned with the idea of scarce resources. He was convinced that overpopulation would exhaust available resources. Since the poor were unlikely to practice restraint, he saw nature's method of natural selection as more promising. Hazardous occupations, disease, wars, famines, and the like would lessen the problem of overpopulation if government simply let nature have its way. Therefore, it was wrong to try to pass Poor Laws that eased the suffering of the poor and allowed them to survive. On the other hand, Malthus was in favor of the British Corn Laws of 1814–15, even though they were a form of protectionism. He insisted that they had increased agricultural prices and profits. This support for protectionist policies resulted in a break with Ricardo, and James and John Stuart Mill.

John Stuart Mill (1806–73). John Stuart Mill, the son of economist James Mill (1773–1836), synthesized the ideas of Smith, Ricardo, and Malthus. Mill endorsed the classical liberal idea of laissez-faire, although he contended that government did had some responsibility for guaranteeing social justice. He thought government also had some responsibility for education but did not endorse the idea of public education. Mill's *Principles of Economy,* written in 1848, became the major economic text for the next half-century. Mill suggested that government could use taxes to redistribute wealth and address the inequalities of capitalism. Though he sometimes called himself a socialist, Mill was rarely radical in his economic thought. Like Malthus, Mill was a strong believer in the dangers of overpopulation and became an advocate for birth control. As a young man, he was arrested for handing out birth-control pamphlets. Mill became the first major political theorist to publicly endorse the rights of women and argued that society was mistaken in limiting itself to the resources of only half the population.

Karl Marx (1818–83). Although he drew on the ideas of classical liberalism as well as French and German thought, Marx rearranged those ideas to develop Marxian SOCIALISM. Marx believed that as alienated workers (the proletariat) rose up against capitalists (the bourgeoisie), they would wrest the means of production from the capitalists and place control in the hands of the STATE. Once the state had served its purpose, it was supposed to "wither away." Unfortunately, when Marx's theories were put into practice in communist countries, the state became totalitarian and hardly withered away. Marxist theory advocated the use of land to serve the public good rather than the interests of individual landowners. Marx advocated a heavy progression of graduated income tax, the abolition of all rights of inheritance, confiscation of all property of emigrants and rebels, a national bank to centralize credit, and a universal commitment to labor.

John Maynard Keynes (1883–1946). The work of Keynes brought about a new way of understanding the role that government should play. He rejected the idea that the government was self-regulating. Instead, Keynes advocated a governmental policy of investment and increased spending and reduced taxes. While Keynesian economics is often associated with Franklin D. ROOSEVELT's (1882–1945) NEW DEAL, a move toward government involvement in the economy was already underway before Keynes played an active role in New Deal policies. After 1938, many Keynesian economists were hired by the Roosevelt administration.

Post-Keynesian economics. By the 1970s, government regulation had changed the way that the market works. In the United States, for example, the FEDERAL RESERVE Board sets the interest rate and controls the supply of reserve money and available credit. The government establishes a minimum wage for workers, which is regulated by Congress as the cost of living increases. The government is also involved in mergers, interstate commerce, international trade, and other aspects of business and the economy.

BIBLIOGRAPHY. Marc Blaug, *Economic History and the History of Economists* (Harvester Press, 1986); Giovanni A. Caravale. *The Legacy of Ricardo* (Basic Books, 1985); Bernard Caravan, *Economics for Beginners* (Pantheon, 1983); Robert L. Heilbroner, *The Worldly Philosophers: The Lives, Times, and Ideas of The Great Economic Thinkers* (Simon and Schuster, 1972); John Maynard Keynes, *The General Theory of Employment, Interest, and Money* (Harcourt Brace & World, 1964); "Major Schools of Economic Theory," www.frbsf.org; Karl Marx and Friedrich Engels, *The Communist Manifesto* (Regnery, 1950); James Medoff and Andrew Harless, *The Indebted Society* (Little Brown, 1996); Louis Putterman, *Dollars and Change: Economics in Context* (Yale University Press, 2001); D.D. Raphael, "Smith," *Three Great Economists,* (Oxford University Press, 1997); Adam Smith, *An Inquiry into the Nature and Causes of The Wealth of Nations* (E. P. Dutton, 1910); Donald Winch, "Malthus," *Three Great Economists* (Oxford University Press, 1997).

ELIZABETH PURDY, PH.D.
INDEPENDENT SCHOLAR

Reliant Energy

RELIANT ENERGY (formerly Houston Industries) was a Houston, Texas, company providing electricity and natural-gas energy services to wholesale and retail customers in the United States and Western Europe. In 2001, Reliant Energy was the fifth-largest investor-owned electric utility in the UNITED STATES and the 67th largest company in the world. The company traced its origins back to the formation of Houston Electric Light & Power, which was granted a franchise to provide electricity to the city in 1882.

Due to restructuring of the Texas energy market, the regulated and unregulated sides of Reliant Energy split into two separate publicly held companies in 2002. The regulated utility side of the business took the name CenterPoint Energy. CenterPoint Energy's lines of business include natural-gas gathering, transmission, distribution, and marketing, electricity-utility operations in the Houston area, and energy-management services to commercial and industrial customers. The company held $19 billion in assets in 2002.

The other newly formed company, Reliant Resources, focused on serving retail and wholesale energy customers in competitive, unregulated markets. Reliant Resources, which retained the Reliant Energy name for marketing purposes, owns electricity generation assets throughout California, the Southwest, the South, the Midwest, and the eastern parts of the country. Reliant Resources held assets worth $20 billion in 2002.

In the early 2000s, the state of California has alleged that the company manipulated the state's wholesale electricity market by withholding power from its California plants. In response to this news and other turbulence in the deregulated power industry, Reliant's credit rating slipped, and the future health of the company is uncertain.

BIBLIOGRAPHY. California Public Utilities Commission, *Report on Wholesale Electric Generation Investigation* (2002); CenterPoint Energy, *CenterPoint Energy Historical Timeline* (2002); Energy Information Administration, *100 Largest Utility Net Generation* (2000); "Global 500: World's Largest Companies," *Fortune* (July 2002).

JAMES PRIEGER, PH.D.
UNIVERSITY OF CALIFORNIA, DAVIS

Repsol-YPF

REPSOL WAS CREATED in 1986 as a Spanish state enterprise. Its PRIVATIZATION started in 1989, becoming fully private in 1997. During this period, it was primarily dedicated to the processing, distribution, and retailing of OIL and gas products, but also expanded into exploration and production in South America and north Africa. The acquisition of Argentine YPF for $13.5 bil-

lion in June 1999, represented a significant expansion that turned Repsol-YPF into the world's eighth-largest oil company. In 2001, it had proven world reserves of oil and gas equivalent to 5.6 billion barrels, produced over 1 million barrels daily and had a daily refining capacity of 1.2 million barrels.

In ARGENTINA and SPAIN, Repsol-YPF dominates the oil and gas sectors accounting for at least 50 percent of transportation, refining capacity, and gas stations in either country.

YPF's history goes back to the discovery of an oil field on Argentine government land in Comodoro Rivadavia in 1907. The Bureau of Mines operated the oil field until nascent oil nationalism in Argentina pushed for the creation of Yacimientos Petroliferos Fiscales (Fiscal Oil Fields) in 1922. General Enrique Mosconi, an ardent advocate of a state monopoly in oil, became its first director (1922–30). From this position, Mosconi promoted the creation of state oil enterprises in other Latin American countries, including MEXICO, where PEMEX would become a state monopoly in 1938. YPF never achieved monopoly status. Foreign companies were edged away from exploration and production, but retained retail privileges, and small domestic companies continued to play a role in all areas of the oil industry.

As part of President Carlos Menem's economic liberalization program, YPF was privatized between 1990 and 1993. Privatization faced opposition in the Argentine Congress and resulted in a reduction of payroll from 50,000 to 10,000 employees. Its more recent acquisition by Repsol has renewed the privatization controversy. Repsol-YPF reported $39 billion in revenue in 2002, making it the 94th largest company in the world.

BIBLIOGRAPHY. Carl E. Solberg, *Oil and Nationalism in Argentina: A History* (Standford University Press,1979); Repsol-YPF, www.repsol-ypf.com; U.S. Energy Information Administration, www.eia.doe.gov; "Global 500: World Largest Companies, " *Fortune* (July 2002).

LEOPOLDO RODRÍGUEZ-BOESTCH
PORTLAND STATE UNIVERSITY

research and development (R&D)

R&D IS A VITAL SET of activities that encompasses the search for scientific invention and the application of ideas to practical processes. The research component comprises the scientific investigation for new knowledge, which may be pure (i.e., guided by the intellectual curiosity of the scientist) or applied (i.e., guided by the needs of a sponsoring body). The development component comprises the commercialization of any scientific breakthrough. The final result, if successful, may be a dramatic innovation or a comparatively minor change to the ways things are already being done. This basic process of invention has been proceeding for thousands of years and has underpinned a great deal of human social and economic development.

R&D is supported by such activities as design, engineering, and learning-by-doing, which are not formally part of R&D, and hence not included in related statistics. While there is a general relationship between GROSS DOMESTIC PRODUCT (GDP) and level of expenditure on R&D, this does not always manifest itself in a positive correlation for economic growth. Countries vary in their ability to provide the macroeconomic stability, network of commercialization, and dissemination of knowledge and efficiency necessary for successful R&D investment.

Given the importance of R&D, governments have long realized it may be better not to allow it to be determined by random distribution of scientists and resources; instead governments have sought to bring together what are now called clusters—or amalgamations of complementary resources such as researchers, laboratory equipment, libraries, industrial facilities, and entrepreneurs—with a view to guiding research and

Research and development, especially in the pharmaceutical industry, is highly skilled and labor-intensive.

stimulating greater production. The first government to make a serious, centralized R&D effort was the French, in the years following the FRENCH REVOLUTION. A more systematic and larger-scale effort was made by the German government in the last years of the 19th century and the beginning of the 20th.

Both these efforts, and others, were motivated by the desire for rapid industrialization, and were spurred by the flow of goods from colonies in the Third World, convenient sources of important industrial inputs. As a result, the focus has generally been upon certain industries considered to be of strategic importance, such as armaments and electronics. More recently, countries such as South KOREA or JAPAN, which have successfully attempted to accomplish rapid industrialization, have focused on consumer products (sometimes by using reverse engineering) to rapidly create an export production capacity. Universities have had a crucial role in R&D, and this has been effectively managed when incentive structures are put in place to encourage university-level research to be developed into industrial applications. However, this can lead to problems with intellectual property ownership when sponsoring companies wish to retain exclusive ownership of the results of applied research, a situation that has frustrated some government-private sector research partnerships in, for example, AUSTRALIA. In a country such as Japan, where scientists are renowned for their ability to develop applications, rather than for pure inventiveness, the majority of R&D activity takes place in commercial concerns in which all the returns can be captured by the firm.

Multinational enterprises (MNEs) take an increasingly important role in the international economy and, as their size and scope increase, so too does their level of diversification in different industries. R&D is necessary to take advantage of the network of activities and resources that such MNEs can mobilize. However, it is likely that the MNE will wish to maintain the core R&D function at the home location.

Somewhat paradoxically, in rapidly changing, technologically advanced, and intensely competitive industries, such as electronics and semi-conductors, R&D partnerships between competing firms are very common, especially in comparatively short-term arrangements that focus on specific projects with designated distribution of returns. Projects often lead to products manufactured quickly and cheaply and at low cost—the profit from such products relies upon the value-added component. In other R&D-intensive industries such as pharmaceuticals, aeronautics, and robotics (in which continuous innovation is required), the very high level of return, required to meet the expenses of lengthy, highly skilled, labor-intensive periods of work, necessitates high retail costs of products.

BIBLIOGRAPHY. David P. Angel and Lydia Savage, "Globalization of R&D in the Electronics Industry: The Recent Experience of Japan," *Geographies of Economies* (Arnold, 1997); David Landes, *The Wealth and Poverty of Nations* (Little, Brown, 1998); OECD, *Science, Technology and Industry Outlook: Drivers of Growth: Information Technology, Innovation and Entrepreneurship* (OECD, 2001); Michael E. Porter, "Clusters and the New Economics of Competition," *Harvard Business Review* (November-December 1998).

JOHN WALSH, PH.D.
SHINAWATRA UNIVERSITY, THAILAND

resource

A biological resource can be as diverse as crops or animals or the production of penicillin molds.

THE CONCEPT RESOURCE is widely used both in economics and management. Generally, it refers to all input factors of production, i.e., goods that are demanded for their usefulness in producing final or intermediary goods. Specifically, one talks about individual classes of inputs such as natural resources, financial resources, human resources, or knowledge resources, all of which are in scarce supply relative to the amount demanded. Time itself is regarded as the ultimately scarce resource, which needs to be optimized by economic agents.

Economics studies the use of exhaustible and renewable resources, their productivity and rate of depletion, and their impact on economic GROWTH. Management theory investigates the employment of resources for the achievement of corporate goals. The resource-based view of the firm, which has become the dominant paradigm of strategic management thought, interprets firms as collections of resources (core competences, know-how, skills, routines, etc.) on which competitive advantages are built.

By pricing resources such that they find their optimum use, which is the core function of a market economy, capitalism is thought to be the economic system that makes the best use of the available resource endowment. Moreover, through the profit system, it provides the appropriate incentives to expand the resource base beyond the one available or known at a particular time. Both effects—the more efficient use of given resources and the expansion of the resource base—are sources of economic growth.

Classification. At a very general level, one may distinguish between exhaustible (or depletable) and renewable resources, the first category being a fund variable based on a given stock (such as minerals or fossil fuels) and the second category being a flow variable (such as sunlight, wind, or surface water). This categorization is related to the distinction between inanimate and biological resources. The latter (for example, crops, forests, and animal populations) use other renewable animate or inanimate resources (such as soil nutrients and solar energy) for their reproduction.

This classification applies also to the social world, where knowledge resources such as innovative ideas or human resources are renewable (though in the short-run they may appear to be in limited supply) while certain raw materials such as gold or bauxite are exhaustible. A further distinction exists between exclusive and non-exclusive resources (i.e., depending on whether or not consumers can be excluded from their consumption or use) and between resources for which rivalry or non-rivalry in consumption holds (i.e., depending on whether more than one consumer can use a resource at any point in time). Furthermore, there is a class of resources (such as beaches or ski slopes) that behave as non-rival resources over a certain range but where congestion sets in once a threshold of users has been reached. Such resources, which are often found in tourism but include also roads and telephone lines, have the economic properties of club goods, for which additional users, by reducing the average cost of using the facility, add to the utility of any one user up to a marginal level whereas additional users beyond this level reduce his utility by imposing congestion costs.

Economic issues. All firms (and households to the extent that they are producers) face, at least in the short-run, resource constraints. This raises the following central questions of resource economics.

1. How scarce are resources in relation to demand, i.e., what are the degrees of their relative scarcity?

2. How should resources best be allocated between alternative uses?

3. At what rate and what price should nonrenewable resources be depleted?

4. Do resources limit economic growth?

The classical economists generally thought of land as a fundamentally limiting factor of production. David RICARDO suggested that the higher-quality (and lower-cost) deposits of exhaustible resources would be exploited first, just as the more fertile agricultural land is cultivated first. Thomas MALTHUS thought that food output was limited to an arithmetic rate of increase whereas the population tended to grow geometrically, which would ultimately lead to declining standards of living.

Neoclassical economic thinking went beyond the limitations of this worldview in two respects: First, it recognized the role of capital and technology in "deepening" scarcer factors of production. LAND, which responded to investment, no longer had any unique significance, and investment in human capital (and in automation) allowed for larger outputs at lower labor inputs. Second, it acknowledged the possibilities of resource discovery and resource substitution as a function of the incentives created by the price system. Capital thus came to be regarded as the only factor truly limiting growth. More recently, it has been argued that even depletable resources would never be fully depleted, because their price can be expected to rise as a function of their increasing scarcity, which will both slow down the depletion rate, and provide incentives to substitute other resources that are available at a lower relative price.

Such arguments still abide by the classical view of increasing costs associated with depletion as a limit to growth. Contrary to this assumption, it has been pointed out that the price of most depletable resources has, over longer periods of time, tended rather to decrease than to increase.

MICROECONOMIC theory suggests that renewable resources are allocated to alternative uses according to the criteria for Pareto-efficiency. A necessary condition for the best allocation of resources is that the marginal product of any resource be the same for all of its alternative uses. Conditions for preserving the necessary minimum for replenishment (such as in fisheries) and for a maximum carrying capacity (such as in wildlife populations) can be defined. The more challenging case is that of formulating conditions for the optimum exploitation of a depletable resource (such as minerals), where intertemporal equilibria depend on factors such as exploration and recycling costs, property rights regimes, and external effects.

Given competitive markets, an optimum allocation between competing uses is achieved automatically. However, market power as under MONOPOLY or monopsony is often thought to lead to different marginal products and thus to misallocation. Furthermore, ignorance of profitable opportunities, lack of factor mobility (e.g., geographical fixation of the labor force or imperfectly competitive financial markets), and institutional constraints (e.g., professional licensing, labor unions, and patent protection) are frequently held to impede the spontaneous occurrence of an optimal allocation of resources. Regulation is often used to achieve a sustainable rate of exploitation, a time path that is meant to be welfare-maximizing over longer periods than market allocation would produce.

An abundance of natural resources is not necessarily a blessing. It has been shown that resource-rich countries tend to experience slower economic growth. They often fall prey to excessive rent-seeking, whereby powerful special interests try to substitute government intervention for the market. Furthermore, resource booms tend to drive up the value of the domestic currency in real terms, thereby dislocating production in other sectors, without a compensating exchange-rate correction when the boom subsides.

BIBLIOGRAPHY. Richard M. Auty, ed., *Resource Abundance and Economic Development* (Oxford University Press, 2001); Anthony C. Fisher, *Resource and Environmental Economics* (Addison-Wesley, 1981); Nicolai J. Foss, ed., *Resources, Firms, and Strategies* (Oxford University Press, 1997); Harold Hotelling, "The Economics of Exhaustible Resources," *Journal of Political Economy* (v.39, 1931); Alan Randall, *Resource Economics* (John Wiley & Sons, 1987); Julian L. Simon, *The Ultimate Resource* (Princeton University Press, 1996).

WOLFGANG GRASSL
HILLSDALE COLLEGE

retail

RETAILING IS THE DISTRIBUTION of products to the final consumer for personal use. It is an indispensable and sophisticated activity in a capitalist economy, and the degree of development of an economy at large can often be measured by the development of its retail sector.

Retailing is counted toward the service sector of an economy. Wholesale and retail businesses together are sometimes referred to as distributive trade. In the statistics of the UNITED STATES, retailing comprises groups 52–59 in the Standard Industrial Classification (SIC) and groups 44–45 in the North American Industrial Classification System (NAICS). In the EUROPEAN UNION (EU), retailing covers divisions 50 and 52 in the Statistical Classification of Economic Activities (NACE). According to the Census of Retail Trade of 1997 (which is part of the Economic Census conducted every five years), there were 1,561,195 retail establishments in the United States (+2.3 percent over 1992), generating sales of $2.546 trillion (+34.7 percent over 1992), using 21,165,111 million paid employees. Survey estimates for retail sales in 2002 amount to $3.266 trillion. Retail sales (including automobiles) in the 15 member countries of the European Union amounted to €1.720 trillion in 1997.

The numbers indicate a strong growth in retail sales but only a slow growth in the number of retail establishments. In the UNITED STATES, the retail sector has, over many decades, experienced a significant growth of average sales per store (1948: $74,000; 1972: $246,000; 1992: $1,242,000; 1997: $2,200,270). This is due to a strong industry concentration. Retailing in the United States, and to some extent also in other developed economies, has increasingly become dominated by large firms. Large retailers (those with sales of more than $10 million) account for just 2.1 percent of all retail firms but 68.0 percent of total retail sales, while small retailers (those with sales less than $1 million) account for 80 percent of all retail firms but only 12 percent of sales. In some retail sectors, the largest four firms account for more than half of total sales (athletic footwear: 65 percent; toys: 58 percent; general merchandisers: 58 percent).

Measured in terms in revenues, WAL-MART, a U.S.-based chain of discount mass merchandisers and warehouse clubs, is the largest company worldwide (sales in 2001: $219.8 billion). The second largest retailer, French chain Carrefour, occupies place 35 on the 2002 *Fortune* Global 500 list (sales in 2001: $62.2 billion), followed by U.S. specialty retailer Home Depot at place 46 (sales in 2001: $53.5 billion).

Retail functions. Retailers are intermediaries in distribution channels that connect producers and consumers. Their function in a capitalist economy is to facilitate exchange and to demonstrate value for buyers and sellers alike. For manufacturers, retailers as intermediaries reduce the costs of distribution by reducing the number of necessary transactions. Under direct distribution, i.e. without intermediaries, four different products to be placed with eight buyers require $4 \infty 8 = 32$ contacts, while a single intermediary reduces this to $4 + 8 = 12$ contacts.

The additional costs of using retailers rather than selling directly to consumers are therefore, in many instances, outweighed by increased efficiency. Retailers increase efficiency also by making products more readily available to target markets. Closeness to the consumer can be a strong competitive advantage.

Retailers not only reduce transaction costs but also help realize value by assuming a number of economic

and marketing functions from producers. They provide information about products, store goods, engage in sales promotion and advertising, take physical (and usually also legal) possession of products, and provide information about consumer demand. For consumers, they provide an assortment of products supplied by different manufacturers that could individually be found only at much higher search costs and offer these at convenient locations and times. Retailers also offer a repeatable mix to customers; with few exceptions (such as street peddlers) they are not one-off traders. In this sense, retailers create customer value in addition to the value derived from the products themselves.

Retail space. Most retailers serve customers within a spatially determined area around their location. With the exception of forms of direct retailing, such as catalog shopping or e-commerce, retailers are engaged in spatial competition, with sales areas spreading around stores as concentric circles. The probability of a particular consumer patronizing a particular store decreases with increasing distance from the store. At the same time, proximity to another store will increase, and halfway between the two store locations the consumer will, all else being equal, have an equal probability of patronizing either store. In reality, of course, the relative attractiveness of either store (as reflected in its assortment, service level, pricing, etc.) will also enter the decision calculus of the consumer and will be weighed against travel costs arising from distance. A consumer's probability of patronizing a retailer and the market share of this store are then related:

$$p_{ij} = f(d_{ik}, a_{ik}), \ k = 1, \ldots, j, \ldots, J \text{ and } M_j = \frac{\sum_i n_i p_{ij}}{\sum_i n_i}$$

where:

p_{ij}: probability of potential customer from location i to patronize retail store

d_{ij}: spatial or temporal distance of potential customer from location i from retail

store j in relation to distances from alternative stores $k \neq j$

a_{ij}: attractiveness of retail store j for potential customer from location i in

relation to attractiveness of alternative stores $k \neq j$

n_i: number of potential customers at location i

M_j: market share of retail store j

Also, the number of shopping trips a consumer will make over a certain period is inversely related to the distance from a retail store. Thus, at greater distances consumers will tend to make fewer trips in order to economize on transaction costs, and average check size will be larger.

Based on this general model, various gravitation models for evaluating the sales potential of retail locations have been elaborated (Jones and Simmons, 2000). The most traditional one is Reilly's Law (published in 1929), which stipulates that the portion of household purchasing power at location i, which is located between cities A and B, that will go to A is proportional to the number of residents at A and the distance between i and A.

Sales areas crucially depend on the type of store. In the United States, where the number of specialty stores has declined, supermarkets generally draw their customers from a smaller area around their location than specialty stores or discounters do. In European cities, which typically have a comparatively larger number of specialty stores but fewer shopping centers or shopping malls, the latter often draw customers from a very wide area while specialty stores supply the neighborhood. A critical determinant of sales areas is also the purchase pattern of residents, particularly the number of shopping trips per week, which in turn depends on factors such as family size and location of residence (rural/suburban/urban).

Retail types. Retailers can be categorized by several criteria, depending on the purpose of classification. Structural and functional criteria of classification comprise ownership type, breadth of assortment, size of establishment, degree of vertical integration, degree of customer contact, modality of customer contact, location, legal form of organization, and operational technique.

The most comprehensive typology of retailers is that used by the Census of Retail Trade in the United States, which places all retailers into more than 80 kind-of-business categories within eight major groups (SIC groups 52–59).

At the highest level in a structural or functional typology of retailing, store retailers (such as department stores or supermarkets) may be distinguished from non-store retailers (including all forms of direct marketing and selling), and from retail organizations (such as book clubs). The retail structures of economies, even in highly developed capitalist countries, show great differences, which are due to economic, cultural, social, legal, and geographic factors. The prevalence of types shifts over time.

In less-developed countries, non-store retailers (such as open-air markets and street vendors) and smaller individual stores predominate. With increasing income levels, the total number of retailers typically decreases while the average size of retail establishments increases (and types such as department stores and shopping malls are introduced). But retail structures are often

quite different even in countries of similar socioeconomic development. In European cities, where agglomeration density is higher and suburban zones are smaller than in typical North American cities, individual specialty stores predominate while shopping malls are still in their infancy and are usually confined to peripheral locations.

Store retailers can further be categorized by the level of service they provide or by classes of store size (usually expressed by increments in sales or number of employees). By increasing service level, they range from self-service stores via self-selection and limited-service stores to full-service stores. Another common classification is by breadth of assortment (i.e., by the number of product lines carried), and by depth of assortment (i.e., the number of items carried in each product line). Different types of store retailers can then be distinguished.

Department stores (such as JCPenney, Macy's or Marshall Fields in the United States, Fortnum & Mason and Harrod's in Great Britain, or Galleries Lafayette and Printemps in France) are large stores that feature many product lines, each line being operated as a separate department managed by specialist buyers or merchandisers. They often embrace the store-in-store model, being organized within (and sometimes across) departments according to major brands, each of which has its own boutique or kiosk.

Supermarkets are relatively large stores with a low-cost and low-margin assortment focusing on food and household products. Discount stores (such as Wal-Mart and K-Mart in the United States and Metro Cash & Carry in Germany) sell standard merchandise at lower prices and lower margins. They pass on to customers advantages from lower purchase prices, lower inventory costs, a lower service level, and a faster merchandise turnover. Specialist discounters and category killers focus on one product category such as toys, home electronics, or shoes, the difference between these retail types being the depth of product lines and the relative share of branded goods.

Off-price retailers are a more recent innovation and offer, as factory outlets, the surplus or discontinued products of particular manufacturers, or, as independent off-price stores (such as Marshalls), of a combination of manufacturers, at prices below the regular retail level. They offer only a minimum of service, in spartan surroundings, and are still largely confined to North America. One type of off-price stores are warehouse clubs (such as Sam's Clubs and Costco in the United States), which sell a broad assortment of brands and store brands only to members at prices typically 20–40 percent below those of supermarkets and discount stores.

Convenience stores are relatively small outlets with a limited assortment of high-turnover convenience products; they are often open every day around-the-clock and may be attached to other businesses such as gas stations. In addition, there are combinations of individual retailers, in the form of shopping centers or shopping malls, a type of retailing that has rapidly gained importance since its inception in the 1950s. Both types (though not smaller malls such as strip malls) require one or more anchor stores to attract customers.

Although it provides only a small share of final consumption, non-store retailing has recently grown faster than retail stores have. The main types of non-store retailing are:

1. System marketing (also known as multi-level selling or network marketing) as practiced by Avon Products or Amway Corp. in many countries

2. Direct selling (through the channels of the telephone, television, mail, or the internet)

3. Automatic vending (through machines)

4. Buying services (i.e., intermediaries which serve a specific clientele) such as the employees or members of an organization.

Retail organizations are associations of retailers (such as voluntary purchasing chains, retailer cooperatives, or franchises) set up to let individual and often smaller retailers benefit from economies of scale in purchasing and administration). They conduct business on organizational (business-to-business) markets.

By legal types, one may distinguish fully owned stores (with ownership of real estate and buildings or only ownership of equipment and inventory) from franchises. Single stores are distinguished from proprietary chains. Individual stores cannot grow beyond a certain size at which they have achieved a maximum penetration of its spatially bounded target market. This is why retail store growth occurs horizontally, by developing chains of same-type stores at multiple locations. Franchises are contractual relations between a franchiser who develops a retail model and independent franchisees who receive marketing services and certain exclusive rights in return for franchise fees. FRANCHISING is an alternative to the expansion of proprietary retail chains. In many countries, automobile dealerships, fast-food restaurants, gas stations, and convenience stores are organized as franchise systems.

Retail evolution. In capitalist economies, the retail sector is typically a very dynamic element. Several theories attempt to explain the dynamism of the sector through specific features of its evolution. The retail life-cycle theory assumes that types of retailing, much like the products they offer, are subject to a life cycle, the phases of which are innovation, growth, maturity, and decline. The exact shape of the cycle may show great interna-

tional variability. Department stores, which developed in the United States in the 19th century and were soon introduced in other industrialized economies, took many decades to reach maturity, as experience was gathered about their optimal organization and marketing.

Catalog merchants developed in the 1870s and 1880s, experienced rapid growth, and have remained in a phase of maturity ever since, with no essential changes to the business model. Newer types such as convenience stores or factory outlets have reached maturity much quicker. In Europe, on the other hand, factory outlets are still in the introduction phase. Some types, such as general stores in the United States, have completed passing through the decline stage and have largely left the market.

In Mediterranean countries, Africa, and Latin America, general stores still have strong market shares and are only slowly being replaced by supermarkets. Some types of retail business such as bazaars in Turkey, North Africa, and the Middle East, have proven very resilient and seem to have been in the maturity phase for decades. Though imported retail types may have taken away some market share, bazaars have reacted by changing their assortment; sales to tourists now make up for what has been lost from selling to locals. In free markets, retail structure adjusts very effectively to changing consumer needs and wants and to changes in real estate value.

Two explanations of retail evolution have attained particular prominence. The wheel-of-retailing hypothesis uses price and service offered to explain how retailers start in the low end of the market and move up to higher segments through the addition of extra services and store features, thus creating a gap in the low end of the market, which gives rise to new entrants (and thus "the wheel turns"). In this way, innovation in the retail sector starts always with deciding how to satisfy consumer wants better at lower prices, and this can be achieved only at a low level of service. Research on the development of the retail sector in many countries, however, has cast doubt on whether stores always increase service levels and costs.

Another explanation, the retail accordion hypothesis, suggests that the pattern of retail evolution has tended to alternate between domination by wide-assortment retailers and domination by narrow-line, specialized retailers. This hypothesis of institutional change implies that both diversification and specialization strategies can succeed under certain circumstances. In the United States, general stores came first; as settlements grew, specialists developed; in the wake of urbanization and of growing incomes, department stores which stocked wide assortments were set up for consumers to satisfy more of their wants at one location and thus save on time. More recently, again, a tendency toward more specialty stores has been noted. Critics of the hypothesis have pointed out that it does not apply to all cases of retail evolution and that is not an explanatory model that lends itself to predictions.

Retail management. Like all management decisions, those of retail managers are driven by the SCARCITY of resources (in retailing mainly shelf space) and the necessity to optimize. The principal retail management decisions (apart from planning decisions such as the choice of location and of store layout and size) are those of choosing, developing and implementing the best retail mix.

· The retail mix includes all factors that can be controlled by a retailer, e.g., physical facilities, merchandising, pricing, promotion, services, purchasing, and personnel. These, in turn, determine consumer perception and influence store choice decisions. The product assortment can be analyzed in terms of the breadth of the assortment (i.e., the number of product lines offered), and the depth of each product line (or the number of distinguishable items).

In retailing, the term stock-keeping unit (SKU) is used for any product that is an inventory item and takes up a slot of shelf space. Retailers manage their business primarily at the level of product forms, i.e., different sizes or package variants of the same product count as different SKUs. An important assortment decision is that of the ratio between branded products (or national brands) and store brands (or private labels). In discount supermarkets (such as Aldi or Sav-A-Lot), store brands typically have a much larger share than in standard supermarkets (such as Kroger or Safeway), and lines tend to be less deep. The business model of discounters relies on a quicker turnover of fewer SKUs (i.e., on the sale of higher-unit volume at lower margins per unit).

Many supermarkets now charge a slotting fee for accepting a new brand, to cover the costs of stocking and listing it. Positioning of products within the store and on shelves is of crucial importance, and retail management has developed rules of optimal location.

Assortment decisions are always made in combination with purchasing and pricing decisions. In some cases, such as generally for food and other convenience products, retailers will order through wholesalers, in other cases directly from manufacturers. Pricing strategies generally have to chose between high-volume, low-markup (market penetration pricing) and lower-volume, higher markup (price skimming). Everyday low pricing, as practiced by Wal-Mart, is an instance of the first strategy. Price tactics, such as promotional pricing and odd-even pricing, are also widely used in retailing.

Retail performance. The economic performance of (store) retailers is measured by ratios such as sales per floor space, gross margin (actual sales price/purchasing cost), and inventory-to-sales. In 2000, for example, the American retail chain Kohl's took in an average of $279 per square foot, compared with $220 for Target and $147 for Dillard's. In the same year, the gross margin of all retailers in the United States was 27.8 percent of sales; it has remained relatively stable for at least a decade. However, there are significant differences according to types of stores and merchandise.

Men's clothing stores average a gross margin of 44.5 percent and furniture stores a margin of 44.1 percent, while that of warehouse clubs and superstores is only 16.7 percent and that of automotive dealers 17.5 percent. The inventory/sales ratio of all retail stores in December 2002, amounted to 1.31. Since unsold inventory is a cost item, retailers want to minimize this ratio (without, at the same time, defaulting on customer requests for readily available merchandise); smaller ratios indicate that merchandise is turned over faster. For motor-vehicle and parts dealers, this ratio is (without seasonal adjustment) as high as 2.07, for food and beverage stores as low as 0.79. Direct product profitability is a measure of an SKU's total handling costs from the time it reaches the warehouse until a customer buys it and takes physical possession. This ratio often has little relation to gross margins, since high-volume SKUs may have high handling costs that reduce their actual profitability. Collection of scanner data allows for the in-store calculation of numerous other metrics that make retail management one of the most sophisticated fields of business.

Retail trends. Some developments that are likely to characterize the retail landscape over the next years are the following:

1. Increasing emphasis on relationship marketing, i.e., on achieving higher customer loyalty by building long-term relationships based on a high level of satisfaction

2. Further retailer domination of marketing channels, as evidenced by larger size and stronger bargaining power of stores, application of advanced technology (such as scanning and electronic data interchange), and a more sophisticated implementation of the marketing concept

3. Further incorporation of wholesaling and even manufacturing functions as vertical integration advances; already now, grocery retailers such as Safeway and Aldi do their own wholesaling while department stores and specialists like Marks & Spencer and The Gap are involved at all levels including product design and quality testing

4. Further increase in the share of store brands in product assortments of supermarkets, and widening of the price gap to national brands

5. Expansion of hybrid forms of retailers, e.g. supermarkets with bank branches

6. Intensification of inter-type competition, e.g. between self-service and full-service stores

7. Increasing shift to non-store retailing, particularly direct sales and internet sales

8. Further integration of "bricks-and-mortar" and "virtual" retailers, as more store-based retailers offer online shopping and retailers with exclusively online-based customers seek a more secure cash-flow

9. Intensification of competition, mainly based on price, in most categories

10. Stagnation or slow reduction of industry concentration, as the share of large chains will likely decline in some markets.

BIBLIOGRAPHY. Barry Berman and Joel R. Evans, *Retail Management: A Strategic Approach* (Prentice Hall, 2000); Patrick M. Dunne, Robert F. Lusch and David A. Griffith, *Retailing* (South-Western, 2002); Avijit Ghosh, *Retail Management* (International Thomson, 1994); Ken Jones and Jim Simmons, *Retail Environment* (International Thomson, 2000); Philip Kotler, *Marketing Management* (Prentice Hall, 2003); Michael Levy and Barton A. Weitz, *Retailing Management* (McGraw-Hill, 2004); James M. Mayo, *The American Grocery Store: The Evolution of a Business Space* (Greenwood, 1993); Peter McGoldrick, *Retail Marketing* (McGraw-Hill, 2002).

WOLFGANG GRASSL
HILLSDALE COLLEGE

Ricardo, David (1772–1823)

DAVID RICARDO WAS a major voice in economics in the final days of the INDUSTRIAL REVOLUTION and continued to dominate the field of British economic history for over 50 years. He was born in London in 1772, the third of 17 children, into a wealthy family of Spanish-Dutch Jews. When Ricardo was 11 years old, his father sent him to Holland for three years to attend Talmud Tora, a special Jewish school. He spent a year studying with tutors after his return, and by the age of 14, Ricardo was serving as an apprentice in his father's brokerage firm. Because his marriage to a Quaker alienated his father, Ricardo was cut off with a legacy of only 800 pounds. He worked hard and, using his extensive understanding of money, Ricardo became a millionaire in his mid-20s. At the age of 42, Ricardo retired to follow intellectual pursuits and enjoy country life on his estate, Gatcomb Park.

Ricardo never went to college and found this fact embarrassing later in his life, but he had an amazing ability to understand complex ideas and translate them into simple terms. Politically, Ricardo became a follower of Jeremy BENTHAM (1748–1832), who believed that the goal of human beings was to pursue happiness and avoid pain. Ricardo rejected his Jewish heritage and became a Unitarian after his marriage, believing that individuals should engage in a search for universal truth rather than limiting themselves to a single creed such as Judaism or Christianity.

In addition to economics, Ricardo studied math, chemistry, geology, and mineralogy on his own, becoming a founder of the British Geological Society. During the course of his intellectual pursuits, Ricardo chanced to read economist Adam SMITH's (1723–90) *Wealth of Nations* and changed the course of economics as well as his own life. Ricardo's critics, such as John Maynard KEYNES (1883–1946), would later claim that Ricardo turned economics in the wrong direction. His supporters, however, argue that Ricardo changed the economist's understanding of political economy.

The focus of Ricardo's study of economics, which he began at the age of 38, was the law of distribution. He wanted to understand how goods were distributed among the various classes of society. Along with most great thinkers of his day, Ricardo believed that resources were scarce. For example, when factory owners received huge amounts of profit, less money was available to be divided among the workers who created the products produced in the factories. Karl MARX, the father of SOCIALISM, traces his economic roots directly to Ricardo's labor theory, claiming that Ricardo promoted the idea that capitalism would have to be destroyed to protect the labor rights of workers.

Early in his intellectual career, Ricardo became friends with two well-known individuals who would influence his life in a number of ways: British economist and philosopher and fellow utilitarian James Mill (1773–1836) became a mentor and political economist Thomas Robert MALTHUS (1766–1834), known for his theories on natural selection, influenced his understanding of economics. Ricardo's first published work on economic theory was a pamphlet, "The High Price of Bullion, A Proof of the Depreciation of Bank Notes," in 1809. The British public called it "The Paper Against Gold" because Ricardo argued that Britain should develop a currency based on metal rather than on gold. His major work was *Principles of Political Economy and Taxation* in 1917 in which he examined various ways to redistribute wealth. Ricardo maintained that the goal of the worker was simply to have enough money to take care of his family at the standard of living to which he was accustomed. Therefore, wages tended to stabilize at this subsistence level. Ricardo believed that investment was the key to personal wealth and invested in funds, land, rents and mortgages. Like Smith, Ricardo wanted to understand how a country could become rich and powerful and still provide happiness and comfort to its citizens.

Ricardo was appointed to a Parliamentary committee created to solve Britain's financial problems and would later serve in the British Parliament from 1819 until his death. Despite his official ties to British institutions, Ricardo was often critical of how the country was run. For example, he claimed that the BANK OF ENGLAND was interested only in huge profits for bank managers and not in serving the interests of the public. Ricardo died in 1923 of a cerebral infection, leaving his wife and seven children an estate of around 750,000 pounds.

BIBLIOGRAPHY. John Bowditch and Clement Ramsland, *Voices of the Industrial Revolution* (University of Michigan Press, 1963); John Wood Cunningham, *David Ricardo: Critical Assessments* (Croom Helm, 1985); "Economists—David Ricardo," www.bized.ac.uk; Paul A. Samuelson, *Economics* (McGraw-Hill, 1973); Pierro Straffa, ed., *The Works and Correspondence of David Ricardo* (Cambridge University Press); David Weatherall, *David Ricardo: A Biography* (Martinus Nuhoff, 1976).

ELIZABETH PURDY, PH.D.
INDEPENDENT SCHOLAR

risk

UNCERTAINTY SURROUNDS, preoccupies, and intrigues us. The future is inherently uncertain: it may promise to be better than today, but who can dismiss the possibility of devastating disasters? A farmer faces the likelihood of a flood or drought, a worker may become unemployed, a firm is never certain about the success of its new product, creditors to a firm may never see their investments again. Uncertainty underlying all these circumstances is the fundamental source of risk faced by decision-makers. Risk is what makes tomorrow so relevant and exciting for today, and managing our future and the risks that surround us is a multibillion dollar industry.

Risk, in economics, measures the impact of probability of a loss or a less desirable outcome on well-being, and is an indispensable component of our decision-making process under uncertainty. Economic analysis of risk seeks answers to the following three basic questions: How does individual behavior respond to uncertainty? How do people value (and price) risk? How do individuals and society manage and mitigate risks? The primary objective behind studying risk is to understand people's choices under uncertainty. This understanding

is, in turn, used to measure and manage risks, and ultimately "to put future at the service of the present," as Peter L. Bernstein puts it.

One fundamental assumption in economics and psychology about human attitude toward uncertainty is that all individuals dislike risk. The standard analysis of risk and its measures build on this key premise—although in gambling situations, whereby addiction and entertainment are involved, this premise is less relevant. This assumption can be demonstrated by the following example: An individual, with a certain amount of initial wealth, is offered to participate in a one-time coin toss (it is a fair coin). If it is heads, she earns $100, otherwise loses $100. This is a "pure risk": with one-half probability she increases her wealth by $100, and with one-half probability her wealth decreases by $100 (her initial wealth is more than $100). There is uncertainty about the outcome but the offer is otherwise fair, and there is no ambiguity (that is, all possible events and their probabilities are known in advance). The fundamental assumption about attitude toward uncertainty suggests that most individuals would decline such an offer. Therefore, by definition, a risk averse individual prefers the certain outcome of keeping her wealth over accepting the pure risk. A risk neutral individual would be indifferent between the certain outcome and the pure risk. A risk lover would prefer the pure risk over the certain outcome.

The price of risk. Suppose we change the scenario slightly and ask: What is the maximum that the person would be willing to pay to avoid the risk (the coin toss)? What is the price of the certain outcome relative to the risk? The answer would determine the risk premium for the given risk, and measures how much the person would be willing to pay to eliminate uncertainty. In our daily lives, all of us are confronted with similar choices. Insuring a car and paying an insurance premium, can be viewed as paying a risk premium to eliminate (at least some of the) undesirable eventualities. Determining a valid measure of risk premium is important, because it allows the markets to price risk in pecuniary terms, and thus allows us to buy and sell, in short, trade risks. This is routinely done in the stock and bond markets, which have specialized to price and trade risky financial assets.

We often speak of increased uncertainty and increased risk, reflecting the fact that uncertainty underlying our assessment of risk may have changed. When risks change, how do they affect the risk premium? Suppose we modify the coin-tossing example above in the following way: if heads, win $200, tails loose $200. Compared to the previous example this has the same expected value (zero) before the coin is tossed. But, now the stakes are raised. Economic theory suggests that a risk-averse individual would find this coin toss even more risky, and thereby should be willing to pay higher risk premium to eliminate uncertainty. In general, a change in underlying uncertainty is deemed to increase risk only when the risk premium also increases.

Pure risks of the sorts mentioned above are rejected because they entail no (risk) premium or welfare gain over the certain outcome. This suggests that individuals would consider a coin toss only when the offer entails a net expected gain over the initial wealth; that is, only when they are properly compensated for the risk. Suppose we revise the offer, increase the gains (in the event of heads), say from $100 to $110, and keep the losses (if tails) at $100. Now the expected gain or return from the coin toss is $10 (but still not certain). Would this offer be accepted?

The significance of such increments in expected return is that eventually there will be a point whereby the individual is indifferent between accepting and declining (certain outcome) the offer. This breakeven point determines the price of this particular risk. Riskier offers must entail higher expected returns (risk premiums), which is the logic underlying the quintessential tradeoff between risk and return.

To study behavior under uncertainty in general contexts, economists have devised an elegant (but also controversial) framework called "expected utility theory." The framework is based on the notion that individuals are risk averse and have a systematic way of ranking the desirability of probabilities associated with future events. While agents have no influence over the probability of these events, their own actions today have a tremendous impact on how each of these events (should they occur) will affect them. These are the consequences or payoffs associated with each event. Expected utility theory postulates that there exists a (utility) function that represents a particular ordering among probability distributions of payoffs by the mathematical expectation of the utility of the payoffs.

For example, for most households, future labor earnings are their primary source of income, but this income is highly uncertain, as well. The unfortunate prospect of unemployment looms large during recessions. The state of unemployment means low (perhaps no) income, and reduced ability to consume goods and services. With this possibility in mind, most households adjust their current actions. Although they cannot change the likelihood of a recession by their own actions, they have a certain level of control over the ultimate outcomes. They may save out of their current income today, and use these savings as buffer stock should they become unemployed. A low saving rate today would mean taking a risk in which the low consumption payoff has a high probability. A high saving rate today would signal that the individual is prepared to postpone immediate gratification, but secure savings that can later be drawn upon.

In fact, by their saving decisions, the individuals reveal their preferences over the likelihood of future payoffs. Expected utility theory suggests that savings decisions would be based on the weighted sum of the utilities from low and high future consumption, where the weights are nothing but the probability of being unemployed and employed.

The uncertainty of risk. Expected utility theory has found extensive applications in many fields of economics. Capital-asset pricing theory in finance studies how future streams of income are discounted and priced today. Since future income streams are uncertain, there is an element of risk, and the entire capital-asset pricing theory can be viewed as determining the appropriate measure of risk for each asset. Consumption smoothing hypothesis in development economics studies how poor households use market and non-market based institutions to mitigate risks such as starvation, and poor health.

Macroeconomists are concerned about the welfare costs of recessions, and these costs ultimately depend on some notion of risk-adjusted welfare.

Two practical issues arise in studying attitudes toward uncertainty. First, although we may agree on the key premise that all individuals are risk-averse, it would be unreasonable to assume that all individuals share the same degree of risk-aversion. Faced with identical risks and under identical circumstances, people make different choices. An appropriate measure of risk should allow for comparing individuals in terms of their aversion to risk. This is possible if an increase in risk-aversion coincides with an increase in the risk premium. Indeed, an individual is said to be more risk-averse if she is willing to pay more to eliminate a given uncertainty.

Second, we might wonder whether all risk-averse individuals agree on the consequences of a change in uncertainty. Unfortunately, a particular change in uncertainty can result in an increase or a decrease in the risk premium depending on the individual. Consequently, while some may dislike the change, others may welcome it. This occurs because with a change in uncertainty while some desirable eventualities may become more likely, others become less likely. These tradeoffs are not valued equally by different individuals, and may lead to different rankings of risks.

When a group of individuals or a society considers the desirability of certain risks, differences in opinion become very important. Risks associated with anthropogenic climate change and genetically modified foods are assessed very differently across and within societies. While both of these activities change the risks we face in the future, relative costs and benefits are valued differently. The intensity of the current debates over these issues partly reflects the difficulty of ranking risks in a unanimous manner.

Another dimension of the future is the unknown. In order to assess the risks associated with our current actions, we must possess some common knowledge of possible future events, and their probabilities. Risk assessment and management start with information gathering, and measurement (statistics). Life insurance is a prime example because premiums are entirely based on life-expectancy calculations. Such calculations have only been possible after systematic data collection and analysis.

Car insurance rates are determined based on historic trends: Young, male drivers have historically had higher accident rates (a risky group). This is unlikely to change in the short run, so all young, male drivers pay higher insurance premiums. But, how much do we know about the future climate of our planet? Our knowledge is imperfect; there are no probabilities or scenarios that all climate scientists seem to agree upon. The notion that all future eventualities and their objective probabilities are known appears far-fetched. However, for the very same reason every bit of information that would allow us to be more precise about the likely future outcomes is tremendously valuable.

Managing risk. Given that risk is such an important part of our reality, and is undesirable, it is understandable that there are many institutions and financial instruments that have been developed to manage them. Since the Neolithic revolution, farmers have faced uncertainty about their future income and thus risks concerning their survival. Today's agricultural technology (and weather) is very different. So are the risks. What has not changed over time, however, is the desire to manage and mitigate these risks. Farmers have, throughout history, designed mechanisms to reduce the impact of risks on individual welfare, even in the absence of perfect knowledge. These mechanisms have varied from simple, but nevertheless effective self-insurance to sophisticated and sometimes complex market-based securities, such as futures contracts and options. The instinctive, but powerful idea behind all these mechanisms is to ensure that "not all the eggs are in one basket."

Since the details of the institutions and instruments that are used to manage risks vary, first consider the simplest case: self-insurance. The basic idea behind self-insurance is that individuals anticipate risks, and their own actions provide cushions for undesirable eventualities without other parties being directly involved. Peasants have developed very effective self-insurance mechanisms. They typically raise crops and livestock simultaneously. Livestock can also be seen as a buffer against the risk of variations in crop yield, because the availability of animals helps regulate the quantity of calories available for human consumption. During a bumper crop year, peasants increase the number of livestock, and existing animals accumulate body weight. When the crop yield is poor, available livestock gives access to additional food by providing meat, and reducing the demand for animal feed, part of which can also be consumed by humans.

While self-insurance mechanisms are simple, they are also costly for individuals. They require substantial buffer stocks or savings that can otherwise be used for current consumption. The value of these savings is especially high for relatively poor individuals and societies. Even in a bumper-crop year, peasants consume low calories and poor households live hand-to-mouth. Self-insurance can be an effective tool for managing risks, but one that requires considerable personal sacrifices, and is sometimes prohibitive.

Human ingenuity has resulted in instruments and mechanisms that reduce such sacrifices, especially when risks are not perfectly correlated across individuals. Perfectly correlated risks occur when all of us become sick simultaneously (epidemics), and when all farmers suffer from a devastating disaster. Such events are (fortunately) rare. Since risks affect different people at different times, it is possible to share them. This circumvents the large sacrifices associated with self-insurance. Risk-sharing takes advantage of the fact that the total resources available to a group of individuals is larger, and that a given risk can be diversified across the group, or shared. Risk-sharing arrangements can be formal contracts, such as car insurance, which involve individuals who are exposed to similar risks. Extended families and communities can share risks through informal arrangements, whereby help is extended to those who need it the most. While these are non-market based institutions, deeply rooted notions of reciprocity ensure enforcement of appropriate risk-sharing.

The principal idea underlying risk-sharing arrangements is also applicable in contexts where particular risk categories are not perfectly correlated. Perfectly correlated risks occur when different events happen simultaneously, when drought, flood, and pestilence all happen at the same time, and when coffee and tea prices are positively correlated. But, if low coffee prices coincide systematically with high tea prices, and vice versa, a farmer who can divide the land between tea and coffee reduces the fluctuations in income, and thus uncertainty. In effect, the farmer diversifies across a given risk category, or "pools" different risks. The same diversification principle has been advocated as the single most important investment strategy.

Of course, some risks are under our own influence. Smoking increases the risk of lung cancer and cardiovascular diseases. By our own actions (not smoking), we can control the risks that we face. However, this very notion of (however imperfect) control over the future renders some risks hard to insure against. Does the availability of car insurance make people more reckless drivers? Surely farmers cannot control the weather, but do they also take excessive risks when the government extends a crop insurance program? Such incentive problems form an important aspect of contemporary risk management practices.

BIBLIOGRAPHY. Peter L. Bernstein, *Against the Gods: The Remarkable Story of Risk* (John Wiley & Sons, 1998); Anne Case, et al., "Symposium on Consumption Smoothing in Developing Countries," *Journal of Economic Perspectives* (v.9/3, 1995); John H. Cochrane, *Asset Pricing* (Princeton University Press, 2001); Christian Gollier, *The Economics of Risk and Time* (MIT Press, 2001); Mark J. Machina and Michael Rothschild, "Risk," *The New Palgrave: A Dictionary of Economics* (v.4, Macmillan Press, 1987); Harry Markowitz, *Portfolio Selection: Efficient Diversification of Investment* (Yale University Press, 1959); William F. Sharpe, Gordon J. Alexander, and Jeffery V. Bailey, *Investments* (Prentice Hall, 1995); Robert Shiller, *Macro Markets: Creating Institutions for Managing Society's Largest Economic Risks* (Clarendon Press, 1993).

TALAN IŞCAN
DALHOUSIE UNIVERSITY, CANADA

Robinson, Joan (1903–83)

JOAN VIOLET ROBINSON was born in Surrey, England. After completion of her studies in economics at Girton College, Cambridge University, she married the young Cambridge economist Austin Robinson in 1926. They had two daughters. After spending a few years in India, Robinson returned to Cambridge and taught there from 1931 until 1971.

Robinson's first important work was "The Economics of Imperfect Competition" (1933). This was a decisive breakaway of economic theory from the assumptions of perfect COMPETITION and an extension of the Marshallian tradition. Later, she became one of the important members of a group of young economists known as the Cambridge Circus, who regularly met for discussion, and played a significant role in the evolving drafts of John Maynard KEYNES' *General Theory of Employment, Interest and Money* (1936). She was a major figure in the Keynesian revolution and produced genuine expositions of Keynes' theory.

Robinson turned her attention to the works of Karl MARX and, in her "Essay on Marxian Economics" (1942), she compares the economic analysis of Marx with mod-

ern economic theory. This was among the first serious studies of Marxian economics.

Published in 1956, Robinson's masterwork, *The Accumulation of Capital*, sought to address the issues related to the long-term growth of income and capital—typical issues of concern within the classical tradition—in a Keynesian framework. This was followed by her work on the growth theory, which in conjunction with the works of Nicholas Kaldor, became known as the Cambridge Growth Theory.

Robinson's work on capital, influenced by Piero SRAFFA (1960), exposed the problems arising from capital aggregation, and its serious ramifications for the neoclassical marginal productivity theory of distribution. This led to a well-known debate between American economists in Cambridge, Massachusetts, and economists in Cambridge, England, which became known as the Cambridge Capital Controversy.

BIBLIOGRAPHY. Geoffrey C. Harcourt, *Some Cambridge Controversies in the Theory of Capital* (Cambridge University Press, 1972); J.M. Keynes, *The General Theory of Employment, Interest and Money* (Macmillan, 1936); Joan Robinson, *The Economics of Imperfect Competition* (Macmillan, 1933); Joan Robinson, *An Essay on Marxian Economics* (Macmillan, 1942); Joan Robinson, *The Accumulation of Capital* (Macmillan, 1956); Piero Sraffa, *Production of Commodities by Means of Commodities* (Cambridge University Press, 1960).

HAMID AZARI-RAD, PH.D.
STATE UNIVERSITY OF NEW YORK, NEW PALTZ

Rockefeller, John D. (1839–1937)

MERGERS BETWEEN OIL giants received significant media coverage in the late 20th century. The giants, EXXONMOBIL, CHEVRONTEXACO, and Amoco are companies that once shared related names. Exxon was once called STANDARD OIL of New Jersey, Mobil was Standard Oil of New York, Chevron was Standard Oil of California, and Amoco was Standard Oil of Indiana. John Davison Rockefeller was the driving force behind the Standard Oil Company, a virtual MONOPOLY that dominated the UNITED STATES oil industry for decades.

John D. Rockefeller was born in Richford, New York. In 1852, Rockefeller attended Owego Academy in Owego, New York. He was very good at mathematics. He attended high school in Cleveland, Ohio from 1853–55, and in the same year learned single- and double-entry bookkeeping, banking, and other business subjects at Folsom Mercantile College.

Rockefeller's business career began as a clerk in a commission sales firm. In 1859, he and a neighbor,

Maurice B. Clark, started a company as commission merchants of grain and other goods. Rockefeller began to apply his precise business style and strong work ethic. It did not take long, however, for Rockefeller to grow weary of being a commission merchant. The rewards were too modest.

In the 1860s, Rockefeller's attention was shifted to the oil industry by the oil boom. He found that the oil from the recently discovered northwestern Pennsylvania wells was of high quality and could be refined into several useful products. Rockefeller also discovered that the oil market was nearly perfectly competitive (an industry with many small buyers and sellers, each being a "price taker"). It only took $10,000 to set up a small refinery, making entry barriers extremely low.

Samuel Andrews, experienced with shale-oil refining, joined the team. The firm of Rockefeller, Andrews, Clark & Company was formed in 1863. In 1865, Rockefeller bought out the Clark interest. In 1866, Rockefeller brought in his brother, William D., and they built another refinery in Cleveland named the Standard Works. They also opened an office in New York City to handle the export business, with William D. in charge. In 1867 Henry M. Flagler, a grain merchant turned oil-barrel manufacturer, became a partner.

By 1868, Rockefeller, Andrews & Flagler ran the largest oil-refining operation in the world. They had their own warehouses and distribution center built in Cleveland. The area's railroad systems (providing substantial rebates) and waterway facilitated transportation. From crude oil they manufactured lubricating oil, gasoline, benzine, and petroleum jelly. They improved their refining methods by careful process analysis, and by treating nearly all waste materials so that they could be used. The volatility of oil product prices prompted Rockefeller and Flagler to adopt "Our Plan" that survives today as the logic of competitive structure. An industry in competitive chaos was analyzed, and eventually consolidated into a form that promoted price stability and economies of scale.

On January 10, 1870, John D. Rockefeller, William D. Rockefeller, Flagler, Andrews, Stephen Harkness (a silent partner in a previous business), and O.B. Jennings (brother-in-law of William D.) established the Standard Oil Company of Ohio. At its inception, Standard Oil held nearly 10 percent of the oil business. The aggressive output of many small companies was driving down oil prices. Rockefeller explored the idea of creating a market that had a few large, vertically integrated firms (OLIGOPOLY in today's parlance). Vertical integration is an arrangement where a company keeps the various stages of production, from underground crude oil to the sale of products to final consumers, within the company.

During 1871, moving the company closer to a MONOPOLY, John D. and his partner, Flagler, decided to consolidate all oil refining firms into one (not a few). This action helped eliminate excess capacity and price-cutting. Consolidation involved assessing the value of a rival refinery, and giving the owner(s) Standard Oil stock in proportion to the value of the company. The more talented owners would enter Standard Oil management. By 1872, Standard Oil began to expand to other areas of the United States through these mergers. The company built its own pipeline, in addition to acquiring the pipelines from other companies. By 1879, Standard Oil controlled about 90 percent of the oil refining in the United States. Rockefeller's tasks became broader as the business grew larger. Standard Oil Trust was formed on January 2, 1882. The 43-year-old John D. Rockefeller was the chief. The trust was capitalized at $70 million, but the true market value was close to $200 million.

By 1890, Standard Oil was set up as a nationwide network that reached almost every locality in America. However, domination of the retail markets helped cause the American public to develop a distaste for the company. The attorney general of Ohio brought a suit against Standard Oil. The company lost the suit, and the trust was dissolved in March 1892. Each trust certificate was to be exchanged for the proportioned share of stock in the 20 component companies of Standard Oil. Interestingly, this had no practical effect on the operation of the company.

As time passed, Rockefeller became very wealthy. At one point, he suffered a partial nervous breakdown from overwork. From his early working days, regardless of how much he was paid, he gave to the Baptist Church and local charities. In 1896, Rockefeller let others take on the day-to-day responsibilities of Standard Oil. He shifted his attention toward major philanthropic activities. One of the most significant of these was a donation made to help create the University of Chicago. The total contribution to the university amounted to $35 million.

The industrial-giant-turned-philanthropist began applying funds to human welfare, and to facilitating the creation of institutions that sought to improve human life. In 1901, Rockefeller founded the Rockefeller Institute for Medical Research. The focus of the organization was to discover the causes, prevention, and cures of disease. Many new scientific techniques in medicine, biology, biochemistry, biophysics, and related disciplines came from its laboratory. The organization thrives today under the title Rockefeller University. Perhaps the Rockefeller creation with the greatest global impact was the Rockefeller Foundation. Established in 1913, the foundation has given significant assistance to public health, medical education, food production, scientific advancement, social research, and countless other fields. Rockefeller established other organizations that promoted education (General Education Board, 1902), and public health (Rockefeller Sanitary Commission, 1902).

Rockefeller's death came on May 23, 1937. His life was an accomplished one, characterized by vigorous entrepreneurship, hard work, and success. Many of his biological descendants have gone on to become prominent Americans. His hard work and investments thrive today through the offspring of the Standard Oil Company, two of which are back together. EXXONMOBIL is now competing in a competitive global oil market. Rockefeller personified American capitalism perhaps more than any individual before or since.

BIBLIOGRAPHY. Ron Chernow, *Titan: The Life of John D. Rockefeller, Sr.* (Random House, 1998); John T. Flynn, *God's Gold: The Story of Rockefeller and his Times* (Harcourt, Brace, 1932); Burton Folsom, Jr., *The Myth of the Robber Barons* (Young America's Foundation, 1991); Allan Nevins, *John D. Rockefeller: The Heroic Age of American Enterprise* (Charles Scribner's Sons, 1940); Keith T. Poole, "Entrepreneurs and American Economic Growth: John D. Rockefeller," voteview.uh.edu; Rockefeller University Archive, www.rockefeller.edu; Daniel Yergin, *The Prize* (Simon & Shuster, 1991).

JOHN SORRENTINO, PH.D.
MAHBUB RABBANI, M.A.
TEMPLE UNIVERSITY

Roman Empire

FROM A SMALL VILLAGE in central Italy dominated by its Etruscan neighbors, came the greatest empire the Western world has known. Legend held that the city of Rome was founded on the Palatine Hill by Romulus, its first king. What is certain is that the empire forged by the energetic, ambitious, and patriotic Romans would be of unprecedented might and durability. Its achievements in government, law, military organization and strategy, engineering, architecture, urban planning, literature, historiography, and oratory serve as models to this day.

At first an aristocratic republic and later a dynastic dictatorship, the Roman Empire often brought long-term and wide-spread stability, peace, commercial activity, and cultural and economic unity to its far-flung dominions. Nevertheless, it also enslaved millions and intermittently produced reigns of unmitigated terror. Although administrative and political skills are often cited as a Roman talent, the unpredictability and brutality of its imperial system was one of its greatest failings. In the end, Rome was a victim of its own excesses. Nevertheless, its achievements are the foundation of Western civilization.

Republic and the rise of empire. The republic was born in 509 B.C.E. when the Romans overthrew their last Etr-

uscan king, the tyrannical Tarquinius Priscus, thereby gaining an aversion to any hint of monarchy and winning independence for their city-state on the banks of the Tiber. Although a republic governed by a senate of elders, inequality remained. The common people, called plebeians, were subservient to the ruling upper class, known as the patricians. The story of the early republic was chiefly the plebeians' successful struggle for representation in the government and expansion of Rome's control over the rest of the Italian peninsula at the expense of its weak and disorganized rivals; thus demonstrating the Roman penchant for military organization, discipline, and diplomacy. Yet, not content with holding sway over Italy, the Romans created great armadas and spread their influence about the Mediterranean. This brought confrontation with Carthage, a formidable military, naval, and trading power of North Africa.

Rome faced the Carthaginian challenge with characteristic determination. The First Punic or Carthaginian War (264–241 B.C.E.) lasted over 20 years and ended with Rome's capture of Sicily. During the Second Punic War (218–201 B.C.E.), in which Rome put almost a quarter of a million men in the field, the young Carthaginian general Hannibal came close to destroying Rome after he crossed the Alps, along with his fearsome war elephants, and attacked northern Italy. After numerous defeats, most particularly at the battle of Cannae in 216 B.C.E. where from 45,000 to 80,000 soldiers were lost, and revolts by conquered territories in southern Italy, Rome persevered and launched an offensive in North Africa, forcing Hannibal to abandon his Italian campaign and return to Carthage. At the battle of Zama outside Carthage in 202 B.C.E., Hannibal's forces were crushed by legions commanded by Scipio Africanus. With its chief Mediterranean rival defeated, Rome was free to mount a series of successful campaigns against the Macedonians in 197 B.C.E. and the Syrians seven years later. After victory in the Third Punic War (149–146 B.C.E.) Carthage was obliterated in 146 B.C.E. Thus, Rome was the unquestioned master of the Mediterranean.

Republican disorder. With Rome's conquests came internal stresses. Its Italian allies demanded equality within the empire, leading to the Social or Italian War of 90–88 B.C.E. The rebellion ended with Roman citizenship, *cives Romanus*, being given to most Italians. Yet power and wealth became increasingly concentrated in the hands of the senatorial class, while the city of Rome experienced rapid population growth, leading to crowded tenements, crime, and unruly mobs manipulated by politicians anxious to garner votes. Such an atmosphere encouraged corruption of the electoral process, and thus distrust of republican institutions and nervousness among the elite.

Tiberius Gracchus and his brother Gaius Gracchus, who each served as tribune, became heroes of the common or equestrian class due to their egalitarian policies of land and tax reform and expanded citizenship for provincials. But when both brothers were assassinated resulting from conservative plots, riots and discontent arose. Finally, martial law was declared under the command of Consul Gaius Opimius. Eventually even the lowest segment of society rebelled. In Sicily and on the peninsula, numerous slave revolts erupted. A gladiator named Spartacus would lead the most notable slave uprising from 73–71 B.C.E. After defeating five Roman armies, Spartacus' slave army was routed by Marcus Licinius Crassus (c. 112–53 B.C.E.), a wealthy and conservative general. In retribution and warning, 6,000 slaves were crucified along the Appian Way.

With continual crises, increasing need for more centralized control of the provinces and armies, and rampant piracy on the sea, the time was ripe for a strong leader. Lucius Cornelius Sulla was the first to assume the mantel. After a victorious campaign against Mithridates in the East, Sulla dared to enter Rome with his legions, dispatched his enemies during a bloody civil war, and imposed a conservative dictatorship (82–79 B.C.E.). Sulla proceeded to reward his soldiers with colonial land, reorganize the senate, reform the courts, reduce the power of the tribunes who represented the common people, and then retired under the illusion that he had achieved the stability Rome required.

Julius Caesar. The late republic produced numerous strong and ambitious leaders who hoped to fill the void left by Sulla. Most notably, Marcus Crassus, victor over Spartacus, and the charismatic Gnaeus Pompeius (Pompey, 106–48 B.C.E.), hero of campaigns against Cilician pirates, Mithridates, and slave rebellions, maneuvered to win the support of the masses and thus, power. While Crassus and Pompey were accomplished generals and political opportunists, neither matched the military genius, political shrewdness, and popular appeal of the young Gaius Julius Caesar (c. 101–44 B.C.E.), heir of a distinguished family that had seen better days.

Caesar was made dictator in 45 B.C.E. for 10 years. This was extended to life in 44 B.C.E. He assumed unprecedented authority and honors, being named *pater patriae* ("Father of the Fatherland") and instituted important reforms, many of which laid the foundation for an imperial system. Yet his rule instilled fear, resentment, and desires to restore the old republic. On the Ides of March (March 15) in 44 B.C.E., conspirators led by Marcus Brutus and Gaius Cassius assassinated Caesar in the senate and unwittingly murdered any hope of restoration of the republic.

Caesar Augustus and the Imperial Order. Marcus Antonius (Mark Antony, c. 82–30 B.C.), Caesar's closest confidant, and the young Gaius Octavius (Octavian, 63 B.C.E.–14 C.E.), Caesar's grandnephew and heir, formed the Second Triumvirate in 43 B.C.E. with Marcus Lepidus as junior partner. After agreeing that Octavian would hold sway in Italy and Antony in the East, and after defeating Caesar's assassins at the Battle of Philippi in 42 B.C.E., Antony and Octavian were soon at odds. At the fateful naval battle of Actium in 31 B.C.E., Octavian was triumphant against Antony and his ally, Queen Cleopatra of Egypt. With Antony and Cleopatra's subsequent suicides, Egypt was made a Roman province.

Octavian claimed both Caesar's name and dream. The senate awarded him the title *princeps* in 28 B.C.E., and he assumed complete command of the army as *imperator*. As tribune, he was the voice of the people, and in 27 B.C.E. he was named Augustus. In 12 B.C.E. he took the position of *pontifex maximus* (chief priest) and was deified in the East. Although retaining the trappings of the republic, such as the senate, the republic was dead. The conservative Augustus then set about reforming Roman society to promote stability and his authority. He appointed senators to secure control of the body, revitalized religion by restoring the temples, promoted morality, encouraged marriage, created the Praetorian Guard to protect the emperor, ended corruption in the governance of the provinces, and established an efficient system of administration. He also expanded the empire to include Galatia in 25 B.C.E., completed the conquest of Spain in 19 B.C.E., added numerous other provinces, and invaded much of western Germania. However, Augustus' ambitions in the Danube-Rhine region were abandoned when Germanic tribes massacred three Roman legions in the Teutoburg Forest in 9 C.E..

The Julio-Claudians. Augustus named his stepson, Tiberius (42 B.C.E.–37 C.E.) his successor. Although less charismatic than Augustus, he set about consolidating the empire. Tiberius' successor and grandnephew Caligula (12–41 C.E.) proved less fortunate. After showing signs of insanity and attempting to force his divinity on the empire, Caligula was assassinated. Caligula's uncle Claudius (10 B.C.E.–54 C.E.) next ruled and expanded the empire into southern Britain, Mauretania, and Thrace, established a professional civil service, and maintained an active public works program, including the port at Ostia. Despite these achievements, Claudius was poisoned in 54 C.E. and was succeeded by his adopted son, the tyrannical Nero (37–68 C.E.), who was accused of causing the burning of Rome in order to clear a site for his new palace. True or not, Nero was deposed and committed suicide before he could be murdered. Thus ended the Julio-Claudian dynasty, and anarchy reigned as various portions of the army installed their choice as emperor. None of these emperors was able to maintain order or authority.

The Flavians. Vespasian (9–79 C.E.), who was proclaimed emperor by the legions in Egypt and Judaea and whose title was accepted by the senate in 69 C.E., founded the Flavian dynasty and provided the strength and stability the empire craved during his 20-year rule. He reformed the army by mixing the legions with soldiers from different localities to inhibit local loyalties, made tax collection fairer, and launched massive public works projects. He rebuilt Rome and began construction of the great Roman Colosseum or Flavian Amphitheater, which became an important political tool as successive emperors strove to surpass their predecessors in bloody spectacles to satisfy the mob. Vespasian's son, Titus (34–81 C.E.), destroyed Jerusalem in 70 C.E. and the rest of the empire was brought under control. The popular Titus succeeded his father in 79 C.E., and completed the Colosseum in 80 C.E.. Titus ruled until his death from plague.

The next five emperors, Nerva, Trajan, Hadrian, Antoninus Pius, and Marcus Aurelius, brought order and took the empire to its greatest height in territory and prosperity. Nerva, chosen by the senate, opened the age of moderation and competent administration. The subsequent four emperors came to power through the wise planning of their predecessors. The last of these "good emperors," Marcus Aurelius (121–180 C.E.), trained from childhood to be emperor, became an enlightened ruler and philosopher, but he confronted plague, rebellion by a general in the East, and Germanic tribes along the Danube frontier in the North.

The Roman economy. Wherever Rome's mighty legions conquered, they built stone roads, chiefly for military purposes and supply, but with secondary benefit to trade and communication. They also constructed ingenious aqueducts, bridges, sewers, amphitheaters, defensive walls, and fortresses, many of which survive. Hence there were benefits to the conquered provinces other than simply the order imposed.

In times of stability and able leadership, the empire fostered peace, commercial activity, and cultural and racial diversity, tolerance, and interchange. The liberal granting of Roman citizenship to conquered peoples most notably shows this general policy of inclusion. Under "good" emperors, currency was stable and taxes relatively fair. Financiers and businessmen appeared, corporations organized shipping, trade routes were established and protected, and iron- and coal-mining encouraged. Cities were founded that expanded commerce, made urban life comfortable for many, and developed regional products for export and markets for import.

At its best, the imperial system provided uniform laws and regulations, supervised critical grain supplies, and permitted development of trade guilds, but there was little industrial innovation and most products were produced in small workshops. The consumerism of the city of Rome encouraged imports from throughout the empire and beyond, but the rich lived in excess, while many others lived in squalor and, at times, as many as one in three inhabitants of the Empire was enslaved, leading to constant fears of slave revolts.

Furthermore, the Roman mob had to be constantly satisfied with handouts, bloody spectacles, and games, and as many as 170 holidays. All this extravagance imposed enormous cost on the treasury and productivity. And the benefits of Roman rule ceased under weak, mad, or tyrannical emperors. But Rome's greatest economic problems came when the empire stopped growing, for its economic strength came from the constant flow of riches and slaves from conquered territories. When the Empire's growth ended, so did the spoils fueling the system.

Division, decline, and fall. Diocletian (c. 245–305 C.E.), who was made emperor by military force in 284, worked to free the government from the military's dominance and created the Tetrarchy, a system whereby he shared power and succession was planned. He completely reorganized the administration of the empire, attempted to stabilize the currency, and fought rampant inflation. He also ruthlessly persecuted Christians.

Upon his retirement in 305, the succession was disorderly despite Diocletian's designs. Strong leadership eventually came under Constantine (c. 274–337 C.E.), who became undisputed emperor after victory at the Battle of Mulvian Bridge in 312. To attempt to regain the empire's stability, Constantine expanded the bureaucracy and divided the empire between East and West, with the Eastern capital, Constantinople, located at Byzantium in 330. He legalized Christianity and accepted the faith on his deathbed. Christianity would eventually become the state religion, and imperial organization would serve as the model for church structure.

Despite the territorial division, the borders of the Western empire proved difficult to maintain. Emperor Valens was even killed in battle with the Goths in 378, a Germanic people who had settled en masse within the imperial borders. The Visigoths sacked Rome itself in 410, and the Vandals did the same in 455. The last Roman emperor, Romulus Augustulus, was deposed in 476 and a Goth, Odovacar, was proclaimed king. The Western Roman Empire was no more.

BIBLIOGRAPHY. Frank C. Bourne, *A History of the Romans* (1966); J.A. Crook, *Law and Life of Rome, 90 B.C.–A.D. 212* (Cambridge University Press, 1967); Matthias Gelzer, *Caesar: Politician and Statesman* (Harvard University Press, 1968); Michael Grant, *The Roman Emperors: A Biographical Guide to the Rulers of Imperial Rome, 31 B.C.–A.D. 476* (Orion, 1997); Michael Kerrigan, *Ancient Rome and the Roman Empire* (DK Publishing, 2001); Christopher Scarre, *Chronicle of the Roman Emperors: The Reign-by-Reign Record of the Rulers of Imperial Rome* (Thames & Hudson, 1995); Chester G. Starr, *The Ancient Romans* (Oxford University Press, 1971); Allen M. Ward, Fritz M. Heichelheim, and Cedric A. Yeo, *A History of the Roman People* (Prentice Hall, 2002).

RUSSELL FOWLER. J.D.
UNIVERSITY OF TENNESSEE, CHATTANOOGA

Romania

A BIT SMALLER THAN the state of Oregon, Romania is located in southeastern Europe and borders Bulgaria, UKRAINE, HUNGARY, Moldova, former Yugoslavia and the Black Sea. Romania has a population of approximately 22.3 million people (2002). Romania's government is organized as a republic, separated into 41 counties. It gained its independence from Turkey May 9, 1877 and was recognized by the Treaty of Berlin on July 13, 1878. Shortly thereafter, on March 26, 1881, Romania declared itself a kingdom. The current republic was officially formed on December 30, 1947. After the monarchy was ousted, a police-state dictator, Nicolae Ceausescu, took power for several decades. In 1989, Ceausescu was executed and the communist party took power until 1996. The government is currently dominated by the Social Democracy party, in conjunction with the ethnic Hungarian minority party.

Romania boasted a 2001 GROSS DOMESTIC PRODUCT (GDP) of $152.7 billion. The GDP real growth rate in the same year was approximately 4.8 percent. Romania has had a difficult transition from communism since 1989; industries and production facilities did not suit the economic environment or the resources of the country. The INTERNATIONAL MONETARY FUND (IMF) is the partial reason for the 4.8 percent growth in 2001.

At the turn of the millennium, Romania had 44.5 percent of its population below the poverty line. Economists point out the country must overcome extensive economic hurdles in order to contend for a position in the EUROPEAN UNION (EU) possibly in 2007. The North Atlantic Treaty Organization expressed interest, at its November 2002, meeting, in adopting Romania into its ranks in 2004. Romania's membership in both of these economic leviathans will present the country with an excellent opportunity to stimulate its struggling economy.

Romania's main industries include textiles and footwear, light-machinery and auto assembly, mining, timber, construction materials, metallurgy, chemicals, food processing, petroleum, and refining. The majority of the labor force (40 percent) is concentrated in agriculture, producing such goods as wheat, corn, sugar beets, sunflower seed, potatoes, grapes, eggs, and sheep. Romania's major trading partner is Italy, providing 19 percent of Romania's imports and receiving 22 percent of Romania's exports.

BIBLIOGRAPHY. *CIA World Factbook* (2002); European Union, europa.eu.int; Lonely Planet World Guide, www.lonelyplanet.com; SFOR Informer Online, www.nato.int/sfor.

ARTHUR HOLST, PH.D.
WIDENER UNIVERSITY

Roosevelt, Franklin Delano (1882–1945)

AS U.S. PRESIDENT from 1933–45, Franklin Delano Roosevelt (FDR) created the foundations of the modern welfare state through his NEW DEAL economic and social reforms. The scion of a wealthy and aristocratic American family, FDR was instilled with a sense of social obligation of the wealthy toward the less fortunate. Early in his political career, FDR supported the fulfillment of this obligation through private institutions and family initiatives. As the Great DEPRESSION of the 1930s deepened, however, FDR forged a new role for government, as guarantor of the economic security of its citizens. Although few economic historians credit FDR's social programs with ending the Depression, the programs did mitigate the suffering of many. The American economy did not fully recover from the Depression, however, until production demand was stimulated by America's entry into WORLD WAR II.

Youth. Roosevelt was born into a prominent family that had resided in New York's Hudson Valley since the 1640s. FDR's mother, Sara Delano, was a sixth-cousin of his father, James Roosevelt. FDR was raised as an only child, though James, who was 26 years older than Sara, was a widower with a grown son. James lived as a country squire on his grand Hyde Park estate and was involved with the family's coal and transportation ventures.

FDR enjoyed a privileged and sheltered upbringing in Hyde Park. He was privately tutored, and spent time in Europe and Campobello (vacation home in Canada) each year. At 14, he was sent to Groton School, a private New England boarding school. Groton's headmaster, Reverend Endicott Peabody, emphasized the social responsibility of his socially elite students to assist the less fortunate. Groton provided FDR's first experience with peers his own age, and he appears to have had difficulty fitting in.

After Groton, FDR hoped to attend the U.S. Naval Academy. However, his parents preferred Harvard University, and that is where he went. Shortly after he began college, in 1900, his father died. At Harvard, FDR made efforts to fit in better than he had at Groton. He joined the Harvard Republican Club and supported nomination of his fifth-cousin Theodore ROOSEVELT as the Republican candidate for U.S. vice president in 1900. Although FDR's grades at Harvard were average, he graduated in only three years. During his third year, FDR became editor of Harvard's daily student newspaper the *Crimson*, and he stayed at Harvard an additional year to oversee publication.

In 1903, he began courting his fifth-cousin-once-removed, Ana Eleanor Roosevelt, the favorite niece of President Theodore Roosevelt (who assumed the presidency after William MCKINLEY's assassination). The two were married March 17, 1905, with the president giving the bride away. In the early years of their marriage, Eleanor gave birth to six (five surviving) children. FDR attended Columbia Law School, but left after passing the New York State Bar exam. He then practiced corporate law with the firm Carter, Ledyard, and Milburn, a job in which he remained restless. Having a different ambition, he mapped out a route to the White House identical to that of his cousin Theodore: New York State legislature, assistant secretary of the Navy, governor of New York, vice president, president.

Public life before polio. In 1910, FDR ran as a Democrat for a seat in the New York state legislature, seeking to represent the predominantly Republican 26th district, Dutchess County. FDR won an upset victory over Republican candidate John F. Schlosser. As state legislator, FDR pursued a progressive, "anti-machine politics" agenda. He championed development of electric power, conservation, women's suffrage, workers' compensation, and maximum-hours legislation. At the same time, FDR obtained his first national recognition by exposing and opposing the corrupt disbursement of patronage appointments by Tammany Hall, the New York Democratic political machine.

The Tammany hall battle brought FDR to the attention of New Jersey Governor Woodrow WILSON. Wilson shared with FDR a vision of progressive government. Both men supported direct election of U.S. senators, regulation of business abuses, and conservation of natural resources. Roosevelt supported Wilson for the Democratic presidential nomination in 1912. In 1913, Wilson's Secretary of the Navy Josephus Daniels appointed FDR assistant secretary of the Navy, a position he held until 1920. As assistant secretary, FDR opposed price-fixing and collusive bidding on the part of defense contractors. He became skilled in handling labor relations and developed a reputation as a friend of organized labor.

In 1920, FDR became widely known through an unsuccessful bid for vice president on the Democratic ticket with Ohio Governor James Cox. He campaigned on progressive ideas and American participation in the League of Nations. Warren HARDING's Republican victory however, pushed FDR out of public life.

After the 1920 election, FDR formed a law firm and became vice-president of a surety bonding firm. In August, 1921, on summer holiday with his family, he contracted polio and many believed it was the end of his political career. Instead, however, it marked a personal and professional turning point. During FDR's illness, his wife Eleanor assumed an active role in the Democratic party. Eleanor's political activity provided a vehicle for FDR's journalist assistant Louis Howe to keep FDR's name in the public eye during his own period of relative inactivity. FDR began a long, and never fully successful road to recovery.

Governor of New York. FDR did not return to national politics again until 1928 when he was instrumental in the nomination of Catholic New York State Governor Alfred Smith as Democratic presidential candidate. In return, Smith successfully supported FDR as successor to the New York governorship. When FDR became governor in 1928, the economy appeared sound. He supported progressive policies such as the development of cheap electrical power, and agricultural reforms to relieve farmers facing falling prices. He remained a friend of organized labor, a relationship cultivated as assistant secretary of the Navy. However, FDR also remained faithful to LAISSEZ-FAIRE market economics.

The 1929 Wall Street crash and subsequent Depression soon led FDR to reconsider his faith in unregulated markets. To avoid failure of an important New York commercial bank, Roosevelt orchestrated a bank merger. The involved businessmen scoffed at his efforts, insisting that a failing bank should go under regardless of the consequences. Roosevelt then appears to have lost faith in business's ability to self-regulate, concluding that BUSINESS CYCLES were not wholly natural events and that perhaps unscrupulous business practices contributed to the depth and length of business-cycle downturns.

As the Depression deepened, FDR became increasingly committed to the view that government should seek to guarantee the economic security of its citizens. He initiated sweeping reforms in New York in support of these beliefs. The National Guard armories were used to house the homeless. Maximum working-hours laws were enacted in order to require employers to "share the work," rather than lay off workers. In addition, FDR created the Temporary Emergency Relief Service, which provided $25 million in public works jobs and direct relief to the unemployed.

In 1932, after two terms as New York governor, FDR ran as the Democratic candidate for president of the

United States. Promising a NEW DEAL for the Depression-stricken American people, FDR overwhelmingly defeated the Republican Herbert HOOVER, who remained committed to laissez-faire economics. In the same election, the Democrats sent large majorities to both houses of Congress.

Presidential years. FDR was sworn into office March 4, 1933. When he took office, approximately 13 million Americans were without work. Banks in 38 states had closed. In his inaugural address, FDR asserted the need for broad executive powers to aid the country against the economic emergency. His first 100 days in office produced a whirlwind of legislation. Two days after taking office, FDR proposed a "bank holiday," and called a special session of Congress. All banks closed. They presented their books to the federal government, which provided emergency funds and promised to reopen only banks with sound finances. This action ended the banking crisis. Notably, the banks were not nationalized.

With this act and the ensuing 100 days, the "Roosevelt Revolution" was underway. The government dramatically entered the lives and business of Americans in ways it had never done before. Although Roosevelt's policies expanded the role of government as protector against the worst excesses of the market, markets remained decentralized. FDR's policies protected and maintained free-market capitalism, despite conservative protests of its destruction.

In 1933, FDR and Congress focused on relief programs. The United States went off the gold standard, providing relief to debtors and exporters. The Civil Works Administration, Home Owners Loan Corporation, Civil Conservation Corps, and the Public Works Administration were all created. These programs brought jobs and relief to millions of desperate Americans.

In 1933 and 1934, Congress continued its efforts to reform business practices through legislation. The Federal Deposit Insurance Company was created to keep banks from failing; the SECURITIES AND EXCHANGE COMMISSION (SEC) was established to regulate the stock exchanges. The Tennessee Valley Authority built dams that provided flood control and inexpensive hydroelectric power, revitalizing the region.

However, the cornerstone legislative enactments of the NEW DEAL, the National Recovery Act (NRA) and the Agricultural Adjustment Act (AAA), both were declared unconstitutional by the U.S. Supreme Court. The NRA authorized labor and management to negotiate legally binding codes of competition regulating hours, wages, and prices within each industry sector. The NRA, which was the first federal statute to recognize the right of unionized workers to collectively bargain, was struck down as unconstitutional in May 1935.

The AAA, which supported farm prices through production control and provided subsidies to farmers who adhered to production quotas, was held unconstitutional in January 1936.

In 1935, three major pieces of legislation helped FDR regain office for a second term. The Social Security Act secured federal payment of old-age pension, and also provided for shared federal-state unemployment compensation and financial assistance for the needy, blind, disabled, and dependent children. The National Labor Relations Act (Wagner Act) secured the right of labor to bargain collectively, and established the National Labor Relations Board. The Works Progress Administration, another New Deal program, paid out millions of dollars per month in work relief between 1935 and 1942.

Despite the New Deal relief and reform efforts of FDR's first term, one-third of the nation's people remained in desperate economic need in the presidential election year of 1936. Nonetheless, FDR was re-elected by a landslide. FDR's second term began, however, with his first major political setback. In an effort to reverse the pro-business conservative philosophy of the Supreme Court that had struck down his NRA and AAA programs, FDR proposed increasing the number of justices on the Court from 9 to 15. By personally selecting the six new justices to be installed, FDR hoped to gain control over the composition of the court, and to ensure that a working majority of justices would sustain New Deal legislation against further constitutional attack. Congress rejected FDR's "court-packing" plan, fearing he was over-reaching his executive power. With this failure, FDR never regained the full support of Congress.

A sharp RECESSION hit in the fall of 1937. Roosevelt was slow to respond with increased federal spending that might have stimulated the economy. By 1938, Republican gains in Congressional elections and Congressional concerns over Roosevelt's handling of the Court, and the recession weakened his ability to get his reform efforts passed.

In 1940, however, FDR was re-elected to an unprecedented third term. The war in Europe had loomed large during the second half of FDR's second term. Shortly into his third term, he convinced Congress to pass the lend-lease program, under which the United States supplied arms to Great Britain. In December 1941, Japan attacked the U.S. Navy at Pearl Harbor, and Germany declared war against the United States. These events brought the country fully into World War II. At home, the war production effort was centralized through governmental boards and agencies such as the War Production Board and National War Labor Board, which controlled prices and supervised the allocation of resources. Ironically, these wartime government production programs, rather than merely being the stimulus to the free markets of capitalism, may ultimately have saved American capitalism and lifted the nation out of the Depression.

After being re-elected to a fourth term in 1944, FDR died April 12, 1945, only weeks before the end of war in Europe. FDR is buried at his home in Hyde Park, New York.

BIBLIOGRAPHY. Paul K. Conkin, "The New Deal Marked the Beginning of the Welfare State," *Franklin D. Roosevelt: Presidents and Their Decisions* (Greenhaven Press, 2001); Carl N. Degler, "The Third American Revolution," *Franklin D. Roosevelt: Presidents and Their Decisions* (Greenhaven Press, 2001); John T. Flynn, "The New Deal Roosevelt Promised *vs.* the One he Delivered," *Franklin D. Roosevelt: Presidents and Their Decisions* (Greenhaven Press, 2001); Frank Freidel, *Franklin D. Roosevelt: A Rendezvous with Destiny* (Little Brown, 1990); William E. Leuchtenburg, *Franklin D. Roosevelt and the New Deal, 1932–1940* (Harper & Row, 1963); Ted Morgan, *FDR: A Biography* (Simon & Schuster, 1985); George A. Wolfskill and John A. Hudson, "Criticism of the New Deal is not Justified," *Franklin D. Roosevelt: Presidents and Their Decisions* (Greenhaven Press, 2001); "American Experience," www.pbs.org.

LINDA DYNAN, PH.D.
INDEPENDENT SCHOLAR

Roosevelt, Theodore (1858–1919)

WHEN AN ASSASSIN'S BULLET killed President William MCKINLEY on September 14, 1901, 42-year-old Vice-President Teddy Roosevelt became the youngest man to hold the office of president. Famous for his energy and enthusiasm, Roosevelt ushered the United States into the 20th century with his bold presidential style, Progressive reforms, and ambitious foreign policy.

Though born into wealth and privilege, Roosevelt's childhood was plagued by poor health. After a year-long European trip and rigorous exercise routines, his health improved. Educated by private tutors for much of his childhood, Roosevelt entered Harvard University in 1876. Following graduation, he married Alice Hathaway Lee, the daughter of a prominent Boston family. The couple moved to New York, where Roosevelt studied law at Columbia University's School of Law before being elected to the New York State assembly in 1884, a position he held until 1885.

However, personal events in Roosevelt's life temporarily sidetracked his political career. On February 14, 1884, Roosevelt lost both his mother to typhoid fever and his wife to complications surrounding the birth of their daughter. Devastated by their deaths, Roosevelt left New York and spent nearly two years on his ranch in the Dakota Territory (what is today South Dakota). He eventually returned to Oyster Bay, New York, in 1886 where he established residency and ran unsuccessfully for mayor on the Republican ticket. Upon his defeat, Roosevelt embarked on a trip to Europe, marrying Edith Carow in London; the couple went on to have five children.

Returning to New York, Roosevelt re-involved himself in politics, both at the state and federal level. In 1897, President McKinley appointed Roosevelt to be assistant secretary to the Navy but he resigned the post the following year with the start of the SPANISH-AMERICAN WAR.

An unabashed nationalist, Roosevelt believed that the Spanish-American War should be waged more aggressively. He formed and became colonel of a volunteer cavalry regiment known as the Rough Riders, and vigorously led his troops to battle. His skirmish victories in Cuba were sensationally reported back to newspaper readers in the United States, and Roosevelt soon became a war hero thrust onto the national stage.

Following the brief war, Roosevelt was elected governor of New York State. As governor, Roosevelt—a Republican who cultivated his own Progressive vision—achieved civil service and tax reforms, and also supported bills to limit the number of working hours for women and children.

This incensed New York's party bosses and they sought ways to move Roosevelt out of his gubernatorial position. At the next Republican National Convention, their efforts secured Roosevelt's place as the vice-presidential nominee under McKinley. Although historians have suggested that Roosevelt was reluctant to campaign for the obscure office of vice president, he proved to be an effective asset to the ticket and the Republicans were elected to White House in 1900. Upon McKinley's death the following year, Roosevelt assumed the presidency.

Roosevelt believed that as president, he was morally and politically obligated to further the interests of the people. He was an enthusiastic capitalist but he supported many of the reforms directed at curing the ills of industrial capitalism in order to protect American democracy from the threat of socialism.

He therefore believed that the government was responsible for assuring honesty in business and extending equal economic opportunities to all. Asserting that his goal was to provide consumers, farmers, laborers, and business interests fair advantages, Roosevelt labeled his economic policy the Square Deal.

Roosevelt was particularly concerned with mediating the interests of business and labor and he quickly earned a reputation for being a "trust-buster." In 1902, Roosevelt initiated an antitrust suit against the Northern Securities Company, a railroad holding company. He achieved the dissolution of the monopoly and celebrated the victory as a sign of the government's power to regulate business.

Roosevelt further established himself as a friend of labor with his mediation of the Anthracite Coal Strike in 1902. By settling the strike, Roosevelt not only broke with his predecessors who had favored business interests over labor, but he also expanded his own executive powers.

Overwhelmingly re-elected in 1904 over Democratic opponent Judge Alton B. Parker, Roosevelt, now serving his own term, vigorously pursued Progressive reforms. In 1906, Roosevelt secured passage of the Pure Food and Drug Act and the Meat Inspection Act, both of which offered consumer protection. Also in 1906, Roosevelt achieved the Hepburn Act, which expanded the powers of the Interstate Commerce Commission.

His commitment to reform legislation extended to natural resources as well. A passionate supporter of the west since his days in South Dakota, Roosevelt made land conservation and the protection of national reserves and forests central to his administration. In 1902, Roosevelt secured the passage of the Newlands Act, which financed irrigation projects. He also encouraged the conservation efforts of the Forest Service and brought environmental issues into the foreground when, in 1908, he summoned a governors' conference to discuss conservation.

Roosevelt's foreign policy initiatives reflected his sense of expanded presidential leadership: He believed that the United States should be a key player in world affairs and built up the army and navy, pursuing aggressive measures abroad. In 1903, he aided Panama in its revolt against Colombia and thereby gained American control over the Panama Canal. One year later, he made the declaration that the United States should be the international guard of all state affairs in the western hemisphere; this policy was known as the Roosevelt corollary to the Monroe Doctrine. (The Doctrine had warned Europe against expanding into the Western Hemisphere.) And it was his interventionist efforts in the Russo-Japanese War, in which he arranged a peace conference between the two countries, which earned him the 1906 Nobel Peace Prize. Through continued diplomacy with Japan in 1907, he also halted the immigration of Japanese laborers to the American West Coast by negotiating what came to be know as the Gentleman's Agreement.

Roosevelt left the White House in 1909 but he did not leave the public spotlight. Dissatisfied with his successor, President William Howard TAFT, Roosevelt ran for president in 1912 on a Progressive ticket known as the Bull Moose Party. Roosevelt's bid for re-election split the Republican votes and secured the victory of Democratic candidate Woodrow WILSON. When the United States entered WORLD WAR I, Roosevelt offered to lead a commission of volunteers into Europe, but Wilson rejected the idea.

Bitter from old age and the tragic death of his son, Quentin, from enemy fire, Roosevelt retired to his home in Oyster Bay, dying there of a coronary embolism. Although in the years before his death his political views had become increasingly liberal and nearly radical, historians have remembered him as "the conservative as progressive."

BIBLIOGRAPHY. Kathleen Dalton, *Theodore Roosevelt: A Strenuous Life* (Knopf, 2002); Richard Hofstader, *The American Political Tradition and the Men Who Made It* (Vintage, 1989); James M. McPherson, ed., "To the Best of My Ability," *The American Presidents* (Dorling Kindersley, 2000); Edward J. Marolda, ed., *Theodore Roosevelt, The U.S. Navy, and the Spanish-American War* (Palgrave, 2001); Edmund Morris, *The Rise of Teddy Roosevelt* (Coward, McCann & Geoghegan, 1979); Edmund Morris, *Theodore Rex* (Random House, 2001).

LINDSAY SILVER
BRANDEIS UNIVERSITY

Royal Dutch Shell

THE ROYAL DUTCH SHELL GROUP was formed in 1907 as a holding company that essentially encompassed the transportation interests of Shell (UNITED KINGDOM) and the production activities of Royal Dutch (the NETHERLANDS), and can trace its origins to the Far East in the 1890s. Royal Dutch Shell is the world's oldest joint venture, with 60 percent of shares held by Royal Dutch and 40 percent by Shell.

By the late 1970s, leading firms in the global petroleum industry were facing strong competitive challenges, including the increasing power of individual nations, and the emergence of new rivals. Royal Dutch Shell's performance began to deteriorate in the 1990s, and they also faced significant public relation problems. First, the proposed disposal of the Brent Spar oil platform in the North Atlantic aroused a huge outcry from environmental groups and forced Shell to change its plans. Second, in late 1995, the Nigerian government executed a prominent activist author, Ken Saro-Wiwa, who had protested Shell's environmental record, and it was widely felt that Shell did not handle the resulting fallout at all well.

In 1998, Shell undertook an ambitious restructuring program, moving from a geographically based organizational structure to a more business-sector orientation in an attempt to shorten decision-making, and improve flexibility and efficiency. In 2001, Royal Dutch Shell was the third-largest petroleum refining company, having been overtaken by EXXONMOBIL and BP, and is ranked eighth on *Fortune* magazine's Global 500 list of the world's largest companies. Shell employs approximately 111,00 people worldwide, with 11 percent in the Netherlands, 9 percent in the United Kingdom, and 23 percent in the United States. In 2002, its global revenue amounted to $179.4 billion, with oil refining accounting for 78.2 percent, and oil exploration (7.9 percent), natural gas (7.3 percent), and chemicals (6.2 percent) making up the rest. Shell has proved reserves of approximately 9 billion barrels of oil.

BIBLIOGRAPHY. R. Grant and K. Neupert, "Organizational Restructuring within the Royal Dutch Shell Group," *Contemporary Strategy Analysis* (Blackwell, 1999); J. Podolny and J. Roberts, *The Global Oil Industry* (Stanford University Press, 1998); www.shell.com.

CATHERINE MATRAVES
ALBION COLLEGE

Russia

A COUNTRY STRETCHING from eastern Europe on the west to the Pacific Ocean in the East and from the Arctic Ocean in the north to the Caucasus mountains and central Asia in the south, Russia has a population of 145 million and a GROSS DOMESTIC PRODUCT (GDP) of $1.2 trillion (in purchasing power). Used to being the second superpower in the world prior to the collapse of the SOVIET UNION in 1991, Russia is struggling in the new century to come to grips with the new reality as it tries to build a permanent free market economy and civic society for the first time in its history.

History prior to 1917. Russia (then the Russian Empire) belonged to a group of countries that started the transition to capitalism in the second half of the 19th century. Rural serfdom was abolished and various other reforms aimed at modernizing the country, that had basically been a feudal monarchy, were implemented during the reign of Emperor Alexander II (1855–81).

Alexander II was assassinated by a radical terrorist group whose proclaimed aim was modernizing Russia. The assassination led to a halt in reforms and to a wave of reaction. In the Russo-Japanese war of 1904–05 a small but rapidly modernizing JAPAN defeated Russia which precipitated a political crisis and a new wave of reforms under Prime Minister Peter Stolypin. Stolypin attempted to modernize the Russian agrarian sector (still the predominant sector of the economy at that time) while also fighting against surging radicalism. He was assassinated in 1911, and the subsequent onset of WORLD WAR I plunged the country, and the monarchy that had ruled it for centuries, into chaos.

In March 1917, Emperor Nikolai II abdicated and a democratic republic was declared. It looked as if Russia might finally make a transition to a market economy and political democracy. But the country was too devastated by war and mismanagement that the new democratic government did little to improve. Hence, when communists challenged the state power in November of the same year, they initially met with little resistance and easily gained control over St. Petersburg (the capital of Russia at that time) and Moscow, ousting the provisional government and establishing the Soviet government.

Communists promised to convene and to honor the decisions of the Constituent Assembly that was supposed to decide upon the future political and economic system of Russia. That promise also contributed to the lack of initial resistance to their takeover. But when the Assembly was elected and convened in early 1918, its majority was distinctly anti-communist. The Soviet government responded by immediately disbanding the Assembly and banning all political opposition to the "dictatorship of the proletariat." The country was plunged into a civil war (with foreign intervention) that completed its devastation.

The Soviet period. The communists won the civil war and established their authority across much of the former Russian Empire by 1922. Seventy-nine years of a communist experiment began.

The official Soviet view was that the communist rule represented a new and more progressive social order than capitalism. The communist revolution and the subsequent totalitarian regime consolidated under the rule of Josef Stalin was, according to some, a reversal to the old, pre-capitalist ways of running the society. The Soviet Union did accomplish industrialization and it also educated its people en masse for the first time in Russian history. On the other hand, it had also reintroduced restrictions on the rural population; peasants in collective farms were not given travel documents allowing them to move out of their villages.

Capitalistic relations, however, had been gradually recuperating ever since the death of Stalin and the abolition of extreme political terror. Since the official Soviet economy continued to be strictly centrally planned, illicit market transactions had to flourish in the underworld. By the time communism started crumbling in the second half of the 1980s, whole regions appeared to have fallen under effective rule of shady businessmen who amassed huge wealth, pulling the strings behind the scene still dominated in appearance by Communist Party leaders. Those were the main forces of internal change that finally brought the communist system down in 1991, while the pressure from the West and the surge of the popular movement for democratic change served as a catalyst of those developments.

The basic institutional structure of the new Russian capitalism.

The fact that the new Russian capitalism, which started in 1992, is deeply rooted in the informal economic system that had been gradually eroding the communist system from inside for at least 35 years, is of utmost importance. In particular, it means that incentives governing the behavior of economic agents are based on mostly informal institutions controlled by interest groups that had been capturing monopolistic rents even before communism collapsed, and that were often formed in alliance with corrupt or semi-criminal structures. Those lower-tier institutions and the informal framework partially inherited from the planned economy have survived the collapse of communism and have been consolidating their grip on the Russian economy and political system ever since. It is this new system of crony capitalism that is largely responsible for the fact that "A decade after the implosion of the Soviet Union in December, 1991, Russia is still struggling to establish a modern market economy and achieve strong economic growth," says the *CIA World Factbook* (2002).

Russian GROSS DOMESTIC PRODUCT (GDP), and especially industrial output, had been contracting in 1991–98 with the accumulated decline in industrial output of over 60 percent, according to official statistics. Despite its vast natural resources (including large deposits of oil, natural gas, strategic minerals, and timber), living standards, again at least by official statistics, also fell dramatically, with 40 percent of the population estimated to be below the poverty line in 1999. The demise of the Soviet Union and the folding-up of the manufacturing industries left Russia heavily dependent on exports of primary resources, particularly oil, natural gas, metals, and timber, which account for over 80 percent of exports.

The economy has been recovering since 1999 but this recovery, besides starting from a very low basis, is also very much dependent on the increase in oil prices and so far remains rather feeble from the long-run perspective. Structural reforms continue to lag behind, the industrial base is increasingly dilapidated and must be replaced or modernized if the country is to achieve sustainable economic growth. Other well-known problems include widespread corruption, lack of a strong legal system, and capital flight.

What went wrong with economic reforms of the 1990s?

When Russia began its transition to a market economy in 1992, the hopes were much higher. The basic ideas behind the reforms introduced after the collapse of communism were appealingly simple. First, price liberaliza-tion and the freeing of economic activity would clear the markets by equilibrating the supply and demand and abolishing the arbitrariness in resource allocation inherent in the state control over production and prices. Privatization would then translate profits and losses of firms into incentives to increase production of goods and services for which there was a large unsatisfied demand, and to curtail the production of those which were not actually demanded by the consumers.

Over a longer term, so it was hoped, this should lead to changes in the industrial structure, bringing production capacity in line with market demand. Macroeconomic stabilization policy was designed to complement privatization. Specifically, the imposition of a hard budget constraint on the government and a harsh ceiling on the creation of new money by the central bank was designed to translate itself into hard budget constraints for firms and reduced rent-seeking activity.

Private firms facing hard budget constraints and free prices would, in theory, change the structure of their investment and production to comply with the preferences of the consumers; thus an efficient resource allocation would result. Finally, opening up of the economy to foreign markets would advance the goals of the reform by:

1. Making it easier for the markets to find equilibrium prices (by imposing upon Russia the structure of relative prices prevailing in market economies)

2. Putting pressure on Russian producers from foreign competitors.

The logic above did produce some results. Especially, freeing of prices balanced short-term supply and demand. Long lines and frustratingly high costs of search for almost all goods and services (both for consumers and for firms) characteristic of the Soviet era have completely become things of the past. Affluent citizens of big cities enjoy the degree of consumption choice they could not even dream of 10 years ago. Those less fortunate do not have the luxury of even standing in line in hope of a subsistence ration. On the macroeconomic side, direct subsidies from the government (and/or the central bank) to firms have been abolished, and the government tries to keep its budget deficit and the creation of money supply under control. Most managers of privatized firms now realize that they can no longer rely on the government to help them get over any difficulties that their firms might run into. There is definitely much more attention paid to costs and quality of supplies and to marketing.

However, all this has not been enough to fundamentally change the allocation of resources and the structure of the Russian economy, and to decisively raise the standard of living of the majority of the population.

The most important problem is that the new Russian capitalism still lacks the mechanism translating the system of free prices and improvement in macroeconomic indicators into real structural changes. The reason is not simply the inertia of the past or some peculiar features of the Russian national character. On the contrary, the present Russian economic woes can be understood very easily in terms of people's rational responses to economic incentives.

The first basic structural reality of the Russian economy is its continued dominance by rent-seeking monopolies. If anything, price liberalization and deregulation of the economy freed those entrenched monopolies from any control over their activities whatsoever. Macroeconomic stabilization programs also had a side-effect of a sharp decline in government revenues and its greater capture by special interest groups.

The capture of the government by special interest groups, that had already begun under the Soviet rule, reached an unprecedented scale in the 1990s. It is true that the economy of those special interest groups (call it the parallel economy) in the former Soviet Union had many features in common with a market economy. In particular, it was completely free from any sort of government intervention (but for the need to bribe or harass government officials), in fact, much "freer" than almost any conventional market economy. However, although the parallel economy helped correct some of the inefficiencies of the planned economy, it was the source of many other inefficiencies, some of them perhaps not less serious than those which it helped to remedy. And it is those inefficiencies that continue to plague the newly emerging Russian capitalism.

The first such inefficiency is the absence of a broad constitutional agreement that would delineate property rights and establish a universal method of exchanging and enforcing those rights. In the official economy of the former Soviet Union, property rights were very strictly delineated and enforced. In the parallel economy, however, there was a strong need for private protection of property rights, that, moreover, had to be done while avoiding the detection from the authorities. The continued state of permanent feud between various private enforcement rings (called the Russian Mafia) involves costs which are unparalleled in normal market economies.

The second source of inefficiency, related to the first, is the high degree of market segmentation. Since the parallel economy had to keep its activities hidden so as to avoid detection, it naturally led to a highly segmented market. The number of participants in each segment of the parallel economy is strictly limited, and the flows of goods, capital, labor and information are severely disrupted. These features are largely inherited today, especially in locally owned businesses.

Third, capitalism relying on pressure groups and private enforcement is, by its nature, oriented toward extracting mostly short-term gain. In particular, it does not have a diversified capital market enabling risk-sharing. This has been the main obstacle to the much-needed radical renovation of industrial capacity. In the special case of a resource-rich Russia, it also means that most economic activity is concentrated in the resource-extraction and export-import sectors, to almost complete neglect of other sectors of potential comparative advantage, especially the human capital-intensive sector. The resulting distortion in profitability accruing to different types of economic activity has detrimental implications for the allocation of human talent.

These inefficiencies of the new Russian capitalism were clearly manifested in a spectacular failure of its privatization program, once hailed as one of the most successful among the economies in transition. Privatized firms have not been transferred to new owners who could put their assets to the most efficient use. Instead, they ended-up under the control of organized crime, which derives its income not from increasing the market value of the firm but from diverting revenues and engaging in asset-stripping.

Oligarchic capitalism? The structure of politico-economic power in today's Russia hinges mainly upon:

1. export of primary resources
2. control over the country's power plants
3. money from the government budget.

It is delineation and re-delineation of control over these sources of wealth which has given an impetus to the open formation of major oligarchic pressure groups, and which constitutes their financial bases.

By using money procured from those sources, oligarchic groups have built up empires that encompass not only industrial enterprises, banks and trading companies, but also political organizations and mass media. Although by most formal criteria Russia is a market economy and a presidential republic with democratic attributes such as the Federal Assembly and Constitutional Court, the reality is quite different. It remains to be seen if Russia will be able to disentangle itself from the grip of oligarchic capitalism and make good use of this latest historic chance to become a modern society.

BIBLIOGRAPHY. Serguey Braguinsky and Grigory Yavlinsky, *Incentives and Institutions: The Transition to a Market Economy in Russia* (Princeton University Press, 2000); *CIA World Factbook*, www.cia.gov (2002); David Hoffman, *The Oligarchs: Wealth and Power in the New Russia* (Public Affairs, 2002); Jerry F. Hough and Michael F. Armacost, *The Logic of*

Economic Reform in Russia (Brookings Institution, 2001); Lawrence R. Klein and Marshall, eds., *New Russia: Transition Gone Awry* (Stanford University Press, 2001).

Serguey Braguinsky, Ph.D.
State University of New York, Buffalo

Russian Revolution

THE RUSSIAN REVOLUTIONS of 1917 took place eight months apart from one another, but were both linked to the crisis Russia experienced in trying to fight WORLD WAR I, and in finding a popularly mandated, effective system of government. The February 1917 Revolution marked the collapse of the old tsarist system of government, an autocracy in which the monarch ruled without a constitution and with an ineffectual parliament. The October 1917 Revolution began the creation of a new order formed by the Bolsheviks, a radical group of Marxists who built the first communist state in history.

By February 1917, the imperial regime of the Romanov dynasty had lost all effective popular support because of the severe strain that Russia experienced during World War I, when the Russian military suffered defeat at the hands of the Central Powers, particularly the German Army. Most historians agree that the Romanovs themselves hastened the destruction of their empire.

For example, Emperor Nicholas II (also called Tsar, from the Russian word for Caesar) tied the success of his reign to the war effort when, against the counsel of his advisers, in 1915 he left Petrograd to take direct command of the war front at military headquarters. The foolhardiness of this decision was magnified when Nicholas II delegated authority for running the government directly to his consort, the Empress Alexandra (or Tsaritsa), even though she had no experience in government affairs. Alexandra suffered from poor health and was devastated that her youngest child Alexis, the heir to the throne, suffered from hemophilia, an incurable disease that kept his blood from clotting. Alexandra found comfort in the peasant Rasputin, whose hypnotic demeanor had a calming effect on Alexis. Even as Rasputin portrayed himself as a holy man, disgust spread throughout Russia that this "mad monk" was actually in control of the government. Indeed, he used his influence with Alexandra to appoint ineffective ministers to important government posts.

By 1917, Russia's government and its under-developed transportation infrastructure were unable to provide enough weapons, ammunition, and supplies for its army. At the same time, Russia's agricultural system was strained by the recruitment of millions of peasants into the army. Wartime inflation and production and transport problems led to a shortage of fuel and food in the cities. The populace of Petrograd, Russia's capital, reached a breaking point in the winter of 1917. On February 23, 1917, women who were waiting in line for rationed bread began a protest that quickly spread among workers, soldiers, peasants, and government officials. Within a week, Nicholas II abdicated in favor of his brother, the Grand Duke Michael, who refused the throne when the government, realizing its own weakness and the unpopularity of the Romanovs, could not guarantee his safety.

With Nicholas's abdication in February 1917, Russia experienced its first revolution of the year, which marked the downfall of the Romanov dynasty and its autocratic form of government. Russia then embarked on a new era that promised a new, constitutionally mandated form of government. Two new governmental authorities arose to fill the vacuum created by the tsarist government's collapse. A Provisional Government was created that had two principal aims. It continued fighting the war on the side of France and England, and it planned for the convening of a Constituent Assembly, or constitutional convention, that was supposed to determine the form of Russia's future political system.

At the same time, striking workers and revolutionaries set up a Petrograd Soviet (Council) of Workers' and Soldiers' Deputies. Hundreds of other soviets were formed across the country, representing soldiers, factory workers, and other groups. The soviets were a type of grass-roots democracy that expressed the opinions of different segments of society and that coordinated revolutionary activity. Thus, after the February Revolution, between the Provisional Government and the soviets, Russia came to be ruled by an unstable system of dual power, in which these two forms of political authority often came into conflict. For example, the Petrograd Soviet passed its Order No. 1, which weakened the Russian Army by granting soldiers the right to elect committees in each military unit, thereby undermining officers' authority and the Provisional Government's attempt to prosecute the war on its own terms.

By October, after conditions on the war front, in the countryside, and in the cities had worsened considerably, the Provisional Government had lost what authority it had held. By attempting to suppress left-wing parties like the Bolsheviks, and by initially showing support for the conservative General Lavr Kornilov to take over the government and establish a right-wing dictatorship, the government pushed revolutionaries into taking action.

Fearing a government crackdown or counter-revolution, Vladimir LENIN decided that the time was right for his party to take power, not in the name of the Bolsheviks, but in the name of the popular soviets. The occasion that they chose was the Second All-Russian Congress of Soviets, a gathering of representatives of hundreds of soviets. On its opening day, October 25, the Bolsheviks took over strategic points in the city, such as roads, railroad stations, telephone and telegraph offices, banks, post offices, and government buildings. Although several hundred people died in the ensuing violence, the Bolsheviks encountered no difficult opposition. Various government ministers were imprisoned and later shot.

After taking power, the Bolsheviks issued five decrees that gained them popular support. The first declaration was an appeal for a "democratic peace" without reparations or territorial annexations. They also abolished the death penalty, a popular move given the Provisional Government's support for executing soldiers who refused to fight. In a country where approximately 85 percent of the population was peasant, they called for distribution of gentry land to the peasants. Also, they appealed for "workers' control" over industry, whereby democratically elected factory committees, not management, would control production. Finally, they declared autonomy for non-Russians in the Russian Empire.

Eventually, the Soviet regime would modify each of these decisions in one way or another: Its 1918 peace treaty allowed Germany to take over large parts of the Ukraine; it allowed selective executions of opponents; it confiscated private farms in a mass collectivization of agricultural lands; it outlawed independent labor unions; and it re-formed the Russian Empire as the Soviet Union, subordinating nationalist aspirations of ethnic minorities to the ideology of communism.

In October 1917, the Bolsheviks still only had control of limited areas of the country, and the elections to the Constituent Assembly, originally planned by the overthrown Provisional Government, took place the following month. When the convention convened on January 5–18, 1918, to determine the future form of Russia's government, the peasant party (the Socialist Revolutionaries) controlled approximately 60 percent of the seats and elected their leader Victor Chernov to chair the assembly. The Bolsheviks won about 25 percent of the seats, with the Kadets (constitutional monarchists) holding about 12 percent and the Mensheviks (moderate Marxists) even less. Lenin, realizing that the convention would be a source of power for the peasant party, disbanded the Constituent Assembly by force after its first session.

In March 1918, the Bolshevik government signed the Treaty of Brest-Litovsk with Germany and paid an enormous price; the Germans occupied vast territories of the Ukraine.

In July 1918, the Bolsheviks carried out an execution of many members of the Romanov dynasty. Russia found itself in a civil war between the Bolsheviks' Red Army and the White Army (supported by foreign mercenaries and monarchists) that sought a restoration of the monarchy. The Bolsheviks' victory helped them to consolidate their October 1917 Revolution and to carry out their vision of the world's first communist state.

BIBLIOGRAPHY. Harold Shukman, ed., *The Blackwell Encyclopedia of the Russian Revolution* (Blackwell, 1988); E. Acton, *Rethinking the Russian Revolution* (Edward Arnold, 1990); E.H. Carr, *The Bolshevik Revolution, 1917–1923* (Edward Arnold, 1985); W.H. Chamberlin, *The Russian Revolution, 1917–1921* (Princeton University Press, 1987); M. McCauley, ed., *The Russian Revolution and the Soviet State, 1917–1921* (Edward Arnold, 1988); A.K. Wildman, *The End of the Russian Imperial Army* (Princeton University Press, 1980–87).

GEORGE KOSAR
BRANDEIS UNIVERSITY

RWE

RHEINISCH-WESTFÄLISCHES Elektrizitätswerk Aktiengesellschaft (RWE) was founded in Essen, GERMANY, on April 25, 1898, when it opened its first electricity plant. More than 100 years later, RWE still operates primarily in the utility industries, acting as a holding company for its many subsidiaries. In recent years, while maintaining focus on its core energy businesses, RWE has also pursued an aggressive growth (via acquisition) and internationalization strategy, particularly across Europe, as trade barriers in services have fallen with the implementation of the EUROPEAN UNION (EU) single European market program.

In Germany, RWE is the market leader in electricity and water- and waste-management, and places second in gas. RWE also operates one of the leading electricity power grids in Europe, and has a commanding global presence in the supply of water. In addition, RWE has a controlling interest in Heidelberger Druckmaschinen (a leading printing systems company worldwide) and Hochtief (a leader in construction and civil engineering). In 2002, total group sales were €46.6 billion. The four core businesses of electricity, gas, water, and environmental services accounted for 51 percent, 12.2 percent, 6.1 percent, and 5 percent respectively. Ranked as the 53rd largest company in the world in 2002, RWE employed 131,765 people worldwide, and return on capital employed was 10.4 percent.

BIBLIOGRAPHY. "Investor Relations," www.rwe.com; "Global 500: World's Largest Companies," *Fortune* (July 2002).

CATHERINE MATRAVES
ALBION COLLEGE